$10, 95

THE
STUDY
OF
BEHAVIOR

Learning, Motivation,
Emotion, and Instinct

THE
STUDY
OF
BEHAVIOR

Learning, Motivation,
Emotion, and Instinct

Edited by John A. Nevin
Columbia University

George S. Reynolds, Consulting Editor
University of California, San Diego

Scott, Foresman and Company
Glenview, Illinois   Brighton, England

ACKNOWLEDGMENTS

The authors would like to thank all sources for the use of their material. The credit lines for copyrighted textual materials appearing in this work are found here; acknowledgments for figures and tables are placed in the reference section at the end of each chapter. These pages are to be considered an extension of the copyright page.

page 4: Excerpt from pp. 4–5 in *Beyond Freedom and Dignity* by B. F. Skinner (Knopf, 1971). Copyright © 1971 by B. F. Skinner. Reprinted by permission of the publisher.

pages 185–86, 241, 242, 282–83: Excerpts from pp. 77, 81, 160, 162, 163, 182–83, 184 in *Science and Human Behavior* by B. F. Skinner (Macmillan, 1953). Copyright 1953 by The Macmillan Company. Reprinted by permission of the publisher.

page 257: Excerpts from pp. 416–17, 427, 428, 429, 432–33 in *Theory of Motivation* by Robert C. Bolles (Harper & Row, 1967). Reprinted by permission of the publisher.

page 282: Excerpt from pp. 292–93 in "An explanation of 'emotional' phenomena without the use of the concept of 'emotion'" by Elizabeth Duffy in *The Journal of General Psychology,* 1941, **25**, 283–93. Reprinted by permission of the publisher.

pages 283, 298: Excerpts from pp. 241–42, 328 in *A Textbook of Psychology,* 2nd ed., by D. O. Hebb (Saunders, 1966). Reprinted by permission of author and publisher.

page 299: Excerpts from pp. 172, 184, 199 in *Social Psychology* by O. Klineberg (Holt, Rinehart and Winston, 1940). Reprinted by permission of the publisher.

Dedicated to William W. Cumming (1927 – 1970) Teacher, Colleague, Friend

PREFACE

This book was originally conceived in 1965 by Dr. George S.
Reynolds as the first of a three-volume series on contemporary
experimental psychology. He laid out the general plan of this volume,
selected the contributing authors, and communicated his own sense of
excitement about the project to all of us. In effect, he proposed that
we do a thorough coverage of our various topics, including enough
introductory material to make the book useful in an intermediate-level
undergraduate course, as well as enough advanced material and
discussion of new directions to challenge more advanced students and
to be of value to the profession at large. Thus, in various ways, each
of the authors has tried to achieve a balance of handbooklike
coverage, innovative discussion of both recent and traditional issues,
and clarity of presentation for students who are just beginning their
studies in experimental psychology. The tension between these
requirements has forced all of us to think through our subject matter
in new ways; hopefully, the results will be beneficial to the serious
beginning student and the professional alike.

Each chapter of this volume stands on its own. Thus, instructors of
undergraduate and graduate courses in learning and animal behavior
can use its contents in whatever order is most suitable to them. For a
general introduction to the field, with an especially clear treatment of
the vocabulary of learning and conditioning, Catania's Chapter 2 will
be valuable not only in conventional courses in the experimental
study of learning, but also in broader courses that deal integratively
with systematic issues in psychology. Undergraduates and graduate
students embarking upon independent study and research in classical
and operant conditioning, with emphases on reinforcement,
punishment, and stimulus control, will find Chapters 3 through 7 by
Terrace, Nevin, and Fantino valuable for comprehensive treatments
of their topics. For students whose interests extend beyond the usual
domain of learning and conditioning, Fantino's Chapter 8 discusses
various theories and empirical approaches to emotion and motivation,
while Burghardt's Chapter 9 provides an extensive treatment of
history and research in ethology. Thus, this volume represents several
important research areas that are crucial for current approaches to the
understanding of behavior.

Inevitably, a volume composed of separate chapters by authors
with different styles and viewpoints will vary in the interpretation of
particular research findings. No attempt has been made to impose
conformity of viewpoint: The science of behavior is far too young to
tolerate orthodoxy. It is our hope that the occasional inconsistencies
in the interpretation of data will serve as a stimulus for research; for
although the present authors may sometimes differ in their approaches

to particular questions, or in their overall orientation, all are dedicated to an objective and experimental analysis of behavior.

Another consequence of attempting a multiauthored volume is that it takes time to assemble. To the authors of these chapters, I owe a debt of gratitude for their patience through the lengthy processes of editing and revision.

Whatever my own substantive chapters may contribute is in large measure due to many stimulating discussions with Professor William W. Cumming, who died in January 1970 at the age of 42, and to whom this book is dedicated. All who knew him and his work feel the loss of his keen insights and his broad knowledge of our field, his stimulating teaching, and his warm, personal concern for his students. Others who have shaped my approach to the study of behavior are Professor W. N. Schoenfeld, who guided my thesis research and taught me to see its findings as a part of a continuum of behavioral processes; and Professor Robert Berryman, who fostered in me a love of laboratory research.

A somewhat different sort of contribution comes from the many students whose questions in my classes have forced reexamination of issues that I thought I understood, and whose research provided a constant source of stimulation and fun. There are too many to name them all, but Robin Welte deserves special mention for her help in clarifying some of the issues and in preparing the adaptations of published data that appear in Chapters 4, 5, and 6.

During the years since Dr. Reynolds initiated this volume, a number of the editorial staff at Scott, Foresman have been intimately involved with it. Of special importance to the project were George Jacobson, who commented extensively on the individual chapters and suggested many valuable revisions; John Cox, who gave important advice on the major editorial decisions that determined the form of this volume; and Linda Peterson, Donna Delaine, and Jerry Hutchins, who patiently saw its text through the many stages of editorial processing to its eventual publication. To all of them, my warmest thanks.

J. A. N.

ABOUT THE AUTHORS

Gordon M. Burghardt

Professor Burghardt received his S.B. and Ph.D. degrees in psychology (biopsychology) from the University of Chicago in 1963 and 1966, respectively. He taught biology at the University of Chicago through 1967 and moved to the Psychology Department at the University of Tennessee at Knoxville in 1968. His current research interests include the analysis of perception, early experience, and social behavior, especially in reptiles and bears, as well as general theoretical issues in ethology.

A. Charles Catania

Professor Catania received an A.B. in 1957 and an M.A. in 1958 from Columbia University, and a Ph.D. in psychology from Harvard University in 1961. After postdoctoral research at Harvard and research in psychopharmacology at the Smith Kline & French Laboratories, he moved in 1964 to University College of Arts and Science, New York University, where he served as department chairman from 1969 through 1972. From 1966 through 1969, he was the editor of the *Journal of the Experimental Analysis of Behavior;* he now continues to serve as review editor of that journal. His research interests, which have included reinforcement schedules (especially concurrent schedules) and the psychology of learning, are currently turning toward language and verbal learning.

Edmund Fantino

Professor Fantino, whose undergraduate major at Cornell University was mathematics, received his Ph.D. in psychology from Harvard University in 1964. He taught at Yale University for three years and then moved to the University of California at San Diego, where he has been since 1967. He is an associate editor of the *Journal of the Experimental Analysis of Behavior*. His current research interests center on choice, conditioned reinforcement, and aversive control, within the framework of both operant conditioning and comparative psychology.

John A. Nevin

Professor Nevin received his B.E. in mechanical engineering from Yale University in 1954 and his Ph.D. in psychology from Columbia University in 1963. He taught at Swarthmore College from 1963 until 1968, with a year's leave for research at Harvard University in 1966–67. He taught at Columbia University from 1968 until 1972, serving as department chairman from 1970 through 1972. He is now at the University of New Hampshire. He is an associate editor of the *Journal of the Experimental Analysis of Behavior*. His current research interests include the effects of reinforcement schedules on stimulus control, conditioned reinforcement, and animal psychophysics.

H. S. Terrace

Professor Terrace received his Ph.D. in psychology at Harvard University in 1961. Since that time he has been a member of the faculty of Columbia University. During 1969–70, he was in residence at the University of Sussex, England, as a Guggenheim Fellow, and during 1972–73, he taught at Harvard as a Visiting Professor. He has served as an associate editor of the *Journal of the Experimental Analysis of Behavior, Learning and Motivation*, and *Animal Learning and Behavior*, and as a member of the editorial board of *Behaviorism*. His current research and writing interests include discrimination learning, conditioned inhibition, ethological contributions to conditioned behavior, and the philosophical bases of behaviorism.

CONTENTS

John A. Nevin

THE
STUDY
OF
BEHAVIOR

Learning, Motivation,
Emotion, and Instinct

PROBLEMS AND METHODS

John A. Nevin
Columbia University

Psychology has been defined in various ways: the study of conscious experience, the science of the mind, the science of behavior. Whatever the definition, though, the immediate subject matter of psychology is behavior. The phenomena of private experience, whether they be characterized as mental or emotional, conscious or unconscious, are inaccessible to direct public observation; the actions of living organisms, on the other hand, can be observed directly and studied in relation to antecedent conditions in the same way as the phenomena treated in other sciences.

Some psychologists study behavior primarily because it may index private processes or events which, although inferred, are taken as the major object of interest. For others, the understanding of behavior can come only from an analysis of the nervous system, and their major concern is with the information that behavior may provide about the operation of physiological processes. For both, the study of behavior is a means to some other end. For still others, though, the behavior of living organisms is of interest in its own right, and is a proper subject matter for study regardless of whether it serves to answer such age-old questions as the nature of mind, or whether its findings prove valuable for the physiologist.

This volume falls squarely within the latter tradition. Its title seems to make reference to processes or entities that are located within the organism and that are not accessible to direct observation. In fact, though, the terms *learning, motivation, emotion,* and *instinct* are used in this volume more as shorthand designations for behavioral relations that are often grouped together for convenience in discussion than as names for inferred entities. It is important throughout the study of behavior to avoid confusing the name for an empirically established relationship between behavior and environment with the name given by our everyday language for an inner event or process. Common sense refers to the emotion of fear, for example, as if it were a thing within a person. In the science of behavior, though, fear is a name for an assemblage of observations, perhaps not well understood, of how organisms act in certain stressful circumstances. We should not be surprised if the connotations of fear, as it refers to the thing of private experience, do not coincide with the properties of behavior revealed by empirical analysis.

Even if this distinction between behavioral relations and inner events is accepted, it may seem reasonable to ask for some definitions. How do we define the set of relations designated by the term *learning*, as opposed to, say, *instinct?* When would we use the term *motivation* rather than *emotion?* Such definitions have often been attempted, usually on the basis of prior theoretical considerations and usually without complete success; that is, they often exclude instances that seem to merit inclusion, and vice versa. Here, no attempt at definition will be made. For the moment, it is enough that the various connotations of the terms in the title serve to indicate the sorts of problems to be treated in this volume.

By and large, the following chapters are concerned with the analysis of fairly simple behaviors that occur repeatedly in the lifetime of an organism. This sort of restriction is necessary to the scientific enterprise. Unless the phenomena of interest can be observed a number of times, it is not possible to ascertain those variables which stand in a causal relation to them—i.e., those variables which regularly precede or accompany their occurrence. Also, unless the phenomena are deliberately simplified by isolation from the complex flow of natural events, there is little chance that lawful causal relations will be discovered.

Another general characteristic of this volume is that most of the research discussed in the following chapters employs animal subjects. There are several reasons for this. First, our central interest is not to study animals in order to make inferences about human behavior, but rather to understand the behavior of all living organisms. This is a vast undertaking that can be approached in many ways. Some psychologists search for behavioral principles that hold across a broad range of species, others concentrate on relations that differentiate among species and thus may give some information about biological or evolutionary factors, while still others work extensively with just one or two species in an attempt to arrive at a detailed understanding of behavior in a setting that is representative of a general case. When humans come under study, observation and interpretation proceed in the same way as they do with infrahuman subjects.

The second general reason for animal research is that there are certain research procedures that cannot be used on human subjects. When the interpretation of data depends crucially on precise control of the subject's past history, or when it is necessary to apply severe deprivation or painful stimulation in order to study the phenomena of interest, human subjects simply cannot be used for obvious ethical reasons.

Implicit in this approach to behavior is the assumption that the principles discovered through the study of simple, recurring responses of humans or animals will lead to an understanding of behavior in complex situations that arise infrequently, and provide the basis for the solution of practical human problems, such as increasing the effectiveness of academic instruction, regulating population growth, or modifying disordered emotional behavior. The need to solve such problems is evident in every aspect of our lives, and it is not at all clear that solutions are forthcoming from other disciplines. As Skinner (1971) has said:

> The application of the physical and biological sciences alone will not solve our problems because the solutions lie in another field. Better contraceptives will control population only if people use them. New weapons may offset new defenses and vice versa, but a nuclear holocaust can be prevented only if the conditions under which nations make war can be changed. New methods of agriculture and medicine will not help if they are not practiced, and housing is a matter not only of buildings and cities but of how people live. Overcrowding can be corrected only by inducing people not to crowd, and the environment will continue to deteriorate until polluting practices are abandoned.
>
> In short, we need to make vast changes in human behavior, and we cannot make them with the help of nothing more than physics or biology, no matter how hard we try. . . .
>
> What we need is a technology of behavior. We could solve our problems quickly enough if we could adjust the growth of the world's population as precisely as we adjust the course of a spaceship, or improve agriculture and industry with some of the confidence with which we accelerate high-energy particles, or move toward a peaceful world with something like the steady progress with which physics has approached absolute zero (even though both remain presumably out of reach). But a behavioral technology comparable in power and precision to physical and biological technology is lacking [pp. 4–5].

It is too early in the history of psychology to judge the value of the approach represented here. Although the range and complexity of behaviors that have been subjected to scientific analysis are steadily growing, and there are numerous instances of the successful application of behavioral principles, our understanding of basic phenomena remains incomplete. The following chapters discuss the ways in which various behavioral processes have been approached experimentally and the general principles suggested by the findings. Some chapters suggest revisions in established approaches based on recent findings or reinterpretations of older data; others point up the complexity of the variables controlling even apparently simple instances of behavior; and still others suggest important limits on widely accepted principles. This process of discovering limits, evaluating complex factors, and revising basic approaches to a problem is the essence of the scientific enterprise. To introduce the principles that have been developed to date and the enduring problems in this area, it will be valuable to provide a brief historical review.

HISTORICAL BACKGROUND

Although mankind must have been concerned with the causes of behavior from the very beginning of social history, the scientific approach to the study of behavior was founded by the French philosopher, René Descartes (1596–1650). Descartes proposed a simple system of classification, grouping all instances of behavior according to their *voluntary* or *involuntary* nature. He sought to account for all involuntary behaviors by showing their dependence on the immediate physical environment. Thus, the withdrawal of a hand from a hot surface was seen as a response to the physical stimulation from the heat source, which acted directly on the body to elicit the movement. The movement was viewed as totally automatic, and not unlike a reaction that could be exhibited by a well-designed mechanical model. Certain human actions, and all behaviors of animals, were said to have this sort of automatic character. Humans, however, were able to influence the actions of their bodies by will. Thus, mental events as well as physical stimuli could serve to initiate action, and behavior was classified according to the nature of its initiation and not the actual movements involved. The distinction between voluntary and involuntary behavior coincided with the philosophical distinction between mind and body, which has endured through several centuries of Western thought. One of Descartes' major contributions to psychology is that by designating a large class of behaviors as involuntary, and by proposing a physical mechanism for their occurrence, he took them out of the domain of philosophy and opened the way for their investigation by scientific methods.

Reflexology

The kind of behavior that Descartes had identified as involuntary or automatic soon became known as *reflex* behavior. A reflex is a relation between a particular stimulus and a particular response that is reliably elicited by the stimulus. The retraction of a limb following a painful stimulation of its extremity and the contraction of the pupil of the eye when exposed to a bright light are common examples of reflexes. Early interest in reflex behavior came from physiologists such as Whytt (1714–1766), Bell (1774–1842), and Magendie (1783–1855). Working with frogs, Whytt demonstrated that hind-limb movement could be elicited by stimulating certain areas of the lower body even after the spinal cord had been severed, thus removing any influence of the brain. Bell and Magendie independently discovered that there were separate sensory nerves, carrying signals from the site of stimulation to the spinal cord, and motor nerves, carrying signals from the cord to the limb. The chemical and electrical nature of these signals was not understood until relatively recently, but that was of little importance in the study of the principles of reflex action.

Whatever the mechanism of neural transmission, the spinal reflex could be treated as a simple behavioral unit, and its analysis proceeded in two ways. One avenue of attack lay in the study of the reflex arc—the pathways that led from receptors via sensory nerves to the spinal cord, and then back from the cord via motor nerves to the muscles. In effect, this was the beginning of physiological psychology—that branch of psychology which is primarily concerned with the mechanisms underlying behavior. Alternatively, the properties of reflex behavior could be studied without further analysis of its mechanism. Once a reflex was isolated, the relations between the response and the eliciting stimulus could be studied with precision. For example, one could determine the minimum intensity of stimulation necessary to produce a response—the *threshold*. At higher intensities, one could examine in detail the way in which the properties of the response depended on stimulation. For example, the *latency* of the response—the time from the onset of stimulation to the occurrence of the response—could be studied in relation to stimulus intensity. As a final example, the eliciting stimuli for different responses could be presented simultaneously or successively in order to examine the *interactions* between reflexes, and thus permit the understanding of increasingly complex sequences of behaviors. In the nineteenth century, this research culminated in the work of Sir Charles Sherrington. His major book, *The Integrative Action of the Nervous System* (1906) clearly demonstrated the power of the experimental method in revealing lawful properties of behavior and in suggesting the basic principles of reflex action.

It is worth pausing here to consider the terms *stimulus* and *response,* which are so fundamental to discussions of behavior. The term *stimulus* refers to that portion of the physical environment which is selected by an experimenter to be presented or withheld, or otherwise varied systematically, in order to ascertain its effects on behavior. The term *response* refers to that portion of all activities of the organism which is selected by the experimenter to be measured and related to the stimulus. Stimuli and responses can be defined operationally without reference to one another, but it is the way in which responses depend on stimuli—the relation between behavior and environment—that is of central interest.

The reflex is one instance of a stimulus-response relationship: An environmental event is presented to an organism, and some particular activity occurs as a result. It is unlikely that any two successive environmental events will be identical in all particulars. For example, the scratch reflex, studied extensively by Sherrington (1906), may be evoked by mechanical or electrical stimulation of the side of a dog whose spinal cord has been transected. There is a broad range of skin areas over which various forms of stimulation will evoke the same response—or at least there will be no systematic relation between the location of the stimulus and the properties of the response. We are thus led to the concept of a *class* of stimuli, all members of which are functionally equivalent in eliciting a response.

One of psychology's enduring problems is to specify the critical aspects of environmental events that determine their inclusion in a stimulus class. The problem may seem trivial with respect to a spinal reflex, but in other areas it is far from trivial. Consider, for example, the problem of determining which aspects of a spoken word lead to its recognition by a listener as the same word, when uttered by a young boy and a mature man and thus varying in pitch and intonation. Problems of this sort are concerned with the isolation of invariant structural relationships within classes of stimuli. The areas of psychology known as perception and cognition deal extensively with such problems; in this volume, they are exemplified by the analyses of attention and conceptual behavior in Chapter 4, and of sign stimuli in Chapter 9.

A parallel problem arises on the response side of the relation in that successive responses will vary if examined closely enough. With reference to the scratch reflex again, successive responses will vary somewhat in the angle through which the leg moves, the rate of movement, and so forth. If there is no systematic dependency of these aspects of the response on details of stimulation, we are led to the concept of a *class* of responses, all members of which are functionally equivalent in their dependency upon a stimulus.

We are then faced with a problem analogous to that of specifying the critical aspects of stimulation: What is it that these responses have in common that determines their membership in a response class? In the case of the spinal reflex, we could probably state an unambiguous definition that could be applied quite mechanically to determine class membership. In other cases, though, the solution is far from obvious: If we ask two people to describe a given event, they are likely to answer in two quite different ways, using different words within different grammatical structures, but each giving an entirely satisfactory description of the event. Thus, both descriptions are members of the same functional class. The problem of ascertaining the common features of these equivalent descriptions is central to the area of psycholinguistics. Within this volume, related problems of what might be termed the structure of behavior are addressed in Chapters 2, 8, and 9.

It is important to understand that the functional relation between the occurrence of instances of a response class and presentations of instances of a stimulus class may be explored without detailed understanding of their properties beyond their membership in those classes. For example, the study of the scratch reflex as a behavioral relation can proceed even though the investigator does not know the sensory process that makes mechanical stimulation and shock equivalent in their effects; it is sufficient that variations in either kind of stimulation lead to similar changes in the response they elicit. Nothing that may be learned about similarities or differences in the ways in which the sensory nerves respond to different kinds of stimulation can alter the validity of the behavioral relations. Indeed, the question of common sensory effects can arise only because of common behavioral effects. In this sense, then, relations between stimuli and responses precede considerations of the properties held in common by all instances of the stimulus or response classes. A complete understanding of behavior obviously requires both kinds of investigation.

Instinctive behavior

Despite the major advances in the study of reflexes, it was clear that the principles of reflex action could account for only a small fraction of the behavior of animals, let alone humans, when their behavior was considered with reference to its natural setting. At the animal level, Darwin (1809–1882) and other naturalists had called attention to elaborate instinctive behavior patterns in many species. One of Darwin's (1859) examples involves the behavior of the young European cuckoo. The European cuckoo lays its eggs in the nests of other species, typically only one egg to a nest. Soon after the cuckoo hatches, it typically ejects its foster siblings, thus obtaining the exclusive attention of the foster parents. The behavior of ejecting other young birds is reliable in that it recurs if one of the birds is replaced, and clearly it is not dependent on prior experience, the expectation of more food, or the like, because it is performed soon after hatching with no opportunity for experience of any sort. Clearly, this is "involuntary" behavior, and it is worthwhile comparing it with reflex behavior. Among the identifying characteristics of reflex behavior was its apparently innate, "wired-in" aspect; that is, reflex behavior appeared not to depend on prior experience, but only on species membership and maturation, so that the properties of a reflex were essentially identical for all individuals of a given species and age. The behavior of the young cuckoo would seem to qualify as reflexive by these criteria. Many other complex patterns of behavior, such as nest-building, mating, the rearing of young, and migration, also seemed analogous to reflexes in that they were similar across individuals and occurred without prior experience. It was therefore tempting to view instinctive behaviors as complex sequences or concatenations of simple reflexes. Moreover, both reflexes and instincts had obvious survival value: Organisms that reflexively escaped from pain, or instinctively threw their foster siblings out of nests, were more likely to survive and reproduce. Thus, involuntary behaviors of this sort were likely to be preserved in the repertoire of a species through the process of *natural selection,* the understanding of which was Darwin's major contribution to science.

However, instinctive behaviors differed from spinal reflexes in that their eliciting stimuli were difficult to characterize. The conditions that led up to the occurrence of instinctive responses appeared to involve complex configurations of environmental events, sometimes including such factors as the actions of other organisms. Consider, for example, the problem of specifying the eliciting stimulus for the behavior of the young cuckoo described here. In many cases, a given stimulus might or might not be sufficient to initiate responding, depending upon a host of other factors. Moreover, some instinctive actions involved a prolonged sequence of responses which, once initiated, tended to go to completion regardless of current stimulating conditions. Thus, it appeared that certain instinctive behaviors had a built-in sequential aspect, perhaps dependent upon internal stimuli.

These matters of stimulus configurations and complex response sequences are, as we have seen, questions of the common elements that determine inclusion in classes; they do not necessarily mean that the functional properties of reflexes and instinctive behaviors are different. Thus, instincts and reflexes could be viewed as similar in their dependence on the biological nature of the organism, but different in the order of complexity of both the stimulus and the response. The analysis of instinctive behavior and the history of theorizing and research in this area are discussed at length in Chapter 9. Accordingly, we will not pursue this development further here, but will turn to the behavioristic tradition, which went on from reflexology to the experimental study of other types of responses in relation to the environment.

Conditioned reflexes

A few reflexologists, most notably Sechenov (1829–1905), rejected the Cartesian dualism of voluntary and involuntary behavior and insisted that all aspects of behavior—including mental activity—could be understood in terms of reflex action. In their view, particular stimuli, sometimes of such low intensity as to elude overt identification, elicited particular responses, which could include small-scale, private responses that for the behaviorist were equivalent to what a mentalist viewed as thought. There was a certain appeal in this sort of approach, because it avoided all the difficulties involved in trying to study ill-defined mental actions and in understanding how a nonphysical event in the mind could alter the course of the thoroughly physical response systems of the body. However, this approach was severely limited: first, because it was not then possible to study such private responses, so that their existence and presumed dependence on environmental events remained hypothetical; and second, because it did not provide any mechanism for variation in the situations that elicited them.

The problem of variation was of central concern to the philosophical and mentalistic tradition of *associationism,* which dated back to Berkeley (1685–1753). Associationism was especially concerned with ways in which successively experienced sensations or ideas could result in the formation of a bond uniting them, so that one sufficed to evoke another. For example, Berkeley suggested that judgments of distance might be understood as resulting from a "constant or habitual connection" between the sensations arising from eye movements and the experience of distance, as when reaching for an object, so that eye movements could come to evoke the idea of distance directly. Later associationists such as James Mill (1773–1836) were concerned with relations that were less likely to be uniform across individuals, but arose through chance conjunction of experiences. Such associations were said to depend on factors such as frequency, recency, temporal proximity, and vividness of the component sensations and ideas; clearly, they were not to be regarded as inborn or independent of experience, as in the case of reflexes. Thus, even if one granted that the events constituting an association could be treated as private stimuli and responses, it was not clear how new associations could be reconciled with the uniformity of reflex action.

The required mechanisms for the acquisition of new reflexes, and their subsequent elimination, were provided by Pavlov (1849–1936). He demonstrated that a previously neutral stimulus could acquire the power to elicit a response through repeated presentations together with a stimulus that naturally elicited the response. His standard experimental subject was a dog with a fistula in a salivary gland, permitting the measurement of the flow of saliva. In a typical experiment, a tone would precede the presentation of meat powder by a few seconds. The dog would normally salivate reflexively when meat powder was presented, and after a few trials it would also salivate when the tone sounded. Pavlov's procedure has come to be called *classical* or *respondent* conditioning (the terms are used interchangeably here). In general, the procedure involves the pairing of a *conditional stimulus (CS)* with an *unconditional stimulus (US)*. As a consequence of this arrangement, the *CS* comes to elicit a *conditional response (CR)* that is similar to the *unconditional response (UR)* elicited by the *US*. In this example, the tone is the *CS* and

the meat powder is the *US;* salivation elicited by the meat powder is the *UR* and the salivation subsequently elicited by the tone is the *CR*.

After a conditional reflex was established, it could be eliminated by a procedure that Pavlov called *experimental extinction.* Briefly, this procedure involved repeated presentations of the *CS,* while withholding the *US*. Under these circumstances, the *CR* would decrease in magnitude and eventually disappear. Thus, Pavlov's research suggested a way of establishing a new reflex relationship between stimuli and responses—a *conditional* reflex, in the sense that its occurrence was conditional upon a specified history of stimulus pairing and response elicitation. Pavlov (1927) reported a substantial body of research concerned with the properties of conditional reflexes (or conditioned reflexes, as they are interchangeably called). Pavlov's methods and findings, and the modern research that has grown out of the tradition of Pavlovian conditioning, are described in detail in Chapter 3.

The problem of voluntary behavior

The category of involuntary behavior proposed by Descartes may be seen as encompassing instinctive behaviors of animals and unconditional and conditional reflexes, the latter of which could account for differences in responding to various stimuli that were acquired within an organism's lifetime. John B. Watson (1878–1958) argued that an analysis of these kinds of behavioral relations could account for the entirety of human behavior, as well as that of animals. Given the existence of unlearned emotional responses such as fear, rage, and love (each entailing a complex pattern of responses in the newborn infant analogous to instinctive behaviors, but more diffuse), together with the existence of motor reflexes such as those involved in crawling, plus the operation of Pavlovian conditioning to establish new reflexes, Watson argued that it would be possible to account in detail for all behavior and indeed to go on to the prediction and control of human behavior without reference to any other processes.

Many psychologists disagreed. For them, one of the most interesting characteristics of behavior was its apparent orientation toward the future, rather than its elicitation by prior stimulation, whether conditioned or unconditioned. As a minor example, consider the selection of clothes one makes in the morning, which seems to be determined by what is likely to happen later in the day—that is, by the sort of human encounters one has planned, such as a job interview. To pursue this example, it is not at all easy to see how job interviews (a complex stimulus class) could have elicited the selection of clean clothes, so that the process of classical conditioning could operate to condition such responses to the stimuli that precede interviews. There may be a lot of classical conditioning going on in situations of this sort, particularly with reference to the sorts of emotional responses that we loosely call anxiety, but it is difficult to understand how preparatory choices can be treated in this sort of framework. On the other hand, it is very easy to account for the selection of clothes for a job interview by referring to factors such as criticism for inappropriate outfits, praise for appropriate ones, and other forms of social pressure, in conjunction with a desire for a job. But what is the status of terms like these in a science of behavior? These factors do not seem to have much in common with eliciting stimuli in conditioned or unconditioned reflexes. Instead they suggest planning on the basis of past experience, future expectations, and long-term goals. We must now face the problem of dealing objectively with behaviors that appear to be intelligently directed toward the future.

To understand how modern psychology has approached this problem, we must go back to Darwin again. With the publication of *The Origin of Species* (1859), Darwin had changed the course of intellectual history by emphasizing the continuity of species, so that human beings could no longer be viewed as specially endowed, except perhaps in degree, with a mental life. If, as nearly everyone uncritically assumed, humans could engage in voluntary activity and plan their behavior on the basis of its expected consequences, animals might do the same. The degree to which different species exhibited intelligent behavior of this sort might provide clues to the nature of mental evolution, just as variations in structure across related species permitted inferences about natural selection. Thus, by the late nineteenth century, a number of researchers became interested in the study of mental processes in animals, with a view to establishing an evolutionary, comparative psychology of intelligence. Modern work within this tradition is discussed in Chapter 9.

The early work of Thorndike (1898) on escape from puzzle boxes grew out of the search for evidence of mental processes in animals, but led to the statement of a fundamental principle of so-called goal-directed behavior that did not imply any form of mental action. In a standard experiment, Thorndike studied the process by which a cat learned to escape from a box by operating a latch. Initially, the cat scrambled about until it hit the release mechanism, which allowed it to run out of the box and obtain food. During subsequent trials, the cat's latency to operate the latch became shorter and shorter, and its movements became smoother and more efficient. The process could be described by saying that the cat initially tried out various responses until one succeeded, and then used its experience in order to gain access to food as soon as possible on each trial. Thorndike viewed matters differently, however. In his view, the consequences of the cat's movements—freedom and food—had served to stamp in a connection between the stimuli of the box and the particular movements that in the past had been followed immediately by release. The stamping in of connections was entirely automatic and independent of any comprehension of the release mechanism and its operation by the latch. Thus, the emphasis was shifted from the purpose of the cat's action to the past consequences of similar actions. Thorndike (1911) termed the underlying principle *The Law of Effect,* which is best stated in his own words:

> The Law of Effect is that: Of several responses made to the same situation, those which are accompanied or closely followed by satisfaction to the animal will, other things being equal, be more firmly connected with the situation, so that, when it recurs, they will be more likely to recur; those which are accompanied or closely followed by discomfort to the animal will, other things being equal, have their connections with that situation weakened, so that, when it recurs, they will be less likely to occur.

Responses that can be modified by their consequences have come to be called *instrumental* or *operant* behavior (the terms are used interchangeably here), and the consequences that are effective in increasing their occurrence are termed *reinforcers*. The term *reinforcement* denotes the process whereby responses are made more likely when they produce reinforcers. The procedures that have evolved from Thorndike's work are called *instrumental* or *operant conditioning*. Chapter 2 discusses Thorndike's experiment in more detail and presents a clear and careful treatment of the vocabulary of reinforcement. For the present, it is sufficient to note that there are two broad classes of reinforcers: *positive reinforcers*, which increase the probability of a specified response when presented contingent upon its occurrence; and *negative reinforcers*, which increase the probability of a specified response that precedes their offset. The former are satisfiers in Thorndike's sense, while the latter are analogous to discomfort in Thorndike's statement, but are presented or removed in a different relation to the response of interest. Thorndike's statement refers to the response-dependent presentation of discomfort, a relationship that we now call *punishment,* while negative reinforcement refers to the removal of discomfort. Chapter 7 deals extensively with modern research on punishment and negative reinforcement. In Thorndike's situation, it is likely that both positive and negative reinforcement were operating: food as a positive reinforcer, and escape from the box as a negative reinforcer. Here, the analysis of the reinforcing event is not at issue: The important contribution was a principle that could account for the apparent goal-directed character of behavior without invoking determination by future goals.

It may be worth pausing again to consider the meanings of the terms *stimulus* and *response* here. First, consider the response. As in the reflex case, the movements involved in operating the latch would be quite likely to vary from one trial to the next. All successful operations of the latch would have one obvious property in common, namely, success. Thus, one possible defining property of the response class is its effect on the environment. But other movements would also occur, including incomplete operations of the latch—movements lacking sufficient force, say, to be effective. Should such movements be included in the response class or not? This question was to become a theoretical issue. As later stated in learning theory, it concerned the question of what was learned: the movements (raising a paw and inserting it in the loop, pulling downward, etc.) or the act of latch operation regardless of the particular movements involved. Chapter 2 provides a detailed discussion of related matters.

Now consider the stimulus, which can be separated into two classes based on temporal relations to the response. One stimulus class is that complex of environmental events involving placement in the puzzle box and the resultant visual, tactile, and olfactory stimulation to which the cat was exposed until it operated the latch; a second stimulus class is that complex of events that follow latch operation. In both cases, there is sure to be some variation from one trial to the next, if only because of variability in the cat's movements. Again, then, we require the concept of stimulus class, except that we now speak of stimuli that precede or accompany the response as belonging to a separate

class from those that follow the response. This separation arises from the possibility of varying them separately and observing different sorts of effects on behavior. If the consequences of behavior are altered—for example, by omitting the food, or disconnecting the latch so that escape cannot occur—it is likely that there will be an irregular increase in latency until the response ceases altogether. The operation of withholding the reinforcer is called *extinction* and is analogous in its effects to withholding the *US* in classical conditioning. By contrast, if one changes the stimuli that precede or accompany the response while escape and food remain available—for example, by tilting the floor of the box, or changing the illumination drastically—an immediate increase in latency is likely to be observed, followed by

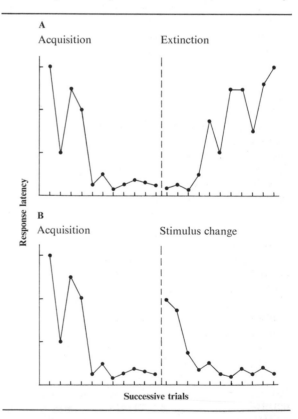

Figure 1.1 Hypothetical data illustrating acquisition of a response in a puzzle-box experiment, followed by extinction (where the response no longer leads to escape and food) in A, or by a change in the stimulus conditions of the box in B. The graphs show how response latency—the time from placement in the box to the occurrence of the response—would vary over successive trials.

decreases as the cat learns to respond under the novel conditions. The extent to which the cat behaves similarly before and after the change in stimulation is a measure of *generalization* between the original and novel conditions. Hypothetical data illustrating the effects of extinction and stimulus change are sketched in Figure 1.1.

Thorndike did not study the effects of extinction and stimulus change in his early work. He did, however, study the changes in behavior that resulted when the location or design of the latch mechanism was altered after a cat had mastered an initial problem, obtaining data much like those shown in Figure 1.1 for stimulus change. Similarities between the properties of antecedent stimuli and the properties of responses are discussed in Chapter 2.

One question that arises here pertains to the class of antecedent stimuli. When the response was "stamped in," in Thorndike's terms, was it equally connected to all of the diverse aspects of stimulation arising from the box? Or only to some aspects? What, in a word, was the effective stimulus class? This is an empirical question, to be answered by analysis in ways to be described in Chapter 4. Whatever the answer, though, the function of the class of stimuli that preceded reinforcement of operant behavior was not clear at the time of Thorndike's research. Were such stimuli to be viewed as elicitors, as in reflexes? Or as conditioned stimuli in the Pavlovian sense? Or was some new sort of relationship involved? This sort of question became a matter of theoretical debate, having to do with differences between classical and instrumental conditioning, and the nature of the basic learning process that was presumed to underlie both kinds of conditioning.

A second sort of question pertains to the class of stimuli that follows responding—the reinforcing stimuli. Although these events follow responding, it is important to appreciate that they still fit our general definition of stimulus: a portion of the physical environment that can be presented or withheld, or otherwise varied by the experimenter. A certain degree of experimental control is lost because the reinforcer can only be presented if a response occurs; however, it need not be presented after every response, nor must it be physically the same throughout the experiment. Systematic variation in the schedule of reinforcement, or in the amount or quality of the reinforcer, can have profound effects on behavior—effects that are related to that portion of the traditional area of motivation which deals with the vigor and persistence of

behavior in relation to its consequences. These matters are considered in Chapter 6. Another question relating to reinforcement asks what it is that all instances of reinforcing stimuli have in common, so that reinforcers can be identified independently of the reinforcement process itself. This issue, which is of central concern to learning theory, is also of enduring interest in the area of motivation and is treated in Chapters 2, 7, and 8.

The rise of behavior theory

During the period from the 1920s through the 1950s several major theories were proposed to encompass the effects of a wide range of experiments and to predict behavior in more complex situations.

E. R. Guthrie

The earliest of these was advanced by Guthrie (1886–1959), who objected to the flavor of subjectivism implicit in Thorndike's Law of Effect (Guthrie, 1935; Smith & Guthrie, 1921). Terms like *satisfaction* and *discomfort* did not seem sufficiently precise or objective; accordingly, Guthrie proposed a general principle that could incorporate both Pavlov's classical conditioning and Thorndike's instrumental conditioning without invoking any additional factors. Briefly, he proposed that whatever stimuli were present when a movement had occurred in the past would, on their recurrence, tend to be followed by that movement; moreover, this effect could occur in a single trial and applied only to the last movement to take place on that trial. If glandular secretion was viewed as a response analogous to muscular movement, it is easy to see how the principle dealt with Pavlovian conditioning. The *US,* food, elicited salivation in the presence of the *CS;* thus, the subsequent occurrence of salivation to the *CS* alone follows directly from the fact that the response had once occurred in the presence of the *CS.* It is perhaps a trifle harder to see how the principle applied to Thorndike's situation, because the cat engaged in all sorts of movements in the presence of puzzle-box stimuli. However, in all cases, the last movement made in the box was the movement required for latch operation, for at that moment the stimulus situation changed as the door opened and the cat ran out. Thus, escape from the box and access to food were treated not as reinforcers, but simply as events that changed the situation, guaranteeing that the last response in the box would be latch operation. The only important aspects of the effects of a response were in what they made the subject do next, and how that action modified the situation. On the basis of this simple contiguity principle, Guthrie argued, one could understand all forms of learned behavior. A good many supplementary assumptions were necessary to achieve this sort of generality, but the bald simplicity of Guthrie's fundamental principle and his ingenuity in extending it to deal with novel experimental procedures remain a source of stimulation and challenge today.

E. C. Tolman

A contemporaneous theorist, Tolman (1886–1959), took a quite different position (e.g., Tolman, 1932, 1938). He argued that organisms learned the relations between prior stimuli, responses, and consequences in a way that permitted behavior to occur when appropriate environmental events coincided with a motivational state or demand for a certain consequence. To give some meaning to this admittedly vague characterization of Tolman's position, consider one of the earliest of the famous *latent learning* experiments. Tolman and Honzik (1930) employed a 14-unit T-maze with doors to prevent retracing and ran separate groups of rats under three conditions. One group found food in the goal-box at the end of the maze on every trial and exhibited progressive improvement in its performance in that the number of erroneous turns decreased systematically from trial to trial. A second group ran without ever receiving food and also exhibited a gradual decrease in errors, but nowhere nearly so large or rapid as the group that always found food. The third group ran without food until the eleventh trial, at which point they found food in the goal-box. On the very next trial, the rats in this third group made the same number of errors as the rats that had found food at the completion of every trial.

These results, which are summarized in Figure 1.2, are not consistent with a Thorndikean stamping-in of connections, because the third group should have exhibited the same reduction in errors with their first reinforcement as did the first group after trial 1. However, the reduction was far greater, suggesting that even in the absence of apparent reinforcement, the rats had learned "what leads to what" and were then able to use this learning when an important consequence was introduced. At the same time, these results are not obviously amenable to Guthrian analysis: Because the doors in each maze unit prevented retracing,

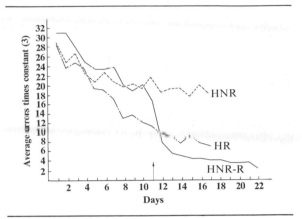

Figure 1.2 Evidence for latent learning in a 14-unit T-maze. Group HNR, hungry with no food reinforcement, exhibits some reduction in errors, while Group HR, hungry with regular food reinforcement, learns much more rapidly. Group HNR-R, run without food until the eleventh trial, exhibits an abrupt reduction in errors immediately after food is introduced. Note that the dependent variable is errors × 3; in a 14-unit maze, seven errors are expected by chance alone, so evidently the subjects were performing worse than chance when the experiment began. (From Tolman & Honzik, 1930.)

the last thing the rats did in each unit was to exit through the correct arm, and hence presumably this was the movement that should have been connected to the stimuli of that unit, equally for all groups.

Many variations in the latent learning paradigm were explored during the course of the next 20 years, each one aimed at answering questions left unresolved by earlier work, but without any clear indication of the necessary and sufficient conditions for producing the result. Chapter 2 discusses this and related experiments that have occasioned considerable controversy over the years since 1930.

C. L. Hull

Perhaps the most ambitious theorist of that period was Hull (1884–1952). Like Guthrie, he proposed a single major principle that could account for all forms of learning if supplemented by a few additional principles. Unlike Guthrie, though, Hull made reinforcement the central principle in his system, and he stated the supplementary principles in an elaborate and highly detailed set of postulates that were given quantitative expression (Hull, 1943,

1951, 1952). There is no need to examine Hull's system in detail here; the central concepts will suffice.

Hull proposed that whenever a given response was closely followed in time by a reduction in a drive or need state, which for him was the *sine qua non* of reinforcement, the stimuli that were present at that time tended, on their recurrence, to evoke the response. This is little more than a restatement of Thorndike's Law of Effect, but Hull intended that it apply to classical as well as instrumental conditioning. Consider, for example, the standard Pavlovian study of conditioned salivation. First the *CS* is presented and followed by the *US,* food, which elicits salivation. Thus, the *CS* is present when a response is evoked, and the ingestion of food leads to a reduction in a drive or need state. The tendency for the *CS* to evoke salivation in its own right is clearly consistent with Hull's principle of reinforcement.

The tendency for a stimulus to evoke a response was termed a *habit,* and the strength of a habit depended on the number of reinforcements. In Hull's view, the habit was not the same thing as actual behavior. An organism could possess a strong habit and still not engage in the response because of the absence of drive (which in effect energized habits into action), or it might respond at substantially below its maximum habit strength because of *inhibition* attributable to response effort, or because of inadequate *incentive* due to insufficient reinforcement. In effect, Hull's and Tolman's theories were similar in that *learning*—habit for Hull, expectancy for Tolman—was not the same as *performance,* which could vary as a result of motivational or other factors. They differed in that Hull asserted that habit could only be acquired through reinforcement, whereas Tolman felt that experience could suffice. This difference turned out to have little significance. Consider, for example, the latent learning experiment by Tolman and Honzik (1930). The fact that there was some reduction in errors for the group that ran without food suggests the possibility of some minimal reinforcement, deriving perhaps from exploration of the maze itself. In Hull's view, the rats could acquire strong habits on the basis of that minimal reinforcement, but perform poorly because of inadequate incentive. The introduction of a potent incentive, food, would then permit the strong habit to emerge into performance. In the absence of an unambiguous specification of what events are to be counted as reinforcers, there is little to choose between an apparently rigid, mechanistic reinforcement theory and a loosely stated expectancy theory in their ability to account for almost any observations.

B. F. Skinner

The fourth major systematist of this period was Skinner (1904–), whose book, *The Behavior of Organisms* (1938), proposed a different sort of approach. Rather than outlining a few abstract principles, such as association by contiguity or reinforcement by drive reduction, or invoking constructs such as habit or expectancy that did not have the dimensions of behavior, Skinner concentrated on the experimental analysis of various functions of stimuli in relation to particular responses. He was the first to make a clear distinction between the roles of the *CS* and *US* in classical- or respondent-conditioning experiments and the stimuli that preceded and followed responding in instrumental or operant conditioning. Similarities and differences between classical and operant conditioning are discussed at length in Chapter 3; here, a brief comparison will suffice.

In the Pavlovian situation, food presentation (the *US*) is contingent only on the prior occurrence of the *CS,* not on the subject's behavior. Moreover, the experimenter is not free to study any response arbitrarily, but is limited to responses similar to those elicited by food, such as salivation. By contrast, in the Thorndikean situation, the experimenter is free to select any response the subject is capable of executing, but cannot present food until the response occurs. Thus, the two conditioning procedures are *operationally* different.

Thorndike's work with the puzzle box involved some stimuli that were present only before and during the occurrence of the response, thus bearing the same sort of temporal relation to latch operation as the Pavlovian *CS* did to salivation. One of Skinner's major contributions was the development of an experimental method that did not necessarily involve stimuli of this sort, and at the same time permitted behavior to occur continuously in time without intervention by the experimenter. Instead of arranging that each response would terminate a trial by allowing escape to food, Skinner kept his subjects enclosed in chambers equipped with levers that could be pressed repeatedly. The only stimulus event that the experimenter could specify was the food pellet that followed lever-pressing. Otherwise, the situation was constant before and after the lever-press, so that there was no antecedent stimulus analogous to the *CS,* and reinforcement was obviously contingent only upon the occurrence of the response.

Skinner's procedure could easily be extended to approximate the Thorndikean situation by arranging that some additional stimulus, such as a light, could be presented whenever food reinforcement was available for lever-pressing. The light was off during periods of nonreinforcement, with the subject remaining in the chamber throughout. In such a situation, onset of the light could be viewed not as eliciting the response, but rather as setting the occasion for reinforcement of the response. Skinner termed stimuli serving functions of this sort *discriminative stimuli*. In the original Thorndike puzzle-box procedure, the stimuli associated with the box could also be viewed as setting the occasion for reinforcement; the fact that the response could not occur at other times, because the subject was not in the box, was incidental.

In Skinner's system, the notion of reinforcement was defined empirically by the observation that certain stimuli reliably served to increase the frequency of the response that preceded their presentation. The question of their other properties was left open. In contrast to Hull's position, drive was not viewed as a state of the organism necessary for reinforcement, but simply as a shorthand designation for the effects of food deprivation, for example, one of which was to increase the rate of food-reinforced responding. Skinner also provided one of the earliest demonstrations of *conditioned reinforcement*, showing that the stimulus that set the occasion for food reinforcement could serve as a reinforcer in its own right.

Thus, a given environmental event could function in various ways in Skinner's system, depending on its relations to behavior. Food, for example, could be viewed as an *eliciting stimulus* for the salivation that followed its presentation, and at the same time as a *reinforcing stimulus* for an operant response that produced food. In like fashion, a light that set the occasion for food reinforcement could serve not only as a *discriminative stimulus* for the food-reinforced response, but also as a *conditional stimulus* eliciting salivation because it preceded food, and perhaps as a *conditioned reinforcer* as well for some other response that produced the light. These various functions of environmental events could combine in complex ways to determine behavior.

Another of Skinner's experimental contributions was the exploration of intermittent reinforcement—that is, conditions under which only certain responses were reinforced, according to some rule.

For example, one might arrange that a response would be followed by food only after a fixed number of unreinforced responses (a fixed-ratio schedule), or that the first response to occur after a set period of time from the preceding reinforcement would be followed by food (a fixed-interval schedule). Skinner accounted for the different effects of schedules of this sort in part by reference to the discriminative function of the lapse of time between responses or reinforcements. This sort of analysis is considered in Chapter 6.

Two-factor learning theory

Distinctions between respondent and operant conditioning were also being forced by parallel developments in the study of *avoidance behavior,* which had its roots in the research of V. M. Bekhterev (1857–1927). In a representative experimental situation, a warning signal would be arranged to precede a shock by a few seconds. If the subject responded by running within that period, the signal would go off and shock would not occur. If, however, the subject delayed too long, shock would be presented and running would be necessary to escape it. It was easy to confuse the situation with a true Pavlovian conditioning experiment: The signal could be viewed as the *CS,* shock as the *US,* running as the *UR,* and anticipatory running when the *CS* came on as the *CR,* which of course was physically similar to the *UR.* However, there were several possible sources of confusion here. When shock was presented and the subject ran, was running elicited by the shock in reflexive fashion, or reinforced (negatively) by termination of the shock? Similarly, did anticipatory running occur because of the contingency between the signal and shock, as in classical conditioning, or because of the consequences of running, namely, offset of the signal and avoidance of the shock?

Careful experimentation led to a separation of these factors: Some studies required a different response to avoid shock from the response that was required to escape from shock, while other studies compared the avoidance situation with a true classical-conditioning procedure in which anticipatory responding did not avoid the shock. This research led to the statement of the two-factor theory of avoidance behavior (Mowrer, 1947). Classical conditioning was indeed taking place in the avoidance experiment, Mowrer argued, but not with respect to the avoidance response itself. Rather, the emotional responses elicited by the shock (fear), were classically conditioned to the warning signal. The "avoidance" response was then reinforced, when it occurred, by the termination of the fear-producing signal; the actual avoidance of the shock was more or less incidental. The history and current status of this research are discussed in Chapter 7, and the evaluation of emotional processes is considered in Chapter 8.

Mowrer (1960) has generalized his thinking to incorporate positive-reinforcement procedures as well as negative reinforcement, and Rescorla and Solomon (1967) have recently reviewed the pertinent experimental work and proposed a further theoretical extension of the two-factor approach to the understanding of behavior. The distinctions between the procedures of classical and operant conditioning, and their combined effects on behavior, are treated in a number of the following chapters.

The problem of motivation

A final theoretical issue that merits brief consideration here has to do with the systematic status of motivation in the study of behavior. Apparently, the need for motivational constructs such as instinctive urges or drives arose because the stimuli that occasioned behavior could not obviously account for its vigor, although they might account for its direction. It was recognized quite early in the study of instinctive behavior that the eliciting stimuli did not actually provide the energy for the responses, because low stimulus intensities could trigger activities involving considerable effort over long periods of time. Thus, early theorizing about instinct, for example by Lorenz (1950), included the notion that energy specific to various forms of behavior could be stored within the organism. This energy could then be released by appropriate stimuli (see Chapter 9 for further discussion of energy theories of instinct).

In like fashion, learned behavior was said to be energized by drives based on deprivation of substances necessary for survival, or by painful stimulation. For example, in Woodworth's (1918) view, the presence of a drive state led to a heightened level of activity; the function of environmental stimuli was to channel this activity into a form that had been reinforced in the past. Thus, the degree of vigor observed in behavior could be ascribed to organismic factors (motivation) other than the relations between antecedent stimuli, responses, and their consequences (learning).

This separation between learning and motivation was difficult to maintain, however. In the Hullian system, for example, deprivation was said to affect behavior through several mechanisms. First, it increased general levels of activity (as in Woodworth's notion of drive as a source of energy); second, it produced the drive state that was necessary for reinforcement by drive reduction; and, finally, it produced internal stimuli that constituted a part of the total environmental stimulation acting when a response was reinforced. These latter functions of drive made it enter into the formation, as well as the energizing, of habits.

As noted briefly earlier, the arrangement of particular relations between behavior and reinforcement could also be interpreted as motivational. In Skinner's (1938) work with free-operant lever-pressing in rats, it was possible to arrange for forceful responding simply by making food reinforcement contingent upon such responding. Thus, the apparent energy exhibited in some situations need not be traced to sources within the subject (see Chapter 6).

Finally, recent formulations of motivation have made extensive use of the notion of learned motivational processes. For example, stimuli that regularly precede reinforcers can acquire the capacity to affect operant behavior, even though there is no specific history of association between the measured operant and the stimulus-reinforcer pairing (see Chapters 4, 5, and 8). Because the effects of stimulus-reinforcer pairings are general to many different behaviors and situations, they have much in common with the general energizing functions commonly identified with motivation. However, their effects are clearly based on a particular history involving the pairing of a stimulus and a reinforcer, much as in Pavlovian conditioning. Whatever the difficulties in separating *a priori* notions of motivation from learning, the general effects of deprivation and stimulation on behavior are important research topics; some representative work in this area is treated in Chapter 8.

OVERVIEW OF THIS VOLUME

In various ways, the chapters that follow address the issues that were raised in this brief historical survey. Chapter 2 discusses the basic procedures that are followed and the observations that are made in the study of behavior. It also stresses the importance of the way in which we speak about behavior. Some studies using certain procedures have traditionally been discussed as examining "learning"; others have not. Perhaps distinctions that arose for historical reasons will fade away if emphasis is placed on continua relating various procedures for presenting stimuli in relation to responses, together with the behavioral relations obtained.

Other chapters follow in this vein. Chapter 3 deals in detail with respondent conditioning and questions whether there is any basis in fact for asserting the existence of a separate process of respondent conditioning. It introduces the notion of the discriminated operant as a behavioral unit, defined by the joint occurrence of antecedent stimulus, response of the organism, and consequent stimulus. This may be the appropriate unit to examine in Pavlovian conditioning. Chapter 4 extends the treatment of the discriminated operant, considering first the complex ways in which antecedent stimuli may control behavior, and then proceeding to show how the stimulus-control paradigm may incorporate certain problems in the areas of attention, perception, and concept formation.

Because so little of the extra-experimental behavior of organisms appears to depend directly on primary reinforcers, the analysis of conditioned reinforcement and a knowledge of its potential generality is essential. Chapter 5 reviews findings in this area from a variety of experimental settings, relating them to the stimulus control of operant behavior and to the Pavlovian conditioning paradigm.

Chapter 6 is concerned with a factor that not only exerts powerful control over behavior, but also can dramatically alter the effects of antecedent stimuli: the schedule of reinforcement. As such, the schedule of reinforcement is not only a useful tool or a parameter of research, but a factor as powerful as the fundamental processes of conditioning and stimulus control.

Although most of the research discussed in earlier chapters involves positive reinforcers, much of life outside the laboratory involves punishment and the avoidance of aversive events. Chapter 7 explores the research and theory in these areas in some detail, concluding that in general punishment is like positive reinforcement in its effects, but opposite in direction. This conclusion, together with current interpretations of avoidance behavior, suggests that there is no need to retain the two-factor theory of avoidance behavior. This is not, however, to say that reinforcing or aversive stimuli do not have effects beyond reinforcement itself. Chapter 8 considers a broad range of phenomena that may accompany strong stimulation, commonly termed *emotional behaviors,* and relates them to phenomena that are said to involve motivation. It argues that there is little advantage in the distinction between or even in the retention of these broad behavioral categories.

Chapter 9 approaches the analysis of behavior from the standpoint of ethology, which concentrates on instinctive behavior in its natural setting. The study of behavior modification in relation to natural, species-specific behaviors may shed some light on apparently paradoxical instances of conditioning, reinforcement, and stimulus control. The concepts of emotion and motivation are also examined here from the ethological viewpoint. Chapter 10 reviews selected topics and serves as a reminder that even in the simplest of settings a number of factors operate in combination to determine behavior.

EXPERIMENTAL METHODS AND REPRESENTATIVE PROBLEMS

The essence of psychological experimentation is the precise specification and control of a situation such that one or a few aspects of the situation can be varied—the independent variables—and one or a few aspects of behavior can be measured—the dependent variables. The outcome of a well-conducted experiment is one or more relationships showing how the dependent variables are determined by the independent variables. If other aspects of the situation vary in some systematic way with changes in the independent variables, the variables are said to be confounded, and the results cannot be ascribed unambiguously to the independent variables. Because behavior is complexly determined by a number of factors, it may be quite difficult to isolate just one variable for study. We now consider a few procedures for isolating the effects of a variable and for understanding its operation in conjunction with other variables.

In some kinds of research, it is common practice to select two independent groups of subjects, drawn at random from a single population, such as a colony of laboratory rats or the students in an introductory psychology class. The subjects are then exposed to situations that are identical in all respects except one: the presence of the independent variable for the experimental group, and its absence for the control group. It is assumed that uncontrolled variables that might affect the outcome, such as individual differences in genetic constitution or environmental history, are distributed equally over the two groups as a result of the random assignment of subjects. Thus, the only systematic difference between groups is the independent variable. The effect of that variable is assessed by statistical comparison of the values of the dependent variables obtained for the experimental and control groups.

Elaborations of this kind of research involve more than two independent groups, where each is exposed to a different value of the independent variable. Work of this sort can indicate not merely whether the variable affects behavior, on the average, but how the effect changes as a function of its experimentally arranged value. Another elaboration of this basic design involves several values of two or more different independent variables. The results of such research can show how the effect of one independent variable depends on the value of another variable. Information of this sort is often essential to reconcile apparently conflicting outcomes of separate, single-variable experiments.

A rather different sort of research design involves the use of a small number of subjects, each of which is exposed successively to all values of the independent variables. Here, one achieves control over individual differences and historical factors by deliberate selection and systematic variation, rather than by randomization across groups. By and large, the use of randomly selected independent groups is most appropriate for the study of variables that affect transitions in behavior, such as the acquisition of a new performance, because a single subject cannot twice acquire the same new performance: The first acquisition experience will obviously affect the second. On the other hand, single-subject designs are especially useful when the research is concerned with the effects of a variable on a stable level of performance. The advantages and limitations of these various kinds of research cannot be discussed in the abstract. Therefore, we will select a few representative problems that illustrate various methods and that raise questions about measurement and the interpretation of data.

Reflexive fighting in response to aversive stimulation

This section will describe an experimental analysis of fighting by paired rats conducted by Ulrich and Azrin (1962). A number of earlier investigators had observed shock-elicited fighting in rats; Ulrich and Azrin examined its determinants in detail. Let us begin with the authors' description of a typical scene in their experimental chamber:

When the Sprague-Dawley rats were first placed in the experimental chamber, they moved about slowly, sniffing the walls, the grid, and occasionally each other. At no time did any fighting behavior appear in the absence of shock. Soon after shock was delivered, a drastic change in the rats' behavior took place. They would suddenly face each other in an upright position, and with the head thrust forward and the mouth open they would strike vigorously at each other [pp. 511–512].

The authors construed fighting as reflexive, because it did not occur before onset of a shock, and when it occurred it was highly stereotyped across individuals, with no need for previous training.

The experimenters recorded a fighting response whenever they observed any striking or biting movements by either animal while the rats were in the stereotyped fighting posture. Two observers kept independent records of fighting, and they agreed on the number of fights within 5 percent. Thus, although the response had to be defined on the basis of human judgment, it is clear that the judgment could be made with consistency.

In this situation, then, the concept of *response* refers to a class of movements, all instances of which lead to an observer's judgment of the fighting posture and striking or biting. Although the *stimulus,* shock, is always the same from the experimenter's standpoint, it is quite likely to vary from one presentation to the next when measured across the bodies of the rats. This is because variations in the way in which the rats stand on the grid will affect their electrical resistance. Such variation is inevitable in the presentation of shock to freely moving animals, although it may be minimized by appropriate design of the shock circuit. In any event, it is the correlation of shock presentations and fighting responses that defines the reflex. One may ask whether there are some experimental variables that affect the likelihood that a response will occur, given a stimulus. Shock intensity is one obvious variable; other variables investigated by Ulrich and Azrin included the frequency of shock presentation and the size of the chamber.

In their investigation of shock intensity, Ulrich and Azrin exposed three pairs of rats to various intensities of shock, always at a frequency of 20 shocks per minute. Shock duration was always 0.5 seconds. Fighting behavior was recorded during 10-minute sessions, where several such sessions were given at each intensity and the sequence of intensities was varied. In this way, the investigators could assess the effects of shock intensity independently of the order in which different intensities were presented. The dependent variable, the proportion of shocks eliciting fighting, is shown as a function of shock intensity for one pair of rats in Figure 1.3A. The data, which are typical of those

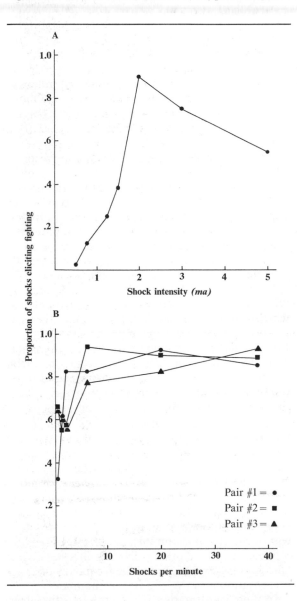

for all three pairs, show that a 2-milliampere (*ma*) shock is optimal for eliciting fighting. The authors noted that lower intensities did not appear to be sufficiently aversive, while higher intensities often evoked other behavior, such as biting at the floor grids, running, or jumping, that was incompatible with fighting.

The optimal shock value was used in the authors' work on shock frequency. They scheduled six different frequencies of shock presentation: 0.1, 0.6, 2.0, 6.0, 20.0, and 38.0 per minute. Three pairs of rats were studied separately, with each shock frequency scheduled during each of three 10-minute sessions. The frequencies were presented in an irregular order, as in the study of shock intensity, to avoid confounding the order of determinations with factors such as sensitivity to shock that might change systematically during continued exposure to the situation. The proportion of shocks eliciting fighting is plotted as a function of shock frequency in Figure 1.3B for each pair of subjects individually. Note that the proportion of shocks eliciting fighting is constant above six shocks per minute. There is a systematic decrease at lower values, but this must be viewed with some caution: Because the sessions were fixed at 10 minutes, the number of opportunities to observe elicitation of the reflex decreased as shock frequency decreased. Thus, the data obtained with infrequent shock may be unreliable simply because they represent small samples. Also, it may be that the first few shocks are relatively ineffective, and some "warm-up" is necessary before fighting is reliably observed. If so, the lower overall probability of fighting at low shock frequencies would result simply because the first few shocks constitute a large proportion of total shocks. To control for this possibility, one might arrange for equal numbers of shocks, presented at different frequencies, in which case there would be large differences in session length, a factor that might also affect fighting.

In the nature of things, the factors of session length and number of shocks must be confounded with shock frequency; that is, one cannot hold both of these specifications of the experiment constant while varying shock frequency. The only way to control for session length and number of shocks is to evaluate their effects directly. Warm-up effects should be visible through close scrutiny of the data for the first few shocks of each session. No warm-up effects are evident in Ulrich and Azrin's records, so this factor can probably be discounted. If the probability of fighting does not change over the course of a protracted session, then variations in

Figure 1.3 Panel A: The proportion of shocks eliciting fighting by a pair of rats, as a function of shock intensity. Shocks were always presented at a rate of 20 per minute. Panel B: The proportion of shocks eliciting fighting as a function of shock frequency. Shock intensity was always 2.0 *ma*. Data are plotted separately for three pairs of rats. (After Ulrich & Azrin, 1962.)

session length can also be discounted. In a separate part of their study, Ulrich and Azrin delivered shock at the rate of 38 per minute for 7.5 hours, and observed virtually no change in the probability of fighting until some 2 hours had elapsed. Thus, data for 10-minute sessions are evidently representative of both initial and prolonged performance, and the only possible question about the functions of Figure 1.3B is the reliability of the data at low shock frequencies. The fact that all three pairs of rats give substantial agreement in their functions, despite the small number of observations per animal at low shock frequencies, suggests that the function form is in fact quite reliable throughout its range.

Given that the data are accepted as portraying the relation between shock frequency and probability of fighting, the question of interpretation arises. Why, it may be asked, does this sort of decrease occur at low shock frequencies? In a science of behavior, the answer to such a question must refer to some other independent observations of behavior that covary with the data to be explained or that can be adduced from other experiments. In this case, Ulrich and Azrin made independent observations that gave some insight into these data Describing the activities of their rats at low shock frequencies, the authors remark:

> Visual observation of the rats revealed that shortly after a shock was presented, the subjects slipped out of the fighting posture and assumed other positions. It was also apparent that fighting in response to shock was more likely if the animals were facing each other at the moment of shock delivery. Thus, the probability of fighting appeared to be lower at the lower frequencies of shock presentation because the rats were at some distance from each other [p. 513].

Observations of this sort suggested the exploration of another aspect of the situation that might alter the positions of the animals relative to each other when shock was presented, namely, the size of the test chamber. Ulrich and Azrin studied fighting by a pair of rats in square chambers ranging from 6 inches by 6 inches, up to 2 feet by 2 feet, using a 2-*ma* shock presented 20 times per minute. They found that the rats fought after 90 percent of the shocks in the smallest chamber, consistent with the observation above, and that the probability of fighting decreased systematically to only 2 percent in the largest chamber. In the authors' words,

> When the rats were only a few inches apart, the shock was likely to cause them to turn and lunge

at each other. At the larger distances, the rats largely ignored each other [p. 517].

Ulrich and Azrin (1962) went on to explore a number of other factors that were related to the occurrence of elicited fighting, including the sex and strain of the rats. Stereotyped fighting was elicited regardless of sex and strain, except that the Wistar strain appeared to be more sensitive to shock than the others studied. The investigators also examined elicited fighting in other species. They observed similar fighting in hamsters (although at a lower shock level, 0.75 *ma*) as in rats; guinea pigs, on the other hand, never exhibited the fighting posture or attack movements. In interspecies pairings, rats were observed to fight with hamsters, but when a rat was paired with a guinea pig, the rat did all the fighting.

Ulrich and Azrin also explored other techniques for delivering electric shock. In the foot-shock situation, both animals necessarily received shock at the same time. In order to shock one animal separately, the investigators implanted electrodes under the skin of one of a pair of rats. When shock was presented, the stimulated rat typically assumed the fighting posture and attacked his unstimulated partner; often, the unshocked rat then assumed the same posture and counterattacked. The authors noted that the full-blown fighting response occurred less often under these conditions than when both rats were shocked.

Finally, the authors investigated other forms of aversive stimulation, including intense heat, cold, and loud noise. They observed fairly frequent fighting when a pair of rats was placed on a preheated floor, but there was no evidence of fighting when the rats were placed on a floor cooled with dry ice, nor in the presence of either continuous or pulsed noise. It would be improper to conclude that fighting cannot be elicited by intense cold or noise: As we have seen in the case of electric shock, fighting depends on the intensity of stimulation, and the failure to obtain fighting with intense cold or noise may have resulted from a failure to approach the optimum intensity level for those forms of stimulation.

All in all, the work of Ulrich and Azrin (1962) stands as a model for the systematic exploration of an intriguing and important behavioral phenomenon. Later research by Ulrich, Azrin, and their co-workers is discussed in Chapter 8, in connection with the experimental analysis of emotion. Aggressive behavior has also been studied extensively by ethologists (cf. Chapter 9), who are primarily concerned with the role of aggression in courtship, mating, dominance, and territoriality in natural settings—in a word, with aggression as an instinctive behavior. The study of aggression in natural settings provides insights into the role of aggression in the evolution of a species and its adaptation to a particular environment, just as laboratory analysis of the sort described above helps us understand the factors that affect aggression within the lifetime of a single organism. Although these approaches may use different methods and different vocabularies in describing their findings, they complement each other in the attempt to understand the determinants of aggression.

Resistance to extinction after regular or intermittent reinforcement

In the experimental study of learning, it is often the case that responding is measured under one uniform set of conditions and is related to some variable to which the subjects were exposed at an earlier time. Although the independent variable is not in effect when the dependent variable is measured, the specification of past conditions is the proper independent variable determining present behavior if all other objective conditions are constant. To illustrate this kind of work, we will consider several experiments that employed different methods for the study of a phenomenon that has intrigued psychologists for over three decades, namely, the fact that operant (or instrumental) responding persists longer when reinforcement is discontinued after intermittent reinforcement than if every response was reinforced during conditioning. The same general finding appears in research on respondent (or classical) conditioning, despite some important differences between respondent and operant behavior during acquisition with intermittent reinforcement (see Chapter 3).

The so-called partial reinforcement extinction effect (*PRE*) has both theoretical and practical importance. In theory, it would seem reasonable that the more consistently a response was reinforced, the stronger it would be; and, moreover, the tendency for the response to persist during extinction would seem a reasonable indication of its strength. Thus, the effect of intermittent reinforcement on resistance to extinction directly contradicts theoretical expectation and as such has been of intense interest to learning theorists.

In practical situations involving behavior modification, the persistence of intermittently reinforced behavior is also important. If we make use of reinforcement techniques in a therapeutic setting to establish some important form of behavior—say, cooperation by an emotionally disturbed child—we do not wish the continuation of that form of behavior to depend crucially on maintained extrinsic reinforcement. Rather, we want to arrange that the behavior will persist long enough outside the therapeutic setting so that the natural advantages of cooperation can act to maintain the behavior. Laboratory analysis of the factors responsible for persistent responding after the termination of reinforcement, and for the generalization of persistence to other stimulus situations, is therefore of general significance.

Two different kinds of procedures have been employed extensively in the study of the *PRE*. One is essentially a version of the Thorndike (1898) puzzle-box procedure, in which the response is simply running from one end of a runway to the other. The subject, a rat, is placed in a start-box at one end of the runway and then released when the experimenter raises a gate. It runs to the other end of the runway, where food may be provided in a goal-box; if there is no food, the rat is confined there briefly. After completion of this sequence, the animal may be returned to the start-box for another trial, or to its home cage to await its next scheduled run. In this *discrete-trials* procedure, then, the experimenter has strict control over the opportunity to run, and the usual measure of behavior is the speed of running.

The second sort of procedure involves the *free-operant* situation originated by Skinner (1938). Typically, a rat is placed in a chamber with a lever continuously available. Depression of the lever may be followed by delivery of a food pellet or not, according to some schedule of reinforcement. Unlike the discrete-trials procedure, the subject may respond at any time, and the response itself is of brief duration. The usual measure of behavior is the rate of lever-pressing—that is, the number of presses made in a fixed period of time. Other dimensions of responding, such as the time it takes to depress and then release the lever, are ignored.

In view of the considerable differences in procedures and measures, it is noteworthy that intermittent reinforcement has similar effects on resistance to extinction in these settings. That is, a group of animals trained with food on only some fraction of the trials in a runway will on the average run more rapidly during the course of a number of extinction trials than a group trained with reinforcement on every trial. Likewise, a group of

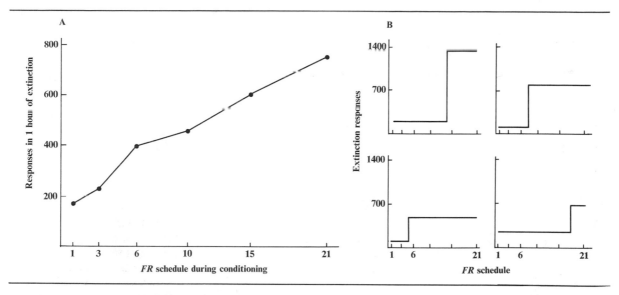

Figure 1.4 Panel A: The average number of responses made during 1 hour of extinction by groups of rats trained on different fixed-ratio *(FR)* schedules. (After Boren, 1961.) Panel B: Some hypothetical functions for individual subjects that, if averaged, would yield a continuous increasing function of the sort exhibited in A.

animals trained in a free-operant setting with food following only some fraction of their responses will make more responses during a fixed period of extinction than a group trained with reinforcement following every response. We will first consider a systematic experiment in the latter setting.

Boren (1961) trained six groups of six rats each on different fixed-ratio *(FR)* schedules of food reinforcement; that is, schedules that arranged reinforcement for a single response after a fixed number of unreinforced responses. Initially, all rats were food deprived and trained to press a lever that presented food following every response until they had received 20 reinforcements. Then, five groups were shifted to fixed ratios of 3 responses per reinforcement for 40 reinforcements, while the remaining group continued to receive food after every response *(FR-1)*. Finally, four groups were shifted to schedules requiring 6, 10, 15, or 21 responses per reinforcement. Each group obtained 500 reinforcements under its final schedule. The relation between terminal performance and the value of the fixed ratio is discussed in Chapter 6; our interest here centers on the rates of responding by these different groups after reinforcement was discontinued. The average number of responses made by each group during 1 hour of extinction showed a systematic increase in relation to the size of the ratio during training; that is, the more responses the subjects had made per reinforcement, the more

responses they emitted in a fixed period of time when reinforcement was discontinued. The relationship is graphed in Figure 1.4A.

Although the order in the average data is gratifying, this relationship may not tell us much about the form of the function for individual subjects, because of the nature of the data-averaging process. Consider the following hypothetical possibility: For all rats, there are only two levels of responding during extinction. Below some value of the fixed ratio, they emit some fairly small number of responses, and above that value of the fixed ratio they emit some other, substantially larger number. The value of the fixed ratio at which the transition occurs from the lower to the higher number of responses varies randomly across rats. Figure 1.4B illustrates four step-functions of this sort. If one samples from these hypothetical functions at high *FR* values, one will obtain a large average number of extinction responses, and if one samples at low *FR* values, the average number will be small. Sampling at intermediate *FR* values will give data from some rats below their point of transition to a high level, while other rats would be above their transition point. The average of their data would be intermediate between the samples from low and high *FR* values. Thus, a continuous average function may result from a discontinuous function with some random variation across subjects.

In order to assess the nature of the relationship

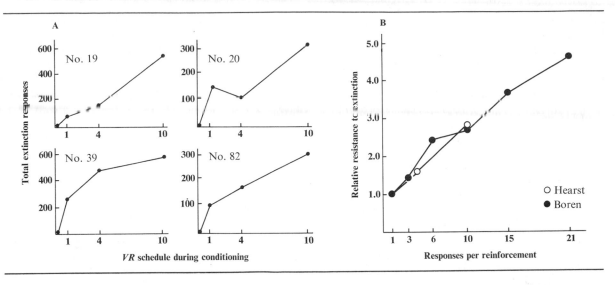

Figure 1.5   Panel A: Number of responses during extinction for four individual pigeons, where each variable-ratio *(VR)* schedule was associated with a distinctive key color during conditioning, and then responses were counted separately in the presence of each color during extinction. (From Hearst, 1961.) Panel B: A comparison of the Boren and Hearst data, expressed in terms of resistance to extinction after training with each ratio schedule, relative to resistance to extinction after regular reinforcement. For both studies, the ratio schedules have been expressed as responses per reinforcement. (Adapted from panel A and Figure 1.4A.)

for individual subjects, it is necessary to explore situations in which a single subject is exposed to each of several different values of the independent variable. An early study of this sort was reported by Hearst (1961). He used four pigeons as subjects and trained them to peck a lighted response key with different variable-ratio *(VR)* schedules of reinforcement arranged in the presence of different key colors. (In variable-ratio schedules, unlike fixed-ratio schedules, the number of responses per reinforcement varies unpredictably from one reinforcement to the next.) Every key-peck was reinforced when the key was one color. When the key was lighted a second color, a variable ratio of four responses was required for reinforcement, and when the key was a third color, a variable ratio of ten responses per reinforcement was in effect. Responses were never reinforced in the presence of a fourth color. Different colors were correlated with these schedules for different subjects, to control for the effects of key color per se. Each color remained on until five reinforcements were obtained, except for the color signaling nonreinforcement, which remained on for 2 minutes. The chamber was darkened for 1 minute between presentations of the different key colors. Each color was presented five times, in an irregular order, during each of 17 sessions. Then, food reinforcement was terminated

and responding during extinction was examined by presenting each of the four key colors in an irregular order for 30-second periods, separated by 10-second periods of darkness. Thus, Hearst's procedure ensured that the subjects would receive equal numbers of reinforcements in the presence of each key color during training, and that equal amounts of time would be available for responding to each color during extinction. This is exactly analogous to Boren's study, which equated numbers of reinforcements for independent groups and then measured extinction responding during a fixed period of time.

Hearst's extinction data were quite clear; as Figure 1.5A shows, each of his four pigeons exhibited an increasing function relating the number of responses to a particular color during extinction to the value of the *VR* schedule correlated with that key color during training. Indeed, Hearst's results are strikingly similar to Boren's findings. To show this in a way that equates for differences in levels of responding across the two studies, the average data for each study have been transformed by dividing the number of responses made during extinction after training on the different intermittent schedules by the number made after training with regular reinforcement. The resulting measure is the resistance to extinction following intermittent reinforcement relative to that following regular reinforcement. Both Hearst's and Boren's data are plotted in Figure 1.5B. The agreement between the results of these studies suggests that, at least in the free-operant situation with ratio schedules of reinforcement, the function for individual subjects trained on each of several schedules is substantially identical to that based on averaged data for independent groups.

As indicated at the beginning of this section, the *PRE* has also been demonstrated in discrete-trial research with rats running in runways. As an example of the systematic exploration of resistance to extinction in the runway, we will consider a study by Wagner (1961) that used separate groups to examine the *PRE* in relation to the duration of training and amount of reinforcement. Wagner employed a 33-inch runway and obtained separate measures of the time required to leave the start-box, running time in the next few inches, and time to enter the goal-box. On reinforcement trials, the rats found food in the goal-box and were allowed 20 seconds to eat. For those groups trained with intermittent reinforcement, food was omitted on 50 percent of the trials, and the rats were simply confined in the goal-box for 20 seconds. Trials were given at the rate of one per day—a drastic difference from the free-operant situation in which successive responses could occur within a fraction of a second. Following training, all rats were given 32 extinction trials, also at the rate of one per day.

Wagner ran eight separate groups of 16 rats each, where each group experienced a unique combination of the independent variables: duration of training, amount of reinforcement, and intermittency of reinforcement. This is known as a factorial design, and it is commonly used to evaluate the interdependence of several variables in the determination of performance. The conditions for the various groups are schematized in Table 1.1.

During the course of training, the different groups achieved quite different speeds in different segments of the alley. In particular, the groups trained for only 16 trials were appreciably slower on all measures than their counterparts trained for 60 trials. In order to take these differences into account, Wagner expressed the speed measures in extinction as a proportion of the speeds attained at the end of training for each group. When the extinction data were examined in this way, the same general conclusions about the effects of amount and percentage of reinforcement held regardless of training duration. Accordingly, extinction after 60 trials will serve to illustrate the

Table 1.1 Experimental Design for the Study by Wagner (1961)

	Duration of training	
	16 trials	60 trials
Regular Reinforcement (100%)	1.0 gram food	1.0 gram food
	.08 gram food	.08 gram food
Partial Reinforcement (50%)	1.0 gram food	1.0 gram food
	.08 gram food	.08 gram food

effects of those variables. Also, roughly similar effects were revealed by each of the three speed measures; accordingly, it will suffice to examine one, the speed of running the final 6 inches to the goal-box.

The course of extinction is shown in Figure 1.6A, which indicates the effects of percentage and amount of reinforcement. The standard *PRE* is indicated by the difference in the persistence of response speed for the 50 percent and 100 percent groups: For both amounts of reinforcement, the 100 percent reinforcement group slows down more rapidly than the 50 percent group. Many other runway studies have obtained similar findings. It is also clear that the difference between the 50 percent and 100 percent groups depends on the amount of reinforcement: There is a greater difference for the 1.0 gram groups than for the .08 gram groups. Thus it appears that the magnitude of the *PRE* depends on the amount of reinforcement, and for two reasons: The smaller amount of food leads to less resistance to extinction for the 50 percent groups, but to greater resistance to extinction for the 100 percent groups. In technical parlance, the amount of reinforcement is said to *interact* with the percentage of reinforcement; that is, the effect of one variable depends on the value of another variable.

To see Wagner's results in a form comparable to those of Boren (1961) and Hearst (1961), the running speeds for each group have been averaged over the course of extinction to give average speed for all 32 trials. In effect, this is what is done when freely emitted responses are counted over a long period of time, because the computation of an average rate for 1 hour ignores systematic differences in rate within that 1-hour period. Wagner's

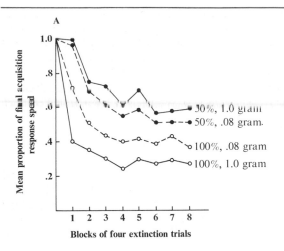

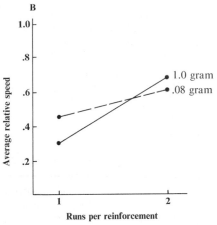

Figure 1.6 Panel A: Speed of running the final 6 inches of a runway during 32 extinction trials, expressed relative to the speed of running at the end of training, averaged for four groups of rats and distinguished by the percentage of trials on which food reinforcement was given and by the amount of food. (After Wagner, 1961.) Panel B: Average running speed throughout extinction, as a function of runs per reinforcement, separated for two amounts of food reinforcement. (Adapted from panel A.)

results are plotted in Figure 1.6B in relation to trials per reinforcement (which is analogous to responses per reinforcement in free responding), separately for the two amounts of reinforcement. In this form, the interaction between amount and percentage of reinforcement is evident in the difference in the slopes of the functions for the two amounts of reinforcement.

Whatever the effects of amount of reinforcement, Wagner demonstrated an effect in the discrete-trials runway situation with independent groups that is comparable to the effects of intermittent reinforcement in the free-operant situation, despite vastly different scheduling and measurement procedures. In the free-operant case, it appeared that there was no important difference between the functions obtained by averaging the data of different groups, or by studying single subjects. It therefore seems reasonable to expect that the *PRE* could be demonstrated with single subjects in the runway by using a method analogous to Hearst's (1961) procedure of correlating different reinforcement schedules with different stimulus conditions. A number of studies have been directed toward this question. Typically, they have arranged that each rat obtained reinforcement after every run in one runway, and after 50 percent of the runs in a distinctively different runway. Runs were alternated irregularly to control for the number of trials or of reinforcements in the two runways. Then, the subjects were run alternately in each runway during extinction. Instead of exhibiting greater resistance to extinction in the runway correlated with partial reinforcement, however, the animals typically slow down at the same rate in both alleys, in the same way as a control group trained with partial reinforcement alone (Amsel, Rashotte, & MacKinnon, 1966). If plotted in the form of Figure 1.6B, the results for the individual subjects would appear as a horizontal line, at the same level as the speed for the partial-reinforcement control group. In effect, these findings demonstrate the *generalization* of the *PRE* from one runway to another.

INTERPRETATION OF EXPERIMENTAL DATA

The analysis of behavior does not stop with the collection of data. All psychologists are interested in interpreting their work in relation to other findings and to theoretical formulations of behavior. To complete this chapter on problems and methods, it is appropriate to consider some approaches to the interpretation of data and the explanation of different outcomes. To exemplify various interpretive approaches, we will consider some accounts of the *PRE* and the difference in the results of single-subject experiments in free-operant and discrete-trial procedures.

Theoretical accounts: Frustration

According to Amsel (1962), the partial reinforcement effect may be understood by reference to frustration induced by nonreinforcement. A subject that has always experienced regular reinforcement during training encounters its first experience of nonreinforcement, and hence frustration, when extinction begins; to the extent that frustration is aversive, responding should be eliminated swiftly in this situation. By contrast, a subject that has experienced nonreinforcement during training on an intermittent schedule has, in effect, been trained to persist in the face of frustration, because further reinforcement has followed the experience of nonreinforcement. When reinforcement is terminated altogether, the resulting frustration is not new, but has been associated with reinforced responding in the past, so that responding persists.

The ability to tolerate frustration, once established in an individual subject by a history of partial reinforcement, should also make frustration after regular reinforcement less effective in reducing responding when extinction begins. Thus, an individual subject trained on both regular and partial schedules should exhibit no difference in resistance to extinction between these conditions and should give data resembling those of a subject trained with partial reinforcement alone, as found by Amsel et al. (1966).

Although it is by no means complete, the foregoing should serve to give the flavor of one of the major theoretical positions dealing with the *PRE* and related phenomena attributable to nonreinforcement. It has intuitive plausibility, and it gains strength as a scientific theory to the extent that it can be applied without contradiction to a wide range of situations, all presumed to involve the frustrative effects of nonreinforcement. However, the theory does not admit direct confirmation, because frustration does not have the dimensions of overt, measurable behavior. Instead, it is said to be a process internal to the organism that is inferred from behavior. Such inferences are gratuitous if based on only a single observation, such as the *PRE*. However, there are a number of other effects of nonreinforcement that may be viewed as independent indices of frustration, including increases in the speed or vigor of responding immediately after nonreinforcement (Chapters 5 and 6), the aversiveness of experimenter-controlled stimuli correlated with nonreinforcement (Chapters 5 and 7), and the elicitation of aggression against another organism when reinforcement is terminated (Chapter 8). To the extent that variables that alter one of these phenomena also affect the others in similar ways, the notion of a common process is supported. For example, it has been suggested that a history of intermittent reinforcement establishes frustration tolerance and thus retards extinction in a situation where regular reinforcement has been obtained. Would it also be true that a prior history of intermittent reinforcement would make aggression less likely after the termination of regular reinforcement? If so, the concept of frustration receives support; but if not, matters become more complex. The theory is unlikely to be abandoned; rather, it may be supplemented by factors that are said to modify the effects of frustration. As soon as two or more inferred processes are available to the theorist, to be combined as needed to account for data after the fact, there is little satisfaction to be derived from a successful account of any behavioral outcome. Good scientific practice requires that the properties of the hypothesized processes be stated exactly, in mathematical form if possible, and that the terms of the theory be identified unambiguously with experimental events. In the absence of such theories, the interpretation of behavior in terms of processes that cannot be evaluated directly is more likely to be valuable in suggesting additional investigations that are of interest in their own right than in confirming or refuting a particular theoretical account.

Empirical accounts: Discrimination

An alternative explanation of the *PRE*, which has been applied to the free-operant situation (Skinner, 1950), points out the similarities and differences in training and extinction conditions. Nonreinforcement would seem to be more discriminable from regular reinforcement than from intermittent reinforcement, because the latter involves some unreinforced responding and a lower density of reinforcement in time than the former. Differences in responding during extinction may be a direct reflection of the discriminability of nonreinforcement, a factor that might be expected to operate similarly for independent groups and the single subjects exposed to several reinforcement schedules during training, thus accounting for the similarity of the Boren and Hearst data in Figure 1.5B. As with frustration, an explanation in terms of the discriminability of extinction has a fair amount of plausibility, and also like frustration effects, it can be inferred from a variety of situations other than extinction, involving behavior maintained by various reinforcement schedules (Chapters 5 and 6). Unlike the construct of frustration, though, discriminability can be evaluated directly in terms of measured behavior. For that reason, it is characterized here as an empirical, rather than a theoretical, concept, although there is indeed some theorizing involved in making the connections between measurements of behavior in different situations.

How might one actually go about evaluating the discriminability of regular reinforcement and extinction in a way that permitted comparisons with the discriminability of intermittent reinforcement and extinction? A number of procedures suggest themselves, all of which involve the explicit use of a reinforcement schedule as a discriminative event indicating the availability of further reinforcement. For example, one could arrange a situation of the following sort in a pigeon chamber equipped with three keys. On each trial, the center key would be lighted for, say, 30 seconds and the bird would be trained to peck it. On half of the trials, reinforcement would be given for pecking; in separate experiments, reinforcement would be either regular or intermittent. On the other half of the trials, extinction would be in effect. Then, at the end of 30 seconds, the center key would be turned off and the side keys turned on, with reinforcement arranged for pecks on the right-hand key only if reinforcement had been given for pecks on the center key during the previous period, and with reinforcement arranged for pecks on the left-hand key if extinction had been in effect during the previous period. Thus, reinforcement or nonreinforcement for pecks on the center key would be serving a discriminative function, setting the occasion for reinforcement of pecks on the right-hand and left-hand keys, respectively. The appropriateness of the bird's pecks at the side keys would provide a direct measure of discrimination between reinforcement and nonreinforcement on the center key. If, as one might reasonably expect, pigeons would discriminate more accurately between regular reinforcement and extinction than between intermittent reinforcement and extinction, the discrimination theory of the PRE would receive direct support.[1]

Parametric analysis

Both of the foregoing approaches have in common the explanation of behavior in one situation by reference to behavior in other situations or to concepts inferred from behavior in other situations. They differ in that the discrimination account invokes measurable aspects of behavior, while the

frustration account is based on a hypothesized intervening process that does not have the dimensions of behavior. A third sort of approach involves direct analysis of aspects of experimental settings that are held constant, but are amenable to variation from one study to another: the *parameters* of the experiment.

In the research reviewed above on the PRE, we have seen that single subjects exhibit a conventional PRE after training with both regular and intermittent reinforcement in the free-operant situation, but not in the discrete-trial runway situation. One could argue that discriminability of reinforcement and extinction conditions is more potent than the generalized effects of frustration in the former case, whereas the effects of frustration predominate in the latter—an argument that might possibly receive support from other observations in ways considered earlier—or one could forego interpretation of this sort and look at parametric differences between the actual experiments. These situations differ in at least two obvious ways: the temporal and spatial properties of the response, and the temporal spacing of responses, which constitute independently manipulable parameters. For example, one may vary the temporal spacing of responses in the usual lever-pressing situation by retracting the lever after each response. As the lever-out interval becomes long and approximates the intertrial intervals commonly used in runway studies, lever-pressing data may come increasingly to resemble runway data. Alternatively, one may arrange for free responding in the runway by permitting the animal to run back and forth freely between the end boxes, giving food on a suitable schedule at either end. These conditions may give rise to data like those generated in the usual free-operant experiments with the lever-press. Some recent developments of this sort are described by Logan and Ferraro (1970).

The essence of parametric analysis is that it relies on continuous variation of parameters to produce a continuum of effects, thereby integrating diverse outcomes of different experiments. One way of conceptualizing further developments in the parametric analysis of extinction effects is to consider the slope of the function relating responding during extinction to the reinforcement schedule during conditioning as a dependent variable in its own right, and to examine the slope of this function in relation to parameters that affect it, as in the earlier discussion of Wagner's (1961) work. As this kind of analysis proceeds, the measure of behavior that serves as the dependent variable becomes

---

[1] This hypothetical procedure is based on the work of Rilling and McDiarmid (1965) on the discriminability of different fixed-ratio schedules; a related procedure is currently being explored by Michael Commons of Columbia University.

progressively more remote from moment-to-moment responding. At the same time, we become less likely to talk about the presence or absence of a particular effect, such as the *PRE*, and instead view this effect as one of several continuously related outcomes that depend systematically on experimental parameters

Finally, as the variables that determine behavioral persistence become more fully understood, the need to invoke factors other than the objective conditions under examination becomes less compelling. As the experimental study of behavior advances, we may look forward to the progressive disappearance of constructs and inferred processes that derive from historical approaches or from common sense. If the reader can suspend his preconceived views of how to interpret behavior while pursuing the topics treated in the chapters that follow, and take a fresh look at behavior in terms of relations between variables, he may derive an exciting appreciation of the complexity and order in the activities of organisms.

REFERENCES

Figure numbers appearing throughout the reference sections are those numbers used in this volume.

Amsel, A. Frustrative non-reward in partial reinforcement and discrimination learning. *Psychological Review*, 1962, **69**, 306–328.

Amsel, A., Rashotte, M. E., & MacKinnon, J. R. Partial reinforcement effects within subject and between subjects. *Psychological Monographs*, 1966, **80**(Whole No. 628).

Boren, J. J. Resistance to extinction as a function of the fixed ratio. *Journal of Experimental Psychology*, 1961, **61**, 304–308. Figure 1.4A: Copyright ©1961 by the American Psychological Association, and reproduced by permission.

Darwin, C. *On the origin of species by means of natural selection, or the preservation of the favored races in the struggle for life*. London, 1859. (Facsimile ed.: Cambridge, Mass., Harvard University Press, 1964.)

Guthrie, E. R. *The psychology of learning*. New York: Harper & Row, 1935.

Hearst, E. Resistance-to-extinction functions in the single organism. *Journal of the Experimental Analysis of Behavior*, 1961, **4**, 133–144. Figure 1.5A: Copyright © 1961 by the Society for the Experimental Analysis of Behavior, Inc., and reproduced by permission.

Hull, C. L. *Principles of behavior*. New York: Appleton-Century-Crofts, 1943.

Hull, C. L. *Essentials of behavior*. New Haven: Yale University Press, 1951.

Hull, C. L. *A behavior system*. New Haven: Yale University Press, 1952.

Logan, F. A., & Ferraro, D. P. From free responding to discrete trials. In W. N. Schoenfeld (Ed.), *The theory of reinforcement schedules*. New York: Appleton-Century-Crofts, 1970. Pp. 111–138.

Lorenz, K. The comparative method in studying innate behavior patterns. *Symposium of the Society for Experimental Biology*, 1950, **4**, 221–268.

Mowrer, O. H. On the dual nature of learning: A reinterpretation of "conditioning" and "problem-solving." *Harvard Educational Review*, 1947, **17**, 102–148.

Mowrer, O. H. *Learning theory and behavior*. New York: Wiley, 1960.

Pavlov, I. P. *Conditioned reflexes*. G. V. Anrep (Trans.) Oxford: The Clarendon Press, 1927.

Rescorla, R. A., & Solomon, R. L. Two-process learning theory: Relationships between Pavlovian conditioning and instrumental learning. *Psychological Review*, 1967, **74**, 151–182.

Rilling, M., & McDiarmid, C. Signal detection in fixed-ratio schedules. *Science*, 1965, **148**, 526–527.

Sherrington, C. S. *The integrative action of the nervous system*. New Haven: Yale University Press, 1906.

Skinner, B. F. *The behavior of organisms*. New York: Appleton-Century-Crofts, 1938.

Skinner, B. F. Are theories of learning necessary? *Psychological Review*, 1950, **57**, 193–216.

Skinner, B. F. *Beyond freedom and dignity*. New York: Knopf, 1971.

Smith, S., & Guthrie, E. R. *General psychology in terms of behavior*. New York: Appleton-Century-Crofts, 1921.

Thorndike, E. L. Animal intelligence: An experimental study of the associative processes in animals. *Psychological Review Monograph Supplement*, 1898, **2**(Whole No. 8).

Thorndike, E. L. *Animal intelligence*. New York: Macmillan, 1911.

Tolman, E. C. *Purposive behavior in animals and men*. New York: Appleton-Century-Crofts, 1932.

Tolman, E. C. The determiners of behavior at a choice point. *Psychological Review*, 1938, **45**, 1–41.

Tolman, E. C., & Honzik, C. H. Introduction and removal of reward, and maze performance in rats. *University of California Publications in Psychology*, 1930, **4**, 257–275. Figure 1.2: Originally published by the University of California Press; reprinted by permission of The Regents of the University of California.

Ulrich, R. E., & Azrin, N. H. Reflexive fighting in response to aversive stimulation. *Journal of the Experimental Analysis of Behavior*, 1962, **5**, 511–520. Figure 1.3: Copyright © 1962 by the Society for the Experimental Analysis of Behavior, Inc., and reproduced by permission.

Wagner, A. R. Effects of amount and percentage of reinforcement and number of acquisition trials on conditioning and extinction. *Journal of Experimental Psychology*, 1961, **62**, 234–242. Figure 1.6A: Copyright © 1961 by the American Psychological Association, and reproduced by permission.

Woodworth, R. S. *Dynamic psychology*. New York: Columbia University Press, 1918.

30 THE NATURE OF LEARNING

THE NATURE OF BEHAVIOR
    Observing the Organism
    Behavioral Hierarchies
    The Classification of Stimuli
    Operations and Processes

THE EFFECTS OF STIMULI
    Eliciting Stimuli and Elicited Responses
    Temporal Effects of Stimuli
    The Nature of Motivation
    The Role of Exercise

THE CONSEQUENCES OF RESPONDING
    The Law of Effect
    The Principle of Reinforcement
    Positive and Negative Reinforcement
    Reinforcement and Punishment
    Neutral Stimuli
    Extinction and Superstition

DIFFERENTIAL REINFORCEMENT AND STIMULUS
CONTROL
    Shaping: Differential Reinforcement of Successive
        Approximations
    Operants: Differentiation and Induction
    Discriminated Operants: Discrimination and
        Generalization
    Differential Elicitation

THE LIMITS OF LEARNING

SUMMARY AND CONCLUSIONS

THE NATURE OF LEARNING

A. Charles Catania
New York University

2

In the study of learning we are concerned with how an organism acquires new ways of behaving. But an organism's behavior can change in many ways, and we may be more willing to count some changes as learning than others. Thus, even the definition of learning is potentially controversial, and in psychology the study of learning has had more than its share of controversies.

One of the lesser but persistent controversies, whether single-celled organisms can learn, illustrates the problem of distinguishing learning from other kinds of behavioral changes. It was once argued, for example, that the *paramecium* could learn, because it had been shown that paramecia would congregate, after several feedings, in a region where food was presented. But this argument abated when it was found that their congregation depended on physical residues from past feedings rather than on past opportunities to eat at that place (Jensen, 1957); the paramecia congregated there because of what was there now, and not because of what had happened there in the past.

Learning in the paramecium was also argued when it was shown that paramecia avoided light after light had been paired with heat. But this argument abated, too, when it was found that paramecia avoid light after they have been heated whether or not light and heat have been presented together (Best, 1954); the paramecia avoided light because that is what heated paramecia do, and not because they had learned something about the relationship between light and heat in these experiments. The question, whether paramecia learn, has remained the same; the answer has changed from time to time.

But what kind of question is this? Certainly the behavior of an individual paramecium can change. Yet something more must be involved, because the same change in behavior might or might not be called an instance of learning, depending on the circumstances that led up to it. The question is partly about paramecia; it is also about the conditions under which we say that an organism has learned.

Consider another example. If we expose paramecia for a time to a somewhat higher temperature than the one at which they have been living, we find that they can survive still higher temperatures that otherwise would have killed them (Beale, 1953). Might not many observers speak of this adaptation to temperature by saying that the paramecia had *learned* to tolerate higher temperatures? And what could we find out about the way in which this temperature adaptation works that would convince them to speak about it differently?

There is no simple or final answer to these questions, but they illustrate that the way in which we speak about behavior deserves as much scrutiny as does the behavior that we investigate. Our aim, therefore, is twofold: We shall examine some properties of behavior, and we shall consider the ways in which these properties can be described. Except by providing examples that are usually regarded as instances of learning, we shall not attempt to define learning itself, for the phenomena of learning are varied even though they share the same name.

THE NATURE OF BEHAVIOR

When we analyze behavior, we have available for study only the properties of the organism's environment and the properties of the organism's behavior. We call these properties *stimuli* and *responses,* but neither is of interest by itself. We study stimuli to determine the ways in which they may affect responses, and we study responses to determine the ways in which they may be affected by stimuli. Thus, one of the essential tasks of the analysis of behavior is to examine the kinds of relationships that can exist between stimuli and responses, and how these relationships can come about.

Observing the organism

The first and easiest thing we can do to find out about an organism's behavior is simply to observe it (cf. ethological methods in Chapter 9). For example, if we were interested in the behavior of a rat, we could place the rat in an open space and then just watch (cf. Bindra, 1961). The rat might remain immobile for a time, but then we might see it walk or run about and occasionally rear up on its hind legs. We might notice it sometimes sniffing or perhaps licking and grooming itself; or the rat might urinate and defecate. If we had set up the necessary recording equipment, we might also be able to note changes in its respiration, heart rate, blood pressure, and other responses that are not easily observed with the naked eye.

We could inventory these and other responses, but our knowledge of the rat's behavior would be severely limited by the restricted character of its environment. If we wished to find out more, we would have to construct an environment that gave the rat more opportunity to engage in different kinds of behavior. For example, we could build an arena around which a number of compartments were located. Each of these compartments could

provide a different set of stimuli. A possible list might include a compartment containing a full food hopper; a compartment containing a drinking tube filled with water; a compartment containing an activity wheel; a compartment containing the entrance to a maze; a small empty compartment; a large empty compartment; a compartment in which the rat's entry turned on a display of lights and patterns on the wall; a compartment in which the rat's entry turned on a recording of noises at a moderate level; a compartment in which the rat's entry turned on a recording of noises at an extremely loud level; a compartment in which the rat's entry turned on a cold shower; a compartment in which the rat's entry turned on a blast of hot air; and, finally, a compartment with an electrified grid floor.

Here again we might expect to observe walking or running, licking or grooming, urination or defecation. But we would also begin to find out about the likelihood with which the rat would engage in other responses that depend more directly on specific stimuli in the environment. The rat would presumably spend some of its time eating from the food hopper, drinking from the drinking tube, running in the activity wheel, or exploring the maze. After a few days it might begin to sleep consistently in the small empty compartment, but perhaps it would spend little time in the large empty compartment. The rat might also spend some time looking and listening in the compartments with lights and with moderate-level noises. And after a few entries, it would probably rarely visit the compartments with loud noises, the cold shower, hot air, or the electrified grid.

Behavioral hierarchies

We can assume that the rat would learn what the entrance to any given compartment leads to, but our main concern would be to assess the likelihood with which the rat would expose itself to the stimuli in different compartments at various times. On this basis, we could describe the rat's behavior in terms of a *hierarchy of responses.* For example, the rat might eat at a particular time of day, and it might usually drink after eating. Thus, at that time eating would be high in the hierarchy and drinking would be next; then other responses, such as running in the activity wheel, would follow. The organization of behavior in terms of the relative likelihoods of different responses has been referred to as a *habit-family hierarchy* (Hull, 1943). As we shall see, one of the essential features of learning is the modification of the positions of different responses in such a hierarchy.

The description of behavior in terms of hierarchies restricted only to those responses we have made available still leaves out some aspects of the organism's behavior. For example, from the rat's behavior in the arena we would find out nothing about its social or its sexual behavior. To study the effects of other rats as stimuli, we would have to add more compartments, some with individual male rats, others with individual female rats, and still others with different-sized groups of rats of one or both sexes.

The classification of stimuli

Nevertheless, on the basis of the rat's behavior in the original arena we could begin to classify some of its responses in terms of the probabilities that the rat engages in them. We would find that over some period of time the rat often puts itself in a position to engage in responses such as eating, whereas it rarely, if ever, puts itself in a position to engage in the jumping and squealing produced by an electrified grid. Stimuli that have these different effects have been distinguished by different names; the former are referred to as *appetitive* or *reinforcing* stimuli, and the latter as *aversive* or *punishing* stimuli.

But such a characterization is not yet complete, because the rat may fail to expose itself to stimuli that are not aversive if those stimuli happen not to be appetitive either. Such stimuli would be referred to as *neutral*. For example, the rat may rarely enter the compartment in which lights and patterns are projected on the wall simply because it is not very likely to engage in looking at such stimuli. Our concern must be not only with the likelihood that the rat will expose itself to different stimuli, but also with the likelihood that it will terminate such exposure once it has begun. At this point, it is necessary for us to intervene; we cannot simply watch the rat. To assess the likelihood that the rat will terminate exposure to the stimuli in any given compartment, we must pick up the rat and place it successively in each compartment and observe how rapidly it leaves. We might perhaps take as a baseline—a point of reference—the time the rat takes to leave the large or the small empty compartments. Relative to this baseline, we would probably find that the rat lingers somewhat longer in the compartments with food and water, but exits much more rapidly from the compartments with loud noise or electric shock.

Our conclusion from such observations is that stimuli, and the various responses for which they provide an opportunity, do not fall neatly into a discrete threefold classification of the environment into appetitive, neutral, and aversive events; rather, the environment provides a continuum of possibilities ranging from those to which the organism is highly likely to expose itself, through those with relatively indifferent effects, to those to which the organism is not only unlikely to expose itself, but which it is highly likely to terminate if so exposed. We might also anticipate that the ordering of these events along the continuum changes from time to time, as when the status of eating changes as a function of the time elapsed since the last meal.

It is important to note that the characteristics of different stimuli cannot be specified independently of the rat's behavior. We know that food is appetitive or reinforcing only by virtue of the rat's behavior with respect to food; and we know that shock is aversive or punishing only by virtue of the rat's behavior with respect to shock. Except on the basis of our observations of behavior, we cannot say what the effects of a given stimulus will be, and we might even change the effects of a particular stimulus by manipulating its properties. For example, the rat might occasionally expose itself to noises at moderate levels in one compartment, but it might rarely expose itself to these noises at more intense levels in another compartment. Thus, we would have to conclude that noises are reinforcing, neutral, or aversive, depending on their level.

Operations and processes

We have indicated that behavior involves relationships among stimuli and responses, and we have seen that these relationships cannot be examined simply by watching an organism. We sometimes must intervene by presenting stimuli to the organism. Once we begin such intervention, we must distinguish between behavioral *operations* and behavioral *processes*. Operations are the experimental procedures that can be imposed upon behavior; processes are the behavioral effects of these procedures.

The elicitation operation

The presentation of stimuli to an organism is the simplest operation, and as a result of this operation on behavior, we may observe changes in the organism's responses. We refer to the presentation of stimuli as an *elicitation* operation, and the effect of this operation is to make particular responses more or less likely. (We will consider some of the effects of the elicitation operation in more detail later.)

The consequential operations of reinforcement and punishment

Some of the most interesting properties of behavior, however, involve not only the effect of environmental events on behavior, but also the effect of behavior on the environment. We can arrange that an organism's behavior has consequences. For example, we could present food to a hungry rat whenever the rat reared up on its hind legs, or we could present shock whenever the rat moved to a certain area of the floor. In these *consequential* operations, discussed later in the sections on reinforcement and punishment, behavior may change not simply because stimuli are presented to the organism, but rather because the stimuli are presented in some relationship to its behavior.

Stimulus-control operations

We can complicate matters even further by superimposing still another operation on elicitation, on reinforcement, or on punishment. We can arrange that the simpler operations are in effect only in the presence of some additional stimulus. We refer to such a procedure as a *stimulus-control* operation. For example, this procedure could be superimposed on elicitation by arranging that food is presented to a rat only when a buzzer sounds, or that shock is presented only when a light is on. Or the procedure could instead be superimposed on the consequential operations of reinforcement or punishment, so that responses will have consequences only in the presence of a particular stimulus: Food might be presented to a rat whenever it rears up on its hind legs, but only if it does so when a green light is on; or shock might be presented whenever the rat moves to a certain region of the floor, but only if it does so when a red light is on. As a result of the stimulus-control operation, the changes in behavior produced by the simpler operations of elicitation, reinforcement, or punishment might come to occur only in the presence of the stimuli correlated with these operations. This outcome is referred to as the behavioral process of *discrimination*.

These several operations, and the behavioral processes that result from them, constitute the main features of experiments on learning and con-

ditioning, and they provide the basic organization of the present chapter. We will first examine briefly some of the effects of the presentation of stimuli, in the elicitation operation. Then we will consider the consequential operations of reinforcement and punishment, in which stimuli are presented as a consequence of the organism's behavior. Finally, we will outline the relationship of these operations to the stimulus-control operation by way of an introduction to the more detailed coverage of some of these procedures in subsequent chapters.

THE EFFECTS OF STIMULI

When we speak of stimuli and responses, we often invoke the vocabulary of the *reflex*. We say that stimuli produce responses, or that behavior is a response to stimuli. This manner of speaking entered into our everyday language, at least in part, as an inheritance from several sources: physiology (e.g., Sherrington, 1906), the conditioned-reflex concepts of Pavlov (1927), and the early behaviorism of Watson (1919). From these sources came the notion that the reflex—the reliable production of a particular response by a specified stimulus—should be considered a unit of behavior; complex behavior and learning would then be reducible to the combination of reflex units.

Many reflexes are familiar: salivation produced by food in the mouth, the knee jerk produced by a tap on the patellar tendon, pupillary constriction produced by bright light, the startle reaction produced by a sudden loud noise, and the postural adjustments produced by a loss of support. The common feature of each of these examples is that a specified stimulus reliably produces a particular response. The reflex itself is neither stimulus nor response; rather, it is the relationship between these two events (cf. Skinner, 1931). Thus, the salivary reflex is defined by the relationship between food in the mouth and salivation. The salivary response, by itself, cannot be spoken of as a reflex, because no eliciting stimulus is specified.

Eliciting stimuli and elicited responses

The concept of the reflex had a tempting simplicity, but it was not found adequate for a thorough description of behavior. Although the contemporary view still deals with behavior in terms of the relationship between stimuli and responses, the reflex is regarded as only one specialized relationship among many. In a reflex, the presentation of a certain stimulus produces a particular response with great reliability. But the stimulus of that reflex may have different effects on other responses, and the response of that reflex may be affected differently by other stimuli. Any stimulus may raise the likelihood of some responses, lower the likelihood of others, and have no effect on still others. Any response may be made more likely by some stimuli, may be made less likely by others, and may be unaffected by still others. To specify completely the relationship between a particular stimulus and a particular response, we must state how likely the response is in the absence of the stimulus and how likely it is when the stimulus is presented.

Consider some examples. If we watch a dog for an extended period of time, we may note that it occasionally moves about, pricks up its ears, or barks. If we present food to the dog, we may see these responses cease and eating begin. If we then shock the dog's foreleg, the dog will stop eating, flex its leg, and perhaps howl. If we present a loud noise instead, the dog might again stop eating, but this time it might prick up its ears and bark. The food, the shock, and the noise simultaneously raise the likelihood of some responses and lower the likelihood of others. Some of the responses might occur with some frequency even in the absence of these stimuli, and none of the responses will necessarily occur every time a given stimulus is presented. Thus, the reflex, in which a particular stimulus raises a specified response from infrequent to virtually certain occurrence, is only one special class of stimulus-response relationship.

A more general description of behavior takes into account the observations that responses may occur with substantial frequencies even in the absence of any identifiable stimuli, and that their frequencies can be modified by stimulus presentation. At any moment in time, the available responses may be characterized in terms of a behavioral hierarchy; when a stimulus is presented, its immediate effect is to modify that hierarchy. For example, when the dog was eating, the effect of shock was to raise leg flexion and to lower eating in their relative positions in the hierarchy.

The situation can sometimes be more complicated. For example, if we give a food pellet to a food-deprived rat, the rat will first eat the pellet. It will then typically drink if water is available (Falk, 1961). Similarly, if a monkey is shocked, it will bite anything nearby into which it can sink its teeth. It will then typically manipulate objects, such as levers, that are available in its chamber (Hutchinson, Renfrew, & Young, 1971). Responses that reliably follow other responses that have been elicited are referred to as *adjunctive* behavior (Falk, 1971). These sequential patterns are additional properties of elicited behavior that must be taken into account.

In summary, then, stimulus presentations provide one operation, called *elicitation*, for modifying behavior. We can change what an organism does simply by presenting stimuli to it. To be able to say how behavior can be modified by presenting stimuli, however, it is not sufficient merely to catalog the effects of different stimuli, because these effects can vary with the number of stimulus presentations and with the spacing of these presentations in time. It is at this point that the elicitation operation becomes relevant to the study of learning: The responding produced by a stimulus at one time may depend on what has happened to the organism at an earlier time.

Temporal effects of stimuli

If we give a rat food pellets and the rat eats them quickly, we are likely to say that the rat was hungry. If we continue to deliver the pellets, the rat eats them more and more slowly until eventually it stops eating completely; at this point we may say that the rat has become satiated. The likelihood with which these stimuli (food pellets) are followed by a particular response (eating) decreases with successive stimulus presentations. This process has been called *satiation,* but it is not limited only to stimuli such as food and water that the organism actually consumes. A variety of other stimuli also have this effect on behavior. A dog will prick up its ears at the presentation of lights or sounds, but if we continue these presentations the dog soon stops responding. A cat will play with a ball of string dangled before it, but eventually the cat moves on to other things. And a child may spend a great deal of time with a new toy, but finally "the novelty wears off."

This process, the decrement in responding with repeated stimulus presentations, has been given different names depending on the stimuli involved. It has been called *satiation* with respect to stimuli that are consumed, but with respect to other stimuli it has more typically been called *adaptation* or *habituation.* Although distinctions among these terms have a long history, sometimes involving physiological concerns, it is not clear that the distinctions have behavioral significance. The phenomenon is illustrated in Figures 2.1A through 2.1C. Responding starts at a different level in each

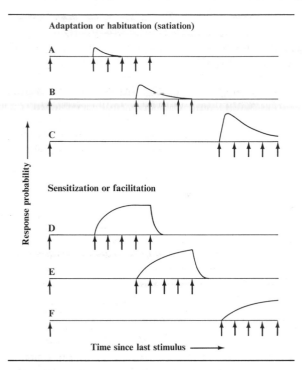

Adaptation or habituation (satiation)

Sensitization or facilitation

Response probability

Time since last stimulus

Figure 2.1 Various temporal effects of the elicitation operation. Arrows indicate stimulus presentations. Effects usually referred to as adaptation or habituation are illustrated in A, B, and C: Responding diminishes with repeated stimulus presentations (with stimuli that are consumed, such as food or water, the phenomenon is typically called satiation). Effects sometimes referred to as sensitization or facilitation are illustrated in D, E, and F: Responding increases with repeated stimulus presentations. In both cases the time since the last stimulus presentation also influences responding. In the former, in which elapsed time is sometimes called the deprivation period, responding increases as time passes without stimulus presentations; in the latter, responding decreases.

of the three examples, but in each case responding declines with successive stimulus presentations.

The process of satiation or adaptation appears to be a characteristic effect of the presentation of most appetitive or reinforcing stimuli, and perhaps also of some stimuli regarded as neutral. Other stimuli have different effects. The first presentation of an electric shock may produce less responding than later presentations (e.g., Badia, Suter, & Lewis, 1966; Hutchinson, Renfrew, & Young, 1971). This process appears to be a characteristic effect of the presentation of stimuli regarded as

aversive or punishing. This basis for distinguishing among different classes of stimuli is also supported by indirect evidence. For example, organisms in experiments involving aversive stimuli (e.g., avoidance) typically go through a warm-up period early in each experimental session; during this time, the aversive stimulus is less effective than it is later in the session.

An increase in elicited responding with successive stimulus presentations does not have a well-established name. It has sometimes been called *sensitization* (but the term has often also applied to cases in which presentations of one stimulus increase the eliciting effect of some other stimulus); the term *facilitation* may also be appropriate. The phenomenon is illustrated in Figures 2.1D through 2.1F. Responding increases at a different rate in each of the three examples, but in each case it increases with successive stimulus presentations.

The processes of adaptation and sensitization will undoubtedly be explored further in future research. For the present, it is sufficient to note that the likelihood with which a particular stimulus produces a specified response depends not only on what the stimulus is, but also on the organism's prior exposure to that stimulus.

Repeated presentations of a stimulus modify the degree to which that stimulus produces responses. But in the subsequent absence of that stimulus, the tendency to respond may return to earlier values. The rat whose eating has ceased after the consumption of many food pellets will eat again if food pellets are withheld for some period of time. The likelihood of its eating and the number of pellets it will eat before stopping depend on how much time has elapsed since it last ate. This property of stimulus presentations is intimately related to the process of satiation or adaptation. The likelihood of responding decreases with repeated stimulus presentations, but increases as time passes since the last stimulus presentation, as illustrated in Figures 2.1A through 2.1C. The operation of withholding stimuli is referred to as *deprivation*. Unfortunately, there is no term that corresponds precisely to the process that results from this operation. Available terms, such as *drive,* often imply inferred states of the organism and tend to draw attention away from the critical events that occurred in the organism's past.

Again, inverse relationships may hold for stimuli that produce sensitization rather than adaptation. For example, responses produced by shock may become less likely as time passes since the last shock (cf. Figures 2.1D through 2.1F). But, again unfortunately, there do not yet exist unambiguous data that would permit such a generalization about behavior. It would simplify the analysis of behavior if the various temporal effects described here were correlated with the appetitive and aversive categories of events that were derived from the behavioral hierarchies discussed earlier (i.e., the organism's likelihood of initiating or terminating different behaviors). But this matter also must await future experimentation.

The nature of motivation

We have indicated that response probabilities can be altered by successive stimulus presentations. This property of behavior provides another means for modifying behavior. Let us return to the rat in the arena. We might note that the rat's eating and drinking are highly likely at a particular time of day, but running in the activity wheel is less so. If, however, we remove the wheel and thereby deprive the rat of an opportunity to run in it, we may find when later presenting the wheel to the rat that it is now more likely to run than it is to eat or drink. The operation of deprivation makes it possible to alter the behavioral hierarchy at a given time. We can make running more likely than eating, or drinking more likely than running, depending on the organism's prior exposure to the stimuli in the presence of which these responses occur. Under each of these different conditions, we may describe the probabilities of different responses in terms of their status relative to other responses in the hierarchy. We shall see later that this kind of description bears on the effects of consequential operations in which responses have an effect on the environment.

In the preceding examples, the significance of stimuli was changed by the conditions under which the stimuli were presented. Such changes are the basic concern of the study of *motivation* (cf. Cofer & Appley, 1964): Stimuli may be made more or less reinforcing, or more or less aversive, depending on such factors as the time elapsed since their last presentation. The significance of stimuli, however, can be changed by operations other than deprivation. In the phenomenon called *imprinting* (see Chapter 9), for example, a stimulus acquires its significance for an organism simply by virtue of its presentation at a particular period in the organism's lifetime. A baby duckling ordinarily sees its mother during the hours after hatching and stays close to its mother thereafter; but if some other moving stimulus is substituted for the mother duck during this critical period after hatching, the duckling may later follow that stimulus rather than its mother (Hess, 1959). Once a stimulus has acquired reinforcing properties through imprinting, following may occur because it has the consequence of keeping this stimulus nearby (Peterson, 1960).

The example of imprinting is of special interest because it illustrates another effect of the elicitation operation. The account of other motivational procedures, such as physiological intervention, is beyond the scope of this chapter, but some methods for altering the significance of stimuli are treated in Chapters 5 and 8.

The role of exercise

We have outlined various effects of stimulus presentations. One last possible effect of the elicitation operation must be mentioned before we move on to the consequential operations of reinforcement and punishment. The effect is not well documented, perhaps because it has been overshadowed by the learning phenomena that we shall consider later. Yet despite the surprising paucity of evidence, it may be of fundamental significance to an analysis of behavior. Early work in learning (e.g., Thorndike, 1913) often referred to the importance of repeated occurrences of a response, described in terms of *laws of exercise* or *practice*. Although the phenomenon has been neglected, it may yet prove to be the case that the repeated production of a response by a stimulus makes that response more likely even in the absence of the stimulus. For example, in a given experimental environment a dog might at first salivate only when food is presented, but after several food presentations the dog may also salivate in the absence of food (e.g., Zener & McCurdy, 1939). Such responding has been called *spontaneous* salivation; it cannot be dealt with as a reflex, because there is no identifiable eliciting stimulus. Another example comes from experiments concerned with aversive stimuli, especially those involving avoidance. These experiments often seem designed to take advantage of the same phenomenon, as when hurdle jumping is chosen as an avoidance response with rats because shock makes rats jump; once jumping has been produced by shock, it is likely to occur at other times when shock is absent. Finally, there is evidence that the pecking of a young chick does not depend only on the eliciting conditions for or the consequences of earlier pecks, but is also affected by how much pecking the chick has already engaged in (Hogan, 1971).

It is only a supposition that this effect of repeated stimulus presentations may be a general property of behavior. If the supposition is correct, the phenomenon will eventually be described, analyzed, and formulated in terms considerably different from the classical laws of exercise or practice. Nevertheless, we cannot overlook the possibility that the elicitation of responses by a stimulus makes these responses more likely even in the absence of the stimulus. In terms that will become more familiar later, the elicitation of a response may raise the likelihood of its subsequent emission. The process, in terms of the operations necessary to produce it, is undoubtedly the simplest that can enter into instances of learning.

THE CONSEQUENCES OF RESPONDING

An organism is not passively driven by stimuli. Stimuli may affect its behavior from moment to moment, but its behavior affects the environment in turn. Merely by moving about, the organism changes the portion of the environment that it confronts. Behavior has consequences, and it is an important fact of behavior that it can be modified by its consequences. A rat that finds food at a particular location is likely to go to that place when deprived of food on subsequent occasions. A rat that encounters electric shock at another location is likely thereafter to stay away from that place.

The operations in these cases involve not simply the presentation of stimuli, but rather the presentation of stimuli in some relationship to behavior. The experimenter arranges the environment so that certain events follow upon certain responses emitted by the organism. A rat may find water in a goal-box after it has negotiated a maze; a pigeon may produce food by pecking on an illuminated disk; a monkey may have an opportunity to look at other monkeys whenever it presses a lever; a child may get candy by putting coins in a vending machine. In each of these cases responses have consequences, and these consequences may make the responses more likely in the future.

The law of effect

The effect of the consequences of responding on subsequent responding was studied experimentally by Thorndike (1898), and it was described in terms of a principle that he called the *Law of Effect*. This law underwent many revisions, but its essence was

that behavior could be strengthened by some consequences and weakened by others. The Law of Effect was based on experiments with animals in *puzzle boxes,* boxes from which the animals could escape by operating a latch. In a typical instance, a hungry cat was placed inside the box with a fish in view on the outside. In its varied activity inside the box, the cat eventually operated the latch and was freed to eat the fish. The conditions were repeated, and over a number of trials the cat learned to operate the latch more and more rapidly. Operat-

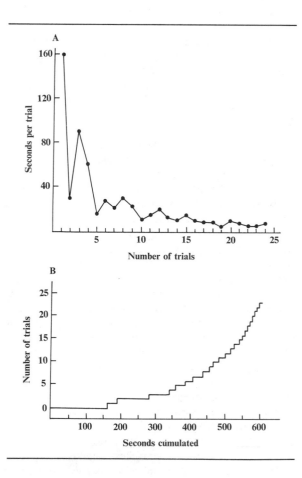

Figure 2.2 Two ways of plotting a learning curve from the performance of a cat in a puzzle box. In A, the time to escape from the box is plotted as a function of trials. In B, the time is cumulated horizontally, and successive trials are represented vertically as cumulative steps. In the first case, the performance is shown as a decreasing but variable temporal measure. In the second case, it is shown as a curve, the steepening slope of which corresponds to the successively more rapid escapes. (From Woodworth & Schlosberg, 1954.)

ing the latch began as a response of low probability, but its probability increased after several occasions on which it gave the cat the opportunity to engage in eating the fish. Sample data from the puzzle box, presented in two ways, are shown in Figure 2.2.

This process, which for a time came to be called *trial-and-error learning,* was examined with different organisms in many variations. A description of the puzzle boxes, mazes, straight alleys, jumping stands, and other apparatus (e.g., Hilgard, 1951) that were used in the study of learning is beyond the scope of the present account. Their designs were often dictated by theoretical concerns, such as whether learning was discrete or continuous, whether the organism learned motor patterns (response learning) or properties of the environment (stimulus learning), or whether the consequences of responding were necessary for learning or only made the organism perform in accordance with what it had learned in other ways. Some of these issues remain matters of experimental and theoretical concern (e.g., Goldstein, Krantz, & Rains, 1965).

Nevertheless, the essential feature of these various experimental designs was that behavior could be made more probable when it had certain consequences. The change in the probability of responding was measured in different ways by different investigators, depending on the apparatus used and the purposes of the experiment. The measures contributed to *learning curves,* graphs that showed how behavior changed in the course of an experiment: the time to escape from a puzzle box as a function of trials; the percentage of correct turns as a function of number of runs through a maze; or the proportion of animals reaching some criterion of successful performance at successive stages of training. But the shape of the learning curve depended so much on which apparatus was used and which measures were taken that no single quantitative description of the progress of learning was satisfactory.

One difficulty was that the performances studied in these learning experiments were complicated. The time course over which entries into blind alleys were eliminated as a rat learned to negotiate a maze did not of necessity show how learning proceeded at one particular choice point of the maze. An average performance measure of the progress of a group of animals was not necessarily representative of the performance of any individual animal in the group. And even a relatively simpler measure, such as the speed of running down a straight alley, could be affected by irrelevant factors such

as the direction the animal was facing when a trial began, odor trails left by other animals, the room available for the animal to slow down at the goal-box without banging its head against the wall, or the way in which the animal was handled between trials when the experimenter returned it from the goal box to the start box of the alley.

A resolution of these problems required at least two experimental innovations: the design of an apparatus in which the organism could repeatedly emit an easily specified response without intervention by the experimenter; and measurement of the responding directly in terms of its rate or frequency, rather than indirectly in terms of other measures that were derived either from complex sequences of responses or from the behavior of groups of organisms. These were the special features of a direction of research initiated by Skinner (1930, 1938; see also Skinner, 1950, 1956).

In a typical arrangement, a food-deprived rat is placed in a small chamber. From one wall protrudes a lever that can be depressed by the rat and a cup into which food pellets can be delivered. Once the rat has come to eat pellets from the cup, the apparatus is arranged so that pellet delivery depends on lever-presses: The lever-press thus provides the rat with an opportunity to eat. In an analogous arrangement for the pigeon, the chamber wall contains a small disk, or key, that can be illuminated from behind and an opening within which a tray of mixed grain can be presented to the pigeon. It then can be arranged that pecks on the key provide the pigeon with an opportunity to eat grain. Under these circumstances, the opportunity to eat can be used to raise the likelihood of the rat's lever-press or the pigeon's key-peck, just as it was used to raise the likelihood of the cat's operation of a puzzle-box latch.

Some of the advantages of these arrangements and the importance of measuring responses in terms of their frequency or rate will be considered again in Chapter 6. For the present, it will suffice to note that what all of these experimental arrangements have in common is that consequences follow upon behavior and that subsequent behavior may be modified by these consequences.

The principle of reinforcement

The lever-presses of a food-deprived rat become more frequent when these lever-presses produce food pellets. This example illustrates the principle of reinforcement, which states that responding increases when it is followed by reinforcing stimuli.

The principle is relatively simple, but during its evolution from Thorndike's early Law of Effect to its current status it has carried with it a number of problems of language and logic (Catania, 1969). These problems must be dealt with before some of the empirical properties of reinforcement can be examined.

The vocabulary of reinforcement

We first consider the vocabulary of reinforcement, which includes the term *reinforcer* as stimulus and the term *reinforcement* as operation. A reinforcing stimulus, such as the food pellet delivered to the food-deprived rat, is called a reinforcer. Reinforcement, however, is neither stimulus nor response. Instead, reinforcement is the operation of presenting a reinforcer when a response occurs. This operation is performed on responses, and we therefore speak of reinforced responses, not organisms. Thus, we may say that the rat's lever-press produced the reinforcer, a food pellet, or that the rat's lever-press was reinforced with a food pellet.

The term *reinforcement* has also often been applied to the process that follows upon the reinforcement operation, namely, the increase in the frequency of the response. This dual usage of the term, as both operation and process, complicates the way in which behavior is described. For example, the statement that a response was reinforced may mean either that the response produced a reinforcer or that the response increased in frequency as a consequence of producing a reinforcer. Although both usages are common in the experimental literature, this chapter will restrict itself to the former usage, that of reinforcement as an operation. The process that follows from this operation is concretely described in terms of changes in the frequency of a response, and thus there is little justification for substituting other terminology for a direct description in terms of changes of frequency (cf. Catania, 1968).

Even if the term *reinforcement* is restricted to an experimental operation, however, this vocabulary leads to some logical difficulties. When a response produces a stimulus and thereby increases in frequency, the stimulus is said to be a reinforcer and the response is said to be reinforced. If we are asked how we know that the stimulus was a reinforcer, we appeal to the response's increase in frequency. If we are then asked why the response increased in frequency, we say that it did so because it was reinforced. It is clear that at some point we will begin repeating ourselves; we cannot at the same time define a reinforcing stimulus in terms of its effect on behavior and the effect on behavior in terms of the reinforcing stimulus.

This problem of circularity in definition can be resolved in a number of ways (cf. Meehl, 1950). It is first important to recognize that the function of the term *reinforcement* is descriptive rather than explanatory. The term names a certain relationship between behavior and environment; it does not explain this relationship. It would be inappropriate, for example, to say that because a response increased in frequency the response must have been reinforced; the increase may have occurred for other reasons (e.g., the response may have been elicited by a stimulus). Instead, we must show that the response increased in frequency because the response produced a stimulus. Once we have done so, we may describe these circumstances by saying that the response was reinforced and that the stimulus was a reinforcer.

We may also make the assumption that the stimulus will continue to serve as a reinforcer in the future, and will reinforce other responses in other situations. This assumption, however, may be incorrect. It is conceivable that certain stimuli may be reinforcers with respect to some responses but not with respect to others. For example, if a rat's lever-pressing leads us to the conclusion that food pellets are reinforcers, it will not necessarily follow that food pellets will increase the frequency with which the rat crosses an electrified grid. Such possibilities, however, are at least susceptible to empirical test, and it remains a well-established fact that the reinforcers used in most experimental situations are effective reinforcers with respect to a variety of responses.

Properties of reinforcers

Although such considerations may buttress the logic of the vocabulary of reinforcement, this formulation still does not provide a means for identifying reinforcers independently of their effects in the reinforcement operation. Without making a particular stimulus a consequence of responding, it is not possible to say whether the stimulus will or will not be a reinforcer. Even those stimuli that have been shown to be reinforcers, such as food and water, may be effective or ineffective depending on deprivation. The delivery of food or water whenever a rat presses a lever will not raise the likelihood of the lever-press if food and water are continuously available even when this response does not occur. (Such circumstances were discussed earlier in terms of *motivation:* We can now define the study of motivation more precisely as a concern with the factors that make stimuli more or less effective as reinforcers or as punishers.)

Reinforcing stimuli exist in great variety. Some reinforcing stimuli are consumed; others are not. Some are effective only if the organism comes into physical contact with them; others are effective even at a distance. Some appear to be effective on the organism's first contact with them; others appear to acquire their reinforcing properties during the organism's lifetime (see Chapter 5). It is therefore not reasonable to expect reinforcers to be identifiable, independently of their behavioral effects, on the basis of any common physical characteristics.

It is possible, however, for the reinforcing properties of a stimulus to be correlated with other behavioral effects of that stimulus. We have already indicated that the probabilities with which stimuli produce responses may vary with successive stimulus presentations, according to the processes of adaptation or sensitization. These processes seem to distinguish classes of stimuli, and it may be that they are related to reinforcing properties.

We have so far spoken of reinforcing stimuli, but the possible involvement of temporal processes such as adaptation in the function of these stimuli suggests that our account will be incomplete if we do not also deal with the responses produced by these stimuli. A rat's lever-press produces food, and the food provides the rat with an opportunity to eat. We know that if we made both the lever and the food available to the rat simultaneously, the rat would be more likely to eat the food than to press the lever.

This kind of observation leads to the conclusion, formulated by Premack (1959), that the probability of a response will increase if it produces a stimulus that provides the organism with an opportunity to engage in a still more probable response. According to this account, food is an effective reinforcer for the food-deprived rat's lever-presses simply because eating is more probable than lever-pressing.

The relativity of reinforcement

Premack has demonstrated this principle in a number of experiments. One of these (Premack, 1962) shows how reinforcers can be reversed by independently varying the probabilities of two re-

sponses. A rat's running in an activity wheel was controlled by engaging or releasing a brake on the wheel, and was measured in terms of the frequency of the wheel's revolution. The rat's drinking from a drinking tube was controlled by introducing the tube into, or removing it from, an opening in a stationary wall on one side of the wheel, and was measured by an electrical system, a drinkometer, that counted licks. After the rat's opportunity to run had been restricted while water remained available, running became more probable than drinking. After the rat's access to the drinking tube was restricted while free running was allowed in the wheel, however, drinking became more probable than running. It was then shown, in each of these cases, that an opportunity to engage in the more probable response could be used to increase the frequency of the less probable response. When running was more probable than drinking, drinking became more frequent if it released the brake on the wheel and allowed the rat to run than if it had no consequence with respect to running. Inversely, when drinking was more probable than running, running became more frequent if it introduced the drinking tube and allowed the rat to drink than if it had no consequence with respect to drinking.

The implication of this demonstration is that reinforcers cannot be defined independently of the responses that are reinforced. Most experiments restrict their attention to responses that occur relatively infrequently and to reinforcers that set the occasion for highly probable responses. Although experimentally both common and convenient, these are special cases. We shall, in subsequent text, refer to these reinforcers simply as stimuli. But we should not forget that, according to this account, reinforcers are relative, not absolute; their important features rest not with their properties as stimuli, but rather with the responses for which they provide an opportunity.

The relativity of the reinforcement relation may be illustrated by considering three different responses instead of only two. Suppose that a food-pellet dispenser is added to the activity wheel and drinking tube of the preceding experiment, and that, by appropriate deprivation operations, eating is made more probable than running, which in turn is made more probable than drinking. Under these circumstances, running would increase in frequency if it produced an opportunity to eat, but at the same time drinking would increase in frequency if it produced an opportunity to run. With respect to eating, running is the reinforced response, but with respect to drinking, an opportunity to run serves as a reinforcer.

We spoke earlier of behavior as a hierarchy. The ranking of responses within this hierarchy varies with the passage of time, with the stimuli that are presented to the organism, and with the organism's opportunity to engage in the different responses that make up the hierarchy. By restricting the organism's opportunity to engage in certain responses in this hierarchy, or, in other words, by deprivation operations, we make these responses more probable and thus may use the opportunity to engage in them to raise the probability of other responses that are lower in the hierarchy. Reinforcement is not an explanation; it is the name of the operation that has this effect.

Positive and negative reinforcement

Earlier in this account, when we suggested ways in which environmental events could be classified, we considered not only the likelihood with which an organism exposed itself to stimuli, but also the likelihood with which the organism terminated such exposure once it had begun. A rat does not ordinarily expose itself to an electric shock, and once shocked it would remove itself from the shock if given an opportunity. This type of stimulus is sometimes called *aversive,* and the termination of an aversive stimulus provides the basis for another type of reinforcement operation.

The termination of a stimulus, like its presentation, may be made a consequence of responding. If this stimulus termination makes the response more probable, the stimulus is said to be a *negative reinforcer* and the operation is called *negative reinforcement*. Positive reinforcement and negative reinforcement, therefore, are distinguished on the basis of whether a stimulus is presented or removed when a response occurs.

Escape and avoidance

The simplest negative-reinforcement operation is sometimes referred to as an *escape* procedure. For an example let us return once again to the rat in the arena. We noted that the rat would soon stop entering the compartment with the electrified grid floor. But the rat may be exposed to the electric shock simply by placing it in that compartment. The construction of the arena then sets the stage for negative reinforcement: The rat may escape from the shock by leaving the compartment. In other words, this apparatus is arranged so that the termination of electric shock is a consequence of the locomotor response of leaving the compartment.

Movement from one place to another has often been the basis for experimental studies of negative reinforcement, but it is possible to substitute responses that are more discrete and more easily measured. For example, if the exit from the compartment is closed, a lever may be introduced that, when pressed, will shut off the shock for a period of time. In this example, as in earlier ones, the principle is the same: A response is allowed to have a particular consequence and thereby may increase in frequency.

Consider then the two cases. In the absence of food, a response that produces food may increase in frequency. In the presence of shock, a response that removes shock may increase in frequency. The parallel is simple and direct. Yet despite the fundamental nature of negative reinforcement in the escape procedure, it has not received as much experimental attention as more complex procedures involving aversive stimuli. The bulk of the literature on negative reinforcement is concerned with avoidance (cf. Herrnstein, 1969; Herrnstein & Hineline, 1966; see also Chapter 7), in which responses in the absence of an aversive stimulus prevent or delay the subsequent presentation of the stimulus. In one avoidance procedure, a neutral stimulus, such as a light, consistently precedes the presentation of a shock, but a response in the presence of the light turns off the light and prevents the subsequent shock presentation. The performance generated by such a procedure is sometimes interpreted in terms of escape from a stimulus, the light, that has acquired aversive properties by virtue of its relationship to the shock.

The reason for the relative neglect of escape in the experimental literature on negative reinforcement is straightforward: Responses such as rats' lever-presses or pigeons' key-pecks that are easily raised in frequency by positive reinforcement are often difficult to affect by negative reinforcement in escape procedures. This difference in the outcomes of positive-reinforcement and negative-reinforcement operations comes about because the temporal relationships among the reinforced response and other responses produced by the reinforcing stimuli are different in the two cases.

The role of elicited responses

In positive reinforcement the reinforcer is absent at the time the reinforced response must occur.

When the response occurs, the reinforcer is presented and other responses produced by the reinforcer may then follow. For example, if the reinforced response is a rat's lever-press and the reinforcer is food, eating cannot occur until the lever-press is completed and the food has been presented; the responses of lever-pressing and eating necessarily occur in succession and do not compete directly with each other.

In negative reinforcement, however, the effective stimulus is present at the time the reinforced response must occur. Only after the response occurs is the stimulus removed. For example, if the reinforced response is a lever-press and the negative reinforcer is shock, the lever-press must occur at a time when the shock is producing other, perhaps incompatible, responses. The shock may directly produce jumping, and it may also raise the probability of responses other than lever-pressing that reduce shock by changing the rat's contact with the electrified grid. These responses remain highly probable so long as the shock is present and thereby reduce the likelihood of the lever-press. When the lever-press occurs, the shock ends along with the responses that it generates. At this point, the responses produced by the shock no longer compete with the lever-press. In the absence of shock, however, the lever-press can no longer be negatively reinforced because it cannot then have the consequence of terminating shock.

This account suggests that an important criterion for distinguishing positive and negative reinforcement is whether responses produced by the reinforcer can occur at a time when they might interfere with the reinforced response. A distinction based on the operation of either presenting or removing stimuli, therefore, may be of questionable utility, for every such operation is simply a change in the organism's environment that might differently affect the likelihood of different responses at different times.

This point is illustrated by an experiment on escape from cold (Weiss & Laties, 1961). The lever-presses of a rat in a cold room were reinforced by the operation of a heat lamp, and lever-presses in the cold thereby increased in frequency. In one respect, this procedure may be spoken of as positive reinforcement, because it involves the presentation of a stimulus, heat, when a lever-press occurs. On the other hand, although cold is nothing more than the absence of heat, it may function as a stimulus through its action on temperature receptors in the rat's skin. Thus, the procedure may also be spoken of as negative reinforcement, because it involves the termination of the stimulus effects of cold when a lever-press turns on the heat lamp.

The conclusion to be drawn from this example is that the distinction between positive and negative reinforcement is to some extent arbitrary. Nevertheless, although there may be cases such as escape from cold in which it is difficult to specify whether the reinforcement operation involves the presentation or the removal of a stimulus, the distinction may have behavioral significance. In this example, it may be important to know what happens to responses other than the lever-press during the reinforcement operation. In the cold, the rat may shiver, huddle in a corner, or engage in other responses that reduce the likelihood that it will press the lever; only after the lever-press is reinforced, when the heat lamp is turned on, does the competition between these other responses and lever-presses end. With respect to response probabilities before and after reinforcement, therefore, this case seems more aptly described as negative than as positive reinforcement.

Reinforcement and punishment

We have so far considered cases in which the consequences of a response raise the likelihood of the response. But there also exist consequences of responding that reduce response likelihood. In fact, the consequences of responding may be represented exhaustively along a continuum ranging from those that substantially raise response likelihood, through those that have little or no effect on response likelihood (discussed later in the section on neutral stimuli), to those that substantially reduce response likelihood.

The vocabulary of punishment

The operation of arranging a response consequence that reduces response likelihood is called *punishment*. The stimulus that is arranged as a consequence is called a *punisher*. For example, if electric shock is presented whenever a rat presses a lever, the lever-press is said to be punished and the shock is said to be a punisher, because the effect of this operation is a reduction in the frequency of lever-presses. Thus, the vocabulary of punishment parallels the vocabulary of reinforcement.

A punisher is a stimulus, and punishment is an operation. But just as the term *reinforcement* has sometimes been applied to processes as well as operations, the term *punishment* has sometimes also served dual functions. In some literature, therefore, the statement that a response was punished may mean either that the response produced a punisher or that the response decreased in frequency as a result of producing a punisher. As with reinforcement, the present account will restrict the application of the term *punishment* to the vocabulary of operations, and the resulting process will be described directly in terms of changes in response frequency or probability.

Another parallel to the vocabulary of reinforcement is that responses, not organisms, are said to be punished. Thus, when a rat's lever-press produces a shock, we may say that the rat was shocked but that the rat's lever-press was punished. Superficially, this distinction may seem both conceptually and grammatically trivial, but it can have a substantial effect on the precision with which we observe and describe behavior.

Consider a case in which a child misbehaves. A parent calls the child, and then, when the child comes, the parent spanks the child. It is convenient to say simply that the parent punished the child. But this manner of speaking makes it all too easy to omit mention of the responses that might be affected by the spanking. The consequence of the child's misbehavior was that the parent called the child, and the parent administered the spanking when the child obeyed the call. Thus, although the spanking may affect the child's future misbehavior, it is more important to note that the parent punished the child's approach at the call. This kind of observation is more likely to be made when it is necessary to be explicit about the punished response (the child's approach to the parent was punished by the spanking) than when a less precise description in terms of the organism rather than the organism's behavior is regarded as acceptable (the child was punished by the spanking). The vocabulary of reinforcing and punishing responses does not prejudge the effects of these operations on behavior; it does not presume that the effects of these operations will be restricted solely to the responses on which the operations are performed. The behavioral effects of these operations can be readily described, however, and it is therefore advantageous to work with a vocabulary of operations that unambiguously states the consequences of behavior.

The effectiveness of punishment

Whether punishment is in fact effective has been a matter of long-standing controversy. The statement that punishment weakened responding was part of the early versions of Thorndike's Law of Effect, but was dropped in later versions. Only in recent years has sufficient evidence accumulated to reinstate punishment as an effective operation for modifying behavior (e.g., Azrin & Holz, 1966; Solomon, 1964). The ways in which punishment can affect responding will be considered in detail in Chapter 7; the present account therefore only briefly outlines some significant features of punishment and its relationship to other operations.

The first difficulty in the analysis of punishment is that a reduction in response frequency can only be studied if the response has some appreciable frequency to begin with. A response that is never emitted cannot be punished. Thus, many experiments on punishment proceed by superimposing this operation on responding that is maintained by reinforcement. In a given experiment, therefore, the effects of punishment may depend in part on how the response is reinforced. For example, a rat's lever-presses may be less affected when they are punished with electric shock if the rat is severely deprived and its presses are reinforced with large food pellets than if the rat is only mildly deprived and its presses are reinforced only with small food pellets.

A second difficulty is that stimuli effective as punishers may affect behavior even when they are not made a consequence of responses. The effect of punishment therefore must be shown to depend on the relationship between responses and punishers, and not simply on the delivery of punishers. For example, a pigeon may peck a key less frequently when occasional shocks are delivered even if the shocks occur independently of key-pecks. Thus, it must be demonstrated that the shocks have a greater effect when they are produced by key-pecks than when they occur independently of key-pecks (cf. Azrin, 1956).

A third difficulty, and the one that has perhaps had the most substantial implications for the historical development of the analysis of punishment, is that the effects of this operation are temporary. Once the frequency of a response has been reduced by punishment, the frequency is likely to return to earlier levels when punishment is discontinued. This impermanence of effect is not a surprising property of a behavioral process and has its equivalent in the impermanence of the effects of reinforcement. As we shall see later in our discussion of extinction, responses that have become more frequent through reinforcement remain so only as long as reinforcement continues; when reinforcement is discontinued they return to earlier levels.

Yet in the evolution of the analysis of punishment, the impermanence of its effects was emphasized; for this reason, punishment long went unrecognized as an operation with fundamental behavioral properties. In fact, effective punishment procedures were sometimes even given a different name, *passive avoidance*. When a response was eliminated by punishment, the organism was often said to be passively avoiding the punisher by withholding the punished response. With this usage, effective punishment procedures could be spoken of in terms of the passive-avoidance vocabulary, while the remaining procedures could be used to defend the claim that punishment was ineffective.

But these presumptions have yielded to experimental findings. Punishment parallels reinforcement, except that the effects of the two operations differ in sign: Reinforcement raises the frequency of the reinforced response, whereas punishment lowers the frequency of the punished response. The effects of both operations diminish in time after the operations are discontinued.

Properties of punishers

In most experiments on punishment, the stimuli that serve as punishers are chosen for their reliable effectiveness with respect to a variety of responses, because such stimuli reveal the effects of punishment most clearly. Electric shock is an example of such a punisher, and it has the additional advantages that it can be accurately measured and that it can be presented at levels that do not injure the organism. Yet such stimuli represent only extreme instances of punishers, and even stimuli that ordinarily serve as reinforcers can become punishers under certain conditions. The self-administration of drugs, for example, may have reinforcing consequences up to a point, but the drugs may become aversive with continued administration (as when too many martinis make the drinker sick, or when a dose of LSD produces a "bad trip").

The implication of this observation is that, like reinforcers, punishers cannot be defined in absolute terms, nor can they be identified in terms of any common physical properties. Rather, the properties of punishers must be assessed in terms of the responses that are punished and their relationship to the responses produced by the punisher.

Let us return once again to the apparatus in which a rat's running in an activity wheel and drinking from a drinking tube can be controlled.

Earlier, we showed how these responses can be used to illustrate Premack's principle of reinforcement, which states that the likelihood of a less probable response can be raised if this response produces an opportunity to engage in a more probable response. This kind of analysis, in terms of response probabilities, has also been extended to punishment (Premack, 1971).

The relativity of punishment

Consider the following modification of Premack's running and drinking apparatus. The activity wheel is ordinarily locked in position, but a motor is attached to it that, when operated, rotates the wheel and thereby forces the rat to run. The operation of the motor can then be made the consequence of some response, such as pressing a lever or drinking from the drinking tube.

The first step in this experiment is to control the relative probabilities of running and drinking. Two conditions can be arranged: Running may be made more probable than drinking by depriving the rat of an opportunity to run but giving it free access to water, and drinking may be made more probable than running by depriving the rat of water but giving it an opportunity to run.

The next step is to make the operation of the wheel a consequence of drinking: Each time the rat drinks, the wheel begins to turn and the rat is forced to run. When running is more probable than drinking, the outcome of this operation is consistent with our earlier discussion of the principle of reinforcement. The probability of drinking increases, and it is therefore appropriate to describe this operation as the reinforcement of drinking by running. When drinking is more probable than running, however, the operation has an opposite effect. The probability of drinking decreases when running is its consequence, and it is appropriate to describe the operation as the punishment of drinking by running. Thus, in this example, a single response, drinking, is either reinforced or punished by a single consequence, enforced running, depending on the relative probabilities of these responses in the behavioral hierarchy.

The potential reversibility of consequences as reinforcers or punishers is not evident from the stimuli used in most experiments on reinforcement and punishment. Reinforcing and punishing stimuli are chosen so that the responses they produce are represented at the extremes of the behavioral hierarchy. The food-deprived rat is more likely to eat, if given an opportunity, than to engage in other responses; and in the typical experiment on rein-forcement with food, eating is made a consequence of responses, such as lever-pressing, that are ordi-narily of relatively low probability. On the other hand, there are few circumstances under which a rat will put itself in a position to engage in the responses produced by shock; and in the typical experiment on punishment with shock, the shock-elicited behavior is made a consequence of re-sponses, such as lever-pressing maintained by reinforcement, that are ordinarily of relatively high probability. These typical experimental arrange-ments obscure the relativity of reinforcement and punishment and the way in which this relativity is based on the positions of different responses in the behavioral hierarchy. It is therefore important to recognize that, although responses may be manipulated by changing their environmental consequences, the effects of these consequences depend on their behavioral properties. An ade-quate account of these properties must deal with the relationship between the responses that pro-duce a particular consequence and the responses that in turn are produced by that consequence.

Aversive stimuli

At various points in our discussion, we have spoken of aversive stimuli, negative reinforcers, and punishers. Each was introduced in a different context. Aversive stimuli were discussed in terms of the effects of elicitation operations, negative reinforcers in terms of consequences that increased the probability of responses, and punishers in terms of consequences that reduced the probability of responses. It would be convenient to assume that each term identifies a different aspect of a single behavioral category of environmental events. Elec-tric shock, for example, may be spoken of as an aversive stimulus, a negative reinforcer, or a pun-isher, depending on the experimental context with-in which it occurs. For many stimuli called aversive, this assumption is probably correct, because each classification has its origins in the relationships among the probabilities of different responses in the behavioral hierarchy. A stimulus that is effec-tive as a negative reinforcer may therefore be ex-pected to be effective as a punisher. It is important to note, however, that the assumption simply pro-vides a convenient categorization. Given the pres-ent state of our understanding of behavior, the correspondence between negative reinforcers and punishers remains a matter for empirical test.

Positive and negative punishment

One last distinction must be made before we close our discussion of the punishment operation. As with positive and negative reinforcers, it is pos-sible to distinguish between positive and negative punishers. The presentation of some environ-mental events, such as electric shock or a rotating wheel that forces a rat to run, may serve as a pun-isher. But responses also may be punished by the termination of a stimulus. For example, the re-moval of food as a consequence of lever-pressing may reduce the likelihood of lever-pressing (and parents sometimes punish misbehavior by with-drawing privileges). This operation therefore may be referred to as *negative punishment*. The effects of this operation, however, have not often been directly studied, because it is difficult to arrange the necessary conditions. For example, if the re-moval of food is made a consequence of a food-deprived rat's lever-press, the rat is more likely to eat than to press the lever; thus, few opportunities to punish the lever-press will arise. Just as studies of negative reinforcement have concentrated on avoidance rather than escape, therefore, studies of negative punishment have concentrated on punish-ment by *time-out from positive reinforcement* (e.g., Ferster, 1958), in which a response is punished by removing a stimulus in the presence of which responses may be reinforced rather than simply by removing the positive reinforcer itself.

Neutral stimuli

We have so far discussed response consequences, called *reinforcers*, that raise the likelihood of re-sponses, and other response consequences, called *punishers*, that reduce the likelihood of responses. But reinforcers and punishers must be defined rel-atively, because a consequence that may serve as a reinforcer for one response may serve as a pun-isher for some other response. We have seen that the stimuli that serve experimentally as reinforcers or punishers are usually chosen for their dramatic effects. Such stimuli, however, represent only ex-tremes along a continuum of behavioral effects. Between these extremes are a range of stimuli that are often called *neutral*, because their effectiveness as reinforcers or punishers cannot be so easily or dramatically demonstrated. Yet such stimuli also can be consequences of responding, and as such may affect subsequent behavior.

Consider some examples. When we reach out for an object on a table, a consequence of the reaching is that our hand comes in contact with the object. When we listen while someone speaks, a consequence of the listening is that we hear what the speaker says. And when we look at a page of a book, a consequence of the looking is that we are able to read the text. Each of these consequences in turn may set the occasion for other responses: Once we have touched an object, we may move it; once we have heard a speaker, we may make a reply; and once we have read one page of a book, we may move on to the next.

In each of these cases, we may describe the consequences of behavior in the vocabulary of reinforcement. We may say that reaching is reinforced by touching, that listening is reinforced by hearing, or that looking is reinforced by seeing. Such an application of this vocabulary is not without precedent (Skinner, 1957), but it will be sufficient for our purposes to speak simply in terms of consequences. We are concerned here not so much with how we raise or lower the likelihood of responses, but rather with how responding comes to be coordinated with environmental events.

Sensory processes as behavior

The role of sensory processes has been a source of long-standing controversy in the study of learning. Theorists took sides on the issue of whether learning was sensory or motor: Did an organism learn relationships among stimuli, or did it learn responses? The issue has not yet been resolved.

Part of the difficulty is with whether sensory processes are to be treated as behavior. The present account assumes that such a treatment is appropriate because it is consistent with the view that the important properties of behavior can be dealt with not in terms of stimuli or responses alone, but rather in terms of relationships among stimuli and responses. Thus, although seeing and hearing are not as easily and unambiguously measured as discrete responses like lever-presses or key-pecks, they are nevertheless part of an organism's behavior. Seeing and hearing depend respectively on visual and auditory stimuli, but they also depend on what the organism does. An organism is not passive in its environment: It sees what it looks at and hears what it listens to. Such behavior can also occur in the absence of the relevant stimuli, as when we speak of attending, searching, imagining, or thinking.

Lights, sounds, and other relatively simple environmental events have often been described as neutral stimuli. The label *neutral* is convenient,

and we use it here for that reason. But, as we shall see, it is a misnomer. Events that can be consequences of behavior cannot be truly neutral, because as consequences they are not likely to be totally without effect on subsequent behavior. It is also difficult to conceive of situations in which all that an organism could do would be without consequence.

The importance of stimuli that were once considered neutral was demonstrated in experiments concerned with a phenomenon called *sensory reinforcement* (see Kish, 1966, for a review). For example, it was shown that a rat's lever-presses increased in frequency if they briefly turned on a light. This effect of the light was both small and transient, but it was nevertheless appropriate to conclude that the light was temporarily effective as a weak reinforcer. These and related phenomena were discussed in terms of *curiosity* or *exploratory behavior* (e.g., Berlyne, 1960), and a variety of demonstrations were added to the experimental literature. It was shown, for example, that a monkey in an enclosed chamber will press a switch if the presses give it an opportunity to look outside the chamber at other monkeys (Butler, 1957).

Such experiments assess the effect of sensory consequences on a response chosen by the experimenter for its ease of measurement. But the inevitable stimulus consequences of the organism's behavior in any environment may affect responding. Simply by moving about, the organism changes the portion of the environment with which it comes in contact; as the organism moves, the things it sees and touches change. The significance of these consequences of behavior is illustrated in an experiment by Held and Hein (1963). Pairs of kittens were raised so that the visual stimulation that one kitten (active) was exposed to as it moved around a circular enclosure was duplicated for a second kitten (passive). The visual stimulation for the active kitten, however, was a consequence of its own movement, whereas that for the passive kitten depended on the active kitten's movements. This was arranged by attaching a harness and pulley system to the active kitten and connecting it, across a lever mounted on a fulcrum in the center of the chamber, to a small compartment within which the passive kitten stood. Thus, the passive kitten, moved about as if in a miniature carousel, saw the same kinds of changes in visual stimuli in the same temporal sequences as those seen by the active kitten, but these changes were not consequences of its own behavior. Despite their equivalent exposures to visual stimuli, the kitten that was passively exposed to visual stimuli by the active kitten's movements was unable to respond appropriately in subsequent tests of visual-motor coordination, although it became able to do so after it was later allowed to move about freely in an illuminated room.

We must conclude, therefore, that the consequences of responding play a critical role in the control of behavior, whether or not we can conveniently categorize these consequences as reinforcing or neutral or punishing stimuli. And if, when we speak of situations in which an organism learns, we cannot say that the organism has learned either stimuli or responses, we can at least usually say that the organism has learned the consequences of its behavior.

Latent learning

A major experimental basis for controversies about the nature of learning came from a phenomenon called *latent learning* (see Thistlethwaite, 1951, for a review). In one experiment on latent learning, food-deprived rats in each of two groups negotiated a maze. The rats in one group found food in the goal-box of the maze, and over successive trials their time to run the maze and their entries into blind alleys gradually decreased. The rats in the other group found no food in the goal-box, and over the same number of trials as the first group their performances gave no evidence of learning. Then the rats in this group were placed in the goal-box and given food there for the first time, and the performances of both groups were again tested. This time there was no substantial difference between the groups. The rats that had previously negotiated the maze without food in the goal-box began to run about as quickly and with about as few entries into blind alleys as did the rats that had found food in the goal-box on all previous trials.

The rats had learned the maze equally well with or without food in the goal-box, so the argument went, and therefore the learning could not be attributed to the effect of food as a reinforcer. But, it was countered, food in the goal-box is not the only possible reinforcer for the rat's running of a maze. Experiments were then performed to assess whether an effective reinforcer might be the removal of the rat from the maze, or its escape from the confinement of blind alleys, or its return to the home cage, where it is fed. While one experiment showed that a particular reinforcer could be effective, another repeated the demonstration of latent learning in such a way that this reinforcer could not account for the phenomenon.

But the argument could not be resolved even in principle, because a rat's negotiation of a maze inevitably involves consequences of responding. At a particular place in the maze, one turn is followed by a blind alley and the other by an opportunity to move further through the maze; at another place, a turn is followed by entry into the goal-box, whether or not the goal-box happens to contain food. The rat's looking, sniffing, touching, and moving through the maze is consequential behavior, even if this behavior is not as easily accessible to the experimenter as correct turns and entries into blind alleys. Whether to call these consequences reinforcers is perhaps nothing more than a matter of preference. But it would be difficult to assert that these consequences were not essential to the processes called learning.

Extinction and superstition

Some responses have consequences that remain fairly constant throughout the lifetime of an organism. Reaching for an object on a table, for example, is usually followed by touching the object. But for many responses, the consequences change. Behavior that is reinforced in childhood may no longer be reinforced when the child has become an adult. And when the consequences of responding change, behavior may change in turn. When a response is reinforced, it increases in frequency; but this effect is not permanent, for when reinforcement is discontinued, the frequency of the response returns to earlier levels.

The discontinuation of reinforcement is called *extinction,* and a response on which this operation is performed is said to be *extinguished.* (Extinction is occasionally confused with forgetting, but an extinguished response is not necessarily forgotten; it simply no longer has the reinforcing consequences it used to have.) As a result of the extinction operation, the likelihood of the response returns toward its level before reinforcement. In this respect, extinction simply demonstrates that the reinforcement operation is temporary in its effect. The decrease in responding during extinction is therefore no more than a part of the process generated by reinforcement, in that the decrease shows how the effects of reinforcement persist over time (cf. Morse, 1966).

Responding during extinction was at one time considered a fundamental measure of the effects of reinforcement. Spoken of as *resistance to extinc-*

tion, such measures as the number of responses emitted during a period of extinction, or the time taken before responding dropped to a specified level, supplemented other measures of responding taken during reinforcement. Thus, if one reinforcement procedure generated more responding after reinforcement was discontinued than another reinforcement procedure, the first procedure was said to have produced the greater resistance to extinction.

Extinction and inhibition

But matters became complicated because the effects of extinction could not be described as only a decline in responding. This decline was typically accompanied by other effects. One of the most prominent of these was the phenomenon of *spontaneous recovery.* After responding had dropped to low levels at the end of one session of extinction, the responding recovered to earlier high levels at the beginning of the next session. Experimental analyses of this and other extinction phenomena led to a variety of accounts of extinction, formulated in terms of inferred processes such as *frustration, interference,* and *inhibition* (cf. Kimble, 1961, Chapter 10). These accounts suggested that responding in extinction did not merely decline passively, but rather was actively suppressed by aversive or inhibitory properties of nonreinforced responding. Phenomena such as spontaneous recovery were taken to indicate that the responding reduced by extinction was in some way "there all the time but inhibited" (cf. Reid, 1958).

Accounts that assumed the active suppression of extinguished responding were criticized on the grounds that they explained the phenomena of extinction in terms of processes or events that were neither observed nor observable. When an extinguished response was said to be inhibited, for example, it was possible to measure the inhibited response but it was not possible to measure directly any processes or events that could be said to do the inhibiting. Other accounts that did not assume suppressive or inhibitory processes were therefore formulated.

One such account suggested that the beginning of a session had special stimulus properties, perhaps derived from the handling of the animal and other pre-experimental conditions, and that the effects of extinction under the different conditions later in the session therefore might not transfer to the beginning of the next extinction session. In one experimental assessment of this account (Kendall,

1965), stimulus conditions were modified during extinction of a pigeon's key-peck. The pigeon's pecks on an illuminated key had previously been reinforced with grain. Extinction was then conducted during 1-minute periods of key-illumination that alternated with 1-minute periods of darkness in the chamber, during which the pigeon did not peck. After pecks on the illuminated key had become infrequent, the key was kept lit continuously; within a few minutes the pigeon again began to peck. Thus, extinction during periodic key-illumination reduced responding, but this effect did not transfer to the continuous key-illumination later in the session. In this experiment, spontaneous recovery might be said to have occurred within the session rather than at its beginning.

Response-stimulus dependencies and stimulus deliveries

Accounts of the nature of extinction and the phenomena that accompany it nevertheless remain controversial. The reason may be that the discontinuation of reinforcement has two effects: A dependency between responses and reinforcers ends, and reinforcers are no longer delivered. The difference between these two effects of the extinction operation may be illustrated by comparing extinction with a satiation procedure, in which the response continues to produce a stimulus but the stimulus becomes ineffective as a reinforcer, and an elicitation procedure, in which the delivery of the reinforcer continues but is independent of the response.

Assume that a food-deprived rat's lever-presses are reinforced with food pellets, and that the rat presses the lever and eats a food pellet once every ten or fifteen seconds. If lever-presses are then extinguished, they no longer produce pellets and the rat no longer eats. As a result, lever-pressing becomes less frequent.

If, instead, the dependency between lever-presses and food pellets is maintained but the rat is no longer food deprived, the rat no longer eats even though presses continue to produce pellets. As a result of this satiation operation, lever-pressing becomes less frequent. It does so, however, not because presses are without consequences, but rather because the consequences are no longer effective as reinforcers.

Consider the third possibility. The rat remains food deprived and the dependency between lever-presses and food pellets is discontinued, but now food pellets are automatically delivered every 10 or 15 seconds. As a result of this elicitation operation, lever-pressing again becomes less frequent. But the effects of the termination of the dependency between responses and reinforcers in this case, unlike those of the extinction operation, are not accompanied by the effect of terminating food.

The distinction between *terminating a dependency* and *terminating the delivery of reinforcers* is important because the effects of these two operations are not necessarily the same. The termination of a dependency is followed by a change in the likelihood of the response for which the dependency was arranged. The termination of the delivery of reinforcers, however, has effects on a broader range of behavior, whether or not the delivery of reinforcers depended on responses. For example, if a food-deprived rat has been eating pellets and the pellets are suddenly made unavailable, the rat will become more active, will perhaps urinate or defecate, and will usually bite or otherwise attack objects in the chamber. If the pellets were produced by lever-presses, the rat may bite the lever (e.g., Mowrer & Jones, 1943); if another organism is in the chamber, the other organism may be attacked (Azrin, Hutchinson, & Hake, 1966); and once such aggressive responses become likely, an opportunity to engage in them may be used to reinforce other responses in turn (Azrin, Hutchinson, & McLaughlin, 1965). Such effects as these are not the direct result of the termination of a dependency; they are side-effects, superimposed on the decline in responding when the dependency is terminated, because this termination is necessarily accompanied by the termination of the delivery of reinforcers.

Analogous problems exist with respect to negative reinforcement and with respect to punishment. Extinction with respect to negative reinforcement in escape from shock, for example, might be assumed to involve termination of the dependency between responses and shock during continued presentation of shock (cf. Herrnstein & Hineline, 1966). More often, however, the simple discontinuation of shock has been spoken of as an extinction operation in the case of negative reinforcement. In this case, there can be no dependency between responses and shock termination, but there also can be no response-independent reinforcing event because the absence of shock can effectively reinforce only if shock is sometimes present.

The termination of punishment is spoken of in terms of *recovery* rather than in terms of *extinction*.

Nevertheless, if responses are punished by shock, the dependency between responses and shocks can be ended by discontinuing the delivery of shocks or by discontinuing the dependency while delivering shocks independently of responses. The first case, but not the second, is analogous to that of extinction with positive reinforcement, because general effects of terminating shock may be superimposed on the specific effects of terminating the dependency. (In neither negative reinforcement nor positive punishment is it clear how the dependency might be maintained while stimulus presentations are discontinued. An operation analogous to satiation in positive reinforcement might be the reduction of shock intensity to a level that makes it ineffective as a negative reinforcer or as a positive punisher, while maintaining the dependency between responses and shock.)

An example is provided by experiments concerned with the maintenance of responding by electric shock (e.g., Kelleher & Morse, 1968). If conditions are arranged so that a monkey's lever-press produces a shock at the end of successive 10-minute intervals, the monkey may come to shock itself regularly by lever-pressing. After each shock the monkey pauses, and then it responds more and more rapidly until it shocks itself again at the end of the next interval. If shock is discontinued, the monkey's lever-pressing ceases. In this performance, shock appears to function as a reinforcer: The monkey responds when its responses produce shock but not when its responses have no consequence. It is also necessary, however, to assess what the monkey does when shocks are delivered independently of its responding. Response-independent shocks elicit lever-pressing in the monkey (e.g., Hutchinson, Renfrew, & Young, 1971). The appropriate comparison is not between response-produced shocks and no shocks at all, but rather between response-produced and response-independent shocks. If lever-pressing occurs less often when shocks are response produced than when they are response independent, it is appropriate to conclude that shock is an effective punisher. In these circumstances, punishment reduces responding, but the eliciting effects of the punisher are so powerful that punishment is not sufficient to eliminate responding; thus, we have the paradoxical finding that the monkey continues to shock itself even though the shocks would no longer be delivered if it stopped responding completely.

This example may have important implications.

We might assume, for example, that a parent who tries to stop a child from crying by punishing the crying will have difficulty simply because the punisher elicits the very response that the parent is trying to suppress. In punishment, therefore, as in reinforcement, we must note that dependencies and stimulus deliveries have separate effects.

In all of these cases, it is of interest to know how response frequency changes when a dependency between responses and consequences ends. But this process has typically been examined during extinction, when the general effects of terminating stimulus presentations are superimposed on the specific effects of terminating the dependency. It is reasonable to ask why this has been the case. To answer this question, we must further consider the effects of response-independent stimulus presentations.

Elicitation operations and superstition

The presentation of a stimulus produces responses, but even if the stimulus is presented without reference to the organism's behavior, it follows responses as well. For example, the response-independent delivery of a food pellet might occur just after the rat rears up on its hind legs, or just after the rat nibbles its tail. And if it happens that the pellet is delivered just after the rat presses a lever, what can distinguish this succession, press followed by pellet, from that in which the press actually produces the pellet? The succession of response and reinforcer may affect subsequent responding as much when this succession occurs accidentally as when it is arranged by the reinforcement operation.

Responding that is raised in likelihood by the accidental succession of responses and reinforcers has been called *superstitious responding* (Skinner, 1948). In the demonstration of an experimental superstition, Skinner presented grain to a food-deprived pigeon at 15-second intervals. Any response that happened to occur just before grain delivery was likely to be repeated, and therefore was likely to be followed by still another grain delivery. Thus, through this accidental succession of responses and reinforcers, a stereotyped pattern of responding tended to develop. Pigeons turned, hopped, or pecked; the responses were different for different pigeons, and even for a single pigeon the pattern often changed gradually over successive grain deliveries. Although it was impossible to anticipate what responses would be affected, it was possible after the procedure had operated for a

while to identify responses that it had made highly probable.

The development of superstitious responding depends at least in part on the temporal spacing of deliveries of the reinforcer, because this spacing determines whether a response that has been made more probable by one accidental pairing with a reinforcer will be likely to occur again just before the next reinforcer is delivered. The effect may also depend on the eliciting properties of the reinforcer, because the reinforcer may directly change the probabilities of responses that occur between successive deliveries. For example, if grain makes pigeons more likely to peck even in the absence of grain, then pecking may be more likely to develop superstitiously than other responses that are unrelated to eating grain (cf. Staddon & Simmelhag, 1971).

Superstitions generated by the accidental succession of responses and reinforcers are a ubiquitous problem in the analysis of behavior, because they may arise whether reinforcers are delivered independently of responses or as a consequence of responses. For example, if one response happens to be followed by a different response that is then reinforced, the reinforcer may affect both responses even though its delivery did not depend on that particular succession of responses.

To illustrate this point, let us now return to the case that led us to the discussion of superstition: The dependency between response and reinforcer is terminated while the delivery of reinforcers is continued. A rat's lever-presses are first reinforced with food pellets; then, lever-presses no longer produce pellets but pellets continue to be delivered, now independently of behavior. Under these circumstances, the rat is likely to continue pressing the lever and, because pellets are still delivered, presses are likely to be followed often by pellets. Thus, lever-pressing may decline only slowly, perhaps eventually to be replaced by other responses, not because a dependency has long-lasting effects even after the dependency is discontinued, but because the superstitious effect of accidental successions of responses and reinforcers to some extent counteracts the effects of terminating the dependency.

We have seen that, although extinction is simple as an experimental operation, its effects are complex. When behavior has consequences, a termination of these consequences affects both the spacing of stimuli in time and the relationship of these stimuli to behavior. An adequate analysis of the transition from reinforcement to extinction must take both of these effects into account.

DIFFERENTIAL REINFORCEMENT AND STIMULUS CONTROL

We have spoken of ways in which behavior can be modified by stimulus presentations in the elicitation operation and by its consequences in the operations of reinforcement and punishment. We have also discussed how these operations affect the relative positions of responses in the behavioral hierarchy. The behavioral hierarchy is a property of the responding with which the organism comes to us. The organism's behavior may be said to consist of a repertory of responses, each of which has a different probability. Yet we cannot restrict our attention only to these responses, because an important feature of the modifications of behavior described as learning is that the organism comes to respond in new ways. As a result of the learning process, the organism emits responses that it was unable to emit before learning began. We must therefore consider how new responses can be added to the behavioral hierarchy or, in other words, how the organism's repertory of responses can be broadened.

We have often used the rat's lever-press or the pigeon's key-peck as examples of responses. But if we simply place a rat in a chamber with a lever or a pigeon in a chamber with a key, these responses will not necessarily occur. And the reinforcement operation cannot have any effect if the response to be reinforced is never emitted. Rather than waiting for the response, therefore, the experimenter may use a procedure called *shaping:* He produces lever-presses or key-pecks by reinforcing behavior that more and more closely approximates these responses.

Shaping: Differential reinforcement of successive approximations

Consider the lever-press. Once the rat has begun to eat food pellets as they are delivered, the experimenter delivers a pellet only when the rat turns toward the lever. After reinforcing two or three movements toward the lever with pellets, the experimenter may reinforce not just any movement toward the lever, but only those movements that include lifting of the forepaws. By this time, the rat spends most of its time near the lever, and the experimenter soon has an opportunity to reinforce contact with the lever. It is no longer necessary to reinforce turns toward the lever, because contacts with the lever more closely approximate lever-pressing and will be repeated once a contact is reinforced. The experimenter therefore may next begin to reinforce only touches on the top surface of the lever, and soon a lever-press occurs. At this point, the experimenter may withdraw, because the apparatus can be automated in such a way that each subsequent lever-press produces a food pellet.

The shaping procedure is based upon *differential reinforcement:* At every stage, some responses are reinforced but others are not. In addition, the criteria for differential reinforcement change, in *successive approximations* to lever-pressing, as responding changes. Two properties of behavior contribute to the effectiveness of this differential reinforcement of successive approximations to a response. The first is that behavior is variable. No two responses are identical, and the reinforcement of one response produces a spectrum of responses that, though similar to the reinforced response, differ from it to some extent in topography or form, and in other properties such as force, magnitude, and direction. Of these responses, some will approximate the response to be shaped more closely than others, and may therefore next be selected for reinforcement. The reinforcement of these responses will be followed in turn by additional responses, some of which will approximate the response to be shaped even more closely. Thus, the spectrum of responses can be gradually altered by reinforcement until the response to be shaped occurs.

This aspect of the shaping procedure, which depends on the specific effect of reinforcers on preceding responses, may at times be supplemented by a second and broader effect of some reinforcers on behavior: The delivery of some reinforcers, such as food, tends to make an organism more active (e.g., Blough, 1958). Thus, both the dependency between responses and reinforcers, in its specific effect on reinforced responses, and the delivery of reinforcers, in its general effect on a variety of responses, contribute to the shaping of new responses. A response greater in force or magnitude and more closely resembling the response to be shaped than the reinforced response may occur not only because reinforcement makes responses similar to the reinforced response more likely, but also because the delivery of a reinforcer makes the organism more active. Once again, both the specific effects of the dependency between responses and reinforcers and the general effects of the delivery of reinforcers must be taken into account.

Operants: Differentiation and induction

A rat may press a lever with its left paw, its right paw, or both paws. Occasionally, it may even press the lever by leaning on it with its chin, biting it, or sitting on it. Each of these responses is different, and even two successive presses with the same paw will not be identical. Nevertheless, all of these responses are called lever-presses. The rat might also make the same movements at the opposite end of the chamber, so that the lever is not depressed. But such movements would not be called lever-presses.

It is therefore not sufficient to speak of behavior only in terms of particular responses. Particular responses are instances of behavior, and because no two responses are in all respects identical, each response can occur only once. The reinforcement of one response produces subsequent responses that more or less resemble the reinforced response, but these responses cannot be exactly the same as the reinforced response. Thus, to speak of behavior effectively we must speak not of single responses but of classes of responses defined by common properties.

Response classes

In experiments on lever-pressing, the lever is attached to a switch that operates whenever the lever is sufficiently depressed. Thus, the common property of all lever-presses is this environmental effect of the presses: Every response that operates the switch qualifies as a lever-press. The definition of response classes in terms of common environmental effects provides the basis for the measurement of responses in the class and for the experimental operations that are imposed on these responses. For example, the experimenter may measure lever-presses by recording from the switch and arrange that all responses within the class of lever-presses are reinforced with food pellets.

But the class of responses measured by the experimenter will not have any behavioral significance unless the effects of the operations imposed on the class are also taken into account. With respect to any response class, it is necessary to ask a fundamental behavioral question: Can the likelihood of responses in this class be modified by their consequences? If so, the class is called an *operant* class; it is a class of responses that is affected by the way in which it operates on the environment. Lever-presses and key-pecks are convenient examples of such classes; as we shall see, however, the behavior that can be spoken of in terms of operant classes is both varied and complex.

Earlier in the study of learning, when operant behavior was called *instrumental* or *voluntary* behavior, it was assumed that the classes of responses that could be modified by their consequences were limited primarily to the skeletal musculature. Other classes of responses, *autonomic responses* such as those of glands and smooth muscles, had not been shown to be modifiable by their consequences. Such responses were elicited by stimuli, and Pavlov's conditioning procedures (see Chapter 3) had shown how new stimuli could come to elicit these responses. There was no evidence at that time that these responses could be modified by reinforcement or punishment.

This view has changed, however, with the demonstration that autonomic responses can be affected by their consequences. The salivary response provides an example. It had been known that salivation occurs spontaneously as well as when it is elicited by a stimulus such as food in the mouth (e.g., Zener & McCurdy, 1939). Thus, it was possible to arrange consequences for spontaneous or emitted salivation, which was measured in drops of fluid brought out from the salivary duct of a dog to an external recording system. But the consequence could not be food delivery, because an effect of food as a reinforcer would not be distinguishable from its effect as an elicitor of salivation. Miller and Carmona (1967) therefore studied salivation in water-deprived dogs with a reinforcer (water) that does not elicit salivation. They found that salivation increased when it produced the delivery of water (positive reinforcement), and that salivation decreased when it prevented the delivery of water (negative punishment). In other words, they showed that this class of responses, measured in drops of saliva, could be modified by its consequences and therefore could be appropriately spoken of as an operant class.

An *operant*, then, is a class of responses that can be modified by its consequences. Just as stimuli cannot be classified independently of their behavioral effects, the definition of response classes depends on the behavioral properties of the responses and not on independent physical or physiological properties. The experimental operation on which the study of these behavioral properties is based is called *differential reinforcement*, or the reinforcement of only those responses that fall within a specified class. The effect of this operation is to make subsequent re-

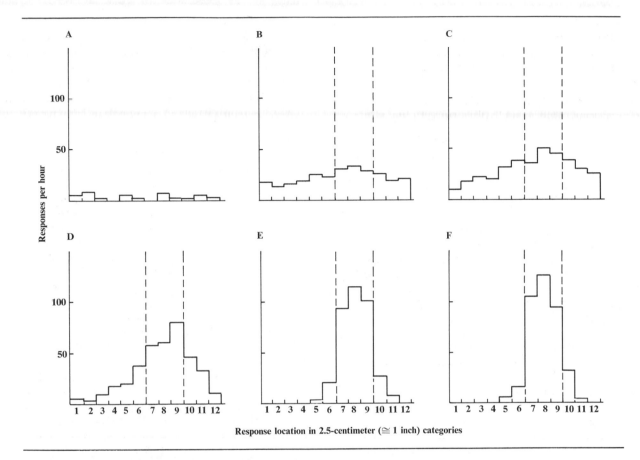

Figure 2.3 Hypothetical data illustrating effects of differential reinforcement on a distribution of responses (insertions of a rat's nose into a 30-centimeter horizontal slot in the chamber wall). Unreinforced responding is shown in A. In B through F, responses at locations 7, 8, and 9 (bounded by dashed vertical lines) are reinforced with food pellets. Induction is illustrated in B; the effects of reinforcement spread to responses across the entire length of the slot. Differentiation is illustrated as responding becomes more and more restricted to the reinforced locations with continued differential reinforcement in C through F. In E and F, the distribution of responses has become stable and corresponds closely to the class of responses that is reinforced.

sponding conform to the boundaries of the specified class. Thus, the essential feature of an operant is the correspondence between the class of responses defined by its consequences and the spectrum of responses generated by these consequences.

An experimental example: Differentiation of response location

The nature of this correspondence can be illustrated with an example. (The data to be presented are hypothetical, but related experiments are reported by Antonitis, 1951, and Gollub, 1966.)

Assume that a food-deprived rat is placed in an experimental chamber in which a horizontal slot 30 centimeters long is located on one wall. Behind the slot are a series of photocells that permit responses to be recorded separately in successive 2.5-centimeter segments (about one inch) whenever the rat inserts its nose in the slot. (These segments will be called locations 1 through 12, reading from left to right along the slot.) On the wall opposite the slot is a cup into which food pellets can be dispensed as reinforcers. The delivery of pellets is accompanied by a loud click, and whenever a pellet is delivered the rat quickly comes to the cup and eats. As it moves about the chamber, the rat may occasionally sniff at the slot and put its nose in it. But in the absence of reinforcement these responses are fairly infrequent, and they do not necessarily have any systematic relationship to the various locations along the slot (see Figure 2.3A).

Suppose now that responses are reinforced, but only at locations 7, 8, and 9. The immediate effect of reinforcement (illustrated in Figure 2.3B) may be a general increase in responding at all locations. This phenomenon is sometimes called *induction:* The effect of reinforcement is not restricted to the reinforced response, but spreads to other, similar responses. In this case, the effect of reinforcing a response at locations 7, 8, or 9 was not limited to responses at these locations, but spread to responses at other locations.

As differential reinforcement continues, however, so that responses at locations 7, 8, and 9 are reinforced while responses at other locations are not, responding at the reinforced locations increases whereas responding at other locations decreases (see Figures 2.3C through 2.3F). Eventually, all but a small proportion of responses occur at locations 7, 8, and 9 (E), and a point is reached at which the continuation of the differential-reinforcement procedure produces no further substantial changes in the distribution of responses across locations (F).

In this example, the distribution of responses comes to conform closely to the boundaries of the response class that has been reinforced. This process is called *differentiation,* and such responding is said to be *differentiated.* An operant class has been established that is defined in terms of the location of responses.

Yet what is to be said of the responses at locations 6 and 10? To be sure, they are outside the boundaries of the class of responses that is reinforced, and according to the strictest interpretation of the defining properties of operants they do not count as responses in the operant class. Such responses have sometimes been spoken of in terms of induction; these responses are so closely related to the reinforced responses along the continuum of location that the effects of reinforcement have spread to them. In this view, responses within the boundaries of the reinforced class are attributed to differentiation, and responses outside the boundaries to induction. But such a distinction seems inappropriate, because responding both inside and outside these boundaries is generated by the same operations and is represented by one continuous distribution.

The resolution of this difficulty comes in recognizing that two different classes of responses are involved. One of these provides the basis for the experimental operation of reinforcement (dashed vertical lines in Figure 2.3). The other represents the performance that comes about as a result of these operations (response distributions in Figure 2.3). It is not necessary to assume that the two must correspond exactly. In fact, for any given class of reinforced responses, the fundamental question concerns the degree to which the behavior produced conforms to the behavior reinforced.

Consider now another example. Once again, responses can be separately measured in successive regions of a slot in one wall of the chamber, but this time the slot is vertical instead of horizontal. To the extent that the rat sometimes puts its nose in the slot as it sniffs about the chamber in the absence of reinforcement, its responses are concentrated in the lower portion of the slot (see Figure 2.4A). The differentiation of responding at the upper end of the slot, therefore, cannot proceed unless responding at the upper end is shaped.

As successive approximations to responses at higher levels are differentially reinforced, the distribution of responses changes, as illustrated in Figure 2.4. At first, all responses at level 5 or higher are reinforced (B). As a result, responding increases at many levels, and some responding occurs at and above level 7 for the first time. At this point, the boundary for differential reinforcement is shifted upward so that only responses at level 7 or higher are reinforced (C). Again, the distribution of responses shifts upward, and responding at the lower levels begins to decrease. The boundary for differential reinforcement is then shifted upward again, to responses at level 9 or higher (D). The distribution of responses shifts further upward, and responding at the lower levels continues to decrease. But the height that the rat can reach is limited, and although the maintenance of differential reinforcement at levels 9 and higher produces some further narrowing of the distribution (E), a point is eventually reached at which continued differential reinforcement at this level produces no further substantial changes in the distribution of responses (F).

In this case, the class of responses that had consequences (responses at levels 9 and higher, which were reinforced) was different from the distribution of responses produced by these consequences (responses ranging up to level 10, but with a maximum at level 8). Responding in this situation clearly has been modified by its consequences, but it seems inappropriate to say that the criterion for

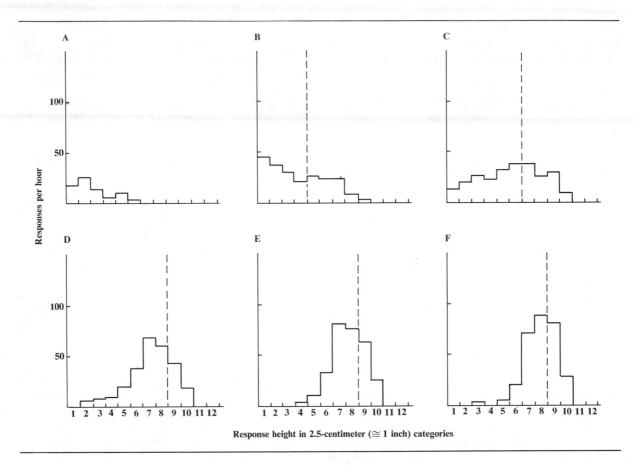

Figure 2.4   Hypothetical data illustrating changes in the distribution of responses (insertions of a rat's nose into a 30-centimeter vertical slot in the chamber wall) with differential reinforcement of successive approximations to higher responses (shaping). Unreinforced responding, concentrated at lower levels, is shown in A. In B, responses at levels 5 and higher (to the right of the dashed vertical line) are reinforced. The resulting distribution of responses includes some responses at levels 7 and higher. In C, and then again in D, the reinforced class is shifted to higher levels. When differential reinforcement of only responses at levels 9 and higher is maintained, in E and F, the distribution of responses becomes stable, but does not correspond closely to the class of responses that is reinforced.

reinforcement is the defining property of the operant class. This criterion provides the basis for an experimental operation, but the behavioral significance of this operation is given by the responding that results. Thus, the defining property of the operant class must instead be behavior: Once the consequential operation of reinforcement has been shown to affect the distribution of responses, this distribution defines the operant class.

These examples have been hypothetical. But it is now possible to consider how these relationships bear on the area traditionally called learning, in which many problems reduce to questions about the correspondences between response classes defined in terms of their consequences and response classes defined in terms of the resulting distributions.

Differentiable properties of behavior

The reinforcement operation inevitably involves differentiation. Responses such as lever-pressing and key-pecking must be at an appropriate location and of a sufficient force, and the hypothetical examples of Figures 2.3 and 2.4 could be repeated by substituting the dimensions of these responses, respectively, for the response dimensions considered in the figures. But responses can vary not only in location and force, but also in topography or form, in duration, and in direction. And since any dimension of responding can be the basis for differential reinforcement, any dimension of responding may provide the defining properties of an operant class.

One dimension of special interest is the separation of responses in time. In the reinforcement of a pigeon's key-pecks, for example, differential reinforcement can be arranged for only those pecks preceded by a 10-second period of no pecking, or for only those pecks emitted so rapidly that at least five pecks occur within a 5-second period of time. In the first case, pecking may decrease, but only because the likelihood of pecks preceded by long pauses increases; the pause must in fact be treated as a component of a complex operant consisting of a pause plus a peck. In the second case, pecking may increase, but only because the high rate itself has been differentially reinforced. The significance of these examples is that the frequency or rate of responding sometimes must be taken as a direct measure of the effects of reinforcement because, like other response properties, it too can be differentiated (cf. Chapter 6). Analyses of differentiation of response rate therefore depend critically on the degree to which the temporal spacing of responses conforms to the temporal spacing that is reinforced.

If a pause plus a peck can be treated as a complex response class, then a pause alone may be treated as a response class also. Consider, for example, the class of all responses consisting of 10 seconds of no pecking. If a reinforcer is delivered after every 10 seconds without a peck, then each peck delays reinforcement by at least 10 seconds. But when a peck prevents or delays the delivery of a reinforcer, the peck is also said to be negatively punished. Thus, the positive reinforcement of a period without responding is equivalent to the negative punishment of responding. The empirical status of this distinction depends at least in part on the properties of "not responding"; should "not responding" be treated as behavior, or as the absence of behavior?

An analogous problem arises in the vocabulary of punishment. If a lever-press produces shock, this response is said to be positively punished. But every response except lever-pressing prevents the delivery of shock. Should the class of all responses but lever-presses therefore be said to be negatively reinforced (we mentioned earlier that some accounts in fact speak of punishment as *passive avoid-*

ance)? On the other hand, if lever-presses escape or avoid shock, then every response except lever-pressing is followed by shock. Should the negative reinforcement in escape or avoidance be spoken of in terms of punishment of the absence of lever-pressing?

It is simpler to speak in terms of discrete responses than in terms of their absence, so that the direct description of the effects of measurable responses such as key-pecks or lever-presses is probably preferable in each of these cases. These examples, however, illustrate the inevitable complementarity of the reinforcement and punishment operations and show how the definition of an operant class can affect the way in which we speak of behavioral operations and processes.

Complex behavior: Maze-learning

We have usually spoken of relatively simple responses, such as lever-presses and key-pecks. But the above account indicates that complex response sequences may also be affected by differential reinforcement and therefore may also be treated as operant classes. It is possible, for example, to treat the negotiation of a maze as a single but complex response. Consider the simplest maze, the T-maze, in which the start-box leads to a single choice point at which a turn either to the left or to the right is followed by some consequence. If the goal-box on the left is empty and the goal-box on the right contains food, a response sequence from start-box to goal-box that includes a right turn will become likely or, in other words, will become differentiated. (It should be noted that long sequences can also be dealt with as a succession of different operants, each having the reinforcing consequence of producing an opportunity to engage in the next, until the sequence is terminated by the delivery of the reinforcer. Such a treatment, which is beyond the scope of the present chapter, is considered in Chapter 5.)

The complexity of differentiating response sequences is illustrated by the *double-alternation problem* (e.g., Hunter, 1928) in maze-learning. At the end of a central alley, a choice point provided an opportunity for a left turn (L) or a right turn (R), but both paths led back to the beginning of the central alley. Thus, the organism could make successive turns at the choice point without being removed from the apparatus. The question was whether a double-alternation sequence (LLRR or RRLL) could be learned. The experiments were directed toward the issue of whether the organism's behavior at one time could control its subsequent behavior, and toward the comparison of the behavior of different species. In fact, the sequence was learned with varying success by different species and by the same species in different experiments. For the present purposes, however, the major point is that the question deals with the correspondence between the sequence of turns that is reinforced and the sequence that is produced by the reinforcement operation.

Except for the length and complexity of the sequence, it differs as a response class from the examples presented earlier primarily in the way in which it can be measured. The possible sequences can be itemized, but they cannot be ordered unambiguously along a single dimension (e.g., is the sequence LLLR, which contains only a single transition from L to R, or the sequence LRLR, which contains equal numbers of L's and R's, more closely related to the reinforced sequence, LLRR?). Within each sequence, the contribution of its components can also be assessed (e.g., do R's occur more frequently than L's because only the last turn in the reinforced sequence, LLRR, is immediately followed by reinforcement?). These problems have parallels in the study of motor skills in humans (e.g., Bilodeau, 1969), which sometimes deals with the acquisition of complex response sequences.

The structure of behavior

Questions about differentiable properties of responding are concerned with the structure of behavior, and the techniques of measurement will vary with the responses under study. In each case the central concern is with the dimensions along which responding conforms to the class of responses that is reinforced. When these dimensions involve structural features of behavior, it is sometimes difficult even to define them. For example, Pryor, Haag, and O'Reilly (1969) produced novel performances in a porpoise by selecting for reinforcement, in each experimental session, a class of responses that had not been reinforced in any previous session. The porpoise came to emit responses, at the beginning of successive sessions, that the experimenters had never seen before. This experiment demonstrated the differentiation of response novelty. The specification of the properties of this operant class, however, is necessarily limited to a description of the criteria for reinforcement.

Another case in point is the grammatical structure of sentences in human verbal behavior.

Grammatical and ungrammatical sentences can undoubtedly have different consequences for the speaker, and sentences can be differentiated into such grammatical classes as active versus passive voice, or declarative versus interrogative. The cases are complicated because the function of a sentence, and therefore the interpretation of its structure, may depend on the conditions under which it is uttered (e.g., Skinner, 1957). Nevertheless, techniques for dealing with the formal properties of grammatical structure are available (e.g., Chomsky, 1963). The paradox is that the development of these techniques has led to controversy over the nature of human language (Chomsky, 1959), on the grounds that the structural properties of grammar in human verbal behavior are incompatible with the processes of differential reinforcement in operant behavior.

Yet verbal behavior is consequential behavior, and the finding that some grammatical structures are more easily learned than others (e.g., McNeill, 1968), or that particular sentences are more or less easily learned depending on their grammatical structure (e.g., Mehler, 1963), is no more of an embarrassment to a behavioral formulation than the finding that a rat can learn a single-alternation sequence (LRLR) more easily than a double-alternation sequence (LLRR), or that a rat's responding may be more easily differentiated along a horizontal slot than along a vertical one. In any of these cases, the problem is empirical: the identification of the dimensions along which responding may come to conform to the class of responses that has consequences. For a given organism, operant classes may be established more easily along some dimensions than along others (at an earlier time, we might have said that some responses are easier to learn than others). Whether these dimensions are simple or complex, intensive or structural, a concern with the analysis of these dimensions must be distinguished from an analysis of the processes that result from the differential consequences of responses along these dimensions: The two concerns are not incompatible; they are complementary, and the analysis of verbal behavior must be deficient if the consequences of verbal behavior are neglected.

Discriminated operants: Discrimination and generalization

The properties with respect to which responses can be differentially reinforced include not only the dimensions of responses but also the dimensions of stimuli in the presence of which these responses occur. For example, a key-peck in the presence of a green light is different from a key-peck in the presence of a red light, and reinforcement can be arranged for pecks in the presence of one light but not the other. Response classes that are established by such differential reinforcement with respect to the properties of stimuli are called *discriminated operants*.

An experimental example: Discrimination of stimulus location

Some characteristics of discriminated operants can be illustrated by a hypothetical example that is closely related to the one presented in Figure 2.3. One wall of the rat's experimental chamber contains a horizontal slot behind which a series of lamps can separately illuminate successive 2.5-centimeter segments of the slot. Beneath the slot is a lever, and a food-pellet dispenser is located on the opposite wall. Assume now that individual lamps are illuminated in irregular order, and lever-presses are recorded during the illumination of each segment. In the absence of reinforcement, lever-pressing will be infrequent and will probably bear no systematic relationship to the segment that is illuminated. In fact, the data might be essentially the same as those shown in Figure 2.3A, the major difference being that the horizontal axis would be labeled *stimulus location* instead of *response location*.

At this point, reinforcement can be introduced for lever-presses, but only when segments 7, 8, or 9 are illuminated. The immediate effect of reinforcement may be to increase lever-pressing during the illumination of all segments, with a result much like that shown in Figure 2.3B. But with continued differential reinforcement with respect to lever-presses during the illumination of only segments 7, 8, and 9, lever-pressing will be likely to increase during the illumination of these segments and decrease during the illumination of the other segments, much as the distribution of responses changed in Figures 2.3C through 2.3E. Eventually, the differential reinforcement would produce a fairly stable pattern of responding during the illumination of the different segments, as in Figures 2.3E and 2.3F, with most lever-presses occurring during the illumination of segments 7, 8, or 9, and with lever-pressing decreasing with increasing distance of illumination from those segments correlated with reinforcement.

In the case of differential reinforcement with respect to stimulus properties, as in this example, the resulting process is called *discrimination* instead

of differentiation, and the spread of the effect of reinforcement from the stimuli correlated with reinforcement to stimuli at other points along the continuum is called *generalization* instead of induction. But the distinction between these two sets of terms is to some extent arbitrary, because in both cases the operation of differential reinforcement is involved and the processes resulting from this operation are similar.

The vocabulary of differentiation and discrimination

One feature distinguishing differential reinforcement with respect to response properties from differential reinforcement with respect to stimulus properties is methodological. In the former, the experimenter measures responses in different classes as they occur; in the latter, the experimenter can control the organism's opportunity to emit responses in different classes by presenting or removing the relevant stimuli. For example, the experimenter could establish a discrimination with respect to locations 4 and 8 by alternately illuminating these two segments and reinforcing lever-presses only during the illumination of segment 8, but never illuminating any of the other ten segments. For this reason, stimuli involved in discrimination procedures are said to *set the occasion* for responses: When a particular stimulus is treated as a property of the responses within a given class, the responses in this class cannot occur if the stimulus has not been presented. (It is appropriate to add the qualification that a stimulus may set the occasion for responding even when a delay is imposed between stimulus and response; when we ask whether the organism's response now is occasioned by some stimulus in the past, we are concerned with the study of *memory*.)

But even this methodological distinction has exceptions. Consider, for example, the differential reinforcement of the spacing of responses in time, briefly discussed in a previous section. If a pigeon's key-pecks are reinforced only when they follow a 5-second period of no pecking, the pigeon may come to space its pecks about 5 seconds apart. This performance may be spoken of as the differentiation of a complex operant consisting of a pause plus a peck. On the other hand, the duration of the pause may be treated as a stimulus property, and the performance may then be spoken of as discrimination with respect to the duration of the preceding pause: Pecks after pauses of less than 5 seconds are not reinforced and become less probable, whereas pecks after pauses of more than 5 seconds are reinforced and become more probable (Catania, 1970).

The distinction here involves the vocabulary with which we describe behavior and not the characteristics of behavioral processes. The operation of differential reinforcement underlies each of these cases. Early in this chapter we indicated that responses and stimuli have little significance unless they are treated in relationship to each other. The present examples illustrate the closeness of these relationships among responses and stimuli. It is not meaningful to speak of responses independently of the environment in which they occur, and even in cases in which the experimenter does not arrange differential reinforcement with respect to stimulus properties, some stimuli in the organism's environment must be relevant to its performance. Lever-presses cannot occur in the absence of levers, and key-pecks cannot occur in the absence of keys. And even those responses that do not depend on special apparatus, such as changes in posture, occur in an environment. Thus the processes of discrimination and generalization, which are considered in more detail in Chapter 4, are similar in their relevance to the phenomena of learning to the processes of differentiation and induction. The fundamental issue again concerns the correspondence between the dimensions on which differential reinforcement is based and the dimensions of the resulting behavior.

The controversy over *place-learning* versus *response-learning* provides an example (e.g., Restle, 1957). If right turns but not left turns are reinforced in a T-maze, the right turns of a rat may be differentiated. It is then possible to ask whether this differentiation is based on a response dimension (right turns as opposed to left turns), or whether it is based on a stimulus dimension (discrimination with respect to the orientation of the maze relative to stimuli outside the maze). If the rat has always approached the choice point from the south, these alternatives can be evaluated by modifying the maze so that the rat approaches the choice point from the north. If the rat turns right, and therefore to the goal-box opposite that in which the reinforcer had previously been delivered, response-learning is said to have been demonstrated. If the rat turns left instead, and therefore to the same goal-box as in earlier trials, place-learning is said to have been demonstrated. The question is whether the rat has learned right turns versus left turns, or east turns versus west turns. In fact, because place-learning cannot occur unless discriminable stimuli

are correlated with turns in a particular direction, the demonstration of place-learning or response-learning depends to some extent on the construction of the maze. If the maze is open, so that the stimuli outside the maze are available (e.g., windows or ceiling lights in the experimental room), place-learning will probably be observed; if the maze is closed, so that external stimuli are unavailable, response-learning becomes predominant. Either outcome can be made more likely than the other. But in both cases, the concern is whether the responding produced by differential reinforcement is to be characterized as an operant class defined by stimulus properties or an operant class defined by response properties.

Discriminable properties of stimuli

Like response properties, the stimulus properties that define the response class of a discriminated operant may be varied and complex. Simple properties of stimuli, such as intensity or visual form, can provide the basis for differential reinforcement. For example, in Lashley's (1930) jumping stand, rats are forced to jump from a platform to one of two displays (e.g., a triangle or a circle). One of these displays drops away when the rat jumps at it, and allows the rat access to food. If the rat jumps at the other display, which is immobile, the rat falls into a net below the stand. The positions of the two stimuli are irregularly alternated from trial to trial. Thus, differential reinforcement is arranged with respect to jumps to one stimulus, and differential punishment with respect to the other. The experimental question is whether responding conforms to the differential consequences in the sense that the rat comes to jump only to the stimulus correlated with reinforcement. In this apparatus, the stimulus properties that control the rat's behavior may be studied.

But differential reinforcement may also be arranged with respect to relationships among stimuli, and with respect to complex properties that are not easily quantified. Pigeons, for example, can be trained to respond to the odd stimulus of several stimuli if all but one of the stimuli are alike, or to respond to the one of several different stimuli that matches a sample stimulus (e.g., Cumming & Berryman, 1965); and in a procedure that might be said to demonstrate *concept formation* in pigeons, they can be trained to respond to pictures that contain a human form but not to pictures in which a human form is absent (e.g., Herrnstein & Loveland, 1964). Thus, the complex dimensions of oddity and matching or of the concept of human form may define discriminated operants (cf. Chapter 4).

Complex behavior: Learning set

The way in which relationships among stimulus properties may come to control responding independently of the specific stimuli that are involved is illustrated by experiments on a phenomenon called *learning set* (Harlow, 1949). Food is located under one of two different objects presented to a food-deprived monkey, and the lifting of this object is therefore differentially reinforced. After the discrimination between these two objects is established, a new pair of objects is presented, with differential reinforcement again arranged with respect to one of them. When this discrimination is established, still another new pair is presented, and so on. As the succession of new stimulus pairs continues, successive discriminations are established more and more rapidly, and eventually the monkey may respond consistently to the stimulus correlated with reinforcement after a single trial with a new pair. A discriminated operant in this situation cannot be described simply in terms of the stimuli of a given pair. Instead, it must be based on the dependency between stimuli and their correlated consequences on successive trials. If the response to a given stimulus is reinforced on the first trial with a new pair, the monkey responds to that stimulus on all subsequent trials. If that response is not reinforced, the monkey responds to the other stimulus on all subsequent trials. These relationships among stimuli, responses, and consequences are the defining properties of the behavior that is established in the phenomenon of learning set and demonstrate the complexity of the dimensions that the analysis of discriminated operants must take into account.

We confront similar problems when we ask about the critical features of letters and words as a child learns to read (e.g., Gibson, 1965). The ease with which a child learns to distinguish letters of the alphabet depends upon relationships among such stimulus properties as symmetry, curvature, and closure. But we cannot simply enumerate critical properties; with respect to some properties, for example, upper-case and lower-case forms of a single letter may differ more from each other than they differ from other letters (cf. e, E, and F; or h, n, and N). An adequate account must deal with both the structural properties of letters as stimuli and the ways in which the child behaves with respect to letters (cf. the analysis of *cognitive* process-

es: Neisser, 1967). Naming the letters in a sequence is different from reading the sequence as a word. The difference is in the child's behavior, and not in the letters as stimuli: In one case, the child responds to the letters as units; in the other, the child responds to a larger unit, the word, in which the letters are components. We may say that the child is *set* to read either letters or words. Thus, this example again demonstrates that stimulus structure cannot be specified without reference to response structure.

The nature of stimulus control

We have emphasized stimulus properties as a basis for differential reinforcement, and discrimination as a behavioral process. It is now appropriate to return to the operations on which this formulation is based. We considered, in an earlier section, the consequential operations of reinforcement and punishment: A response is followed by a consequence. But we also noted more recently that differential reinforcement with respect to stimulus properties depends on the presentation of stimuli. Thus, to deal most generally with differential reinforcement we must superimpose another operation, the *stimulus-control* operation, on the consequential operations of reinforcement and punishment: In the presence of a stimulus, a response is followed by a consequence. In these three terms, *stimulus-response-consequence,* we exhaustively characterize the fundamental relationships of operant behavior. It remains therefore to come full circle and return to the elicitation operation, to briefly consider its relationship to the operation of stimulus control.

Respondents: Differential elicitation

We defined operants in terms of their environmental effects, but classes of responses can also be defined in terms of the stimuli that produce them. Such classes are called *respondents* and correspond to what we spoke of earlier as elicited or reflexive behavior. Thus, salivation produced by food in the mouth is a respondent class. This class must be distinguished from salivation produced by acid in the mouth, which is a different respondent class, and from spontaneous salivation, which may be treated as an operant class because it is emitted rather than elicited.

We spoke of the production of responses by stimuli as the elicitation operation. There is no procedure corresponding to the differential reinforcement of response properties for the elicitation operation, because the properties of the responses in a respondent class are determined by the eliciting stimuli presented to an organism. Thus, although new operants can be created by shaping, respondents are more limited in their potentiality for modification.

There is, however, a procedure corresponding to differential reinforcement with respect to stimulus properties. Just as the stimulus-control operation can be superimposed on the operations of reinforcement or punishment, so also it can be superimposed on the operation of elicitation: A discriminative stimulus can set the occasion on which an eliciting stimulus is presented (Catania, 1971). We may call such a procedure *differential elicitation;* the elicitation operation is arranged only in the presence of a particular stimulus.

Respondent conditioning

The most familiar cases come from the demonstration of *respondent conditioning* in Pavlov's (1927) *conditioned-reflex* experiments. (Respondent conditioning has also often been called *classical* or *Pavlovian* conditioning, and is explored in detail in Chapter 3.) For example, a dog is held on a stand by a harness, a bell rings, and then food is placed in the dog's mouth. Food, which elicits salivation, is presented at the sound of the bell but not at other times. Thus, the bell is a stimulus in the presence of which the elicitation operation, the delivery of food, is arranged. The bell is referred to as a *conditioned* (or *conditional*) *stimulus*, and the food as an *unconditioned* (or *unconditional*) *stimulus*. As a result of this procedure, the dog may begin to salivate at the sound of the bell, and a *conditioned* (or *conditional*) *reflex* is then said to be established.

A contemporary example involving a motor rather than a glandular response is provided by Brown and Jenkins (1968). The key in a pigeon chamber is illuminated at irregular intervals. After several seconds of illumination, the feeder is operated. Thus, the key-illumination sets the occasion on which eating is elicited by food. In this procedure, pigeons come to peck the key after several successions of key-illumination and food. This phenomenon has been referred to as *auto-shaping* of the key-peck, and it has been given several interpretations. One is that the key-peck gradually evolves as a superstitious response; another is that it occurs because food raises the likelihood of pecking even when food is absent, and this response therefore comes to be emitted in the presence of the

stimulus correlated with food presentations. The essential point is that these procedures illustrate the operation of *differential elicitation*, elicitation in the presence of a discriminative stimulus.

Stimulus classes in conditioning

The superimposition of the stimulus-control operation on the elicitation operation need not be restricted to reinforcers as eliciting stimuli. It can also be extended to stimuli with relatively neutral properties and to stimuli with aversive properties. For example, in experiments on the phenomenon of *sensory preconditioning* (Brogden, 1939), one stimulus sets the occasion on which a second stimulus is presented; a bell may be sounded only in the presence of a light. Subsequently, a conditioned reflex is established in which the bell functions as the conditioned stimulus (e.g., the bell may set the occasion for salivation). The light is then presented to examine whether, by virtue of its earlier relationship to the bell, the light will also control responding. Demonstrations of sensory preconditioning bear the same kind of relationship to the operation of differential elicitation as demonstrations of latent learning bear to the operation of reinforcement.

Differential elicitation involving aversive stimuli has been referred to as *defensive conditioning*. For example, a light may set the occasion on which shock is presented, and responses in the presence of the light and their relationship to the responses elicited by shock may then be examined. In a related procedure concerned with a phenomenon called *conditioned suppression* or *anxiety* (see Chapter 8), the effects of the light are examined on an ongoing baseline of reinforced responding.

Response properties in conditioning

In both differential elicitation and differential reinforcement with respect to stimulus properties, responding comes to be concentrated in the presence of discriminative stimuli. In the first case, responding is produced by the elicitation operation, and in the second case, by the reinforcement operation. But in both cases the superimposition of a stimulus-control operation has similar effects; thus, the discriminative processes generated by this operation may be closely related (cf. Chapter 3). Many experiments have been concerned with the relationship between operant and respondent processes, and the success or failure of particular experiments has been taken as evidence that operant processes are in some way reducible to respondent processes, or that respondent processes are in some way reducible to operant processes, or that the two processes are completely independent. The outcomes of particular experiments, however, may depend critically on the relationship between elicited and reinforced responses. This dependency can be illustrated by comparing two experiments concerned with the operant or respondent properties of salivation.

In the classical Pavlovian experiment, salivation was elicited by food, and the subsequent elicitation of salivation by a conditioned stimulus that consistently preceded food was taken as evidence that a new respondent class, salivation elicited by the conditioned stimulus, had been established. It was possible to argue, however, that the relationship between salivation and the conditioned stimulus came about accidentally, and that salivation was subsequently maintained, as in a superstition procedure, because salivation in the presence of the conditioned stimulus was consistently followed by food (e.g., Smith, 1954). To evaluate this kind of possibility, Sheffield (1965) conducted an experiment to determine whether the addition of consequences to this procedure could modify salivation. Specifically, food was presented to a dog in the presence of a conditioned stimulus, but the food presentation was omitted whenever the dog salivated in the presence of the conditioned stimulus. This procedure, an example of negative punishment referred to as *omission training,* did not eliminate salivation; salivation did not come under the control of its consequence, the omission of food. Once salivation occurred in the presence of the conditioned stimulus, food was omitted; as a result salivation decreased on subsequent trials. But in trials without salivation, food was again presented, and thus salivation was reinstated by the succession of the conditioned stimulus and food. A new cycle of food omissions and decreased salivation then began.

In an earlier section, however, we considered an experiment by Miller and Carmona (1967). In that study, salivation was reduced when it had the consequence of reinforcement omission. The difference was that the reinforcer was water. We therefore must conclude that the relative effectiveness of eliciting and reinforcing operations must depend to some extent on the compatibility of reinforced responses and elicited responses. In the Sheffield experiment, the absence of salivation was reinforced by the presentation of food, which then elicited salivation; the reinforced absence of saliva-

tion and the elicited salivation were clearly incompatible, and reinforcement was not demonstrably effective. In the Miller and Carmona experiment, however, the absence of salivation was reinforced by the presentation of water, which does not elicit salivation; thus, there was no incompatibility between the reinforced response (the absence of salivation) and the response elicited by the reinforcer. In this case, reinforcement was effective.

Multiple functions

These examples illustrate a general concern in the analysis of behavior: the problem of *multiple function.* We have dealt with stimuli in elicitation, reinforcement, and stimulus control. But a given stimulus in a particular procedure is unlikely to have only one of these functions. A discriminative stimulus may also function as a reinforcer, and a reinforcing stimulus may also function as an elicitor. Although we understand some of the properties of these separate functions, our understanding of their effects in combination is limited. Progress in the analysis of learning phenomena will therefore depend in part on our ability to characterize the interactions among stimulus functions.

THE LIMITS OF LEARNING

The preceding account has emphasized the classification of learning phenomena in terms of behavioral operations. But when an experimental procedure is imposed upon an organism, there is no guarantee that the procedure will be effective. A procedure that leads to learning with one organism may not do so with other organisms, and an organism that learns under one procedure may not do so under other procedures. Such findings do not invalidate the classification, because the classification is simply a way of naming phenomena and relating them to one another. It would be otherwise, however, if learning were assumed to be based on a single process that acted across all organisms and all procedures.

In its historical development, the psychology of learning examined the experimental outcomes of various behavioral procedures; each procedure, in its turn, was assigned importance in proportion to its demonstrable effectiveness. The experimental findings available at different times led to theoretical formulations in which principles of association and contiguity, rules of respondent conditioning, or laws of reinforcement were singled out for dominant roles, sometimes to the extent that one or another was regarded as the exclusive and fundamental basis for learning. Such formulations, however, were inevitably open to challenge and controversy, because no single process could exhaustively account for the phenomena of learning. Learning theories became more precise, but progressive refinements were necessarily accompanied by restrictions of the range of phenomena to which the theories could be applied. Recognition of the limits of learning was implicit in these restrictions.

When the limits of learning can be readily traced to the sensory or motor capacities of an organism, they pose no problems. We are not surprised, for example, if certain stimuli are more capable of controlling responses in some species than in others. The pigeon is capable of visual discriminations that are impossible for the bat, and the bat is capable of auditory discriminations that are impossible for the pigeon, simply because these organisms have different sensory systems. Different response capabilities also do not worry us. We can attribute different modes of flight in pigeons and bats to such anatomical differences as wing structure. The examples are obvious but not trivial. They illustrate the extent to which we take the limitations of an organism's sensory and motor capacities for granted. We are not likely even to ask about flight in the rat, as we might with the bat or the pigeon; we know well enough why rats cannot fly.

Like sensory and motor capacities, the capacity of various stimuli to reinforce differs across species. Before the relativity of reinforcement was recognized, however, it was difficult to deal with findings in which established reinforcers for a species failed to have their characteristic effects. Several cases were described by Breland and Breland (1961). In a demonstration with raccoons, for example, food reinforcers were delivered when a raccoon picked up coins from the ground and deposited them in a container. But after the procedure had continued for some time, the raccoon began to spend its time rubbing the coins together instead of releasing them into the container. This finding did not invalidate the principle of reinforcement; rather, it demonstrated a property of the raccoon's behavior. A raccoon ordinarily rubs and washes its food before eating it, but the coins apparently provided a better opportunity for this behavior than the food that was used to reinforce the raccoon's performance. In this situation, rubbing was sufficiently more probable than eating that food was not an effective reinforcer; we may therefore presume that an opportunity for rubbing could have been

used to reinforce other responses, perhaps including eating.

When the relativity of reinforcement was recognized, it was no longer sufficient simply to identify the effective reinforcers for a given species. Reinforcers also had to be defined in terms of the response to be reinforced. In a given species, an effective reinforcer with one response is not necessarily an effective reinforcer with others. Thus, the limits of learning cannot be specified separately in terms of stimuli and in terms of responses; it is also necessary to consider limitations on the kinds of relationships that can be established between stimuli and responses in a given species.

An example is provided by experiments on food aversion in the rat (Revusky & Garcia, 1970). If a rat becomes sick after eating a particular food, the rat ordinarily stops eating that food; thus, eating can be punished by its systemic consequences even though these consequences may follow the eating only after a substantial delay. The properties of this kind of punishment were studied by allowing thirsty rats to drink sweetened water in the presence of noise and light. In one group of rats, drinking was followed by electric shock. In a second group, drinking was followed by levels of X-irradiation that later produced sickness. In subsequent tests with sweetened and unsweetened water, rats that had been shocked drank less in the presence of noise and light, but rats that had been X-irradiated drank less sweetened water whether or not noise and light were present. When the aversive stimulus was shock, the rats learned its relationship to external events such as noise and light. When the aversive stimulus was the delayed systemic effect of X-irradiation, the rats learned its relationship to the taste of the water that they had recently consumed. In other words, the immediate effects of shock punished drinking in the presence of noise and light, but the delayed effects of X-irradiation punished the drinking of sweetened water. This example, which is treated under the topic of attention in Chapter 4, demonstrates that rats are predisposed to learn different relationships among stimuli and responses in different situations (cf. Seligman, 1970). Thus, it is not sufficient to say for a given species that some responses or some stimuli are more easily learned than others; an account of the limits of learning must also deal with relationships among stimuli and responses.

The list could be extended. Recent research has examined the role of reinforcement and delayed systemic consequences in the development of food preferences and of the specific hungers that follow dietary deficiencies (Rozin & Kalat, 1971), the effect of species-specific defense reactions that are elicited by aversive stimuli on the development of avoidance performance (Bolles, 1970), and the nature of behavior that cannot be attributed to the accidental succession of a response and a reinforcer in the development of performance during a superstition procedure (Staddon & Simmelhag, 1971). These examples, which are also discussed in Chapter 9, deal with the boundaries within which various operations are effective, but in so doing they do not alter the defining properties of behavioral processes. If a phenomenon turns out to be less general than we once believed, it does not follow that we should begin to call it by a different name.

If it were maintained that the sole principle of learning is demonstrated by a given experimental operation, such as elicitation or reinforcement or stimulus control, then the discovery of conditions that limited the effectiveness of that operation would challenge its generality as a basis for learning. But it is now recognized that the various operations are all important in their different ways. Thus, the discovery of the limitations of each is an integral part of, rather than a critical challenge to, the analysis of learning phenomena.

SUMMARY AND CONCLUSIONS

We have presented the phenomena of learning in terms of experimental operations. We first considered the effects of the simplest operation, elicitation or the presentation of stimuli. Responses are produced by stimuli, and the probability of these responses can be modified not only by stimulus presentations but by the temporal patterning of these presentations. The elicitation operation also may have other effects: Elicited responses may become more probable even in the absence of the eliciting stimulus, and stimulus presentations may affect responses that they follow in the phenomenon of superstition.

But just as stimuli may be followed by responses, responses may be followed by stimuli, and the treatment of the consequential operations of reinforcement and punishment therefore dealt with the effects of response consequences. On the basis of the effects of these operations, we distinguished among positive reinforcement, negative reinforcement (or escape and avoidance), positive punishment, and negative punishment (or omission training). In addition, the treatment of phenomena such

as sensory-motor learning and latent learning demonstrated the importance of the less dramatic consequences, sometimes misleadingly called neutral, that are not usually classified as reinforcers or punishers.

Reinforcement and punishment were distinguished on the basis of whether response consequences produced increases or decreases in responding, but we noted that the distinction between the positive and negative cases of these operations was to some extent arbitrary. The positive and negative cases could not be treated consistently in terms of whether response consequences involved the presentation or removal of stimuli. Instead, these cases were treated in terms of the temporal relationship between the reinforced or punished responses and other responses that were produced by these operations.

The final operation, stimulus control, is an operation that can be superimposed on either the elicitation operation or the consequential operations of reinforcement and punishment. When superimposed on elicitation, this operation generates the processes that have been spoken of as respondent conditioning; special cases include sensory preconditioning, in which the eliciting stimulus is neutral, and defensive conditioning, in which the eliciting stimulus is aversive. When superimposed on consequential operations, the stimulus-control operation generates discrimination procedures. We considered here only the case of discrimination with respect to positive reinforcement, but the analysis can be extended to punishment and to the neutral consequences of latent learning as well.

These operations exhaust the behavioral relationships that can be established among stimuli and responses. A particular concern was therefore the characterization of the dimensions along which stimuli and responses can vary: This concern was treated in the discussion of the processes of differentiation and discrimination and it was shown that the relevant dimensions included not only such relatively simple dimensions as intensity, location, and topography, but the complex dimensions of stimulus and response relationship and structure. The analysis of structure is different from the analysis of the functions of stimuli and responses, and it is essential to the definition of response classes.

One conclusion to be drawn from this account is that behavior is best represented in terms of a continuum of processes instead of in terms of dichotomized categories. Reinforcement and punishment are not independent processes, but are extremes on a continuum ranging from those consequential operations that raise the probability of responses, through those that have no effect on the probability of responses, to those that lower the probability of responses. Positive and negative reinforcement are not independent processes, but differ with respect to the magnitude of the eliciting and discriminative effects of the stimuli that are present during the reinforcement operation. Differentiation and discrimination are not independent processes, but differ only with respect to whether the operation of differential reinforcement emphasizes response properties or stimulus properties. And the effects of differential reinforcement and differential elicitation are not independent processes, but are related in that the stimulus-control operation modifies the respond-ing that is generated by the reinforcement or elicitation operations on which it is superimposed.

In all of this, the term *learning* has receded into the background, and it may well be that it has outlived its usefulness. Behavioral hierarchies can be modified, new responses can be shaped, and discriminations can be established. These are phenomena of behavior, and part of our understanding of these phenomena depends on how accurately we can speak of them. The present vocabulary is not without ambiguities, and it will undoubtedly change. But in its emphasis on behavioral operations and behavioral processes, it adheres closely to what is done and what is seen in experiments on behavior. And this adherence may be essential to our progress, for it is not useful to say that an organism has learned unless we can also say what it has learned, and how.

REFERENCES

Antonitis, J. J. Response variability in the white rat during conditioning, extinction, and reconditioning. *Journal of Experimental Psychology,* 1951, **42,** 273–281.

Azrin, N. H. Some effects of two intermittent schedules of immediate and non-immediate punishment. *Journal of Psychology,* 1956, **42,** 3–21.

Azrin, N. H., & Holz, W. C. Punishment. In W. K. Honig (Ed.), *Operant behavior: Areas of research and application.* New York: Appleton-Century-Crofts, 1966. Pp. 380–447.

Azrin, N. H., Hutchinson, R. R., & Hake, D. F. Extinction-induced aggression. *Journal of the Experimental Analysis of Behavior,* 1966, **9,** 191–204.

Azrin, N. H., Hutchinson, R. R., & McLaughlin, R. The opportunity for aggression as an operant reinforcer during aversive stimulation. *Journal of the Experimental Analysis of Behavior,* 1965, **8,** 171–180.

Badia, P., Suter, S., & Lewis, P. Rat vocalization to shock with and without a *CS. Psychonomic Science,* 1966, **4,** 117–118.

Beale, G. H. Adaptation in paramecia. In R. Davis & E. F. Gale (Eds.), *Adaptation in microorganisms.* (Third Symposium of the Society for General Microbiology.) Cambridge: Cambridge University Press, 1953. Pp. 294–305.

Berlyne, D. E. *Conflict, arousal, and curiosity.* New York: McGraw-Hill, 1960.

Best, J. B. The photosensitization of paramecia aurelia by temperature shock. *Journal of Experimental Zoology,* 1954, **126,** 87–99.

Bilodeau, E. A. (Ed.) *Principles of skill acquisition.* New York: Academic Press, 1969.

Bindra, D. Components of general activity and the analysis of behavior. *Psychological Review,* 1961, **68,** 205–215.

Blough, D. S. New test for tranquilizers. *Science,* 1958, **127,** 586–587.

Bolles, R. C. Species-specific defense reactions and avoidance learning. *Psychological Review,* 1970, **77,** 32–48.

Breland, K., & Breland, M. The misbehavior of organisms. *American Psychologist,* 1961, **16,** 681–684.

Brogden, W. J. Sensory preconditioning. *Journal of Experimental Psychology,* 1939, **25,** 323–332.

Brown, P. L., & Jenkins, H. M. Auto-shaping of the pigeon's key-peck. *Journal of the Experimental Analysis of Behavior,* 1968, **11,** 1–8.

Butler, R. A. The effect of deprivation of visual incentives on visual exploration motivation in monkeys. *Journal of Comparative and Physiological Psychology,* 1957, **50,** 177–179.

Catania, A. C. Glossary. In A. C. Catania (Ed.), *Contemporary research in operant behavior.* Glenview, Ill.: Scott, Foresman, 1968. Pp. 327–349.

Catania, A. C. On the vocabulary and the grammar of behavior. *Journal of the Experimental Analysis of Behavior,* 1969, **12,** 845–846.

Catania, A. C. Reinforcement schedules and psychophysical judgments: A study of some temporal properties of behavior. In W. N. Schoenfeld (Ed.), *The theory of reinforcement schedules.* New York: Appleton-Century-Crofts, 1970. Pp. 1–42.

Catania, A. C. Elicitation, reinforcement, and stimulus control. In R. Glaser (Ed.), *The nature of reinforcement.* New York: Academic Press, 1971. Pp. 196–220.

Chomsky, N. Review of B. F. Skinner's *Verbal behavior. Language,* 1959, **35,** 26–58.

Chomsky, N. Formal properties of grammars. In R. D. Luce, R. R. Bush, & E. Galanter (Eds.), *Handbook of mathematical psychology.* Vol. 2. New York: Wiley, 1963. Pp. 323–418.

Cofer, C. N., & Appley, M. H. *Motivation. Theory and research.* New York: Wiley, 1964.

Cumming, W. W., & Berryman, R. The complex discriminated operant: Studies of matching-to-sample and related problems. In D. I. Mostofsky (Ed.), *Stimulus generalization.* Stanford: Stanford University Press, 1965. Pp. 284–330.

Falk, J. L. Production of polydipsia in normal rats by an intermittent food schedule. *Science,* 1961, **133,** 195–196.

Falk, J. L. The nature and determinants of adjunctive behavior. *Physiology and Behavior,* 1971, **6,** 577–588.

Ferster, C. B. Control of behavior in chimpanzees and pigeons by time out from positive reinforcement. *Psychological Monographs,* 1958, **72,** (8, Whole Number 461).

Gibson, E. J. Learning to read. *Science,* 1965, **148,** 1066–1072.

Goldstein, H., Krantz, D. L., & Rains, J. D. *Controversial issues in learning.* New York: Appleton-Century-Crofts, 1965.

Gollub, L. R. Stimulus generalization of response-position in the rat. *Psychonomic Science,* 1966, **6,** 433–434.

Harlow, H. F. The formation of learning sets. *Psychological Review,* 1949, **56,** 51–65.

Held, R., & Hein, A. Movement-produced stimulation in the development of visually guided behavior. *Journal of Comparative and Physiological Psychology,* 1963, **56,** 872–876.

Herrnstein, R. J. Method and theory in the study of avoidance. *Psychological Review,* 1969, **76,** 49–69.

Herrnstein, R. J., & Hineline, P. N. Negative reinforcement as shock-frequency reduction. *Journal of the Experimental Analysis of Behavior,* 1966, **9,** 421–430.

Herrnstein, R. J., & Loveland, D. H. Complex visual concept in the pigeon. *Science,* 1964, **146,** 549–551.

Hess, E. H. Imprinting. *Science,* 1959, **130,** 133–141.

Hilgard, E. R. Method and procedures in the study of learning. In S. S. Stevens (Ed.), *Handbook of experimental psychology.* New York: Wiley, 1951. Pp. 517–567.

Hogan, J. A. The development of a hunger system in young chicks. *Behaviour,* 1971, **39,** 128–201.

Hull, C. L. *Principles of behavior.* New York: Appleton-Century-Crofts, 1943.

Hunter, W. S. The behavior of raccoons in a double-alternation temporal maze. *Journal of Genetic Psychology,* 1928, **35,** 374–388.

Hutchinson, R. R., Renfrew, J. W., & Young, G. A. Effects of long-term shock and associated stimuli on aggressive and manual responses. *Journal of the Experimental Analysis of Behavior,* 1971, **15,** 141–166.

Jensen, D. D. Experiments on learning in paramecia. *Science,* 1957, **125,** 191–192.

Kelleher, R. T., & Morse, W. H. Schedules using noxious stimuli: III. Responding maintained with response-produced electric shocks. *Journal of the Experimental Analysis of Behavior,* 1968, **11,** 819–838.

Kendall, S. B. Spontaneous recovery after extinction with periodic time-outs. *Psychonomic Science,* 1965, **2,** 117–118.

Kimble, G. A. (Ed.) *Hilgard and Marquis' Conditioning and learning*. (2nd ed.) New York: Appleton-Century-Crofts, 1961.

Kish, G. B. Studies of sensory reinforcement. In W. K. Honig (Ed.), *Operant behavior: Areas of research and application.* New York: Appleton-Century-Crofts, 1966. Pp. 109–159.

Lashley, K. S. The mechanism of vision. I. A method for rapid analysis of pattern vision in the rat. *Journal of Genetic Psychology*, 1930, **37**, 453–460.

McNeill, D. On theories of language acquisition. In T. R. Dixon & D. L. Horton (Eds.), *Verbal behavior and general behavior theory*. Englewood Cliffs, N.J.: Prentice-Hall, 1968. Pp. 406–420.

Meehl, P. E. On the circularity of the law of effect. *Psychological Bulletin*, 1950, **47**, 52–75.

Mehler, J. Some effects of grammatical transformations on the recall of English sentences. *Journal of Verbal Learning and Verbal Behavior*, 1963, **2**, 346–351.

Miller, N. E., & Carmona, A. Modification of a visceral response, salivation in thirsty dogs, by instrumental training with water reward. *Journal of Comparative and Physiological Psychology*, 1967, **63**, 1–6.

Morse, W. H. Intermittent reinforcement. In W. K. Honig (Ed.), *Operant behavior: Areas of research and application.* New York: Appleton-Century-Crofts, 1966. Pp. 52–108.

Mowrer, O. H., & Jones, H. M. Extinction and behavior variability as functions of effortfulness of task. *Journal of Experimental Psychology*, 1943, **33**, 369–385.

Neisser, U. *Cognitive psychology.* New York: Appleton-Century-Crofts, 1967.

Pavlov, I. P. Conditioned reflexes. G. V. Anrep (Trans.) London: Oxford University Press, 1927.

Peterson, N. Control of behavior by presentation of an imprinted stimulus. *Science*, 1960, **132**, 1395–1396.

Premack, D. Toward empirical behavior laws: I. Positive reinforcement. *Psychological Review*, 1959, **66**, 219–233.

Premack, D. Reversibility of the reinforcement relation. *Science*, 1962, **136**, 255–257.

Premack, D. Catching up with common sense or two sides of a generalization: Reinforcement and punishment. In R. Glaser (Ed.), *The nature of reinforcement*. New York: Academic Press, 1971. Pp. 121–150.

Pryor, K. W., Haag, R., & O'Reilly, J. The creative porpoise: Training for novel behavior. *Journal of the Experimental Analysis of Behavior*, 1969, **12**, 653–661.

Reid, R. L. The role of the reinforcer as a stimulus. *British Journal of Psychology*, 1958, **49**, 202–209.

Restle, F. Discrimination of cues in mazes: A resolution of the "place-versus-response" question. *Psychological Review*, 1957, **64**, 217–228.

Revusky, S., & Garcia, J. Learned associations over long delays. In G. H. Bower (Ed.), *The psychology of learning and motivation*. Vol. 4. New York: Academic Press, 1970. Pp. 1–84.

Rozin, P., & Kalat, J. W. Specific hungers and poison avoidance as adaptive specializations in learning. *Psychological Review*, 1971, **78**, 459–486.

Seligman, M. E. P. On the generality of the laws of learning. *Psychological Review*, 1970, **77**, 406–418.

Sheffield, F. D. Relation between classical conditioning and instrumental learning. In W. F. Prokasy (Ed.), *Classical conditioning: A symposium*. Appleton-Century-Crofts, 1965. Pp. 302–322.

Sherrington, C. S. *The integrative action of the nervous system.* New Haven: Yale University Press, 1906.

Skinner, B. F. On the conditions of elicitation of certain eating reflexes. *Proceedings of the National Academy of Sciences*, 1930, **16**, 433–438.

Skinner, B. F. The concept of the reflex in the description of behavior. *Journal of General Psychology*, 1931, **5**, 427–458.

Skinner, B. F. *The behavior of organisms*. New York: Appleton-Century-Crofts, 1938.

Skinner, B. F. "Superstition" in the pigeon. *Journal of Experimental Psychology*, 1948, **38**, 168–172.

Skinner, B. F. Are theories of learning necessary? *Psychological Review*, 1950, **57**, 193–216.

Skinner, B. F. A case history in scientific method. *American Psychologist*, 1956, **11**, 221–233.

Skinner, B. F. *Verbal behavior*. New York: Appleton-Century-Crofts, 1957.

Smith, K. Conditioning as an artifact. *Psychological Review*, 1954, **61**, 217–225.

Solomon, R. L. Punishment. *American Psychologist*, 1964, **19**, 239–253.

Staddon, J. E. R., & Simmelhag, V. L. The "superstition" experiment: A reexamination of its implications for the principles of adaptive behavior. *Psychological Review*, 1971, **78**, 3–43.

Thistlethwaite, D. A critical review of latent learning and related experiments. *Psychological Bulletin*, 1951, **48**, 97–129.

Thorndike, E. L. Animal intelligence: An experimental study of the associative processes in animals. *Psychological Monographs*, 1898, **2**, 109.

Thorndike, E. L. *The psychology of learning.* New York: Teachers College, 1913.

Watson, J. B. *Psychology from the standpoint of a behaviorist.* Philadelphia: Lippincott, 1919.

Weiss, B., & Laties, V. G. Behavioral thermoregulation. *Science*, 1961, **133**, 1338–1344.

Woodworth, R. S., & Schlosberg, H. *Experimental psychology.* (Rev. ed.) New York: Holt, Rinehart & Winston, 1954. Figure 2.2: Copyright 1938, 1954 by Holt, Rinehart and Winston, Inc. Copyright © 1966 by Mrs. Greta Woodworth Herron, Svenson Woodworth, William Woodworth, and Virginia Woodworth. Reprinted by permission of Holt, Rinehart and Winston, Inc.

Zener, K., & McCurdy, H. G. Analysis of motivation factors in conditioned behavior: I. Differential effect of change in hunger upon conditioned, unconditioned, and spontaneous salivary secretion. *Journal of Psychology*, 1939, **8**, 321–350.

CLASSICAL CONDITIONING

3

H. S. Terrace
Columbia University

Questions about mind are everywhere, poor doctor. Why do your arms and feet
obey your will, while your liver does not? How does thought take place in your
fragile brain? What is matter? Your peers have written ten thousand volumes
on this subject. All they have found are a few of its qualities which children
know as well as you.

Voltaire (1769)
Philosophical Dictionary

Classical conditioning is a procedure for creating a new reflex (*S2* elicits
R2). This is accomplished by repeatedly presenting a stimulus (*S2*) prior
to the occurrence of an existing reflex (*S1* elicits *R1*). The temporal contiguity between *S1* and *S2* at once places this aspect of classical conditioning in the venerable tradition of associationist and empiricist philosophies
(e.g., Aristotle, ca. 350 B.C.; Hartley, 1749; Locke, 1690). The principles of
classical conditioning per se did not emerge full blown, however, until
Pavlov (1906, 1927), the eminent Russian physiologist, integrated the
principles of association with the more recently developed principles of
reflexology. What resulted was an associationist psychology whose unit of
analysis was the acquired reflex rather than the idea.

Pavlov's work on acquired reflexes also broadened considerably the
domain of adaptive mechanisms of the kind described earlier by Darwin
and by Spencer. Prior to Pavlov, only inborn reflexes were recognized as
examples of how an organism's behavior could help it adapt to particular features of the environment. Thus, Pavlov's description of how
innate responses come to be controlled by stimuli other than those which
initially elicited them was a major supplement to the Darwinian theory
of biological adjustment. The principles of classical conditioning also
provided a basis, heretofore lacking, for a completely deterministic
analysis of behavior.

Even though Pavlov was a gifted observer of behavior, his systematic
studies of the classically conditioned reflex were concerned more with
unraveling the physiology of the cerebral cortex than with establishing
the classically conditioned reflex as a unit of behavioral analysis. The
behavioral implications of the concept of classical conditioning received
little attention until Watson (1916, 1919) brought Pavlov's work to the

Preparation of this chapter was supported in part by National Science Foundation Grant
GB 8111X and National Institutes of Health Grant HD–00930–08.

attention of American psychologists as part of his promotion of behaviorism. Watson (1925) felt so confident about the potential of Pavlov's methods for establishing new reflexes that he concluded: "Give me a dozen healthy infants, well-formed, and my own specified world to bring them up in and I'll guarantee to take any one at random and train him to become any type of specialist I might select—doctor, lawyer, artist, merchant, chief and, yes, even beggarman and thief, regardless of his talents, penchants, tendencies, abilities, vocations, and the race of his ancestors" [p. 104].

It is now a matter of history that neither Pavlov's hope of understanding the activity of the cerebral cortex via the study of classical conditioning, nor Watson's hope of establishing a system of behavior based solely on the analytic unit of the conditional reflex (e.g., Watson, 1919, 1925) were to materialize in accordance with their expectations. Pavlov's metaphorical descriptions of how the cerebral cortices function have yet to prove fruitful. Watson's blueprint for synthesizing all of human behavior on the basis of inborn and classically conditioned reflexes was incomplete because it neglected to consider behavior that was conditioned as a result of its consequences.

As described in Chapter 1, this second type of conditioning was initially investigated by Thorndike in his work on escape from puzzle boxes. Since then, it has been studied by many psychologists and has been given various names: "trial-and-error" or "success" learning, "problem-solving," "instrumental conditioning," and "operant conditioning." These names have different connotations, depending on their historical usage in reference to different experimental settings by psychologists of various theoretical persuasions. However, all these terms have in common the notion of a dependency between a specified response and a consequent stimulus. This sort of dependency, and the behavioral processes to which it gives rise, has been discussed at length in Chapter 2. Here, the term *instrumental conditioning* will be used to designate procedures that involve such a dependency, in contrast to *classical conditioning,* which, at least in terms of experimental operations, does not involve any dependency between a response and a consequent stimulus. Instead, classical conditioning involves a dependency between a prior stimulus and an eliciting stimulus (in the terminology of Chapter 2, this is a *stimulus-control* operation superimposed upon an elicitation operation).

When discussion turns to the kinds of responses that may be conditioned by these two procedures, it will be necessary to distinguish between *operants* —that is, responses that are freely emitted, in the sense that no eliciting stimulus can be identified— and *respondents,* which are occasioned by specific eliciting stimuli. This chapter will be concerned in part with the relations between different classes of responses and different conditioning procedures that are effective in modifying behavior.

The delineation of a second type of conditioning not only reduced the domain of behaviors to which the principles of classical conditioning could apply, but it also raised some important and yet unresolved questions that must be answered before we can feel secure about how we characterize classical conditioning. These questions include: Which paradigm, classical, instrumental, or possibly some combination of the two, was responsible for a particular instance of conditioned behavior? Which of the two procedures is more effective in establishing a conditioned response? Might classical conditioning be an artifact of instrumental conditioning?

Many psychologists have come to appreciate that a pure instance of classical or instrumental conditioning is difficult, if not impossible, to produce (e.g., Kimble, 1961, pp. 78–81) and have begun instead to consider the two types of conditioning as interacting processes (e.g., Rescorla & Solomon, 1967; Schoenfeld, 1966). The principles of classical conditioning have nevertheless made a fundamental impact on modern psychology. The purposes of this chapter are to describe these principles, to assess the current state of our knowledge of classical conditioning, and to describe some of the possible relations between classical and instrumental conditioning.

PAVLOV'S STUDY OF SALIVARY CONDITIONING

The systematic study of classical conditioning originated with Pavlov's investigation of the *psychic secretion* of saliva (Pavlov, 1906, 1927). During the course of his research on the dog's digestive and salivary reflexes, for which he received the Nobel prize in 1904, Pavlov noted that salivation sometimes occurred upon his entering the laboratory room in which a particular dog was studied. This salivation, which occurred before food powder had been placed in the dog's food dish, at first annoyed Pavlov because it interfered with his measurement of the salivation elicited by food that was actually in the dog's mouth.

Pavlov soon realized that he could not attribute these apparently spontaneous instances of psychic secretion to the dog's thoughts or emotions, because each dog appeared to salivate in response to some particular exteroceptive stimulus. Thus, the phenomenon of psychic secretion appeared reflexive in nature. Pavlov concluded that psychic secretion was not a capricious event and that it could be studied with the same rigor that he had applied to the study of inborn digestive reflexes.

One of the problems that Pavlov studied in his original investigations of the stomach and salivary glands was the relationship between what was fed to the dog and the nature and the amount of the resulting gastric or salivary secretion. In these studies Pavlov could clearly specify the stimulus that produced a particular secretory response, which allowed him, as well as other investigators, to duplicate the stimulus situation in subsequent experiments with different subjects. This was not, however, true in the case of the psychic salivation that followed Pavlov's entrance into the room. Pavlov did not know whether his footsteps, the opening of the door, his coat, his beard, or some other stimulus was responsible for the dog's salivation. Nor was he sure why some dogs salivated at the sight of food in the food dish instead of on his entering the room. Pavlov also did not understand why psychic secretion did not occur reliably within individual dogs. He hypothesized that the variations he observed had to do with certain features of the earlier history of each dog.

Pavlov had tested this hypothesis by insuring that he could specify clearly the stimulus responsible for eliciting salivation. Thus Pavlov's experiments made use of fairly simple stimuli, such as pure tones, buzzes, or the ticking of a metronome. He conducted these experiments in a building whose foundations were surrounded by straw and whose interior walls were more than a foot thick. As an extra safeguard against extraneous sounds from outside the building or from other experiments, each laboratory was isolated from other laboratories in all directions.

A modern version of the typical arrangement used in Pavlov's laboratory is shown in Figure 3.1. A dog, partially restrained by a harness, was placed on a stand. A minor operation had been performed earlier to divert the dog's saliva, which would normally flow from the parotid gland to the mouth, into a tube leading through the cheek. Also shown are devices for presenting food and the stimuli.

The acquisition of a conditional response

An experiment performed by Anrep (1920), a collaborator of Pavlov's, illustrates the conditioning of the salivary response. Prior to the start of the

Figure 3.1 Apparatus for the conditioning of a salivary response in a dog. (From Shapiro, 1959.)

experiment, the dog was familiarized with the experimental situation. At the start of the experiment Anrep noted that the tone did not elicit salivation, while food placed directly in the mouth did. We can state, therefore, that the reflex, food elicits salivation, was at greater-than-zero strength, while the reflex, tone elicits salivation, was at zero strength.

After noting the initial magnitudes of the salivary response to the tone and to food in the mouth, Anrep employed the following procedure. The tone was sounded for 5 seconds. The food dish was filled approximately 2.5 seconds after the tone had been turned off. A period of silence followed, and a new trial was started when the tone-followed-by-food sequence was again initiated. The values of the intertrial interval ranged between 5 and 35 minutes. Over a period of 16 days, 50 tone-food trials were presented.

Following every tenth trial, Anrep presented the tone for a period of 30 seconds. No food was presented on these trials to insure that whatever salivation occurred could be attributed unequivocally to the presentation of the tone alone. On each subsequent test trial Anrep recorded the number of drops of salivation and the latency of each response. The results are shown in Figures 3.2 and 3.3. In Figure 3.2 we see that the number of drops of salivation elicited by the tone increased from an initial value of zero to an asymptotic value of approximately 60 drops. In Figure 3.3 we see that the latency of the tone-elicited salivary response steadily decreased to an asymptotic value of less than 2 seconds.

As a result of pairing tone and food, the tone-followed-by-salivation reflex was increased from a value of zero to a value greater than zero. The increase in the strength of one reflex (tone elicits salivation), as a result of its being followed by a second reflex (food elicits salivation), is what is meant by classical conditioning.

Pavlov referred to the originally ineffective stimulus as a *conditional* stimulus (*CS*) to emphasize that the presentation of food was conditional upon the prior occurrence of this stimulus. In referring to it as the conditional stimulus, Pavlov also sought to draw attention to the fact that the only way in which the originally ineffective stimulus could be made to elicit salivation was by pairing it with food. In his description of Anrep's experiment, Pavlov referred to food as the *unconditional* stimulus (*US*) to indicate that no additional conditions were necessary for the elicitation of salivation by food placed in the mouth. The sequence of the conditional stimulus followed by salivation was called a conditional reflex. Unfortunately, the

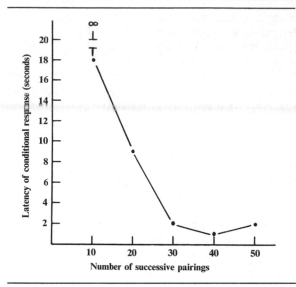

Figure 3.3 Latency of the conditional salivary response as a function of the number of pairings of the *CS* and the *US*. (From Anrep, 1920.)

terms *conditional* and *unconditional* have been modified in translation into *conditioned* and *unconditioned,* respectively (Dykman, 1967; Galanter, 1966; Gantt, 1966). With hopes of conveying Pavlov's original meaning, we will follow his original terminology.

Processes of conditioning

In addition to describing the sufficient conditions for establishing conditional reflexes, Pavlov (1927) also described how conditional reflexes were weakened or abolished in *extinction*, how the tendency to respond to one conditional stimulus *generalized* to other stimuli, and how a *discrimination* between two or more conditional stimuli could be formed.

Extinction

"The phenomenon of a rapid and more or less progressive weakening of the reflex to a conditional stimulus which is repeated a number of times without reinforcement may be appropriately termed experimental extinction of conditional reflexes" [Pavlov, 1927, p. 49]. Pavlov thus described the weakening of a conditional reflex by the repeated presentation of the *CS* without the *US*. A graphic illustration of the weakening of the conditional reflex as represented by a lengthening of the latency

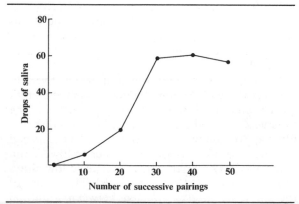

Figure 3.2 Magnitude of the conditional salivary response as a function of the number of pairings of the *CS* and the *US*. (From Anrep, 1920.)

of the conditional response and a decrease in its magnitude is shown in Figures 3.4 and 3.5.

The use of an extinction procedure does not necessarily result in the permanent weakening of the conditional reflex. Pavlov (1927) observed that when "left to themselves, extinguished conditional reflexes spontaneously recovered their full strength after a longer or shorter interval of time" [p. 58]. This process, which Pavlov referred to as *spontaneous recovery,* required no further presentation of the unconditional stimulus. Data illustrating spontaneous recovery are shown in Table 3.1. In both instances, we see that the salivary reflex in-

Table 3.1   Spontaneous Recovery

Time during extinction session	Secretion of saliva in *cc*'s
11:33 A.M.	1.0
11:36 A.M.	0.6
11:39 A.M.	0.3
11:42 A.M.	0.1
11:45 A.M.	0.0
11:48 A.M.	0.0
Interval of 2 hours	
1:50 P.M.	0.15
Data obtained by Dr. Babkin	
1:42 P.M.	8
1:52 P.M.	3
2:02 P.M.	0
Interval of 20 minutes	
2:22 P.M.	7
Data obtained by Dr. Eliason	

(From Pavlov, 1927.)

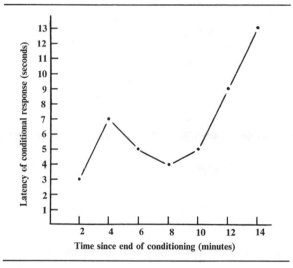

Figure 3.4   Latency of the conditional salivary response during extinction. (From Pavlov, 1927.)

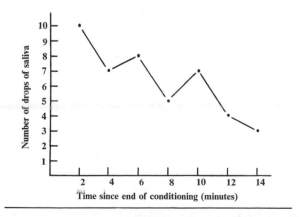

Figure 3.5   Magnitude of the conditional salivary response during extinction. (From Pavlov, 1927.)

creased from zero strength at the end of the first extinction period to a greater-than-zero value following a period of time during which neither the conditional nor the unconditional stimulus was presented.

Generalization

After establishing a conditional reflex, in which the conditional stimulus was a 1000-*Hertz* (*Hz*) tone, Pavlov (1927) observed:

Many other tones spontaneously acquired similar properties, such properties diminishing proportionally to the intervals of these tones from the one of 1000 *Hz*. Similarly, if a tactile stimulation of a definite circumscribed area of skin is made into a conditional stimulus, tactile stimulation of other skin areas will also elicit some conditional reaction, the effect diminishing with increasing distance of these areas from the one for which the conditional reflex was originally established [p. 113].

Table 3.2 shows some data collected by Anrep that illustrate Pavlov's second example. The values in Table 3.2 are averaged data from a single subject. They were obtained following the presentation of a tactile stimulus to various parts of the body after a conditional salivary response to stimulation of the thigh was established. All the data shown in Table 3.2 were collected during extinction in order

Table 3.2   Generalization Data

Location of stimulation	Number of drops of salivation (cc)
Hind paw	33
Thigh (area to which U/S was presented)	53
Pelvis	45
Middle of trunk	39
Shoulder	23
Foreleg	21
Front paw	19

(Anrep, as reported in Pavlov, 1927.)

to minimize the possibility that the dog would learn to discriminate between the original conditional stimulus and the test stimuli.

Discrimination learning

If the conditions shown in Table 3.2 were permanent, the conditional reflex would appear to be more of a detriment than an advantage to the organism in adapting to its environment. It is usually the case, however, that an organism learns to respond almost exclusively to a stimulus that precedes the unconditional stimulus and not to respond to other related stimuli that are not followed by the unconditional stimulus. By using the *method of contrasts,* which calls for the successive alternation of two or more stimuli in an irregular series, Pavlov studied the way in which an organism learns to respond differentially to the stimulus that is followed by the presentation of the *US.* In the simplest case, only one of these stimuli is correlated with the unconditional stimulus. This stimulus is usually referred to as $CS+$ and the stimulus that is not followed by the presentation of the unconditional stimulus is referred to as $CS-$. Since, by definition, $CS-$ is never followed by the *US,* the $CS-$ condition is identical to the experimental extinction previously discussed. Over the course of successive presentations of $CS+$ and $CS-$ the strength of the response to $CS-$ steadily decreases.

It is important to note that all classical-conditioning procedures, including those which only employ $CS+$, train a discrimination between the conditional stimulus and its absence. This is true

Table 3.3   The Formation of a Discrimination

Time	Stimulus applied during 30 seconds	Salivary secretion recorded by divisions of scale (5 divisions = 0.1 cc) during 30 seconds	Remarks
	Experiment of February 15, 1917.		
3:13 P.M.	Object rotating clockwise	27	Reinforced
3:25 P.M.	Object rotating counter-clockwise	7	Not reinforced
	Experiment of February 16, 1917.		
1:04 P.M.	Object rotating clockwise	24	Reinforced
1:14 P.M.	Object rotating clockwise	26	Reinforced
1:25 P.M.	Object rotating clockwise	27	Reinforced
1:34 P.M.	Object rotating counter-clockwise	10	Not reinforced
	Experiment of February 17, 1917.		
2:45 P.M.	Object rotating counter-clockwise	12	Not reinforced
	Experiment of February 18, 1917.		
2:48 P.M.	Object rotating clockwise	19	Reinforced
3:33 P.M.	Object rotating counter-clockwise	34	Not reinforced
	Experiment of February 20, 1917.		
3:07 P.M.	Object rotating counter-clockwise	26	Not reinforced
3:28 P.M.	Object rotating clockwise	26	Reinforced
	Experiment of February 21, 1917.		
3:00 P.M.	Object rotating counter-clockwise	12	Not reinforced

The strength of the reflex that is undergoing differential inhibition now diminishes progressively with small fluctuations until it reaches a permanent zero.

(Gubergritz, as reported in Pavlov, 1927.)

because, by definition, the *CS* occurs during, but not between, trials. Since the frequency of the conditional response is greater in the presence of the *CS* than in its absence, we can say that in every successful experiment on classical conditioning the subject has learned to discriminate between the presence of the *CS* and its absence.

An experiment performed by Gubergritz (in Pavlov, 1927) illustrates the acquisition of a discrimination between two exteroceptive stimuli. In this experiment an object rotating in a clockwise direction served as *CS+,* while the same object rotating in the opposite direction served as *CS−.* Over the course of discrimination training, the magnitude of the response to *CS−* decreased in an irregular manner until, as noted at the bottom of Table 3.3, the strength of the response to *CS−* reached a zero value.

GENERAL PRINCIPLES OF CLASSICAL CONDITIONING
Unconditional stimuli

By definition, all unconditional stimuli elicit certain responses. These responses may involve organs innervated by either the skeletal or the autonomic nervous systems. It is also possible to produce an unconditional response by bypassing surgically the peripheral nervous system and stimulating the brain or spinal cord directly. For example, direct stimulation of the *lateral cerebellar lobe* (Brogden & Gantt, 1937), the *dorsal columns* of the spinal cord (Loucks & Gantt, 1938), and the *motor cortex* (Doty & Giurgea, 1961; Wagner, Thomas, & Norton, 1967) can serve as effective unconditional stimuli.

In addition to eliciting behavior, unconditional stimuli may also function as reinforcing stimuli (cf. Chapter 2). Food, for example, elicits salivation, but it can also function as a *positive reinforcer:* Behavior instrumental in obtaining food is typically strengthened. Electric shock can elicit leg flexion, but it can also function as a *negative reinforcer:* Behavior followed by shock is typically weakened. On the other hand, if some response is instrumental in eliminating or reducing the probability of occurrence of the negative reinforcer, or in diminishing its intensity, that response is typically strengthened.

Direct stimulation of the central nervous system deserves special consideration as an unconditional stimulus. Doty and Giurgea (1961) and Wagner, Thomas, and Norton (1967), among others, have reported that direct stimulation of

the motor cortex can serve as an unconditional stimulus. Whether or not such stimulation also functions as a reinforcing stimulus—either positive or negative—cannot be stated unequivocally at the present time. As we shall see later, however, the study by Wagner et al. (1967) indicates that direct stimulation of the motor cortex may have rewarding properties. A partial, but representative, list of unconditional stimuli and the responses they elicit is shown in Table 3.4.

The potentially dual functions of unconditional stimuli—eliciting and reinforcing—pose a number of important questions about the nature of classical conditioning. As we shall see later, certain generalizations concerning classical conditioning are not equally valid for both positive and negative unconditional stimuli. It may, therefore, be important to distinguish between *classical reward conditioning,* where the *US* can function as a positive reinforcer, and *classical defense conditioning,* where the *US* can function as a negative reinforcer (cf. Spence, 1956).

The potentially dual functions of unconditional stimuli are exceedingly difficult to separate during

Table 3.4 Some Unconditional Stimuli and Some of the Responses They Elicit

Stimuli	Responses
Dry food or acid in the mouth	Salivation
Food in the mouth	Gastrointestinal secretions
Food in the throat	Swallowing
Light	Blocking of EEG alpha rhythm
	Change in skin resistance (*GSR*)
	Pupillary reflex
Electric shock	Vasomotor reactions
	Change in respiration
	Withdrawal movements
	Locomotion
Morphine in the bloodstream	Nausea, vomiting, and so on
Increase water intake	Diuresis
Patellar blow	Knee jerk
Shock, sound, air puff	Eyelid reflex
Rotation	Eye movements
Heat	Salivation
Stimulation of motor cortex	Flexion of various limbs

(After Kimble, 1961.)

a conditioning experiment (cf. Kimble, 1961, pp. 78–81). Consider, for example, what takes place when an experimenter attempts to condition leg flexion in the dog. In a typical procedure the experimenter presents a buzz for a few seconds, and then he shocks the dog via electrodes firmly attached to its leg. After a number of pairings of the buzz and the shock, the dog begins to lift its leg during the interval between the onset of the buzz and the onset of the shock (cf. Liddell, 1934). There are at least two interpretations of what has transpired. From the classical conditioning point of view, the effect of the pairings of the buzz and the shock was that the buzz elicited a flexion similar to the leg flexion that was elicited by the shock. From an instrumental conditioning viewpoint, the dog learned to lift its leg in order to minimize either the discomfort of having its leg suddenly flexed or the pain produced by the shock, although the dog cannot escape or avoid the shock completely. An instrumental conditioning interpretation assumes that the buzz functions as a *discriminative stimulus* in the presence of which leg flexion can minimize the noxious effects of shock.

To carry this example one step further, suppose that the experimenter was also recording the *galvanic skin response (GSR)* and that he observed reliable changes in skin resistance following the onset of the buzz. Since there is no obvious way by which a change in skin resistance could reduce the discomfort of a sudden flexion of the leg or of the electric shock, it might seem appropriate to interpret the reliable occurrence of a *GSR* following the buzz as an example of classical conditioning that was free of the effects of instrumental conditioning. But as Smith (1954) has argued, the *GSR* elicited by the buzz may be an artifact of the leg-flexion response that was brought on by the buzz.

Various attempts have been made to clarify this issue, most of which have centered on techniques which prevent the occurrence of a skeletal response by the administration of *curare* (a drug which leads to paralysis of muscles) prior to the conditioning procedure. These experiments will be discussed in greater detail toward the end of this chapter; by that time we will have considered other issues relevant to the relation between classical and instrumental conditioning. For the present, however, it is important to note that the elicitation of a skeletal response typically requires a stimulus that might also function as a negative reinforcer. The presence of a negative reinforcer may establish contingencies that lead to *instrumental escape* or *avoidance responses,* which in turn may evoke autonomic activity.

A similar situation exists in the case of conditioning based on positive unconditional stimuli. At first glance the effects of positive and negative unconditional stimuli may appear distinguishable on the basis of the kinds of responses they elicit. It may be tempting to argue that negative unconditional stimuli elicit activity in both the skeletal and the autonomic nervous systems, whereas the effects of positive unconditional stimuli (e.g., food placed directly in the stomach) may be restricted to the autonomic nervous system. However, Pavlov (1927) and Zener (1937) have noted that the signaled presentation of food may result in anticipatory chewing movements along with salivary or other digestive responses. These observations prompted Smith (1954) to suggest that conditioned salivation might be evoked by chewing brought on by *S2.*

Conditional stimuli

Stimuli can be classified as exteroceptive, interoceptive, or proprioceptive (Sherrington, 1906). An *exteroceptive* stimulus is a stimulus that impinges upon an external receptor, for example, the eye, ear, skin, or nose. Light and sound energy are the most common examples of exteroceptive stimuli. (Sherrington actually distinguished between exteroceptors and telereceptors. Exteroceptors included all receptors on the surface of the body that respond to contact stimulation; telereceptors included all receptors that respond to distant stimuli. This distinction, however, has seldom been invoked subsequently. We will therefore follow the widely accepted practice of combining exteroceptors and telereceptors into one category.)

Interoceptive stimuli are stimuli that impinge upon internal organs innervated by the autonomic nervous system. The warming of the stomach mucosa or the mechanical stimulation of the intestinal walls are examples of interoceptive stimuli. *Proprioceptive* stimuli, which result from movement of the muscles and joints, have not been studied in experiments on classical conditioning primarily because of the experimenter's inability to manipulate them independently of the subject's behavior.

Effective conditional stimuli have also been produced by directly stimulating the central nervous system or an *afferent* nerve (Loucks, 1934). Loucks (1938) and Doty, Rutledge, and Larsen (1956) have shown that direct stimulation of various areas of the cortex can serve as an effective conditional stimulus.

In most classical-conditioning experiments, *S2*

is an exteroceptive stimulus of a constant value (e.g., a pure tone or a flashing light). Some experiments, however, have used more complex extero ceptive S2s (e.g., forms or words used by Menzies, 1937). A considerable number of experiments on classical conditioning have also made use of interoceptive stimuli. Four basic conditioning paradigms emerge from the possibilities that either S1 or S2 can be exteroceptive or interoceptive: exteroceptive-exteroceptive conditioning, exteroceptive-interoceptive conditioning, interoceptive-exteroceptive conditioning, and interoceptive-interoceptive conditioning (cf. Razran, 1961). Most of the material to be discussed in this chapter is derived from experiments in which both S1 and S2 are exteroceptive. The reader interested in the conditioning of interoceptive organs can find numerous examples and references in Bykov (1957) and Razran (1961).

The nature of a conditional response is always determined by the nature of the unconditional stimulus. Thus, the responses listed in Table 3.4 are also representative of the kinds of conditional responses that have been studied.

Most experiments in classical conditioning, especially those performed in the United States, usually focus on a particular conditional and unconditional response. Thus, a study of salivary conditioning typically records the latency and the magnitude of the conditional and the unconditional responses and nothing else. Examination of Table 3.4 (which is far from complete), however, reveals that a particular unconditional stimulus elicits a cluster of responses. It is therefore not very surprising that those studies that have attempted to measure the response of different *effectors* have reported the establishment of numerous conditional responses (cf. Liddell, 1934). Typical contemporary Russian experimental arrangements for conducting conditioning experiments in which various responses are simultaneously observed are shown in Figures 3.6 and 3.7.

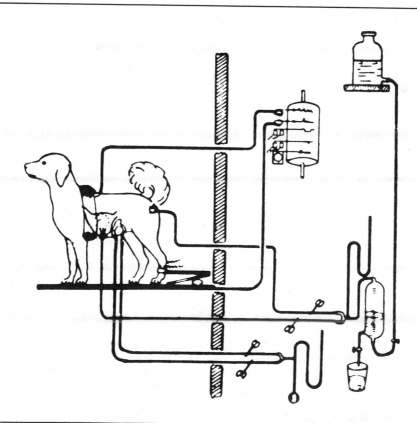

Figure 3.6 Experimental arrangement for conditioning dogs in a Russian laboratory (Ayrepetyants). Apparatus included facilities for stimulating ileocelum, rectum, stomach, and hind leg and for recording activity of ileocecal region, respiration, paw movement, and intragastric pressure. (From Razran, 1961.)

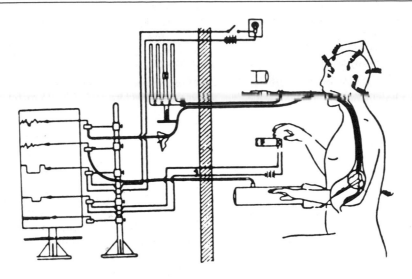

Figure 3.7 Experimental arrangement for studying conditioning in humans in a Russian laboratory. Apparatus records EEG, volume of blood vessels, blinking, visual sensitivity, and subjects' report of interoceptive and visual sensations. (From Razran, 1961.)

The results of the relatively few experiments that have studied the simultaneous development of different conditional responses indicate that this strategy should be applied more extensively in studies of classical conditioning. However, this has not been true of the typical American classical-conditioning experiment. From what can be gathered from translations of Russian experiments, it seems that Russian researchers have developed many techniques for the simultaneous recording of different responses (e.g., Bykov, 1957; Israel Program, 1960; Razran, 1961; Sokolov, 1963). Indeed, it appears that the most striking difference between the Russian and American approaches to the study of classical conditioning is best characterized by the American preoccupation with the parametric details of a particular response system that has been conditioned by a particular paradigm, as opposed to the Russian concentration on a qualitative unraveling of the nature of classical conditioning. While it is clear that a complete emphasis of either of these approaches would be unwise, it would seem that American research on classical conditioning could benefit from a heavier concentration of qualitative studies, particularly those involving the simultaneous recording of responding in different systems. Especially important is the simultaneous recording of operant responses during the establishment of classically

conditioned responses. The need for such research will become more apparent as we consider such questions as:

1. Given that both operant and classically conditioned responses are established during classical-conditioning training, does either the classical or the operant response typically occur earlier? A related question is whether classical conditioning is an artifact of instrumentally conditioned responses? This question would be answered in part by noting whether instrumentally conditioned responses occurred regularly prior to the classically conditioned response.

2. Are there reliable differences between the development of classically conditioned responses in different response systems? Gantt (1953, 1958, 1960), for example, has noted that certain autonomic responses are more easily conditioned than motor responses and that these autonomic responses show a greater resistance to extinction. Gantt referred to these differences in the rate of conditioning and extinction as *schizokinesis*. Razran (1961), on the other hand, reports that many interoceptive responses are more difficult both to condition and to extinguish than motor or salivary responses.

3. To what extent is our ability to condition a particular response related to the status of other

conditional responses? Runquist and Ross (1959), for example, measured changes in heart rate and skin conductance as well as eyelid closure during standard conditional eyeblink training. They found that the conditional eyeblink response can be more easily established in subjects who exhibited large changes in heart rate and skin conductance during training.

Varieties of classical conditioning
Higher-order conditioning

Classical conditioning has been shown to occur in situations in which an unconditional stimulus is not directly involved. Pavlov (1927, pp. 33–34), for example, described an experiment performed by Frolov in which an ineffective stimulus (*CS2*) was followed by an effective conditional stimulus (*CS1*). After a number of pairings of *CS2* and *CS1*, the former elicited a response similar to that elicited by *CS1*. Pavlov referred to this phenomenon as *higher-order conditioning*. For example, the tick of a metronome, which elicits salivation as a result of its having been previously paired with food, was preceded by a light. The light initially elicited no salivation. After a number of pairings of the light and the sound of the metronome without any presentations of food, the light alone elicited salivation. This process cannot, however, be extended indefinitely. There is no evidence from the organisms studied so far that more than three conditional stimuli, counting backward from the unconditional stimulus, can be established through higher-order conditioning.

An unconditional stimulus functioning as a conditional stimulus

Classical conditioning can also occur when two unconditional reflexes occur in close temporal contiguity. In these instances, the nature of at least one of these reflexes is modified. A simple demonstration has been described by Pavlov (1927): An electric shock delivered to the foot was followed by food. After a number of pairings of electric shock and food, the frequency of leg flexion, the original response to the shock, declined, and the strength of the reflex, electric shock elicits salivation, increased.

A definition of classical conditioning

The examples of classical conditioning that have been discussed thus far include experiments in which (a) a stimulus which originally could elicit no salivation (e.g., a tone) was paired with food, (b) a stimulus which could not elicit salivation (e.g., a light) was paired with a stimulus that could elicit salivation as a result of a prior conditioning history (e.g., a tone), and (c) two unconditional stimuli are paired (e.g., electric shock and food). Accordingly, we will define classical conditioning as the increase in the strength of a reflex from a zero or near-zero value as a result of the occurrence of that reflex in close temporal contiguity with a stronger reflex. The initially weak reflex is referred to as *S2-R2*, the stronger as *S1-R1*. In most cases, *S1* and *R1* refer to the unconditional stimulus (*US*) and the unconditional response (*UR*), respectively, and *S2* and *R2* refer to the conditional stimulus (*CS*) and the conditional response (*CR*), respectively. It should be noted, however, that *S1* can refer to an effective *CS* (cf. higher-order conditioning) and that *S2* and *R2* can refer to a *US* and *UR*, respectively, as in the case of the modification of an unconditional response by the successive elicitation of two unconditional reflexes.

This definition specifies the minimal conditions of classical conditioning. There still remain, however, a number of questions that need to be answered. These concern the nature of the conditional response, the necessity of contiguity between *S1* and *S2*, the proper control conditions, the effects of varying the temporal relation between *S1* and *S2*, and the influence of concurrent instrumental conditioning.

The nature of the conditional response
Stimulus substitution theory

Pavlov (1927) viewed the conditional reflex as an adaptive mechanism which served to broaden the conditions under which inborn, unconditional reflexes would occur. Thus, Pavlov, and subsequently many other psychologists, seemed to imply that conditional and unconditional responses were equivalent. This view, which has become known as the *stimulus substitution* theory of classical conditioning (cf. Hilgard & Marquis, 1940, pp. 75 ff.), states that the *CS* comes to function as the *US* as a result of its having been paired with the *US*. Given that the *CS* functions as the *US*, one would expect the response elicited by the *CS* to be the same as that elicited by the *US*. However, a wide variety of experiments have shown that the stimulus substitution theory is untenable. In this section we will consider two general classes of experiments: The first is concerned with topographical comparisons of the *CR* and the *UR;* the second type of experiment examines the *CR* as a component of a complex of responses established by the conditioning procedure.

Beginning with Pavlov, the main concern of most psychologists performing the typical salivary-conditioning experiment was the number of drops of saliva that followed each presentation of the *CS* and the *US.* Typically, the amount or rate of salivation elicited by the *CS* was less than that elicited by the *US.* Indeed, the typical finding in the classical-conditioning literature is that the magnitude of the *CR* is smaller than the magnitude of the *UR* and the latency of the *CR* is longer than the latency of the *UR* (see Hull, 1934, pp. 427–431, for a summary of these studies). The difference between the magnitudes of the *CR* and the *UR* is not a serious problem since it is conceivable that the quantitative differences between the *CR* and the *UR* could be related to differences in the intensities of the *CS* and the *US.*

However, qualitative differences between the *CR* and the *UR* present a different problem. Pavlov noted, in a somewhat anecdotal manner, that the chemical compositions of the *CR* and the *UR* differed: The *CR* was less viscous and had a lower constituency of organic material than did the *UR.* This finding has been confirmed by a number of Russian investigators (e.g., Moldavskia, 1928).

Other studies of the difference between the *CR* and the *UR* in various response systems have substantiated Pavlov's observations of the difference between conditional and unconditional salivation. We will first consider the conditional eyeblink response, which has become the most widely studied classically conditioned response in the human and the most popular subject of study in American classical-conditioning laboratories.

In a typical eyelid-conditioning experiment, the subject is seated in a comfortable chair with an experimental apparatus which presents both the *CS* and the *US* mounted on his head. This device can also detect the occurrence of an eyeblink and record its latency and magnitude. A typical record of the development of what is presumed to be a conditional eyeblink response is shown in Figure 3.8. One problem is that not all eyeblinks occurring during the *S2-S1* interval can be accepted as conditional responses. Figure 3.8 shows tracings from photographic records of the eyeblink responses of a single human subject. The reason one cannot be certain that the tracings shown in Figure 3.8 represent a conditional response will become clear once we consider differences between the char-

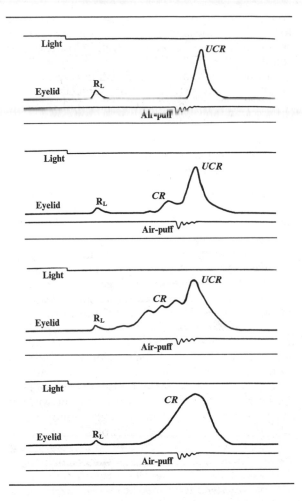

Figure 3.8 Tracings of photographic records of the eyelid response of a single human subject. Top record shows reflex closure to light and the unconditional response to an air-puff. The second and third records show conditional responses to the light. The fourth record shows a conditional response that prevents the air-puff from reaching the eye. This response could be classified as an avoidance response. (From Hilgard & Marquis, 1940.)

acteristics of an actual conditional eyeblink and other eyeblinks that may be recorded during a conditioning session.

The *US* in eyelid-conditioning experiments is typically a puff of air directed at one eye (see Gormezano, 1966, pp. 397–401, for technical details); the *UR* is an eyeblink whose latency is approximately 50 milliseconds; and the *CS* is a low-intensity flash of light. In many instances the *CS* elicits an unconditional eyeblink before the pairing of the *CS* and the *US* has begun. The reflex blink to

A

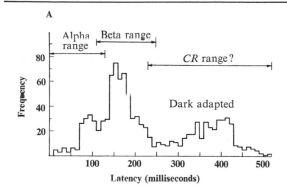

B

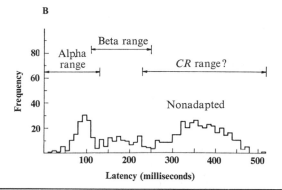

Figure 3.9 Latency distributions of eyelid closures evoked by the *CS* during an eyelid-conditioning experiment under conditions of dark adaptation (A) and light adaptation (B). (From Grant & Norris, 1947.)

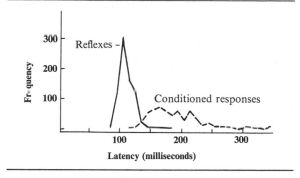

Figure 3.10 Distributions of latencies of eyelid responses categorized according to unconditional and conditional responses. (From Hilgard, 1931.)

the *CS*, which is called an *alpha response,* has a modal latency of 70 milliseconds and a range of 50–120 milliseconds (Grant & Adams, 1944).

Another complication results from the standard procedure for recording the eyeblink by photographing the response in a darkened room. During the experiment the subject becomes dark adapted. Under these conditions the range of latencies of the unconditional response to the light, which is called a beta response, is 120–240 milliseconds. The modal latency of the eyeblink to the *CS* following dark adaptation is 150 milliseconds (Grant & Norris, 1947). The difference in the latencies of the alpha and beta responses undoubtedly reflects differences between reaction times based on rod-mediated and cone-mediated vision.

After a number of trials on which the flash of light is followed by the puff of air, the flash of light itself begins to elicit an eyeblink whose latency is typically 250–450 milliseconds. A frequency distribution showing the relative frequency of alpha, beta, and conditional responses following the conditioning of the eyeblink under dark-adaptation conditions is shown in Figure 3.9A. A frequency distribution of the same responses obtained under light-adaptation conditions is shown in Figure 3.9B. Figure 3.9 should be compared with the results of an earlier study performed by Hilgard (1931) on eyelid conditioning, which are shown in Figure 3.10. Hilgard's study was performed under conditions which allowed dark adaptation to take place. The dashed curve, which shows the relative frequency of conditional responses as a function of latency, indicates that many of the responses that Hilgard classified as conditional responses may have been beta responses.

The delineation of the beta response and its causes led to the subsequent discovery that beta responses retard the development of a conditional eyeblink response (Grant & Norris, 1947). Apparently, the *refractory* period of the beta response, which typically occurs at approximately 160–170 milliseconds following the onset of the *CS*, interferes with the development of the conditional response.

Another complication in specifying the conditional eyeblink response arises from the occurrence of *voluntary* responses, which are presumably normal eyeblinks or avoidance responses. The range of the latency of a voluntary response is approximately 200–500 milliseconds. Voluntary responses tend to differ from conditional eyeblink responses in that voluntary responses show a shorter latency, a sharper and more prolonged closure of the eye, and a longer duration than do conditional responses (Kimble, 1964; Spence & Ross, 1959; Spence & Taylor, 1951). These differences can be seen in Figures 3.11 and 3.12. Figure 3.11 shows tracings of conditional and voluntary eyeblink responses. Figure 3.12 shows records of alpha, conditional, voluntary, and unconditional eyeblink responses. Of special interest is the third line of each record in Figure 3.12, which shows the first derivative of eyelid movement. A comparison of the first derivatives of the conditional (record 2) and the voluntary (record 3) responses shows the different characteristics of conditional and voluntary responses. On the basis of the distinctions shown in Figures 3.11 and 3.12, Spence and his co-workers where able to exclude "voluntary responders" from the population of college students that they studied (e.g., Spence & Taylor, 1951) and thereby obtain less variable data on the acquisition of the conditional eyeblink response.

The data on the latency and the magnitude of alpha, beta, voluntary, and conditional eyeblinks indicate that the occurrence of an eyeblink following the CS hardly provides assurance that a conditional response has been established. These data and the records shown in Figure 3.8, which describe the development of the conditional eyeblink response, also indicate that Pavlov's, and later Watson's, view that the conditional response could be considered as simply a substitute for the unconditional response is no longer tenable.

An experiment on human cardiac conditioning performed by Notterman, Schoenfeld, and Bersh (1952) provides another important example of the difference between conditional and unconditional responses. In this experiment, the unconditional stimulus was a mild electric shock delivered to the left hand. The conditional stimulus was a pure tone. Using an *electrocardiograph,* the experimenters recorded the heart rate of the subjects following the presentation of each tone and shock. The unconditional response to the shock was an acceleration of the heart rate. The conditional response to the tone, however, was a deceleration of the heart rate. Other studies (e.g., Westcott & Huttenlocher, 1961; Zeaman & Smith, 1965) have shown that the difference in the form of the CR and the UR in the human cardiac-conditioning experiment may be related to corresponding respiration differences. This possibility does not, however, detract from the generalization that the CR and the UR are different responses and that, in some instances, the CR and the UR may deviate in opposite directions from a baseline value.

Interactions between different conditional responses established by the same conditioning procedure

Zeaman's experiments (cf. Zeaman & Smith, 1965) on human cardiac conditioning showed that the pairing of light and shock resulted in the conditioning of a breathing response in addition to the conditioning of the cardiac response. This should hardly come as a surprise, since it is well known that negative reinforcers such as electric shock elicit many unconditional responses, including the galvanic skin response, pupillary contraction, and others (Ax, 1953; Lacey, 1956; Lacey & Lacey, 1958; Lindsley, 1951; see also Table 3.4). In focusing on only one response during a conditioning procedure, other reactions to a stressful stimulus are excluded, as has been demonstrated in a series of experiments performed by Liddell and his associates (e.g., Liddell, 1934; Liddell, James, & Anderson, 1934; Moore & Marcuse, 1945). Although these experiments were concerned mainly with the conditional leg flexion in sheep, Liddell also recorded breathing rate, cardiac responding, and general activity. The US in these studies was electric shock delivered to the leg, and the CS was typically a light. One interesting observation that Liddell reported was the occurrence of the conditional leg flexion prior to the appearance of the conditional cardiac and breathing responses. As we will see later, this observation, which has been confirmed by other investigators (e.g., de Toledo & Black, 1966), poses a problem for those theories which state that autonomic responses mediate the acquisition of skeletal responses. An example of typical polygraph records is shown in Figure 3.13.

The finding that many responses become con-

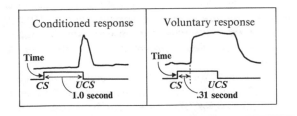

Figure 3.11 Tracings of photographic records of eyelid responses. Left-hand tracing shows a characteristic form of involuntary response; right-hand tracing shows a characteristic form of voluntary response. (From Kimble, 1964.)

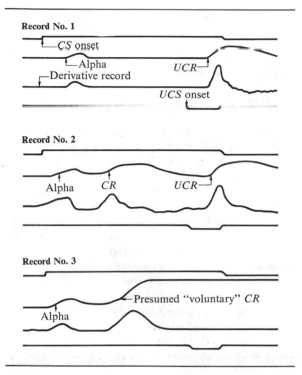

Figure 3.12 Tracings of records of the human eyelid response during a conditioning experiment. The third line of each record shows the first derivative of eyelid movement. (From Gormezano, 1966.)

ditioned during a conditioning procedure is by no means restricted to those procedures which use negative reinforcers. Pavlov and others (e.g., Zener, 1937) have shown that the pairing of a stimulus with food not only increases the frequency of the conditional salivary response, but increases the frequency of the subject's approach to the food tray and tongue and jaw movements as well. It should also be recalled that Pavlov noted that various digestive reflexes were also conditioned by the procedure he used to condition the salivary response.

Nonassociative factors in conditioning

The observation that the strength of the reflex *S2-R2* increases following the pairing of *S1* and *S2* cannot always be accepted as evidence that a conditional response has been established. In addition, it must be demonstrated that the increase in the strength of the reflex *S2-R2* can be attributed unequivocally to the *pairing* of *S1* and *S2*. Those factors responsible for increases in the strength of

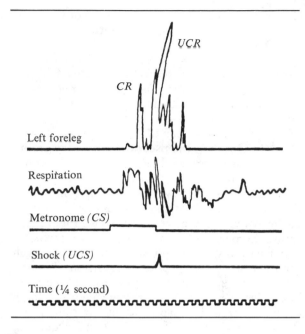

Figure 3.13 Recordings of conditional leg flexion and respiration responses in sheep. (From Liddell, 1934.)

S2-R2 that are not due to the pairing of *S1* and *S2* have been referred to as *nonassociative* factors. In this section we will consider some of these factors and discuss the ways in which their effects can be demonstrated and controlled.

Pseudoconditioning

The term *pseudoconditioning* appears to have been coined by Grether (1938), who observed that the mere presentation of an unconditional stimulus, for example, a loud noise produced by an explosion, was sufficient to insure that *S2* would elicit a response similar to the *UR*, that is, a startle response. To produce pseudoconditioning, *S1* (which has always been a negative reinforcer) is presented a number of times without *S2*. Afterwards, *S2* is presented for the first time. *S2* is followed by a response that resembles the response elicited by *S1*. This response is referred to as a pseudoconditioned response because *S2* was never paired with *S1*.

An instructive experiment comparing the pseudoconditioning procedure with a procedure in which both *S1* and *S2* were presented during training was performed by Harris (1941). In this experiment, *S1* was an electric shock delivered to the finger and *R1* was a finger-withdrawal response.

Harris used four groups of subjects. For Group 1, a standard conditioning procedure was used in which S2, a loud tone, preceded the onset of S1 by 4.75 seconds. For Group 2, the sequence of stimuli was reversed: S2 followed S1 by 4.75 seconds (see the discussion of *backward-conditioning procedures* later in this chapter). Harris referred to Group 3 as a random-presentation group because S1 and S2 were not paired in any systematic manner. For Group 4, the pseudoconditioning group, only S1 was presented. During this phase of training, each group received 80 presentations of S1. Groups 1–3 also received 80 presentations of S2. Each group was subsequently tested on 10 trials during which only S2 was presented. Figure 3.14 shows the percentage of test trials during which a finger-withdrawal response occurred in each group. Initially, the highest proportion of conditional responses occurred in the case of the pseudoconditioning procedure. By the end of the tenth extinction trial, however, the group trained with the regular forward-conditioning procedure (S2-S1) showed the highest proportion of finger-withdrawal responses.

It is important to note that S2 elicited finger withdrawal following training under the backward-conditioning and random-presentation procedures as well as following training under the pseudocon-

ditioning procedure. In both instances it seems doubtful that the finger-withdrawal response is a true conditional response. The frequency of occurrence of the finger-withdrawal response declined abruptly in the case of the backward and random groups, just as it did in the case of the pseudoconditioning group.

A similar result was obtained by Spooner and Kellogg (1947) following an attempt to condition the finger-withdrawal response using a backward-conditioning procedure. Spooner and Kellogg also noted that the latency of the finger-withdrawal response of the backward-conditioning group was longer than the latency of the finger-withdrawal response of the forward-conditioning group. It appears, therefore, that the response obtained by backward and random procedures may be a pseudoconditioning effect. It also appears as if some of the effect of the forward-conditioning procedure, especially during the first few trials of the Harris study, may be a pseudoconditioning effect.

A dramatic and theoretically significant example of a pseudoconditioning effect in a standard eyelid conditioning procedure was provided by a study performed by Kimble, Mann, and Dufort (1955). In this study, S2 was paired with S1 on the first 20 trials. S2 was then omitted on the following 30 trials. During the last 10 trials, S2 was again paired with S1. A control group was given trials on which S2 was paired with S1 throughout training. The increased frequency of the eyeblink response during those trials on which S2 was omitted and the absence of any difference between the groups in the frequency of responding at the end of training indicate that the eyeblink continued to be conditional on those trials during which only S2 was presented. This, by definition, would be pseudoconditioning.

Later studies (e.g., Champion, 1961; Goodrich, Ross, & Wagner, 1959; McAllister & McAllister, 1960) have failed to confirm the Kimble, Mann, and Dufort result. In these studies, the omission of S1 resulted in a weaker CR than did the continuous pairing of S2 and S1. With the exception of the Kimble, Mann, and Dufort study, however, none of these studies used a procedure in which there was an interval during which neither S2 nor S1 was presented. The Kimble, Mann, and Dufort study showed that the CR of the group, which received only S1 presentations during trials 21–50, had a greater frequency of occurrence than the CR of the group for which neither S1 nor S2 were presented during trials 21–50. It appears, therefore, that even though unpaired presentations of S1 are not always

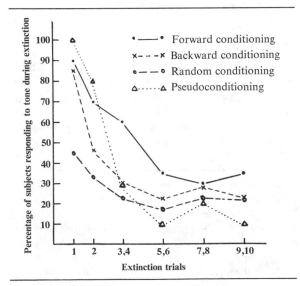

Figure 3.14 Percentage of subjects responding to a tone during extinction following training on forward, backward, random, and pseudoconditioning. (From Harris, 1941.)

as effective as *S2-S1* presentations, unpaired presentations are better than the absence of any stimulation.

Kimble (1961, pp. 63–64) has argued that the term *pseudoconditioning* may have dissuaded psychologists from studying this effect systematically. One approach to the study of pseudoconditioning that warrants further study is the possibility that pseudoconditioning results from stimulus generalization between *S1* and *S2* and hence represents a true conditioning phenomenon. This possibility is supported by the results of a study performed by Wickens and Wickens (1942) in which the authors drew attention to the sudden onset of *S1* and *S2* as the common feature that may serve as a basis for generalization from *S1* to *S2*. According to this view, pseudoconditioning effects are similar in nature to our being startled by any sudden stimulus of moderate intensity following a previous exposure to a sudden intense stimulus.

Wickens and Wickens trained two groups of rats to escape from shock. For one group, the onset of the shock was sudden; for the second group, the onset of the shock was gradual. Each group was then divided into two subgroups, each of which was tested with a light that was presented either suddenly or gradually. Fifteen of the 19 rats from the two groups for which the nature of stimulus onset during escape training and testing were similar made an escape response during the test trials. On the other hand, only 3 of the 18 rats of the two groups characterized by dissimilar types of stimulus onset during escape training and testing made an escape response during the test with the light. Even though Wickens and Wickens studied an escape response, which may be more an operant than a classically conditioned response, their results suggest that pseudoconditioning may be due to stimulus generalization between *S1* and *S2*.

Habituation

A characteristic of many response systems is a temporary reduction of the strength of a response following the repeated elicitation of that response. This phenomenon has been referred to as *adaptation* in the physiological literature and as *habituation* in the literature on conditioning. Habituation has been observed in classical-conditioning experiments in the cases of both the conditional and the unconditional stimulus. It is especially important to consider this factor when the experimental design consists of a series of test trials in which the preconditioning effects of the conditional and the unconditional stimuli are evaluated.

An experiment by Taylor (1956) on the eyeblink response illustrates the effect of habituation in the case of the unconditional stimulus. Four groups of subjects were used in this experiment. Three of these groups were given 50 preliminary trials during which only the unconditional stimulus was presented. The pressure values of the air-puffs, in millimeters of mercury, which varied across these groups were 80, 30, and 15. *S2* was not presented to the subjects of the fourth group during this stage of the experiment. Each of the four groups was then given 50 conditioning trials during which the air-puff was preceded by *S2*, a light. The results indicated that the strength of the conditional eyeblink response varied inversely with the pressure of *S1* during the habituation phase of the experiment. Similar results have been reported by Kimble and Dufort (1956) in the case of eyelid conditioning, and by Seward and Seward (1934) in the case of the *GSR* response to shock. Other investigators, however, have reported no habituation to the *UCS*. Prokasy, Hall, and Fawcett (1962), for example, reported no diminution of the amplitude of the *GSR* during the course of 20 presentations of electric shock. Similarly, Landis and Hunt (1939) observed that some components of the startle response do not habituate.

Habituation to the *CS* has been observed in a wide variety of studies. Grant (1939) and McAllister (1953a) have reported a gradual decrease in the frequency of the alpha eyelid response following repeated presentation of the *CS*. Notterman, Schoenfeld, and Bersh (1952) reported adaptation of the heart-rate response (deceleration) following successive presentations of a tone.

Sensitization

It is often the case in studies of classical conditioning that a response which resembles the conditional response can be elicited by *S2* without any pairing between *S2* and *S1* or without any prior presentation of *S1*. As we have seen, an unconditional response to *S2* is called an *alpha response*. This does not normally pose a serious problem since alpha responses often habituate. In some instances, however, the presentation of *S1* restores or augments the alpha response. Thus, for sensitization to occur, the effects of habituation must be overcome. The augmentation of the alpha response as a result of the presentation of the unconditional stimulus has been referred to as *alpha conditioning* or *sensitization*. In many cases, an alpha response can be distinguished from a conditional response by its latency or magnitude.

An experiment performed by Grant and Adams (1944) provides a clear demonstration of sensitization during eyelid conditioning. One group (an alpha-conditioning group) was given a pretest of 4 trials with $S2$ (a light) alone, a conditioning series of 40 trials on which $S2$ was followed by $S1$ (a corneal puff of air), and a posttest of 4 trials with $S2$ alone. The same procedure was followed by a second group (an adaptation control group), except that 40 trials with $S2$ alone were given instead of the 40 trials on which the light-puff combination were presented. On the basis of an analysis of eyelid responses during the pretest, an alpha response was defined as an eyeblink whose latency fell between 50 and 100 milliseconds. The relative frequency of alpha responses was much higher for the alpha conditioning group (approximately 50 percent) than for the adaptation control group (approximately 15 percent).

Control procedures

Our purpose in considering the phenomena of pseudoconditioning, habituation, and sensitization was to distinguish between associative and non-associative factors in the study of classical conditioning. Given that classical conditioning refers only to the effects of pairing the conditional and the unconditional stimuli, it is important to distinguish between the consequences of pairing and the consequences of presenting the conditional and the unconditional stimuli separately.

The basic strategy that has been followed in attempts to determine the contribution of non-associative aspects of classical conditioning has been to compare the performance of a group for whom the conditional and the unconditional stimuli have not been paired with the performance of a different group for whom these stimuli have been paired. More often than not, however, these control groups raise as many additional problems as they were intended to resolve. For example, suppose one wanted to distinguish between alpha and conditional responses. This becomes an important problem in situations in which the latency and magnitude of the alpha response is difficult to distinguish from the latency and magnitude of a conditional response, as in the case of the GSR or the cardiac response. One approach would be to present $S2$ by itself during a series of trials prior to the pairing of $S2$ and $S1$. This procedure would be practical only when one is certain that the con-

ditioning procedure does not result in sensitization. While, as a result of adaptation, the alpha response may diminish during such a series of $S2$ presentations, a single presentation of $S1$ may restore it. In order to determine whether sensitization has occurred, a discrimination procedure may be used. Since the alpha response to $CS+$ ($S2$ followed by $S1$) and $CS-$ ($S2$ alone) should be the same, the possibility of sensitization is essentially the same on both kinds of trials. Conditioning in this situation would be demonstrated by the difference between the frequency of responding to $CS+$ and $CS-$.

The contribution of sensitization in classical conditioning has also been studied by using a control group for whom $S1$ and $S2$ alternate in some irregular manner but never in temporal contiguity with each other. The difference between the performance of this control group and a group for whom the $S2$ and $S1$ were paired is the measure of how much conditioning has taken place.

To determine the magnitude of pseudoconditioning effects, various experimenters have used a control group in which $S1$ is presented alone. The frequency of a response on subsequent $S2$ trials indicates the magnitude of a pseudoconditioning effect as compared to the frequency of a response to $S2$ following a series of $S2$-$S1$ pairings. In using this procedure it should be remembered that the effects of habituation to $S2$ must also be taken into account.

A problem common to all of the control procedures that have been used in conjunction with experiments on classical conditioning was brought into sharp focus by Prokasy (1965) and Rescorla (1967). Rescorla argued that all attempts to break up the dependency between $S1$ and $S2$ in controlling for nonassociative factors set up an alternative relationship whereby the presentation of $S2$ implies that $S1$ will not occur. This procedure could establish $S2$ as an *inhibitory* stimulus. Both Prokasy and Rescorla argue that the only neutral control procedure for nonassociative factors is one where there is a truly random relationship between $S2$ and $S1$—an arrangement in which the presentation of $S2$ provides no information whatsoever as to whether or not $S1$ will occur.

Temporal relations between conditional and unconditional stimuli

The definition of classical conditioning emphasizes the temporal contiguity between two reflexes as the fundamental requirement for conditioning.

The temporal relation between the stimuli of these two reflexes can be specified according to whether *S2* precedes *S1* and the value of the time interval between the onsets of *S2* and *S1*. Once the relation between *S1* and *S2* has been specified, it is also necessary to specify the duration of *S2* and the value(s) of the intertrial interval between successive presentations of *S2*.

As we have seen, those procedures in which *S2* precedes *S1* are forward-conditioning procedures. Backward conditioning applies to those procedures in which *S1* precedes *S2*. We will first consider the various types of forward-conditioning procedures that have been used. Generally speaking, forward-conditioning procedures are the only ones that have proved effective in establishing a conditional reflex.

Each pairing of *S2* and *S1* is usually referred to as a *trial*. The value of the intertrial interval between presentations of *S2* is usually varied to maximize the possibility that the *CR* can be attributed to the onset of *S2* and not to the subject's ability to time the intertrial interval. The value of the minimum intertrial interval is usually selected on the basis of how much time is needed for the conditional response to return to its baseline value. Thus, in the case of the salivary or the galvanic skin responses, the minimum intertrial interval is usually longer than 2 minutes; in the case of the conditional eyeblink response, the minimum intertrial interval has assumed values as low as 5 seconds (e.g., Prokasy & Whaley, 1961, 1963).

Forward conditioning

1. Simultaneous conditioning. The most widely used forward-conditioning procedure is one where the onset of *S2* occurs 5 seconds or less prior to the onset of *S1*. In such a simultaneous-conditioning procedure, *S2* may either terminate at the onset of *S1* or be continued through the offset of *S1*. Both variations of the simultaneous procedure are shown below in Figure 3.15, lines A and B.

Simultaneous conditioning has been shown to be the most effective forward-conditioning procedure under a large variety of experimental conditions. It is often used as a point of departure for studies of the effects of some of the other forward-conditioning procedures.

The value of 5 seconds as upper limit of the *S2-S1* interval in the definition of simultaneous conditioning appears to derive from Pavlov's observation that *S2-S1* intervals that did not exceed 5 seconds had similar effects on the ease of establish-

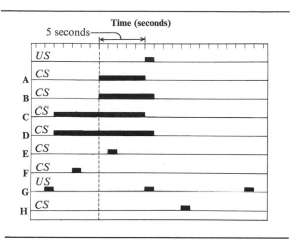

Figure 3.15 Schematic representation of forward-conditioning (lines A & B), delayed-conditioning (lines C & D), trace-conditioning (lines E & F), temporal conditioning (line G), and backward-conditioning (line H) procedures.

ing the conditional salivary response. It is doubtful, however, that the value of 5 seconds has special significance in the case of response systems that have shorter latencies and more rapid recovery, e.g., the eyeblink.

2. Delayed conditioning. In a delayed-conditioning procedure, the onset of *S2* occurs more than 5 seconds before the onset of *S1*, as shown in lines C and D of Figure 3.15. In the delayed procedure, *S2* is continued until the onset of *S1* (line C) or through the offset of *S1* (line D). Initially, the latency of the conditional response is small, but as training continues, the latency of the conditional response increases. According to Pavlov, this is due to the inhibition of the conditional response during the early portion of the *S2-S1* interval (Pavlov, 1927, Lecture VI).

3. Trace conditioning. This term refers to a procedure in which *S1* and *S2* are separated by an interval during which neither stimulus is present. If the interval between the onset of *S2* and *S1* is less than 5 seconds, the procedure is referred to as *short-trace conditioning* (Figure 3.15, line E). If this interval is more than 5 seconds, the procedure is referred to as long-trace conditioning (Figure 3.15, line F).

4. Temporal conditioning. In the case of temporal conditioning, *S1* is presented after a fixed interval of time has elapsed. There is no explicit *S2* (cf.

Figure 3.15, line G). The result is that a conditional response comes to occur prior to each presentation of *S1*.

The result of this temporal-conditioning procedure may be a special case of the trace-conditioning procedure in the sense that *S1* may function as both an unconditional and a conditional stimulus. In trace conditioning, the subject presumably learns that *S1* follows *S2* after a fixed period of time; in temporal conditioning, the subject presumably learns that *S1* occurs after a certain interval has elapsed since the last presentation of *S1*.

It is instructive to compare the temporal-conditioning procedure with the procedure that Skinner (1948) used to establish *superstitious* responding. From an operational point of view, the procedures are identical. In both cases, food is delivered after a fixed interval of time, regardless of what the subject is doing. Skinner observed that the main consequence of presenting food to a hungry pigeon every 15 seconds was to strengthen whatever the pigeon was doing (e.g., turning, bowing) just prior to the presentation of food. Skinner concluded that reinforcement was just as effective when the contingencies between a response and a reinforcing stimulus were adventitiously determined by the environment as when they were specified by the experimenter. The temporal-conditioning procedure and the procedure for producing a superstitious response are identical operationally, and they both result in an increase in the strength of some response just prior to the delivery of food. We will pursue the interesting theoretical implications of the relation between temporal conditioning and superstitious conditioning later in a full comparison of classical and instrumental conditioning.

Backward conditioning

Pavlov (1927, p. 27) and many other psychologists who have studied classical conditioning have stated that conditioning does not take place when *S2* follows *S1* (Figure 3.15, line H). The few exceptions in which a conditional response was observed following a backward-conditioning procedure have been attributed to pseudoconditioning (e.g., Harris, 1941) or to the possibility that *S1* was still effective when *S2* was presented (e.g., Guthrie, 1935, pp. 45–46). We have already considered a situation (Harris, 1941) in which the initial effect of a backward-conditioning procedure was almost as potent as the effect of a forward-conditioning procedure, which, in turn, was not quite as pronounced as the effect of a pseudoconditioning procedure. Recall,

however, that by the tenth trial of the Harris study, the effect of the backward-conditioning procedure was essentially the same as the effect of a random-conditioning procedure.

Wolfle (1932) attempted to backward condition finger withdrawal and showed a small effect. On approximately 10 percent of the test trials, a conditional response was obtained. However, a replication of this study (Spooner & Kellogg, 1947) showed that the latency of the withdrawal whose frequency was increased by the backward-conditioning procedure (approximately 200 milliseconds) was much smaller than the latency of the withdrawal that was strengthened by various forward-conditioning procedures (approximately 700 milliseconds). Spooner and Kellogg also showed that with continued training the frequency of finger withdrawal increased under forward-conditioning training, while the frequency of these responses decreased under backward-conditioning training.

The optimal interval between S1 and S2

In our survey of the different possible temporal relations between *S1* and *S2*, we noted that simultaneous conditioning appeared to be the most effective of the forward-conditioning procedures. In Pavlov's research on the development of the conditional salivary response, the particular value of the *S2-S1* interval in the simultaneous-conditioning procedure did not appear to make much difference in the establishment of a conditional response as long as *S1* followed *S2* within 5 seconds of the onset of *S2*. Subsequent work, however, indicated that in the case of a *phasic* response, such as the eyeblink or finger withdrawal, the effectiveness of the simultaneous-conditioning procedure depended rather more critically on the value of the *S2-S1* interval.

The relative effectiveness of different *S2-S1* intervals was systematically studied by Wolfle (1930, 1932), who used forward-conditioning intervals ranging from 0.0 to 3.0 seconds, and backward-conditioning intervals ranging from −0.5 to −1.0 seconds. The results of these studies and those of a replication performed by Spooner and Kellogg (1947) are shown in Figure 3.16. The optimal interval under Wolfle's training procedure appears to be between 0.33 and 0.66 seconds. Spooner and Kellogg's replication of the Wolfle study indicated that an *S1-S2* interval of 0.5 seconds was optimal.

An excellent study by Hansche and Grant (1960) on the optimal *S2-S1* interval in the case of eyelid conditioning also showed that 0.55 seconds was

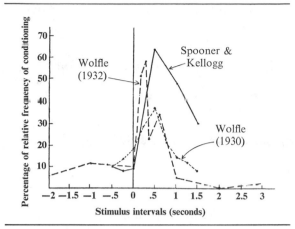

Figure 3.16 Relative frequency of the conditional eyelid response as a function of the interval between the *CS* and the *US,* as observed in studies by Wolfle (1930, 1932) and Spooner and Kellogg (1947). (From Spooner & Kellogg, 1947.)

the optimal interval among a group of intervals whose values were 0.15, 0.35, 0.55, and 0.75 seconds. McAllister (1953b) and Boneau (1958) have shown that shifting from a short to a long interval during the course of eyelid conditioning decreased performance, in some cases to the level that the *CR* would have assumed had the longer interval been used all along. A number of other studies (summarized by Kimble, 1961, Table 13, pp. 156–157) have corroborated the value of approximately 0.5 seconds as the optimal *S2-S1* interval. Systematists, notably Clark L. Hull, felt that 0.45 seconds was the exact value of the optimal interval.

The generality of approximately 0.5 seconds as an optimal interval is, however, still an open question. Various considerations indicate that this value is specific to those response systems where an unconditional stimulus also functioned as a negative reinforcer and where only one conditional stimulus was used. In a discrimination where a *CS*+ is alternated with a *CS*−, the value of the optimal interval is considerably longer than 0.5 seconds.

The fact that *S1* was a negative reinforcer in all of the systematic studies of the *S2-S1* interval means that pseudoconditioning, sensitization, and unrecognized instrumental conditioning may have affected the outcomes. For example, in the Spooner and Kellogg and in the Wolfle studies, it is surprising that little conditioning occurred when the *S2-S1* interval exceeded 1.5 seconds. When *S2* precedes the onset of shock, it is probable that the

subjects attempted to be in the best position to minimize the effect of shock. When the *S2-S1* interval was 1 second or less, a finger withdrawal may have seemed to the subject to be an effective way to minimize the shock. In the case of longer *S2-S1* intervals, however, the subject may have restrained himself during the *S2-S1* interval and prepared to withdraw his hand when he received the shock.

No systematic studies have been performed to date on the optimal value of the *S2-S1* interval in establishing a phasic conditional response where the unconditional stimulus is a positive reinforcer. At present there are no techniques available for performing such a study. If, however, such an experiment could be performed, the relatively longer latencies of *UR*s elicited by positive reinforcers (as compared with the latencies of *UR*s elicited by negative reinforcers) suggests that the optimal value of the *S2-S1* interval might be longer than 0.5 seconds.

The nature of the conditional response is yet another factor that may detract from the generalization that the optimal value of the *S2-S1* interval is 0.5 seconds. We have already noted that Pavlov felt that the value of the *S2-S1* interval did not matter as long as this interval did not exceed 5 seconds. It seems likely that the optimal value for the *S2-S1* interval may be considerably longer for responses whose latency and duration are longer than the latency and duration of the typical skeletal response.

Experiments in which a differential-reinforcement procedure was used generally show that the optimal *S2-S1* interval is longer than 0.5 seconds, even in the case of eyelid conditioning. Hartman and Grant (1962a), for example, reported that the asymptote of discrimination performance of a conditional eyelid response increased with the *S2-S1* interval. The intervals used in Hartman and Grant's experiments were 400, 600, 800, and 1000 milliseconds. Grings, Lockhart, and Dameron (1962) report similar findings with even longer *S2-S1* intervals in the case of a conditional galvanic skin response in mentally defective subjects.

Partial reinforcement

It has been widely demonstrated that the contingency between a conditional and an unconditional stimulus (classical conditioning) or between a response and a reinforcing stimulus (instrumental conditioning) results in the strengthening of certain responses, and that abolishing these contingencies results in the weakening of the behavior that was conditioned. Given these facts, it should be easy to appreciate the puzzling nature of reports that a contingency that called for the omission of the unconditional or the reinforcing stimulus on a substantial number of trials resulted in an increase in response strength. In 1938, Skinner (Chapter 4) demonstrated that failing to reinforce every response (a rat's lever-press) did not result in a decrease in the rate of responding. Skinner also demonstrated that the resistance to extinction of a response maintained on a schedule that reinforced only a small proportion of responses was substantially greater than the resistance to extinction of a response that had been maintained by a schedule that allowed every response to be reinforced.

Humphreys (1939, 1940) subsequently showed similar effects in the case of eyelid conditioning. The omission of the unconditional stimulus (a puff of air) on 50 percent of the trials did not decrease the strength of the conditional response. Humphreys also showed that the resistance to extinction of the conditional response was greater after a conditioning procedure in which the unconditional stimulus occurred on 50 percent of the trials than after a conditioning procedure in which the unconditional stimulus occurred on all of the trials.

But the apparent similarity of the effects of partial reinforcement in instrumental and classical conditioning was short-lived. Although a large variety of experiments have confirmed the effects of partial reinforcement that were described by Skinner, Humphreys' observation of the paradoxical effects of partial reinforcement on classical conditioning and extinction has not been confirmed by others.

Acquisition of a conditional response under a schedule of partial reinforcement

According to Pavlov (1927, pp. 384–386), the omission of the unconditional stimulus on more than two thirds of the trials makes conditioning impossible. While some subsequent studies (e.g., Grant & Schipper, 1952) performed after Humphreys' experiments have shown that conditioning is not only possible, but is unimpaired with partial reinforcement, the general finding is that partial reinforcement retards the acquisition of the conditional response (Razran, 1955, 1956). In particular, various well-controlled studies of the conditional eyeblink have systematically shown deleterious effects of partial reinforcement during conditioning (e.g., Grant & Hake, 1951; Grant, Schipper, & Ross, 1952; Hartman & Grant, 1960, 1962b; Reynolds, 1958; Ross, 1959).

Ross' (1959) study provides a good illustration of the relative effects of continuous and partial reinforcement on the performance of a classically conditioned response. It is important to note that in Ross' study both *S2* and *S1* were presented on nonreinforced trials. However, the value of the *S2-S1* interval was 2.4 seconds, a value shown to result in virtually no conditioning (McAllister, 1953a). The results described here have been confirmed in other studies (e.g., Runquist, 1963) in which *S1* was omitted on nonreinforced trials.

Ross' study was concerned primarily with the acquisition of a classically conditioned eyelid response. Accordingly, unlike other studies of partial reinforcement which have addressed themselves to resistance to extinction following a relatively short acquisition period, Ross' study used a relatively long acquisition period. The five experimental groups that served in the study are summarized in Table 3.5.

Two conditions of reinforcement (100 percent and 50 percent) were used. Group C received 200 trials at 100 percent reinforcement; Group P received 220 trials at 50 percent reinforcement; Group C 100 P received 100 trials at 100 percent reinforcement followed by 100 trials at 50 percent

Table 3.5 Experimental Groups of Ross' (1959) Study

Experimental group	Number of trials			Total number of trials	Total number of reinforcements
	100% reinforcement	50% reinforcement	100% reinforcement		
C	200	—	—	200	200
P	—	220	—	220	110
C 100 P	100	100	—	200	150
C 20 P	20	100	—	120	70
P 40 C	—	40	80	120	100

reinforcement; Group C 20 P received 20 trials at 100 percent reinforcement followed by 100 trials at 50 percent reinforcement. Finally, Group P 40 C started off with 40 trials at 50 percent reinforcement and was then switched to 80 trials at 100 percent reinforcement.

The asymptotic curves for each of these groups are shown in Figure 3.17. Inspection of the acquisition curves of Groups C and P show that performance throughout conditioning and asymptotic performance was substantially higher following 100 percent reinforcement than following 50 percent reinforcement. The performance of those groups shifted to partial reinforcement (C 100 P and C 20 P) dropped markedly. The asymptotic performance of both of these groups was indistinguishable from the performance of the partial group (Group P) after the equivalent number of trials. Group P 40 C, which was given 80 continuous trials after 40 partial trials, equaled the performance of Group C after 120 trials.

The differences in the performances of these groups cannot be attributed to the different number of presentations of $S1$ given to each group. Figure 3.18, which contains the acquisition curves based on the number of trials during which $S1$ was presented, shows the same performance differences that were seen when acquisition was analyzed in terms of the number of training trials.

Resistance to extinction of a classically conditioned response following partial reinforcement

Experiments which have studied the resistance to extinction of a classically conditioned response have generally confirmed Humphreys' (1939) observation of more responding during extinction following partial reinforcement than following continuous reinforcement. Hartman and Grant's (1960) study of the resistance to extinction of the conditioned eyelid response serves as a good illustration. All subjects of this experiment were given a total of 40 reinforcements. The percentage of reinforced trials varied across four groups of subjects as follows: 25, 50, 75, and 100 percent. The acquisition and extinction curves for each group are shown in Figure 3.19. As was the case in Ross' (1959) study, the asymptotes of the acquisition curves varied with the percentage of reinforced trials. During extinction, the magnitude of the decrement in performance during the first extinction session varied with the proportion of rein-

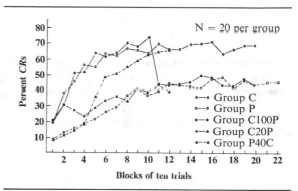

Figure 3.17 Mean percentage of conditional eyelid responses in successive blocks of 10 trials for each of the experimental groups in Ross' (1959) study.

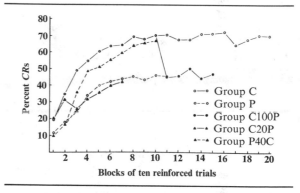

Figure 3.18 Mean percentage of conditional eyelid responses in successive blocks of 10 reinforced trials for each of the experimental groups in Ross' (1959) study.

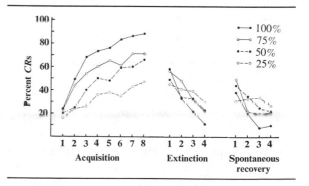

Figure 3.19 Percentage of conditional eyelid responses for successive eighths of acquisition and successive quarters of extinction and spontaneous recovery sessions for the four experimental groups of Hartman and Grant's (1960) study.

forced trials during acquisition. It was also the case that the overall level of responding during extinction varied inversely with the percentage of reinforced trials during acquisition.

In the case of classical conditioning, partial reinforcement appears to have an adverse effect during conditioning. Resistance to extinction following partial reinforcement, however, is greater than that following regular reinforcement. At present, there is no theoretical formulation to account for either the different effects of partial reinforcement on acquisition or the resistance to extinction in the case of classical conditioning. Nor is there an adequate explanation of the different effects of partial reinforcement on the acquisition of instrumentally conditioned and classically conditioned responses.

THE RELATIONS BETWEEN CLASSICAL AND INSTRUMENTAL CONDITIONING

Thus far, we have examined in detail a number of variables that affect the acquisition and maintenance of a classically conditioned response. It should be apparent that our picture of the necessary and sufficient conditions for the establishment of a classically conditioned response is very inadequate. Two major questions for which we have only limited answers are: How applicable to different response systems and unconditional stimuli are the empirical generalizations drawn thus far? and How does what we have referred to as a classically conditioned response relate conceptually to what we know about the conditioning of operants?

In the case of a response system like eyelid conditioning, the framework of a parametric system for describing classical conditioning has been roughly sketched. However, it is not clear how representative the data on eyelid conditioning are of other response systems such as salivary or heart-rate conditioning.

Even if we were more secure about our store of empirical knowledge of different response systems and unconditional stimuli, we would still not be in a position to distinguish classical and instrumental conditioning on anything more than an operational level. Indeed, our ability to distinguish classical and instrumental conditioning on even an operational level is not as decisive as some have hoped. For example, we have previously noted that the operations used in temporal and superstitious

conditioning are the same. Yet temporal conditioning is referred to as an example of classical conditioning and superstitious responding is referred to as an example of operant behavior.

Ironically, as our knowledge of instrumental conditioning increases, it appears that the domain of classical conditioning decreases; and the notion that classical conditioning is a fundamental and independent type of conditioning becomes more and more doubtful. The large overlap between classical and instrumental conditioning makes it mandatory that the relation between what is known about these two types of conditioning be examined carefully if we are to delineate classical conditioning. This is the main concern of the remainder of this chapter. Those readers interested in pursuing a general treatment of the various parameters of classical conditioning should consult Gormezano's (1966) and Beecroft's (1966) authoritative reviews as well as Hull's (1934) elegant review of the older literature.

Operational distinctions between classical and instrumental conditioning

Operationally, classical and instrumental conditioning may be distinguished on the basis of the relations associated with certain stimuli and a response. Classical conditioning involves the relation between a conditional stimulus and an unconditional stimulus, whereas instrumental conditioning involves the relation between an arbitrary response and a reinforcing stimulus.

Our purpose in distinguishing between an unconditional stimulus and a reinforcing stimulus is to start our discussion of the relations between classical and instrumental conditioning with the assumption that there is no overlap between these two classes of stimuli. Once we have identified the characteristics of these classes of stimuli, it should be simpler to specify similarities and differences that exist between unconditional and reinforcing stimuli.

Historically, there has been little or no distinction between unconditional and reinforcing stimuli. Pavlov, for example, referred to the unconditional stimulus as a reinforcing stimulus. Other theorists, often for different reasons, have also followed Pavlov's lead of not distinguishing between unconditional and reinforcing stimuli (e.g., Estes, 1950; Guthrie, 1935; Hull, 1929). It should, therefore, be no surprise that these men did not distinguish between classical and instrumental conditioning.

A second group of theorists has taken the position that the consequences of classical- and instrumental-conditioning procedures are fundamentally different (e.g., Miller, 1948; Mowrer, 1947; Schlosberg, 1937; Skinner, 1938). However, recently the distinction has become somewhat blurred, and there has been a noticeable change from a belief in two kinds of conditioning to a reliance on only one kind of conditioning. The interested reader should consult the papers of Herrnstein (1969), Rescorla and Solomon (1967), and Schoenfeld (1966).

Those who have argued that classical and instrumental conditioning involve different processes have often distinguished between them on grounds other than the stimulus and response relations that characterize each procedure. The most influential of these additional distinguishing characteristics have been (a) the class of responses affected by classical and instrumental conditioning, and (b) the nature of the events that serve as unconditional and reinforcing stimuli.

Classical- and instrumental-conditioning procedures distinguished with respect to the response classes they effect

The most widely cited basis for distinguishing between classical and instrumental conditioning, other than by the operations that characterize each paradigm, has been the nature of the response effected by each of these paradigms. The most influential of these classificatory schemes are summarized in Table 3.6.

Although the distinctions listed in Table 3.6 do not exhaust the ways in which different response systems have been related to instrumental- and classical-conditioning paradigms, they amply illustrate the nature and the logic of such distinctions. In each case, the logical relation between a particular binary classification and the distinction between classical and instrumental conditioning is the same. It is assumed that the paradigm listed at the head of each column applies only to those types of responses listed beneath that heading. Thus, it is assumed that only elicited and autonomic responses can be classically conditioned, and that the domain of instrumental conditioning is restricted to emitted and skeletal responses. In discussing these distinctions, we will attempt first to define them and then to amplify the discussion in Chapter 2 of the exceptions to the exclusive relationships specified in Table 3.6.

Autonomic versus skeletal nervous system effectors

The distinction between responses by organs innervated by the autonomic and skeletal nervous systems is the least ambiguous of those specified in Table 3.6. The autonomic and skeletal nervous systems have been traditionally distinguished on the basis of (a) the location and organization of the centers of the central nervous system that control each system, (b) the organs that each system innervates, (c) the type of neurohumor that transmits nervous impulses across synapses and at neuro-effector junctions, and (d) the nature of the feedback from organs innervated by the skeletal and autonomic nervous systems. All of these distinctions and the exceptions to the above generalizations have been extensively documented in various standard physiological texts (e.g., Grossman, 1967; Ruch & Patton, 1965). Most of the exceptions to the criteria used to distinguish between the autonomic and the skeletal nervous systems are of little concern, but one generally accepted by psychologists does require elaboration here, because it appears to be erroneous. This is the often-stated generalization that, unlike the skeletal nervous system, the autonomic nervous system does not provide direct feedback to the central nervous

Table 3.6   Response Criteria for Distinguishing Between Classical and Instrumental Conditioning

Classical conditioning	Instrumental conditioning	Source
Autonomic effectors	Skeletal effectors	Keller & Schoenfeld, 1950; Mowrer, 1947; Skinner, 1953
Respondents	Operants	Skinner, 1938
Involuntary responses	Voluntary responses	Galanter, 1966; Skinner, 1953
Diffuse emotional responses	Precise adaptive responses	Schlosberg, 1937

system. It appears that this distinction is especially responsible for the assertion that autonomically innervated organs cannot be conditioned instrumentally. Various sources, however, have presented evidence of afferent fibres running from autonomic organs to the central nervous system (e.g., Ochs, 1965).

Two types of exceptions to the distinction drawn in Table 3.6 are possible. Either some members of the response classes listed under *classical conditioning* can be instrumentally conditioned or some of the response classes listed under *instrumental conditioning* can be classically conditioned. We will first consider the evidence concerning the question of whether autonomic responses can be conditioned instrumentally.

Can autonomic responses be conditioned instrumentally?

Two reports that autonomic responses could not be brought under operant control appear to have retarded research in this area (Mowrer, 1938; Skinner, 1938). More recently, however, a number of investigators have shown that, under a wide variety of conditions, various autonomic responses can be conditioned with instrumental procedures. Among the earliest studies to report positive results was a series of experiments by Kimmel and his associates, who studied the *GSR* (Fowler & Kimmel, 1962; Kimmel & Baxter, 1964; Kimmel & Kimmel, 1963; see Kimmel, 1967, for a summary of these experiments). It is also apparently possible to condition changes in heart rate with an instrumental avoidance paradigm (Shearn, 1962).

The observation that the frequency of an autonomic response can be increased if a reinforcing stimulus follows the occurrence of that response can be interpreted in a number of ways. All but one of these interpretations, however, affirm that autonomic responses can be brought directly under instrumental control. The alternative account maintains that the conditioning procedure affects certain skeletal responses and that the autonomic response then increases in frequency as a by-product of the skeletal response (cf. Smith, 1954). For example, the conditioning of an increase in blood pressure with an instrumental procedure—positive reinforcement following each such increase—could result from reinforcement of the subject's general activity (operant behavior), which then elicits an increase in blood pressure. To make matters more complicated, it may be possible to reinforce a human subject's thoughts, which then

elicit an increase in blood pressure. With non-humans, where the concept of thinking strikes some as inappropriate, a mediational mechanism involving skeletal responses has been proposed (e.g., Guthrie, 1935; Lawrence, 1963; Schoenfeld & Cumming, 1963).

Such arguments are difficult to refute. Skinner (1938, pp. 112–115), for example, suggested that sticking a pin in one's own arm (or thinking of a pin prick) in order to raise blood pressure would qualify as an operant-respondent chain rather than as evidence of autonomic conditioning. Extrapolating this point of view, blushing and other evidences of an emotional (mainly an autonomic) response can be elicited by thinking, as the world's greatest actors have so delightfully demonstrated.

Two main experimental strategies have been employed in attempts to answer these criticisms of demonstrations of the instrumental conditioning of autonomic responses. The most widely used seeks to immobilize the subject during conditioning by paralyzing his skeletal musculature. The other approach asks whether skeletal responses condition more rapidly than autonomic responses in situations where one expects both kinds of responses to become conditioned.

1. Paralysis of skeletal musculature. Paralysis of the skeletal musculature is accomplished by administering *curare* and other related drugs which selectively block the transmission of nerve impulses across the *motor endplates* of skeletal muscles. Breathing, which is in part controlled by skeletal muscles, must be maintained by artificial respiration for as long as curare is effective. It is apparently possible for human subjects to maintain consciousness and to think under curare (Smith, Brown, Toman, & Goodman, 1947). Thus, it should be noted that, while the administration of curare may eliminate gross overt responding, it is entirely possible that covert responding may still occur. Black (1965), in fact, has shown that dosages of curare which eliminated overt responding did not eliminate even the covert responding detectable by electromyographic recording of muscular activity.

N. E. Miller (1969) and his students have demonstrated that various autonomic responses can apparently be conditioned as a result of an instrumental procedure while the subject is under curare. Miller observed that "paralyzing the animal with curare not only greatly simplifies the problem of recording visceral responses without artifacts introduced by movement, but also apparently it makes it easier for the animal to learn, perhaps because paralysis of the skeletal muscles removes sources of variability and distraction" [p. 435]. In most of these studies, the level of curare was sufficient to eliminate all muscular activity, including activity which usually can only be detected electromyographically.

Trowill (1967) demonstrated either a small increase or a small decrease in the heart rate of curarized rats (a 5 percent change from the baseline rate) when the change was followed by reinforcing electrical stimulation of the brain. Miller and DiCara (1967) produced substantially greater changes in heart rate in the same preparation by shaping the desired change. They were also able to train a discrimination that called for the change in heart rate only during the presence of a discriminative stimulus.

In another experiment, DiCara and Miller (1968a) demonstrated that changes in heart rate in curarized rats can be conditioned as the response in avoidance and escape procedures. A decrease (or, in some instances, an increase) in heart rate allowed the rat to avoid or to escape from a mild electric shock. In the discriminated avoidance procedure, one stimulus was present when shocks could be avoided or escaped, and a second stimulus was present when shocks were not programmed. Shock was delivered to the rat's tail. Heart rate was recorded under three conditions: (1) in the presence of a signal that was correlated with programmed shocks, (2) in the presence of a different (safe) signal indicating that no shock would occur, and (3) on "blank" trials when neither shock nor a discriminative stimulus was programmed. The results of this experiment are shown in Figure 3.20. As training progressed, the stimulus present when the avoidance-escape procedure was in effect evoked the greatest change in heart rate. At the other extreme, the change in heart rate was minimal during the safe signal.

The use of curare, in appropriate dosages, can preclude the possibility that actual and visible movements mediate the apparently operant conditioning of autonomic responses. But even if peripheral skeletal mediators were definitely excluded, it would still be possible to invoke more central mediating responses. We have noted, for example, that even during paralysis a human subject can think about emotional events which could result in peripheral autonomic events. At the present time, there is no clear way to rule out thoughts or central nervous system mediators when an autonomic response is strengthened as a result of an instrumental contingency between that

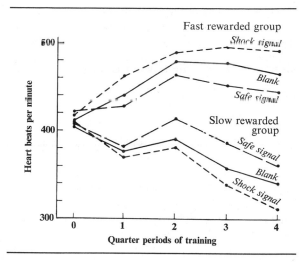

Figure 3.20 Changes in heart rate resulting from the instrumental-conditioning paradigm. (From DiCara & Miller, 1968a.)

response and a reinforcing stimulus. On the other hand, until the nature of the controlling mediators that are presumed to operate in successful attempts to condition autonomic responses as operants are more precisely specified, this sort of distinction between classical and instrumental conditioning will remain metaphorical.

2. Instrumental conditioning of opposing autonomic responses. Another strategy employed in dealing with the criticism that changes induced by instrumental conditioning in autonomic responding are artifacts of instrumentally conditioned skeletal responses takes as its point of departure the *parallel* activation pattern of the sympathetic nervous system. Given that the sympathetic nervous system generally acts in a parallel manner, any skeletal mediator would presumably result in the activation of a cluster of autonomic responses. If, in the same organism, it could be shown that different instrumental contingencies resulted in an increase in the frequency of one autonomic response but a decrease in the frequency of another synergistic autonomic response, it would be difficult to imagine a single skeletal mediator that could produce autonomic changes in opposite directions.

An experiment illustrating this approach was performed by Miller and Banuazizi (1968). After demonstrating that the intestinal response of a curarized rat could be conditioned instrumentally to contract or to relax, the experimenters proceeded to condition changes in heart rate and changes in the intestinal response within the same rat. All subjects in this experiment were completely paralyzed by curare, maintained by artificial respiration, and rewarded by electrical stimulation of the brain. Half of the subjects were conditioned to relax the intestine; the remaining half were conditioned to contract the intestine. These two groups were divided into subgroups which were rewarded for either an increase or a decrease in heart rate. The results are shown in Figure 3.21. Neither of the groups rewarded for a change in intestinal response (Figure 3.21A) showed any change in heart rate. At the same time, however, large changes in the intestinal response were produced. Conversely, when either an increase or decrease in heart rate was conditioned, there was no change in the intestinal response (Figure 3.21B).

3. Which occurs first: Conditioned autonomic or conditioned skeletal responses? For a variety of theoretical reasons, many experimenters have sought to monitor skeletal and autonomic responses in situations where members of each response class become conditioned. An interesting procedure, adopted in a number of different laboratories (e.g. Shapiro, 1961; Williams, 1965; Wolf, 1963), is the simultaneous recording of salivation and a lever- (or panel-) press that is reinforced with food. In all of these experiments, the intermittent schedule that was used insured that reinforcement would be widely distributed over time and that skeletal responding would occur in a particular temporal pattern. For example, on a *fixed-interval (FI)* schedule, which reinforces the first lever-press that occurs after *t* seconds have elapsed since the previous reinforcement, the rate of responding accelerates during the interval from a zero value to some maximal value that occurs just prior to the end of the interval (Shapiro, 1961). On a *fixed-ratio (FR)* schedule of reinforcement, which reinforces every *n*th response, one typically observes a pause following reinforcement followed by responding at a constant rate until the next reinforcement is delivered (Williams, 1965; Wolf, 1963). In all of these experiments, the pattern of responding characteristic of an *FR* or an *FI* schedule was observed first in the case of the skeletal response and afterward in the case of the salivary response. It was also the case that, following a postreinforcement interval during which no skeletal responding occurred and food-elicited salivation decreased to a baseline level, the onset of skeletal responding preceded the resumption of salivary responding.

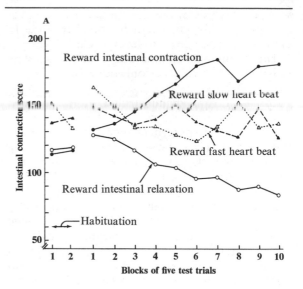

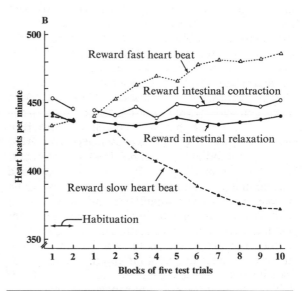

Figure 3.21 Intestinal-contraction (A) and heart-rate (B) scores over five trial blocks. In A, increases or decreases in the intestinal contraction rate were conditioned instrumentally. In B, increases or decreases in heart rate were conditioned instrumentally. (From Miller & Banuazizi, 1968.)

On other schedules, however, a different sequence of events was observed. Shapiro (1962) observed that following training on a *differential reinforcement of low rate (DRL)* schedule, which reinforces only those responses that are preceded by a period of nonresponding of at least t seconds, salivation typically preceded the occurrence of a panel-press by dogs

Yet another relation between panel-pressing and salivation was reported by Ellison and Konorski (1964, 1965), who trained dogs to press a panel on an *FR* schedule of reinforcement. Once the ratio was completed, the stimulus condition was changed and food was delivered 8 seconds later. By using this procedure, Ellison and Konorski completely separated panel-pressing and salivation in time.

Gantt and Dykman (1957) and Black (1959) studied the development of a conditioned heart-rate response in dogs that were trained to perform an operant skeletal response to avoid electric shock. Both experimenters reported that heart-rate conditioning occurred prior to the acquisition of the avoidance response. On the basis of these and other studies (see Rescorla & Solomon, 1967, pp. 165–169, for an extensive review of this area), it is clear that one cannot conclude that a conditioned skeletal response develops prior to a conditioned autonomic response in a situation in which both kinds of responses eventually become conditioned. Indeed, the best way to characterize the results of experiments that have simultaneously recorded skeletal and autonomic responses is by noting that no consistent pattern of priority has been observed.

Can skeletal responses be classically conditioned?

Thus far we have dealt with only one half of the question of whether classical and instrumental conditioning can be distinguished on the basis of the responses that can be conditioned by each paradigm. We have seen that the weight of recent evidence seems to indicate that autonomic responses can be conditioned instrumentally, i.e., they can be reinforced. We must, therefore, conclude that autonomic responses do not fall within the exclusive province of classical conditioning. An analogous conclusion can be drawn in the case of the classical conditioning of a skeletal response. Here again, however, there are problems of interpretation.

Schlosberg (1928) reported the conditioning of the patellar reflex (knee jerks) in human subjects, a reflex that appears to be completely under the control of the skeletal nervous system. Eyelid conditioning in humans is another more widespread example of the classical conditioning of a skeletal response. It is important to note that in both of these instances the eliciting stimulus may prove to be a noxious event. While there is no strong evidence to support this conjecture in the case of the patellar reflex in humans (all we have is the report by some of Schlosberg's subjects that the patellar tap was unpleasant), there is ample evidence which indicates that the air puff or the electrical shock used to elicit eye closure in eyelid-conditioning experiments is an aversive event. Logan (1951), Kimble, Mann, and Dufort (1955), and Hansche and Grant (1965), for example, have shown that the eyelid response could be conditioned by an instrumental avoidance procedure in which an eyelid closure canceled the presentation of the *US*.

If it can be demonstrated that the unconditional stimulus is also an aversive stimulus, one must ask whether the response that is conditioned might not function to minimize the aversive effects of the *US* and thus be strengthened instrumentally. A promising technique for studying this problem has been described by Wagner, Thomas, and Norton (1967) in connection with a study of cortical unconditional stimuli. The experimenters gave their subjects a choice between presentations of the normal *CS-US* sequence and the *US* presented alone. In the first case, the *CS* would be followed by the *CR*, after which the *US* would elicit the *UR*. In the second case, only the *UR* would occur. If the *CR* functions to attenuate the magnitude of the *UR* or in some way reduce the aversiveness of the *US*, one would expect subjects to opt for the condition in which the *CS* precedes the *US*. This is, in fact, what Wagner et al. observed. While such a demonstration by itself is not solid evidence that the *US* is aversive, it would be interesting to apply this procedure in other situations where a skeletal response has been increased in frequency following training on a classical-conditioning paradigm.

Another skeletal response, which has been studied by many investigators of classical conditioning, is the leg-flexion response that is elicited by electric shock (e.g., Bekhterev, 1913; Liddell, 1934, 1956). Unfortunately, many of these studies did not distinguish between a classical-conditioning contingency, where electric shock (the *US*) is always presented following the presentation of the *CS*, and avoidance or escape contingencies, where the occurrence of a leg flexion following the onset of the *CS* resulted in the cancellation of the shock (avoidance) or allowed the subject to terminate the shock (escape). But even when neither the probability of the occurrence of the *US* nor its duration is altered by the occurrence of the *CR*, it is possible to argue that the *CR* was strengthened instrumentally because it served to attenuate the effects of the *US*.

Respondent versus operant response classes

The distinction between classical and instrumental conditioning in terms of *operants* and *respondents* was first suggested by Skinner (1938): "Behavior that is correlated with specific eliciting stimuli may be called respondent behavior" [p. 20]. An operant is defined as a response for which "no correlated stimulus can be detected upon occasions when it has been observed to occur" [p. 21]. Skinner, however, makes it very clear that his distinction between operants and respondents is isomorphic with the distinction between skeletal and autonomic responses. Indeed Skinner (1953) and Keller and Schoenfeld (1950) termed classical and instrumental conditioning synonymous with respondent and operant conditioning, respectively, as well as with autonomic and skeletal conditioning. Autonomic responses, according to Skinner, are concerned with the internal commerce of the organism, while skeletal responses are concerned with organism-environment interactions (Skinner, 1938, p. 112; 1953, pp. 113–115). Operants affect the environment in a way that respondents cannot.

Other distinctions between classical and instrumental conditioning in terms of *involuntary* and *voluntary* responses (Galanter, 1966, pp. 10 ff.; Skinner, 1953, p. 115), or in terms of *diffuse preparatory responses* and *precise adaptive responses* (Schlosberg, 1937), appear to add little to those already suggested by the autonomic-skeletal and operant-respondent distinctions. Voluntary and involuntary responses cannot be defined independently of instrumental- and classical-conditioning procedures. Galanter (1966), for example, defines the following relationship between voluntary and involuntary responses and operants and respondents: "We shall assign the words *operant* to voluntary acts and *respondent* to involuntary acts. . . . Operants are acts affected by their outcomes; respondents are acts that are not affected by their outcomes" [p. 10]. Later, Galanter, following the lead of Skinner, exclusively relates classical conditioning with involuntary responses and instrumental conditioning with voluntary responses. In the same paper in which he distinguished between diffuse-preparatory and precise-adaptive responses, Schlosberg (1937) acknowledged that this distinction could be reduced to the distinction between autonomic and skeletal responses.

Classical and instrumental conditioning as distinguished by the types of stimuli that serve as unconditional and reinforcing stimuli

We have seen thus far that a distinction between classical and instrumental conditioning cannot be made unequivocally on the basis of either paradigm's having exclusive control over a particular kind of response. One possible basis for distinguishing between these paradigms is the nature of the events that serve as unconditional and reinforcing stimuli. Our main concern in discussing the nature of the unconditional and reinforcing stimuli will be to determine to what extent they can function in only one capacity.

At first glance, it may appear that all primary reinforcers can function as unconditional stimuli for at least some autonomic response, but that the converse may not be true. The evidence relevant to this generalization is too meager to allow a strong conclusion. Perhaps the most promising examples of stimuli that can function as unconditional, but not as reinforcing, stimuli are interoceptive stimuli (e.g., the warming of the stomach mucosa, or an increase in the pressure applied to a portion of the intestine), which Bykov (1957) and others (summarized in Razran, 1961) have studied in classical-conditioning paradigms. Unfortunately, the best arguments that such stimuli cannot function as reinforcing stimuli are the absence of any demonstration to the contrary and the fact that we are apparently unconscious of the activity of our interoceptive organs.

It has been argued that the unconscious nature of interoceptive stimuli provides them with special status as unconditional stimuli (Razran, 1961). We will assume that the term *unconscious* applies to those stimulus consequences of a response that cannot be rendered effective as discriminative stimuli following differential reinforcement (cf. Skinner, 1957). However, in the absence of any studies attempting to differentially reinforce human subjects with respect to the presence or absence of an interoceptive stimulus, we cannot be that certain that human subjects cannot be made conscious of the responses of their interoceptive organs. Even if we could not be made conscious of the activity of our interoceptive organs, it is not clear how this characteristic of interoceptive responses can distinguish between reinforcing and unconditional stimuli. Human subjects are often not conscious of the positive reinforcers for which they work (e.g., Greenspoon, 1955; Verplanck, 1962). Similarly, in negative-reinforcement studies it is clear that instrumental conditioning occurs without the subject's awareness of the presence or absence of the aversive event. Lindsley (1957), for example, demonstrated that human subjects could be conditioned to bring their fingers together to avoid a loud noise even while they were asleep.

Other examples of unconditional stimuli which have not been used in instrumental-conditioning paradigms are a blow to the patellar tendon (e.g., Schlosberg, 1928) and stimulation of the motor cortex (Doty & Giurgea, 1961; Wagner, Thomas, & Norton, 1967). We have previously noted, however, that in both of these cases it appears that the unconditional stimuli cannot be considered neutral in the sense that they will not reinforce operant behavior. While some of Schlosberg's subjects indicated that they had a "neutral" attitude toward the patellar tap, others did not, and it is not clear whether a subject's report should be accepted as sound evidence of the neutrality of such stimulation. In the case of brain stimulation of the motor cortex, we have noted that if a subject is given a choice between a presentation of a *US* that is preceded by the *CS* and an unsignaled presentation of the *US,* he prefers the signaled *US* (Wagner, Thomas, & Norton, 1967). Although this cannot be accepted as an unequivocal demonstration of the reinforcing nature of the unconditional stimulus per se (as opposed, for example, to some informational properties of the *CS*), it suggests that stimulation of the motor cortex cannot be accepted as an example of an unconditional stimulus free of any primary reinforcing properties.

Are there primary reinforcing stimuli that cannot function as unconditional stimuli? A number of candidates quickly suggest themselves. It is interesting to note, however, that these same stimuli are the ones often cited as evidence that primary reinforcers do not always reduce drive. These stimuli include light onset (Kiernan, 1964), the opportunity for a confined monkey to see certain objects (e.g., electric trains, Butler, 1953, 1957), the opportunity for a monkey to manipulate certain objects (Harlow, 1950), the opportunity to run in a running wheel (Hundt & Premack, 1963), and brain stimulation (Olds & Milner, 1954). One must caution, however, that the argument that these events cannot

function as unconditional stimuli is based more on intuitive notions than on empirical observations. Light onset and moving electric trains, for example, undoubtedly produced *orienting reflexes* (cf. Sokolov, 1960, 1963). Whether this is true of the opportunity to manipulate objects or to run on a running wheel is less clear. In the case of brain stimulation, it has been demonstrated that in some instances (e.g., Malmo, 1965) the same stimulation that serves to condition the operant, lever-pressing, may not suffice as an unconditional stimulus in a heart-rate conditioning situation. And, finally, any stimulus that affects an organism's behavior elicits the activity in the nervous system that is necessary for its effect. In this strict sense, no perceived stimuli are neutral.

Is classical conditioning distinctive?

Even if the minor exceptions just mentioned prove to be valid examples of reinforcing stimuli that do not function as unconditional stimuli, it should not divert our attention from the significance of the large class of stimuli that function as both reinforcing and unconditional stimuli. As mentioned earlier, it can be shown in most classical-conditioning experiments that the conditional response may enhance or somehow modify the reinforcing quality of the unconditional stimulus. Thus, each time a classical-conditioning paradigm is used, we must ask whether the observed changes in behavior are due to classical or to instrumental conditioning. A logically analogous question should, of course, also be raised in evaluating the outcome of every experiment with an instrumental-conditioning paradigm. We will first consider alternative interpretations of the outcomes of classical-conditioning experiments.

In a typical salivary-conditioning experiment, the basic datum is an increase in the frequency of the salivary response in the presence of the *CS* following the pairing of the *CS* and the *US*. To what extent are we sure that these results can be accounted for by the principles of classical conditioning? It will be instructive to consider first a number of other interpretations, none of which require the concept of classical conditioning.

An experiment performed by Miller and Carmona (1967) demonstrated that the salivary response can be brought under instrumental control. In this experiment, different groups of water-deprived dogs were trained to either increase or decrease their rates of salivation. The consequence of a change in the rate of salivation was the presentation of water reinforcement. The results are shown in Figure 3.22. As training progressed, there was a clear change in the rate of salivation for each group. While the subjects of this experiment were not given curare (Miller, 1969, p. 435, reports that curare led to copious amounts of continuous salivation), we may be in a reasonably sound position to accept this as a demonstration of the direct instrumental conditioning of the salivary glands, given the results of similar experiments in which the subjects had been given curare. It is interesting to note that the decision to use water as a reinforcer for water-deprived dogs was based on the unsuccessful results of an experiment in which food was used with food-deprived dogs. Originally, food was contingent upon a change in the rate of salivation. Miller (1969, p. 435) reports that he and Carmona switched from food to water reinforcement partly because of strong and persistent unconditional salivation elicited by food (see also Chapter 2).

The possibility that salivation is instrumentally conditioned during a typical classical-conditioning paradigm can be brought into sharper focus by comparing the procedures used in a temporal-conditioning experiment (e.g., Pavlov, 1927, p. 41) and the procedures that are used in the experiment on superstition (e.g., Skinner, 1948). We have noted previously that a temporal-conditioning procedure calls for the presentation of the US at fixed-time intervals. The result is a conditional response that occurs prior to the presentation of the US. The

procedure for developing a superstitious response calls for the presentation of the reinforcing stimulus following a fixed-time interval (Herrnstein, 1966; Skinner, 1948). The result is an increase in the frequency of occurrence of whatever the organism was doing prior to the presentation of the reinforcing stimulus. The only difference between the procedure for developing a superstitious response and a standard instrumental conditioning procedure is that in the former case the experimenter does not specify what response must occur if reinforcement is to be presented. The demonstration that regular presentations of a positive reinforcer can strengthen certain responses shows that the *Law of Effect,* which states that the frequency of a response is increased when followed by a positive reinforcer, is not concerned with whether the response in question met the experimenter's specification.

The similar outcomes of temporal conditioning and superstition procedures pose an important question relevant to the interpretation of classical conditioning. What basis do we have for not asserting that Pavlov's dogs were superstitiously salivating to obtain food in a manner comparable to the way in which Skinner's pigeons engaged in bowing or other ritualistic behavior to obtain food? We have seen that the salivary response, as well as other autonomic responses, can be conditioned as operants. Furthermore, since food normally elicits salivation, the baseline level of salivating is increased above its normal level during the typical salivary-conditioning experiment. Thus, the salivary response is at high strength prior to the presentation of food. The continued occurrence of the salivation-food sequence should further increase the level of salivation. According to this interpretation, the function of the conditional stimulus is a discriminative one. As a result of discrimination training between those stimulus situations followed by food (the CS) and those that are not, the CS presumably also functions to restrict the occurrence of salivation to the intervals following the onset of the CS.

We are now in a position to specify three different interpretations of what happened in Pavlov's experiment on conditioned salivation. Again, the reader is reminded that none of these interpretations require the concept of classical conditioning.

1. The increase in the frequency of salivation is an artifact of skeletal chewing movements known to occur following the presentation of the CS. In this case, the CS would be considered a discriminative stimulus in the presence of which chewing is

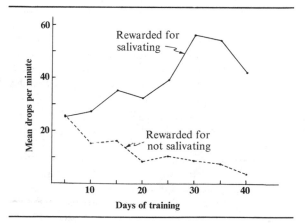

Figure 3.22 Magnitude of the salivary response over successive days and training of dogs that were conditioned to salivate or not to salivate for water reinforcement. (From Miller & Carmona, 1967.)

followed by food reinforcement. This point of view (originally stated by Smith, 1954) maintains that the increase in salivation is an artifact of chewing movements which are under the stimulus control of *S2*.

2. Salivation was conditioned instrumentally. The consequence of salivating is an increase in the palatability and the digestibility of food. This interpretation, which derives from Hebb (1956) and Bekhterev (1913) in the case of negative unconditional stimuli, is consistent with our earlier observation that autonomic responses can be conditioned when reinforcement is arranged by the experimenter.

3. The increase in the frequency of salivation represents an operant superstition. Under this interpretation, anything the dog does prior to the delivery of food is reinforced. Thus, just as a pigeon engages in ritualistic behavior following a procedure that presents food reinforcement independently of what the pigeon does, it is assumed that salivation in the dog is a superstitious response in that food reinforcement is not contingent upon salivation. This interpretation, like the preceding one, is strengthened by the observation that autonomic responses can be instrumentally conditioned.

These interpretations all maintain that a classical-conditioning procedure insures that motor responses and/or salivation are conditioned instrumentally. They also assume some stimulus control by the *CS*. Stimulus control (cf. Chapter 4) refers to the extent to which an antecedent stimulus determines the probability of the occurrence of a response (Terrace, 1966, p. 271). In all three cases, it is clear that the response presumed to be conditioned instrumentally is under stimulus control in the sense that the probability of its occurrence is higher in the presence of the *CS*.

Since an antecedent stimulus is a necessary ingredient of any instrumental-conditioning interpretation of what happens during training by a classical-conditioning procedure, it is apparent that both the classical and instrumental conditioning interpretations of the outcome of a classical-conditioning training procedure involve the same sequence of events. These are shown in Table 3.7. In the discussion that follows, we will focus our attention on the first three terms and ignore the consequences of the unconditional and the reinforcing stimuli.

Table 3.7 draws attention to an obvious, yet often ignored, feature that the results of classical- and instrumental-conditioning experiments have in common. In both cases a conditioned response has been brought under stimulus control. This situation, however, has been more or less ignored at the expense of other considerations in descriptions of instrumental and classical conditioning. For example, psychologists concerned with classical conditioning typically use as their point of departure the fact that the response that was brought under the control of the conditional stimulus is similar to the unconditional response. This is presumed to be different from the situation in instrumental conditioning where there is no necessary relation between the response that has been strengthened and the unconditional response to the reinforcer. If this is true, however, it is only because most experimenters have focused on recording only one response in a conditioning experiment. We have noted previously that whenever an experimenter records from numerous response systems (e.g., Zener, 1937) he is likely to observe the conditioning of operants that are similar in topography to the unconditional response to the reinforcing stimulus (e.g., turning toward the food, chewing).

In experiments on instrumental conditioning, the control of the discriminative stimuli is usually ignored, especially during acquisition. In defining the operant, Skinner (1938, pp. 19–21) stated that the occurrence of the conditioned operant did not depend on the value of any particular antecedent stimulus. However, Skinner did note that some stimulus (designated s) was part of the sequence of events that preceded a conditioned operant, $s: R$ elicits S^R. It is undoubtedly the case, however, that the value of s is important in determining the probability of an operant. An interesting example is what

Table 3.7 Sequence of Stimulus and Response Events in Classical and Instrumental Conditioning

	S1	*R1*	*S2*	*R2*
Classical conditioning:	Conditional stimulus	Conditional response	Unconditional stimulus	Unconditional response
Instrumental conditioning:	Discriminative stimulus	Conditioned operant	Reinforcing stimulus	Unconditional response

happens when one cleans an experimental chamber (Eckerman, Lanson, & Cumming, 1968). This can result in the marked disruption in the performance of a strongly conditioned operant. Even more to the point is the obvious fact that the sight of the lever or the key is important in the case of the conditioned operant. Yet the contribution of such stimuli has not been the subject of experimental study, nor have these stimuli been incorporated into the formulation of the conditioned operant. This is quite understandable in the context of the issues to which Skinner addressed himself in distinguishing between the conditions necessary to produce classical and instrumental conditioning. Since Skinner's (1938) formulation of these two types of conditioning, however, it has become abundantly clear that the conditioned operant does not occur in a stimulus vacuum. The fact that the experimenter does not specifically present a stimulus in conjunction with the contingency between a response and reinforcement does not of course mean that attendant stimuli do not gain control over the conditioned operant. Experiments by Morse and Skinner (1957, 1958) and Brown and Jenkins (1968) indicate that, just as Skinner's original experiment on superstition showed that an explicit contingency is not necessary in strengthening a response, an explicit relation between a stimulus and a conditioned operant is not necessary to establish stimulus control over that operant.

Even though the procedure for operant conditioning does not specify that a discriminative stimulus be present during conditioning, it seems impossible to conceive of a situation where certain stimuli that were present while an operant was conditioned did not acquire some degree of stimulus control over that operant. Thus, just as a classical-conditioning procedure explicitly establishes stimulus control by the *CS* (by virtue of the *CS*'s having been alternated with its absence), it appears as if stimulus control over operant behavior is also established during instrumental conditioning.

When one considers the *trial procedure* (cf. Jenkins, 1965), as opposed to the *free-operant procedure* (cf. Ferster, 1953) that is commonly used in studies of operant behavior, the role of the antecedent stimulus becomes quite explicit (e.g., Jenkins, 1961; Terrace, 1963). Indeed, with the exception of the contingency between the response and the reinforcing stimulus, the sequence of events in a trial procedure (discriminative stimulus: response followed by reinforcing stimulus) is the same as in a classical-conditioning experiment (conditional stimulus elicits conditional response;

unconditional stimulus). Following Skinner's usage, we will refer to the sequence, discriminative stimulus: response followed by reinforcing stimulus, as a *discriminative operant*.

Until the recent work of Miller and others on the operant conditioning of autonomic responses, the choice between the traditional conditional reflex and the discriminative-operant interpretations of what happens during classical-conditioning training was hardly an issue. Indeed, the discriminative-operant interpretation of the behavior changes following training on a classical-conditioning paradigm would not have stood close scrutiny, since it was widely accepted that an autonomic organ could not be conditioned with the instrumental paradigm. Even from the present vantage point, it is hardly the case that the discriminative-operant model of classical conditioning can be considered on an equal basis with the traditional reflex model. It may turn out, however, that our inability to make a strong case for the discriminative-operant model stems more from a lack of supporting evidence than from available evidence capable of refuting this model.

Our review of the basis on which operants and respondents can be distinguished revealed that the response class that could be influenced by each procedure can no longer differentiate between classical and instrumental conditioning. While it is yet to be established that all response systems that have been studied in classical-conditioning experiments can be conditioned instrumentally, the success that has been achieved to date in the case of salivation (Miller & Carmona, 1967), heart rate (DiCara & Miller, 1968a), the galvanic skin response (Fowler & Kimmel, 1962; Kimmel & Baxter, 1964), intestinal contraction (Miller & Banuazizi, 1968), and vasoconstriction and vasodilation (DiCara & Miller, 1968b) certainly augurs well for the possibility that other autonomic effectors can be conditioned in that fashion as well. We have also seen that the nature of the stimulus that is contingent upon the presentation of a prior stimulus in the case of classical conditioning, and upon the prior occurrence of a response in the case of instrumental conditioning, does not provide a criterion for clearly distinguishing between the classical- and instrumental-conditioning paradigms.

Perhaps the best bases that are currently available for distinguishing between classical- and instrumental-conditioning paradigms have to do with the effects of partial reinforcement and differences in the topography of the responses that are conditioned. We have seen that the acquisition of a response in a classical-conditioning paradigm is retarded when the unconditional stimulus is presented on a partial schedule. Although it may eventually prove possible to account for the different effects of partial reinforcement on acquisition in terms of the size of the response unit, no adequate theory along these lines has been posed to date.

Another criterion for distinguishing between a response that has been conditioned by classical, as opposed to instrumental, conditioning is the detailed topography of the response. We have seen, for example, that a classically conditioned eyelid closure differs from an operant eyelid closure in terms of its (a) latency, (b) magnitude, (c) duration, and (d) rate of closure. Systematic data from other responses conditioned by both classical and instrumental procedures are not yet available.

The rather minor differences of response topography and the effects of partial reinforcement must be placed in balance with many characteristics that both classical and instrumental conditioning have in common. In addition to the similarities we have noted, such as response classes that can be conditioned and the nature of the reinforcing event, these include (a) spontaneous recovery (Ellson, 1938; Pavlov, 1927; Skinner, 1938); (b) stimulus generalization (Guttman & Kalish, 1956; Hovland, 1937a, 1937b); (c) discrimination (Gynther, 1957; Pavlov, 1927; Skinner, 1938); (d) conditioned inhibition (Brown & Jenkins, 1967; Pavlov, 1927); (e) induction (Jenkins, 1961; Pavlov, 1927; Reynolds, 1961); (f) higher-order conditioning (Pavlov, 1927; Skinner, 1938, pp. 245 ff.; see also Cowles, 1937; Wolfe, 1936; Chapter 5); and numerous other characteristics which have been summarized by Kimble (1961, pp. 78–98).

It is especially interesting to note that most of the phenomena that are common to classical and instrumental conditioning are also related to the concept of stimulus control (e.g., generalization, induction, conditioned inhibition, higher-order conditioning). However, since both classical and instrumental conditioning share the same minimal sequence of an antecedent stimulus, a response, and a reinforcing or unconditional stimulus, it should be no surprise that many phenomena associated with control by an antecedent stimulus are common to both.

Two factors or one?

The dwindling number of criteria for distinguishing between classical and instrumental conditioning, and our recognition of an increasing number of points of overlap between them, pose a clear threat to the viability of *two-factor learning theory*. However, before we talk seriously of abandoning two-factor theory, which has dominated psychology for the last 30 years or so, we must first ask ourselves what better theory is available. At present, there are no promising new candidates. Many of the considerations discussed in this chapter seem to point to a *one-factor theory*, which describes how the probability of a response can be increased in the presence of an antecedent stimulus. It should be remembered, however, that one of the main reasons for the lack of acceptance of one-factor theories (e.g., Estes, 1950; Guthrie, 1935) was the lack of suitable experimental techniques for working within the framework of these theories.

Even if one-factor theory were able to stimulate more experiments, it would still prove difficult to dislodge two-factor theory. Undoubtedly, the main source of resistance would be the thought that the conditional reflex may no longer prove useful as a unit of analysis of conditioned behavior. Such an admission would indeed appear to abandon one of the major cornerstones of modern psychology. It may turn out, however, that the unit of the conditional reflex, which was seized upon avidly by American psychologists after Watson popularized the conditional reflex (Kimble, 1961, pp. 14–21), raises more problems than it solves. Its main weaknesses are that it draws attention to the discredited stimulus-substitution model of conditioning and that it does not recognize the reinforcing function of the *US*.

That the concept of the conditional reflex was so widely accepted even in the absence of much supporting experimental data is not very surprising when one considers that this concept at once tied together the traditions of *associationism*, *reflexology*, and *natural selection*. In addition, the concept of the conditional reflex allowed psychologists to take seriously for the first time the argument that all behavior was determined. A completely deterministic point of view, however, no longer encounters the resistance it did at the turn of the century. This would undoubtedly be the case even if the concept of conditional reflex were no longer one of the central units of learning theory.

It appears that the best strategy to follow at present is to concentrate on the terms that are common to both classical and instrumental conditioning and to study the necessary and sufficient conditions for the acquisition of a conditioned response in the presence of an antecedent stimulus. Research of this nature is notably lacking. This situation is owing in part to the difficult nature of such research. It is hard to study acquisition over a prolonged period of time and, unlike most steady-state experiments, every variation of procedure requires the study of a new organism. It may, therefore, be unfair to criticize the weak empirical foundation of one-factor theory. There appears to be a widespread lack of firm empirical knowledge regarding the acquisition of a conditioned response, respondent or operant. Aside from the difficult nature of such research, it may be the case that psychologists have shied away from the study of acquisition per se, since it usually occurs no matter how crude or how elegant a procedure the experimenter employs. It seems certain, however, that until systematic data on acquisition are obtained we will continue to find it difficult to formulate just what occurs as a result of pairing a neutral stimulus with an unconditional stimulus.

SUMMARY AND CONCLUSIONS

Classical conditioning was defined as a procedure for creating a new reflex by presenting a stimulus prior to the occurrence of an existing reflex. The principles of classical conditioning, first enunciated by Pavlov, tied together the principles of reflexology and association and also provided a conceptual framework for twentieth-century learning theory. Pavlov's psychological formulation of such phenomena as acquisition, extinction, generalization, and discrimination learning, among others, still serve as a basis for much research on learning.

Pavlov's description of the sufficient conditions for the establishment of a classically conditioned response left many questions unanswered. These included (a) the relation between the conditional and the unconditional response, (b) how to distinguish between a conditional response that could be attributed to pairing of the *CS* and the *US* and responses whose strength was modified by the repeated presentations of either the *CS* or the *US*, and (c) the relation between classical conditioning and instrumental conditioning, a second type of conditioning that achieved widespread systematic recognition long after psychologists had turned to classical conditioning as a basis of describing acquired behavior.

A review of the literature on the relationship between the *CR* and the *UR* showed that the *CR* and the *UR* differ in many respects. Thus, stimulus substitution theory, which holds that the *CS* comes

to serve as a substitute for the *US*, was shown to be untenable. Furthermore, when one examines a broad range of responses in a classical-conditioning experiment, it is observed that many responses are conditioned following the pairing of the *CS* and the *US*. These include skeletal responses as well as autonomic responses.

A detailed analysis of the kinds or responses that are observed in a typical eyelid-conditioning experiment reveal that, in addition to the conditional response, it is possible to distinguish alpha, beta, and voluntary responses. Since the frequency of some of these responses is increased by merely presenting the *US*, it is necessary to perform control experiments. Such experiments allow responses resulting from nonassociative factors to be distinguished from responses resulting from the pairing of the *CS* and the *US*. As examples of nonassociative factors, pseudoconditioning, sensitization, and habituation were discussed and techniques for controlling for these phenomena were described. A common feature of these control procedures is that the *US* is never paired with the *CS*. Since this makes it possible for the *CS* to function as an inhibitory stimulus, it may prove necessary to modify the traditional control procedures by having a random relation between the *CS* and the *US*.

A comparison of classical and instrumental conditioning revealed that there were no criteria—either operational or functional—that could distinguish consistently between these phenomena. The operations for producing temporal conditioning and for producing superstitious conditioning are identical. Yet temporal conditioning is described as an example of classical conditioning and superstition is described as an example of instrumental conditioning. Functionally, response class and the nature of the stimulus that follows the *CR* were shown to be unable to distinguish between classical and instrumental conditioning. Recent demonstrations of the instrumental conditioning of autonomic responses ruled out the possibility that the types of responses each procedure is capable of conditioning can distinguish between instrumental and classical conditioning. A comparison of reinforcing and unconditional stimuli revealed no way in which they could be distinguished. Finally, it was noted that since the *US* can also function as a reinforcing stimulus, the possibility that instrumental conditioning can occur is present in every classical-conditioning experiment.

Another similarity between instrumental and

classical conditioning is that both procedures result in stimulus control with respect to an antecedent stimulus. Thus both classical and instrumental conditioning have in common the sequence: *S1-R-S2*, where *S1* is a cue and *S2* is a reinforcing stimulus. It was suggested that the three terms *S1 R S2* constitute the basic unit of analysis of what we call classical and instrumental conditioning. It was also suggested that future research should be directed toward understanding the acquisition of conditioned behavior in the presence of an antecedent stimulus and that such research should cover a broad range of response systems and reinforcing stimuli.

REFERENCES

Anrep, G. V. Pitch discrimination in the dog. *Journal of Physiology*, 1920, **53**, 367–385. Figures 3.2 and 3.3: Reproduced by permission of the Editorial Board of *The Journal of Physiology*.

Aristotle. *De memoria et reminiscentia* (ca. 350 B.C.). J. I. Beare (Trans.) In W. D. Ross (Ed.), *The Works of Aristotle Vol. 3*. Oxford: Clarendon Press, 1931. Also in R. J. Herrnstein & E. G. Boring (Eds.). *A source book in the history of psychology*. Cambridge, Mass.: Harvard University Press, 1965. Pp. 2–7.

Ax, A. F. The physiological differentiation between fear and anger in humans. *Psychosomatic Medicine*, 1953, **25**, 433–442.

Beecroft, R. S. *Classical conditioning*. Goleta, Calif.: Psychonomic Press, 1966.

Bekhterev, V. M. *La psychologie objective*. Paris: Alean, 1913.

Black, A. H. Heart-rate changes during avoidance learning in dogs. *Canadian Journal of Psychology*, 1959, **13**, 229–242.

Black, A. H. Cardiac conditioning in curarized dogs: The relationship between heart rate and skeletal behaviour. In W. F. Prokasy (Ed.), *Classical conditioning: A symposium*. New York: Appleton-Century-Crofts, 1965. Pp. 20–47.

Boneau, C. A. The interstimulus interval and the latency of the conditioned eyelid response. *Journal of Experimental Psychology*, 1958, **56**, 464–471.

Brogden, W. J., & Gantt, W. H. Cerebellar conditioned reflexes. *American Journal of Physiology*, 1937, **119**, 277–278.

Brown, P. L., & Jenkins, H. M. Conditioned inhibition and excitation in operant discrimination learning. *Journal of Experimental Psychology*, 1967, **75**(2), 255–266.

Brown, P. L., & Jenkins, H. M. Auto-shaping of the pigeon's key-peck. *Journal of the Experimental Analysis of Behavior*, 1968, **11**, 1–8.

Butler, R. A. Discrimination learning by rhesus monkeys to visual-exploratory motivation. *Journal of Comparative and Physiological Psychology*, 1953, **46**, 95–98.

Butler, R. A. The effect of deprivation of visual incentives on visual exploration motivation in monkeys. *Journal of Comparative and Physiological Psychology*, 1957, **50**, 177–179.

Bykov, K. M. *The cerebral cortex and the internal organs*. W. H. Gantt (Trans. and Ed.) New York: Chemical Publishing, 1957.

Champion, R. A. Interpolated *UCS* trials in *GSR* conditioning. *Journal of Experimental Psychology*, 1961, **5**, 108–146.

Cowles, J. T. Food-tokens as incentives for learning by chimpanzees. *Comparative Psychological Monographs*, 1937, **14**, No. 71.

De Toledo, L., & Black, A. H. Heart-rate changes during conditioned suppression in rats. Paper presented at the meeting of the Eastern Psychological Association, New York, April 1966.

DiCara, L. V., & Miller, N. E. Changes in heart rate instrumentally learned by curarized rats as avoidance responses. *Journal of Comparative and Physiological Psychology*, 1968, **65**(1), 8–12. (a) Figure 3.20: Copyright © 1968 by the American Psychological Association, and reproduced by permission.

DiCara, L. V., & Miller, N. E. Instrumental learning of vasomotor responses by rats: Learning to respond differentially in the two ears. *Science*, 1968, **159**, 1485–1486. (b)

Doty, R. W., & Giurgea, C. Conditioned reflexes established by coupling electrical excitation of two cortical areas. In J.

Delafresnaye (Ed.), *Brain mechanisms and learning*. London: Blackwell Scientific Publications, 1961. Pp. 133–151.

Doty, R. W., Rutledge, L. T., Jr., & Larsen, R. M. Conditioned reflexes established to electrical stimulation of cat cerebral cortex. *Journal of Neurophysiology*, 1956, **19**, 401–415.

Dykman, R. A. On the nature of classical conditioning. In C. Brown (Ed.), *Methods in psychophysiology*. Baltimore: Williams and Wilkins, 1967. Pp. 234–290.

Eckerman, D. A., Lanson, R. N., & Cumming, W. W. Acquisition and maintenance of matching without a required observing response. *Journal of the Experimental Analysis of Behavior*, 1968, **11**, 435–441.

Ellison, G. D., & Konorski, J. Separation of the salivary and motor responses in instrumental conditioning. *Science*, 1964. **146** (Whole No. 3647), 1071–1072.

Ellison, G. D., & Konorski, J. An investigation of the relations between salivary and motor responses during instrumental performance. *Acta Biologiae Experimentalis Sinica*, 1965, **25**(4), 297–315.

Ellson, D. G. Quantitative studies of the interaction of simple habits: I. Recovery from specific and generalized effects of extinction. *Journal of Experimental Psychology*, 1938, **23**, 339–358.

Estes, W. K. Toward a statistical theory of learning. *Psychological Review*, 1950, **57**, 94–107.

Ferster, C. B. The use of the free operant in the analysis of behavior. *Psychological Bulletin*, 1953, **50**, 263–274.

Fowler, R. L., & Kimmel, H. D. Operant conditioning of the *GSR*. *Journal of Experimental Psychology*, 1962, **63**, 563–567.

Galanter, E. *Textbook of elementary psychology*. San Francisco: Holden-Day, 1966.

Gantt, W. H. Principles of nervous breakdown: Schizokinesis and autokinesis. *Annals of the New York Academy of Science*, 1953, **56**, 143–163.

Gantt, W. H. (Ed.) *Physiological bases of psychiatry*. Springfield, Ill.: Charles C. Thomas, 1958. Pp. 12–21.

Gantt, W. H. Cardiovascular component of the conditional reflex to pain, food, and other stimuli. *Physiological Review*, 1960, **40**, 266–291.

Gantt, W. H. Conditional or conditioned, reflex or response? *Conditional Reflex*, 1966, **1**, 69–73.

Gantt, W. H., & Dykman, R. A. Experimental psychogenic tachycardia. In P. H. Hoch & J. Zubin (Eds.), *Experimental psychopathology*. New York: Grune & Stratton, 1957. Pp. 12–19.

Goodrich, K. P., Ross, L. E., & Wagner, A. R. Effect of interpolated *UCS* trials in eyelid conditioning without a ready signal. *Journal of Experimental Psychology*, 1959, **58**, 319–320.

Gormezano, I. Classical conditioning. In J. B. Sidowski (Ed.), *Experimental methods and instrumentation in psychology*. New York: McGraw-Hill, 1966. Pp. 385–420. Figure 3.12: Copyright © 1966 by McGraw-Hill Book Company, and reproduced by permission.

Grant, D. A. A study of patterning in the conditioned eyelid response. *Journal of Experimental Psychology*, 1939, **25**, 445–461.

Grant, D. A., & Adams, J. K. "Alpha" conditioning in the eyelid. *Journal of Experimental Psychology*, 1944, **34**, 136–142.

Grant, D. A., & Hake, H. W. Dark adaptation and the Humphreys random reinforcement phenomenon in human eyelid conditioning. *Journal of Experimental Psychology*, 1951, **42**, 417–423.

Grant, D. A., & Norris, E. B.   Eyelid conditioning as influenced by the presence of sensitized beta responses. *Journal of Experimental Psychology*, 1947, **37**, 423–433. Figure 3.9: Copyright 1947 by the American Psychological Association, and reproduced by permission.

Grant, D. A., & Schipper, L. M.   The acquisition and extinction of conditioned eyelid responses as a function of the percentage of fixed-ratio reinforcement. *Journal of Experimental Psychology*, 1952, **43**, 313–320.

Grant, D. A., Schipper, L. M., & Ross, B. M.   Effect of intertrial interval during acquisition on extinction of the conditioned eyelid response following partial reinforcement. *Journal of Experimental Psychology*, 1952, **44**, 203–210.

Greenspoon, J.   The reinforcing effect of two spoken sounds on the frequency of two responses. *American Journal of Psychology*, 1955, **68**, 409–416.

Grether, W. F.   Pseudo conditioning without paired stimulation encountered in attempted backward conditioning. *Journal of Comparative Psychology*, 1938, **25**, 91–96.

Grings, W. W., Lockhart, R. A., & Dameron, L. E.   Conditioning autonomic responses of mentally subnormal individuals. *Psychological Monographs*, 1962, **76**, 39.

Grossman, S. P.   *A textbook of physiological psychology.* New York: Wiley, 1967.

Guthrie, E. R.   *The psychology of learning.* New York: Harper & Row, 1935.

Guttman, N., & Kalish, H. I.   Discriminability and stimulus generalization. *Journal of Experimental Psychology*, 1956, **51**, 79–88.

Gynther, M. D.   Differential eyelid conditioning as a function of stimulus similarity and strength of response to the *CS*. *Journal of Experimental Psychology*, 1957, **53**, 408–416.

Hansche, W. J., & Grant, D. A.   Onset versus termination of a stimulus in eyelid conditioning. *Journal of Experimental Psychology*, 1960, **59**, 19–26.

Hansche, W. J., & Grant, D. A.   A comparison of instrumental reward and avoidance training with classical reinforcement technique in conditioning the eyelid response. *Psychonomic Science*, 1965, **2**, 305–306.

Harlow, H. F.   Learning and satiation of response in intrinsically motivated complex puzzle performance by monkeys. *Journal of Comparative and Physiological Psychology*, 1950, **43**, 289–294.

Harris, J. D.   Forward conditioning, backward conditioning, and pseudoconditioning, and adaptation to the conditioned stimulus. *Journal of Experimental Psychology*, 1941, **28**, 491–502.

Hartley, D.   Observations on man, his frame, his duty, and his expectations, London and Bath, 1749. In R. J. Herrnstein & E. G. Boring (Eds.), *A source book in the history of psychology.* Cambridge, Mass.: Harvard University Press, 1965. Pp. 348–355.

Hartman, T. F., & Grant, D. A.   Effect of intermittent reinforcement on acquisition, extinction, and spontaneous recovery of the conditioned eyelid response. *Journal of Experimental Psychology*, 1960, **60**, 89–96. Figure 3.19: Copyright © 1960 by the American Psychological Association, and reproduced by permission.

Hartman, T. F., & Grant, D. A.   Differential eyelid conditioning as a function of the *CS-UCS* interval. *Journal of Experimental Psychology*, 1962, **64**, 131–136. (a)

Hartman, T. F., & Grant, D. A.   Effects of pattern of reinforcement and verbal information on acquisition, extinc-

tion, and spontaneous recovery of the eyelid *CR*. *Journal of Experimental Psychology*, 1962, **63**, 217–226. (b)

Hebb, D. O.   The distinction between "classical" and "instrumental." *Canadian Journal of Psychology*, 1956, **10**, 165–166.

Herrnstein, R. J.   Superstition: A corollary of the principles of operant conditioning. In W. K. Honig (Ed.), *Operant behavior: Areas of research and application.* New York: Appleton-Century-Crofts, 1966. Pp. 33–51.

Herrnstein, R. J.   Method and theory in the study of avoidance. *Psychological Review*, 1969, **76**, 49–69.

Hilgard, E. R.   Conditioned eyelid reactions to a light stimulus based on the reflex wink to sound. *Psychological Monographs*, 1931, **217**, 49.

Hilgard, E. R., & Marquis, D. G.   *Conditioning and learning.* New York: Appleton-Century-Crofts, 1940. Figure 3.8: Copyright 1940 by Appleton-Century-Crofts, Inc., and reproduced by permission of Appleton-Century-Crofts, Educational Division, Meredith Corporation.

Hovland, C. I.   The generalization of conditioned responses: I. The sensory generalization of conditioned responses with varying frequencies of tone. *Journal of General Psychology*, 1937, **17**, 125–148. (a)

Hovland, C. I.   The generalization of conditioned responses. II. The sensory generalization of conditioned responses with varying intensities of tone. *Journal of Genetic Psychology*, 1937, **51**, 279–291. (b)

Hull, C. L.   A functional interpretation of the conditioned reflex. *Psychological Review*, 1929, **36**, 498–511.

Hull, C. L.   Learning: II. The factor of the conditioned reflex. In C. Murchison (Ed.), *A handbook of general experimental psychology.* Worcester, Mass.: Clark University Press, 1934. Pp. 382–455.

Humphreys, L. G.   The effect of random alternation of reinforcement of the acquisition and extinction of conditioned eyelid reactions. *Journal of Experimental Psychology*, 1939, **25**, 141–158.

Humphreys, L. G.   Extinction of conditioned psychogalvanic responses following two conditions of reinforcement. *Journal of Experimental Psychology*, 1940, **27**, 71–75.

Hundt, A. G., & Premack, D.   Running as both a positive and negative reinforcer. *Science*, 1963, **142**, 1087–1088.

Israel Program for Scientific Translations.   *The central nervous system and behavior: Selected translations from the Russian medical literature.* Bethesda, Md.: National Institutes of Health, 1960.

Jenkins, H. M.   The effect of discrimination training on extinction. *Journal of Experimental Psychology*, 1961, **61**, 111–121.

Jenkins, H. M.   Measurement of stimulus control during operant conditioning. *Psychological Bulletin*, 1965, **64**, 365–376.

Keller, F. S., & Schoenfeld, W. N.   *Principles of psychology.* New York: Appleton-Century-Crofts, 1950.

Kiernan. C. C.   Positive reinforcement by light. *Psychological Bulletin*, 1964, **62**, 551–557.

Kimble, G. A. (Ed.)   *Hilgard and Marquis' Conditioning and learning.* (2nd ed.) New York: Appleton-Century-Crofts, 1961. Table 3.4: Copyright © 1961 by Appleton-Century-Crofts, Inc., and reproduced by permission of Appleton-Century-Crofts, Educational Division, Meredith Corporation.

Kimble, G. A.   Categories of learning and the problem of definition: Comments on Professor Grant's paper. In A. W. Melton (Ed.), *Categories of human learning.* New York:

Academic Press, 1964. Pp. 32–45. Figure 3.11: Copyright© 1964 by Academic Press, Inc., and reproduced by permission.

Kimble, G. A., & Dufort, R. H.   The associative factor in eyelid conditioning. *Journal of Experimental Psychology*, 1956, **52**, 386–391.

Kimble, G. A., Mann, L. I., & Dufort, R. H.   Classical and instrumental eyelid conditioning. *Journal of Experimental Psychology*, 1955, **49**, 407–417.

Kimmel, E., & Kimmel, H. D.   A replication of operant conditioning of the *GSR*. *Journal of Experimental Psychology*, 1963, **65**, 212–213.

Kimmel, H. D.   Instrumental conditioning of autonomically mediated behavior. *Psychological Bulletin*, 1967, **67**(5), 337–345.

Kimmel, H. D., & Baxter, R.   Avoidance conditioning of the *GSR*. *Journal of Experimental Psychology*, 1964, **68**, 482–485.

Lacey, J. I.   The evaluation of autonomic responses: Toward a general solution. *Annals of the New York Academy of Science*, 1956, **67**, 123–164.

Lacey, J. I., & Lacey, B. C.   Verification and extension of the principle of autonomic response stereotype. *American Journal of Psychology*, 1958, **71**, 50–73.

Landis, C., & Hunt, W. A.   *The startle pattern*. New York: Johnson Reprint, 1939.

Lawrence, D. H.   The nature of a stimulus: Some relationships between learning and perception. In S. Koch (Ed.), *Psychology: A study of a science*. Vol. 5. *Process areas*. New York: McGraw-Hill, 1963. Pp. 179–212.

Liddell, H. S.   The conditioned reflex. In F. A. Moss (Ed.), *Comparative psychology*. New York: Prentice-Hall, 1934. Figure 3.13: Copyright 1934 by Prentice-Hall, Inc., and reproduced by permission.

Liddell, H. S.   *Emotional hazards in animals and man*. Springfield: Ill.: Charles C Thomas, 1956.

Liddell, H. S., James, W. T., & Anderson, O. D.   The comparative physiology of the conditioned motor reflex: Based on experiments with the pig, dog, sheep, goat, and rabbit. *Comparative Psychology Monograph*, 1934, **11**, 51.

Lindsley, D. B.   Emotion. In S. S. Stevens (Ed.), *Handbook of experimental psychology*. New York: Wiley, 1951. Pp. 473–516.

Lindsley, O. R.   Operant behavior during sleep: A measure of depth of sleep. *Science*, 1957, **126**, 1290–1291.

Locke, J.   An essay concerning human understanding: In four books. London, 1690. In R. J. Herrnstein & E. G. Boring (Eds.), *A source book in the history of psychology*. Cambridge, Mass.: Harvard University Press, 1965. Pp. 14–17.

Logan, F. A.   A comparison of avoidance and nonavoidance eyelid conditioning. *Journal of Experimental Psychology*, 1951, **42**, 390–393.

Loucks, R. B.   A technique for faradic stimulation of tissues beneath the integument in the absence of conductors penetrating the skin. *Journal of Comparative Psychology*, 1934, **18**, 305–313.

Loucks, R. B.   Studies of neural structures essential for learning: II. The conditioning of salivary and striped muscle responses to faradization of cortical sensory elements and the action of sleep upon such mechanisms. *Journal of Comparative Psychology*, 1938, **25**, 315–332.

Loucks, R. B., & Gantt, W. H.   The conditioning of striped muscle responses based upon faradic stimulation of dorsal roots and dorsal columns of the spinal cord. *Journal of Comparative Psychology*, 1938, **25**, 415–426.

Malmo, R. B.   Comment on the exchange of theoretical notes between Smith and Black and Lang. *Psychological Review*, 1965, **72**, 240–241.

McAllister, W. R.   Eyelid conditioning as a function of the *CS-UCS* interval. *Journal of Experimental Psychology*, 1953, **45**, 417–422. (a)

McAllister, W. R.   The effect on eyelid conditioning of shifting the *CS-UCS* interval. *Journal of Experimental Psychology*, 1953, **45**, 423–428. (b)

McAllister, W. R., & McAllister, D. E.   The influence of the ready signal and unpaired *UCS* presentations on eyelid conditioning. *Journal of Experimental Psychology*, 1960, **60**, 30–35.

Menzies, R.   Conditioned vasomotor responses in human subjects. *Journal of Psychology*, 1937, **4**, 75–120.

Miller, N. E.   Studies of fear as an acquirable drive: I. Fear as motivation and fear reduction as reinforcement in the learning of new responses. *Journal of Experimental Psychology*, 1948, **38**, 89–101.

Miller, N. E.   Learning of visceral and glandular responses. *Science*, 1969, **163**, 434–445.

Miller, N. E., & Banuazizi, A.   Instrumental learning by curarized rats of a specific visceral response, intestinal or cardiac. *Journal of Comparative and Physiological Psychology*, 1968, **65**(1), 1–7. Figure 3.21: Copyright © 1968 by the American Psychological Association, and reproduced by permission.

Miller, N. E., & Carmona, A.   Modification of a visceral response, salivation in thirsty dogs, by instrumental training with water reward. *Journal of Comparative and Physiological Psychology*, 1967, **63**(1), 1–16. Figure 3.22. Copyright © 1967 by the American Psychological Association, and reproduced by permission.

Miller, N. E., & DiCara, L. V.   Instrumental learning of heart-rate changes in curarized rats: Shaping, and specificity to discriminative stimulus. *Journal of Comparative and Physiological Psychology*, 1967, **63**(1), 12–19.

Moldavskia, E. A.   The activity of the salivary glands in the dog during conditioned and unconditioned heat reflexes. *Fiziologicheskii Zhurnal SSSR*, 1928, **11**(5), 393–411.

Moore, A. U., & Marcuse, F. L.   Salivary, cardiac, and motor indices of conditioning in two sows. *Journal of Comparative Psychology*, 1945, **38**, 1–16.

Morse, W. H., & Skinner, B. F.   A second type of superstition in the pigeon. *American Journal of Psychology*, 1957, **70**, 308–311.

Morse, W. H., & Skinner, B. F.   Some factors involved in the stimulus control of operant behavior. *Journal of the Experimental Analysis of Behavior*, 1958, **1**, 103–107.

Mowrer, O. H.   Preparatory set (expectancy)—a determinant in motivation and learning. *Psychological Review*, 1938, **45**, 62–91.

Mowrer, O. H.   On the dual nature of learning: A reinterpretation of "conditioning" and "problem-solving." *Harvard Educational Review*, 1947, **17**, 102–148.

Notterman, J. M., Schoenfeld, W. N., & Bersh, P. J.   Conditioned heart-rate responses in human beings during experimental anxiety. *Journal of Comparative and Physiological Psychology*, 1952, **45**, 1–8.

Ochs, S.   *Elements of neurophysiology*. New York: Wiley, 1965.

Olds, J., & Milner, P.   Positive reinforcement produced by electrical stimulation of septal area and other regions of rat brian. *Journal of Comparative and Physiological Psychology*, 1954, **47**, 419–427.

Pavlov, I. P.   The scientific investigation of the psychical faculties or processes in the higher animals. *Science*, 1906, **24**, 613–619.

Pavlov, I. P.   *Conditioned reflexes*. G. V. Anrep (Trans.) Oxford: The Clarendon Press, 1927. Tables 3.1, 3.2, 3.3, and Figures 3.4 and 3.5: Reproduced by permission of The Clarendon Press, Oxford.

Prokasy, W. F.   Classical eyelid conditioning: Experimenter operations, task demands, and response shaping. In W. F. Prokasy (Ed.), *Classical conditioning: A symposium*. New York: Appleton-Century-Crofts, 1965. Pp. 208–225.

Prokasy, W. F., Hall, J. F., & Fawcett, J. T.   Adaptation, sensitization, forward and backward conditioning, and pseudoconditioning of the *GSR*. *Psychological Reports*, 1962, **10**, 103–106.

Prokasy, W. F., & Whaley, F. L.   The intertrial interval in classical conditioning. *Journal of Experimental Psychology*, 1961, **62**, 560–564.

Prokasy, W. F., & Whaley, F. L.   Intertrial interval range shift in classical eyelid conditioning. *Psychological Reports*, 1963, **12**, 55–58.

Razran, G.   Operant vs. classical conditioning. *American Journal of Psychology*, 1955, **68**, 489–490.

Razran, G.   Extinction reexamined and reanalyzed: A new theory. *Psychological Review*, 1956, **63**, 39–52.

Razran, G.   The observable unconscious and the inferable conscious in current Soviet psychophysiology: Interoceptive conditioning, semantic conditioning, and the orienting reflex. *Psychological Review*, 1961, **68**(1), 81–147. Figures 3.6 and 3.7: Copyright © 1961 by the American Psychological Association, and reproduced by permission.

Rescorla, R. A.   Pavlovian conditioning and its proper control procedures. *Psychological Review*, 1967, **74**(1), 71–80.

Rescorla, R. A., & Solomon, R. L.   Two-process learning theory: Relationships between Pavlovian conditioning and instrumental learning. *Psychological Review*, 1967, **74**, 151–182.

Reynolds, G. S.   An analysis of interactions in a multiple schedule. *Journal of the Experimental Analysis of Behavior*, 1961, **4**, 107–117.

Reynolds, W. F.   Acquisition and extinction of the conditioned eyelid response following partial and continuous reinforcement. *Journal of Experimental Psychology*, 1958, **55**, 335–341.

Ross, L. E.   The decremental effects of partial reinforcement during acquisition and the conditioned eyelid response. *Journal of Experimental Psychology*, 1959, **57**, 74–82. Table 3.5 and Figures 3.17 and 3.18: Copyright © 1959 by the American Psychological Association, and reproduced by permission.

Ruch, T. C., & Patton, H. D.   *Physiology and biophysics*. Philadelphia: Saunders, 1965.

Runquist, W. N.   Performance in eyelid conditioning following changes in reinforcement schedule. *Journal of Experimental Psychology*, 1963, **65**, 616–617.

Runquist, W. N., & Ross, L. E.   The relation between physiological measures of emotionality and performance in eyelid conditioning. *Journal of Experimental Psychology*, 1959, **57**, 329–332.

Schlosberg, H.   A study of the conditioned patellar reflex. *Journal of Experimental Psychology*, 1928, **11**, 468–494.

Schlosberg, H.   The relationship between success and the laws of conditioning. *Psychological Review*, 1937, **44**, 379–394.

Schoenfeld, W. N.   Some old work for modern conditioning theory. *Conditional Reflex*, 1966, **1**(4), 219–223.

Schoenfeld, W. N., & Cumming, W. W.   Behavior and perception. In S. Koch (Ed.), *Psychology: A study of a science*. Vol. 5. *Process areas*. New York: McGraw-Hill, 1963. Pp. 213–252.

Seward, J. P., & Seward, G. H.   The effect of repetition on reactions to electric shock. *Archives of Psychology*, 1934, **168**, 1–103.

Shapiro, M. M.   Classical salivary conditioning in dogs. Unpublished doctoral dissertation, Indiana University, 1959. Figure 3.1: Reproduced by permission.

Shapiro, M. M.   Salivary conditioning in dogs during fixed-interval reinforcement contingent upon lever-pressing. *Journal of the Experimental Analysis of Behavior*, 1961, **4**, 361–364.

Shapiro, M. M.   Temporal relationship between salivation and lever-pressing with differential reinforcement of low rates. *Journal of Comparative and Physiological Psychology*, 1962, **55**, 567–571.

Shearn, D. W.   Operant conditioning of heart rate. *Science*, 1962, **137**, 530–531.

Sherrington, C. S.   *The integrative action of the nervous system*. New Haven, Conn.: Yale University Press, 1906.

Skinner, B. F.   *The behavior of organisms: An experimental analysis*. New York: Appleton-Century-Crofts, 1938.

Skinner, B. F.   Superstition in the pigeon. *Journal of Experimental Psychology*, 1948, **38**, 168–172.

Skinner, B. F.   *Science and human behavior*. New York: Macmillan, 1953.

Skinner, B. F.   *Verbal behavior*. New York: Appleton-Century-Crofts, 1957.

Smith, K.   Conditioning as an artifact. *Psychological Review*, 1954, **61**, 217–225.

Smith, S. M., Brown, H. O., Toman, J. E. P., & Goodman, L. S.   The lack of cerebral effects of d-Tubocurarine. *Journal of the American Society of Anesthesiology*, 1947, **8**(1), 1–14.

Sokolov, E. N.   Neuronal models and the orienting reflex. In M. A. B. Brazier (Ed.), *Central nervous system and behavior*. New York: Josiah Macy, 1960. Pp. 187–276.

Sokolov, E. N.   *Perception and the conditioned reflex*. S. W. Waydenfeld (Trans.) New York: Macmillan, 1963.

Spence, K. W.   *Behavior theory and conditioning*. New Haven: Yale University Press, 1956.

Spence, K. W., & Ross, L. E.   A methodological study of the form and latency of eyelid responses in conditioning. *Journal of Experimental Psychology*, 1959, **58**, 376–385.

Spence, K. W., & Taylor, J. A.   Anxiety and strength of the *UCS* as determiners of the amount of eyelid conditioning. *Journal of Experimental Psychology*, 1951, **42**, 183–188.

Spooner, A., & Kellogg, W. N.   The backward-conditioning curve. *American Journal of Psychology*, 1947, **60**, 321–334. Figure 3.16: Reproduced by permission of the University of Illinois Press.

Taylor, J. A.   Level of conditioning and intensity of adaptation stimulus. *Journal of Experimental Psychology*, 1956, **51**, 127–130.

Terrace, H. S.   Discrimination learning with and without errors. *Journal of the Experimental Analysis of Behavior*, 1963, **6**, 1–27.

Terrace, H. S.   Stimulus control. In W. K. Honig (Ed.), *Operant behavior: Areas of research and application*. New York: Appleton-Century-Crofts, 1966. Pp. 271–344.

Trowill, J. A.   Instrumental conditioning of the heart rate in the curarized rat. *Journal of Comparative and Physiological Psychology*, 1967, **63**, 7–11.

Verplanck, W. S.   Unaware of where's awareness: Some verbal operants—notates, moments, and notants. In C. W. Eriksen (Ed.), *Behavior and awareness*. Durham, N.C.: Duke University Press, 1962. Pp. 130–158.

Wagner, A. R., Thomas, E., & Norton, T. Conditioning with electrical stimulation of motor cortex: Evidence of a possible source of motivation. *Journal of Comparative and Physiological Psychology*, 1967, **64**(2), 191–199.

Watson, J. B. The place of the conditioned reflex in psychology. *Psychological Review*, 1916, **23**, 89–116.

Watson, J. B. *Psychology from the standpoint of a behaviorist*. Philadelphia: Lippincott, 1919.

Watson, J. B. *Behaviorism*. New York: Norton, 1925.

Westcott, M. R., & Huttenlocher, J. Cardiac conditioning: The effects and implications of controlled and uncontrolled respiration. *Journal of Experimental Psychology*, 1961, **61**, 353–359.

Wickens, D. D., & Wickens, C. D. Some factors related to pseudoconditioning. *Journal of Experimental Psychology*, 1942, **31**, 518–526.

Williams, D. R. Classical conditioning and incentive motivation. In W. F. Prokasy (Ed.), *Classical conditioning: A symposium*. New York: Appleton-Century-Crofts, 1965. Pp. 340–357.

Wolf, K. Properties of multiple conditioned reflex type II activity. *Acta Biologiae Experimentalis Sinica*, 1963, **23**, 133–150.

Wolfe, J. B. Effectiveness of token-rewards for chimpanzees. *Comparative Psychological Monographs*, 1936, **12**, No. 60.

Wolfle, H. M. Time factors in conditioning finger withdrawal. *Journal of General Psychology*, 1930, **4**, 372–378.

Wolfle, H. M. Conditioning as a function of the interval between the conditioned and the original stimulus. *Journal of General Psychology*, 1932, **7**, 80–103.

Zeaman, D., & Smith, R. W. Review and analysis of some recent findings in human cardiac conditioning. In W. F. Prokasy (Ed.), *Classical conditioning: A symposium*. New York: Appleton-Century-Crofts, 1965. Pp. 378–418.

Zener, K. The significance of behavior accompanying conditioned salivary secretion for theories of the conditioned response. *American Journal of Psychology*, 1937, **50**, 384–403.

STIMULUS CONTROL

John A. Nevin
Columbia University

In the last chapter, the concept of stimulus control was employed to unify the procedures and phenomena of classical and operant conditioning, despite the diverse distinctions that have arisen during the study of these processes. Here, we pursue the concept of stimulus control and make contact with psychological problems outside the domain of conditioning as it is usually defined. A few simple examples will serve to introduce this topic.

Throughout our lives, our behavior is influenced by similarities and differences in the environment. When driving a car along an unfamiliar street, we stop at a traffic light even though we have never seen a light at exactly that height or location relative to the road and even though the exact physical properties of its red light differ in many ways from other red lights we have seen. This is an instance of the *generalization* of behavior to a novel situation that is similar in some ways to previously experienced events. Indeed, without generalization, instruction would be fruitless, because the stimulation experienced during training can never be reproduced exactly in all its rich detail.

In this particular example, generalization is appropriate to the situation, but that may not always be the case. When a small child has had some experience with a friendly, playful dog, he is likely to approach strange dogs in the same way, inviting play. Sooner or later, he may come into contact with a dog unaccustomed to rough play with children and be frightened by the dog's barking and snapping. The immediate consequence of an unpleasant experience of this sort is usually *generalized avoidance* of all dogs, but in due course the child will learn which dogs are likely to be friendly and which are not, and he will behave differently in the presence of different animals. Such differences in behavior under different stimulus conditions exemplify *discrimination*, which is typically the outcome of experience, with success dependent on appropriate responding in each condition.

The purpose of these examples is to indicate the major concern of this chapter: the control of learned behavior by antecedent and concurrent environmental stimuli, as a joint function of the physical specification of the stimuli and the subject's past history. The emphasis on learning distinguishes this inquiry from other branches of psychology which also consider the stimulus as a determinant of behavior. Such

Preparation of this chapter was supported in part by U.S. Public Health Service Grant MH-16252 to Columbia University.

reflexes as the contraction of the pupil when a bright light is directed into the eye are clearly dependent on the physical properties of the stimulus, but do not depend on the subject's history. As soon as the reflex is studied within the classical-conditioning paradigm, so that pairing with an arbitrary neutral stimulus comes to affect behavior, then the question of learning becomes relevant.

The emphasis on antecedent stimuli serves to distinguish the subject matter of this chapter from the determination of behavior by reinforcement. Behavior can be controlled quite precisely by its consequences, during both *acquisition* and *maintenance*, in ways which depend on the nature of the consequences and their scheduled relation to responding (cf. Chapters 6 and 7). It will become clear that control by reinforcement cannot be ignored in the analysis of generalization and discrimination, but it is important that we recall and continue to distinguish clearly two kinds of control on the basis of the temporal relations between stimulus and response. In the case of reinforcement (or punishment), the stimulus is presented after the response under study. Generalization and discrimination, however, involve stimuli which are presented before the response occurs, although in many situations the stimuli may remain present during and after the response.

This separation may not always be so obvious. For instance, in the study of conditioned reinforcement (Chapter 5), it is frequently the case that a stimulus is presented after the occurrence of one response and before the next response in a sequence. It is then necessary to speak of the reinforcing function of the stimulus with respect to the first response and its discriminative function with respect to the second response. Another case that is particularly difficult to treat is that of *imprinting* (cf. Chapter 9). Some birds, for example, tend to follow and approach objects to which they have been exposed during a brief *critical period* early in their lives. The general tendency to behave in this way appears to be an unlearned, species-specific characteristic of those birds, but the particular object chosen depends on the history of exposure to objects during the critical period. Furthermore, following occurs after the object is presented, suggesting a discriminative relation, but it can be shown independently that the imprinted stimulus is an effective reinforcer. Thus, imprinting involves a complex interaction of unlearned response tendencies, maturation, and learning including discriminative and reinforcing functions of stimulation.

Although the exclusion of a discussion of complex cases like imprinting may seem arbitrary, this chapter will confine itself to situations in which the behavior of interest has been established by reinforcement—that is, *operant behavior*. This restriction has the advantage of freeing the experimenter from the limitations imposed by the study of reflexive behavior or more complex species-specific behaviors. In the latter cases the choice of the phenomenon largely determines the response that must be studied and the stimuli that may be employed. Research on operant behavior permits the experimenter to choose among a variety of stimulus dimensions or modalities and to select responses and reinforcers on the basis of experimental convenience. The interest then centers on stimulus-response relations which are at least qualitatively similar, regardless of the choice of stimulus, response, or reinforcer, so that a general understanding of the determinants of behavior may be achieved. As we will see, such a goal lies in the fairly distant future, but encouraging progress is being made in several problem areas.

A final, somewhat arbitrary, restriction on the contents of this chapter should be noted. Because of the extensive use of the *free operant* and positive reinforcement in the experimental analysis of behavior, the emphasis here will be on studies of this type. Occasionally, findings from studies employing *discrete trials* or from experiments with negative reinforcement will be cited to provide support or to raise questions about the relations under consideration.

GENERALIZATION, DISCRIMINATION, AND STIMULUS CONTROL: METHODS AND BASIC PHENOMENA

The related behavioral processes of generalization and discrimination have traditionally been viewed as fundamental to an understanding of complex stimulus control, conceptual behavior, and other topics to which this chapter is addressed. Accordingly, it is necessary to begin with a fairly detailed discussion of research designed to study generalization and discrimination within the unifying framework of stimulus control.

Stimulus generalization of a free operant

The empirical phenomenon of generalization is the finding that a response conditioned in the presence of one stimulus also occurs in the presence of other, physically different, although related, stimuli. Typically, the strength of the generalized response, measured by its *latency, probability, amplitude,* or *rate,* is less than in the original training stimulus, and the decrement in responding is continuously related to the difference between the training stimulus and generalization-test stimuli. This relation defines the *gradient of stimulus generalization.* For convenience, the training stimulus will be designated $S+$, and the stimuli employed in the generalization test will be denoted $S_1, S_2, S_3, \ldots, S_n$, in order of increasing physical difference from $S+$.

The empirical fact of generalization is not in doubt, but the experimental determination of a generalization gradient is complex. Consider, for example, a situation in which rats have been trained to run in a runway with food as reinforcement, while a tone $(S+)$ is present. To evaluate generalization, one must conduct test trials with tones $S_1, S_2, S_3, \ldots, S_n$ and measure running speed. A single observation with each tone will not suffice, because the natural variability of running speed is likely to give a most irregular function. A series of trials at each test stimulus is therefore required, or else one must determine an average gradient from data for many rats, each receiving only a single test with one of the test stimuli.

Consider the problems in either case. If repeated trials are used, the experimenter must either continue to give food reinforcement or face the fact that running speed will decrease with continued testing. The temporal sequence of $S_1, S_2,$ and S_3 may determine a gradient directly; even if the sequence is *counterbalanced,* one still faces the problem of averaging speed on early and late trials, which are known not to come from a homogeneous sample. On the other hand, if food reinforcement is continued in the presence of $S+$, the generalization test is actually just the early portion of a discrimination experiment in which reinforcement is differentially associated with $S+$, and systematic changes in gradient slope may be expected as testing continues. This problem may be avoided if food reinforcement is given in the presence of all stimuli, but in this case $S_1, S_2,$ and S_3 become training stimuli in their own right and complete generalization is virtually certain.

Resorting to separate groups of rats, each tested for one trial with $S_1, S_2,$ or S_3 alone, solves these problems but raises others. Suppose that some animals generalize completely and others do not generalize at all—that is, they simply don't run in

the presence of tones other than $S+$. Averaging their data may yield an orderly gradient of intermediate running speeds, but this is obviously a statistical artifact, providing no information about the process of generalization for an individual organism (cf. Chapter 1).

Much of the early research on generalization may be criticized on one or another of these grounds. Improved research methods became available when some properties of intermittent reinforcement of free-operant behavior were understood. The free operant has the advantage of yielding a sensitive and reliable measure—the rate of responding—which may remain virtually unaffected for several hundred responses when reinforcement is terminated after training on an intermittent schedule of reinforcement. Guttman and Kalish (1956) reasoned that these properties of the free operant would permit repeated determinations of response rate in $S+, S_1, S_2, \ldots, S_n,$ without contamination by reinforcement and without serious weakening of the response by nonreinforcement. The use of this technique, with pigeons as subjects, was suggested by earlier reports by Skinner (1950) and Brush, Bush, Jenkins, John, and Whiting (1952).

Guttman and Kalish used 24 pigeons as subjects. The birds were maintained at 80 percent of their normal free-feeding weights, a deprivation procedure that has become quite standard in research with pigeons, to insure the effectiveness of food reinforcement. The pigeons were trained in a chamber which included a grain magazine, a house light for general illumination, and a response key that could be illuminated from behind with light composed of a narrow band of wavelengths. The experimenters were able to present lights ranging from 450 to 640 nanometers (*nm*) at their central wavelength, with bandwidths of 14 to 24 *nm*. Lights of this sort yield highly saturated hues, with apparent differences in brightness depending on the hue presented. There was no attempt to adjust for brightness in this early work, although such adjustment has become a standard feature of later research with pigeons and the wavelength continuum.

The birds were divided into four groups according to the wavelength projected on the key during training: 530, 550, 580, or 600 *nm*. Initially, the birds were trained to eat from the grain magazine and then to peck the key by the method of *successive approximations* (see Chapter 2). After two sessions of training during which every peck was reinforced, the schedule of reinforcement was changed so that an average of 1 minute elapsed between reinforcements. This is known as a *variable-interval (VI)* 1-minute schedule (see Chapter 6 for discussion of reinforcement schedules). During this *VI* training, illumination of the key and house light was interrupted for 10 seconds every 60 seconds to accustom the birds to responding under conditions that would prevail during the generalization test. Generalization testing was conducted with food no longer available after stable *VI* performances were established. The test consisted of 30-second presentations of each of 11 different wavelengths on the key. Presentations were separated by 10 seconds of darkness to allow the experimenters time to record the number of responses made during the previous period and to set the apparatus to a different wavelength. The 11 wavelengths were presented in 12 different random sequences, so that responding in the presence of each wavelength was measured repeatedly during the course of extinction. To establish a generalization gradient, responses in the presence of each wavelength were totaled at the end of testing and plotted as a function of the wavelength value.

The research method worked handsomely. Orderly gradients were obtained from individual subjects, and although there was a fair amount of variation in the details of the individual gradients, their general character was not affected by averaging. The average gradient for the group trained with *S+* at 580 *nm*, shown in Figure 4.1, is representative. The data have been transformed to show the number of responses made in the presence of S_1, S_2, ..., S_n, as a proportion of the number of responses made in the presence of *S+* during the test. When generalization gradients are transformed in this way, they are termed *relative* gradients, while a plot of the actual numbers of responses would be termed a gradient of *absolute* generalization.

It is instructive to compare the relative gradient obtained by Guttman and Kalish (1956) with a similarly transformed gradient obtained in a study by Blough (1967). Blough's experiment was similar in that pigeons served as subjects and food reinforcement was given on a *VI* schedule for key-pecking in the presence of *S+* (582 *nm* in this case). The experiments differed in that the generalization stimuli, separated by 2 *nm*, were also presented in an irregular series during training, and reinforcement was never scheduled in their presence. Training lasted for several weeks, and the data in Figure 4.1 are based on responding by a single bird during the final 28 sessions of training. When these final data were collected, reinforcement was excluded

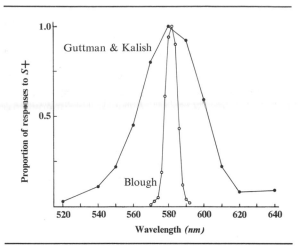

Figure 4.1 Generalization gradients of responding by pigeons to lights of different wavelengths. The outer gradient, from Guttman and Kalish (1956), is based on average data for six pigeons trained to respond to 580 *nm*, without explicit discrimination training. The steep inner gradient, from Blough (1967), is for a single pigeon which had undergone extensive training with reinforcement for responding to 582 *nm* and extinction at all other wavelengths. Both sets of data have been transformed into relative gradients to facilitate comparison.

during some *S+* presentations, so that the *S+* rate could be measured without contamination by the presentation of food. Control of key-pecking by wavelength is obviously much more precise in Blough's study than in the Guttman and Kalish experiment.

Traditionally, Blough's procedure would be classed as a discrimination experiment, because training involved maintained reinforcement in the presence of *S+* with extinction in the presence of all other stimuli. Guttman and Kalish are said to have studied generalization because they trained with *S+* alone and tested during extinction with novel values of the stimulus continuum. Since Blough's data show that pigeons are capable of distinguishing wavelengths quite precisely, one may be led to ask why Guttman and Kalish's birds responded to such a broad range of wavelengths. The answer to such a question usually invokes a theoretical process of generalization that is assumed to be internal to the subject, and one may then attempt to understand the relation between this process—inferred from the generalization data—and the findings of discrimination experiments. On the whole, this theoretical approach has added rather little to our understanding of the data, and an alternative approach will be pursued here.

Although *generalization* and *discrimination* are convenient shorthand terms used to designate different procedures or to emphasize different aspects of the data, the distinction may obscure some continuous relations between the data of these studies. Consider some of the procedural differences. In Blough's study, periods of reinforcement were interspersed throughout periods of nonreinforcement in the presence of many different stimuli, whereas Guttman and Kalish's birds did not experience nonreinforcement in the presence of other stimuli until testing began. It may be that gradient slopes are affected by alternating reinforcement and extinction, even if extinction is carried out in the presence of stimuli other than those used in generalization testing. Another obvious difference is total training time, which may affect gradient slopes quite apart from other factors. Considering the procedures and data in this way leads one to ask not about an inferred generalization process, but rather how various experimental parameters may affect gradient slopes. The distinctions between generalization and discrimination become a good deal less clear when matters are viewed in this way, and therefore it seems appropriate to adopt the relatively neutral term, *stimulus control*, to designate the way in which responding is related to a stimulus continuum.

Measurement considerations

Before proceeding with a discussion of some parametric determinants of stimulus-control gradients, it is necessary to deal with certain questions of measurement. Many variables are likely to affect both the rate of responding and the slope of the gradient during a stimulus-control test. When two aspects of behavior change at the same time, it becomes difficult to make comparisons. To illustrate the problem, imagine that the four gradients in Figure 4.2 were obtained after different training procedures. In the case of the absolute gradients in panel A, gradients 1 and 3 have the same slopes, while gradient 2 is steeper and gradient 4 is shallower. It could be argued that gradient 4 only appears shallow because of a *floor effect;* that is, S_1-responding cannot fall below zero. A relative transformation might seem more appropriate in this case. However, the relative gradients in panel B reverse the ordering of the slopes of gradients 1 and 4, while gradients 2 and 3 become identical. How is one to choose?

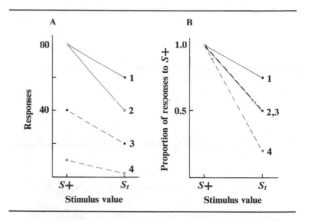

Figure 4.2 Hypothetical gradients expressed as numbers of responses to $S+$ and a generalization stimulus, S_1, in panel A and transformed into relative gradients in panel B. Note that the transformation leads to quite different conclusions about slope comparisons.

The only reasonable answer is to choose that transformation which gives invariant data with respect to some presumably irrelevant variable, and at the same time leads to agreement across different experiments. For instance, if several subjects are studied on each procedure, there will surely be some differences in their data. Which transformation will minimize individual differences in slope, and at the same time lead to replicable findings? There cannot be any generally correct answer here, but to illustrate the point, consider the Guttman and Kalish data again. The data obtained during generalization testing were broken down into successive quarters of extinction and were also divided according to whether a given subject was ranked in the top, middle, or bottom of the entire group on the basis of total responses emitted during the test.

The resulting average gradients are presented in Figure 4.3, which suggests that gradients become shallower as extinction progresses and that gradients are shallowest for the subjects with the lowest response totals. When these data are transformed into relative gradients, however, it appears that the gradient becomes slightly, but systematically, steeper during extinction, whereas there is little consistent difference between high, middle, and low responders (see Figure 4.4). This provides support for the relative transformation, since it minimizes individual differences and at the same time reveals a systematic effect that has been reported in several other generalization experiments involving different species and experimental para-

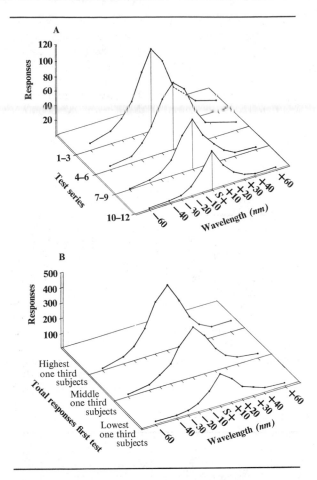

Figure 4.3 Averaged generalization gradients obtained by Guttman and Kalish (1956), combined for all groups to illustrate the effects of different levels of responding. Panel A presents gradients obtained during successive fourths of the generalization tests; panel B presents gradients from separate groups of subjects ranked according to their total responding during the test.

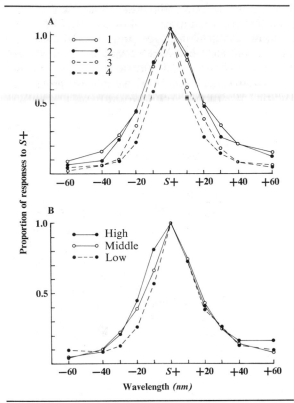

Figure 4.4 Relative gradients based on the Guttman and Kalish (1956) data presented in Figure 4.3. Relative gradients for successive fourths of testing are displayed in panel A, and relative gradients for high-, middle-, and low-responding groups are displayed in panel B.

digms. For example, Wickens, Schroder, and Snide (1954) have reported that the gradient for the classically conditioned galvanic skin response in humans becomes steeper during testing, and Hearst (1969) has observed the same trend in gradients for lever-pressing by rats after both shock-avoidance and food-reinforcement training. Friedman and Guttman (1965) have provided further confirmation of the steepening of relative gradients during extinction after several different training procedures.

Other questions of measurement arise when one considers the dependent variable—rate of respond-ing—more carefully. It might be that the subjects always respond steadily, but the spacing between responses depends on the stimulus; or it might be that if the subject responds, the spacing between responses is always the same, but the proportion of time spent responding in this stereotyped way depends on the stimulus. The calculated average response rate might be the same either way, but quite different behaviors are implied.

One study which makes the point quite clearly has been reported by Cumming and Eckerman (1965). They trained pigeons in a special chamber equipped with a 10-inch key, designed so that pecks at 20 different locations could be recorded separately. In the presence of a high level of illumination, the birds obtained food at variable intervals for pecking between 1.5 and 2.5 inches from the right-hand end of the key. In the presence of a low level of illumination, the same reinforcement schedule was in effect for pecking between 7.5 and 8.5 inches from the right-hand end of the key. These two levels of illumination were presented alternately until the subjects came to respond predominantly at the appropriate key-locations. A generalization test was then conducted involving three levels of illumination lying between the training values, as well as the two training intensities. As shown in Figure 4.5, the birds did not shift their modal response location continuously at intermediate intensities. Rather, they responded primarily at the two locations reinforced during training, with the

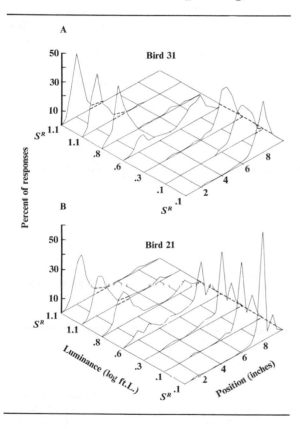

Figure 4.5   Distributions of key-pecking along a 10-inch key by two pigeons. The birds were reinforced for pecking near the right-hand end of the key when the illumination was bright (1.1 log ft.L.) and near the left-hand end of the key when the light was dim (.1 log ft.L.). Distributions obtained at the end of training are at the extremes of the plots, labled S^R. Distributions obtained during a generalization test with the training illumination levels and three intermediate levels are arrayed according to illumination level. Note the bimodal distribution of responding for both subjects at .6 and .8 log ft.L. (From Cumming & Eckerman, 1965.)

proportion of pecks at each location depending on the illumination of the key. If one were to compute an average key-location, there would be a continuous function relating responding to key-illumination, but inspection of the actual raw data makes it obvious that such a function would be an averaging artifact. Similar findings in other procedures involving two response classes, each reinforced in the presence of a different stimulus, have been reported by Migler (1964) and Migler and Millenson (1969).

The relevance of these findings to the Guttman and Kalish and Blough gradients becomes clear if one imagines that a pigeon in a single-key, free-operant situation actually has two classes of behavior available: key-pecking and not key-pecking. It may be that the pigeon divides its time between these behaviors in a way that depends on the stimulus, resulting in an orderly gradient relating average response rate to the stimuli. Because of the problems involved in specifying and measuring not-key-pecking behavior, it is difficult to validate this speculation. However, analysis of interresponse-time distributions (Blough, 1963, 1969; see also Chapter 6) suggests that this may indeed be an appropriate description of behavior during a generalization test.

Accurate characterization of the dependent variable will certainly become crucial if and when quantitative theories become available for combining gradients obtained in different experiments to predict the results of new studies. For the present, most investigators are willing to settle for qualitative agreement across experiments. As long as the measured number of key-pecks is at least ordinally related to the proportion of time spent responding, agreement of this sort may be achieved. The reader should, however, keep this matter in mind when interpreting the results of the studies to be considered in this chapter.

Variables affecting gradients after training with $S+$ alone
Duration of training

The method devised by Guttman and Kalish (1956) has been used by Hearst and Koresko (1968) to study the effects of duration of training and maintenance of a performance on the slopes of gradients. They trained pigeons to peck a key with a vertical line and then gave 2, 4, 7, or 14 sessions of *VI* training to two sets of independent groups. Line orientation was varied during extinction to determine stimulus-control gradients. Both absolute and relative gradients became steeper as a function of increased training, although one sub-group trained for only 2 sessions exhibited a steeper relative gradient than either the 4- or 7-session sub-groups in one portion of the study. On the other hand, Margolius (1955) found that gradients became less steep with increasing training. His study differed in several ways, using rats in a discrete-trial runway procedure, rather than the free-operant procedure. The rats receiving the most training obtained appreciably fewer total reinforcements and emitted fewer responses than the birds in Hearst and Koresko's least-trained group.

Despite the differences among these studies, it is instructive to consider them together. Early in training, there may be little tendency to generalize to novel stimuli. Indeed, this failure of generalization is often a source of irritation to an experimenter attempting to establish a new response to several stimuli or key positions. As training progresses, gradients evidently become less steep up to a point and then become steeper again. (In the Hearst and Koresko study, this point was presumably reached between the second and fourth sessions of *VI* training.) This sort of nonmonotonic relation has also been suggested by Kimble (1961, p. 335) in his analysis of generalization of the galvanic skin response. To obtain a more satisfactory picture of the effects of training, it will be necessary to explore a wider range of the independent variable with free-operant procedures designed to obtain reliable data from individual subjects after brief training, or to extend the duration of training in discrete-trial experiments.

Schedule of reinforcement during training

In a closely related study, Hearst, Koresko, and Poppen (1964) used the same basic methodology to investigate the effects of the schedule of reinforcement on stimulus control. Pigeons were trained to peck a key on which a vertical line was projected, and they were then tested with lines of different orientation. In one portion of their study, different groups were trained for equal numbers of sessions with variable-interval schedules averaging .5, 1, 2, 3, and 4 minutes between food reinforcements. Standard stimulus-control tests in extinction revealed gradients that became systematically shallower as the intervals between food reinforcements increased. The same relation has been obtained by Haber and Kalish (1963) on the wavelength continuum. Hearst et al. (1964) were also concerned with the effects of different reinforcement con-

tingencies on stimulus control. In a separate experiment, they trained pigeons on a schedule that made food available for key-pecking only if a certain period of time had elapsed since the previous peck. (This schedule is termed *DRL* for *differential reinforcement of low rates* of responding. Its properties are discussed and compared with *VI* schedules in Chapter 6.) For one group of pigeons, a pause of 6 seconds was required, and for another group, 10 seconds was required. Under these conditions, it was possible for reinforcement to be quite frequent, even though the response rate was low. Despite reinforcement frequencies comparable to those obtained on the short *VI* schedules, both absolute and relative stimulus-control gradients were consistently shallower than those obtained after training with frequent *VI* reinforcement. Hearst et al. argued that this finding was the result of increased dependence on internal cues that were important for timing behavior in the *DRL* situation. Because these cues would be present within the subject regardless of the value of line tilt, flat gradients would be expected.

Another study of reinforcement schedules as determinants of gradient slopes has been reported by Thomas and Switalski (1966). In their study, pairs of pigeons were trained at the same time with food reinforcement for key-pecking in the presence of a 550 *nm* key-light. For one bird, a *variable-ratio* (*VR*) schedule was in effect: Reinforcement was presented after an unpredictable number of responses, averaging 40. When the *VR* requirement was completed by the first bird, reinforcement was also made available for a second bird in a separate chamber. In this way, both subjects received identical numbers of reinforcements in time, but the schedule for the second bird was in effect a variable-interval schedule with intervals dictated by the behavior of the first bird. This technique for equating reinforcement frequencies is known as *yoking*. In Thomas and Switalski's study, the birds on the *VR* schedule responded about twice as fast as their yoked partners. After stable responding was well established, both groups of birds were given standard stimulus-control tests, with wavelength varied during extinction. The absolute and relative gradients for birds trained on *VR* were less steep than those for the yoked birds, even though their rate of responding in the presence of 550 *nm* fell to the same level as that of the yoked birds fairly early during testing.

It is not likely that the high rates generated by *VR* schedules involve such heavy dependence on internal cues as *DRL*, in which timing is essential for reinforcement. Similarly, it is not at all obvious that the internal-cues explanation is applicable to the pigeons receiving relatively infrequent *VI* reinforcement in Hearst, Koresko, and Poppen's experiment. Nevertheless, all of these conditions appear to produce shallower gradients than frequent *VI* reinforcement. Whatever the interpretation, these findings demonstrate the importance of a variable that is usually ignored in the study of stimulus control. It would be valuable to know how the contingencies of reinforcement interact with other determinants of stimulus control, such as length of training, degree of motivation, or differential reinforcement, so that the findings of diverse experiments could be integrated more successfully.

Effects of deprivation

Motivation is a traditional parameter of research on learned behavior, and a number of studies have been concerned with the effects of this variable on stimulus-control gradients. Common sense might lead us to expect that the higher the level of a subject's drive, the more a response should generalize to novel stimuli, but the experimental findings are far from clear on this point. A standard method for controlling hunger drive with pigeons is to vary the subject's body weight. Using the Guttman and Kalish methodology, Thomas and King (1959) trained pigeons to peck a 550 *nm* key at 80 percent of their free-feeding weights and then shifted different groups of birds to 90, 70, or 60 percent, keeping some birds at 80 percent. When the new body weights were achieved, wavelength gradients were obtained. Both absolute and relative gradients indicated that the slopes were steepest for the 80 percent birds, suggesting a nonmonotonic relation between drive and stimulus control. To determine whether this finding might have resulted from the fact that only the 80 percent birds did not experience a change in drive level, they repeated a portion of the study with training at 70 percent of free-feeding weight and confirmed the earlier data. However, the finding has not proven to be replicable. Kalish and Haber (1965) employed a very similar training and testing procedure with pigeons, and found that high drive produced the steepest gradients. This is exactly contrary to intuitive expectation (as well as failing to conform to the Thomas and King findings). However, their relative gradients suggested that drive level had little systematic effect. Several other studies have shown that relative gradients are not systematically affected by drive (e.g., Coate, 1964; Newman & Grice, 1965; Thomas, 1962), although some workers have obtained effects in the expected direction (e.g., Jenkins, Pascal, & Walker, 1958; Kawashima, 1964). There is little point in attempting to reconcile the discrepant results in this area until parametric analysis indicates those variables responsible for the presence or absence of motivational effects.

Acquisition of differential responding

Before attempting to understand the effects of differential reinforcement for responding in the presence of two or more stimuli on stimulus-control gradients, it is necessary to consider how differential reinforcement acts to establish differential responding during discrimination training.

Methodological issues

The process of discrimination learning has typically been studied by confronting an organism with two stimuli and reinforcing choices of one stimulus only. A traditional method employs the *Lashley jumping stand*, from which a rat jumps across a gap to one of two different cards. The correct card ($S+$) leads to a platform with food reinforcement; the incorrect card ($S-$) is locked in place, so that errors lead to a bump on the nose followed by a fall into a net below. Variants of this basic technique employ two alleys painted different colors, diverging from a common choice point; a pair of objects on a tray with food beneath one of them; or two adjacent keys illuminated with different patterns or colors. All these *simultaneous discrimination* procedures have in common the availability of two stimuli and two responses on every trial. When the subject learns to respond to $S+$, its performance may be the result of any one of several possible stimulus-response relations. For example, the subject may have come to respond to $S+$ without regard for the location or characteristics of $S-$; or not to respond to $S-$, but rather to select any other stimulus available; or a combination of these. Moreover, responding may be based on the properties of the individual stimuli or on the total configuration (e.g., turn left if the left alley is darker than the right alley). The analysis of those features of the situation which actually control responding is complicated by the fact that the standard measure of performance—percent of choices of $S+$—combines both the tendency to respond to $S+$ and the tendency not to respond to $S-$.

A lot of recent work on discrimination learning has employed *successive* discrimination procedures in which the organism is confronted with either $S+$ or $S-$ alone. This procedure has the advantage of insuring effective exposure to both stimuli and permitting separate measures of responding to $S+$ and $S-$ throughout the acquisition of differential responding. With intermittent reinforcement of a free operant, sufficient resistance to extinction can be established to permit the determination of stimulus-control gradients after a history of differential reinforcement.

At the same time, free-operant procedures have raised methodological problems. If $S+$ and $S-$ alternate regularly in time, the subject may learn to respond differentially on the basis of passage of time or the change in stimulation, without being controlled by the properties of the stimuli themselves. Also, once a response in the presence of $S+$ has obtained reinforcement, the stimuli correlated with reinforcement (e.g., the taste of food, the proprioceptive accompaniments of chewing and swallowing, etc.) may themselves function as discriminative stimuli to control further responding. Indeed, the subject need only respond occasionally until food is obtained, and then respond rapidly until no food is forthcoming for a while, in order to give evidence of a "discrimination" without any explicit discriminative stimuli. Other potential methodological problems in free-operant work have been discussed by Jenkins (1965b).

To exemplify methods for minimizing these problems and to provide representative data on acquisition of a free-operant successive discrimination, consider the following unpublished experiment by Nevin. Pigeons were trained to peck at a red key with a white line tilted 20 degrees from vertical. Initially, food was given for every response. When key-pecking was well established, food was scheduled at variable intervals averaging 1 minute. After two more sessions, the average interval between reinforcements was increased to 3 minutes. Then, the session was divided into 32 periods, each lasting 2.5 minutes and separated by 4 seconds with the key darkened. The *VI* 3-minute schedule was in effect only during a randomly selected half of these periods. Because of the long intervals in the *VI* schedules, reinforcement did not occur during every positive period, and the stimulus on the key during negative periods did not differ from $S+$. When performance became stable, response rates during positive periods were no greater than during negative periods, indicating that the procedure had effectively prevented

discrimination on the basis of cues such as reinforcement and/or the passage of time. Finally, the stimulus correlated with negative periods was changed from 20 to 60 degrees from vertical. Differential responding was established rapidly, with a systematic decrease in rate during presentations of $S-$ and increases during $S+$ (see Figure 4.6). This increase is of special interest because it occurred without any alteration in the schedule of reinforcement. The phenomenon, known as *behavioral contrast*, is discussed later. For now, it suffices to note that contrast is a frequent accompaniment of differential reinforcement in the presence of $S+$ and $S-$.

Errorless discrimination learning

Although data of the sort presented in Figure 4.6 are typical, it is possible to employ special training procedures to ascertain which aspects of the pro-

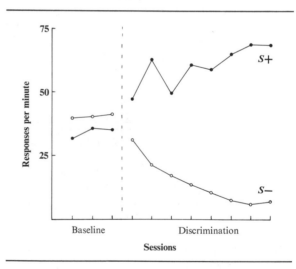

Figure 4.6 Acquisition of differential responding by pigeons to a 20-degree slanted line ($S+$) and a 60-degree slanted line ($S-$) after training with irregular alternation of intermittent reinforcement and extinction in the presence of the 20-degree line. During the last three sessions of baseline training, response rates during periods of reinforcement availability are indicated by filled circles, while responding during periods of nonreinforcement is indicated by unfilled circles. Note that there was no evidence of discrimination on the basis of reinforcement scheduling during baseline training, but as soon as periods of reinforcement and extinction were correlated with different stimuli, differential responding emerged rapidly. The data are averages for four pigeons. (Nevin, unpublished data.)

cedure and results are crucial for the establishment of differential responding. For example, the occurrence and gradual elimination of responding in the presence of $S-$ has been viewed as essential to the formation of a discrimination (Keller & Schoenfeld, 1950, p. 119). However, Terrace (1963a, 1966a) has demonstrated that if $S-$ is introduced gradually, it is possible to establish a discrimination without any $S-$-responding at all. Terrace's original experiment was conducted with pigeons trained to peck a red key ($S+$) for food reinforcement on a VI 30-second schedule. As soon as keypecking was established, the key was darkened for 5 seconds ($S-$) at regular intervals. No reinforcement was given if the birds pecked during this time, but since birds tend not to peck dark keys, no responses occurred. The duration of the dark-key $S-$ was gradually increased to 30 seconds. Next, the $S-$ duration was again reduced to 5 seconds, and the intensity of a green light during $S-$ periods was gradually increased until it was as bright as $S+$. Finally, the duration of $S-$ at full brightness was increased to 30 seconds. After completion of this training, the birds were still responding at a moderate rate in the presence of $S+$ and had rarely, if ever, responded during presentations of $S-$. This performance was maintained for 28 sessions.

To appreciate the results, it is necessary to contrast the performance of these "errorless" birds with those trained in a more conventional fashion. Terrace (1963a) trained another group for 14 sessions with reinforcement on a VI schedule in the presence of $S+$ and then abruptly introduced $S-$ at full brightness and duration. These birds made several thousand responses in the presence of $S-$, and their response rates increased during $S+$, resulting in a pattern of acquisition similar to that shown in Figure 4.6.

Terrace referred to these conditions as *early-progressive* and *late-constant*, respectively, to designate the timing and manner of introduction of $S-$. He also investigated the *early-constant* condition, in which the green $S-$ was introduced at full intensity and duration as soon as key-pecking was established, and the *late-progressive* condition, in which $S-$ was introduced progressively, as for the "errorless" group, but after 14 sessions of training. Birds trained on these conditions made an intermediate number of responses to $S-$, indicating that both the early and the progressive aspects of errorless training were important for the striking effects obtained.

Comparison of the early and late groups confirms the earlier suggestion that there is relatively little generalization to novel stimuli early in training. The importance of progressively narrowing the $S+$-$S-$ difference in establishing a difficult discrimination had also been noted before (e.g., Lawrence, 1952). Terrace's major contribution was in isolating the function of unreinforced responding to $S-$. His experiment not only demonstrated that extinction was not necessary for the establishment of precise differential responding, but also that training with extinction had interesting side effects. The usual increase in $S+$ rate (contrast) did not occur in the absence of errors, and observation of the birds indicated quite different patterns of behavior during presentation of $S-$. Birds that had made errors flapped their wings and turned away from the key, while birds that learned without errors simply waited quietly in front of the key.

The importance of unreinforced responses to $S-$ has been demonstrated with particular clarity by Terrace (1963b). He trained pigeons to discriminate vertical and horizontal lines without errors by superimposing the lines on red and green backgrounds and then fading out the backgrounds. The pigeons had learned the original red-green discrimination without errors. For two other groups, the transition from red-green to vertical-horizontal was abrupt, so that errors occurred during the vertical-horizontal phase of the study. When the birds were returned to the original red-green discrimination, it was found that those which made errors during vertical-horizontal training now made errors on the red-green problem, even though they had originally been trained without errors. Birds which accomplished the transition without errors continued to exhibit errorless performances when returned to the red-green discrimination. Terrace's data suggest a continuous relation between the number of errors on the vertical-horizontal problem and the number of errors in the subsequent red-green test. This result suggests that the precision of stimulus control by $S+$ depends not only on the manner of introduction of $S-$, but also on the history of responding. Apparently, unreinforced responding on one stimulus dimension is sufficient to increase responding to stimuli on another dimension.

Response-independent reinforcement and stimulus control

During initial exposure to a standard discrimination-training procedure, the subject responds and obtains reinforcement in the presence of $S+$ and responds but does not obtain reinforcement in the presence of $S-$. Since Terrace's work has demonstrated that a discrimination may be formed without responding to $S-$, it is not entirely unreasonable to ask whether a discrimination may be formed without responding to $S+$ either. The basic question is whether the correlation of $S+$ and reinforcement, in the absence of any specified responding, suffices to establish control over an arbitrary response which is subsequently made available to the subject. An early study bearing on this question was carried out by Estes (1948). More recently, Morse and Skinner (1958) have performed a similar experiment with pigeons, which will serve as reference here.

These experimenters began by presenting food to pigeons when the chamber was illuminated with red light $(S+)$ and withholding food when the illumination was green $(S-)$. For some subjects, the colors were reversed. Food was presented at variable intervals during $S+$ without regard for the subjects' behavior, and the response key was covered. After 20 sessions of this response-independent correlation of $S+$ and food, the chamber was lighted with white light, the key was uncovered, and the birds were trained to peck the key for food reinforcement. After 6 sessions of training with variable-interval reinforcement in the presence of white light, food was discontinued and red and green lights were presented alternately. During the first extinction session, three out of four subjects made more key-pecks in the presence of the stimulus formerly correlated with response-independent food reinforcement than in the presence of the alternated color. All four exhibited differences in that direction during a second extinction session. This result suggests that it is not necessary to reinforce a particular response to $S+$ during training in order to obtain control over that response during subsequent testing. Indeed, the result runs directly counter to expectations based on the likely course of events during original training. Intermittent presentation of reinforcement in the absence of any contingency on a specified response is quite likely to establish some *superstitious* pattern of behavior as a result of accidental correlations of particular movements and reinforcement. Any superstitious behaviors which may have been established in the presence of $S+$ would probably be incompatible with key-pecking, so that their occurrence would lower the rate of key-pecking during subsequent testing.

A series of studies by other workers have confirmed and extended this finding. Bower and Kaufman (1963) have demonstrated that a stimulus correlated with response-independent reinforcement can control responding established under altered deprivation and reinforcement conditions, and Bower and Grusec (1964) have shown that such a correlation of stimuli with differential reinforcement can have durable effects on subsequent discrimination learning with a specified response. There is no question but that the correlation of stimuli and reinforcers suffices to provide control of operant behavior by those stimuli. The control is not nearly so strong as that established with response-dependent reinforcement, but it is important for an understanding of the minimal conditions for establishing stimulus control.

Differential reinforcement and gradients of stimulus control

Errorless discrimination training and response-independent reinforcement procedures unquestionably have interesting effects on differential responding. Conventional discrimination training can also have potent effects on stimulus-control gradients.

Sharpening stimulus control

A standard citation on this question is the experiment by Jenkins and Harrison (1960) on auditory frequency generalization in pigeons. After training to peck a key in the presence of a 1000-Hertz (Hz) tone $(S+)$, two groups of pigeons were distinguished according to whether training continued in the presence of $S+$ alone or whether $S+$ alternated with $S-$ (absence of tone). After comparable training, both groups received tests for stimulus control by tone frequency. The group which had been trained with $S+$ alone exhibited no stimulus control at all: The gradients were almost perfectly flat. The group which had experienced differential reinforcement in the presence and absence of tone exhibited sharply peaked gradients on the frequency continuum (see Figure 4.7). This procedure differs from most investigations of stimulus control in that $S-$ was not on the dimension subsequently tested for control. Nevertheless, it appears that some explicit differential training with auditory stimuli was crucial for the development of stimulus control by tone.

An extension of this finding has been described by Switalski, Lyons, and Thomas (1966). They began by training pigeons with VI reinforcement in the presence of a 555 nm key-light and then administered a standard extinction test to determine an

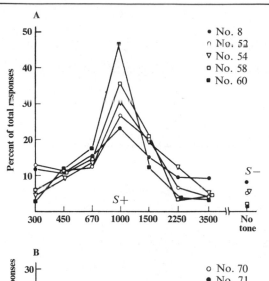

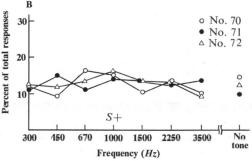

Figure 4.7 Gradients of responding by pigeons to tones of different frequency after training with reinforcement in the presence of 1000 *Hz*. For the birds represented in panel A, 1000 *Hz* alternated with extinction in the absence of tone during training; the birds represented in panel B had no experience of differential reinforcement before the test for stimulus control. (From Jenkins & Harrison, 1960.)

initial wavelength gradient. Half of the subjects received further training with 555 *nm* as *S+*, alternated with extinction in the presence of a white vertical line on a dark key. The other half obtained reinforcement on a *VI* 1-minute schedule for pecking both 555 *nm* and the vertical line. A final test revealed steeper wavelength gradients for those birds receiving differential-reinforcement training and shallower gradients for those trained with non-differential reinforcement, compared with the initial gradient. As in the Jenkins and Harrison study, control by a stimulus continuum was modified by training with a stimulus that could not be defined on that continuum.

A further step in this development has been re-ported by Honig (1969). He demonstrated that pigeons trained with differential reinforcement in the presence of green and blue key-lights subsequently exhibited steeper gradients of control by line orientation than did birds trained with non-differential reinforcement in blue and green. Thus, it is apparently possible for differential reinforcement on one continuum to sharpen stimulus control on an independent continuum.

In all this work, training and test stimuli were in the same modality, either auditory or visual. Rheinhold and Perkins (1955), working with rats in a runway, obtained data suggesting that the stimuli correlated with differential reinforcement need not even be in the same modality as those subsequently tested for control. It would be useful to obtain further information on this question.

The peak shift

The majority of studies of differential reinforcement and stimulus control have examined the effects of training with two stimuli on a continuum on subsequent stimulus control by that continuum. For example, Hanson (1959) trained separate groups of pigeons with a 550-*nm* key-light as *S+*, alternating with 555, 560, 570, or 590 *nm* as *S−*. After differential responding was established, the birds were tested for stimulus control by the wavelength continuum. Compared with the Guttman and Kalish gradient obtained after nondifferential training with 550 *nm*, Hanson's gradients were shifted away from *S−* (see Figure 4.8). Note that the shifted gradients were elevated in terms of total responding, and steeper not only in the region between *S+* and *S−*, but also beyond the peak. The phenomenon has been replicated on the line-tilt continuum by Bloomfield (1967), working with pigeons, and by Pierrel and Sherman (1960), working with rats and auditory intensity. This so-called peak shift has recently received a good deal of empirical and theoretical attention and is worth analyzing in some detail.

The elevation of the gradient peak may be seen as an instance of behavioral contrast, which was noted during acquisition of a successive discrimination (see Figure 4.6). Also, the studies reviewed here suggest that the sharpening of the gradient may result from differential reinforcement per se, without regard to the value of *S−*. The fact that all of Hanson's gradients are quite similar in height and slope supports these interpretations. Only the shift, then, represents something new in our survey. The magnitude of the shift, as measured by the pro-

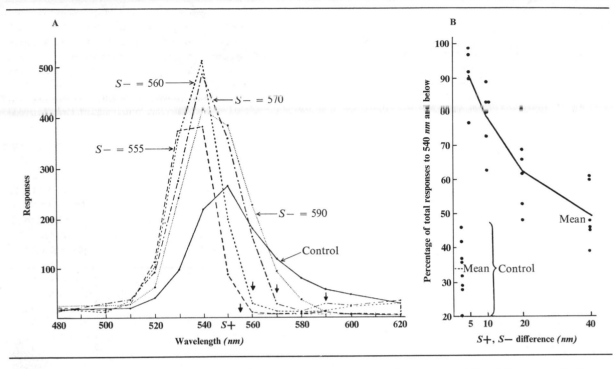

Figure 4.8   Panel A: Gradients of responding to wavelength by pigeons after training with reinforcement in the presence of 550 *nm* (S +) and extinction in 555, 560, 570, or 590 *nm*. The gradients of these separate groups are to be contrasted with that of a control group, trained with 550 *nm* alone. Panel B: The percentage of responses in the gradients at the left which occurred to wavelengths of 540 *nm* or less, as a function of the wavelength difference between $S+$ and $S-$ during training. (From Hanson, 1959.)

portion of responses to wavelengths shorter than $S+$, depends systematically on the value of $S-$ (see Figure 4.8B). Therefore, it is reasonable to look for factors which increase responding as a function of the separation of a stimulus from $S-$.

Stimulus control of not-responding

It is possible that $S-$ controls not-responding in the same way that $S+$ controls responding. For example, if an organism is trained not to respond in the presence of one stimulus, changing to another stimulus may lead to less not-responding; that is, more responding. Although this sounds peculiar, the empirical finding has been demonstrated in several studies. For example, Honig, Boneau, Burstein, and Pennypacker (1963) trained two groups of pigeons with a blank white key as $S+$ and a black vertical line on a white key as $S-$. After differential responding was well established, they gave a stimulus-control test with varying line orientation. There was a systematic increase in responding as the orientation departed increasingly from $S-$. Two other groups, trained with $S+$ and

$S-$ reversed, exhibited the expected gradient with maximum responding at $S+$. Gradients from both pairs of groups are presented in Figure 4.9. The groups differed considerably in terms of total responding during the test, but it is clear that the gradients for the groups with the black line as $S-$ look like inversions of the gradients for groups with the line as $S+$.

An important feature of gradients like this, indicating stimulus control of not-responding, is that they are obtained along a continuum which is independent of that defined by $S+$ and $S-$. Logically, it would appear that varying the orientation of a line does not make the stimulus any more or less similar to a blank key. In fact, however, a subject's behavior may not correspond to that expectation. Suppose the pigeon only looks at the top half of the key when it pecks. For the pigeon, then, a vertical line would be very different from a blank key, while a horizontal line would be effectively identical to a blank key. Lines slanted 45 degrees either way would be intermediate between the vertical line and blank key. The elevated responding to stimuli which are increasingly distant from $S-$

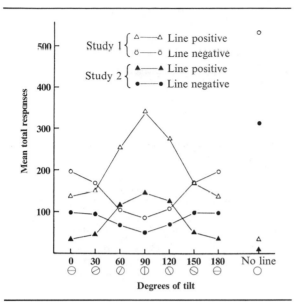

Figure 4.9 Gradients of stimulus control by line orientation following training with a vertical line as $S+$ and a blank key as $S-$ (line positive) or the vertical line as $S-$ and the blank key as $S+$ (line negative). The data are averaged separately for two groups of pigeons that were studied in successive replications of the experiment and that differed only in their total response outputs. (From Honig, Boneau, Burstein, & Pennypacker, 1963.)

may therefore be explained in terms of increasing similarity to $S+$, rather than decreasing similarity to $S-$.

Whatever the logic of stimulus similarity, therefore, it is probably worth giving each subject a preliminary test to see whether it does indeed treat the continua involved as independent. For example, after training with a blank key only as $S+$, one might administer a stimulus-control test with lines of different orientations to see whether the bird responds equally to all slants.

Although no published studies involve the preliminary test for independence, it is unlikely that stimulus control of not-responding is artifactual. As one way of controlling for varying similarity between $S+$ and stimuli on the test continuum, Jenkins and Harrison (1962) employed two different values of tone frequency as $S-$, while absence of tone served as $S+$. They obtained elevated responding at tone frequencies lying both outside the range between the $S-$ values and in between the two $S-$ frequencies. It is exceedingly unlikely that results of this sort can be explained by effective similarity to $S+$. Also, there are a number of ex-

perimental variables that determine whether or not the U-shaped gradients are obtained within experiments using the same $S+$ and $S-$ for all conditions. These studies will be reviewed later.

Stimulus control of not-responding by a dimension of $S-$, after discrimination training with $S+$ on a different dimension, has been identified with the concept of *inhibition* by Jenkins (1965a), and gradients of the sort obtained by Honig et al. (1963) are commonly viewed as demonstrating inhibitory stimulus control. For the present, this usage will be avoided, and the concept of inhibition will be discussed later. It suffices to note here that gradients of stimulus control of not-responding by $S-$ and of responding by $S+$ can be combined to explain the peak shift. In Hanson's experiment, for example, a wavelength between $S+$ and $S-$ will control both responding and a competing tendency not to respond. At a wavelength similarly spaced on the other side of $S+$, there will be less tendency not to respond, and therefore a greater net amount of responding. Responding to $S+$ itself may be lower than at wavelengths more remote from $S-$ under these conditions.

Relations between behavioral contrast, peak shift, and stimulus control of not-responding

It is not clear exactly how one ought to combine gradients of responding and not-responding to predict the postdiscrimination gradient in detail. For the present, there is at least reasonable qualitative agreement in several sets of findings. That is, there are a number of situations in which variables affecting the peak shift also affect gradients of not-responding.

First, Guttman (1959) has demonstrated that training with VI 1-minute reinforcement in the presence of $S+$ and VI 5-minute reinforcement in the presence of $S-$ produces a peak shift away from $S-$. It is not entirely appropriate to refer to a stimulus as $S-$ if it is correlated with reinforcement, but Guttman's data argue that relatively infrequent reinforcement may be functionally equivalent to extinction in this respect. Terrace (1968) has reported a further analysis of this result. In his study, one group of pigeons was trained with VI 1-minute reinforcement in the presence of both 550 and 573 *nm*, while a second group obtained VI 5-minute reinforcement in the presence of both wavelengths. After 10 training sessions, both groups received further training with VI-1 in the presence of 573 *nm* and VI-5 in the presence of 550 *nm*. Thus, the first group experienced a reduction in the frequency of reinforcement correlated with 550 *nm*, while the second group did not. Both groups came to respond differentially, with higher rates in the presence of 550 than 573 *nm*. All birds in the first group gave evidence of behavioral contrast. In a final stimulus-control test, only the first group exhibited gradients consistently peaked at 586 *nm* (peak shift).

In a closely related study, Weisman (1969) trained two groups of pigeons in similar fashion with a blank green key and a white vertical line on a green key as stimuli. One group experienced *VI* 1-minute reinforcement in the presence of both stimuli, while *VI* 5-minute schedules were correlated with both stimuli for the second group. After this nondifferential-reinforcement training, both groups were shifted to *VI*-1 in the presence of the green key and *VI*-5 in the presence of the vertical line. When line orientation was varied, only the group that had experienced a reduction in the frequency of reinforcement correlated with the line (and gave evidence of a correlated contrast effect in responding to green) exhibited consistent stimulus control of not-responding by line orientation.

A second pair of studies by Terrace (1968) and Weisman (1969) used the same sets of stimuli as in the previously described studies, with a *DRL* schedule of reinforcement in the presence of one of the stimuli and a *VI* 1-minute schedule in the other. Terrace obtained evidence of peak shift away from the stimulus correlated with the *DRL* schedule, at least in those birds exhibiting behavioral contrast, and Weisman found gradients of not-responding centered about the stimulus correlated with the *DRL* schedule. All of Weisman's birds gave evidence of contrast. These results are of interest for several reasons. First, they delineate some of the conditions necessary for production of peak shift and stimulus control of not-responding, and both suggest that extinction is not a necessary condition for either effect. Second, they suggest a correlation between these effects and contrast.

In another portion of Terrace's (1968) study, *VI* 1-minute reinforcement was given for key-pecking in the presence of both 586 *nm* and 561 *nm*, and 561 *nm* was also correlated with mild punishing shock. Behavioral contrast was observed during training, and stimulus-control gradients gave evidence of peak shift.

A third pair of studies on this question employed extinction in the presence of *S*−, but varied the way in which extinction was programmed. Honig, Thomas, and Guttman (1959) trained pigeons with variable-interval reinforcement in the presence of a 550 *nm* key-light. After 10 training sessions, the wavelength on the key was changed to 570 *nm* for one group of pigeons, and extinction was in effect continuously for 40 minutes. A second group also received a total of 40 minutes of extinction in the presence of 570 *nm* (*S*−), but this was alternated irregularly in 1-minute periods with reinforcement in the presence of 550 *nm* (*S*+). In a subsequent stimulus-control test, peak shift occurred only for subjects that experienced *S*+ and *S*− in alternation; birds trained with continuous extinction in the presence of *S*− had gradients peaked at *S*+. Again, Weisman has provided the corresponding data on stimulus control of not-responding (Weisman & Palmer, 1969). After nondifferential reinforcement with respect to a blank green key and a green key with a vertical white line, one group of birds received massed extinction in the presence of the white line, while a second group underwent discrimination training with the green key as *S*+ and the white line as *S*−. Only the latter group gave any evidence of stimulus control of not-responding by line orientation. Again, the agreement across experiments is perfect. It is not possible to measure contrast during massed extinction training, because *S*+ is never presented, but in both studies the absolute level of responding to *S*+ during the stimulus-control test was lower after massed extinction than after discrimination training.

As we have seen, the formation of a discrimination normally involves the reduction of the rate of responding in the presence of *S*− as a result of extinction. A correlated increase in response rate in the presence of *S*+ (contrast) is usually observed. It is also possible to accomplish a substantial reduction in the rate of responding by presenting reinforcement if the measured response does not occur for some fixed period of time. This is known as a *differential reinforcement of other behavior (DRO)* schedule (see Reynolds, 1961a). In the pigeon, a discrimination may be formed by alternating stimuli correlated with variable-interval reinforcement and *DRO*. If the frequency of reinforcement provided by the *DRO* schedule is appreciably greater than that arranged by the *VI* schedule, contrast does not occur (Reynolds, 1961a). Therefore, *DRO* schedules provide another method for investigating the relations between contrast and related stimulus-control phenomena.

In a study by Nevin (1968), pigeons were trained with *VI* 3-minute reinforcement for key-pecking during presentation of a blank white key, which alternated irregularly with a black vertical line on a white key. In the presence of the line, various *DRO* schedules of reinforcement were in effect during different experimental conditions, ranging from 180 reinforcements per hour to zero (extinction). When the frequency of reinforcement correlated with the vertical line was greater than that provided by the *VI* schedule correlated with the blank key, there was no evidence of contrast during blank-key periods, and subsequent tests for stimulus control by line orientation revealed flat gradients of not-responding. Shallow but reliable gradients of not-responding similar to those in Figure 4.9 were obtained after training with extinction in the presence of the vertical line. Nevin's findings are consistent with the results of Yarczower, Gollub, and Dickson (1968), who found that the peak shift did not occur after training with a *VI* schedule in the presence of 550 *nm,* which alternated with a *DRO* schedule providing about three times as many reinforcements per hour in the presence of 570 *nm.*

Errorless discrimination training, which was discussed earlier, provides another method for establishing differential responding without contrast. Terrace (1966b) demonstrated that if pigeons learned a discrimination between a line (*S+*) and a uniform 550 or 580 *nm* key-light (*S−*) without responding to *S−,* there was no evidence of a gradient of not-responding: The subjects did not respond at any wavelength. Pigeons that made many responses to *S−* during training exhibited gradients of not-responding on the wavelength continuum. Terrace (1964) had previously demonstrated the usual peak shift after training with *S+* and *S−* on the wavelength continuum if the pigeons responded to *S−* during training, but there was no peak shift if the discrimination had been trained without errors.

In summary, a consistent picture emerges: Those conditions which produce rate increases in the presence of *S+* during discrimination training (contrast) are also likely to produce peak shifts away from *S+* after training on the dimension controlling responding and gradients of not-responding about *S−.*

Inhibition and stimulus control

The findings summarized above may be organized around the concept of *inhibition.* The concept was used early in the study of reflexive behavior, and it may be understood by considering an example from this work. One of the preparations studied by Sherrington (1906) involved severing the spinal cord of a dog and suspending the animal so that both hind legs hung unsupported. Under these conditions, the spinal dog exhibits the so-called *mark-time reflex* in which the hind legs swing alternately back and forth. The eliciting stimulus for this response is extension of the legs by gravity. If the dog's tail is stimulated, the movement stops abruptly, even though the way in which the legs are suspended has not been altered (see Figure 4.10). This phenomenon is an instance of inhibition: the cessation of some ongoing behavior resulting from the application of an additional stimulus. Note that the kymograph tracing in Figure 4.10A shows that when stimulation of the tail terminates, responding resumes immediately with a greater amplitude and rate than before. In a reflex preparation, this is known as *positive induction,* or perhaps more graphically as *postinhibitory rebound.*

A rather different pattern results when the stimulus condition responsible for the reflex is removed. Figure 4.10B shows what happens when a support is placed beneath the dog's paws. The reflex stops at once, and when it resumes after removal of the support, there is no evidence of rebound. Thus, inhibition (as opposed to mere removal of the eliciting stimulus) is characterized in part by the rebound phenomenon which follows. Similar observations of *postinhibitory rebound* have been made in single-neuron recordings within several sensory systems and in classical conditioning of the salivary response.

There is a sense in which behavioral contrast is directly analogous to the postinhibitory rebound. Contrast is ordinarily observed in situations involving successive presentations of *S−* (which controls a low rate of responding) and *S+* (which controls a moderate, maintained rate). The increase in responding to *S+* during alternated presentations of *S+* and *S−* may be interpreted as a rebound following the inhibitory effects of *S−.* The transient character of the rebound, showing a maximal effect immediately after termination of the inhibiting stimulus, also has its parallel in the free operant. Boneau and Axelrod (1962), Catania and Gill (1964), and Nevin and Shettleworth (1966) have shown that the rate of responding in the presence of *S+* is highest immediately after exposure to *S−.* By programming reinforcement on a *DRO* schedule in the presence of a stimulus correlated with low response rate, Nevin and Shettleworth (1966) found that the effect was attributable not to the low response rate, but rather to the absence of reinforcement in *S−.* Therefore, by analogy with the rebound effect in a reflex preparation, it appears that a stimulus correlated with

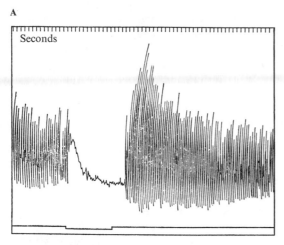 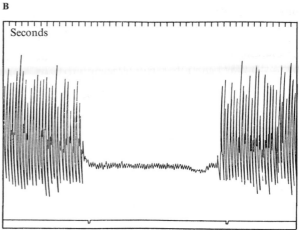

Figure 4.10 Kymograph records of the *mark-time reflex* in a spinal dog. Each upward movement of the center pen corresponds to a flexion of the hind leg. In record A the reflex was arrested by stimulating the dog's tail while the lower pen was down. Note the enhancement of both amplitude and rate of the reflex when the tail stimulation was discontinued. In record B the reflex was arrested by supporting the paws during the time between marks on the bottom line. Note the absence of rate or amplitude changes in this case. (From Sherrington, 1906.)

extinction may be regarded as possessing inhibitory properties.

This conclusion must be qualified by noting that errorless discrimination training apparently circumvents the inhibitory effects of nonreinforcement. Also, it must be qualified by noting apparent inhibitory effects with maintained reinforcement. As we have seen, contrast, peak shift, and gradients of not-responding may result from a reduction in response rate without changes in reinforcement frequency, as in research with *DRL* schedules by Terrace (1968) and Weisman (1969; see also Weisman, 1970, on *DRO* with equated frequency of reinforcement). Also, it is not at all clear that the reduction in the rate of an operant by changing a stimulus from $S+$ to $S-$ is the same sort of operation as adding an inhibitory stimulus while an eliciting stimulus is still acting, as in the Sherrington (1906) reflex demonstration. However, the analogy between the postinhibitory rebound and behavioral contrast, coupled with the frequent correlation between contrast and stimulus-control gradients of not-responding, suggest that it may well be appropriate to think of these gradients as reflecting the operation of an active inhibitory process conditioned to $S-$, diminishing in strength as stimulus conditions depart increasingly from $S-$.

The utility of the construct of inhibition depends

on its ability to integrate research findings with various procedures. A different method for measuring inhibitory control of operant behavior has recently been described by Brown and Jenkins (1967). They trained pigeons on a direct analog to the procedure introduced by Pavlov (1927) to demonstrate inhibitory control of conditioned salivation. The pigeons were first trained to peck the right-hand half of a split key when the key was red and the left-hand half when the key was green. Then, a tone was introduced on half of the green trials, and reinforcement was withheld when the tone was present, so that the birds now had two $S+$s—red and green—and the combination of green-plus-tone as $S-$. Since the tone was differentially correlated with nonreinforcement and controlled a low rate, it might be expected to have inhibitory properties. To test for this possibility, Brown and Jenkins conducted an extinction test employing the three stimulus conditions used in training and also the novel combination, red-plus-tone. During the test, the birds pecked far less when the tone was on than when it was off, both when the key was green and when it was red. If they did peck, though, they pecked the formerly correct half of the split key, indicating that the finding could not be attributed to a failure to discriminate red and green when the tone was present. A control group demonstrated that the effect could not be attributed to the sheer novelty of the red-tone compound. Therefore, it appeared that the tone, presented in compound with a stimulus which normally controlled a high rate of responding, served to inhibit the behavior, and the amount of inhibition could be measured by the decrement in responding produced by the tone.

To demonstrate inhibition in this way, which is formally analogous to the demonstrations of inhibition of reflex behavior and conditioned respondents, Brown and Jenkins (1967) had to devise a procedure which is quite different from the simple successive $S+$-$S-$ discrimination experiment. It would be of great interest to determine whether the inhibitory control in their study would be affected by the same variables as the gradients of not-responding obtained after successive-discrimination training. For example, if the tone signaled availability of reinforcement contingent upon not-responding, a pigeon would presumably learn not to respond in the presence of green-plus-tone. As described above, Nevin (1968) found that contrast did not occur and gradients of not-responding were flat if reinforcement was given contingent upon not-responding in the presence of a vertical line. These observations suggest the absence of inhibition, even though the rate of responding in the presence of the vertical line was low. In the Brown and Jenkins situation, would a tone which signaled reinforcement for not pecking green transfer to control not pecking red? If so, the Brown and Jenkins transfer effect and the results of standard successive-discrimination training procedures would be difficult to organize in terms of a single inhibitory process.

Hearst, Besley, and Farthing (1970) have recently provided an extensive review of experiments bearing on the concept of inhibition. They identify the inhibitory function of a stimulus with its ability to reduce rates of responding when presented in combination with stimuli that have been correlated with reinforcement for responding (Brown & Jenkins, 1967). They point out that this definition of inhibition may be more general than one based on demonstrations of inhibitory stimulus control— the U-shaped gradients indicating stimulus control of not-responding. Perhaps most importantly, they suggest new methods for the exploration of inhibitory phenomena. Experiments that provide simultaneous determination of response reductions and gradient slopes would be most valuable in further investigations of the role of inhibition in stimulus control.

SUMMARY AND THEORETICAL INTERLUDE

We have seen stimulus-control gradients ranging from the horizontal functions relating key-pecking to tone frequency (Jenkins & Harrison, 1960) to the precise control by wavelength obtained by Blough (1967). Within this range, a continuum of gradient slopes could be generated by varying the duration of training and the schedule of reinforcement in the presence of $S+$ and by the use of differential reinforcement with stimuli on or off the test continuum. We have also seen that stimuli correlated with extinction may gain control over the nonoccurrence of a response. Blough's results may be understood as the outcome of all those variables favoring precise stimulus control: extended differential training with VI reinforcement in $S+$, and extinction in the presence of all other stimuli. The Jenkins and Harrison results, at the other end of the continuum of possible stimulus-control findings, present a different sort of problem: Why was there no evidence of stimulus control after training with $S+$ alone, even though it was evident from the data of the differentially trained subjects that pigeons are capable of distinguishing tone frequency? Or, more generally, under what circumstances may a potentially effective stimulus continuum fail to exert any control over behavior?

The question may be placed in its historical context by considering the assumptions of the Hull-Spence theory of generalization (Hull, 1943; Spence, 1937). These theorists asserted that reinforcement of a response increased its *habit strength* —that is, its tendency to occur in the presence of the stimuli acting at the time of reinforcement. Habit strength also increased, but to a lesser extent, in the presence of other stimuli. The spread of habit strength depended on the difference between stimuli, but was assumed to be the same for all continua if they were scaled in psychological units, such as the *just noticeable difference.*

At the same time, nonreinforcement in the presence of $S-$ established a gradient of inhibition for that habit. It was assumed that the excitatory and inhibitory effects associated with any stimulus on the continuum could be combined by algebraic summation to determine the net habit strength. The example used by Spence (1937) is reproduced in Figure 4.11. It should be clear that the model accounts readily for peak shift, but not for the correlated contrast effects. The interested reader should work out examples with linear or concave gradients rather than Spence's hypothesized con-

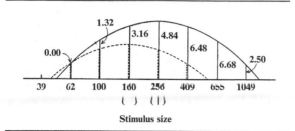

Figure 4.11 Theoretical curves of excitation and inhibition produced by differential reinforcement with a 256-cm² figure as $S+$ and a 160-cm² figure as $S-$, as proposed by Spence (1937). The ordinate represents an arbitrary scale of habit strength, which is positive for $S+$ (solid line) and negative for $S-$ (dashed line). Net habit strength at each figure size on the continuum is given by algebraic summation of the excitatory and inhibitory effects. Note that the maximum net habit strength is not at $S+$, but is displaced to larger figures, away from $S-$. (From Spence, 1937.)

vex gradients in order to appreciate the properties of this simple and influential model.

The Jenkins and Harrison data raise problems in connection with this formulation. Taken at face value, the theory asserts that training in the presence of a single stimulus suffices to produce an orderly decremental stimulus-control gradient. Clearly, that was not true for birds trained with $S+$ alone. The fact that discrimination training between the presence and absence of $S+$ gave steep gradients does not fit into the theory, because any theoretical inhibitory gradient around $S-$ would not lie along the tone-frequency continuum and should not interact with the $S+$ gradient. However, other "incidental" stimuli must be taken into account. As Hull (1929, 1952) observed, there are many stimuli present when a response is reinforced, and the theory assumed that all stimuli acquired the ability to evoke the habit. Therefore, the slope of an empirical gradient will depend on the extent to which responding is controlled by other stimuli which are present during training and testing.

In the Jenkins and Harrison study, for example, the visual aspects of the chamber (e.g., key-position and key-illumination) are also present during reinforcement, and a failure of control by tone frequency may be interpreted as resulting from relatively complete control by other aspects of the environment, which of course remain constant during testing. The fact that steep gradients were obtained

after discrimination training with respect to presence versus absence of tone may be understood by noting that under these conditions only the tone bears any consistent relation to reinforcement, so the other stimuli may lose their controlling power.

Working within the Hull-Spence tradition, Wagner, Logan, Haberlandt, and Price (1968) have performed a series of studies bearing on this question. In one experiment, rats were trained in a discrete-trial lever-pressing situation with a light present on every trial in compound with one of two tones. Trials were terminated by a lever-press, or after 5 seconds if no lever-press occurred. Reinforcement was available in 50 percent of the trials. Two groups were distinguished according to the correlation between tones and reinforcement. For the correlated group, reinforcement was always available in trials with tone A and never with tone B. For the uncorrelated group, reinforcement was available on 50 percent of the trials with both tone A and tone B. The main interest of the study was in the control of responding by light, which is functionally equivalent to the incidental apparatus cues in the Jenkins and Harrison study. For the correlated group, tones bear a consistent relation to reinforcement, while light does not, whereas light and tones are equally inconsistent for the uncorrelated group. To evaluate the control of responding by light alone, test trials were interspersed among the training trials during the final stages of training. The correlated group exhibited very little tendency to respond to light alone, but the uncorrelated group responded nearly as often as to the light-tone compounds. This finding was supported by other studies using different conditioning procedures. The result is clearly consistent with the notion that incidental stimuli present during reinforcement will control responding if no other stimuli bear a more consistent relation to reinforcement. The control by incidental stimuli may mask the effects of the stimulus manipulated by the experimenter.

A very different view has been expressed by Lashley and Wade (1946). They argued that a dimension of stimulation did not exist for an organism until established by experience of differential reinforcement with respect to that dimension. Training with a single stimulus should give a flat stimulus-control gradient, not because of the relative potency of other stimuli, but because the subject fails to associate reinforcement of key-pecking with that dimension at all. The flat gradients obtained by Jenkins and Harrison after training with $S+$ alone and the steepening effect of differential reinforcement are consistent with the Lashley and Wade position, although strictly speaking it should have been necessary to give discrimination training with respect to frequency, rather than presence versus absence of tone, to satisfy the Lashley and Wade assumptions.

The opposite problem is raised by the numerous findings of orderly wavelength or orientation gradients after training with $S+$ alone. Procedurally, these experiments were identical with the method used by Jenkins and Harrison for the group that failed to exhibit gradients. For the Hullian theorist, these orderly gradients after single-stimulus training raise the question of why some experiments led to relatively potent control by $S+$ and others did not. On the other hand, the appearance of orderly gradients after training with $S+$ alone would appear to contradict the Lashley and Wade hypothesis directly. However, the Lashley and Wade view leads one to seek variables which are not ordinarily dealt with in the Hullian framework, such as the subject's pre-experimental history, or other factors implicated in selective attention to certain aspects of stimulation.

INTERPRETING FAILURES OF STIMULUS CONTROL

When a stimulus that is present during reinforcement of a response does not gain control over responding, in the sense that variations in the stimulus have no effect on responding, one may speak of a failure of stimulus control. One possible reason for such failures is that the organism lacks the necessary sensory receptors; one would not, obviously, expect control by visual stimuli in blind subjects. The question of whether an organism has the necessary receptors is not always so clear, though. For example, there do not seem to be any special receptors for X rays, and for some time it appeared that organisms could not detect their presence. Recently, Smith (1970) and his associates have demonstrated stimulus control by X rays in several species and have shown that X-ray detection is mediated by the olfactory system. Possibilities of this sort always arise, and one should not be too quick to attribute a failure of stimulus control to an inability to detect the stimulus. Here, we will concentrate on failures of stimulus control when the stimuli are known to be readily detectable, as in the Jenkins and Harrison study with pure tones.

Effects of pre-experimental exposure to the stimulus continuum

Following Lashley and Wade's suggestions, it is easy to imagine that pigeons have experienced differential reinforcement with respect to color of grain or orientation of perches and bars in their home cages, so that orderly stimulus-control gradients may be obtained along these continua, whereas Jenkins and Harrison's birds had probably never heard pure tones before participating in the experiment. Perhaps this lack of prior experience and/or differential reinforcement was responsible for the failure of stimulus control in their study. Obviously, some controlled experimentation would be preferable to this sort of speculation. There is only a limited amount of data that is directly relevant here, but it is important to consider these data in some detail.

The first attempts to control the pre-experimental histories of subjects in stimulus-control experiments were reported by Ganz and Riesen (1962) and Peterson (1962). Ganz and Riesen reared four monkeys in the dark. When the monkeys were mature, they were trained to press a key for VI reinforcement in the presence of a single wavelength of light ($S+$), which alternated with extinction in the absence of light ($S-$). A separate group of four monkeys was similarly trained after normal rearing. Wavelength gradients were obtained during tests on seven successive days, with reinforcement in $S+$ interspersed. The results are shown in Figure 4.12 for individual subjects, based on total responses during the seven test sessions. If anything, the dark-reared monkeys exhibit *steeper* gradients than those with experience in making visual discriminations, despite equivalent experience of differential reinforcement with respect to presence versus absence of light during the experiment proper. The gradients obtained during the first test session were, on the average, a bit shallower for the dark-reared than for the experienced monkeys, but steep gradients developed in the second test session. Since this steepening may have resulted from the small amount of differential reinforcement experienced during the first test session, the results are not definitively opposed to the Lashley and Wade hypothesis, but the extremely rapid development of steep gradients argues that pre-experimental history may be of little significance in determining stimulus control.

A very different result was obtained by Peterson (1962). He compared wavelength gradients ob-

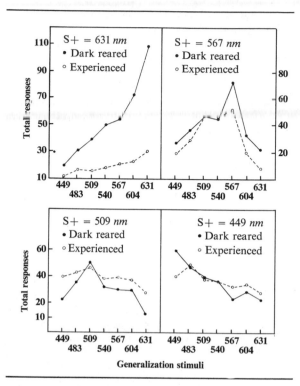

Figure 4.12 Generalization of responding on the wavelength continuum after training at various values of $S+$ for four monkeys that were reared in the dark and consequently had no pre-experimental history of wavelength discrimination, and four monkeys that were normally reared and thus had experience with visual discriminations. The results are total responses over the course of seven training and testing sessions. (From Ganz & Riesen, 1962.)

tained from Peking ducklings after rearing and key-peck training in the presence of monochromatic sodium vapor light with those obtained from a group given similar training after normal rearing. He found that monochromatic rearing led to almost perfectly flat gradients, while the normally reared ducklings exhibited standard peaked wavelength gradients similar to those obtained from pigeons with uncontrolled pre-experimental histories. Since rearing in monochromatic light prevents the subject from making discriminations on the basis of wavelength, this study is entirely consistent with the Lashley and Wade hypothesis that experience with the test continuum is a necessary condition for peaked gradients. However, two more recent studies have complicated the picture. Rudolph, Honig, and Gerry (1969) have reported

a series of experiments in which monochromatic-reared quail and chickens gave wavelength gradients that were quite comparable to those of normally reared birds after training with an $S+$ alone. Tracy (1970) has shown that the wavelength gradients of ducklings are seriously confounded by apparently unlearned tendencies to respond to wavelengths in the green range. He obtained shallower (but not flat) gradients after monochromatic rearing than after normal rearing, and he found that much of the difference could be explained by wavelength preferences. Thus, studies comparing restricted and normal rearing do not lead to any simple conclusions. This area clearly needs a great deal of work, hopefully with other stimulus continua in addition to wavelength.

The problem of attention

An alternative approach to the failure of stimulus control after training with $S+$ alone invokes the concept of *attention*. Although somewhat imprecisely defined, the concept may be valuable in suggesting avenues of attack. It could be argued that in Jenkins and Harrison's study, differential reinforcement with respect to presence and absence of tone forced the birds to attend to auditory stimuli. On the other hand, the fact that Guttman and Kalish's pigeons pecked directly at a localized spot of light may have forced attention to the visual aspects of the key, thus leading to a fairly steep wavelength gradient in the absence of explicit differential reinforcement. Although there is some intuitive plausibility in this account, there remains a need to define attention more precisely and to ascertain what variables determine attention to different stimuli.

As noted above, there are many aspects of stimulation present when a response is reinforced. *Attention* may be defined by the empirical observation that some but not all of these stimulus dimensions control responding when varied independently during a stimulus-control test. It is not always clear that the receptors are exposed to all aspects of stimulation. For instance, a rat may run in a runway with its eyes closed. Failure to demonstrate control of running by light in this situation would obviously be ascribed to the fact that the receptors were never exposed to the stimuli. Many "two-stage" theories of discrimination learning (e.g., Wyckoff, 1952) assume, quite reasonably, that observing responses—that is, orientation toward the stimuli—must precede stimulus control. But the notion of attention implies something more. A straightforward example has been reported by Reynolds (1961b). He trained two pigeons with a white triangle on a red field as $S+$, and a white circle on a green field as $S-$. After the birds were thoroughly trained, a special sort of stimulus-control test was conducted during extinction. The key was illuminated with one of the four elements of the training stimuli: white triangle or white circle on a dark key, or a uniform red or green key. One of the birds made nearly all its responses when the white triangle was presented, and the other concentrated nearly all its pecking on the uniform red key. Since the colors and forms were projected directly onto the response key, it is unlikely that idiosyncratic receptor orientation could explain the results. It must be assumed that the birds saw both dimensions, but attended exclusively (and unpredictably) to one dimension of $S+$.

This sort of result is by no means universal. Butter (1963) trained pigeons to peck a key with a vertical band of 550 *nm* light as $S+$. After training with $S+$ alone, a standard stimulus-control test was given in which both the wavelength and the orientation of the band were varied. Orderly decremental gradients were obtained on both dimensions, demonstrating that both aspects of $S+$ controlled responding in this instance.

The differences between Butter's and Reynolds' findings may be sought in various features of the experiments, such as the choice of stimulus dimensions and the subjects' histories. Johnson and Cumming (1968) have investigated these variables in a situation closely related to that studied by Reynolds (1961b). In their first experiment, pigeons were trained with a vertical line on a green key as $S+$ and a horizontal line on a red key as $S-$. After the discrimination was well established, a stimulus-control test of the sort used by Reynolds was administered, with colors and lines presented separately during extinction. Both birds responded predominantly to green, demonstrating selective control by color rather than line when the two dimensions were redundant. Johnson and Cumming went on to study this phenomenon by giving various kinds of pretraining with lines or colors alone. They found that 10 sessions of pretraining with a vertical line as $S+$ and a horizontal line as $S-$, before training with line-color compounds, sufficed to reverse the selective control by color observed in their first experiment, with most responding occurring in the presence of the vertical line during a final test. Also, they found that this effect was dependent on the intensity of the lines

during pretraining: If the lines were projected on the key at low intensity during pretraining, selective control by color resulted during subsequent training with compound stimuli. This result was obtained despite clear evidence that the pigeon was able to discriminate line orientation at the low pretraining intensity. Thus, it is possible to conclude that *selective attention* may be modified by a history of discrimination training with one element of a compound as $S+$.

A study by Garcia and Koelling (1966) suggests an important limitation on the modifiability of selective attention. Although their techniques are quite different from any encountered elsewhere in this chapter, it is appropriate to review their work here. They conducted an experiment in which thirsty rats could obtain flavored water by licking at a drinking tube. Each contact of the rat's tongue with the tube operated a sensor and activated a flashing light and a clicker. For one group of rats, exposure to this "bright, noisy, tasty" water was paired immediately with electric shock; for a second group, shock was delayed; a third group was treated with X rays, which are known to have aversive effects on rats, while they drank from the tube; for a fourth group, *lithium chloride,* which tastes like salt but has toxic effects, was added to the water. In alternating sessions, the rats drank plain water (the dark, quiet, tasteless kind) and no shock, X-ray, or lithium chloride treatment was administered. Within three to five sessions, there was clear evidence of stimulus control: Little drinking occurred when the light, click, and taste were all present at once. To ascertain which elements of the stimulus compound correlated with shock or irradiation were effective in suppressing drinking, Garcia and Koelling gave stimulus-control tests like those in Reynolds' (1961b) study. Bright, noisy water and tasty water were presented separately to each group of rats. The shock groups drank normally with tasty water, but licking was suppressed when it produced light and click. The irradiated rats and those given lithium chloride during training did just the reverse. The results of this study are summarized in Figure 4.13. All groups exhibited selective attention, but the nature of the aversive stimulus apparently determined which elements of the compound would acquire control.

As Garcia and Koelling note, it is appropriate in the natural environment for a rat to associate internal discomfort, such as that resulting from irradiation or poisons, with taste. (When someone feels sick, he is apt to say, "It must have been something

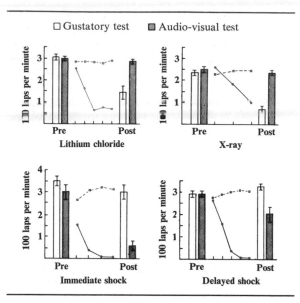

Figure 4.13 Histograms indicating the amount of water consumed when a distinctive taste was present (gustatory test), or when each lick produced a click and a flash of light (audiovisual test). The histograms at the left indicate little or no disruption of drinking before training, during which taste, light, and click were paired with an aversive stimulus, while plain water was not correlated with aversive consequences. The curves in the center illustrate the acquisition of suppression of drinking to the taste-light-click compound, while the intake of plain water was unchanged. The histograms at the right indicate selective control of reduced drinking by either taste or light plus click, depending on the nature of the aversive stimulus employed during training. (From Garcia & Koelling, 1966.)

I ate.") Conversely, external pain is appropriately associated with exteroceptive stimuli. (When someone burns a hand by touching a pot while tasting some cooking food, he avoids the pot, not the food.) The authors argue that these stimulus-selective mechanisms are not the result of arbitrary conditioning histories, but rather have developed through natural selection because of their survival value. However, it is also likely to be true that systematic correlations between taste and sickness or between visual stimuli and pain have occurred during the life of the normal organism, whereas the reverse correlations are unlikely. It remains to be seen whether the selective effects isolated by Garcia and Koelling can be modified by special rearing conditions in the same sort of way that Johnson and Cumming (1968) modified selection

of different visual dimensions by preliminary training.

Since Garcia and Koelling's work, a number of other demonstrations of the same sort have been reported. Rozin and Kalat (1971) have reviewed these developments and argued that gustatory stimuli, consummatory responses, and poisons all pertain to a feeding system that may have quite different properties from those of other systems, such as those involving exteroceptive cues, defense reactions (see Chapter 7), and pain. If this argument is correct, it is probably best not to think of Garcia and Koelling's results in terms of selective attention, but rather in terms of the selection of different learning mechanisms based on the different reinforcers involved. The ethological approach to behavior presented in Chapter 9 will be an essential adjunct to the analysis of stimulus control as work of this sort proceeds.

Even when responses are chosen arbitrarily and maintained by conventional laboratory procedures, there is evidence that different degrees of control by a stimulus can operate within a single organism at the same time, depending on the behavior under control. An elegant demonstration of this has been provided by Hearst (1965). He trained monkeys to press a lever on a *Sidman avoidance schedule* (see Chapter 7) in order to postpone an aversive electric shock, and at the same time arranged for food reinforcement of chain-pulling on a *VI* 2-minute schedule. (In the terminology of schedules of reinforcement, these are *concurrent* schedules, discussed in Chapter 6.) After 10 sessions of exposure to the concurrent schedules, all conducted with illumination of the chamber at its highest available level, stimulus-control tests were conducted by varying illumination, with both shock and food excluded. Separate gradients were determined for lever-pressing and for chain-pulling. For all subjects, the gradient for the avoidance response was nearly flat, while the concurrently obtained gradient for the food-reinforced response was fairly steep.

This result might not be too startling if the two gradients were obtained at different times or with different groups of subjects. It could then be argued, as Hearst (1965) does, that internal cues play a relatively greater role in avoidance than they do in food-reinforced responding. Indeed, there is a good deal of plausibility in this argument, since the Sidman avoidance schedule does not involve exteroceptive warning stimuli, and explanations of performance on this schedule lean heavily on inferred internal stimuli (e.g., Anger,

1963; see Chapter 7). These internal stimuli would still be present at all values of chamber-illumination, and could therefore completely mask control by illumination. The problem with this explanation is that whatever internal stimulation may be involved in avoidance responding must also be present while the subject engages in food-reinforced chain-pulling. If continued presence of these internal stimuli is invoked to explain the absence of control by illumination in the case of the avoidance lever-press, surely the same principle must hold for chain-pulling. Instead, it is as if the subject can simultaneously attend to light (and ignore internal cues) with its chain-pulling hand, and ignore light while attending to internal stimuli with its lever-pressing hand. In other words, attention seemed to be conditional upon the performance being controlled.

CONDITIONAL STIMULUS CONTROL

In most of the material considered so far, stimulus control was studied in situations involving a simple response, and interest centered on changes in the rate of responding when the stimulus took on different values. The question to be considered next is whether stimulus-control functions of this sort can themselves be brought under stimulus control.

To exemplify this sort of relation, consider some of the data reviewed above on differential reinforcement and stimulus control. Several studies demonstrated that a group of subjects which experienced differential reinforcement on one continuum exhibited steeper stimulus-control gradients on a different continuum than did a separate group which had not experienced differential reinforcement. Suppose, now, that these two conditions could be realized within a single subject by exposure to two different environmental conditions, one correlated with differential reinforcement and the other correlated with equal reinforcement for responding to two stimuli. In this case, one might expect each subject to give steeper gradients in the former condition than in the latter. Operationally, such a finding may be described as stimulus control over the stimulus-control gradient itself.

A study by Honig (1969) investigated the situation outlined here. He trained pigeons to peck a key for food reinforcement in the presence of two different tones, 2500 *Hz* and 1000 *Hz*. In the presence of one tone, designated the *TD* tone, three

vertical lines on a white background were projected on the key to serve as $S+$; correlated with a *VI* schedule of food reinforcement, and a blank white key served as $S-$. In the presence of the other tone, designated the *VI* tone, the same *VI* schedule was in effect during *both* of the visual stimuli. Thus, the *TD* tone was correlated with differential reinforcement in the presence and absence of vertical lines, while the *VI* tone was correlated with equal reinforcement. After extended training, the birds learned to respond at approximately equal rates to the stimuli during the *VI* tone, while responding infrequently to $S-$ when the *TD* tone was on. Finally, a stimulus-control test was given, with variations in both line orientation and tone frequency. The major finding, consistent for all subjects, was that the line-orientation gradient obtained during presentations of the *VI* tone was shallower than the gradient obtained in the presence of the *TD* tone. This demonstration of conditional control over the slope of a gradient is an important advance in the analysis of stimulus control, suggesting that a stimulus-response relationship may itself be taken as a dependent variable and manipulated within a single subject in a manner analogous to the manipulation of discrete responses.

Another instance of conditional stimulus control is the *matching-to-sample* experiment. In a standard matching situation, the subject is confronted with a sample (or standard) stimulus, and then with two comparison stimuli, one of which is physically identical to the standard. Choices of the matching stimulus are reinforced, while responses to the nonmatching stimulus are extinguished. A series of studies of the behavior of pigeons in this situation has been described by Cumming and Berryman (1965). In their work, the stimuli were different colors illuminating the three response keys. For instance, on some trials, the center key was green. When the pigeon pecked it, the two side keys were illuminated, one green and the other red or blue. The center-key color, the location of the matching side key, and the color of the nonmatching key were randomized from trial to trial, but in all cases reinforcement was available for responses to the matching side key. Consider a trial on which one side key was green and the other was red. In a standard *simultaneous discrimination,* either red or green would be designated $S+$ and the other $S-$. In the matching situation, however, green is $S+$ if the center key is green, and red is $S+$ if the center key is red. Thus, unlike a standard discrimination, the relation between a side-key color and reinforcement is conditional upon the center-key color, and the center-key color may be regarded as a stimulus selecting which of several side-key discriminations will occur.

Under the conditions employed by Cumming and Berryman, pigeons have no difficulty learning the matching performance or its converse, *oddity,* in which reinforcement is contingent upon choosing the side key which differs from the center key. It could be argued that no conditional stimulus-control relations are required in these situations. For instance, the birds might simply have acquired a set of discriminations such as: Green on the left, green in the center, and red on the right constitute a compound $S+$ for pecking the left key (or, for oddity, the right key). The same number and kind of discriminations would be involved in both matching and oddity. Detailed examination of the course of acquisition revealed some differences, however. When first exposed to the matching situation, pigeons took up *position preferences* and only abandoned them when correct matching performance developed. That is, the period before the emergence of correct performance was not characterized by random responding, but rather by consistent (although 50 percent incorrect) choices of one side key. This sort of systematic presolution behavior has often been observed during the early stages of simultaneous-discrimination learning and has figured prominently in early theorizing about stimulus control (for review, see Riley, 1965). Its relevance here is that comparable position preferences did not develop during the presolution period in oddity training. Rather, when pigeons were first exposed to the oddity situation they tended to select the correct stimulus with somewhat more than chance probability from the outset.

In addition to the differences observed early in acquisition, Cumming and Berryman (1965) found that matching was more easily disrupted by a drug, *sodium pentobarbital,* at low doses than was oddity. Neither of these differences would be expected if, in both situations, the birds had simply learned to respond to a set of compound $S+$s. Cumming and Berryman argued, therefore, that matching and oddity involved an additional stimulus-control function, which was to be sought in the different conditional relations between the stimuli and reinforcement.

An extension of these conditional discriminations has been described by Nevin and Liebold (1966). Using red and green keys, they scheduled reinforcement for choices of the odd key color when a yellow light above the keys was lighted. When the yellow light was off, reinforcement was scheduled on the matching key. In this situation, correct choices were conditional on both the color of the center key and the presence or absence of the yellow light. The pigeon learned to perform at high levels of accuracy after about 50 hours of training. Nevin and Liebold investigated the possibility that the matching and oddity performances were under separate stimulus control by injecting the bird with various doses of sodium pentobarbital. They replicated the differential sensitivity of the matching performance which had been demonstrated in separate drug experiments by Cumming and Berryman (1965). Accordingly, this experiment demonstrated *higher-order conditional stimulus control,* which involved the control of functional classes of stimulus-response relations: matching and oddity.

A further demonstration of complex stimulus control over the matching performances of pigeons has been reported by Mintz, Mourer, and Weinberg (1966). They arranged for food reinforcement to occur after every tenth correct match, rather than after every correct choice as in the usual experiment. Under these conditions, pigeons tend to make errors immediately after reinforcement, with their matching accuracy gradually increasing as trials progress toward the next available reinforcement (Nevin, Cumming, & Berryman, 1963). Mintz, Mourer, and Weinberg added a row of stimulus lights next to the response keys, which were successively illuminated with each correct response, so that there were exteroceptive stimuli functioning like counters to indicate proximity to reinforcement. After their birds were thoroughly trained, they administered test trials in which the stimulus lights that normally came on just before reinforcement were presented immediately after a reinforcement. All birds exhibited increases in accuracy on these trials, suggesting that the pilot lights had gained control over the accuracy of the matching performance. This result is essentially similar to Honig's (1969) finding that stimuli correlated with differential reinforcement control steeper gradients than stimuli correlated with nondifferential reinforcement, in that the pilot lights which came on late in the sequence of trials between reinforcements were closely correlated in time with differential reinforcement of correct matching.

To summarize, several studies have demonstrated the possibility of stimulus control over the slope of a generalization gradient, the selection of a complex performance—matching or oddity—and the accuracy of performance. Note that in all of these examples of conditional stimulus control, the presence or absence of some background stimulus condition affects some property of responding that cannot be defined at any moment in time by the simple occurrence or nonoccurrence of a response to a particular element of the situation. Rather, it affects a relationship between particular stimuli and responses. We often talk of a person as insightful or obtuse, attentive or inattentive, careful or sloppy, intending to convey something about his personal style that goes beyond the particulars of his actions. The observations that give rise to these judgments are sets of relations between environmental events and changes in behavior of exactly the sort that we have been considering in experiments involving pigeons pecking keys in relatively simple settings. The demonstration of stimulus control over functional relations between stimuli and responses, or functional classes of behavior such as matching and oddity, goes a long way toward bringing the laboratory analysis of stimulus control into contact with complex human behavior.

ACQUISITION AND ANALYSIS OF CONCEPTS

Conceptual behavior has been defined as generalization within classes of stimuli and discrimination between classes (Keller & Schoenfeld, 1950, p. 155). For example, we say that a child understands sex differences because he says *man* for mature males, regardless of their age, skin color, hair length, or clothing, but says *woman* in the presence of females who may be quite similar to males on these irrelevant dimensions. It is very difficult to ascertain just which features of those multidimensional stimuli constituting mature males and females are crucial for his behavior; presumably, they are features which happen to be highly correlated with the differences in anatomy and reproductive function. We assume that the child has been differentially reinforced by the adult members of his verbal community for correct identifications of sex, and this has resulted in both broad generalization within the set of stimuli that are equivalent with respect to reinforcement and precise stimulus control with respect to dimensions that are correlated with differential reinforcement.

The concepts of sameness and difference

Experimental analogs of conceptual behavior are fairly easy to establish, and with the use of animals it is possible to study the necessary and sufficient conditions for obtaining the complex stimulus-control relations that we call concepts. An interesting example has been reported by Robinson (1955), who used chimpanzees as subjects in a situation requiring discrimination based on sameness. During training, pairs of objects were presented on a tray in the standard *Wisconsin General Test Apparatus* (WGTA). Food was available under the pair of objects that were physically identical, but never under pairs of objects that differed. Training was initiated with various combinations of circle, square, and triangle; for example, two circles mounted side by side served as $S+$, while a square and triangle side by side were $S-$. All six chimpanzees mastered these problems, averaging 83 percent correct choices in the final training trials. They were then given 20 test trials, during which novel pairs of objects were presented. Reinforcement was continued during testing, with the position of food varying randomly from trial to trial. All six chimpanzees gave evidence of transfer, responding most of the time to the pair of objects that was the same. On the average, 78 percent of their responses on these test trials were made to the pair of objects that were the same. The following major points should be understood. First, the subjects presumably learned the concept of sameness. After training with circles, squares, and triangles, they went on to respond appropriately during testing to objects as diverse as insulators, sink stoppers, and scouring pads. This performance exemplifies the essence of conceptual behavior: transfer to novel instances on the basis of features that are the same as those correlated with reinforcement in the past. Second, the concept of sameness demonstrated in this study is of special interest because it is not definable on the basis of properties of any single object, but requires an abstraction of relations between two objects.

Pigeons have also been used to study discriminations based on sameness and difference. Honig (1965) extended Robinson's work by training birds in a two-key situation to peck one key if both keys were lighted with the same wavelength and the other key if the wavelengths differed by 40 *nm*. Eight wavelengths covering the range from 500 to 570 *nm* in 10-*nm* steps were used during training. For example, if 550 *nm* lights were projected on both keys, reinforcement was available after a variable interval for pecking the left key. After reinforcement, the key colors changed, so that, for example, 550 *nm* was on the left-hand key and 510 *nm* on the right-hand key. In this case, reinforcement was available after a variable interval for pecking the right-hand key. A total of 16 pairs of wavelengths were presented in a random order, with the longer wavelength light appearing equally often on the left and right when the keys were different. Three methodological features of the procedure should be noted. First, changing stimuli after each reinforcement prevented the subjects from using reinforcement itself as a cue for continuing to respond on a key. Second, a *changeover delay* was in effect, so that responses to the correct key were reinforced only if at least 4 seconds had elapsed since the last peck at the incorrect key, to prevent the subject from obtaining reinforcement for performances that were not based on the stimuli, such as simply alternating between keys. Third, each of the training wavelengths was correlated with reinforcement equally often on both keys, so that the birds could not base their responding on particular wavelengths or positions.

Following extensive training, the subjects were exposed to a stimulus-control test in which all possible pairs of stimuli in the range from 500 to 570 *nm* (in 10-*nm* steps) were presented. These included the training pairs, of course, and also included novel pairs differing in wavelength separation by various amounts. The percentage of responses to the key that had been correct during training when the key lights were the same was recorded for all pairs of wavelengths over the 70-*nm* range. The results, in Figure 4.14, show that all birds exhibited orderly gradients along the dimension of wavelength *difference;* that is, the training conditions apparently sufficed to establish control by the abstract relation of degree of difference between stimuli.

In further work within the same general paradigm, Honig (1965) trained discriminations based on large versus small wavelength differences, with reinforcement scheduled on one key if the key lights differed by 20 *nm* and on the other key if they differed by 80 *nm*. Again, orderly gradients were obtained along the wavelength-difference continuum, and virtually perfect transfer was obtained when wavelengths lying between the

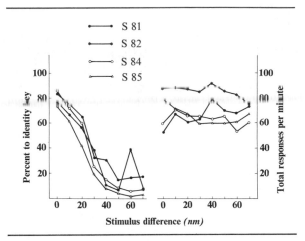

Figure 4.14 Gradients showing the tendency of pigeons to respond to a key correlated with reinforcement when two keys were identically lighted during training, as a function of the difference between wavelengths of the key-lights. The pigeons had also obtained reinforcement during training for pecking the second key when the key-lights differed by 40 *nm*. The functions at the right show that total responding to the two keys was the same at all wavelength difference values, so that the only aspect of performance affected by stimulus difference was the distribution of pecks to the two keys. (From Honig, 1965.)

training wavelengths were presented for the first time. These findings indicate that, at least within the wavelength continuum, pigeons can learn the concepts of sameness and difference and come under the control of the degree of difference between the wavelengths on the keys. Related data have been obtained in a different experimental setting by Malott and Malott (1970), where only one pair of colors was employed during training.

Conceptual behavior of this sort has not been demonstrated in pigeons after training on matching-to-sample or oddity, however. In Cumming and Berryman's (1965) work, a test for transfer to yellow was given after standard matching or oddity training with red, green, and blue lights. In no instance was there evidence of transfer; that is, the birds evidently did not acquire the concepts of matching and oddity in general. Perhaps in these situations pigeons require training with more different stimuli before transfer will occur. This problem does not seem to arise with chimpanzees, however. Nissen, Blum, and Blum (1948) trained their subjects with a cup or a box as the standard stimulus and a cup and a box as comparison stimuli.

(Note that two objects are the minimum possible to define matching.) Food was always under the matching comparison object. After the chimpanzees had mastered this problem, they were tested with 77 new object combinations. All seven chimpanzees performed well above the chance level, choosing the matching object on an average of 85 percent of the test trials. Here, the minimal stimulus conditions necessary to define the task were evidently sufficient to establish the concept of matching.

Learning sets

Commonly, infrahuman subjects require experience with a large number of stimulus conditions exemplifying the concept before conceptual behavior can be demonstrated. In Honig's (1965) work, exposure to eight pairs of wavelengths equally spaced on the wavelength-difference continuum was arranged within single sessions, and tests were conducted only after this training was complete. Alternatively, one may arrange for exposure to a set of stimulus conditions sequentially and observe the acquisition of the concept as a function of exposure to successive instances. As an example of this sort of analysis, consider the work of Moon and Harlow (1955) on the acquisition of the oddity concept. They trained 16 rhesus monkeys on a series of 256 oddity problems. On each problem, a given set of objects—for example, circle on the left, circle in the center, and triangle on the right— was presented for six successive trials. The particular object under which food was available, and its location to the left or right of center, varied systematically from trial to trial within the six trials constituting a problem. The probability of choosing the odd object on the first trial of each problem served as a measure of the degree to which the oddity concept had been mastered, since the subject's choice on these trials could not, of course, be based on experience of reinforcement within that problem. At the beginning of training, the subjects were not performing at a level much better than chance. By the end of training, however, they were choosing the correct (odd) object on 90 percent of the first trials of each problem. This method clearly demonstrates the gradual acquisition of the oddity concept through repeated measurement of transfer to new problems.

The emergence of correct performance on early trials of each new problem of a discrimination task of this sort is evidence for the formation of a *learning set*—a tendency to solve each problem swiftly

on the basis of some general principle or strategy acquired during training.

Moon and Harlow also examined their monkeys' tendencies to respond on the basis of stimulus conditions other than the oddity relation which defined reinforcement availability. For example, tendencies to respond on the basis of the tray position most recently correlated with reinforcement were found to remain low and roughly constant throughout training, while tendencies to choose objects previously correlated with reinforcement were initially high and declined systematically with training. Responding based on conditions other than that defining the availability of reinforcement have been termed *error factors* by Harlow and Hicks (1957), who have argued that the acquisition of stimulus control is in large part the result of elimination of these error factors.

Error-factor analysis is particularly appropriate to situations of the sort studied by Moon and Harlow (1955), in which subjects are trained on a series of discrimination problems and the common dimension of all problems acquires control, because it is the only dimension consistently correlated with reinforcement. The analysis is less applicable to simple stimulus control situations of the sort treated earlier. Taken literally, the error-factor approach would suggest that in a successive discrimination between $S+$ and $S-$ the subject learns not to respond in the presence of $S-$ or, stated otherwise, to respond if any stimulus other than $S-$ is present. However, variations away from $S+$ on a dimension independent of $S-$ ordinarily lead to systematic decrements in responding, indicating that the subject has also learned something about responding to $S+$. Moreover, Terrace's (1963a, 1966a) work indicates that stimulus control may be established without occurrence of any errors.

Whatever the general value of error-factor analysis, it provides a useful way of thinking about the development of a concept. In effect, it suggests that we learn to generalize among members of a class by finding out about aspects of stimuli which exclude them from the class, rather than by inducing a few defining features of the class. To translate this into the language of a stimulus-control experiment, the acquisition of a concept should also be facilitated by multiplying the number of conditions in which responding is extinguished or only inconsistently reinforced.

Although no systematic investigation of this sort has been conducted with animals, an intriguing finding reported by Herrnstein and Loveland (1964) is relevant here. They trained pigeons to detect human beings in photographs chosen from a collection of 35-mm color slides by arranging for reinforcement in the presence of photographs containing human beings $(S+)$, which alternated with photographs that did not include people $(S-)$. Over 1200 slides were available, of which 80 were used per daily session. After extensive training, the birds gave evidence of having acquired the concept *person* by pecking at high rates in the presence of novel slides that contained people and at low rates when no people (or parts of people) were visible. This performance emerged despite the fact that, in the experimenters' words,

> Many slides contained human beings partly obscured by intervening objects: trees, automobiles, window frames, and so on. The people were distributed throughout the pictures: in the center or to one side or the other, near the top or bottom, close up or distant. Some slides contained a single person; others contained groups of various sizes. The people themselves varied in appearance: they were clothed, semi-nude, or nude; adults or children; sitting, standing, or lying; black, white, or yellow [p. 550].

The essence of their finding is that the pigeons apparently came under the control of a set of stimuli which could not be specified physically by the experimenters, but rather was defined by the experimenters' own responses in categorizing slides. Presumably, this is how children learn concepts, but understanding of this process is much more likely to be achieved with animals. For example, one can control the subject's pre-experimental exposure to the stimuli to be employed and then proceed to examine the acquisition of conceptual behavior with various amounts of exposure to simple or complex instances of either positive or negative stimuli. Studies of this sort may bring the most subtle aspects of conceptual behavior within the domain of an experimental analysis of behavior.

SENSATION, PERCEPTION, AND STIMULUS CONTROL

Sensation and perception are traditional topics in psychology that are usually treated quite separately from generalization and discrimination learning. However, it is evident that behaviors based on sensory or perceptual processes fall under the general heading of stimulus control, in the sense that they depend crucially on antecedent and current environmental stimuli. This chapter cannot deal fully with these extensive topics; however, it can at least indicate the logical and experi-mental continuity of sensation, perception, and stimulus control.

Psychophysics and sensory sensitivity

One of the oldest and best developed areas of psychology, psychophysics, is concerned with the determination of functions describing how an organism's sensitivity to stimulation changes as a function of properties of the stimulus. Although this chapter has emphasized the effects of variables such as reinforcement contingencies and training procedures, the changes in behavior that result from changes in stimulation also depend on the physical properties of the stimuli themselves. To take a well-known example, humans are able to make refined visual discriminations on the basis of wavelength when a light is projected at fairly high intensities into the *fovea*, but not when dim lights are projected into the periphery of the eye. In stimulus-control terms, the slope of a wavelength gradient depends on the intensity and retinal location of the stimulus. Indeed, it is exactly this sort of finding which has led to the duplicity theory of vision. Psychophysical analysis of differential responding to precisely controlled visual stimuli has been coordinated with careful research on the anatomy, photochemistry, and electrophysiology of the retina to give a fairly complete picture of the operation of the visual system. Since the physiological research is usually conducted on infrahuman subjects, it is of interest to obtain behavioral data from members of the same species to give a complete picture of sensory function.

The most basic behavioral data in psychophysics are obtained within experimental procedures designed to determine the minimum intensity of stimulation required for detection of the presence of the stimulus—that is, the *absolute threshold*. With humans, the procedure is fairly straightforward. Taking auditory sensitivity as an example, one would begin by describing the experiment to the subject, placing headphones over his ears, and asking him to press a button whenever he heard a tone. One might begin by presenting fairly weak but audible tones, gradually decreasing the intensity until the subject no longer pressed the button. Then, to make precise determination of threshold, one might select a set of several intensities, spanning the range from one which was easily detected down to one which was never reported during preliminary testing. Each of these intensities would be presented a number of times in an irregular order, and the number of button-presses at each intensity would be recorded. This procedure is known as the *method of constant stimuli,* and the typical result is a *psychometric function* in which response probability is an increasing function of stimulus intensity. The relation of this sort of function to a stimulus-control gradient follows from the assumption that the instructions establish a high probability of pressing the button when tones are heard clearly and of refraining in the absence of a tone. The probability of button-pressing changes continuously as tone intensity increases, just as the average rate of responding is related to the value of stimuli between $S+$ and $S-$ after discrimination training.

Although the analogy between the psychometric function and a stimulus-control gradient may seem clear, it is instructive to consider how one might proceed to determine a psychometric function for an animal. Suppose one were simply to arrange for reinforcement in the presence of a readily detected tone and nonreinforcement in its absence. Differential responding to presence and absence of tone would be expected to develop after some training, and one could then present tones of varying intensity and measure the resulting gradient. As we have seen, however, the gradient slope would be certain to depend on a host of variables, and one could not claim to have measured the detectability of the tones, rather than the effects of these other variables.

Most researchers who have been concerned with behavioral evaluation of animal sensory systems have chosen to use maintained reinforcement procedures, which are more similar to Blough's (1967) work mentioned earlier than to the usual extinction test for stimulus control. As an example, consider the technique used by Gourevitch and Hack (1966) to study auditory sensitivity in rats. To control the subject's position in the sound field at the moment of stimulus onset, they required the rats to produce brief tones by touching a nose key. Tones followed every twelfth nose-contact on the average, and the intensity of the tone varied from trial to trial in an irregular sequence. Reinforcement was available for pressing a lever while the tone was on, but never otherwise. In essence, this is a situation with multiple $S+$s (all values of tone intensity) and one $S-$ (silence). It is interesting to consider a problem here which has not come up before. Suppose that the subject touches the nose key, produces a tone that is so weak that it is not detected, but nevertheless the subject goes over and presses the lever. Reinforcement will then occur in the presence of a condition indiscriminable from silence, which

should increase the tendency to press the lever in the absence of tone. To evaluate this tendency, the experimenter may present periods of silence on exactly the same schedule as tones, and assess the subject's probability of pressing the lever during these "catch trials." As long as this probability remains low, the experimenter can proceed with reasonable confidence that the subject is in fact basing its lever-pressing on the presence of tones. (It may be worth noting here that exactly the same

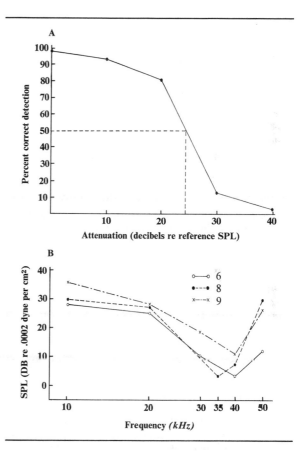

Figure 4.15 Panel A shows the probability of responding by a rat in a psychophysical experiment concerned with the absolute threshold of hearing. A tone of constant frequency was presented at different intensities chosen randomly from trial to trial. The tones were specified in terms of attenuation from a fixed reference level, so that the probability of detecting the tone decreased as attenuation increased. Thresholds were estimated by interpolation at 50 percent correct detections and plotted as a function of the frequency of the tone for three subjects in panel B to show how auditory sensitivity depended on tone frequency. (From Gourevitch & Hack, 1966.)

precautions are necessary with human subjects, to be sure that they are not responding on the basis of uncontrolled apparatus noises or trial-warning signals.) Gourevitch and Hack (1966) succeeded in establishing low response probabilities in the absence of tones and obtained psychometric functions of the sort shown in Figure 4.15A. The abscissa scale is expressed in units of attenuation from a strong signal, so that response probability declines as the abscissa values increase. As the dashed lines indicate, the tone intensity that would occasion lever-pressing on 50 percent of the presentations was estimated from the graph and used as a measure of threshold. Thresholds were determined in this way at each of several tone frequencies and then plotted as a function of frequency as shown in the audiograms in Figure 4.15B.

In essence, this function relates a measure of stimulus control (the 50 percent point in this instance) to a parameter of the stimulus that controls responding. Functions of this sort are the basic data of psychophysics.

It is important to understand that the psychometric functions from which the audiogram was derived are dependent on the reinforcement schedule and other conditions of the experiment as well as the frequency of the tone. Any aspect of the situation which increases the tendency to press the lever will elevate the entire psychometric function and lead to a different estimate of threshold. Using a very similar procedure, Nevin (1970) has shown that the tendency to emit false reports on catch trials and the slope of the psychometric function between strong and weak signals may be manipulated by varying the probability of reinforcement in the presence of signals of different intensities. In studies of animal sensory systems, then, the psychometric function is similar to the stimulus-control gradients reviewed earlier in this chapter; its slope and location depend on both stimulus and reinforcement variables.

The measurement of perceptual phenomena

As a final example of the application of stimulus-control methods to the analysis of psychological processes, consider the area of *perception*. In perception studies it is presumed that the subject's responses are not directly dependent on the physical stimuli presented to him, but on the internal events produced by those stimuli. For example, in much human work, the observer is asked to make a verbal statement about how a stimulus appears to him, rather than what it is. When we look at a perspective drawing, we agree that one object looks farther away than another; in fact, of course, both objects are represented by lines in a two-dimensional plane, and the "correct" answer on the basis of the physical specification of the drawing must be that the two objects are in the same plane. Presumably, our responses indicating apparent depth or distance in a perspective drawing are the generalized result of a history of reinforcement in the three-dimensional world, where we often have to make depth or distance judgments on the basis of perspective cues.

Although perception studies with human subjects seem quite straightforward, because one can simply ask a person what he sees, in fact they involve complex assumptions. To make this clear, it is instructive once again to consider how one might study a perceptual phenomenon in animals. The dramatic *aftereffects* of *spiral movement* will serve as an illustration.

It is well known that exposure to a slowly rotating spiral produces an aftereffect opposite in direction to the movement of the spiral. If the spiral is rotated so that it appears to expand, objects viewed immediately afterward appear to shrink, and vice versa. Scott and Powell (1963) devised a method for demonstrating and measuring this aftereffect in a monkey. They began by training their subject to discriminate between expanding and contracting circles, which were presented on a cathode-ray tube facing the monkey. Two levers were available, with food reinforcement following responses on the left-hand lever if the circle was contracting, and on the right-hand lever if the circle was expanding. Each lever-press terminated the trial, and every other correct response was reinforced. Mild shock followed an incorrect response. After extensive training the monkey performed almost perfectly on this task. Then the spiral was introduced, and the subject was trained to fixate it steadily by presenting the circle after steady fixation for at least 10 seconds. During this phase of training, the spiral was always motionless, but discrimination training with respect to expansion or contraction of the circle continued. The rate of expansion or contraction of the circle varied from trial to trial, taking on values ranging from easily discriminated expansion, through zero change, to easily discriminated contraction. Finally, testing was conducted on sessions which alternated with continued training. On some test trials, the spiral was motionless, as in training, and the food and shock contingencies remained in effect. On other test trials, the spiral rotated in one direction or the other. If it turned clockwise, the spiral appeared to expand, and if it turned counterclockwise, it appeared to contract. The expected movement aftereffect, then, would be apparent contraction of the circle after exposure to clockwise rotation of the spiral, and the monkey would be more likely to press the left-hand lever. Conversely, the monkey would be expected to press the right-hand lever, indicating apparent expansion of the circle, after seeing counterclockwise rotation of the spiral. However, there is a serious question of what to do about food and shock on these test trials. Suppose the spiral rotated clockwise and the monkey was then presented with a circle which, physically, was expanding slowly. In terms of the stimulus, the right-hand lever should be defined as correct. However, if the circle subjectively appeared to contract, the monkey's training should lead it to press the left-hand lever. If reinforcement is scheduled on the right-hand lever and shock on the left, the experimenter is, in effect, telling the monkey to base its responding on the physical properties of the circle rather than reporting its subjective appearance. On the other hand, if reinforcement is scheduled on the left-hand lever and shock on the right, which might be "correct" on the basis of the experimenter's own judgment of apparent shrinkage under these conditions, the experimenter is reinforcing responses indicating the expected aftereffect. The obvious way out of this dilemma—to test during experimental extinction—is not useful here because extinction would then be differentially associated with conditions in which the spiral was rotating. The subject would be quite likely to cease responding whenever a trial began with a rotating spiral under such conditions.

Scott and Powell opted for a compromise between these possibilities. They continued reinforcement availability for every other correct response during testing, where the correctness of the response was defined on the basis of the physical change in the test circle, but discontinued shock for incorrect responses except under conditions in which the circle was changing rapidly, so that conditions most likely to produce an aftereffect would not provide punishment for responses indicating the aftereffect. Their results, shown in Figure 4.16, provide a beautiful demonstration of the aftereffect. Over much of the range tested, the subject was more likely to press the right-hand lever (indicating apparent expansion) after exposure to counterclockwise spiral rotation than after exposure to a motionless spiral. The subject

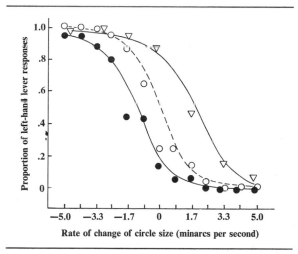

Figure 4.16 Data demonstrating an aftereffect of spiral movement perceived by a monkey. The monkey had been trained to press the left-hand lever if a circle was contracting and the right-hand lever if it was expanding. The unfilled circles show performance when a spiral, which preceded the circle on each trial, was motionless. The triangles show responding on trials which began with exposure to a moving spiral that appeared to expand. Under these conditions, the monkey responded predominantly on the left-hand lever, indicating apparent contraction of the circle, even when the circle was objectively expanding. The reverse occurred on trials following exposure to an apparently contracting spiral, as shown by the filled circles. The magnitude of the aftereffect may be measured by the lateral displacement of the functions at 50 percent left responses. (From Scott & Powell, 1963.)

also pressed the left-hand lever, indicating apparent contraction, more often after exposure to clockwise rotation than to a motionless spiral. The aftereffect of motion may be measured by the lateral displacement of the functions at 50 percent left responses. The authors note that the measured aftereffect is somewhat smaller than that measured in comparable work with humans, and it may be that the maintenance of reinforcement for responses based on the physical characteristics of the test circle was responsible for limiting the effect. Perhaps even more important in this regard is the use of punishment for responses indicating an aftereffect when the circle was changing rapidly.

By now, hopefully, the reader will be asking himself whether the human perceptual data are not similarly biased. Remember, this sort of situation, which is common in research with human subjects, is essentially a generalization test for stimulus control in the absence of differential reinforcement. As we have seen, the stimulus-control gradient can be altered considerably by variables other than the stimuli, most notably by a past history of differential reinforcement (which is rarely controlled in humans).

Procedural variables are certain to play an important part in any experiment, but it is not suggested that the processes studied in perceptual research are nothing more than procedural artifacts. A perceptual process is revealed by a functional relation showing the dependence of a behavioral measure on a parameter of stimulation. In our example of sensory research with animals, we saw that the auditory threshold could be measured and related to tone frequency. The absolute value of the measured threshold at each frequency would be quite likely to depend on procedural details, but the form of this function—i.e., the minimum at 35 kHz and the abrupt rise above 40 kHz— would be unlikely to vary with the details of the procedure, at least not after stimulus control by auditory intensity was well established. In the work by Scott and Powell (1963), it might well be that the numerical estimate of the aftereffect would depend on the particulars of training and testing, but functions relating the size of the aftereffect to the rotation rate of the spiral might prove to be quite similar across procedures. Invariances of this sort are the goal of empirical research in any area, and they are commonplace in research on human sensory processes. Hopefully, similar functional invariances will be discovered within other areas of research on stimulus control as experimental analysis progresses.

SUMMARY AND CONCLUSIONS

Stimulus control has been defined operationally by the way in which responding changes when an antecedent stimulus is varied. The traditional gradient of stimulus generalization is the simplest example of stimulus control. Differential responding to two or more stimuli as a result of discrimination training is another. Although conventionally these examples are treated separately, they may be seen as continuously related instances of stimulus control, differing in the number of stimuli employed during training and the schedules of differential reinforcement associated with them. The effects of these and other variables on the slopes of stimulus-control gradients were reviewed in some detail to suggest that any particular gradient is the result of the combined action of many factors, so that no underlying generalization process can be isolated.

Explicit differential reinforcement has several effects which may shed light on some processes involved in stimulus control. If differential responding to $S+$ and $S-$ in a successive discrimination results from a history of extinction in the presence of $S-$, the following effects are reliably observed:

1. Response rate to $S+$ increases (behavioral contrast).
2. The peak of the gradient on the $S+$-$S-$ continuum is shifted away from $S-$.
3. Variations in a dimension of $S-$, which is independent of $S+$, leads to increases in responding, indicating stimulus control of not-responding.

These effects are highly correlated; that is, variations in differential-reinforcement procedures that eliminate one of these effects are quite likely to eliminate the others. Of special interest is the absence of any of these effects if a discrimination is formed without responding to $S-$. To the extent that the correlation of these findings holds up, they may be understood in terms of an inhibitory process conditioned to $S-$ as a result of unreinforced responding in its presence.

Even under equivalent training conditions, some stimulus dimensions gain control over responding while others do not. Which dimensions control behavior may be assessed in stimulus-control tests which vary several dimensions independently during extinction. The demonstration of selective control by some features of the environment, but not by others (even though the subject is potentially sensitive to them), defines the phenomenon of attention. Under some circumstances, it is possible to establish experimental control over attention by manipulations in the subject's history of reinforcement.

Ordinarily, stimulus control is assessed by examining the rate or probability of responding in the presence of various stimuli. In more complex situations, responding to a particular stimulus may be made dependent on some prior stimulus. In such cases, it is appropriate to speak of conditional stimulus control, in which the conditional stimulus acts to determine a stimulus-response relation, rather than a particular rate of responding. Conditional control has been demonstrated over the slope of a generalization gradient, the selection of a complex performance (matching or oddity), and the accuracy of a matching performance.

Responding may also be brought under the control of stimulus variables which can be stated in abstract terms, such as sameness or difference. In such cases, responding often generalizes to novel instances of particular stimuli bearing the same abstract relationship to each other as the stimuli employed during training. This sort of generalization is the essence of conceptual behavior. Thus, the concepts and methods of stimulus-control research may be brought to bear on such processes as attention, abstraction, and conceptualization, which have traditionally been viewed as higher mental processes, inaccessible to direct behavioral analysis.

Finally, sensory and perceptual processes may be treated within the context of stimulus control. The study of refined sensory discriminations such as the absolute threshold raises no special problems for the experimenter, because the subject's task is well defined and differential reinforcement can be scheduled throughout training and testing. Perceptual processes differ in that the experimenter cannot define the stimuli that control behavior in advance. Therefore, it is necessary to evaluate perception by testing for stimulus control during extinction. In this respect, the traditional problem areas of perception, attention, and conceptualization are related in their analysis within the framework of stimulus control.

REFERENCES

Anger, D. The role of temporal discriminations in the reinforcement of Sidman avoidance behavior. *Journal of the Experimental Analysis of Behavior*, 1963, **6**, 477–506.

Bloomfield, T. M. A peak shift on a line-tilt continuum. *Journal of the Experimental Analysis of Behavior*, 1967, **10**, 361–366.

Blough, D. S. Interresponse time as a function of continuous variables: A new method and some data. *Journal of the Experimental Analysis of Behavior*, 1963, **6**, 237–246.

Blough, D. S. Stimulus generalization as signal detection in pigeons. *Science*, 1967, **158**, 940–941. Figure 4.1B: Copyright © 1967 by the American Association for the Advancement of Science, and reproduced by permission.

Blough, D. S. Generalization gradient shape and summation in steady state tests. *Journal of the Experimental Analysis of Behavior*, 1969, **12**, 91–104.

Boneau, C. A., & Axelrod, S. Work decrement and reminiscence in pigeon operant responding. *Journal of Experimental Psychology*, 1962, **64**, 352–354.

Bower, G., & Grusec, T. Effect of prior Pavlovian discrimination training upon learning an operant discrimination. *Journal of the Experimental Analysis of Behavior*, 1964, **7**, 401–404.

Bower, G., & Kaufman, R. Transfer across drives of the discriminative effect of a Pavlovian conditioned stimulus. *Journal of the Experimental Analysis of Behavior*, 1963, **6**, 445–448.

Brown, P. L., & Jenkins, H. M. Conditioned inhibition and excitation in operant discrimination learning. *Journal of Experimental Psychology*, 1967, **75**, 255–266.

Brush, F. R., Bush, R. R., Jenkins, W. O., John, W. F., & Whiting, J. W. M. Stimulus generalization after extinction and punishment: An experimental study of displacement. *Journal of Abnormal and Social Psychology*, 1952, **47**, 633–640.

Butter, C. M. Stimulus generalization along one and two dimensions in pigeons. *Journal of Experimental Psychology*, 1963, **65**, 339–346.

Catania, A. C., & Gill, C. A. Inhibition and behavioral contrast. *Psychonomic Science*, 1964, **1**, 257–258.

Coate, W. B. Effect of deprivation on postdiscrimination stimulus generalization in the rat. *Journal of Comparative and Physiological Psychology*, 1964, **57**, 134–138.

Cumming, W. W., & Berryman, R. The complex discriminated operant: Studies of matching-to-sample and related problems. In D. Mostofsky (Ed.), *Stimulus generalization*. Stanford, Calif.: Stanford University Press, 1965. Pp. 284–330.

Cumming, W. W., & Eckerman, D. A. Stimulus control of a differentiated operant. *Psychonomic Science*, 1965, **3**, 313–314. Figure 4.5: Reproduced by permission of author and publisher.

Estes, W. K. Discriminative conditioning: II. Effects of a Pavlovian conditioned stimulus upon a subsequently established operant response. *Journal of Experimental Psychology*, 1948, **38**, 173–177.

Friedman, H., & Guttman, N. Further analysis of the various effects of discrimination training on stimulus generalization gradients. In D. Mostofsky (Ed.), *Stimulus generalization*. Stanford, Calif.: Stanford University Press, 1965. Pp. 255–267.

Ganz, L., & Riesen, A. H. Stimulus generalization to hue in the dark-reared macaque. *Journal of Comparative and Physiological Psychology*, 1962, **55**, 92–99. Figure 4.12: Copyright © 1962 by the American Psychological Association, and reproduced by permission.

Garcia, J., & Koelling, R. A. Relation of cue to consequence in avoidance learning. *Psychonomic Science*, 1966, **4**, 123–124. Figure 4.13: Reproduced by permission of author and publisher.

Gourevitch, G., & Hack, M. H. Audibility in the rat. *Journal of Comparative and Physiological Psychology*, 1966, **62**, 289–291. Figure 4.15: Copyright © 1966 by the American Psychological Association, and reproduced by permission.

Guttman, N. Generalization gradients around stimuli associated with different reinforcement schedules. *Journal of Experimental Psychology*, 1959, **58**, 335–340.

Guttman, N., & Kalish, H. I. Discriminability and stimulus generalization. *Journal of Experimental Psychology*, 1956, **51**, 79–88. Figures 4.1A, 4.3, and 4.4: Copyright © 1956 by the American Psychological Association, and reproduced by permission.

Haber, A., & Kalish, H. I. Prediction of discrimination from generalization after variations in schedule of reinforcement. *Science*, 1963, **142**, 412–413.

Hanson, H. M. Effects of discrimination training on stimulus generalization. *Journal of Experimental Psychology*, 1959, **58**, 321–334. Figure 4.8: Copyright © 1959 by the American Psychological Association, and reproduced by permission.

Harlow, H. F., & Hicks, L. H. Discrimination learning theory: Uniprocess vs. duoprocess. *Psychological Review*, 1957, **64**, 104–109.

Hearst, E. Approach, avoidance, and stimulus generalization. In D. Mostofsky (Ed.), *Stimulus generalization*. Stanford, Calif.: Stanford University Press, 1965. Pp. 331–355.

Hearst, E. Stimulus intensity dynamism and auditory generalization for approach and avoidance behavior in rats. *Journal of Comparative and Physiological Psychology*, 1969, **68**, 111–117.

Hearst, E., Besley, S., & Farthing, G. W. Inhibition and the stimulus control of operant behavior. *Journal of the Experimental Analysis of Behavior*, 1970, **14**, 373–409.

Hearst, E., Koresko, M. B., & Poppen, R. Stimulus generalization and the response-reinforcement contingency. *Journal of the Experimental Analysis of Behavior*, 1964, **7**, 369–380.

Hearst, E., & Koresko, M. B. Stimulus generalization and amount of prior training on variable interval reinforcement. *Journal of Comparative and Physiological Psychology*, 1968, **66**, 133–138.

Herrnstein, R. J., & Loveland, D. H. Complex visual concept in the pigeon. *Science*, 1964, **146**, 549–551.

Honig, W. K. Discrimination, generalization, and transfer on the basis of stimulus difference. In D. Mostofsky (Ed.), *Stimulus generalization*. Stanford, Calif.: Stanford University Press, 1965. Pp. 218–254. Figure 4.14: Copyright © 1965 by the Board of Trustees of the Leland Stanford Junior University, and reproduced by permission.

Honig, W. K. Attention and the modulation of stimulus control. In D. Mostofsky (Ed.), *Attention: Contemporary theory and analysis*. New York: Appleton-Century-Crofts, 1969. Pp. 193–238.

Honig, W. K., Boneau, C. A., Burstein, K. R., & Pennypacker, H. S. Positive and negative generalization gradients obtained after equivalent training conditions. *Journal of Comparative and Physiological Psychology*, 1963, **56**, 111–116.

Figure 4.9: Copyright © 1963 by the American Psychological Association, and reproduced by permission.

Honig, W. K., Thomas, D. R., & Guttman, N. Differential effects of continuous extinction and discrimination training on the generalization gradient. *Journal of Experimental Psychology,* 1959, **58,** 145–152.

Hull, C. L. A functional interpretation of the conditioned reflex. *Psychological Review,* 1929, **36,** 498–511.

Hull, C. L. *Principles of behavior.* New York: Appleton-Century-Crofts, 1943.

Hull, C. L. *A behavior system.* New Haven, Conn.: Yale University Press, 1952.

Jenkins, H. M. Generalization gradients and the concept of inhibition. In D. Mostofsky (Ed.), *Stimulus generalization.* Stanford, Calif.: Stanford University Press, 1965. Pp. 55–61. (a).

Jenkins, H. M. Measurement of stimulus control during discriminative operant conditioning. *Psychological Bulletin,* 1965, **64,** 365–376. (b)

Jenkins, H. M., & Harrison, R. H. Effect of discrimination training on auditory generalization. *Journal of Experimental Psychology,* 1960, **59,** 246–253. Figure 4.7: Copyright © 1960 by the American Psychological Association, and reproduced by permission.

Jenkins, H. M., & Harrison, R. H. Generalization gradients of inhibition following auditory discrimination learning. *Journal of the Experimental Analysis of Behavior,* 1962, **5,** 434–441.

Jenkins, W. O., Pascal, G. R., & Walker, R. W., Jr. Deprivation and generalization. *Journal of Experimental Psychology,* 1958, **56,** 274–277.

Johnson, D. T., & Cumming, W. W. Some determiners of attention. *Journal of the Experimental Analysis of Behavior,* 1968, **11,** 157–166.

Kalish, H. I., & Haber, A. Prediction of discrimination from generalization following variations in deprivation level. *Journal of Comparative and Physiological Psychology,* 1965, **60,** 125–128.

Kawashima, T. The effect of drive on stimulus generalization. *Japanese Psychological Research,* 1964, **6,** 88–95.

Keller, F. S., & Schoenfeld, W. N. *Principles of psychology.* New York: Appleton-Century-Crofts, 1950.

Kimble, G. A. (Ed.) *Hilgard and Marquis' Conditioning and learning.* (2nd ed.) New York: Appleton-Century-Crofts, 1961.

Lashley, K. S., & Wade, M. The Pavlovian theory of generalization. *Psychological Review,* 1946, **53,** 72–87.

Lawrence, D. H. The transfer of a discrimination along a continuum. *Journal of Comparative and Physiological Psychology,* 1952, **45,** 511–516.

Malott, R. W., & Malott, K. Perception and stimulus generalization. In W. Stebbins (Ed.), *Animal psychophysics.* New York: Appleton-Century-Crofts, 1970. Pp. 363–400.

Margolius, G. Stimulus generalization of an instrumental response as a function of the number of reinforced trials. *Journal of Experimental Psychology,* 1955, **49,** 105–111.

Migler, B. Effects of averaging data during stimulus generalization. *Journal of the Experimental Analysis of Behavior,* 1964, **7,** 303–307.

Migler, B., & Millenson, J. Analysis of response rates during stimulus generalization. *Journal of the Experimental Analysis of Behavior,* 1969, **12,** 81–87.

Mintz, D. E., Mourer, D. J., & Weinberg, L. S. Stimulus control in fixed ratio matching-to-sample. *Journal of the Experimental Analysis of Behavior,* 1966, **9,** 627–630.

Moon, L. E., & Harlow, H. F. Analysis of oddity learning by rhesus monkeys. *Journal of Comparative and Physiological Psychology,* 1955, **48,** 188–194.

Morse, W. H., & Skinner, B. F. Some factors involved in the stimulus control of operant behavior. *Journal of the Experimental Analysis of Behavior,* 1958, **1,** 103–107.

Nevin, J. A. Differential reinforcement and stimulus control of not-responding. *Journal of the Experimental Analysis of Behavior,* 1968, **11,** 715–726.

Nevin, J. A. On differential stimulation and differential reinforcement. In W. Stebbins (Ed.), *Animal psychophysics.* New York: Appleton-Century-Crofts, 1970. Pp. 401–423.

Nevin, J. A., Cumming, W. W., & Berryman, R. Ratio reinforcement of matching behavior. *Journal of the Experimental Analysis of Behavior,* 1963, **6,** 149–154.

Nevin, J. A., & Liebold, K. Stimulus control of matching and oddity in a pigeon. *Psychonomic Science,* 1966, **5,** 351–352.

Nevin, J. A., & Shettleworth, S. J. An analysis of contrast effects in multiple schedules. *Journal of the Experimental Analysis of Behavior,* 1966, **9,** 305–315.

Newman, J. R., & Grice, G. R. Stimulus generalization as a function of drive level, and the relation between two measures of response strength. *Journal of Experimental Psychology,* 1965, **69,** 357–362.

Nissen, H. W., Blum, J. S., & Blum, R. A. Analysis of matching behavior in chimpanzees. *Journal of Comparative and Physiological Psychology,* 1948, **41,** 62–74.

Pavlov, I. P. *Conditioned reflexes.* G. V. Anrep (Trans.) Oxford: The Clarendon Press, 1927.

Peterson, N. Effect of monochromatic rearing on the control of responding by wavelength. *Science,* 1962, **136,** 774–775.

Pierrel, R., & Sherman, J. G. Generalization of auditory intensity following discrimination training. *Journal of the Experimental Analysis of Behavior,* 1960, **3,** 313–322.

Reynolds, G. S. Behavioral contrast. *Journal of the Experimental Analysis of Behavior,* 1961, **4,** 57–71. (a)

Reynolds, G. S. Attention in the pigeon. *Journal of the Experimental Analysis of Behavior,* 1961, **4,** 203–208. (b)

Rheinhold, D. B., & Perkins, C. C., Jr. Stimulus generalization following different methods of training. *Journal of Experimental Psychology,* 1955, **49,** 423–427.

Riley, D. A. *Discrimination learning.* Boston: Allyn & Bacon, 1965.

Robinson, J. S. The sameness-difference discrimination problem in chimpanzees. *Journal of Comparative and Physiological Psychology,* 1955, **48,** 195–197.

Rozin, P., & Kalat, J. W. Specific hungers and poison avoidance as adaptive specializations of learning. *Psychological Review,* 1971, **78,** 459–486.

Rudolph, R. L., Honig, W. K., & Gerry, J. E. Effects of monochromatic rearing on the acquisition of stimulus control. *Journal of Comparative and Physiological Psychology,* 1969, **140,** 57–59.

Scott, T. R., & Powell, D. A. Measurement of a visual motion aftereffect in the rhesus monkey. *Science,* 1963, **140,** 57–59. Figure 4.16: Copyright © 1963 by the American Association for the Advancement of Science, and reproduced by permission.

Sherrington, C. S. *The integrative action of the nervous system.* New Haven: Yale University Press, 1906. Figure 4.10: Copyright 1906 by Yale University Press, and reproduced by permission.

Skinner, B. F. Are theories of learning necessary? *Psychological Review*, 1950, **57**, 193–216.

Smith, J. C. Conditioned suppression as an animal psychophysical technique. In W. Stebbins (Ed.), *Animal psychophysics*. New York: Appleton-Century-Crofts, 1970. Pp. 125–159.

Spence, K. W. The differential response of animals to stimuli differing within a single dimension. *Psychological Review*, 1937, **44**, 430–444.

Switalski, R. W., Lyons, J., & Thomas, D. R. Effects of interdimensional training on stimulus generalization. *Journal of Experimental Psychology*, 1966, **72**, 661–666.

Terrace, H. S. Discrimination learning with and without "errors." *Journal of the Experimental Analysis of Behavior*, 1963, **6**, 1–28. (a)

Terrace, H. S. Errorless transfer of a discrimination across two continua. *Journal of the Experimental Analysis of Behavior*, 1963, **6**, 223–232. (b)

Terrace, H. S. Wavelength generalization after discrimination learning with and without errors. *Science*, 1964, **144**, 78–80.

Terrace, H. S. Stimulus control. In W. K. Honig (Ed.), *Operant behavior: Areas of research and application*. New York: Appleton-Century-Crofts, 1966. Pp. 271–344. (a)

Terrace, H. S. Discrimination learning and inhibition. *Science*, 1966, **154**, 1677–1680. (b)

Terrace, H. S. Discrimination learning, the peak shift, and behavioral contrast. *Journal of the Experimental Analysis of Behavior*, 1968, **11**, 727–741.

Thomas, D. R. The effects of drive and discrimination training on stimulus generalization. *Journal of Experimental Psychology*, 1962, **64**(1), 24–28.

Thomas, D. R., & King, R. A. Stimulus generalization as a function of level of motivation. *Journal of Experimental Psychology*, 1959, **57**, 323–328.

Thomas, D. R., & Switalski, R. W. Comparison of stimulus generalization following variable-ratio and variable-interval training. *Journal of Experimental Psychology*, 1966, **71**, 236–240.

Tracy, W. K. Wavelength generalization and preference in monochromatically reared ducklings. *Journal of the Experimental Analysis of Behavior*, 1970, **13**, 163–178.

Wagner, A. R., Logan, F. A., Haberlandt, K., & Price, T. Stimulus selection in animal discrimination learning. *Journal of Experimental Psychology*, 1968, **76**, 171–180.

Weisman, R. G. Some determinants of inhibitory stimulus control. *Journal of the Experimental Analysis of Behavior*, 1969, **12**, 443–450.

Weisman, R. G. Factors influencing inhibitory stimulus control: Differential reinforcement of other behavior during discrimination training. *Journal of the Experimental Analysis of Behavior*, 1970, **14**, 87–91.

Weisman, R. G., & Palmer, J. A. Factors influencing inhibitory stimulus control: Discrimination training and prior nondifferential reinforcement. *Journal of the Experimental Analysis of Behavior*, 1969, **12**, 229–237.

Wickens, D. D., Schroder, H. M., & Snide, J. D. Primary stimulus generalization of the *GSR* under two conditions. *Journal of Experimental Psychology*, 1954, **47**, 52–56.

Wyckoff, L. B., Jr. The role of observing responses in discrimination learning. Part 1. *Psychological Review*, 1952, **59**, 431–442.

Yarczower, M., Gollub, L. R., & Dickson, J. F. Some effects of discriminative training with equated frequency of reinforcement. *Journal of the Experimental Analysis of Behavior*, 1968, **11**, 415–423.

5

CONDITIONED REINFORCEMENT

John A. Nevin
Columbia University

Stimulus control, the subject of Chapter 4, concerns the effects on responding of the stimuli that precede and accompany responding. Reinforcement, conditioned or unconditioned, concerns the effects on responding of the stimuli that follow, and depend upon the responding. For example, suppose that a person throws a light switch in a dark room. If we inquire into the person's tendency to throw the switch under various degrees of darkness—the stimuli that precede and accompany his response—we ask about stimulus control. But if we inquire into the effects of illumination that follows the response on the person's tendency to throw the switch, we ask about reinforcement.

The reinforcers selected for study in the behavior laboratory are usually important to the bodily health of the subjects. Food, water, and escape from pain are common examples. In contrast, most daily actions of humans and animals are only remotely related to such biologically important consequences; the immediate outcomes of responding have much less obvious significance. To use a common example, signs of attention from a parent can be very important in establishing many kinds of behavior in a child. If attention is commonly accompanied by candies or relief of discomfort, a child will learn a variety of ways to attract attention—some desirable, some less so, but all strengthened by their success in producing attention. On the other hand, if attracting attention has often resulted in parental disapproval and punishment, a child will learn to keep quiet or out of sight. Thus, either producing or avoiding attention may be strengthened, depending on the events with which attention is associated.

Because attention's reinforcing effect on behavior is not intrinsic, but rather conditional upon a history of association with other events, attention is called a *conditioned reinforcer*. An understanding of the process through which events become reinforcing, and the conditions that determine the effectiveness of conditioned reinforcement, is of considerable importance in the analysis of behavior.

Preparation of this chapter was supported in part by U.S. Public Health Service Grant MH-08515 to Swarthmore College.

Given all the complexities of the natural and social environment, it is often difficult to determine whether any given instance of behavior should be accounted for by appeal to conditioned reinforcement. Moreover, important events in the past history of the organism may be unknown, so that any attempt to understand the necessary historical conditions for conditioned reinforcement is doomed to failure if we study behavior in its normal setting. Accordingly, this chapter will be confined to laboratory research, usually conducted with animal subjects in highly restricted experimental environments, which attempts to isolate conditioned reinforcement for the purpose of determining the conditions under which it is established and the mode of its action on behavior.

The process of conditioned reinforcement is inferred from two related observations. First, one must demonstrate that the event in question is in fact reinforcing. If the event—a stimulus—is presented immediately after a particular bit of behavior—a response—the organism's tendency to respond again must increase. The stimulus, then, is operationally defined as a *positive reinforcer*. If, instead, a stimulus is terminated when a response occurs, and the organism's tendency to make the response again increases, the stimulus is defined as a *negative reinforcer*.

Having demonstrated that a stimulus is a reinforcer, either positive or negative, it must then be shown that its reinforcing effect depends on an explicit conditioning procedure. For example, suppose it can be demonstrated that a rat will increase its rate of pressing a bar or lever if each bar-press produces a 1-second tone (i.e., the tone is positively reinforcing). Before the tone is identified as a *conditioned* reinforcer, we must be sure that its effect is the result of having been associated with a known positive reinforcer. The tone may function as a reinforcer in its own right, in virtue of its sensory qualities and/or its scheduled relation to responding. To control for these possibilities, it might be shown that the rate of bar-pressing to produce the tone remained very low until the rat was fed every time the tone sounded. In general, we speak of conditioned reinforcement when two conditions are satisfied: (1) The stimulus in question must have a history of association with a known reinforcer; and (2) the stimulus must be shown to increase the probability of a response which produces it (if associated with a positive reinforcer), or a response which terminates it (if associated with a negative reinforcer), relative to responding in appropriate control conditions.

CONDITIONED REINFORCEMENT DURING EXPERIMENTAL EXTINCTION

Many psychologists feel that the action of conditioned reinforcers is best studied when all other sources of reinforcement have been removed from the experimental situation. In general, then, the pairing of primary reinforcement with the stimulus to be tested as a conditioned reinforcer must be discontinued before its reinforcing effect is evaluated. Under such conditions, experience dictates a gradual weakening of the effects of conditioning (extinction), so that the conditioned reinforcer is evaluated while it is losing its strength.

Positive conditioned reinforcement

We turn now to a detailed examination of an experiment which attempted to evaluate positive conditioned reinforcement by using a previously neutral stimulus (S_1) to strengthen a response during extinction. This study (Bersh, 1951) was concerned with the role of the number of pairings of S_1 with a primary reinforcer (S^R). If the acquisition of conditioned reinforcing properties by S_1 bears any resemblance to other learning processes, the effectiveness of S_1 as a conditioned reinforcer (S^r) should be an increasing function of the number of pairings. Bersh sought to determine the form of this function over the range of 10 to 120 pairings, with rats as subjects.

For several days before experimentation, the rats were fed once every 24 hours, so that their hunger would be stable from day to day. The experiment consisted of four distinct phases. First, the subjects were simply placed in a chamber with a bar and a food magazine for six daily 45-minute sessions. If they pressed the bar, a light came on for 1 second. This phase determined the rate of bar-pressing before any conditioning had taken place. Technically, such responding is called *operant-level* responding. Bersh made up six groups of ten rats each, matched on the basis of their final operant levels, so that the mean number of responses in the last two sessions of Phase I was between 38.5 and 38.8 for all groups.

In the second phase of the study, bar-pressing was followed by S_1 (a 3-second light), and S^R (food) was presented after the light had been on for 1 second. Phase II served two purposes: It strengthened the bar-pressing response and at the same time paired the light with food. Various groups of rats were allowed to press the bar for light and food 10, 20, 40, 80, or 120 times. A sixth group received 120 food reinforcements with a delay of 1 second after bar-pressing, but never had the light paired with food.

At the end of this training, the groups differed considerably in bar-pressing rates, because they had received different amounts of training. Accordingly, in Phase III the bar-press was extinguished for six 30-minute sessions without light or food. This period of extinction sufficed to eliminate differences between groups, and bar-pressing returned to near its Phase I operant level.

Finally, in Phase IV the 1-second light was again made available for every bar-press. If the light were S^r, it would be expected to recondition the bar-press. Figure 5.1 shows the relation between the number of bar-presses in Phase IV and the number of light-food pairings in Phase II. The ordinate value at zero pairings is the median number of responses for the group that had received 120 reinforcements but no light in Phase II. Responding in Phase IV may be compared with operant level in the last two sessions of Phase I, or with final extinction rates in Phase III. Such comparisons use the subjects as their own controls, by taking two measures of their behavior under different conditions. Alternatively, responding may be compared with that of the group which never experienced light paired with food. All comparisons suggest that the number of bar-presses to produce the light in Phase IV was an increasing function of the number of pairings in Phase II.

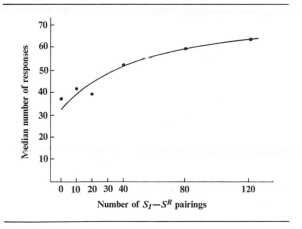

Figure 5.1 The median number of bar-presses in two 45-minute test sessions, where each response produced a 1-second light, as a function of the number of light-food pairings during bar-press training. (From Bersh, 1951.)

But does this permit the conclusion that the effectiveness of S^r increased with the number of pairings? Consider first the other possible functions of S_1, especially its discriminative functions. In Phase II bar-pressing produced food when it also produced light; in Phase III bar-pressing produced neither food nor light. This process should make response-produced light a discriminative stimulus $(S+)$ for further bar-pressing. Thus, when the light was again produced by responding in Phase IV, additional responses may be attributable to the fact that S_1 functioned as a discriminative stimulus and possibly not as an S^r at all.

Intuitively, we can think of the situation in this way: Phase IV was more similar to Phase II, in which S^R was available, than to Phase III, in which S^R was not available. Numerous studies of stimulus control have shown that the rate of responding in a test situation tends to increase as a function of increasing physical similarity between the test stimulus and that which accompanied reinforcement. If the amount of generalization between Phase II and Phase IV is related to the number of reinforcements in Phase II (see Chapter 4), one need not conclude that the function in Figure 5.2 is descriptive of conditioned reinforcement.

There is a second sense in which S_1 is an $S+$. In Phase II approaching the magazine was reinforced with food only in the presence of light. When the rat presses the bar in Phase IV and turns on the light, the light should function as $S+$ for approaching the food magazine. If the food magazine is near the bar, the rat's movements in the vicinity of the magazine may result in additional bar-presses. Thus, S_1 may function in either of two ways as $S+$ to produce bar-pressing.

Another source of difficulty arises from the finding that general activity may be enhanced in the presence of a stimulus that has been previously paired with food, as demonstrated by Gilbert and Sturdivant (1958). They gave rats food sprayed with oil of anise and later found that the animals were more active in an anise-scented tilt box than rats that had not had anise on their food. In Bersh's (1951) experiment, the light may have functioned similarly to raise the general level of activity, and bar-pressing may have resulted from this activity in and of itself. Again, the effects of S_1 as a discriminative stimulus for magazine-approach or as a stimulus for general activity may be functionally related to the number of pairings. Since it is not at all clear how the other effects of S_1 would interact with its apparent effect as a conditioned reinforcer, no conclusions about the relation between number

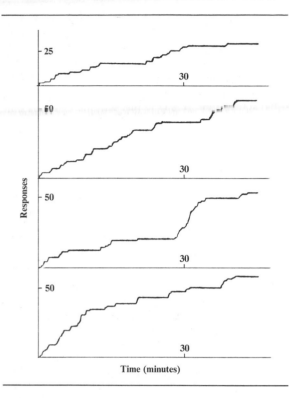

Figure 5.2 Cumulative records of bar-pressing by four rats, where each bar-press was followed by the sound of the food magazine but no food. The bar-press had no prior history of reinforcement. (From Skinner, 1938.)

of pairings and conditioned reinforcement can be drawn.

Yet another factor which may increase bar-pressing during extinction is the very fact that primary reinforcement is no longer given. A number of studies have shown that nonreinforcement in a situation formerly associated with regular reinforcement actually enhances responding, presumably as a result of the familiar emotion known as *frustration*. Perhaps the best known experimental demonstration of this frustration effect was performed by Amsel and Roussel (1952). They trained rats in a double runway, with food reinforcement given when the rats had run the first half of the runway and again at the end of the second half of the runway. When reinforcement at the end of the first half was discontinued, running speeds in the second half increased markedly. This has been interpreted as a general energizing effect of nonreinforcement. It is also widely assumed that frustration resulting from nonreinforcement is

aversive; indeed, some theories of extinction are based on the notion that organisms will avoid stimuli that are associated with extinction (Amsel, 1962).

The frustrative effect of nonreinforcement is relevant for conditioned reinforcement in two ways. First, when S_1 was presented for bar-pressing, and the rat then moved to the magazine for food, the absence of food may have resulted in the enhanced general activity characteristic of frustration. It may be that the increased rate of bar-pressing resulted from this increase in activity. Second, once the rat experienced nonreinforcement in the presence of S_1 the stimulus may actually have acquired aversive rather than reinforcing properties. This question will be considered again later in this chapter. For now, it suffices to note that the removal of primary reinforcement during the test for conditioned reinforcement may have effects which seriously complicate the evaluation of conditioned reinforcement.

These uncertainties of interpretation introduce a temptation to dismiss the notion of conditioned reinforcement altogether. However, other methods of studying conditioned reinforcement have been used, and they may avoid these difficulties. We can bypass the first problem by pairing S_1 with S^R without requiring a bar-press. Since the bar-press is never followed by food, increases above operant level when the response produces S_1 cannot be attributed to discriminative control of the response by S_1. In fact, one of the earliest demonstrations of conditioned reinforcement used this so-called new response method. It was described by Skinner in *The Behavior of Organisms* in 1938.

Skinner studied rats in a chamber with a lever and an automatic pellet dispenser. Preliminary procedures included food deprivation, a period of adaptation to the apparatus, and the periodic discharge of food from the magazine with the lever disconnected so that presses were ineffective. Skinner's (1938) description of this demonstration follows:

> The usual preliminary procedure was carried out with four rats, as a result of which they came to respond readily to the sound of the magazine by approaching the food tray. Sixty combined presentations of the sound and food were given. On the day of conditioning the magazine was connected with the lever but was empty. For the first time in the history of the rat the movement of the lever produced the (hitherto always reinforced) sound of the magazine, but no responses were

ultimately reinforced with food. The four result-ing curves are given [see Figure 5.2]. The sound of the magazine serves to reinforce the response to the lever so that a considerable number of responses are made [p. 82].

The number of responses was substantially greater than the number expected in a comparable period of operant-level responding. Accordingly, it appears that the lever-press was reinforced by the magazine sound alone.

Skinner's procedure does not exclude the possibility that the magazine sound may increase lever-pressing by its effects on general activity in the vicinity of the magazine. In order to control for these effects of S_1, it is necessary to exclude S_1 itself from the test situation. It is possible to do this, because reinforcement is expected to establish a certain resistance to extinction that can be measured some time after the termination of reinforcement. Thus, if S_1 is in fact S^r, a response that has produced S_1 should be more likely to occur than a response that has not produced S_1, even after S_1 is no longer available.

An experiment by Crowder, Gay, Fleming, and Hurst (1959) was based on this reasoning. In the first phase of their study, hungry rats were given 100 presentations of food. Each pellet was preceded by S_1, a 1-second buzzer-light combination. After this training, the rats were separated into two groups for Phase II. One group, the experimental rats, could press a lever to produce S_1. Each rat in the second group was paired with an experimental rat and received S_1 whenever its experimental partner pressed the lever, regardless of its own behavior. This is the useful yoked control technique, which we have encountered before in this volume. In this case, the yoked rats experienced S_1 at times uncorrelated with lever-pressing. Phase II ended after the experimental rats had produced S_1 20 times. On the following day, in the third phase of the experiment, all rats were given a 50-minute session with the lever available, but S_1 was never presented. The experimental rats consistently made more lever-presses than their yoked part-ners, indicating that S_1 had functioned as S^r during Phase II. The response differences between the two groups cannot be attributed to any other function of S_1, because it was not present when the difference was observed.

In the study, a fairly high operant level was needed in Phase II, so that the subjects would be exposed to S_1. There is usually a good deal of variability in both the frequency and topography of operant-level responding; this variability may ob-

scure weak S^r effects. A well-established response may be less variable. One may avoid the difficulties in interpretation of S^r with established responses, such as those considered in Bersh's (1951) study, by manipulation of the contingency between the response and the stimulus to be tested. For example, Kelleher (1961) trained two pigeons to peck a key on a 5-minute fixed-interval schedule of reinforcement (*FI*-5), with the distinctive sound of the magazine accompanying availability of grain reinforcement. The key-peck was then extinguished by withholding food. During extinction, the magazine sound was presented either following a fixed number of responses (*FR*) or after a short period without a response (*DRO*). On a *DRO* schedule, reinforcement is presented regularly in time, every t seconds, unless a response occurs. Each response postpones the next reinforcement t seconds from the response. Under both conditions, the magazine sound occurred much more frequently than in training on *FI*-5, but the rates of responding were very different. Fairly steady low-rate responding was maintained under a 10-second *DRO* requirement; when the schedule was changed to *FR*, response rates increased rapidly to a level roughly double that maintained under *DRO*. This effect could be reversed several times within a single session. Generalization from training on *FI*-5 clearly cannot account for this difference, and the maintenance of low rates by *DRO* is opposed to the expected effects of general activation. Kelleher noted that the rates and patterns of responding were generally similar to those produced by comparable schedules of S^R, thus providing evidence of the functional similarity of conditioned and unconditioned reinforcement.

Negative conditioned reinforcement

Thus far we have considered the strengthening of a response which produces a stimulus that has been paired with a positive primary reinforcer, such as food or water. If a stimulus has been associated with the onset of a negative primary reinforcer (S^{-R}) such as a painful electric shock, it may become a negative conditioned reinforcer (S^{-r}), which will strengthen a response that permits the subject to escape from it.

A well-known demonstration of negative conditioned reinforcement, performed by Miller (1948), used a *discrete-trials* technique in which the experimenter controls the animal's opportunity to respond by removing the subject from the apparatus, or otherwise blocking the response. A common measure of responding in such procedures is the time from beginning of a response opportunity (a trial) to the occurrence of the response. This interval is termed the *latency* of the response. Miller used the reciprocal of the latency (speed) as the measure.

Rats served as subjects in a two-compartment shuttle box, the halves of which were separated by a door. One compartment was painted white and had a grid floor for administering shock; the other compartment was black and had a smooth floor. The procedure involved five phases: First, the rats were placed in the shuttle box with the door open and were allowed to wander freely. No preferences for either half were noted. Next, the rats were placed in the white compartment and shocked briefly every 5 seconds while the door remained closed. At the end of 60 seconds of this treatment, the rats were given continuous shock and the door was dropped, allowing them to escape into the black compartment. Nine additional escape trials were given, and all subjects learned to escape rapidly from the white compartment.

In the third stage of the experiment, shock was discontinued and the rats were simply placed in the white compartment and allowed to escape to the black compartment. They continued to run rapidly into the black compartment, even though S^{-R} no longer occurred.

The fourth stage of the experiment required the rats to make a new response to open the door and permit escape. Sixteen trials were given in which door opening depended on a turn of the wheel in the white compartment. Thirteen of the 25 subjects succeeded in turning the wheel within 100 seconds after placement in the white box; the remaining 12 crouched, urinated, defecated, bit at the floor grid, and exhibited other signs of high emotionality, but did not turn the wheel. After 100 seconds without responding they were removed. The 13 rats which made the response, did so with increasing speed on successive trials (see Figure 5.3). Escape through the open door usually followed the wheel-turn immediately.

Finally, the wheel-turn was made ineffective, and the rats were required to press a bar in order to drop the door. Under these conditions, the wheel-turning response extinguished, while the speed of bar-pressing increased in a manner virtually identical to the strengthening of wheel-turning in the previous phase. These effects, also shown in Figure 5.3, clearly indicate that escape from the white box was reinforcing; in other words, the box functioned as S^{-r}.

In this demonstration, shock served two functions. It was a *UCS* eliciting pain and a variety of diffuse autonomic nervous system responses associated with strong emotion. The white box clearly became an effective *CS* for at least some portion of these responses, producing the crouching and emotionality described by Miller. Shock also functioned as S^{-R} in establishing the operant behavior of escaping into the black box. Since escape was possible only when the door was open, the sight and sound of the door being dropped could

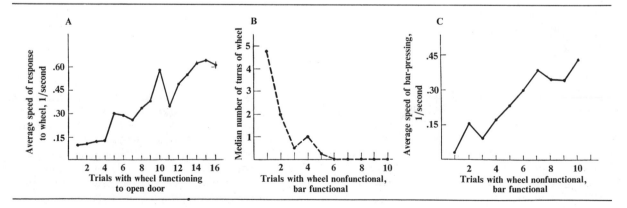

Figure 5.3 Panel A: Learning to turn a wheel to escape from a white box which had a history of association with shock. Each point is the average speed for the 13 rats which made the response. Panel B: Extinction of wheel-turning when a bar-press, rather than wheel-turning, was required for escape from the white box. Data are medians for 13 rats. Panel C: Learning to press the bar to escape from the white box, while the original wheel-turning response was undergoing extinction. Data are average speeds for 13 rats. (From Miller, 1948.)

function as $S+$ for running toward and through the door.

The interpretation of conditioned reinforcement in this study is fairly straightforward. In the fourth and fifth phases of the experiment, turning the wheel or pressing the bar resulted in lowering the door, a well-established cue for escape from the white box. Thus the $S+$ function of dropping the door removed the rat from the situation so that no further responding could occur. In addition, the emotionality produced by the white box resulted in crouching and other behavior that competed with, rather than facilitated, the operant being studied. Thus, neither the $S+$ nor the CS functions of stimulation could be regarded as contributing to wheel-turning or bar-pressing. Neither of these responses was ever strengthened by escape from shock (S^{-R}), so there was no generalization from original training for these responses. Therefore, the function of the white box as S^{-r} is not confounded with its other functions.

Comparison of positive and negative conditioned reinforcement

There has been a widespread feeling among experimental psychologists that positive and negative conditioned reinforcement are quite different phenomena. One reason for this belief seems to be the rather small and transitory effects usually obtained with positive conditioned reinforcement, compared with the powerful and durable effects of negative conditioned reinforcement.

The effects of negative conditioned reinforcement are usually studied within the setting of classical avoidance experiments (see Chapter 7), in which the subjects are presented with an aversive stimulus (usually shock) preceded by a warning stimulus of some sort. If a designated response occurs after the onset of the warning stimulus, but before shock, the shock is not delivered, and usually the warning stimulus is turned off. Many investigators have preferred to account for the acquisition and maintenance of avoidance behavior by reference to the warning stimulus as S^{-r}, rather than to reinforcement resulting from the nonoccurrence of shock, since the nonoccurrence of something does not have any obvious stimulus properties. A number of studies have shown that avoidance behavior is not only acquired rapidly, but is also highly resistant to extinction when shock is turned off permanently (e.g., Solomon, Kamin, & Wynne, 1953). Although not all studies of avoidance behavior yield such enduring con-

ditioning, the fact remains that most reported studies in which S^{-r} is involved indicate powerful effects, while most reported studies of positive conditioned reinforcement have yielded weak and transitory effects. Moreover, these effects are often confounded with other aspects of the experimental procedure. In an article primarily concerned with higher-order conditioning of respondents, Razran (1955) summarized a common view of positive conditioned reinforcement:

> As an isolated force, secondary reinforcement is, too, as any mere inspection of the data of its several experiments reveals, very impermanent, very extinguishable, and quite ancillary and immediately dependent upon primary reinforcement [p. 330].

The difficulties involved in establishing strong and durable positive conditioned reinforcement that will not be confounded by other stimulus functions are not insuperable. Kelleher's (1961) study, reviewed above, is a clear demonstration of the power of schedules of positive conditioned reinforcement. Another important demonstration, described by Zimmerman (1959), was based on a two-phase procedure involving discrete trials in a runway. In the first phase, food-deprived rats were released from the start-box 2 seconds after a buzz sounded. Initially, food was available at the far end of the runway on every trial. As the running response became well established, the availability of food was gradually reduced so that, by the end of training, it was given only every fourth or fifth trial on the average. After 93 training trials, the second phase began during which the food reinforcement was terminated altogether and a bar was inserted in the start-box. When the bar was pressed, the same buzz sounded and the door opened 2 seconds later, allowing the rat to enter the runway. Over the course of 5 bar-pressing sessions, the number of bar-presses required to open the door on each trial was gradually raised to 20, the level at which it was maintained for 6 to 10 additional sessions. A response pattern typical of fixed-ratio reinforcement schedules developed and was maintained for several sessions, with initial latencies becoming very long after the tenth session. The performance of one rat is shown in Figure 5.4.

An identically trained control group was used to determine whether bar-pressing could be attributed to general activation resulting from confinement in the start-box. During the second phase of the experiment, buzz and release from the start-box were given on a schedule matched to that of

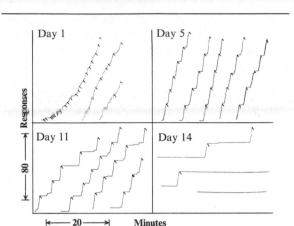

Figure 5.4 Cumulative records of bar-pressing by a rat to gain access to a runway, which was formerly associated with food. The number of bar-presses to produce the conditioned reinforcer was gradually increased during the first session; thereafter, the requirement was 20 responses per trial. (From Zimmerman, 1959.)

the experimental rats, if the control rats had not responded for 10 seconds. Each bar-press postponed release for 10 seconds. This group did little bar-pressing, demonstrating that the effect depended on the contingency between bar-pressing and release. A second control group received similar exposure to the runway in Phase I, but did not receive food at any time. This group also showed little tendency to press the bar in Phase II, demonstrating that a history of primary reinforcement in the runway was necessary to establish durable bar-pressing.

Replications by other experimenters have indicated that bar-pressing was not reinforced by the buzz, functioning as S^r, but depended rather on escape from the start-box (e.g., Wike, Platt, & Knowles, 1962). However, this possibility was adequately controlled in Zimmerman's own work. His demonstration must be accepted as evidence of a strong and durable S^r, although the necessary conditions for his result have not been fully specified.

Note the similarity between Zimmerman's and Miller's demonstrations. Both workers began by ensuring that running from one compartment to another would be rapid and highly resistant to extinction. Then, with no further primary reinforcement, they established a new response by allowing it to produce the discriminative stimulus ($S+$) for running. As Skinner (1938) described the pro-

cedure, "the process is that of adding an initial member to a chain of reflexes without ultimately reinforcing the chain" [p. 82]. A sequence of responses is called a *chain* if each response of the sequence produces the discriminative stimulus for the next response. In Skinner's demonstration, the magazine sound was the $S+$ for the response of magazine-approach. When the bar-press produced the sound, it set the occasion for approach, which had been reinforced by food in the past. In Miller's demonstration, door opening was the $S+$ for escape from the white box; turning the wheel or pressing the bar dropped the door and set the occasion for escape, which had been reinforced by shock termination. Finally, in Zimmerman's demonstration, the buzz and door opening was the $S+$ for running down the runway, a response that had a history of intermittent food reinforcement.

In these and many other experiments which explicitly establish some form of behavior by using primary reinforcement, an essential part of the conditioned reinforcing effect may consist of the emission of the next member of the chain: approaching the magazine, dashing out of the white box, or running down the runway. In Skinner's research the magazine-approach behavior was not specifically studied, but in Miller's and Zimmerman's work it was possible to examine the relations between successive members of the chain during testing for conditioned reinforcement. It is interesting to note that in both cases, running, which had a history of primary reinforcement, extinguished before the added initial member of the chain. Miller (1951) describes the course of extinction in one of his experiments as follows:

At first the rats dash to the far end of the black compartment. Gradually they begin to stop sooner. Finally they fail to go through the door after pressing the bar [p. 451].

Zimmerman (1959) says that

The runway performance of all four experimental animals during the development and maintenance of the bar-pressing behavior followed a common pattern. On the first two test days the performance was characteristic of that at the conclusion of training, when food reinforcements were being received intermittently. Opening the starting door caused the animal to run to the goal box promptly. On the third test day, approximately the fourth hour of bar-pressing, the runway behavior began to deteriorate. Occasionally, now, the animal would fail to enter the goal box and would return to the starting box; after the eighth day this disrupted performance became the rule. . . . The animals, after shooting out of the box, would now often stop short in the runway only a few inches from the starting door. . . . However, reduction of the runway chain to this vestige had no apparent effect on the stability of the bar-pressing performance for a long time [pp. 356–357].

These observations, both made after intermittent primary reinforcement increased the resistance to extinction of the second member of the chain, suggest a strong functional similarity between positive and negative conditioned reinforcement.

MAINTENANCE OF CONDITIONED REINFORCEMENT

In the studies considered thus far, primary reinforcement was excluded from the experimental situation before the test for conditioned reinforcement was conducted. The purpose of this procedure, of course, is to give a measure of conditioned reinforcement that is not contaminated by the direct effects of primary reinforcement on the response under study. A disadvantage of this class of procedures, equally obvious, is that the conditioned reinforcing effect of S_I is undergoing extinction while the measurement is being made. There is nothing about conditioned reinforcement which necessitates the use of extinction procedures, and a number of experimenters have worked out techniques for studying conditioned reinforcement in situations where the association between S_I and S^R is maintained while the conditioned reinforcing effect of S_I is evaluated. We will consider two general classes of experimental procedures: In one, there is no contingency between the behavior under study and the pairing of S_I and S^R; in the second, such a contingency exists, and its effects must be considered in the analysis.

Response-independent maintenance in a U-maze

The importance of maintained pairing of S_I and S^R was clearly demonstrated in a study by Saltzman (1949), which introduced an experimental technique that has come to be used in many studies of conditioned reinforcement. It differs from the procedures considered earlier in that the effectiveness of S_I as S^r is measured by the subject's preference for S_I when allowed to make either a response followed by S_I or a different response followed by some other stimulus (S_0).

After depriving his rats of food, Saltzman trained four groups in a straight runway. Half the subjects in each group received food in a white goal-box, the other half in a black goal-box. Training differed for the four groups as follows: Group 1 received 25 trials with food on every trial; Group 2 received 25 food reinforced trials with 14 nonreinforced trials interspersed at random, all trials involving the same goal-box; Group 3 received 25 food-reinforced trials in one goal-box, with 14 randomly distributed nonreinforced trials using the other goal-box; and Group C was a control group trained identically to Group 1. In effect, this training gave all groups the same number of pairings of S_I, the white or black box, with S^R. For Group 2, the pairing was intermittent; for Group 3, S_I could function as $S+$ for entering the box and approaching the food dish, while the other goal-box color was $S-$.

During their last training session, all rats were given three trials in a U-shaped maze with gray goal-boxes at the ends of both arms. The purpose of this test was to determine any unconditioned preferences for one side or the other.

To determine whether S_I could function as S^r, all animals were given 15 trials in the U-maze; the goal-box that had been associated with food during runway training was placed on the nonpreferred side of the maze, and the other goal-box was placed on the opposite side. No food was available for this test, except to Group C, which was tested in the U-maze with identical goal-boxes but with food on the nonpreferred side. If S_I had become a conditioned reinforcer, the rats of Groups 1, 2, and 3 would be expected to reverse their original preferences and learn to go to the side with S_I. Selection of the S_I arm of the maze on at least 8 of the 15 trials would indicate that such learning had taken place. This score could be compared with that of Group C, which learned the maze for primary reinforcement. The mean numbers of choices of the side leading to the box formerly associated with food, or to food for Group C, are summarized in Table 5.1 (Experiment I). These results suggest that the goal-box had become S^r for all three groups and that its effectiveness could be enhanced by intermittent pairing or discrimination training. It is interesting to note that the latter procedure, used with Group 3, was as effective as food reinforcement.

In a second experiment, Saltzman gave exactly the same training to three more groups of rats, but testing differed in that food-reinforced runway trials were interpolated between U-maze test trials.

Experiment I		Experiment II
Group 1	8.3	11.5
Group 2	9.0	10.4
Group 3	10.7	11.6
Group C	10.0	—

Table 5.1 The average number of turns out of 15 trials in a U-maze toward a goal-box that had been associated with food in a runway. In Experiment I, the U-maze test was conducted after termination of pairing of food with the goal-box; in Experiment II, trials with food in the runway were interpolated between test trials in the U-maze. Group C learned the maze for food reinforcement. (After Saltzman, 1949.)

The results, shown in Table 5.1 (Experiment II), indicate that continued pairing with S^R during testing produced U-maze learning that was at least as good as that with food reinforcement for all three groups, and completely overcame the differences in previous training history. Since this pairing occurred quite independently of the behavior in testing, the U-maze choices cannot be explained on the basis of confounding effects of primary reinforcement.

Despite its effectiveness in Saltzman's study, the usefulness of this technique in extended studies is doubtful. Consider the sequence of stimuli to which the subjects were exposed: On runway trials running was reinforced with food, but on maze trials the rats did not obtain food. The maze should therefore function as $S-$ for running, with the result that after prolonged training on alternated runway and maze trials, the rats should simply stop running in the maze.

Concurrent scheduling of primary and conditioned reinforcement

Zimmerman (1963) has described a related procedure in which it appeared that responding could be maintained indefinitely by S^r. In his experiment, a pigeon was confronted with two response keys. Pecking the left-hand key produced 4 seconds' access to grain on a variable-interval schedule with a mean interval between reinforcements of 3 minutes (VI-3). Pecking the right-hand key produced all the stimuli associated with availability of grain—the sound of the magazine, illumination of the feeder light, and darkening of the key and house lights—but was never followed by S^R, since the operation of the grain magazine was so brief (0.5 seconds) that the bird could not con-

sume any food. Furthermore, the schedule of reinforcement on the right-hand key was entirely independent of the schedule of food reinforcement on the left-hand key: regardless of what the bird did on the right-hand key, pecking the left-hand key was reinforced with food on an average of every 3 minutes. This general procedure is known as a *concurrent* schedule of reinforcement (see Chapter 6).

Initially, the schedules on the two keys were both VI 3-minutes. Both pigeons exhibited low but steady rates of responding on the right-hand key, which produced only S^r. Zimmerman reported that behavior of this sort could be maintained for months of daily experimentation, as long as food was available for pecking the left-hand key. However, when the left-hand key response no longer produced food, thus breaking the pairing between S_l and S^R, the right-hand key response extinguished rapidly.

In experimental situations of this sort, it is possible that one response may be strengthened by an accidental relation to the delivery of S^R. Suppose that the bird has pecked the left-hand key several times and has not received reinforcement. It then pecks the opposite key once or twice, finally switching back to the left-hand key, and food is presented. It seems likely that this food reinforcement would strengthen not only pecking the left-hand key, but also the immediately preceding behavior: pecking the right-hand key and switching. As such, pecking the right-hand key would be an example of *superstitious behavior*, responding that was strengthened by reinforcement through chance arrangements in the experiment, and not because of an experimentally programmed contingency. To demonstrate that pecking the right-hand key was in fact maintained by S^r and not by a superstitious contingency with S^R on the left-hand key, Zimmerman varied the schedule of reinforcement on the right-hand key while keeping a constant VI-3 schedule of reinforcement on the left. Among the schedules he examined were extinction (i.e., pecking the right-hand key had no effect) and FR-10, in which every tenth peck on the right-hand key produced S^r. When extinction was programmed for responding on the right-hand key, the rate on that key fell to near zero; when FR-10 was programmed, responding on the right-hand key increased and took on a characteristic fixed-ratio pattern, with pauses after each presentation of S^r followed by steady responding at a fairly high rate. The fact that the level and pattern of responding on the right-hand key could be altered by changing the right-hand key schedule, while the left-hand key schedule remained constant, is a clear demonstration of the independence of these two responses. Thus, it appears that the effectiveness of the magazine operation as a conditioned reinforcer could be maintained indefinitely by occasional pairings of the magazine stimuli with food, without any confounding by a contingency, either superstitious or programmed, between the response being studied and food.

Further research with a related procedure has been reported by Zimmerman, Hanford, and Brown (1967). Food-deprived pigeons were presented with grain reinforcement every 3 minutes on the average, but only if they had not pecked the response key within 6 seconds. If food was scheduled to be presented less than 6 seconds after a key-peck had occurred, the presentation was postponed until 6 seconds without a key-peck had elapsed. At the same time, it was arranged that key-pecking would sometimes produce all the stimuli correlated with grain for 0.5 seconds, but food could not be obtained on these occasions because a transparent shutter blocked access to the grain magazine. Thus, pecking produced S^r, while S^R followed some behavior other than key-pecking.

The response key was illuminated alternately for 24-minute periods with blue and yellow light. When the key was blue, pecking produced S^r on a VI 1-minute schedule. When the key was yellow, a different VI schedule was in effect. This is termed a *multiple* schedule of reinforcement (see Chapter 6), a procedure which has been employed extensively with primary reinforcement. The S^r schedule in the presence of yellow was variously VI-1, VI-3, VI-6, VI-12, or extinction—that is, S^r was never available. However, it should be kept in mind that the same schedule of grain presentation was programmed throughout both blue and yellow, without regard for the schedule of S^r for key-pecking. Each S^r schedule remained in effect until performance became stable. For all pigeons, the rate of key-pecking in the presence of yellow was directly related to the frequency of S^r provided by the VI schedule. This result, averaged for the four pigeons, is displayed in Figure 5.5. This systematic dependency of response rate on the S^r schedule demonstrates that key-pecking was in fact maintained by S^r, and not indirectly by S^R. Throughout the experiment, grain could be obtained with a 6-second delay after key-pecking, but since this contingency was constant, there should have been no systematic variation in responding if S^R were a major determinant of performance.

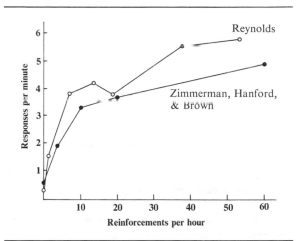

Figure 5.5 The average rate of key-pecking by pigeons to produce grain magazine stimuli, but no food, as a function of the number of times per hour the magazine stimuli were available on VI schedules. Magazine stimuli and food were given every 3 minutes on the average, but only if no key-peck had occurred for 6 seconds. (After Zimmerman, Hanford, & Brown, 1967.) Average response rates by pigeons for food reinforcement in a similar experiment with VI schedules have been divided by ten and plotted for comparison of function forms. (After Reynolds, 1963.)

In addition, this relationship suggests that the frequency of S^r affects performance in much the same way as the frequency of S^R in other experiments. Reynolds (1963) studied the effects of frequency of food reinforcement in multiple VI schedules with pigeons as subjects (for a description, see Chapter 6). Average response rates on the varied schedule in his Experiment I are also plotted in Figure 5.5. There is considerable similarity in the forms of the two functions. Thus, the work of Zimmerman and his associates has demonstrated that primary and conditioned reinforcement are functionally similar in at least two ways: The pattern of responding depends on the type of S^r schedule, and the average rate of responding depends on the frequency of S^r in the same way as in schedules of primary reinforcement.

Token reinforcement

Another method for maintaining the strength of a conditioned reinforcer is known as *token reinforcement*. In this work, the subject, usually a chimpanzee, is first trained to insert poker chips into a vending machine that dispenses food, thus effectively pairing the poker chips with food. The poker chips are then used as S^r to establish or maintain a variety of behaviors. Typically, the subject works for poker chips in one portion of the procedure and later exchanges them for food under different stimulus conditions. The effect of the poker chips as S^r is maintained by continued pairing with S^R, even though this pairing may take place in a situation quite different from that in which the reinforcing effect of the tokens is assessed. Indeed, Wolfe (1936) has shown that token-reinforced behavior may be maintained satisfactorily even though the exchange of tokens for food is delayed for an hour or more, provided that the subjects are allowed to keep the tokens and handle them during the delay interval. The whole procedure has much in common with Saltzman's (1949) second experiment in which opportunities to exchange tokens for food are interpolated between tests of the reinforcing effectiveness of the tokens. There is, however, one very important difference: The chimpanzees working for tokens cannot receive S^R unless they perform appropriately on test trials and earn the requisite number of tokens to gain access to the vending machine. To make token reinforcement analogous to Saltzman's work, the subjects might be given some fixed number of tokens to use in the "Chimp-o-mat" regardless of the number earned in the test session. No experiments of this sort seem to have been performed; it would be interesting to see if the tokens would be as effective in maintaining test performances under these conditions as in the usual procedure.

In addition to demonstrating that tokens would serve as effective reinforcers despite long delays before exchange is permitted, Wolfe (1936) found that his chimpanzees would work nearly as hard for tokens (with immediate exchange) as for food; that they would discriminate between tokens that would operate the vending machine and those that would not; and that they would choose a token giving access to two pieces of food rather than an alternative that produced only one piece of food in exchange.

All of Wolfe's test procedures involved well-established responses. Cowles (1937) extended his work to several standard learning problems, such as selecting one of several alternative positions, visual discriminations of size and color, and spatial delayed responses. In the latter situation, the subject watches while the experimenter places a token in one of two identical boxes and then covers the boxes for a delay period. After the delay period,

during which the subject has no differential cues to the location of the token, the experimenter allows the subject to choose one of the boxes. Correct choices are reinforced by the token. Under these conditions, Cowles' subjects learned the appropriate performance rapidly, with delays ranging from 1 second to 2 minutes. Performance was better when the tokens could be exchanged for food immediately than when a delay was imposed, and food reinforcement was only slightly more effective than tokens with immediate exchange. To control for the effects of token manipulation, Cowles trained his subjects to exchange tokens of one color for food, while tokens of another color could not be exchanged. He then tested the chimpanzees on the delayed-response task with a food token in one box and a nonfood token in the other. Performance was worse than under conditions with the food token alone, but was still well above chance. As Cowles notes, there may have been considerable generalization between the food and nonfood tokens.

In summarizing his work, Cowles (1937) says,

> Each of the five problems . . . was mastered by at least one animal who had not previously received food directly in the learning apparatus or even in the room in which the apparatus was located. . . . Furthermore, entire habits . . . may be completely learned in one session with food-tokens as the sole differential reinforcing agents, prior to any reception of food reward [pp. 80–81].

These token-reinforcement studies clearly meet the criteria for positive conditioned reinforcement: Their effects cannot be attributed to confounding by the behavior required for S^R, since exchange occurred after testing sessions were completed, often in a separate room and after extensive delays; and the reinforcing effects depend on a history of association with S^R and cannot be ascribed to unconditioned reinforcement by, say, the opportunity to manipulate tokens.

More recently, a series of experiments by Kelleher has brought reinforcement scheduling techniques to bear on research with token reinforcers. Using chimpanzees as subjects, Kelleher (1957) employed multiple schedules (see Chapter 6) to demonstrate that two quite different performances could be established in the presence of successive stimuli if different schedules of token reinforcement for lever-pressing were in effect. In the presence of a stimulus associated with S^r for every 20 responses (FR-20), the subjects either paused or responded steadily until S^r was presented. During presentations of the alternated stimulus, associated with S^r after a fixed interval of 5 minutes (*FI*-5), rates were initially low and increased throughout the 5-minute period. These patterns are typical of *FR* and *FI* schedules of primary reinforcement. On both schedules, the average response rates were low at the beginning of each session and increased as the session progressed.

In this and other research, Kelleher required his subjects to accumulate a specific number of tokens before they could exchange them for food. Under these conditions, the number of tokens currently possessed by the chimpanzee could take on discriminative properties: Large numbers of tokens would be a part of the stimulus complex associated with food availability, while small numbers were never followed closely by food. This discriminative effect of the number of tokens received might account for the low rates early in the session. In one experiment, Kelleher (1958b) required his subjects to accumulate 50 tokens on an *FR*-125 schedule before exchange was permitted. Again, he observed that responding was erratic early in the session, with pauses sometimes lasting as long as 2 hours. To determine whether these pauses depended on the number of tokens in the subjects' possession, he gave 50 free tokens at the beginning of a session and found that the initial pauses and erratic responding were almost completely eliminated. This is clear evidence that the number of tokens in the chimpanzees' possession had acquired discriminative control over responding. Early in the session this discriminative effect would oppose the action of the tokens as S^r, while late in the session it would combine with the S^r effect to increase response rates. Thus, it appears that although the reinforcing effect of the tokens cannot be explained by their discriminative function, it is necessary to take this discriminative function into account when attempting to evaluate the strength of the tokens as S^r.

In addition to providing discriminative stimulation, the possession of tokens clearly had other effects as well. In describing his observations of his chimpanzees, Kelleher (1958b) says,

> Informal observations indicated that the Ss were very inactive at the start of each session. They became extremely active when they had numerous poker chips, and continually manipulated several poker chips with one hand. Often, they held several poker chips in their mouths and rattled these against their teeth by vigorous head movements. All this activity was accompanied by

high rates of responding as well as the screaming and barking which usually occurred during daily feedings in the home cages [p. 288].

This state of heightened activity in the presence of stimuli associated with food has been suggested as a possible source of confounding in extinction tests for conditioned reinforcement. Its effects on responding must be taken into account together with the discriminative and reinforcing effects of the tokens.

Chained schedules of reinforcement

Token-reinforcement procedures are easily seen as instances of *chaining*. Consider the case in which a chimpanzee is required to earn a single token and may then exchange it immediately for food. The sequence of stimuli and responses may be diagramed like this:

$$S_2 \rightarrow R_2 \rightarrow S_1 \rightarrow R_1 \rightarrow S^R$$

where S_2 represents the test situation, R_2 is the response that produces tokens, S_1 represents the token plus access to the vender, R_1 is token insertion, and S^R is food. In this situation, it is clear that the token is a critical part of the compound which serves as $S+$ for the final food-reinforced response; it is also, of course, S^r for the test task. Technically, this pattern is called a *heterogeneous* chain, since the two successive responses are of different form. The chains considered earlier in this chapter were also heterogeneous, involving, for instance, bar-pressing to produce a stimulus in the presence of which the subject's magazine-approach would be reinforced with food.

Exactly the same analysis can be applied to *homogeneous* chains, in which the subject is required to emit the same response several times in succession, under different stimulus conditions, to receive S^R. For example, a pigeon might be required to peck an orange key to change its color to blue, and then to peck the blue key to receive food. Simple chains of this sort may be very useful in the analysis of conditioned reinforcement if various schedule requirements are imposed in the presence of orange and blue. For example, 1 minute after the presentation of food reinforcement, the first peck at the orange key would change the key from orange to blue. Then, in the presence of blue, food would be made available for the first peck occurring after the passage of 1 minute. The key would turn orange again after the presentation of food, and the cycle would start over again. The blue key may be regarded as S^r for pecking the orange key on *FI*-1, and as $S+$ for the fixed-interval schedule of food reinforcement. Functionally, the procedure is quite similar to token-reinforcement situations in which the test task is an *FI* 1-minute schedule and a 1-minute exchange delay is imposed. This chaining procedure can be set up with organisms of nearly any species, requiring only that the subject be able to execute some simple response repetitively. It is of special interest because it makes available sensitive measures of the discriminative and reinforcing functions of the component stimuli. For instance, one may examine the rate and pattern of responding in the presence of both orange and blue as a function of the schedules of reinforcement, or other variables which may affect S^r.

As in the case of token reinforcement, there is a contingency between responding in S_2 and the eventual receipt of food in S_1. In the preceding example, if the pigeon never responds in orange, it will never be exposed to blue and consequently will never receive food. It is possible that this indirect contingency with S^R is responsible for responding in S_2, rather than the effects of S_1 as S^r.

To evaluate this possibility, a procedure is needed in which the same contingencies prevail, but there is no change in stimulation when the subject completes the first component of the chain. A reinforcement schedule of this sort is called a *tandem* schedule. The effects of tandem and chained schedules have been compared by Gollub (1958). Among the schedules he studied were sequences of *FI*-1 schedules, as in the preceding example. One of Gollub's pigeons was trained on a tandem schedule in which food was given after two 1-minute fixed-interval requirements in succession. The key was always illuminated with S_1. When the performance appeared stable, a novel key color was introduced as S_2 during the first component. At first, there was a decrease in response rate during S_2, followed by an increase to a level above that which was maintained by the tandem schedule. A typical fixed-interval pattern of responding appeared in S_2. Gollub attributed these changes to two factors. First, rate of responding decreased in S_2 because it functioned as $S-$: Food was never available in its presence. Then, rate increased as S_1 acquired strength as S^r. It would seem that S_1 would already have some strength as S^r, since it had been paired with reinforcement throughout training on the tandem schedule; thus it may be more reasonable to account for the rate increase in terms of acquisition of the fixed-interval

performance in S_2 with continued exposure to the contingencies of reinforcement.

Gollub's comparison of chained and tandem schedules would appear to have isolated the conditioned reinforcing effects of S_1. However, the differences between performances on tandem and chained schedules may not always be in this direction, even though S_1 is a conditioned reinforcer in the chain. For example, consider the likely course of events on a tandem *FI-FR* schedule, one in which the first response after a fixed interval initiates a ratio requirement, which must be completed for reinforcement. Under such a schedule it is likely that a high rate of responding will prevail when reinforcement is delivered (see Chapter 6). A high rate of responding in the *FI* component is likely to result. If a new stimulus, S_2, is now introduced during the *FI* component, the contingencies between responding and reinforcement in the two components are quite different. Since *FI* schedules usually produce moderate rates, responding in the *FI* component may decrease even though S_1 is an effective reinforcer. The purpose of this example is simply to suggest caution in the evaluation of the functions of S_1 in chained schedules.

Referring again to the performance of Gollub's pigeon on chain *FI* 1-minute, *FI* 1-minute, there is another possible source of strength for key-pecking in the presence of S_2 which should be controlled. To the extent that S_1 and S_2 are physically similar, responding in S_2 may result from stimulus generalization. To control for this possibility, one may employ a reinforcement schedule involving the same stimuli but without the contingency between responding in S_2 and the presentation of S_1. For example, Ferster and Skinner (1957) trained a pigeon on a multiple schedule with a 1-minute *FI* schedule in S_1 alternated with extinction in S_2. The extinction periods were programmed for variable periods lasting an average of 1 minute each. After the pigeon had learned to respond at a high rate in S_1 and a very low rate in S_2, the procedure was changed to a chained schedule by introducing a contingency between pecking in S_2 and the presentation of S_1. On this chain *VI* 1-minute, *FI* 1-minute schedule, the rate of responding in S_2 gradually increased. The difference in rate between multiple and chained conditions indicates the effect of the contingency and excludes the possibility that responding in S_2 is attributable to simple stimulus generalization.

-The multiple schedule used by Ferster and Skinner effectively forced the subject to discriminate between S_1 and S_2. Another technique for insuring discrimination is to use a heterogeneous chain. For instance, a pigeon might be required to peck one key in the presence of an orange light in order to turn on a blue light on an adjacent key. Food would then be presented for responding on the blue key. Any failure of the pigeon to discriminate the component stimuli would be made obvious by the occurrence of inappropriate responses, such as continued pecking on the orange key after presentation of blue.

Before leaving the topic of chained schedules, it is interesting to consider the effects of longer chains. Gollub (1958) exposed pigeons to chained *FI* schedules of up to five components, after various kinds of preliminary training. Regardless of the training given, he found that responding was not maintained in components far removed from the terminal reinforcement. For one of his subjects, the length of the chain was gradually increased from two 30-second *FI* components to five such components. The results are summarized in Figure 5.6. The low rates of responding in the presence of the early component stimuli (S_5 and S_4) were the result of extremely long pauses, sometimes exceeding 1 hour, between responses made in the presence of these stimuli. Within each cycle of stimuli between food reinforcements, performance changed in a fashion quite similar to the within-session changes in behavior maintained by token reinforcement, described by Kelleher (1958b).

Although tandem or multiple control procedures make it clear that S_1 may be effective as S^r in a two-component chain, the status of earlier stimuli in longer chains is less clear. These stimuli are always associated with nonreinforcement and therefore may function as $S-$ to control such low response rates that S^r effects could not be seen. As in the case of token reinforcement, interactions between the various stimulus functions must be taken into account in evaluating conditioned reinforcement.

In summary, it is fairly easy to maintain behavior during the first component of a two-component chain by presenting the second-component stimulus, which is associated with primary reinforcement, contingent upon the response in the first component. To obtain a measure of S^r in this situation is not easy, however. One must take into account at least the following factors: (1) The first-component stimulus is correlated with the non-availability of S^R, and this relationship may depress responding; (2) responding during the first component may be maintained in part by the contingency between responding and the eventual

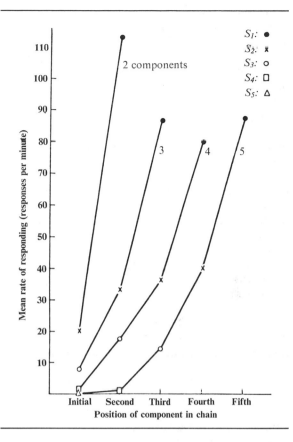

Figure 5.6 The average rate of responding by a pigeon in successive components of chained fixed-interval schedules, with a fixed-interval 30-second contingency in each component. Initially, the chain consisted of two components; additional stimuli and components were added one at a time at the beginning of the chain, so that the relation between any given stimulus and primary reinforcement was the same regardless of length of the chain. (From Gollub, 1958.)

delivery of S^R; (3) responding during the first component may be attributable in part to generalization between the first- and second-component stimuli. Taken together, these difficulties suggest that the isolation of S^r in chained schedules is no less a problem than in the more widely used extinction procedures. The advantage of chained schedules is that variations of the basic procedure can all be conducted with the same subject while primary reinforcement is maintained, so that measures of behavior under stable conditions may be compared.

Conditioned reinforcement in second-order schedules

Another procedure for the study of conditioned reinforcement has developed recently from complex schedules of reinforcement, known as second-order schedules. In effect, second-order schedules arrange a schedule of intermittent primary reinforcement for the completion of a second schedule requirement. Suppose, for example, that a brief tone is presented for bar-pressing on a 30-second fixed-interval schedule, and the tone is paired with food after every fifth such interval. This situation is closely analogous to a simple schedule requiring five consecutive responses for reinforcement (*FR*-5), except that in this case the "response" is the entire pattern of behavior within each 30-second interval, ending with the tone. Because the tone is paired with food, it is presumably a conditioned reinforcer, and its reinforcing effect can be measured by the rate and pattern of responding within the 30-second intervals.

Such a second-order schedule is similar to Gollub's (1958) chained schedule previously described, in which five consecutive 30-second fixed-interval schedules, each in the presence of a distinctive stimulus, preceded food delivery. Its most important difference is that the subject always responds in the presence of the same stimulus condition, S_2, and each interval ends with the same stimulus presentation, S_1. Thus, within the cycle of five intervals between primary reinforcements, there is no differential stimulation to complicate the measurement of conditioned reinforcement.

It is easy to arrange various control procedures to assess the role of conditioned reinforcement in maintaining the performance on a second-order schedule. For instance, Findley and Brady (1965) trained a chimpanzee to press a button on a very high fixed-ratio requirement for food reinforcement under two alternating conditions. In the presence of a red light, the subject had to respond 4000 times for food, which was presented in a magazine illuminated by a flashing light. In the presence of a green light, 4000 responses were also required, but every 400th response was followed by a flash of the magazine light. In the green condition, then, the chimpanzee was on a second-order schedule in which the *FR*-400 performance was reinforced on *FR*-10. The contingency between responding and food reinforcement was identical in the green and red conditions, but the differences in performance were striking. In the red condition, the chimpanzee usually waited more than 20 minutes before starting to respond, and occasionally stopped responding in the middle of the ratio. In the green condition, initial pauses rarely exceeded 4 minutes and were followed by responding at a high, steady rate until food was received. Evidently, performance on this demanding ratio schedule was markedly enhanced by the magazine light as S^r.

The frequency of reinforcement on ratio schedules depends on the rate of responding: The higher the rate, the more reinforcements the subject can receive per unit of time. To keep primary-reinforcement frequency constant while evaluating conditioned reinforcement in second-order schedules, it is necessary to use interval schedules, as in a study by Kelleher (1966). In one portion of his experiment, pigeons were required to peck a blue key to complete fifteen 4-minute fixed-interval schedules to obtain food. Food was always preceded by 0.7 seconds of white light on the response key. When the white light was also presented at the end of each 4-minute interval, the pigeons exhibited the standard fixed-interval pattern of responding within each interval. When the light was presented only in the final, food-reinforced interval, there was relatively little change in the total output of responding between food reinforcements, but the fixed-interval pattern was lost. This difference in the pattern of responding could be attributed to the conditioned-reinforcement effect of the white key-light. However, it is possible that the white key-light was acting in another way, providing some informative feedback to the subject by indicating the completion of each interval. The behavioral effects of feedback of this sort have received very little study and are not well understood. To separate the role of feedback from conditioned reinforcement, Kelleher (1966) programmed a different stimulus—darkening of the key for 0.7 seconds—at the end of each of the first 14 intervals, with white light and food at the end of the fifteenth interval. The darkened key had never been paired with primary reinforcement before. Under these conditions, responding was maintained throughout the period between food reinforcements, but the characteristic fixed-interval pattern of responding within each component was lost. Thus, it appeared that the brief stimulus at the end of each interval had to be paired with food in order to maintain the fixed-interval performance, demonstrating that the white light was functioning as S^r.

A number of more recent experiments on second-order schedules have demonstrated effects similar to Kelleher's (1966) findings: When a brief stimulus is scheduled at fixed intervals, and is intermittently paired with primary reinforcement, a characteristic fixed-interval pattern of responding is maintained, suggesting the operation of conditioned reinforcement. However, a number of studies have also demonstrated similar rates and patterns of responding when a stimulus is presented periodically but is not paired with primary reinforcement. These latter findings are clearly contrary to our definition of conditioned reinforcement. A recent paper by Stubbs (1971) demonstrates effects of this sort and provides a thorough review of the relevant literature.

Such findings raise important questions about the control of behavior by periodic stimuli, but they do not invalidate the concept of conditioned reinforcement as it applies to the effects of brief stimuli in second-order schedules. Rather, they indicate the need for further study of experimental conditions involving identical temporal schedules of S_I and S^R, but differing in the pairing relations between S_I and S^R. In one relevant study, Nevin (1969) trained rats to respond on one lever to produce a light on a 30-second fixed-interval schedule. A single response on a second lever turned off the light and also produced water in half of the light periods at random. The light went off, and the *FI* 30-second interval started again, if the second lever was not pressed within 2 seconds of light onset. This is a second-order schedule in which a simple chain *FI* 30-second, *FR*-1 performance is reinforced 50 percent of the time. It generates a characteristic *FI* performance on the first lever, as in Kelleher's (1966) study, but also provides an explicit discriminatively controlled second response equivalent to approaching the food magazine. For Group 1, after performance stabilized, a buzz was introduced together with the light, but only if water was available. For a Group 2, the buzz was also introduced, but only if water was not available. Thus, for both groups the light was still presented every 30 seconds, so that patterns of responding on the first lever were similar, and both groups were exposed to the sound of the buzzer and received water every 60 seconds on the average. The only difference in procedure was that the buzz was always followed by water for Group 1 and was never followed by water for Group 2. With respect to the second lever, then, the buzz was $S+$ for Group 1 and $S-$ for Group 2.

When the buzz was introduced, both groups learned the second-lever discrimination at the same rate; that is, the probability of pressing the second lever given light alone (which was $S-$ for Group 1) or light-plus-buzz (which was $S-$ for

Group 2) decreased to near-zero levels over the course of the same number of sessions. However, there was a threefold increase in first-lever response rates for Group 1, while the rates of Group 2 did not change. This large increase in responding to produce a stimulus paired with primary reinforcement, with all other factors equated, would seem to be a clear demonstration of conditioned reinforcement in fixed-interval second-order schedules. It may be that the use of an explicit second-lever response encouraged discrimination between paired and unpaired stimuli, and that such discrimination is essential for the demonstration of conditioned reinforcement in second-order schedules.

Maintenance of behavior by negative conditioned reinforcement

As in the case of positive reinforcement, it is possible to arrange for continued pairing of a negative primary reinforcer, such as electric shock, with a stimulus being evaluated as S^{-r}. This pairing could be accomplished under conditions which exclude any contingency between behavior and shock delivery, as in the work of Saltzman (1949) and Zimmerman (1963) with positive reinforcers, or under conditions which are analogous to chained schedules. An example of the latter, and a procedure for determining the effects of the contingency between responding and shock, have been described by Dinsmoor (1962).

His procedure is best understood by referring to Figure 5.7. In the presence of a distinctive signal—a tone or a light—brief electric shocks were presented to rats in a standard operant-conditioning apparatus. When the signal was on, these shocks were scheduled to occur at variable intervals, without regard to the behavior of the rat. Thus, the signal could function as S^{-r}. The rats had a bar available, and bar-pressing could turn off the signal after a variable period of time measured, from onset of the signal. Turning off the signal also prevented the occurrence of further shocks. The signal remained off for a fixed period of time; 60 seconds appeared to be the most effective period of time-out from the signal. When the frequency of shocks in the presence of the signal was varied, all three of Dinsmoor's subjects exhibited a direct relationship between their rate of bar-pressing and the average number of shocks per minute in the presence of the signal. This function is shown in Figure 5.8.

These data might be interpreted to mean that the effectiveness of the signal as S^{-r} was an increasing function of shock frequency. However, as in the

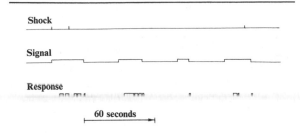

Figure 5.7 A diagram of a procedure for the study of negative conditioned reinforcement. Shocks are presented to a rat in the presence of a signal at variable intervals, independent of bar-pressing. After a variable time after signal onset, a bar-press terminates the signal and the associated shock schedule for a fixed period of time. As a control for the reinforcing effects of reducing the frequency of shocks, the procedure is run in the same way, but the signal is never actually presented. (From Dinsmoor, 1962.)

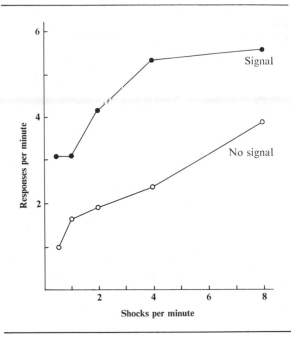

Figure 5.8 Rate of bar-pressing by rats to terminate a signal in the presence of which shock was given at variable intervals, as a function of the frequency of shock. The "no signal" function describes performance on the same procedure but with no signal, so that the only effect of responding was to terminate an irregular series of shocks. The signal, or shock series, remained off for 60 seconds. Data are means for three rats. (After Dinsmoor, 1962.)

case of chained schedules, there was a contingency between responding and shock: The bar-press not only served to shut off the signal, but also reduced the total number of shocks, relative to what the rat would have received if no responding occurred. Accordingly, it is possible that bar-pressing was strengthened by its success in reducing the frequency of shocks. To evaluate the effect of the signal, Dinsmoor programmed an equivalent of the tandem-schedule procedure. The relationship between programmed shocks and responding remained the same, but the signal was never presented. Responding during periods in which the signal would have been present was recorded and is also plotted in Figure 5.8 as a function of shock frequency. It is clear that a substantial amount of responding could be maintained simply by allowing the bar-press to reduce the number of shocks, and the function relating that behavior to shock frequency parallels that obtained when the signal was present. The difference between the heights of these functions reflects the contribution of negative conditioned reinforcement by termination of the signal.

PARAMETERS OF POSITIVE CONDITIONED REINFORCEMENT

The experiments discussed in the preceding sections have made two things clear. First, conditioned reinforcement can be a powerful factor in establishing and maintaining operant behavior. Second, the procedures for making a stimulus function of S^r, that is to say, pairing it with primary reinforcement and presenting it contingent upon a response, often lead to confounding with other stimulus functions and/or the contingencies of primary reinforcement. Ideally, the S^r function should be isolated, so that a "pure" measure can be derived. In fact, though, behavior is complexly determined by many factors, and although it may be shown that conditioned reinforcement is an important factor, no pure measure can be derived.

One goal of the science of behavior is to go beyond the mere demonstration of processes such as conditioned reinforcement, to ascertain how they depend on experimental variables. How can this goal be achieved without unambiguous measures? The only answer is to study the effects of a variable in a variety of procedures, all involving conditioned reinforcement in various ways, and to look for agreement across experiments. Variables that determine the magnitude of a behavioral effect are called *parameters*. This section will focus on parameters that have been studied in several different kinds of settings, so that the generality of their effects may be assessed. The reader should consult Wike (1966) for further treatment of these and related problem areas.

Number of pairings with primary reinforcement

One experiment on number of pairings (Bersh, 1951) has already been considered in some detail. A more recent study by Miles (1956) used the same basic technique with rats as subjects, examining resistance to extinction with and without S_1 after every bar-press. Miles had a control group, extinguished without S_1, matched with every experimental group. Different groups were allowed to receive 0, 10, 20, 40, 80, or 160 reinforcements during training, with a light and a click serving as S_1. The results are plotted in Figure 5.9. The difference between responding with and without S_1 increases as a function of number of pairings while the ratio measure remains substantially constant. However, the ratio measure is independent of number of pairings, including zero pairings. In the absence of independent data on the contribution of generalization from the training situation, one cannot be sure that the difference in fact reflects the effects of S^r.

A quite different method was used in the study of this parameter by Hall (1951). He trained rats to run in a runway for food reinforcement presented in a distinctively painted goal-box, and interpolated trials in the runway with a different goal-box and no food. Three groups of rats received 25, 50, or 75 reinforcements in one goal-box, with 15, 30, or 45 unreinforced trials interspersed. The test for conditioned reinforcement employed a U-maze, with the goal-box formerly associated with food at one end and the goal-box formerly associated with nonreinforcement at the other end. All rats were given 15 trials in the U-maze without food. The results indicated that the tendency to choose the goal-box formerly associated with food was an increasing function of the number of reinforcements.

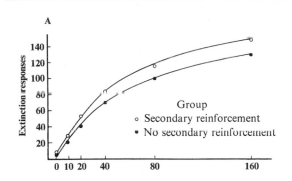

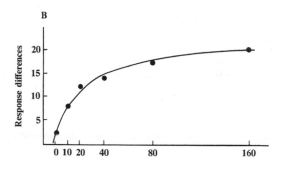

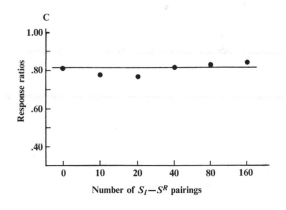

Figure 5.9 Panel A: The median numbers of bar-presses in extinction by rats given S_1 after every bar-press (secondary reinforcement), and those without S_1 (no secondary reinforcement). Each pair of groups received different numbers of S_1-S^R pairings during bar-press training. Panel B: Differences between median responses in extinction with S_1, and those without. Panel C: Ratios of median responses in extinction without S_1 to those with S_1. (From Miles, 1956.)

The training procedure in Hall's experiment clearly permitted a discrimination between the box associated with food $(S+)$ and that associated with extinction $(S-)$. Since the amount of discrimination training was confounded with the number of pairings, it may be that the results reflect an increasing tendency to avoid $S-$ rather than an increase in the effectiveness of S^r.

In summary, none of the data on the effect of number of pairings unambiguously indicates the effect of this parameter. However, the fact that all three studies indicate the same effect is at least suggestive of an increasing relation between number of pairings and the effectiveness of S_l as S^r.

Magnitude of primary reinforcement

Another variable of systematic importance in conditioning is the magnitude of reinforcement delivered when a desired response is made. This variable has been studied extensively in the runway and in the free-operant situation (see Chapter 6). It seems reasonable to expect that the amount of S^R paired with S_l during training will determine the effectiveness of S_l when it functions as S^r; at the very least, some amount greater than zero is required.

A number of studies have focused on this question. In one early study, D'Amato (1955b) investigated S^r in a T-maze with rats after training in a runway with food reinforcement. On some training trials the rats received five pellets of food in a white goal-box; on other trials, they received single pellets in a black goal-box (the colors were reversed for half the rats to control for black-white preference). After 70 training trials, the rats were tested in the T-maze with the white box on one side and the black box on the other. In 15 test trials in the T-maze, the rats turned toward the box formerly associated with the larger reinforcement an average of 8.80 times, with 18 of the 20 rats indicating a preference for that goal-box. Statistically, these results are highly significant, and they suggest that a stimulus paired with a larger magnitude of reinforcement is a stronger positive conditioned reinforcer than a stimulus paired with a smaller amount.

A study reported by Hopkins (1955) raised some doubt of the generality of this conclusion. Hopkins trained six groups of rats in a black-white discrimination apparatus with different weights of food reinforcement for each group. Amounts of food ranged from .05 grams to 2.40 grams for

correct choices of white, and one group had its food impregnated with saccharine, an effective reinforcer for rats despite its lack of nutritive value (Sheffield & Roby, 1950). After 60 training trials, during which all groups learned to choose the black compartment reliably, a T-maze test with white and black goal boxes but no food was conducted. All groups gave evidence of preferring the white box, which had a history of pairing with S^R, but there was no evidence that the extent of their preferences was affected by the amount of food or the addition of saccharine.

This negative result suggests that the conditions of training and testing may be important determinants of the role of magnitude of S^R. In D'Amato's study, all rats were exposed to two substantially different amounts of S^R in training; in testing, the stimuli associated with these different amounts were pitted against each other. By contrast, Hopkins' subjects experienced only one value of S^R, and in testing they had to choose between a chamber in which they had been reinforced and one in which they had never been reinforced. Training methods of the type used by D'Amato have come to be known as the *differential* method, while Hopkins' procedure is called the *absolute* method.

Other data on this parameter are available from other kinds of experiments involving conditioned reinforcement. For example, Wolfe (1936) found that his chimpanzees consistently preferred tokens that produced two pieces of food in a vending machine over tokens that produced only one piece of food, a result analogous to that of D'Amato. On the other hand, in a second-order schedule of reinforcement, Kelleher (1966) found that the rates and patterns of responding attributed to conditioned reinforcement declined only slightly when the duration of food reinforcement was reduced by a factor of ten for several sessions.

The discrepancies among these experiments have an analogy in studies of magnitude of primary reinforcement in simple operant-conditioning situations. Catania (1963) has shown that a pigeon's response rate is insensitive to duration of food reinforcement when the subject is trained for several sessions with a single duration, but is quite sensitive when the subject has two different durations available concurrently for different responses. Similarly, conditioned reinforcers associated with different magnitudes of primary reinforcement appear to be about equally effective if the subject is exposed to only one conditioned reinforcer in training and testing, but exert a strong differential effect if the subject has more than one conditioned reinforcer available in a choice situation.

An exception to this generalization appears in the research with rats on reinforcement by sucrose solutions. Guttman (1953) has shown that higher rates of bar-pressing are maintained by intermittent reinforcement with high concentrations of sucrose than with low concentrations, even though the subjects are only exposed to a single value of the sucrose concentration. Butter and Thomas (1958) used S^r to condition a new response during extinction and showed that the conditioned reinforcing effect of a stimulus paired with a high concentration of sucrose for one group of rats was greater than that of a stimulus paired with a lower concentration for another group. These results suggest that, in general, the magnitude of primary reinforcement will affect the strength of a conditioned reinforcer only in those experimental situations where magnitude of reinforcement is itself effective in controlling behavior.

Delay of primary reinforcement

A third variable of general importance in the study of learning is the interval between stimulation and reinforcement. Both the interval between *CS* and *UCS* in respondent conditioning and the delay of reinforcement for operant behavior have been studied extensively and have been shown to affect the rate of acquisition of conditioned responses.

There are two parametric studies which used extinction procedures to relate the strength of S^r to the delay between the stimulus and S^R in training. Jenkins (1950) used a trace-conditioning procedure with rats as subjects (see Chapter 3). The interval between offset of 3-second buzz and presentation of food was varied for five independent groups of rats over the range from 1 to 81 seconds. After 80 to 100 paired presentations of food and buzz, a lever was made available and a 3-second buzz was presented when the rats pressed the lever. Testing continued for twelve 30-minute sessions. A control group was identically trained and tested, except that the buzz was omitted in training.

The experiment by Bersh (1951) differed in that the stimulus remained on throughout the delay interval. To establish control levels of responding and to permit accurate matching of the groups of rats, Bersh started by giving his subjects six 45-minute sessions to determine operant levels of bar-pressing. During these sessions each bar-press

produced a 1-second light. The bar was then removed for the training phase of the experiment, and the rats were given 160 pairings of light and food, with the interval from light onset to food presentation being varied from 0 to 10 seconds for the different groups. The light remained on for 2 seconds after delivery of the food pellet. After completion of this training, the lever was inserted again and the rats were given three 45-minute sessions in which bar-pressing produced a 1-second light, as in operant-level determinations.

The results of these experiments are summarized in Figure 5.10. In order to make the levels of responding comparable, data from both Jenkins' and Bersh's experiments are expressed as responses per hour. Delay intervals from Jenkins' study are plotted as time from onset of the buzz to S^R, rather than offset, as in his original presentation. A logarithmic scale has been used to compress the

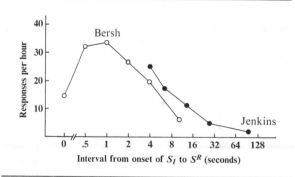

Figure 5.10 Conditioned reinforcement as a function of the time from onset of a stimulus to presentation of food. In Bersh's (1951) experiment, groups of rats were exposed to pairings of light and food, with the light remaining on until after food was delivered. The measure of conditioned reinforcement is the number of bar-presses in two 45-minute sessions where each bar-press was followed by light, minus the number of bar-presses in two 45-minute sessions of operant level. In Jenkins' (1950) experiment, groups of rats were presented with food at various times after offset of a 3-second buzz. The measure of conditioned reinforcement is the number of bar-presses in twelve 30-minute sessions where each bar-press was followed by the buzz, minus the number of responses made by a control group which had not experienced the buzz-food association. In both cases, this difference was expressed in responses per hour, and intervals are given on a logarithmic scale.

range of the independent variable. The mean number of responses per hour emitted by Jenkins' control rats during the 6 hours of testing, and the mean number of responses per hour given by Bersh's subjects during the final sessions of operant level, have been subtracted from their results. Both experiments found a systematic decrease in amount of bar-pressing when the interval between S_1 and S^R in training was increased beyond 1 second; Bersh's data also indicate a decline in effectiveness of S^r for very short intervals. In neither experiment can the intervals be stated with precision, since the time at which the subjects actually made contact with the food during training was not under experimental control.

The agreement in the slope of these functions is striking, considering the differences in method. Bersh's design used groups of rats as their own controls, while Jenkins made comparisons with an independent control group. Bersh's subjects experienced different durations of light in training and testing. For instance, his 10-second group had 12 seconds of light on each presentation in training, but only 1 second of light followed each bar-press. Through the use of the trace technique, Jenkins was able to hold stimulus duration constant throughout training and testing. Bersh excluded data after the first two sessions of testing, because of the apparent loss of differential effectiveness of the light as S^r in the third test session. Jenkins noted a similar tendency of his delay gradient to become shallower with continued testing, but included all 12 test sessions in the final results. Given these procedural differences, it is impossible to determine whether there are any quantitative differences in establishment of S^r by trace- or delay-conditioning procedures; however, it is clear that S^r depends systematically on the delay between S_1 and S^R in training. It is interesting to note that maxima in the vicinity of 0.5 seconds are often reported in studies of the *CS-UCS* interval in respondent conditioning (Chapter 3). Comparison with functions describing the acquisition of instrumental responses under various delays of reinforcement is difficult because of the importance of the method of training and the stimulation provided in the delay interval (Grice, 1948). However, a number of studies agree that acquisition is increasingly retarded by increasing delay of S^R.

Comparable results have been obtained in token-reinforcement studies. In particular, Cowles (1937) found that the accuracy of performance on a delayed-response task was reduced when a

period of time elapsed between receipt of the token and its exchange for food.

One may also study the effects of the interval between onset of S_1 and presentation of S^R in chaining procedures. Ferster and Skinner (1957) trained two pigeons on a chained schedule with a *VI* 3-minute schedule in the presence of S_2 followed by a fixed interval in the presence of S_1 terminating with food reinforcement. Three values of the fixed interval—2, 5.5, and 7.5 minutes—were used, each value of the *FI* remaining in effect until responding stabilized. In general, the rate of responding during presentations of S_2 decreased and became more variable when the *FI* in S_1 was lengthened, suggesting a reduction in effectiveness of S_1 as a conditioned reinforcer.

It should be noted here that the conditioned reinforcing effect of S_1 in a chained schedule with a fixed interval in the final component does not appear to depend on the behavior that occurs in the presence of S_1. Ferster (1953) trained a pigeon on chain *VI*-1, *FI*-1 until responding on the *VI* to produce S_1 was stable. He then arranged for the presentation of food at the end of each 1-minute presentation of S_1, regardless of whether the pigeon pecked the key. When the contingency on pecking was removed, the rate of responding in the presence of S_1 gradually fell to low levels, but the rate of responding on the *VI* schedule in S_2 remained constant. This result has been replicated by Ferster and Skinner (1957) and Neuringer (1969). It suggests that the important factor in chained schedules is the time from onset of S_1 to the presentation of S^R.

As a final example, Stubbs (1969) has explored the effects of delay between S_1 and S^R in a second-order schedule of reinforcement and found that the effect of S_1 as S^r decreased as the delay lengthened. Thus, the interval between onset of S_1 and presentation of S^R has powerful and consistent effects over a wide variety of experimental procedures.

Intermittency of primary reinforcement

Intermittency of reinforcement has been studied extensively in two rather different situations. In one, the main interest is in resistance to extinction as a function of the intermittency of primary reinforcement during training. Most of this research has employed discrete-trial methods, with intermittency determined by the ratio of reinforcements to trials. The general finding of such experiments is that intermittently reinforced behavior is much more resistant to extinction than continuously reinforced behavior (Chapter 1). If conditioned reinforcement is functionally similar, one would expect that the effect of S^r in an extinction test would be more durable after intermittent association of S_1 with S^R during training.

The other main line of research on intermittency of reinforcement has been concerned with the maintenance of free-operant behavior by various schedules of reinforcement. Here, the primary interest has been in analyzing the relations between rates and patterns of responding and the schedule maintaining the behavior (see Chapter 6). The overall intermittency of reinforcement is determined by the ratio of reinforcements to responses or by the number of reinforcements per unit of time. There has been considerable interest in evaluating the conditioned reinforcing effect of a stimulus as a function of the reinforcement schedule programmed in its presence, as indicated in the review by Kelleher and Gollub (1962). In this section, we will consider the role of intermittency of reinforcement in the establishment of conditioned reinforcers, as measured by extinction tests, and in the effectiveness of conditioned reinforcers under maintained conditions.

A representative extinction study has been reported by Klein (1959). He trained rats to run a runway, with the stimulus to be tested as S^r (a distinctive goal-box, black or white) present on every trial, but with food reinforcement on only some fraction of the training trials. Six independent groups received reinforcement on random schedules making food available from 100 percent to 20 percent of the 120 training trials. Following this training, the effectiveness of the goal-box as S^r was tested with a T-maze procedure requiring the subjects to choose between the goal-box in which they had been reinforced and a neutral gray box. The rats showed an increasing tendency to choose the box associated with food as the percentage of reinforced training trials decreased. The results clearly showed intermittent pairing with S^R acted to increase the strength of S^r in this choice procedure. Note that this effect is opposed to that expected on the basis of number of reinforcements: The 100 percent group received 120 reinforcements, while the 20 percent group received only 24. This suggests that intermittency of pairing is a powerful determinant of the strength of S^r.

The generality of this effect may be limited to the absolute method of training, however.

D'Amato, Lachman, and Kivy (1958) obtained data similar to Klein's when comparing 50 percent and 100 percent reinforcement for independent groups in a similar training and testing procedure. In a second experiment, they gave a single group of rats 100 percent reinforcement in one goal-box and 50 percent reinforcement in a distinctively different goal-box. They then tested the rats in a T-maze situation requiring them to choose between the two goal-boxes, and found a reliable preference for the goal box associated with 100 percent reinforcement. Thus, it appears that the effects of intermittent pairing of a stimulus with S^R depend on the particular condition employed.

In a free-operant study, Fox and King (1961) presented either continuous or intermittent pairing of a buzz with S^R in the absence of the bar, followed by a bar-press learning test. When every bar-press produced the buzz in testing, rats that had been trained with continuous buzz–S^R pairings made as many bar-presses as those trained with intermittent pairings. However, when the buzz was presented on an intermittent schedule of reinforcement during testing (*FI* 1-minute), rats having a history of intermittent pairing of buzz and S^R made many more bar-presses than those trained with continuous pairing. In this study, it appeared that the schedule in testing was an important determinant of the effectiveness of a variable applied in training. It is evident that one cannot generalize about the effects of intermittent pairing of S_1 with S^R without detailed consideration of the training and testing procedures.

The maintenance of conditioned reinforcement under various conditions of primary reinforcement scheduling has been studied with chained schedules. As indicated in an earlier section, chained schedules do not isolate the effects of conditioned reinforcement unless comparisons are made with performances on multiple or tandem schedules as controls. Recently, several experimenters have developed a technique for obtaining quantitative measures of S^r which may not require such controls. The technique is complicated, involving the concurrent availability of two chained schedules. In a typical experiment, a pigeon faces two response keys illuminated with white light. Pecking the left-hand key may change the key color from white to green on a *VI* 1-minute schedule; the right-hand key is darkened when the left-hand key is green. Alternatively, pecking the right-hand key may change the key color from white to red on a *VI* 1-minute schedule; the left-hand key is darkened when the right-hand key is red. Then, in the presence of green on the left or red on the right, food reinforcement is made available on different schedules. For instance, food might be available on a *VI* 15-second schedule in green and a *VI* 30-second schedule in red. These schedules would remain in effect for a fixed number of reinforcements or a fixed period of time, and then both keys would be white again. Operation of the procedure is indicated in Figure 5.11.

The way in which these concurrent chained schedules are usually programmed permits the subject to obtain all available reinforcements by distributing its responses equally over the two keys. Usually, the actual number of reinforcements received on the two keys is about equal. Accordingly, any departure from equal responding to the left or right when the keys are white is a measure of the differential effectiveness of green or red as S^r.

Early experiments within this situation have been described by Autor (1969) and Herrnstein (1964). Autor performed three separate experiments, each with different kinds of reinforcement schedules in the second components of the concurrent chained schedules. In his first experiment, one key always led to a *VI* 15-second schedule of

reinforcement in the second component; the schedule on the other key was varied from *VI* 3.75-seconds to *VI* 60-seconds. In the second experiment, variable-ratio schedules were used. The second-component schedule on one key was held constant at *VR*-40, while the other key was associated with schedules ranging from *VR*-16 to *VR*-100. In the third experiment, variable-interval schedules were used, as in the first experiment, but the pigeons were required *not* to peck the key during the second component in order to receive reinforcement. This procedure effectively controlled for the possibility of generalization of responding between the first and second component on the same key. The first-component schedules were always equal but independent *VI* 1-minute schedules. The various second-component schedules were kept in effect until responding stabilized.

In analyzing his data, Autor determined the number of reinforcements actually received per unit of time during the second components and the number of reinforcements actually received per response. The former is determined by the variable-interval schedules, but is free to vary in ratio schedules; the latter is determined by the variable-ratio schedules, but varies with response rate on variable-interval schedules. He then calculated the ratio of reinforcements per unit of time, or per response, on one key relative to the sum of reinforcements per unit of time or per response on both keys, and termed that the relative density of reinforcement. Perhaps an example would be useful here. Suppose that, in the course of a single session, the following results were obtained for responding in the second component:

	Left (red)	Right (green)
Responses	300	500
Elapsed time (minutes)	5	10
Reinforcements	20	20

The number of reinforcements per response on the left is 1/15; that on the right is 1/25. Accordingly, the relative density of reinforcement on the left, in terms of responses, is

$$\frac{1/15}{1/15 + 1/25} = 0.63.$$

The number of reinforcements per minute on the left is 4; that on the right is 2. Accordingly, the

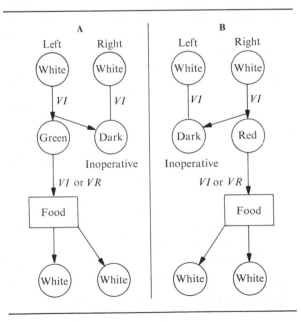

Figure 5.11 Pictorial representation of the concurrent chained schedule procedure. Panel A indicates the sequence of events when responses on the left-hand key are reinforced. Panel B represents the analogous sequence on the right-hand key. (From Fantino, 1969.)

relative density of reinforcement on the left in terms of time is

$$\frac{4}{4 + 2} = 0.67.$$

After determining the relative density of reinforcement in the second component for the various schedules used, Autor calculated the relative responding during the first component for each pair of second-component schedules. Suppose that, in the course of the session used as an example above, the subject pecked the left-hand key 900 times and the right-hand key 600 times while both keys were white. The relative number of responses on the left-hand key would be

$$\frac{900}{900 + 600} = .60.$$

The relative number of responses on one key in the first component was found to be very simply related to the relative density of reinforcement on that key in the second component. Averaged data are shown in Figure 5.12. There is almost perfect matching between relative responding and relative reinforcement density. It makes no difference, in this study, whether time or responses are used in calculating the density of reinforcement.

The experiment by Herrnstein (1964) separated these specifications of reinforcement density by programming variable-ratio schedules in the second component on one key and variable-interval schedules in the second component on the other key. When the experiment was completed, he calculated the relative reinforcement densities in terms of time and in terms of responses. When calculations were based on time, the relative rate of responding during the first component was approximately equal to the relative frequency of reinforcement in the second component, with good agreement among subjects and rather little variance around the matching line. By contrast, when responses were used in the calculation of relative reinforcement density, the data exhibited greater variance around the best-fitting straight line, and there was less agreement among subjects in the slope of the line. Herrnstein examined his data in a variety of ways and concluded that first-component responding was indeed attributable to conditioned reinforcement. In a choice situation of this sort, then, pigeons prefer the conditioned reinforcer associated with more frequent primary reinforcement, as did the rats in D'Amato, Lachman, and Kivy's (1958) second experiment. Furthermore, pigeons match the proportion of choices

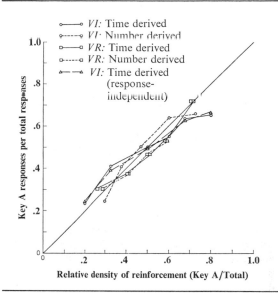

Figure 5.12 The proportion of all first-component pecks on one key as a function of the relative density of reinforcement on that key in the second component of the procedure described in Figure 5.11. The results are averages for groups of two or three pigeons. The diagonal line indicates perfect matching of relative responding and relative reinforcement. For the calculation of relative density of reinforcement, see text. (From Autor, 1969.)

of that conditioned reinforcer to the proportion of primary reinforcements available per unit of time spent in its presence.

The generality of the matching relation has recently been called into question by Fantino (1969). He explored variations in the initial-link schedules of concurrent chains like Autor's (1969) or Herrnstein's (1964) and demonstrated systematic departures from matching: If the initial links were short, the pigeons responded more often to produce the stimulus associated with relatively frequent reinforcement than the matching relation would predict; if the initial links were long, they responded to that key less often than expected. Fantino summarized these and other findings in the concurrent-chain situation by showing that the relative effectiveness of S_1 as S^r in a maintained choice procedure depended on the relative reduction in the average time to primary reinforcement signalled by S_1. This formulation encompasses much of the available data and suggests the basic importance of temporal variables, in agreement with the preceding material on the effects of delay of primary reinforcement.

OTHER PARADIGMS FOR CONDITIONED REINFORCEMENT

A stimulus associated with the presentation of positive primary reinforcement will normally function as a positive conditioned reinforcer. Similarly, a stimulus associated with the presentation of negative primary reinforcement is expected to become a negative conditioned reinforcer. What are the effects of stimuli associated with the removal, rather than the presentation, of primary reinforcement?

In the initial discussion of positive conditioned reinforcement during extinction, it was noted that the termination of primary reinforcement might be viewed as leading to the emotional state of frustration—a state which intuitively seems aversive. It is assumed that frustration can be conditioned to the stimuli in whose presence it occurs (Amsel, 1962). If so, a stimulus associated with presentations of food during training and the absence of food during testing might be either positively or negatively reinforcing, depending on various details of the experimental setting. To isolate the negative conditioned reinforcing effect of a stimulus associated with the nonavailability of food, one may arrange that a particular stimulus is consistently associated with the absence of food throughout training, while food is given in the presence of other stimuli. Because of this consistent correlation with the absence of food, the stimulus should become maximally aversive, so that a response which terminates or avoids that stimulus may be strengthened.

The converse relation can be stated for negative primary reinforcers. Intuitively, again, the removal of an aversive stimulus is not merely an absence of pain, but is accompanied by a sense of relief. If this emotional state is positively reinforcing, a stimulus associated with the offset of a negative primary reinforcer may acquire the properties of a positive conditioned reinforcer. That is, a response that produces the stimulus may be strengthened. Mowrer (1960) has discussed relations of this sort, and their importance for behavior theory, at length.

The problem of negative conditioned reinforcement based on removal of positive reinforcement has been reviewed by Leitenberg (1965), while the question of whether a positive conditioned reinforcer may be established by pairing with termination of an aversive event has been reviewed by Beck (1961), LoLordo (1969), and Siegel and Milby (1969). All of these reviews point out difficulties in the interpretation of the experimental findings of the same sort as were considered in connection with positive conditioned reinforcement at the beginning of this chapter. However, there are enough demonstrations of reinforcing effects to suggest that conditioned reinforcers can be established by the removal of primary reinforcers. To give a sense of the difficulties in this research, we will examine one experiment using extinction techniques and one using maintained pairing with the primary reinforcing event in each of these problem areas.

Removal of positive primary reinforcement

Wagner (1963) demonstrated that a stimulus associated with extinction of food-reinforced behavior in a runway could function as S^{-r} in a hurdle box. His subjects were trained in pairs to run a runway for food reinforcement that was available on only 50 percent of the trials. For the experimental rat, these extinction trials were accompanied by an interrupted light and noise; the yoked control rat was merely exposed to this compound stimulus in a separate cage and received no differential stimulation on runway trials. By the end of 116 training trials, the experimental subjects ran more slowly in the presence of the noise and light than in their absence, indicating that the stimulus compound functioned as $S-$.

After this training, 16 trials were given in a hurdle box with the same noise and light present. When the rats crossed the hurdle, the noise and light were turned off. Speed of hurdle crossing from the onset of the stimuli was measured and found to be appreciably greater for the experimental than for the control rats. Moreover, the control rats slowed down over the course of the 16 test trials, while the running speed of the experimental rats was maintained. This finding suggests that the light-noise compound functioned as a negative conditioned reinforcer because of its history of association with nonreinforcement in the runway. However, there was no control for the sheer activation of behavior that may have resulted from stimuli correlated with nonreinforcement, which Wagner demonstrated with an independent group of rats in an activity cage.

The maintainance of negative conditioned reinforcement by a stimulus associated with nonreinforcement has been studied by Ferster (1958, Experiment IV). Using chimpanzees as subjects in a two-key chamber, he made food reinforcement available on a *VI* 3-minute schedule for responses on the right-hand key. Periods of food availability lasted 45 seconds and alternated with 3-minute periods in which all lights in the chamber were off and reinforcement was not available. Responses on the left-hand key during periods of food availability could postpone the 3-minute blackouts. Postponements of 1, 2, 5, and 10 minutes from occurrence of each response on the left-hand key were programmed for several sessions each. The delivery of food for responses on the right-hand key was prevented for 7 seconds after each response on the left-hand key to avoid accidental strengthening of the left-hand key response by food. Responding on the left-hand key was maintained satisfactorily, even though there were no immediate consequences of that response. In general, the rate of responding on the left-hand key increased when the postponement was reduced, as in similar experiments on shock avoidance (see Chapter 7). Thus, it appeared that the left-hand key response was maintained by avoidance of the blackout, which was correlated with the non-availability of food reinforcement, suggesting that the blackout was a negative conditioned reinforcer.

Before this conclusion can be accepted with confidence, however, one important control would be needed. If the chimpanzees failed to respond on the left-hand key, they would receive only 12 minutes of food availability, or an average of 4 food reinforcements, in a 1-hour period. If they successfully avoided the blackout for an entire hour, they would receive 20 food reinforcements. It is quite possible that this difference in the availability of food reinforcement, rather than the function of the blackout as S^{-r}, was responsible for the maintained behavior on the left-hand key. Before maintained procedures of this sort can isolate the role of negative conditioned reinforcement, some control for the contingencies between the avoidance response and the overall frequency of primary reinforcement is necessary.

Removal of negative primary reinforcement

The reviews by Beck (1961), LoLordo (1969), and Siegel and Milby (1969) attest to the difficulty of studying the effects of stimuli associated with the removal of negative primary reinforcers. Of the studies they cite, few give clear evidence for the establishment of positive conditioned reinforcement by removal of S^{-R}. Murray and Strandberg (1965) have reported one of the clearest demonstrations. They began by training three groups of rats to escape shock by pressing a bar in a standard experimental chamber. A buzz sounded continuously during shock. For Group 1 alone, a panel above the bar was illuminated for 3 seconds after each escape response. After all the rats had turned off shock ten times, they were tested in a runway with which they had no previous experience. A buzz was turned on when the start-box door was raised and turned off when the rat entered the goal-box. Rats of Group 1, which had been trained with the light after each shock-escape response, received a similar 3-second light in the goal-box. Rats of Group 2 also received light in the runway goal-box; Group 3 never received light.

The results indicated that the light was effective as a positive conditioned reinforcer. Rats of Group 1 ran for many more trials in the runway before meeting an extinction criterion than did Group 2, indicating that a history of association with removal of shock was necessary to obtain a reinforcing effect with the light. Group 1 also ran more than Group 3, indicating that the results could not be attributed to reinforcement by termination of the buzz. It is particularly impressive that the light was able to reinforce a new response—running—in a situation quite different from that used in training. In this respect, the study is similar to Wagner's (1963) experiment, which tested for conditioned reinforcement in a hurdle box after training in a runway.

The maintenance of positive conditioned reinforcement by a stimulus associated with termination of shock has been studied by Dinsmoor and Clayton (1963, 1966). In their more recent study, rats were briefly trained to press a bar to turn off shock. A variable number of responses, averaging three, was required to terminate the shock. They were then required to press the bar, on the same schedule, to produce noise; noise and shock were terminated 30 seconds after onset of the noise. In one experiment, offset of shock was postponed if the rats pressed the bar during noise; in a second experiment, there was no contingency on responding in the presence of noise. In both cases, substantial rates of bar-pressing resulted after the onset of shock and before noise, while rates after noise onset were fairly low. When the onset of noise and termination of shock were made independent of bar-pressing, rates declined markedly, but returned to their former levels with reinstatement of the contingency.

Dinsmoor and Clayton argue that this study

demonstrates the conditioned reinforcing effect of the noise; however, they did not evaluate the contingency between bar-pressing and the eventual termination of shock. Since this primary reinforcing event was delayed by at least 30 seconds after the noise-producing bar-press, its effect may have been small. However, the situation is closely analogous to a chained schedule of positive primary reinforcement, where, as we have seen, it is necessary to evaluate the effects of responding early in the chain on the ultimate delivery of primary reinforcement. Hopefully, this work will be extended with other procedures analogous to those which maintain pairing of a stimulus with the presentation of positive primary reinforcement.

THE GENERALITY OF CONDITIONED REINFORCEMENT

These demonstrations of negative conditioned reinforcement (by a stimulus associated with removal of positive reinforcement) and of positive conditioned reinforcement (by stimuli associated with removal of negative reinforcement) raise questions about many of the studies described earlier. For example, when a pigeon responds on a two-component chained schedule, responding in the presence of S_2 produces S_1, and responding in the presence of S_1 produces food. In this situation, S_2, which is associated with nonavailability of food, could function as a negative conditioned reinforcer, while S_1, which is associated with food, could function as a positive conditioned reinforcer. When the pigeon pecks the key in the presence of S_2 and produces S_1, it is not clear to what degree responding depends on escape from S_2 or presentation of S_1.

The same sort of question can be raised in connection with Miller's (1948) demonstration of negative conditioned reinforcement. The rats learned to press a bar which permitted them to run from the white box, in which they had been shocked, into a black box, which was associated with offset of shock. Is the effect best described as negative reinforcement by escape from white, or positive reinforcement by access to black?

Questions of this sort boil down to something like this: Can a conditioned reinforcer strengthen behavior in a context of stimulation different from that in which it was paired with primary reinforcement? In the chained-schedule example, would S_1 maintain responding if some novel stimulus were substituted for S_2? Or would escape from S_2 be reinforcing if responding produced a stimulus other than S_1? Would Miller's rats have escaped as readily from the white box if they had never been exposed to the black box during pairing of shock with the white box? Or would they learn to press a bar in a wire cage in order to get access to a black box?

These are all questions of the trans-situational generality of conditioned reinforcement. The problem is closely related to the apparent circularity in the definition of reinforcement and the Law of Effect. If a reinforcing event is defined only in terms of its ability to strengthen behavior, and then the change in behavior is explained solely in terms of such reinforcement, the circularity is evident. The usual escape from this circle is to identify reinforcing events in one situation, and then use this identification to aid in the explanation of behavior in some new situation. Exactly the same reasoning applies in the case of conditioned reinforcement.

Trans-situational tests for conditioned reinforcement

Experimental tests for conditioned reinforcement may involve situations that differ in several ways from the training situation. Generally, a new response is required within a situation that is otherwise identical to that used in pairing. For instance, Skinner (1938) and Zimmerman (1959) used stimuli that had been paired with food to strengthen bar-pressing in rats when the bar-press had no previous history of reinforcement. Miller (1948) was able to strengthen one new response—wheel-turning—and then extinguish it and strengthen another new response—bar-pressing—when these responses led to escape from a stimulus paired with shock. Thus, there is no question but that the effects of conditioned reinforcement can generalize to new responses, even in the absence of continued pairing with primary reinforcement.

Positive conditioned reinforcers may also be effective in establishing new temporal patterns of responding when presented according to a schedule of reinforcement. For instance, Zimmerman (1963) made a conditioned reinforcer available on a fixed-ratio schedule after extensive training on a variable-interval schedule, and observed typical fixed-ratio behavior under the new contingency. This study represents an example of the generalization of conditioned reinforcement to a new schedule.

The generality of conditioned reinforcement may also be tested in stimulus situations which differ markedly from those in training. For example, Saltzman's (1949) demonstrations of positive conditioned reinforcement in a U-maze after training in a runway, and the use of token reinforcers to train position habits or color discriminations, are of this sort. Recent work by McAllister and McAllister (1965) with negative conditioned reinforcers provides another instance. They placed rats in a distinctive box and paired light with electric shock. They then placed the rats in a different box, presented the same change in illumination, and turned off the light when the rats jumped a hurdle and entered another box. The speed of hurdle jumping increased systematically under these conditions, indicating that the light was a negative conditioned reinforcer for a new response despite the change in the stimulus situation. The experiments by Wagner (1963) on negative conditioned reinforcement by stimuli associated with extinction and by Murray and Strandberg (1965) on positive conditioned reinforcement by stimuli associated with the offset of shock also used different apparatus and a new response in testing. In summary, it appears that conditioned reinforcement can strengthen a variety of behaviors under conditions which depart to a considerable extent from the context in which the conditioned reinforcer was established.

Perhaps we should note here that if this kind of trans-situational generality could not be demonstrated, conditioned reinforcement would be of restricted interest. In the natural world, organisms are exposed to constantly changing environmental conditions. If the effects of conditioned reinforcement could not manifest themselves under changed conditions, the concept would be of little value in the explanation of behavior outside the controlled conditions of the laboratory.

The role of motivation

One of the conditions that we have not considered is the motivational state of the organism. It is necessary to deprive the experimental subject of certain stimuli in order to make the stimuli positively reinforcing. An obvious example is that food will have no strengthening effect on a response unless the subject is sufficiently deprived of food to approach and consume it. Food deprivation may be said to create a hunger drive within the subject. In the case of negative reinforcers, the presentation of a strong stimulus such as an electric shock or a loud noise may be said to create a drive state of pain or discomfort. These internal effects are rarely measured in behavioral experiments. For our purposes, drive is perhaps best considered as a convenient term for the diverse effects of deprivation or strong stimulation, which may be specified by reference to the operations performed by the experimenter. The question we must now ask is whether conditioned reinforcement depends on these operations, as they may affect the state of the organism.

There are several experiments indicating that positive conditioned reinforcers can operate under deprivation conditions which differ radically from those in training. For example, Estes (1949) trained rats to approach a water dipper whenever the dipper mechanism sounded; during this training, the rats were deprived of water for 22 hours, but had continuous access to food. After dipper-approach was well established, a lever was introduced and each bar-press resulted in presentation of the water dipper, but without water. Some groups of rats learned the new response under 22 hours water deprivation, as in training; others learned it after 22 hours of food deprivation, during which time they had continuous access to water. The rats that were hungry but water-satiated acquired the new response in much the same way as those tested under thirst, but gave about 25 percent fewer total responses during the 30-minute test session. Estes repeated the experiment, requiring a response on a second lever to produce water during training, and obtained much the same result. Although the dipper sound may not have been quite as effective for rats tested under hunger as it was for those tested under thirst, it clearly had a reinforcing effect for both groups.

The ability of a positive conditioned reinforcer to transfer from thirst to hunger drives, and vice versa, has also been demonstrated by D'Amato (1955a). He trained water-deprived rats in a runway with water in a distinctive goal-box. He then satiated the rats on water, deprived them of food, and conducted a T-maze test. The rats responded to the former goal-box an average of 8.80 times in 15 trials. In a second experiment, the reverse procedure was used. Food-deprived rats were trained with food reinforcement in the runway and were then satiated on food and deprived of water. In the T-maze test, they chose the former goal-box on an average of 8.70 out of 15 trials. Since both results were significantly above chance, these two quite different experiments suggest that positive conditioned reinforcers can be at least minimally effective under drive conditions differing from those used in pairing S_1 with primary reinforcement.

An exception to this generalization has been suggested by Pliskoff and Tolliver (1960). After depriving rats of food and training them to press a lever for dry food pellets on fixed-ratio schedules of reinforcement, a second lever was made available, which the subjects could press to produce a 5-minute period in which food was not available. This period was accompanied by a tone and general illumination of the chamber. Presumably, silence and darkness, which were correlated with food availability, could function as positive conditioned reinforcers. Under normal deprivation conditions, with continuous access to water, the rats rarely pressed the lever that produced light and tone. However, under conditions of severe water deprivation, all four rats increased their rates of responding to produce light and tone. These data suggest that the stimuli associated with availability of dry food had acquired aversive properties: Responding that terminated those stimuli was strengthened.

This experiment differs in several ways from those of Estes and D'Amato, most notably in that dry food was available during testing, both food and water deprivation were employed, and the presumed positive conditioned reinforcing effects of the stimuli associated with food availability were never explicitly demonstrated. However, the possibility that alterations in drive might reverse the sign of a conditioned reinforcer is of considerable interest, and it deserves further investigation with other experimental techniques.

In a thorough parametric investigation of the effects of food deprivation, Miles (1956) subjected rats to a procedure described earlier. He trained rats under 20 hours of food deprivation to press a lever for food, with a stimulus preceding each food pellet. After all rats had received comparable training, they were divided into six groups and deprived of food for various periods of time before a bar-press extinction test. Each deprivation group was divided in half; one subgroup extinguished with S_1 following each bar-press, and the other extinguished without S_1. The results are shown in Figure 5.13. The amount of bar-pressing by both classes of subgroups increased systematically with increasing deprivation; the difference between subgroup medians increased; and the ratio of the medians remained constant over the entire deprivation range. It is interesting to note the similar-

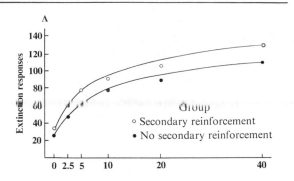

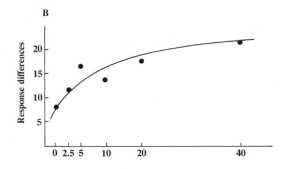

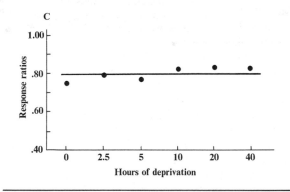

Figure 5.13 Panel A: The median numbers of bar-presses by rats during an extinction session with S_1 after every bar-press (secondary reinforcement), or without S_1 (no secondary reinforcement), as a function of hours of food deprivation before that session. Panel B: The difference between the median numbers of extinction responses with and without S_1. Panel C: The ratio of the median number of extinction responses without S_1 to the median number of responses with S_1. Each pair of groups had received S_1 and food for bar-pressing at 20 hours of food deprivation. (From Miles, 1956.)

ity of these results to those in Figure 5.9, which illustrates the effects of number of pairings.

Whether one concludes that the effect of S_1 as S^r varies with deprivation level depends, of course, on the separation of S^r from discriminative effects of S_1 and on the measure chosen. The major conclusion of this study is that conditioned reinforcement can apparently act to increase resistance to extinction even under drive levels drastically different from those used in training, including zero deprivation.

The possibility that conditioned reinforcers might be effective for satiated rats has been investigated by Seward and Levy (1953) in a complex procedure involving discrimination training in both a runway and a choice apparatus, followed by testing in a T-maze. During training, the rats were water deprived and given water reinforcement; testing was conducted with thirst thoroughly satiated. Seven sessions of three test-trials each were alternated with sessions of further training in the runway under water deprivation. The T-maze test results indicated that the rats increased their tendency to turn to the former goal-box even in the absence of thirst.

A related study using bar-pressing has been reported by Wenrich (1964). He established a buzz as S^r by presenting it immediately before release from the start-box of a runway; in the course of training, intermittency was introduced by sometimes sounding the buzzer without release. At this point, a bar was inserted into the start-box and bar-pressing was established with the buzz as S^r. Bar-pressing was never followed by release from the box or food. The bar-press was effective in producing the buzz only if a light was on ($S+$); if the light was off ($S-$), bar-pressing had no effect. (Light and dark were reversed for half the rats.) Runway trials with food in the absence of the bar were interspersed with this discrimination training to maintain the strength of the buzz as S^r. Finally, four sessions consisting of twenty 1-minute test periods were conducted; light and dark alternated regularly, with the buzz following every bar-press in light. Two of these sessions were conducted with normal food deprivation, and two were conducted after 45 minutes' access to food (which presumably sufficed to satiate hunger). All seven rats responded more often in $S+$ than in $S-$, under both deprivation and satiation, although the levels of responding were appreciably higher when the rats were deprived. This study indicates that a simple successive discrimination may be established in rats with a new response,

using S^r alone, and that the discriminative stimuli continue to control responding in states of satiation as well as in deprivation conditions.

Other studies have failed to confirm the ability of conditioned reinforcement to strengthen behavior in satiated subjects, and the necessary conditions for obtaining the effect cannot be stated with precision. However, it may be worth noting that both Seward and Levy's study and Wenrich's procedure involved discrimination training before the satiation tests; also, both studies maintained the pairing of S_1 with S^R during testing for S^r effects.

In the case of negative primary reinforcement, the operational equivalent of satiation—the absence of drive—is to withhold the negative reinforcer itself. All experiments that pair shock with S_1 and then demonstrate the strengthening of a response that terminates S_1 in the absence of shock, are, in effect, demonstrating the generality of negative conditioned reinforcement across drive conditions. Miller's (1948) demonstration was of this sort, and numerous later studies have confirmed the finding that stimuli associated with presentation of shock function as negative conditioned reinforcers in the absence of further shock.

Generalized conditioned reinforcement

In the studies just reviewed, a stimulus paired with a primary reinforcer under one set of conditions was then shown to be effective as a conditioned reinforcer when the required response, the experimental context, or the drive state of the subject was varied. In the world outside the laboratory, conditions vary not only when behavior is being strengthened by conditioned reinforcement, but also while the stimulus is being paired with primary reinforcement. Skinner (1953) has suggested that this variability may provide exceptionally effective conditioned reinforcement. If a stimulus is paired with several different primary reinforcers under appropriate conditions of deprivation, and if it precedes reinforcement within a variety of situations, it may become completely generalized; that is, it may exert powerful strengthening effects in any new situation, regardless of how it differs from conditions during pairing. The reasoning is that, in Skinner's words, "if a conditioned reinforcer has been paired with reinforcers appropriate to many conditions, at least one appropriate state of deprivation is more likely to prevail upon a later occasion" [1953, p. 77]. Further, Skinner suggests that "eventually, generalized reinforcers are effective even though the primary reinforcers upon which they are based no longer accompany them" [p. 81]; that is to say, generalized reinforcers may be extremely durable in extinction.

The concept of generalized reinforcement is an exciting extension of conditioned reinforcement, but laboratory analysis is lacking. In one demonstration, Nevin (1966) trained rats in a variety of experimental situations with food or water reinforcement under the appropriate deprivation state. A buzz always preceded primary reinforcement. After extensive training, the rats were satiated on both food and water and placed in a novel situation to determine the effectiveness of the buzz as a generalized conditioned reinforcer. In the first test session, the rats acquired a preference for responding on a lever that produced the buzz; in a second test session, they learned to respond differentially in the presence of a light ($S+$) that was correlated with availability of the buzz. However, the overall level of responding declined throughout both test sessions. The buzz had no effect in a third test session. Thus, although this study demonstrated a high degree of generality of conditioned reinforcement, using a new response in a novel situation in the absence of either training motivation and using two different tests for conditioned reinforcement, the effects were neither large nor durable. Nor were they compared with the effects of conditioned reinforcement after a history of pairing with a single reinforcer within a single training situation.

Earlier, Wike and Barrientos (1958) had shown that a goal-box associated with food and water is a more effective reinforcer for rats in a T-maze than a goal-box associated with food or water alone; however, the effect was small and depended on food or water deprivation at the time of testing. Similarly, Kanfer (1960), in a token-reinforcement study with human subjects, found that tokens associated with different prizes were more effective in maintaining performance than tokens associated with a single kind of prize; however, there was no test for generality.

Working with autistic children as subjects, Ferster and DeMyer (1962) established tokens as generalized reinforcers by arranging that they were necessary to operate a number of different reinforcing devices. For example, the tokens could be used to operate a pinball machine, a television set, a phonograph, a candy vending machine, an electric train, a slide viewer, or another vending machine that dispensed trinkets or parts of the child's lunch. The coins were then shown to be effective reinforcers for a key-pressing response on *FR*-15 schedule; subsequently, various performances requiring discriminated responding, including matching-to-sample (see Chapter 4), were established through differential reinforcement with the tokens.

Although there is no question about the powerful conditioned reinforcing effects in Ferster and DeMyer's work, they were not concerned with experimental comparisons with token reinforcement based on only one reinforcing device. They simply wanted to establish a potent reinforcer that could be administered conveniently, so that their analysis of autistic behavior could proceed.

In summary, there is at present little reason to believe that pairing a stimulus with more than one kind of primary reinforcer within a variety of experimental settings will enhance its generality or durability as a conditioned reinforcer. Nevertheless, this possibility deserves further investigation. Knowledge of the conditions for the establishment of potent, durable, and general conditioned reinforcers could be important for the understanding human behavior in a normal environment.

THEORIES OF CONDITIONED REINFORCEMENT

So far, this chapter has concentrated on the operation of conditioned reinforcement in various situations, and on the variables which determine its effectiveness. No attempt has been made to answer the question of the minimal conditions that must be satisfied in order to establish a stimulus as a conditioned reinforcer beyond the suggestion that some form of association with primary reinforcement is necessary. Nor has any attempt been made to propose a general theory of the mechanism of conditioned reinforcement from which one might predict the effectiveness of the conditioned reinforcer. In conclusion, this chapter will examine some experimental attempts to isolate the minimal conditions for the establishment of conditioned reinforcement, and some theoretical attempts to provide a systematic account of the data in this area.

The conditioned reinforcer as a discriminative stimulus or as CS

When food is presented to an organism in the presence of a stimulus, the organism engages in a variety of behaviors including approach to the food magazine, seizing the food pellet, chewing, salivating, swallowing, and the like. At least some portion of this activity—salivation, for instance— may be classically conditioned to the stimulus, while other portions that are more obviously operant in nature, such as approach to the magazine, may be discriminatively controlled by the stimulus. In an early attempt to integrate conditioned reinforcement into a general behavior theory, Hull (1943) suggested an intimate connection between these behaviors and secondary reinforcement.

> Stimuli which acquire secondary reinforcing power seem always to acquire at the same time a conditioned tendency to evoke an associated reaction. The available evidence indicates that as such stimuli lose through extinction the power of evoking this reaction, they lose in about the same proportion their power of secondary reinforcement. It is probable also that the reverse is true; that a stimulus gradually acquires its powers of secondary reinforcement as it acquires the power of evoking the reaction conditioned to it [pp. 97–98].

That is, in order to predict the effectiveness of a stimulus as a conditioned reinforcer, one has only to determine the strength of the response made in its presence.

Hull did not distinguish between the operant behavior occasioned by the stimulus as a discriminative stimulus and the respondent behavior elicited by the stimulus as a *CS*. Usually, a stimulus paired with the presentation of food will take on both functions. Although discussion in Chapter 3 suggests that the distinction is no longer useful, its history may be instructive. Schoenfeld, Antonitis, and Bersh (1950) attempted to separate these functions by presenting a light after rats had pressed a bar to produce food, taking care that the onset of light did not occur until the rats had seized the food and started eating. They reasoned that the light could act as a *CS*, since the rats were engaged in chewing and swallowing for several seconds during and after the light. However, the light could not serve as a discriminative stimulus in the sense that there was no opportunity for extinction in the absence of light, since the rats had already made contact with the food before the light came on. In a careful test, they found that presentation of the light did not serve to recondition the bar-press after several sessions of extinction; in other words, the light was not a conditioned reinforcer. This result led to the statement of the *discriminative-stimulus hypothesis* of conditioned reinforcement (Keller

& Schoenfeld, 1950): "In order to act as an S^r for any response, a stimulus must have status as an S^D [discriminative stimulus] for some response" [p. 236].

This hypothesis is weakened by the fact that it was not demonstrated that the rats, hungry and devouring their food, ever saw the light. It has also been questioned experimentally by indications that it is possible to establish a conditioned reinforcer without any overt behavior in its presence. This can be done by pairing a stimulus with a primary reinforcer that can be administered independently of the subject's behavior. For example, electrical stimulation of the brain can have powerful reinforcing effects and can be given by the experimenter without requiring anything equivalent to approach or consummatory behavior on the part of the subject.

In order to examine this situation, Stein (1958) implanted electrodes in areas of the brain which generally have positive reinforcing effects. In the first phase of his study, the rats were given six 1-hour sessions in a two-lever chamber, with all responses on one lever followed by a 1-second tone. Then, the rats received 400 paired presentations of tone and brain shock: Tones lasted 1 second, with stimulation administered during the last 0.5 seconds. The levers were removed from the chamber during this phase. The tone was then tested for its effects as S^r in the absence of further brain shock by inserting the levers and allowing all responses on one lever to produce the tone as before. Finally, the rats were allowed to press a bar to obtain brain stimulation directly, to determine whether the electrodes were in positively reinforcing sites. Results for the two-lever test were separated according to whether or not the brain stimulation was an effective reinforcer in the final phase of the study. Those rats for which brain stimulation was positively reinforcing exhibited an increase in rate and a preference for the tone-producing bar, where no preference was apparent during operant-level determinations. By contrast, neither effect appeared in the data of those rats for which brain shock was neutral. This is clear evidence that the tone functioned as S^r. The findings have been replicated and extended to intermittent pairing by Knott and Clayton (1966).

In discussing the relations between his data and the discriminative-stimulus hypothesis, Stein (1958) says,

> The operations that imparted secondary reinforcing properties to the tone in the study described in this report (that is, the pairings with

brain shock) did not provide, at the same time, the conditions favorable to its development as a discriminative stimulus. This is because the effective delivery of the brain-shock reward requires no (operant) response on the part of the animal, in contrast to conventional reward situations, which involve approaching and consummatory behavior. In a case such as this, it is hard to see how particular responses could have been selectively reinforced with brain shock in the presence of the tone to permit the formation of a discrimination. Furthermore, the brevity of the interval between tone and brain shock (0.5 second) would make the development of superstitious behavior in response to the tone unlikely. No evidence of such behavior was indicated by observation [p. 467].

The possibility remains that it is not operant behavior under stimulus control that determines the effectiveness of conditioned reinforcement, but rather some respondents elicited by the stimulus as a result of classical conditioning. The experiment by Schoenfeld, Antonitis, and Bersh (1950) did not exclude this possibility either. Although it is true that the light, presented after the rats began to eat, might not, even if seen by the rats, have been a discriminative stimulus, it might not have become an effective *CS* either. To study the relations between classically conditioned respondents and conditioned reinforcement for operant behavior, it is necessary to make concurrent measurements of both classes of behavior. Research of this sort has been reported by Ellison and Konorski (1964), among others, but no firm conclusions about conditioned reinforcement have emerged from this work (see also Chapter 3).

In connection with Stein's experiment, it is far from clear that one could isolate and measure respondent behavior elicited by the brain stimulation and conditioned to the tone. Brain shock does not usually elicit any obvious unconditioned responses, although Malmo (1965) has reported classical conditioning of heart-rate changes elicited by stimulation of the brain. It remains to be determined whether the strength of any single respondent conditioned to a stimulus paired with primary reinforcement can serve to predict the conditioned reinforcing effect of that stimulus.

Conditioned reinforcement as a source of information

Stein's (1958) research suggests that in order to establish a stimulus as a conditioned reinforcer, it is sufficient to pair the stimulus with primary re-

inforcement; no operant behavior in the presence of the stimulus is necessary. Egger and Miller (1962, 1963) have proposed that simple pairing is not by itself sufficient, but that the stimulus must be presented in a fashion that provides the organism with information about the imminence of primary reinforcement. *Informative* predictors of reinforcement are expected to acquire greater reinforcing power than *redundant* stimuli, and *reliable* predictors will be more effective than *unreliable* stimuli. Egger and Miller suggest that the informativeness and reliability of the stimuli are evident from their scheduled relations to reinforcement. Consider the situation diagramed as Procedure A in Figure 5.14. A stimulus (S_2) is presented for 2.0 seconds; another stimulus (S_1) is presented for 1.5 seconds; and both end with delivery of food (S^R). S_2 is said to provide information about imminent reinforcement, while S_1 is redundant in this case. Egger and Miller predict that S_2 will be the more effective conditioned reinforcer.

This is contrasted with Procedure B in Figure 5.14, where S_2 is sometimes presented alone, with-

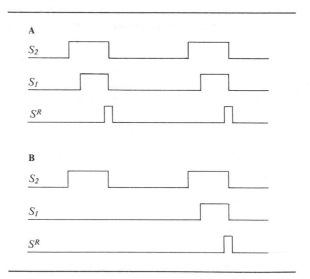

Figure 5.14 Schematic representation of the training procedures used by Egger and Miller (1962) to study conditioned reinforcement as a function of its reliability and information value in predicting primary reinforcement. In Procedure A, S_1 is redundant, since S^R always follows S_2 and S_1 provides no additional information. In Procedure B, however, S_1 is informative and is a more reliable predictor of S^R than is S_2, which is occasionally presented alone. (After Egger & Miller, 1962.)

out S_1 or S^R. In this case, S_1 is informative rather than redundant and is a more reliable predictor of S^R than is S_2. Egger and Miller hypothesized that S_1 should be a more effective reinforcer for subjects trained on Procedure B than on Procedure A. By similar reasoning, S_2 should be more effective after training on Procedure A, where it is a reliable predictor, than on Procedure B, where it is unreliable.

Egger and Miller (1962) tested these hypotheses by training two groups of rats to press a bar for food, and then, with the bar removed, they exposed one group to Procedure A and the other to Procedure B. For half the rats in each group, S_2 was a tone and S_1 was a flashing light; for the other half, the stimuli were reversed. In a subsequent test, these groups were subdivided. The bar-press was extinguished for 10 minutes and then reconditioned with either S_2 or S_1 alone. The main results are summarized in Table 5.2, which gives the mean number of bar-presses in testing for S_1 or S_2, depending on whether the subjects were trained on Procedure A or Procedure B. It appears that S_2, which was informative for Group A, was more reinforcing for that group than the redundant stimulus S_1. Also, S_1 was more effective for Group B, for which it was informative, than for Group A. (This result did not reach statistical significance, but was subsequently confirmed by Egger and Miller, 1963). Finally, S_2 was more effective for Group A, for which it was a reliable predictor, than for Group B, for which it was unreliable. The hypotheses based on informativeness and reliability were, therefore, well substantiated.

One of these results is contrary to other information about conditioned reinforcement. For Group A, onset of S_1 was closer in time to S^R than onset of S_2, so that S_1 should have been the stronger reinforcer. It is quite possible, however, that the subjects did not attend to S_1 in Procedure A. The phenomenon of selective attention is familiar in everyday experience and can be demon-strated in the animal laboratory in studies of stimulus control (see Chapter 4). When a compound stimulus is used as an $S+$, one member of the compound may gain exclusive control of the discriminated operant. Among the variables determining which member gains control, the modality of stimulation is undoubtedly important; for instance, unless relatively intense, tones may not be as effective as lights of moderate brightness for some species. Indeed, Egger and Miller (1962) note that their rats responded more for light than for tone when these stimuli were compared without regard to temporal order or training procedure. Another important determinant of attention may be temporal priority, the variable which was said to determine redundancy for Group A. Whether the concepts of attention and information will prove to be empirically separable is not clear, but for the moment an explanation of the results in terms of attention seems plausible.

A more accurate characterization of the concept of information is that it reduces uncertainty. To see this, an experimental example may be helpful. Suppose that an organism is exposed to a situation in which periods of intermittent reinforcement and nonreinforcement alternate irregularly. Under such conditions, there is uncertainty concerning the momentary probability of reinforcement. If, however, different stimuli are correlated with periods of reinforcement ($S+$) and extinction ($S-$), the uncertainty is resolved: $S+$ signals reinforcement, while $S-$ signals nonreinforcement. If information concerning the availability of reinforcement is itself reinforcing, it should be possible to establish and maintain a new response which has as its only consequence the production of $S+$ or $S-$; that is, without altering the basic schedule of primary reinforcement.

A response which serves only to produce discriminative stimuli is called an *observing* response, because it can be viewed as analogous to the behavior of looking for stimuli that may guide subsequent behavior. A number of studies (e.g., Kelleher, 1958a; Wyckoff, 1969) have demonstrated that arbitrary new responses can be established and maintained under such circumstances. Moreover, these studies have demonstrated that the observing behavior depends on the correlation of the stimuli with differential reinforcement: When this correlation is eliminated by arranging for equal reinforcement schedules in the presence of both stimuli, so that the stimuli no longer reduce uncertainty, the observing response extinguishes. Note that such results do not fit with a simple

Training procedure		S_2	S_1
	A	115.1	65.8
	B	76.1	82.6

Table 5.2 The average number of bar-presses in an extinction test, when bar-pressing produced either S_1 or S_2. For rats trained on Procedure A, S_2 was informative and S_1 was redundant. S_1 was informative for rats trained on Procedure B. (After Egger & Miller, 1962.)

account in terms of pairing, because even when there is no *differential* reinforcement, the stimuli remain paired with reinforcement.

A particularly well-defined situation in which to study the reinforcing effects of information has been devised by Bower, McLean, and Meacham (1966), based on earlier work by Prokasy (1956). In the study by Bower et al., pigeons were confronted with two response keys. If the birds pecked the left-hand key, it was lighted yellow and a fixed-interval schedule of food reinforcement of either 10 or 40 seconds was in effect. The 10- and 40-second intervals were arranged with equal frequency in an unpredictable order. If the birds pecked the right-hand key, the same schedules of food reinforcement were arranged, but the key was red if the 10-second interval was in effect, or green if the 40-second interval was scheduled. Thus, the birds could choose between unsignaled *FI* schedules on the left-hand key and the identical signaled schedules on the right-hand key. The degree of preference for the right-hand key would indicate the reinforcing effect of the reduction of uncertainty concerning which interval length was scheduled.

All birds in the Bower et al. study exhibited overwhelming preferences for the right-hand key. Control procedures eliminated the possibility that the preference was based on key position or variation in key color. Similar preferences for signaled ratio schedules, as opposed to the same unsignaled schedules, have been obtained by Hendry (1969). Earlier, Prokasy (1956) had demonstrated that rats preferred to enter an arm of a maze where the color was correlated with reinforcement or extinction rather than an arm where color was uncorrelated with an identical alternation of reinforcement and nonreinforcement. Thus, the phenomenon has considerable generality.

In order to interpret the preference for signaled schedules in terms of information, rather than by reference to an averaging process whereby the combined conditioned reinforcing effect of two stimuli correlated with different schedules is greater than that of a single stimulus correlated with both schedules, it is necessary to manipulate the information content of the stimuli. Bower et al. (1966) reduced the informativeness of the stimuli by arranging that 80 percent of the fixed intervals on both keys were 40 seconds long, while 20 percent were 10 seconds long. Because this reduced the uncertainty concerning which interval was coming up, the addition of red or green provided a smaller reduction of uncertainty than in the former

procedure, so that the preference for the signaled schedules should have decreased. However, there was no change in preference. Hendry (1969) also failed to affect preference with a similar manipulation. Thus, strictly speaking, there is no evidence of a relation between the amount of reduction of uncertainty and the reinforcing effect of stimuli correlated with different reinforcement schedules. Until such a relation is demonstrated, the information hypothesis of conditioned reinforcement remains just that—a hypothesis with considerable promise for integrating research in this area, but not clearly superior to other accounts.

The cue-strength theory of conditioned reinforcement

The findings of studies of observing responses, or of preferences for signaled versus unsignaled reinforcement schedules, are amenable to a rather different interpretation that relates to the discriminative functions of the stimuli. Although Stein's (1958) demonstration of conditioned reinforcement based on pairing with brain stimulation cast serious doubt on the generality of the discriminative-stimulus hypothesis, and neither Stein (1958) nor Egger and Miller (1962, 1963) considered overt behavior in the presence of a stimulus as a determinant of its conditioned reinforcing effect, there are many experiments that demonstrate a systematic relationship between the discriminative and reinforcing functions of a stimulus. A theory which attempts to specify the nature of this relationship has been proposed by Wyckoff (1959). He suggested that the conditioned reinforcing effect of a stimulus is an increasing function of its *cue strength,* where the conditioned reinforcing effect is measured by the probability of a response that produces the stimulus, and cue strength is measured by the probability of a response in its presence. In qualitative terms, this simply means that conditioned reinforcement by S_1 depends on the strength of the discriminated operant controlled by S_1: The higher the probability of the discriminated response, the stronger will be the conditioned reinforcing effect.

Wyckoff suggested that the function relating conditioned reinforcement to cue strength must be positively accelerated over some of its range. This assertion is based on the results of experiments such as those of Bower et al. (1966) and Prokasy (1956), in which it was shown that the combined conditioned reinforcing effect of stimuli associated with frequent and infrequent reinforcement was greater than that of a single stimulus associated with both reinforcement schedules. The general form of the function, and the reasoning that relates it to these experiments, is shown in Figure 5.15.

Data relevant to Wyckoff's formulation are available from many experiments on the relation between the discriminative and reinforcing functions of stimuli. This relation is best studied in a chain, when separate measures of behavior before and after presentation of the stimulus are readily available. An extinction study by Notterman (1951), using independent groups of rats in a two-component runway, provided data supporting Wyckoff's (1959) analysis, but the maintenance of conditioned reinforcement in chained schedules would seem to be especially appropriate. The rate of responding during the terminal component of a two-component chain would be taken as the mea-

sure of cue strength of S_1, and the rate of responding during the preceding component would serve to measure conditioned reinforcement by S_1. In many situations, these measures may covary.

An example is provided by Fischer and Fantino's (1968) investigation of the effects of deprivation on chained schedule performances of pigeons. After extended training on chain *VI* 45-seconds, *VI* 45-seconds, rates of key-pecking were determined at four different levels of body weight. As body weight increased, response rates decreased during both components. When initial-component performance is related to terminal-component performance, a function of the sort suggested by Wyckoff (1959) is generated (see Figure 5.16). Fischer and Fantino present data suggesting that the degree of curvature may depend on the amount of training and the exact procedure used to vary deprivation.

As Kelleher and Gollub (1962) have pointed out, the cue-strength formulation cannot deal with chained schedules of reinforcement where a low response rate in the presence of S_1 is produced by the reinforcement contingency. For example, a pigeon will respond at moderate rates in S_2 to produce an S_1 correlated with differential reinforcement of low rate (Ferster & Skinner, 1957), or with response-independent reinforcement (Ferster, 1953). In both cases, the rate of the measured response may be lower in S_1 than in S_2. To incorporate these results into the cue-strength formula-

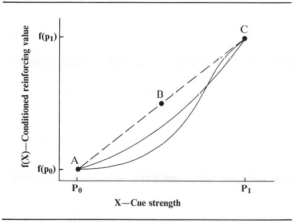

Figure 5.15 The general function form proposed by Wyckoff (1959) to relate the conditioned reinforcing effect of a stimulus to its cue strength—the probability of response in its presence. In observing response experiments, subjects sometimes receive one stimulus, with cue strength P_1, and sometimes another, with cue strength P_0, for the same response. The conditioned reinforcing effects of these stimuli are indicated by the heights of the points A and C, respectively, and their combined reinforcing effects lie on the line from A to C, say at B. The results of these experiments indicate that the combined reinforcing effect of two such stimuli is greater than that of a single stimulus associated with an intermediate cue strength. In terms of Wyckoff's theory, this means that the effects of intermediate cue strengths must lie below the straight line ABC connecting the effects of P_1 and P_0. Two acceptable function forms are shown. (From Wyckoff, 1959.)

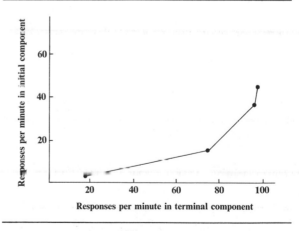

Figure 5.16 Rate of responding during the initial component of a two-component chained schedule, in relation to the rate of responding during the terminal component. The data were obtained at four different levels of deprivation. (After Fischer & Fantino, 1968.)

tion, one would have to assume that S_1 had become a strong cue for low-rate responding, or for some behavior other than pecking the key. Defining and measuring the probabilities of such behavior in some rational way is a very difficult problem, and to do so after the fact makes the predictions of the cue-strength theory trivial.

Another difficulty with the prediction of conditioned reinforcement in chained schedules by cue strength is that a number of experiments have failed to find any relation between rates in S_1 and S_2 when the frequency of reinforcement in S_1 is varied. For example, Herrnstein (1964) found that the frequency of reinforcement in S_1 was a powerful determinant of responding in S_2, but there was no relation between rates of responding in the two components.

In these studies, which provide measures appropriate for treatment by the cue-strength formulation, but where the results do not obviously support it, performance in the presence of S_1 was controlled by various schedules of reinforcement. Each schedule of reinforcement implies various contingencies which are potent determinants of performance (see Chapter 6). Because of this control by the contingencies of reinforcement, the rate or probability of responding in the presence of S_1 may not provide a sensitive measure of the effectiveness of S_1 as a discriminative stimulus. Even if it were sensitive, it could be argued that the measure is not appropriate. The effectiveness of a stimulus in occasioning some behavior is not measured by the absolute level of performance in its presence, but rather by the way in which perfor-

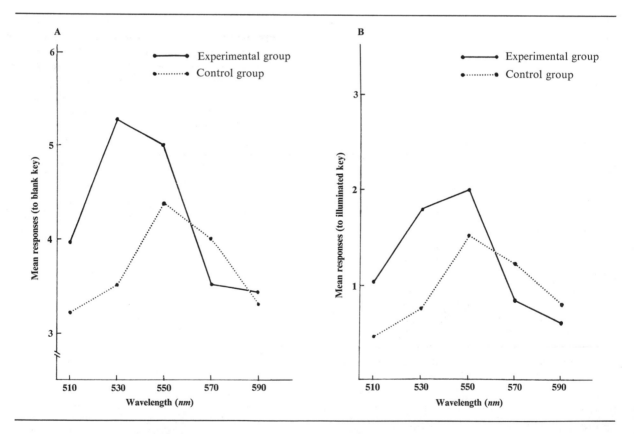

Figure 5.17 Panel A: Generalization of conditioned reinforcement in pigeons, as measured by the average numbers of responses in 30-second test periods, related to the wavelength of light presented for 2 seconds after each peck. Panel B: The average number of responses by pigeons during the 2-second light presentations. Pecking the lighted key was not required at any stage of training, so these responses represent superstitious behavior discriminatively controlled by the light associated with food. The experimental group was trained with food in the presence of a 550-*nm* light, and no food in the presence of a 570-*nm* light; the control group was exposed to only the 550-*nm* light and food. (From Thomas & Caronite, 1964.)

mance changes when the stimulus is changed, as in studies of stimulus control.

The history of discrimination training is an important determinant of the effects of variations in the stimulus. For example, discrimination training between two stimuli on a continuum affects the slope and location of the gradient of stimulus generalization—the tendency to respond in the presence of stimuli that are physically similar to $S+$ in training (see Chapter 4). This relation has been studied with respect to conditioned reinforcement by Thomas and Caronite (1964). They trained two groups of pigeons to peck a dark key to produce, on a variable-interval schedule, a 2-second light with a wavelength of 550 *nm*. At the end of 2 seconds, food was presented with no contingency on responding to the lighted key. One group received extensive training on this procedure. The second group received either the 550-*nm* light, paired with food, or a 570-*nm* light, which was never paired with food, for a comparable period of training.

An extinction test was then conducted, such that each peck at the dark key turned on a 2-second light, but food was never presented. A 1-second blackout followed each light presentation. The wavelength of the light was maintained at one value for 30 seconds and then changed randomly to some other value for 30 seconds, and so on throughout extinction, so that the pigeons had equal opportunity to produce lights of 510, 530, 550, 570, or 590 *nm*. The results of this test are shown in panel A of Figure 5.17, which gives the mean number of pecks on the dark key, per 30-second period, to produce these various lights. Both groups exhibit orderly generalization gradients. For the experimental group, which received discrimination training, the maximum of the gradient is elevated and shifted away from 570 *nm*, relative to the gradient of the control group. This kind of shift is commonly found in generalization gradients following discrimination training.

Although there was no contingency on pecking in the presence of the light during training, the pigeons often pecked the lighted key, apparently because of the accidental correlation between such pecks and food. These pecks were also recorded during the conditioned reinforcement test, and may be taken as indicative of the discriminative or cue function of the light. Gradients of responding in the presence of the various wavelengths are given for both groups in panel B of Figure 5.17. Comparison of the gradients for the reinforcing effect of the light and the discriminative effect of

the light suggests an excellent correlation in general form.

To present these data in the form suggested by Wyckoff, the rate of pecking on the blank key in number of responses per second has been calculated and plotted against the rate of responding to the illuminated key at each wavelength for both groups (see Figure 5.18). The function is quite shallow, with a fivefold change in cue strength producing only a twofold change in the effect of conditioned reinforcement as measured in this experiment. It is interesting to observe that both the experimental- and control-group data fall along the same line. There is no way of determining the expected rate of pecking in the absence of any light presentation in this experiment, so the conditioned reinforcing effect of lights of different wavelengths cannot be evaluated with reference to control levels of responding. However, the existence of a single relation for both groups provides strong support for the cue-strength theory.

To summarize this section, there is a great deal of evidence that variables which affect the strength of an operant in the presence of a stimulus also alter the effectiveness of a stimulus as a conditioned reinforcer, and in much the same way. In some experiments, there is evidence of a covariation in reinforced and discriminated responding according to the function form proposed by Wyckoff (1959). A covariation in two measures of behavior does not, of course, imply a causal relation between them; rather, both measures of behavior may change because of some other process. Stein's

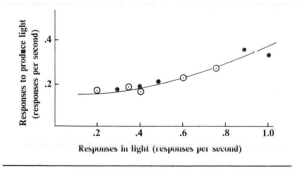

Figure 5.18 Rate of responding to produce light of a given wavelength as a function of the rate of responding in the presence of that light. The plot is based on the generalization test results in Figure 5.17. Filled circles represent the data of the experimental group; unfilled circles represent those of the control group. (After Thomas & Caronite, 1964.)

(1958) data on conditioned reinforcement with brain stimulation clearly argue against the dependency of conditioned reinforcement on discriminated operant behavior. It is suggested, then, that discriminated responding in the presence of a stimulus which has been correlated with primary reinforcement may reflect, at least in part, the effects of the basic pairing operation on which conditioned reinforcement also depends.

Interactions of operant behavior and classical conditioning

A substantial number of experiments have indicated that the procedure of pairing a stimulus with reinforcement may enable that stimulus to exert control over any operant behavior, in the absence of discrimination training for the response under investigation (see Chapter 4). An early experiment by Estes (1948) will serve to illustrate this effect. In the first phase of his study, rats were given paired presentations of a 1-minute tone and food, with no specific response required for reinforcement. He then trained the rats to press a lever for food reinforcement on a fixed-interval schedule in the absence of tones. Finally, he discontinued food reinforcement altogether and presented the tone for 10-minute periods during extinction of bar-pressing. Despite the fact that the tone could not have served as an $S+$ for bar-pressing, since the response was established after tone-food pairings, a marked increase in rate of pressing was observed in the presence of the tone. This is not, of course, an effect of conditioned reinforcement since the tone was presented independently of responding and remained on regardless of the rats' behavior.

This increase in rate in the presence of a stimulus correlated with response-independent food reinforcement has been observed in a number of experiments. It may be that the enhancement of operant behavior by such a stimulus would provide a more satisfactory prediction of the conditioned reinforcing effect of that stimulus than any other measure of behavior, especially in extinction tests. Operants such as magazine-approach or responding in the terminal component of a chained schedule, and conditioned respondents such as salivation, are deficient for several reasons. First, operant behavior is determined in part by the contingencies of reinforcement, complicating evaluation of the effectiveness of a stimulus as a discriminative stimulus. However, the effect of pairing a stimulus with reinforcement can be demonstrated in test situations that do not involve any explicit contingencies. Second, one cannot always identify a specific respondent elicited by the primary reinforcer paired with a stimulus, as in Stein's (1958) research with brain stimulation, and consequently one cannot determine the effectiveness of the stimulus as a CS. However, the effect of that stimulus on separately established operant behavior does not require the identification of any such responses.

The effect of a stimulus on an arbitrary operant may be especially interesting in connection with trans-situational tests for conditioned reinforcement. For instance, a tone paired with food when a rat is food deprived may later function as a conditioned reinforcer when the rat is satiated and placed in a novel chamber without a food tray. Under circumstances of this sort, it would be very difficult to find any behavior evoked by the stimulus within the test situation from which to predict the effectiveness of conditioned reinforcement: food-magazine approach could not occur, and conditioned salivation would be unlikely. However, an independent group of subjects could be trained to perform some unrelated operant for food reinforcement while food deprived and then receive tone-food pairings. The enhancement in responding produced by response-independent presentations of the tone in the test chamber, while these rats were satiated, might serve to predict the conditioned reinforcing effect of the tone.

Basically, the present suggestion is quite similar to Hull's (1943) proposal, as quoted earlier, of a relation between conditioned reinforcement and the "conditioned tendency to evoke an associated reaction"; however, the associated reaction is not specified except in terms of the effects of a stimulus paired with response-independent reinforcement on operant behavior.

In empirical terms, this suggestion requires the isolation of variables which determine the magnitude of the effect when a stimulus is presented independently of responding, and the effectiveness of conditioned reinforcement when stimulus presentation is contingent upon responding. The discovery of conditions in which these effects covaried would open many new lines of investigation in this difficult research area.

SUMMARY AND CONCLUSIONS

When a stimulus is paired with an effective reinforcer, that stimulus acquires the capacity to reinforce operant behavior. Four relationships among stimuli and reinforcers, and their conditioned reinforcing effects, were discussed: (1) Behavior may be strengthened if it produces a stimulus associated with presentation of positive primary reinforcement; (2) behavior may be strengthened if it terminates a stimulus associated with presentation of negative primary reinforcement; (3) behavior may be strengthened if it terminates a stimulus associated with removal of positive primary reinforcement; and (4) behavior may be strengthened if it produces a stimulus associated with removal of negative primary reinforcement.

A number of investigations regarding the first relationship have shown that the effectiveness of positive conditioned reinforcement is directly related to the frequency or amount of primary reinforcement given in its presence. The relationship is clearest when the subject is allowed to choose between two different conditioned reinforcers, each associated with different amounts of frequencies of primary reinforcement. The frequency relationship may be reversed when the subject is tested in extinction with only one conditioned reinforcer. The effectiveness of a stimulus as a conditioned reinforcer is inversely related to the delay between onset of the stimulus and presentation of primary reinforcement. Parametric analysis of the other cases of conditioned reinforcement are generally lacking.

In all cases, measurement of the reinforcing effect of the stimulus is complicated by the fact that relations among the response under study, the stimulus being evaluated, and the primary reinforcing event associated with the stimulus may provide other sources of strength for responding. Commonly, the tendency to respond may be increased by the discriminative functions of the stimulus, and in maintained pairing procedures, by the relations between responding and the primary reinforcer itself. Enough experiments have controlled or eliminated these sources of strength to leave little doubt about the reality of the process of conditioned reinforcement. Most important in this connection are demonstrations of the generalization of conditioned reinforcement to novel situations, involving responses without prior histories of reinforcement.

The largest and most important segments of human behavior do not seem to be related to obvious primary reinforcers such as food, water, or escape from pain. Therefore, behavior theorists who wish to account for human behavior in terms of principles developed in the conditioning laboratory make frequent use of the concept of conditioned reinforcement. An opposed theorist who wishes to invoke other principles is likely to argue that conditioned reinforcement is an inadequate explanatory concept because of its inability to sustain high levels of performance without frequent pairing with primary reinforcement. This objection to a universal explanation of human behavior by conditioned reinforcement may be just. However, our understanding of effective primary reinforcers for human beings is probably inadequate. The reinforcing effects of stimulation by, and manipulation of, the environment are widely recognized and may account for much of our behavior. Long and complicated chains of behavior terminating in such reinforcers may well involve conditioned reinforcement in maintained pairing conditions like those examined in studies of token reinforcement or second-order schedules of reinforcement. Thus, an understanding of conditioned reinforcement and its integration into a comprehensive behavior theory may have considerable relevance to the understanding of complex human behavior.

REFERENCES

Amsel, A. Frustrative nonreward in partial reinforcement and discrimination learning: Some recent history and a theoretical extension. *Psychological Review,* 1962, **69,** 306–328.

Amsel, A., & Roussel, J. Motivational properties of frustration: I. Effect on a running response of the addition of frustration to the motivational complex. *Journal of Experimental Psychology,* 1952, **43,** 363–368.

Autor, S. M. The strength of conditioned reinforcers as a function of frequency and probability of reinforcement. In D. P. Hendry (Ed.), *Conditioned reinforcement.* Homewood, Ill.: Dorsey Press, 1969. Pp. 127–162. Figure 5.12: Copyright © 1969 by The Dorsey Press, and reproduced by permission.

Beck, R. C. On secondary reinforcement and shock termination. *Psychological Bulletin,* 1961, **58,** 28–45.

Bersh, P. J. The influence of two variables upon the establishment of a secondary reinforcer for operant responses. *Journal of Experimental Psychology,* 1951, **41,** 62–73. Figures 5.1 and 5.10A: Copyright 1951 by the American Psychological Association, and reproduced by permission.

Bower, G., McLean, J., & Meacham, J. Value of knowing when reinforcement is due. *Journal of Comparative and Physiological Psychology,* 1966, **62,** 184–192.

Butter, C. M., & Thomas, D. R. Secondary reinforcement as a function of the amount of primary reinforcement. *Journal of Comparative and Physiological Psychology,* 1958, **51,** 346–348.

Catania, A. C. Concurrent performances: A baseline for the study of reinforcement magnitude. *Journal of the Experimental Analysis of Behavior,* 1963, **6,** 299–300.

Cowles, J. T. Food-tokens as incentive for learning by chimpanzees. *Comparative Psychology Monographs,* 1937, **14,** No. 5.

Crowder, W. F., Gay, B. R., Fleming, W. C., & Hurst, R. W. Secondary reinforcement or response facilitation? IV. The retention method. *Journal of Psychology,* 1959, **48,** 311–314.

D'Amato, M. R. Transfer of secondary reinforcement across the hunger and thirst drives. *Journal of Experimental Psychology,* 1955, **49,** 352–355. (a)

D'Amato, M. R. Secondary reinforcement and magnitude of primary reinforcement. *Journal of Comparative and Physiological Psychology,* 1955, **48,** 378–380. (b)

D'Amato, M. R., Lachman, R., & Kivy, P. Secondary reinforcement as affected by reward schedule and the testing situation. *Journal of Comparative and Physiological Psychology,* 1958, **51,** 737–741.

Dinsmoor, J. A. Variable-interval escape from stimuli accompanied by shocks. *Journal of the Experimental Analysis of Behavior,* 1962, **5,** 41–47. Figures 5.7 and 5.8: Copyright © 1962 by the Society for the Experimental Analysis of Behavior, Inc., and reproduced by permission.

Dinsmoor, J. A., & Clayton, M. H. Chaining and secondary reinforcement based on escape from shock. *Journal of the Experimental Analysis of Behavior,* 1963, **6,** 75–80.

Dinsmoor, J. A., & Clayton, M. H. A conditioned reinforcer maintained by temporal association with the termination of shock. *Journal of the Experimental Analysis of Behavior,* 1966, **9,** 547–552.

Egger, M. D., & Miller, N. E. Secondary reinforcement in rats as a function of information value and reliability of the stimulus. *Journal of Experimental Psychology,* 1962, **64,** 97–104. Figure 5.14: Copyright © 1962 by the American Psychological Association, and reproduced by permission.

Egger, M. D., & Miller, N. E. When is a reward reinforcing? An experimental study of the information hypothesis. *Journal of Comparative and Physiological Psychology,* 1963, **56,** 132–137.

Ellison, D. G., & Konorski, J. Separation of the salivary and motor responses in instrumental conditioning. *Science,* 1964, **146,** 1071–1072.

Estes, W. K. Discriminative conditioning: II. Effects of a Pavlovian conditioned stimulus upon a subsequently established operant response. *Journal of Experimental Psychology,* 1948, **38,** 173–177.

Estes, W. K. Generalization of secondary reinforcement from the primary drive. *Journal of Comparative and Physiological Psychology,* 1949, **42,** 286–295.

Fantino, E. Choice and rate of reinforcement. *Journal of the Experimental Analysis of Behavior,* 1969, **12,** 723–730. Figure 5.11: Copyright © 1969 by the Society for the Experimental Analysis of Behavior, Inc., and reproduced by permission.

Ferster, C. B. Sustained behavior under delayed reinforcement. *Journal of Experimental Psychology,* 1953, **45,** 218–224.

Ferster, C. B. Control of behavior in chimpanzees and pigeons by time-out from positive reinforcement. *Psychological Monographs,* 1958, **72,** 1–38. (No. 461)

Ferster, C. B., & DeMyer, M. K. A method for the experimental analysis of the behavior of autistic children. *American Journal of Orthopsychiatry,* 1962, **32,** 89–98.

Ferster, C. B., & Skinner, B. F. *Schedules of reinforcement.* New York: Appleton-Century-Crofts, 1957.

Findley, J. D., & Brady, J. V. Facilitation of large ratio performance by use of conditioned reinforcement. *Journal of the Experimental Analysis of Behavior,* 1965, **8,** 125–129.

Fischer, K., & Fantino, E. The dissociation of discriminative and conditioned reinforcing functions of stimuli with changes in deprivation. *Journal of the Experimental Analysis of Behavior,* 1968, **11,** 703–710. Figure 5.16: Copyright © 1968 by the Society for the Experimental Analysis of Behavior, Inc., and reproduced by permission.

Fox, R. E., & King, R. A. The effects of reinforcement scheduling on the strength of a secondary reinforcer. *Journal of Comparative and Physiological Psychology,* 1961, **54,** 266–269.

Gilbert, T. F., & Sturdivant, E. R. The effect of a food-associated stimulus on operant-level locomotor behavior. *Journal of Comparative and Physiological Psychology,* 1958, **51,** 255–257.

Gollub, L. R. The chaining of fixed-interval schedules. Unpublished doctoral dissertation, Harvard University, 1958. Figure 5.6: Reproduced by permission.

Grice, G. R. The relation of secondary reinforcement to delayed reward in visual discrimination learning. *Journal of Experimental Psychology,* 1948, **38,** 1–16.

Guttman, N. Operant conditioning, extinction, and periodic reinforcement in relation to concentration of sucrose used as reinforcing agent. *Journal of Experimental Psychology,* 1953, **46,** 213–224.

Hall, J. F. Studies in secondary reinforcement: I. Secondary reinforcement as a function of the frequency of primary reinforcement. *Journal of Comparative and Physiological Psychology,* 1951, **44,** 246–251.

Hendry, D. P. (Ed.) *Conditioned reinforcement.* Homewood, Ill.: Dorsey Press, 1969.

Herrnstein, R. J. Secondary reinforcement and rate of primary reinforcement. *Journal of the Experimental Analysis of Behavior*, 1964, **7**, 27–36.

Hopkins, C. O. Effectiveness of secondary reinforcing stimuli as a function of the quantity and quality of food reinforcement. *Journal of Experimental Psychology*, 1955, **50**, 339–342.

Hull, C. L. *Principles of behavior.* New York: Appleton-Century-Crofts, 1943.

Jenkins, W. O. A temporal gradient of derived reinforcement. *American Journal of Psychology*, 1950, **63**, 237–243. Figure 5.10B: Reproduced by permission of the University of Illinois Press.

Kanfer, F. H. Incentive value of generalized reinforcers. *Psychological Reports*, 1960, **7**, 531–538.

Kelleher, R. T. A multiple schedule of conditioned reinforcement with chimpanzees. *Psychological Reports*, 1957, **3**, 485–491.

Kelleher, R. T. Stimulus producing responses in chimpanzees. *Journal of the Experimental Analysis of Behavior*, 1958, **1**, 87–102. (a)

Kelleher, R. T. Fixed-ratio schedules of conditioned reinforcement with chimpanzees. *Journal of the Experimental Analysis of Behavior*, 1958, **1**, 281–289. (b)

Kelleher, R. T. Schedules of conditioned reinforcement during experimental extinction. *Journal of the Experimental Analysis of Behavior*, 1961, **4**, 1–5.

Kelleher, R. T. Conditioned reinforcement in second-order schedules. *Journal of the Experimental Analysis of Behavior*, 1966, **9**, 475–485.

Kelleher, R. T., & Gollub, L. R. A review of positive conditioned reinforcement. *Journal of the Experimental Analysis of Behavior*, 1962, **5**, 543–597.

Keller, F. S., & Schoenfeld, W. N. *Principles of psychology.* New York: Appleton-Century-Crofts, 1950.

Klein, R. M. Intermittent primary reinforcement as a parameter of secondary reinforcement. *Journal of Experimental Psychology*, 1959, **58**, 423–427.

Knott, P. D., & Clayton, K. N. Durable secondary reinforcement using brain stimulation as the primary reinforcer. *Journal of Comparative and Physiological Psychology*, 1966, **61**, 151–153.

Leitenberg, H. Is time-out from positive reinforcement an aversive event? A review of the experimental evidence. *Psychological Bulletin*, 1965, **64**, 428–441.

LoLordo, V. M. Positive conditioned reinforcement from aversive situations. *Psychological Bulletin*, 1969, **72**, 193–203.

Malmo, R. B. Classical and instrumental conditioning with septal stimulation as reinforcement. *Journal of Comparative and Physiological Psychology*, 1965, **60**, 1–8.

McAllister, W. R., & McAllister, D. E. Variables influencing the conditioning and the measurement of acquired fear. In W. F. Prokasy (Ed.), *Classical conditioning.* New York: Appleton-Century-Crofts, 1965. Pp. 172–191.

Miles, R. C. The relative effectiveness of secondary reinforcers throughout deprivation and habit-strength parameters. *Journal of Comparative and Physiological Psychology*, 1956, **49**, 126–130. Figures 5.9 and 5.13: Copyright © 1956 by the American Psychological Association, and reproduced by permission.

Miller, N. E. Studies of fear as an acquired drive: I. Fear as

motivation and fear-reduction as reinforcement in the learning of new responses. *Journal of Experimental Psychology*, 1948, **38**, 89–101. Figure 5.3: Copyright 1948 by the American Psychological Association, and reproduced by permission.

Miller, N. E. Learnable drives and rewards. In S. S. Stevens (Ed.), *Handbook of experimental psychology.* New York: Wiley, 1951. Pp. 435–472.

Mowrer, O. H. *Learning theory and behavior.* New York: Wiley, 1960.

Murray, A. K., & Strandberg, J. M. Development of a conditioned positive reinforcer through removal of an aversive stimulus. *Journal of Comparative and Physiological Psychology*, 1965, **60**, 281–283.

Neuringer, A. J. Delayed reinforcement versus reinforcement after a fixed interval. *Journal of the Experimental Analysis of Behavior*, 1969, **12**, 375–383.

Nevin, J. A. Generalized conditioned reinforcement in satiated rats. *Psychonomic Science*, 1966, **5**, 191–192.

Nevin, J. A. The maintenance of conditioned reinforcement. *Transactions of the New York Academy of Sciences*, 1969, **31**, 686–696.

Notterman, J. M. A study of some relations among aperiodic reinforcement, discrimination training, and secondary reinforcement. *Journal of Experimental Psychology*, 1951, **41**, 161–169.

Pliskoff, S., & Tolliver, G. Water-deprivation-produced sign reversal of a conditioned reinforcer based on dry food. *Journal of the Experimental Analysis of Behavior*, 1960, **3**, 323–329.

Prokasy, W. F. The acquisition of observing responses in the absence of differential external reinforcement. *Journal of Comparative and Physiological Psychology*, 1956, **49**, 131–134.

Razran, G. A note on second-order conditioning and secondary reinforcement. *Psychological Review*, 1955, **62**, 327–332.

Reynolds, G. S. Some limitations on behavioral contrast and induction during successive discrimination. *Journal of the Experimental Analysis of Behavior*, 1963, **6**, 131–139. Figure 5.5B: Copyright © 1963 by the Society for the Experimental Analysis of Behavior, Inc., and reproduced by permission.

Saltzman, I. J. Maze learning in the absence of primary reinforcement: A study of secondary reinforcement. *Journal of Comparative and Physiological Psychology*, 1949, **42**, 161–173.

Schoenfeld, W. N., Antonitis, J. J., & Bersh, P. J. A preliminary study of training conditions necessary for secondary reinforcement. *Journal of Experimental Psychology*, 1950, **40**, 40–45.

Seward, J. P., & Levy, N. Choice-point behavior as a function of secondary reinforcement with relevant drives satiated. *Journal of Comparative and Physiological Psychology*, 1953, **46**, 334–338.

Sheffield, F. D., & Roby, T. B. Reward value of a non-nutritive sweet taste. *Journal of Comparative and Physiological Psychology*, 1950, **43**, 471–481.

Siegel, P. S., & Milby, J. B. Secondary reinforcement in relation to shock termination: Second chapter. *Psychological Bulletin*, 1969, **72**, 146–156.

Skinner, B. F. *The behavior of organisms.* New York: Appleton-Century-Crofts, 1938. Figure 5.2: Copyright 1938 by Appleton-Century-Crofts, Inc., and reproduced by permission of Appleton-Century-Crofts, Educational Division, Meredith Corporation.

Skinner, B. F. *Science and human behavior*. New York: Macmillan, 1953.

Solomon, R. L., Kamin, L. J., & Wynne, L. C. Traumatic avoidance learning: The outcomes of several extinction procedures with dogs. *Journal of Abnormal and Social Psychology*, 1953, **48**, 291–302.

Stein, L. Secondary reinforcement established with sub-cortical stimulation. *Science*, 1958, **127**, 466–467.

Stubbs, D. A. Contiguity of briefly presented stimuli with food reinforcement. *Journal of the Experimental Analysis of Behavior*, 1969, **12**, 271–278.

Stubbs, D. A. Second-order schedules and the problem of conditioned reinforcement. *Journal of the Experimental Analysis of Behavior*, 1971, **16**, 289–313.

Thomas, D. R., & Caronite, S. C. Stimulus generalization of a positive conditioned reinforcer: II. Effects of discrimination training. *Journal of Experimental Psychology*, 1964, **68**, 402–406. Figures 5.17 and 5.18: Copyright © 1964 by the American Psychological Association, and reproduced by permission.

Wagner, A. R. Conditioned frustration as a learned drive. *Journal of Experimental Psychology*, 1963, **66**, 142–148.

Wenrich, W. W. The tact relation: An experiment in verbal behavior. *Journal of General Psychology*, 1964, **71**, 71–78.

Wike, E. L. *Secondary reinforcement*. New York: Harper & Row, 1966.

Wike, E. L., & Barrientos, G. Secondary reinforcement and multiple drive reduction. *Journal of Comparative and Physiological Psychology*, 1958, **51**, 640–643.

Wike, E. L., Platt, J. R., & Knowles, J. M. The reward values of getting out of a starting box: Further extensions of Zimmerman's work. *Psychological Record*, 1962, **12**, 397–400.

Wolfe, J. B. Effectiveness of token-rewards for chimpanzees. *Comparative Psychology Monographs*, 1936, **12**, 1–72. (No. 60)

Wyckoff, L. B. Toward a quantitative theory of secondary reinforcement. *Psychological Review*, 1959, **66**, 68–78. Figure 5.15: Copyright © 1959 by the American Psychological Association, and reproduced by permission.

Wyckoff, L. B. The role of observing responses in discrimination learning. In D. P. Hendry (Ed.), *Conditioned reinforcement*. Homewood, Ill.: Dorsey Press, 1969. Pp. 237–260.

Zimmerman, D. W. Sustained performance in rats based on secondary reinforcement. *Journal of Comparative and Physiological Psychology*, 1959, **52**, 353–358. Figure 5.4: Copyright © 1959 by the American Psychological Association, and reproduced by permission.

Zimmerman, J. Technique for sustaining behavior with conditioned reinforcement. *Science*, 1963, **142**, 682–684.

Zimmerman, J., Hanford, P. V., & Brown, W. Effects of conditioned reinforcement frequency in an intermittent free-feeding situation. *Journal of the Experimental Analysis of Behavior*, 1967, **10**, 331–340. Figure 5.5A: Copyright © 1967 by the Society for the Experimental Analysis of Behavior, Inc., and reproduced by permission.

THE MAINTENANCE OF BEHAVIOR

6

John A. Nevin
Columbia University

The ways in which behavior is changed by the basic operations of classical conditioning and differential reinforcement have been reviewed in the early chapters of this volume. But change in behavior is only a small part of the story. Once learned, responses and patterns of behavior tend to be maintained. This chapter deals with a major factor in the maintenance of behavior—the schedule of reinforcement. Schedules, which were encountered in all of the preceding chapters because they are so fundamental, are rules for selecting which among the many occurrences of a response will be reinforced. A detailed study of schedules of reinforcement and their effects is fundamental to an understanding of behavior.

This chapter is concerned only with *positive* reinforcement; performance under maintained *negative* reinforcement is discussed in Chapter 7. Of particular interest are those conditions intermediate between the standard learning situation, in which reinforcement is given regularly for each response, and extinction, in which reinforcement never occurs. Conditions of this sort are known collectively as *intermittent reinforcement*.

Intermittent reinforcement is more characteristic of the real world than is the regular reinforcement procedure of the learning laboratory. A hungry animal in the wild does not always find food in the same place, and a driver's attempts to start his car are not always successful. Unless there is a change in the animal's environment, or in the ignition system of the car, the conditions of reinforcement will persist through many repetitions of the same behavior. Under maintained conditions of this sort, the behavior of interest is likely to assume some characteristic pattern or frequency of occurrence. The hungry animal may visit one place three times as often as another, day in and day out, in its search for food; and the average number of times the driver tries the starter switch before giving up and pushing his car may also be quite constant from day to day.

In order to analyze such performances in the laboratory, it is desirable to work within a simple experimental situation which provides a maximum of control over extraneous variables, and in which the conditions of interest can be specified and varied with precision. Moreover,

Preparation of this chapter was supported in part by U.S. Public Health Service Grant MH-08515 to Swarthmore College.

the behavior under study must be sensitive to these conditions and should be conveniently and reliably measurable. An experimental technique which has become quite standard in many psychological laboratories involves the use of animal subjects, enclosed in chambers to insure precise environmental control. The subjects are trained to make some simple manipulative response, such as depressing a lever, pulling a chain, or pecking at a key. Usually, the response is a *free operant*—free in that it may occur at any time, without the constraints imposed by removing the subject from the experiment between trials, and operant in that it operates to produce reinforcing consequences, usually food. The relations between the response under study and its consequences are readily arranged with simple programming equipment, and the behavior can be recorded automatically in a variety of ways.

As an example of the establishment and maintenance of free-operant behavior, consider the following situation. A mature rat was deprived of water except for a 15-minute period at the same time daily. Twenty-two hours after its last access to water, the rat was placed in a small chamber equipped with a lever and a water dipper. Each operation of the dipper made a drop of water available to the rat. The rat was first trained to drink from the dipper and was then trained to press the lever by allowing each lever-press to operate the dipper. The response was readily acquired, and by the end of an hour the rat was pressing the lever with a swift, discrete motion, moving to the dipper and drinking, and then returning to the lever, in a rather stereotyped fashion. Over the course of the next few sessions—each lasting 50 minutes and conducted 22 hours after the last access to water—the frequency with which lever-pressing produced water was gradually reduced until an average of 2 minutes elapsed between water presentations. The intervals varied from 30 seconds to 6.5 minutes and changed unpredictably after each reinforcement. After ten daily sessions of this procedure, the rat started pressing the lever as soon as the session began and continued throughout the session at a steady, moderate rate. Further training produced no change in performance, other than small daily fluctuations in the total number of responses. This behavior, then, represents stable performance, maintained in a steady state by the conditions of reinforcement.

The performance was recorded in the form of a *cumulative record*—a tracing made by a pen that stepped upward with each lever-press, while the paper moved continuously to the left in time. Two records for the eleventh and twelfth sessions of training are shown in Figure 6.1. The stability of the performance is shown by the approximate constancy of the slopes of these records, both within each session and from one session to the next. Note that there is little if any change in slope immediately after reinforcement (indicated by the diagonal marks).

This method of recording obscures detail to some extent, but quantitative measurement confirms this apparent constancy in performance. There were 231 and 229 responses in sessions 11 and 12, respectively, yielding an average rate of 4.6 responses per minute for both sessions. Thus, the average interval between responses was 1/4.6 minutes, or 13 seconds. The average time between the presentation of water and the next response was measured separately and found to be 17 seconds. Therefore, allowing a few seconds for drinking, the presentation of reinforcement had essentially no effect on the average time to the next response. This rough invariance is by no means typical of maintained performances, but it is worth considering as an extreme form of behavioral constancy, in which the event on which performance depends has no effect on the momentary tendency to respond.

This example has been considered at some length because it is quite typical of the procedures used to establish an operant and then maintain it at a stable level with intermittent positive reinforcement. Maintained performances of this sort are studied for two somewhat different reasons. First, they may provide sensitive and reliable behavioral baselines from which the effects of a host of vari-

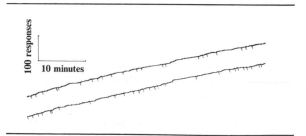

Figure 6.1 Cumulative records of a stable lever-pressing performance by a rat. Lever-presses produced a dipper of water every 2 minutes on the average. Water presentations are indicated by the diagonal marks. The upper record is from the eleventh session of training, and the lower record is from the twelfth session. (Nevin, unpublished data.)

ables may be measured. Such performances are often used in studying the physiology of food or water motivation, or the effectiveness of different reinforcing stimuli (e.g., Teitelbaum, 1966). In connection with the previous example, one might study the effects on response rate of prolonged water deprivation or saline injections, the amount of water given per reinforcement, or the sweetness or salinity of the water. This procedure would be especially useful for such work, since very little water would actually be consumed by the subject and the amount would be about the same in each session, regardless of the response rate.

Maintained performances are also used to assess the effects of emotional conditioning by presenting a stimulus associated with an unavoidable shock while the subject is engaged in lever-pressing (e.g., Kamin, 1965). Other behavioral processes which can be studied conveniently with maintained free-operant behavior are punishment and conditioned reinforcement. As a final example, standard techniques in the study of animal sensory systems require the maintenance of an operant performance which is sensitive to small changes in discriminative stimuli (e.g., Blough, 1966).

In such research the investigator's interest in the maintained performance is incidental to his primary goal; the conditions of reinforcement used to maintain a sensitive, stable baseline are regarded as tools. Like any other laboratory instrument, however, the properties of the baseline behavior need to be understood in some detail if errors of measurement and interpretation are to be avoided. For this reason alone, a study of how the conditions of reinforcement act to determine performance would be worthwhile.

There is a more general reason for the study of maintained performances: The processes determining steady-state behavior are assumed to be common to all aspects of learned behavior. Systematic formulations of learning have not been notably successful in accounting for the data of acquisition and extinction, even though these phenomena are regarded as basic; learning theories have rarely been extended to deal with maintained performances at all. An alternative approach to the systematization of learned behavior is first to try to build an adequate theory of steady-state performance and then to try to incorporate the phenomena with which traditional theories of learning have started. It is quite likely that maintained performances will prove simpler to systematize than the immensely complex aspects of behavior in transition. If such a system can be achieved, the additional assumptions needed to incorporate acquisition and extinction may be fairly straightforward.

The success of this approach to the study of learning via the steady state cannot, of course, be predicted before the attempt is made. This chapter will review some of the findings about maintained performances and their determinants and will suggest some possible interrelations among them, in the hope of facilitating the construction of a satisfactory system in the not-too-remote future.

SCHEDULES OF REINFORCEMENT

The conditions of reinforcement in steady-state experiments must now be considered in some detail. Our special interest is the vast array of conditions that are intermediate between regular reinforcement and extinction, that is, conditions in which responses are sometimes followed by reinforcement, and sometimes not. A *schedule of reinforcement* is simply a specification of which responses will be reinforced. An extensive treatment of reinforcement schedules, with numerous examples of their effects on behavior, is given by Ferster and Skinner (1957). More recently, Morse (1966) has written a systematic review of the accumulating literature on schedules of reinforcement. In this chapter we will not attempt to exhaust the field, but will consider a few of the more commonly studied schedules and how their effects may be analyzed.

Some schedules specify a reinforced response by counting the number of responses since some event, usually the last reinforcement. The simplest schedule to arrange is the *fixed-ratio (FR)* schedule, in which every nth response is regularly followed by reinforcement, while all other responses go unreinforced. The *variable-ratio (VR)* schedule, in which the number of responses required for reinforcement changes irregularly after each reinforcement, is closely related. An *FR* schedule is wholly specified by the number of responses per reinforcement. A *VR* schedule should specify each required number and its programmed position in the sequence. In practice, though, if the sequence is unpredictable it suffices to specify the average number of responses per reinforcement and the progression used to generate the sequence. For example, an arithmetic *VR*-30 schedule might consist of requirements of 10, 20, 30, 40, and 50 responses in an irregular order. Ratio schedules control the number of responses per reinforcement, but do not impose any direct restrictions on the time between reinforcements.

Another class of schedules, based on time intervals, specifies the time since the last reinforcement before a response will be reinforced. A *fixed-interval* (*FI*) schedule imposes a regular and constant period of nonreinforcement after each reinforced response. The first response to occur after this period is reinforced, and another period of nonreinforcement begins. The number of responses occurring in this period is not specified by the schedule and has no effect on the eventual presentation of reinforcement. In a *variable-interval* (*VI*) schedule the length of time without reinforcement varies irregularly after each reinforcement. Specification of these schedules is similar to ratio schedules: For *FI,* a statement of the interval length suffices, whereas a specification of the progression of intervals and their mean value is customary for *VI* schedules.

These four basic schedule classes—*FR, VR, FI,* and *VI*—fall into a simple and obvious classification system: Reinforcement is programmed on the basis of responses or of time since a preceding reinforcement, the program being either constant or variable from one interval to the next. From this simple beginning, matters can (and will) become exceedingly complicated. For example, it is possible to devise schedules that are intermediate between ratio and interval schedules (see the discussion of *interlocking* schedules later in this chapter), and it is easy to see that fixed schedules are continuously related to variable schedules by the amount of variability between successive reinforcements. Thus, the four-way classification really serves only to identify extremes or typical cases along various conceptual continua. Moreover, a schedule may begin with some event other than a prior reinforcement—a designated response, for example. That response may itself be specified by a schedule, and more than one schedule may be combined to designate the response eventually to be reinforced. The work of Ferster and Skinner (1957) attests to the diversity of behaviors that may be generated and maintained by such complex schedules and suggests methods for the analysis of these behaviors. As will be seen, the performances maintained by even the simplest schedules of reinforcement are sufficiently complex to puzzle students of behavior, and it is to these performances that we now turn.

Some representative cumulative records of lever-pressing performances by rats on *FR*-45, *VR*-45, *FI* 1-minute, and *VI* 1-minute schedules are shown

in Figure 6.2. These samples are taken from the 47th and 48th sessions of training in a situation much like that described for Figure 6.1. The rats were deprived of water for 22.5 hours before each experimental session, and lever-pressing was reinforced with a drop of water. Each rat received preliminary training with regular reinforcement, followed by a gradual increase in the schedule requirement; the final schedule value was placed in effect after several such training sessions.

Consider first the record for *FR*-45 and note that, in general, a pause follows each reinforcement, which occasionally may be quite long. Once responding begins, however, the requirement of 45 responses is met with a sustained burst of lever-pressing, with a high average rate and rather little variability.

Compare this sort of performance with that maintained on an arithmetic *VR*-45 schedule. Once again, the records consist of alternations between high-rate bursts of lever-pressing and pauses of variable length. Unlike the *FR* records, however, pauses are not correlated with reinforcements.

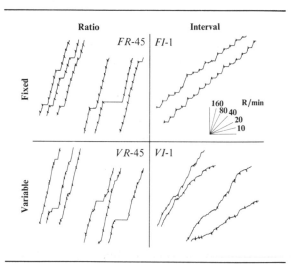

Figure 6.2 Cumulative records of lever-pressing by rats on various schedules of reinforcement. Water was presented after every 45th response (*FR*-45), after every 45th response on the average (*VR*-45), for the first response occurring 1 minute after the previous reinforcement (*FI*-1), or at variable times averaging 1 minute after the previous reinforcement (*VI*-1). Water presentations are indicated by diagonal marks. The left-hand records in each panel are taken from the 47th session of training, and the right-hand records are taken from the 48th session. (Nevin, unpublished data.)

Long pauses are as likely to appear in the middle of sustained runs of responses as they are to occur immediately after reinforcement.

In both cases, then, performance is fairly well characterized as consisting of two states: sustained high-rate responding and no lever-pressing at all, with abrupt transitions from one state to the other. In the *FR* case, pauses seem to occur only after reinforcements, while the pauses are distributed irregularly throughout the sessions on *VR*.

Records of performance on *FI*-1 are presented in Figure 6.2. Again, there is a marked pause after each reinforcement, followed by a transition to a fairly steady, moderate rate of responding. The rate while responding is somewhat variable from one interval to the next, but appears quite constant within each interval. Occasionally there is a gradual acceleration in rate within an interval, known as a *scallop*. This scalloped pattern may be quite pronounced under some conditions (e.g., panel A of Figure 6.14), but may disappear under other conditions so that the pattern of responding resembles *FR* performance, as in some intervals of the present example. Note, however, that when the rat responds, the rate is appreciably lower than with *FR*-45.

The cumulative records of responding on *VI* 1-minute are in marked contrast to the others. Responding is maintained throughout the intervals between reinforcements, but undergoes wide fluctuations from moment to moment. On the average, the rate is similar to that maintained on *FI*-1. The average number of responses per hour during the 44th through 48th sessions of training on *FI*-1 was 1727, while the average for the same sessions on *VI*-1 was 2505 responses per hour. These values may be compared with the averages for the same sessions on *FR*-45 (6289 responses per hour) and on *VR*-45 (5795 responses per hour). Evidently, similarities in average rates of responding may mask important qualitative differences in performance, as between *FI* and *VI*. Conversely, gross differences in average rates may lead one to ignore some qualitative similarities in performance, as between *FR* and *FI*.

As exemplified here, the terminal performances produced by the fixed, cyclic schedules, whether interval or ratio, consist of a distinct pause in responding after each reinforcement, followed by a rather abrupt shift to a steady rate of responding. This rate is relatively constant from one cycle to the next. The variable schedules, on the other hand, produce performances with no apparent systematic variation between reinforcements. *VR*

performance is characterized by a fairly constant rate while responding, interrupted irregularly by pauses of varying length, while *VI* performance may vary considerably in rate while responding. The ratio schedules, whether fixed or variable, generate substantially higher rates than the interval schedules.

The performances illustrated here are quite typical of those reported throughout the experimental literature with other schedule values and with species other than rats. The next few sections of this chapter will consider various ways in which these characteristic performances may be understood.

EFFECTS OF THE SCHEDULE PARAMETERS

In the examples just described, the values of the ratio or interval schedules were chosen for convenience, to illustrate typical performances. Although the general nature of maintained performance is the same over a wide range of values, or *parameters* of these schedules, there is considerable evidence that the quantitative features of performance depend systematically on the schedule parameters.

Average response rates on interval schedules

Consider, first, the length of the fixed interval and how one might study its effects on performance. A typical experiment would keep one schedule value in effect for a number of sessions until responding was satisfactorily stable, and then change to a new value. After steady-state performances had been obtained with each subject on each of several different schedule values, a redetermination of an earlier value might be used to evaluate the reversibility of the effect of the schedule. Alternatively, independent groups of subjects may be used, each group being trained exclusively on a different schedule.

An early experiment of the first sort was performed by Skinner (1938, Chapter 4). Each of four rats was exposed to each of four *FI* schedules in a different order, with reexposure to the original *FI* value at the end of the experiment. All four subjects responded at rates inversely related to the value of the *FI*. The average data are in remarkably good agreement with a study of *FI* schedules by Wilson (1954). He used the second technique mentioned earlier, training six separate groups of six rats each at *FI* values of 6, 4, 2, and 1 minutes, and 20 and 10 seconds, until they had obtained 240 reinforcements. The function relating the final average rate for each group to the programmed *FI* value is given in Figure 6.3A, together with the average function from Skinner's experiment.

These two functions are replotted in Figure 6.3B,

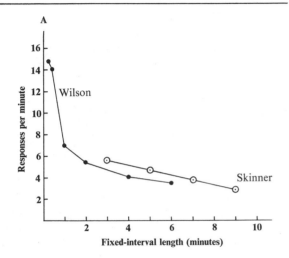

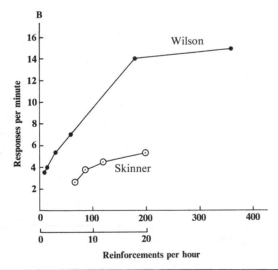

Figure 6.3 Panel A: Average rates of responding as functions of the fixed interval between reinforcements, as determined for separate groups by Wilson (1954) and for individual subjects by Skinner (1938). Panel B: The same data, replotted as functions of the number of reinforcements per hour. Note that separate abscissa scales are employed to spread out the functions obtained by Wilson and Skinner.

with the abscissa transformed into reinforcements per hour. As a result of this transformation, the functions are negatively accelerated: As the frequency of reinforcement goes up, equal increases in reinforcement frequency produce smaller increments in rate. Similar functions have been obtained with *VI* schedules of reinforcement by Clark (1958), working with independent groups of rats (see Figure 6.22), and by Catania and Reynolds (1968), working with pigeons in single-subject experiments.

Rate of responding under ratio reinforcement

The effects of ratio size on responding maintained by *FR* schedules are more complex than related effects with interval schedules. Boren (1953, 1961) studied the effects of this schedule parameter on rates of lever-pressing by rats, using both independent groups and single-subject methods (see Chapter 1 for discussion of other aspects of Boren's study). In one portion of his study, six groups of six rats each were trained on *FR* values of 1, 3, 6, 10, 15, and 21 until they had obtained 500 reinforcements during the course of ten sessions. Their average rates were calculated for the final two sessions and are shown as function I in Figure 6.4A. In a separate part of his study, Boren exposed rats to different *FR* schedules in the following order: 3, 8, 15, 26, 36, 15, and 3. Training continued on each schedule until performance stabilized. Average response rates were determined for the last two sessions on each schedule and are plotted in Figure 6.4 as function II. The extra points at *FR*-3 and *FR*-15 are recoveries of earlier performance. They are remarkably close to the earlier results. The agreement between the results for single subjects and independent groups indicates that the function relating average rates to the value of an *FR* schedule is independent of the experimental method.

Although the average rate of responding on *FR* schedules bears a consistent relation to the value of the *FR* schedule, matters become more complex when the *FR* performance is broken down into its two obvious components: the pause after reinforcement, and the rate once responding has started, which is termed the *running rate*. In Boren's (1953) single-subject research, the average rate of responding on short *FR* schedules was recoverable after exposure to larger ratios, but the components of performance were not recoverable. For example, the pause after reinforcement was longer and the running rate higher during reexposure to *FR*-15 than in the original determination. Felton and

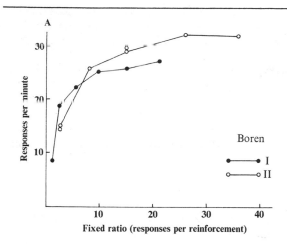

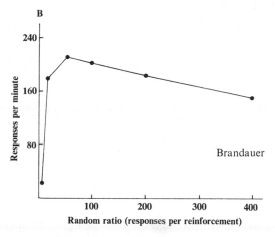

Figure 6.4 Rate of responding on ratio schedules as a function of the number of responses required per reinforcement. Panel A: Lever-pressing by rats on fixed-ratio schedules. Function I shows average data for independent groups, and function II plots average data for single subjects exposed to each value of the ratio in increasing order, with repetition of *FR*-3 and *FR*-15. (From Boren, 1953.) Panel B: Average rate of keypecking by pigeons on random-ratio schedules. (After Brandauer, 1958.)

Lyon (1966) studied these components of *FR* performance in pigeons on *FR* schedules ranging from 50 to 150. They found that the pause increased and running rate decreased with increases in the *FR* value. As a result, the average rate decreased markedly. In their study, both pause length and running rate were recoverable when the schedule was changed back to *FR* 50.

Taken together, the studies of Boren and of Felton and Lyon suggest a nonmonotonic function relating average rate to the value of the *FR*. Such a relation has been obtained using variable, rather than fixed, ratios by Brandauer (1958). He trained pigeons on a procedure that made reinforcement equally likely for every response. For example, if the probability of reinforcement was 0.10, every tenth response on the average was reinforced. Technically, this is termed a *random ratio* schedule. As the average number of responses per reinforcement required by the schedule increased, the average rate of responding first increased, up to a value of 50 responses per reinforcement, and then decreased. The average results for three pigeons are shown in Figure 6.4B. Thus, unlike interval-schedule performance, the average rate of responding on ratio schedules is evidently not a monotonic function of the size of the ratio.

The pause after reinforcement

Despite this difference in average rate functions, the pause after reinforcement bears a simple relation to both *FI* length and *FR* size. Figure 6.5 summarizes the results of an experiment by Sherman (1959) on *FI* schedules (panel A), and Felton and Lyon's (1966) experiment on *FR* schedules (panel B). In Sherman's study, five pairs of rats were trained for 60 sessions on different *FI* schedules: 10 seconds, 30 seconds, 1 minute, 2 minutes, and 4 minutes. On all schedules, final performances were much like the *FI* 1-minute performance in Figure 6.2. The average interval between the occurrence of reinforcement and the next response was calculated for each subject for a single session near the end of training. As shown in the figure, there was excellent agreement between subjects, and a linear relation describes the results quite well. Schneider (1969) has obtained similar data with pigeons on *FI* schedules ranging from 16 to 512 seconds. In Felton and Lyon's experiment, the average interval between reinforcement and the next response was determined for each bird on each *FR* value. Again, there is a direct relation between pause length and the schedule requirement for each subject.

The similarity of these functions may arise from a common process. An *FI* schedule obviously precludes the possibility of reinforcement immediately after a prior reinforcement. Numerous studies of discrimination learning show that when an exteroceptive stimulus, such as a light or a tone, is correlated with a period of nonreinforcement, it comes to control a near-zero rate of responding

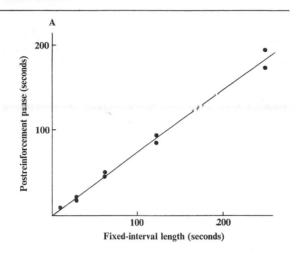

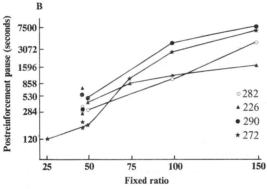

Figure 6.5 The pause after reinforcement on fixed-interval schedules (panel A) and fixed-ratio schedules (panel B). The fixed-interval data were obtained with independent groups of rats by Sherman (1959); the fixed-ratio data were obtained with individual pigeons trained at each ratio schedule by Felton and Lyon (1966). Note the logarithmic ordinate scale in panel B.

(Chapter 4). Stimuli associated with time after a reinforcement, although internal to the subject, function similarly to control a low rate of responding at that time. The duration of these internal stimuli signaling nonreinforcement may be directly related to the time between reinforcements specified by the schedule.

FR schedules do not specify a time between reinforcements. However, a minimum interval between reinforcements is imposed by the time required to complete the ratio, so that as in the case of *FI* schedules, stimuli associated with short times after reinforcement are also associated with nonreinforcement. These temporal stimuli control low

rates, as in *FI* schedules. As the size of the *FR* increases, the duration of the period of nonreinforcement must necessarily increase, leading to increases in the length of the pause after reinforcement.

This interpretation suggests that there is essentially no difference between fixed-ratio and fixed-interval schedules in determining the length of the pause. That is, under comparable experimental conditions, the pause after reinforcement should bear the same relation to the time between reinforcements whether the latter is controlled by the experimenter, as in *FI* schedules, or determined by the subject, as in *FR* schedules. A study by Berryman and Nevin (1962) provides data bearing on this question. The experimenters were interested in reinforcement schedules intermediate between *FI* and *FR*, called *interlocking* schedules. To understand these schedules and their relation to *FI* and *FR*, it is helpful to consider a diagrammatic representation of reinforcement schedules proposed by Skinner (1958). This representation uses a form similar to the cumulative record to describe the time and number of responses since a preceding reinforcement that are required before availability of the next reinforcement. For example, panel A of Figure 6.6 represents an *FR* schedule. The horizontal line describes the fact that reinforcement is available after *n* responses, regardless of the time required to emit those responses. Panel C represents an *FI* schedule by means of a vertical line, signifying that reinforcement is available after *t* seconds, regardless of the number of responses made during that time. An interlocking schedule is represented in panel B. Here, the number of responses required

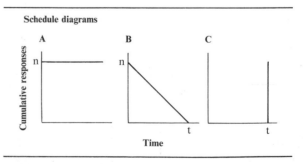

Figure 6.6 Diagrams for a fixed-ratio schedule of *n* responses per reinforcement (A), a fixed-interval schedule of *t* seconds (C), and an interlocking schedule (B) in which the number of responses required for reinforcement decreases as a linear function of time since the preceding reinforcement. (After Skinner, 1958.)

for reinforcement decreases linearly as time passes since the last reinforcement, so that the subject may obtain reinforcement frequently by responding at a high rate, or may wait until t seconds have elapsed and receive reinforcement for a single response, or give any intermediate performance. If the parameter t is increased, the interlocking schedule line becomes more nearly horizontal and approximates an *FR* schedule. Conversely, if the parameter n is increased, the line becomes more nearly vertical and approximates an *FI* schedule.

Berryman and Nevin trained rats on an *FR* schedule, an *FI* schedule, and four intermediate interlocking schedules until performances were stable. They obtained performances varying continuously in running rate and pause after reinforcement as functions of the schedule parameters. The length of the average pause after reinforcement is related to the average time between reinforcements in Figure 6.7. Only on the *FI* schedule was this value controlled by the experimenters; on all other schedules it depended on the subjects' performances. Although there was considerable variability in performance from one schedule to another and across subjects on any given schedule, the results are adequately described by a linear function passing through the origin. To a first approximation, then, performance on fixed, cyclic schedules of reinforcement is characterized by a pause after reinforcement which is a constant fraction of the time between reinforcements, regardless of whether reinforcement is programmed on a ratio schedule, an interval schedule, or an intermediate interlocking schedule.

Performances on *VR* and *VI* schedules, such as those portrayed in Figure 6.2, generally do not exhibit consistent pausing after reinforcement. This observation is in accord with the present interpretation, in that variable schedules sometimes arrange for reinforcement very soon after a previous reinforcement. Thus, postreinforcement stimuli are not consistently correlated with nonreinforcement, and hence should not come to control near-zero response rates.

Patterns of responding between reinforcements

This way of looking at schedule performance suggests that the tendency to respond shortly after a reinforcement should be related to the frequency with which reinforcement is available at that time. *FR* and *FI* schedules exclude reinforcement altogether, while in conventional *VR* and *VI* schedules

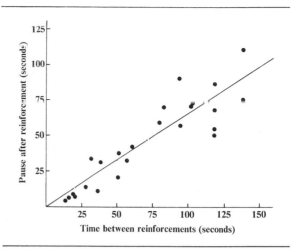

Figure 6.7   The pause after reinforcement as a function of the average time elapsing between reinforcements on a fixed-ratio schedule, a fixed-interval schedule, and four interlocking schedules. The data points are for four individual subjects exposed to each schedule. (After Berryman & Nevin, 1962.)

it may be fairly frequent. Clearly, the frequency of reinforcement at any given time after a previous reinforcement can be varied experimentally by constructing special kinds of variable schedules. For example, Catania and Reynolds (1968) trained pigeons to peck a key for food reinforcement on an *FI* 240-second schedule. After performance stabilized, reinforcement was given occasionally on *FI* 30-seconds. Under one condition, 1 out of every 20 *FI* cycles was 30 seconds long, and the remainder where 240 seconds. Thus, the relative frequency of reinforcement for a key-peck 30 seconds after a previous reinforcement was .05. Under another condition, the 30-second interval alternated irregularly with the 240-second interval, so that the relative frequency of reinforcement at 30 seconds was .50. Note that these schedules were, in effect, minimal *VI* schedules, composed of only two intervals that were programmed with different relative frequencies.

To record the pattern of responding within the intervals between reinforcements, Catania and Reynolds counted the number of pecks in successive 10-second periods after reinforcement. The recording apparatus automatically reset to the first period after each reinforcement, regardless of whether a 30-second or a 240-second interval was in effect. Rate of responding in each 10-second period was then calculated. The results for one pigeon are shown in Figure 6.8A. On *FI*-240, the average rate of responding increased steadily throughout the interval, with a very low rate during the first 30 seconds. Note that this average pattern could result from pauses of variable length, followed by a steady terminal response rate; it does not imply a tendency for rate to increase steadily within individual *FI* periods. The initial rate increased markedly when the relative frequency of reinforcement at 30 seconds was .05, and still further when it was .50. The relation between rate of responding between 20 and 30 seconds after reinforcement, and the relative frequency of reinforcement at 30 seconds, is shown in panel B for two birds.

The study just described is only one of a number performed by Catania and Reynolds (1968), all concerned with the rate of responding during the time after reinforcement and its relation to changes in the relative frequency of reinforcement in time. Their work demonstrates that control of response rate by reinforcement is not unique to short post-reinforcement times, but extends also to long periods. In general, then, it appears that the pattern of responding in time depends on the pattern of reinforcement in time, with the typical *FI* pattern of pausing followed by a fairly abrupt transition to a steady rate as an extreme case.

Experimental comparison of interval and ratio schedules

Now, let us reconsider how the schedule values may have determined the different rates maintained by interval and ratio reinforcement in the examples of Figure 6.2. The rats on *FI* 1-minute and *VI* 1-minute received about 60 reinforcements per hour, as determined by the schedules. The rats on *FR*-45 and *VR*-45 received 139 and 129 reinforcements per hour, respectively. These values could not have been predicted in advance, since they depended on the response rates. However, the resulting differences in reinforcement frequency may be important. As has been shown, more frequent reinforcement produces higher average response rates, at least in part because of reductions in the pause after reinforcement. It may be that the differences in reinforcement frequency suffice to explain the higher rates on ratio schedules.

To isolate this factor, it is necessary to give precisely equal frequencies of reinforcement to different subjects—one on an interval schedule and the other on a ratio schedule. This equality is not easy to arrange, because reinforcement frequency depends directly on performance on ratio schedules, and thus cannot be controlled by the experi-

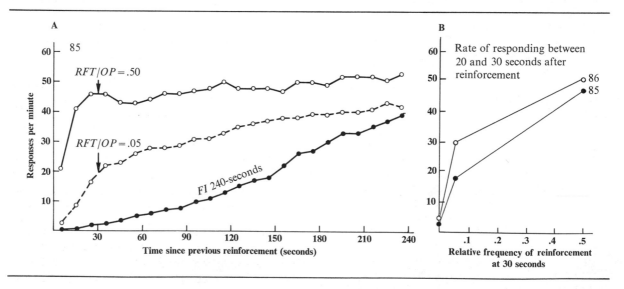

Figure 6.8   Panel A: Responding by a pigeon on an *FI* 240-second schedule, showing the effect of the introduction of reinforcement on *FI* 30-seconds in 1 out of 20 intervals (.05) or 10 out of 20 intervals (.50). Responding was measured in 10-second periods after each reinforcement. *RFT/OP* refers to the probability of reinforcement at 30 seconds. Panel B: Responding by two pigeons between 20 and 30 seconds after reinforcement as a function of the relative frequency of reinforcement at 30 seconds. (After Catania & Reynolds, 1968.)

menter. One technique for insuring equal rein- forcement frequency is to use a *yoked control*. In such an experiment, the performance of one sub- ject is used to program reinforcement for another, working at the same time in a separate chamber. For example, one subject may receive food rein- forcement for responding on a *VR* schedule. Each time it obtains a reinforcement, the yoked subject is allowed to obtain reinforcement for its next re- sponse. In essence, the yoked subject is on a *VI* schedule in which the successive intervals are determined not by a timer but by the subject on the *VR* schedule. This arrangement guarantees identi- cal numbers and patterns of reinforcement in time, while retaining the essential difference between ratio and interval scheduling: One subject must complete a certain response requirement, while for the other, a certain period of time must elapse be- fore reinforcement is available.

This experiment has been performed by Ferster and Skinner (1957, pp. 399–405) with pigeons as subjects. After training to equate the two birds' rates on a *VI* schedule, one was shifted to a *VR* schedule and the other received yoked *VI* rein- forcement as just described. Over the course of several sessions, the bird on the *VR* schedule in- creased its rate markedly, to an average level of two to three responses per second. The yoked bird, receiving an identical frequency of reinforcement, averaged about one response per second. Thus, reinforcement frequency cannot account for the differences in performance on *VR* and *VI* schedules.

This experiment has been repeated by Killeen (1969) with pigeons on various *FR* schedules. Yoked birds received reinforcement on an *FI*-like basis, although the intervals were not precisely constant. In general, the results were the same as those of Ferster and Skinner.

It is also possible to compare interval and ratio schedules within the same subject, to eliminate in- dividual differences. To do this, a *VR* schedule and a *VI* schedule may be programmed alternately on two different response keys, each associated with a distinctive stimulus condition. The values of both the *VR* and *VI* schedules are varied over wide ranges to produce stable performances under a variety of obtained frequencies of reinforcement. Data of this sort have been obtained by Herrnstein (1964) in a study involving a complex sequence of reinforcement schedules (described in detail in Chapter 5). For our present purposes, it is suf- ficient to note that the *VR* rates were consistently above *VI* rates at comparable frequencies of rein-

forcement, thus confirming the conclusions from the yoked-control experiments.

CONTINGENCIES RESULTING FROM REINFORCEMENT SCHEDULES

If the difference between ratio and interval per- formances cannot be explained by reference to the obtained frequency or pattern of reinforcement, how is it to be understood? Remember that the only contact between the subject and the schedule is in the occasional production of a reinforcer by a response. To see how this occasional contact acts on responding, it is necessary to consider the re- lations between responding and reinforcement im- plied by the schedule. These implied relations are known collectively as the *contingencies* of rein- forcement.

Relations between response rate and reinforcement frequency

The time between reinforcements, or the average number of reinforcements per hour, de- pends directly on performance in ratio schedules: The faster the subject responds, the more fre- quently it obtains reinforcement. Assuming the existence of some variability in performance, instances of high-rate responding will produce reinforcement sooner (or more often) than in- stances of low-rate responding. The continued application of this differential frequency of rein- forcement for higher rates should operate to sus- tain high rates.

No such differential reinforcement for high rates of responding is present in interval schedules, how- ever. An upper limit is imposed on the frequency of reinforcement by the programmed intervals, and even very low rates will achieve this frequency if responses are spaced to occur near the times of reinforcement availability. In principle, the rate could fall to a single response per reinforcement without a change in obtained reinforcement fre- quency, if responding were timed perfectly. In fact, of course, timing is not perfect on *FI* sched- ules, and the use of variable intervals precludes such timing, so that the obtained frequency of rein- forcement will decrease somewhat at very low response rates.

This, then, is a likely reason for the difference between interval and ratio performances: Upward changes in rate on ratio schedules produce more frequent reinforcement, whereas rate increases above a certain minimum have no effect on reinforcement frequency in interval schedules.

Differential reinforcement of interresponse times

The foregoing explanation invokes a rather gross property of responding—the average rate—and rather remote consequences—a reduction in the average time between reinforcements. It assumes that rats and pigeons are sensitive to changes in the average frequency of reinforcement in time, even though the particular intervals between reinforcements may vary considerably about the average. An explanation based on behavior at the moment of reinforcement itself may be more reasonable.

Reinforcement may be presumed to affect not only the reinforced response itself, but also the immediately preceding response and the time separating them—the *interresponse time (IRT)*. If the temporal spacing of responses is itself a conditionable aspect of free-operant behavior, then reinforcement following a short *IRT* should increase the frequency of such *IRT*s, and hence raise the rate of responding. Conversely, if reinforcement follows a long *IRT*, it should tend to lower the response rate.

There is considerable evidence that the selective reinforcement of *IRT*s has a dramatic effect on free-operant behavior. It is easy to arrange for a response to be reinforced only if that response terminates an *IRT* greater than or less than some particular duration. Suppose, for example, the experimenter requires that 20 seconds or more must elapse from the preceding response in order for the next response to be reinforced, but every response meeting that requirement produces reinforcement. Such a schedule is termed *differential reinforcement of low rate* of responding (*DRL*). Performance on such a schedule is best described by constructing a frequency distribution of the *IRT*s. For instance, all *IRT*s less than 2.0 seconds are scored in the first class interval, all *IRT*s from 2.00 to 3.99 seconds in the second, all *IRT*s from 4.00 to 5.99 seconds in the third, and so forth. In such a distribution, the variability of performance and the proportion of *IRT*s meeting the requirement for reinforcement are readily seen.

A representative performance by a rat on a *DRL* 20-second schedule of water reinforcement is presented in this fashion in Figure 6.9A. The data are taken from an extensive study of *DRL* performances by Malott and Cumming (1964). This dis-

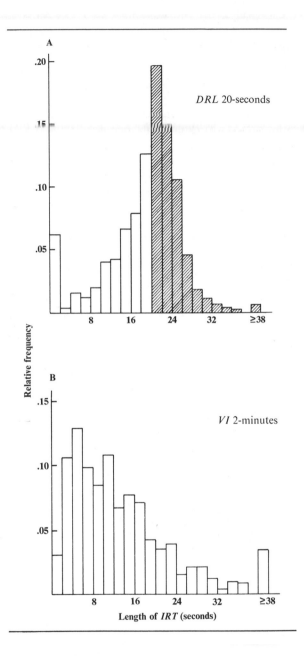

Figure 6.9 Panel A: The distribution of times between successive responses, recorded in 2-second class intervals, when every response following a previous response by 20 seconds or more was reinforced (*DRL* 20-seconds). The shaded area indicates reinforced responses. (From Malott & Cumming, 1964.) Panel B: The distribution of interresponse times, similarly recorded, for the performances depicted in Figure 6.1, when responses were reinforced every 2 minutes on the average.

tribution is based on pooled data for five sessions after prolonged training on this and related *DRL* schedules. Note that the modal *IRT* is just above the requirement for reinforcement, and the distribution is sharply peaked. A second mode appears at the shortest class interval. This second mode is quite characteristic of *DRL* performances.

It may be instructive to compare this *IRT* distribution with one resulting under variable-interval reinforcement. The performance shown in Figure 6.1, which was maintained by a *VI* 2-minute schedule, was similar to the *DRL* performance in its low, steady rate, and the range of *IRTs* was similar. A distribution of all *IRTs* in the two cumulative records of Figure 6.1 was constructed, using 2-second class intervals. This distribution is shown in Figure 6.9B. Comparison with panel A shows that the *VI* performance is much more variable in its *IRTs*, with its mode occurring at 4 to 6 seconds. A number of factors may be responsible for this difference in variability. First, a response may be reinforced following an *IRT* of any length on a *VI* schedule, while the *DRL* schedule imposes a strict contingency on *IRT* length. Second, all *IRTs* above 20 seconds led to reinforcement on the *DRL* schedule, while on the *VI* schedule responses were reinforced intermittently regardless of the preceding *IRTs*. Malott and Cumming (1964) found that the variability of *IRTs* on a *DRL* schedule increased when only a fraction of the responses meeting the schedule requirement was reinforced. The importance of these factors is difficult to determine, given the difference in apparatus, experimental procedure, and training time. The comparison is intended simply to suggest that regular reinforcement of responses following long *IRTs* can produce rather precise control of the *IRT* distribution relative to the distributions obtained under other schedules maintaining similar rates.

This precision of control is not confined to long *IRTs*, as in a *DRL* schedule. Similar contingencies may be arranged for short *IRTs* by establishing an upper as well as a lower limit for *IRTs* qualifying for reinforcement. For example, one might require that a response terminate an *IRT* greater than 2 seconds, but less than 3 seconds, to qualify for reinforcement. Schedules of this sort are called *pacing* schedules. They have been studied systematically by Malott and Cumming (1964) with rats as subjects, and by Shimp (1967) with pigeons. Their studies demonstrated that selective reinforcement of responses in a narrow band of *IRTs* can control both the average rate of responding and the form of the *IRT* distribution.

Contingencies on *IRTs* in ratio and interval schedules

Ratio and interval schedules, as they are usually programmed, do not specify any explicit contingency on interresponse time. Nevertheless, the operation of these schedules indirectly provides for differential reinforcement of responding after different *IRTs*. Consider a hypothetical example of performance on a short *VI* schedule—say, a *VI* 30-second schedule composed of the following intervals: 10, 20, 30, 40, and 50 seconds. On such a schedule, an *IRT* greater than 50 seconds is certain to be followed by reinforcement, regardless of which interval happens to be programmed when the response occurs. On the other hand, an *IRT* of 5 seconds is sure to be followed by reinforcement only if it is initiated within 5 seconds of reinforcement availability. Since the schedule is composed of five intervals, there are five 5-second periods during which the *IRT* must be initiated if the terminal response is to be reinforced. The total time during which these five reinforcements are scheduled is simply the sum of the intervals: 10 + 20 + 30 + 40 + 50 = 150 seconds. Assuming a random arrangement of the intervals, and random initiation of different *IRTs* within each interval, the probability of reinforcement for a response terminating a 5-second *IRT* is given by the time during which the *IRT* must be initiated to receive reinforcement, divided by the total time during which it may be initiated. In the present example, this figure is 25/150 or 0.17. As *IRT* length increases, the probability of reinforcement increases according to the function labeled *VI* 30-seconds in Figure 6.10. This sort of increasing, negatively accelerated function, reaching 1.00 at the longest programmed interval, is characteristic of *VI* schedules generally.

The function for *FI* schedules, assuming random initiation of different *IRTs*, is simply a linear function rising from 0 to 1.00 at the value of the *FI*. The assumption of randomness is dubious on *FI* schedules, however, and no function is plotted.

On ratio schedules, all *IRTs* are equally likely to be followed by reinforcement, since the availability of reinforcement does not change in any way with the passage of time. This constancy depends on the assumption of random initiation of different *IRTs* at different positions within the ratio. This assumption may be inappropriate for *FR* performances, but it is probably acceptable for *VR* schedules. The function for *VR*-10 is included in Figure 6.10 for comparison. Also shown is the function for *DRL*

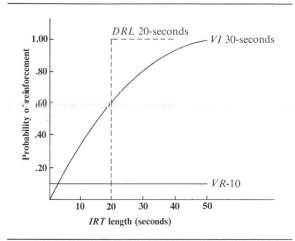

Figure 6.10 The probability of reinforcement for interresponse times of various lengths on a *DRL* 20-second schedule, a variable-ratio schedule of 10 responses per reinforcement, and a *VI* 30-second schedule. (Nevin, unpublished data.)

20-seconds. On the latter schedule, the probability of reinforcement jumps abruptly from 0 to 1.00 at 20 seconds, and, as we have seen in Figure 6.9, it produces quite precise control of *IRT*s. The *VI* function may be thought of as producing effects intermediate between those for *VR* and *DRL*: *VI* schedules favor longer *IRT*s, but not with such precision as the *DRL* schedule. Clearly, these different functions should produce high rates on *VR*, intermediate rates on *VI*, and low rates on *DRL*, which are the usual results.

Although the relations between *IRT* length and reinforcement on different schedules are clear enough, and differences in average response rates seem to conform to these relations, relatively little is known about the effects of reinforcement probability on different *IRT*s within a given schedule. In particular, do the probabilities of occurrence of different *IRT*s conform to the probabilities of reinforcement arranged by the schedule?

This question was raised by Anger (1956) in a study of performance after extended training on a *VI* schedule. To carry out his analysis, Anger introduced a statistic which has gained widespread use, and which must be understood before considering his findings. Termed *interresponse times per opportunity (IRTs/OP)*, the statistic estimates the conditional probability of responding in an *IRT* class interval, given that the *IRT* is greater than the lower limit of that interval. This condi-

tional probability is needed to evaluate the momentary response tendency because of the sequential nature of responding in time. Suppose, for example, that we observe a small number of *IRT*s in the class interval between 12 and 16 seconds. This small number could arise either because the subject had little tendency to respond at that time, as might occur on a *DRL* 30-second schedule, or because it responded at a very high rate, so that virtually all *IRT*s were less than 12 seconds and there were very few opportunities for longer *IRT*s to occur. To evaluate the subject's tendency to respond between 12 and 16 seconds after a previous response, one must consider responses in that class interval relative to the number of opportunities the subject actually had to respond in that interval—that is, relative to the number of *IRT*s that are at least 12 seconds long.

To understand the *IRTs/OP* statistic, and to show how it may reveal a somewhat different picture of performance from the standard *IRT* distribution, consider the hypothetical sample of responding given by the *IRT* distribution in Figure 6.11. The sample consists of 640 interresponse times, divided into 4-second class intervals. Half of all the *IRT*s fall into the first class interval, with decreasing numbers falling into each successive interval. The calculated relative frequency of response in each interval is tabulated in panel A and graphed in panel B. This picture of responding suggests that the subject becomes less and less likely to make a response terminating an *IRT* as the time since the last response increases.

The subject has 640 opportunities to respond in the 0- to 4-second interval—one after each response—and it responds in that interval 320 times, giving a conditional probability of 0.50. Only 320 opportunities remain to give an *IRT* greater than 4 seconds. Of those 320 opportunities, 160 result in responses between 4 and 8 seconds. Therefore, the conditional probability of responding in that interval is 0.50—exactly the same as between 0 and 4 seconds, although the absolute and relative frequencies of responding in that interval are much smaller. The same sort of relationship prevails throughout the observed range of *IRT*s, up to the final class interval which pools all *IRT*s longer than 20 seconds. The conditional probability of responding in this final category is necessarily 1.00. The conditional probability of responding in each interval before the "dump" category is plotted in panel C, to indicate that a correction for the decreasing numbers of opportunities to respond at long times after reinforcement reveals a constant

A

IRT class	Number of IRTs	Number of OPs	Relative frequency	IRTs/OP	Probability of reinforcement	Number of reinforcements
0–4	320	640	.500	.500	.067	21
4–8	160	320	.250	.500	.200	32
8–12	80	160	.125	.500	.333	26
12–16	40	80	.063	.500	.440	18
16–20	20	40	.031	.500	.546	11
> 20	20	20	.031	—	—	—

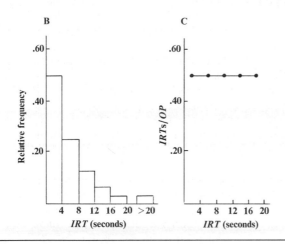

Figure 6.11 A hypothetical distribution of interresponse times, indicating the calculation of the relative frequency of each response time (panel B) and the conditional probability of responding in each class interval (termed *IRTs/OP* and illustrated in panel C). Also tabulated are the probabilities of reinforcement in each class interval taken from the *VI* 30-second schedule of Figure 6.10 and the resulting numbers of reinforcements obtained (panel A).

tendency to respond in each class interval. The advantages and disadvantages of the *IRTs/OP* statistic are considered at length by Anger (1956), and further discussion is unnecessary here. Instead, we will examine his results and their relations to the *VI* schedule contingencies.

During the first 5 of 38 2-hour training sessions on *VI* 5-minutes, Anger's rats exhibited substantially flat *IRTs/OP* functions of the sort shown in Figure 6.11. With continued training, there was

a systematic change, so that *IRTs/OP* decreased as a function of *IRT* length for all subjects. The results for the final 10 sessions of training are given for each subject in Figures 6.12A through 6.12D, replotted from Anger's (1956) data. Clearly, the momentary tendency to respond did not correspond to the probability of reinforcement, which increased with increasing *IRT* length. Rather, it may have depended on the frequency of reinforcement. The numbers of reinforcements obtained per hour for responding in each *IRT* class are also shown in panels A through D, and a fair correspondence between *IRTs/OP* and obtained reinforcement frequency is apparent.

Anger demonstrated that even when the momentary tendency to respond was constant, as in the early stages of training, the obtained frequency of reinforcement decreased with increasing *IRT* length. To see this aspect of *VI* schedules, consider the hypothetical distribution of *IRTs* given in connection with Figure 6.11, and the *VI* schedule of reinforcement described in Figure 6.10. To determine the probability of reinforcement in the first *IRT* class interval, 0 to 4 seconds, assume that the average *IRT* in that class is 2 seconds; then from Figure 6.10, the probability of reinforcement is .067. Similarly, for the 4 to 8 second interval, assume a mean of 6 seconds, leading to a probability of reinforcement of .20. Probabilities of reinforcement for the other class intervals were determined similarly and are listed in Figure 6.11A. The number of reinforcements obtained in each class interval is given directly by multiplying the number of responses by the probability of reinforcement. The results of this calculation for each interval are also listed in panel A. This shows that the frequency of reinforcement decreases as a function of *IRT* length beyond the 4- to 8-second class interval.

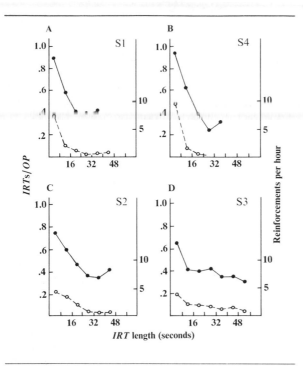

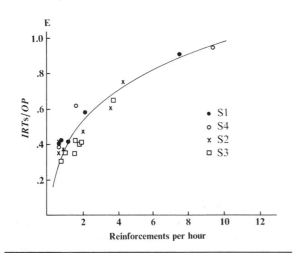

Figure 6.12 Panels A, B, C, and D: The conditional probability of responding (*IRT*s/*OP*) in 8-second class intervals, as a function of the length of the interresponse time, after prolonged training on a *VI* 5-minute schedule. Each panel represents an individual rat. Also indicated in each panel are the numbers of reinforcements obtained per hour in each class interval. Panel E: The resulting relation between *IRT*s/*OP* and the obtained numbers of reinforcements per hour for each rat. (After Anger, 1956.)

The essence of Anger's argument is that the decreasing *IRT*s/*OP* at long *IRT*s after prolonged training is the result of the decreasing frequency of reinforcement experienced even when the conditional probability of responding was constant, upon initial exposure to the procedure. The shift in *IRT*s/*OP* produced by differential reinforcement frequency, in turn, leads to a further change in the distribution of reinforcement frequencies. To describe the end product of this interaction, Anger's results for the final ten sessions of training on *VI*-5 (Figures 6.12A through 6.12D) have been replotted in Figure 6.12E to show the relation between *IRT*s/*OP* in each class interval and the frequency of reinforcement obtained in that interval. Although there are substantial differences between subjects in the *IRT*s/*OP* functions, a single increasing, negatively accelerated function describes the relation between *IRT*s/*OP* and reinforcement frequency for all four rats.

The relationship shown here is the result of both the programmed schedule of reinforcement and the subjects' behavior: Changes in their *IRT* distributions necessarily change both the *IRT*s/*OP* and the obtained reinforcement frequencies. However, the form of the function is not forced. It is easy to construct other function forms, and the reader who wishes to be sure of understanding this material might do well to try working out hypothetical *IRT* distributions that lead to other relations. It should be noted that the hypothetical data of Figure 6.11 exemplify a different relation between *IRT*s/*OP* and reinforcement frequency: *IRT*s/*OP* are constant and independent of the frequency of reinforcement. Therefore, the data of Figure 6.12 imply the operation of a behavioral process rather than a forced correlation.

The generality of the relationship is not known at present. Working with pigeons in situations that involved selective reinforcement of different *IRT*s at different frequencies, Shimp (1968) and Staddon (1968) have obtained data that are consistent with the function suggested by Figure 6.12. However, Blough and Blough (1968) found that the *IRT* distributions of pigeons responding on *VI* schedules did not seem to conform in any simple way to the obtained frequencies of reinforcement. Moreover, demonstrated sequential dependencies between different *IRT* classes complicate analysis (Williams, 1968). The data in this area of research on maintained performances are orderly enough to encourage further research, but the findings are likely to be complex.

Experimental manipulation of the relation between *IRT*s and reinforcement

It has been shown that the probability of reinforcement increases as a function of time since the last response on interval schedules as they are usually programmed. It is possible to alter this relationship by imposing a *limited hold* on the availability of reinforcement. For example, with a limited hold of 3 seconds, the subject must respond within 3 seconds of reinforcement availability or the reinforcement is canceled. This procedure means that responses are followed by reinforcement only if they fall within a 3-second period. The probability of reinforcement does not increase with *IRT* length beyond 3 seconds, but remains constant at the proportion of time in the schedule during which reinforcement is held. In our sample *VI* schedule with intervals of 10, 20, 30, 40, and 50 seconds, totaling 150 seconds, a 3-second limited hold would restrict reinforcement availability to 15 seconds—3 seconds after each interval. The probability of reinforcement for *IRT*s longer than 3 seconds is therefore 15/150 or .10, exactly as in a *VR*-10 schedule (see Figure 6.10).

On an interval schedule with limited hold, then, long *IRT*s are treated exactly as on a ratio schedule. If the differential reinforcement of long *IRT*s is a factor in the maintenance of lower rates on standard interval schedules than on ratio schedules, a limited hold should lead to rate increases, even though there is no consequent increase in reinforcement frequency. Ferster and Skinner (1957) have demonstrated that this effect occurs with pigeons responding for food reinforcement on *VI* schedules.

An extensive program of research on interval schedules with limited hold has been described by Schoenfeld and Cumming (1960) and their co-workers. Their basic schedule consists of the regular alternation in time of a period in which the first response is reinforced (t^D) and a period in which responding is never reinforced (t^Δ). Figure 6.13 gives an example of the operation of this program with t^D t^Δ 15 seconds. In effect, the resulting schedule is like a standard *FI* 30-second schedule with a 15-second limited hold (which is so long as to have no effect on a well-trained subject). The basic variables of the system are the cycle length, $t^D + t^\Delta$, and the length of t^D.

Hearst (1958) and Clark (1959) have studied the effects of reducing t^D while holding the cycle length constant. Both experiments used pigeons as sub-

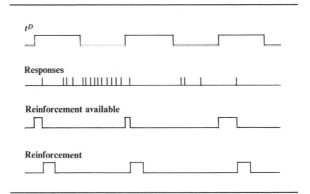

Figure 6.13 The operation of a t^D-t^Δ schedule. The first response in each t^D period is reinforced, and all other responses are unreinforced. t^D and t^Δ alternate regularly in time, without regard for the time at which reinforcement is actually obtained.

jects and demonstrated continuous increases in rate, coupled with the acquisition of a fixed-ratio character in the pattern of responding, as the value of t^D became very small. Some of Clark's (1959) cumulative records of responding by pigeons on a schedule with a 2-minute cycle length and various values of t^D are shown in Figure 6.14. As t^D becomes smaller, the maintained performance is characterized by increasingly abrupt transitions from pausing to responding, and the rate of responding is dramatically increased. Note that this effect occurred without any concomitant increase in the frequency of reinforcement; indeed, there was a decrease in the number of reinforcements obtained per session at short t^D values. Although it is not clear that these schedules can duplicate ratio performances in all aspects, it is evident that restrictions on the availability of reinforcement in time can produce major changes in the performances maintained by interval schedules.

Varying the cycle length while holding constant the ratio of t^D to cycle length is equivalent to varying the length of an interval schedule. We have seen that response rate is inversely related to the length of an interval schedule, but what happens when the cycle length becomes very short—much shorter than the average *IRT*? Under these conditions, where a response is reinforced only if it coincides with t^D, each response has a constant probability of reinforcement equal to the ratio $t^D / t^D + t^\Delta$. This is of course similar to the conditions imposed by *VR* schedules, as shown in Figure 6.10. Therefore, re-

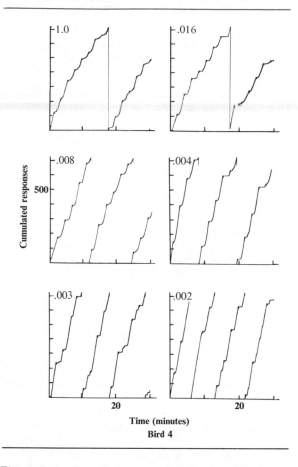

Figure 6.14 Cumulative records of key-pecking by a pigeon on t^D-t^Δ schedules. The sum of t^D and t^Δ was always 2 minutes. The proportion of the cycle in t^D is indicated in each panel. Reinforcements are indicated by diagonal marks. (From Clark, 1959.)

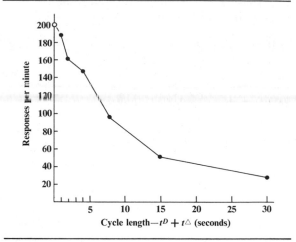

Figure 6.15 Average rate of responding by pigeons as a function of the sum of t^D and t^Δ, where t^D was always equal to 1/20 of the cycle length. The point at .001 seconds was interpolated from Brandauer's (1958) data in Figure 6.4, for a value of 20 responses per reinforcement. (After Schoenfeld & Cumming, 1957.)

ductions in cycle length should also lead to ratio-like performance.

The effects of cycle length have been explored by Schoenfeld and Cumming (1957) with pigeons as subjects. They held the ratio t^D/t^D+t^Δ constant at 0.05 and varied the cycle length from 30 seconds to 0.94 seconds. The average rate of responding maintained at each cycle length is shown in Figure 6.15. Also plotted at a cycle length of 0.001 seconds is the average rate interpolated from Brandauer's (1958) data (see Figure 6.4) for a probability of reinforcement of 0.05. The strong relation between cycle length and response rate in this figure is presumably due both to changes in the frequency and distribution of reinforcements and the ratio-like

contingencies imposed on *IRT*s by the reduction in t^D length. To separate these variables, a yoked control group might be useful.

The use of limited hold reduces the differential reinforcement for long *IRT*s in interval schedules. Conversely, it is possible to provide differential reinforcement of long *IRT*s in a fixed-ratio schedule by requiring that the final *IRT* exceed some short value. Ferster and Skinner (1957) have studied performances of pigeons on schedules of this kind. For example, after 160 responses spaced in any way (*FR*-160), the first response following an *IRT* greater than 2 seconds was reinforced (*DRL*-2). Some examples of a characteristic performance on this schedule after prolonged training on simple *FR*, and gradual increase of the *DRL* requirement from a fraction of a second, are shown in Figure 6.16. This performance is of great interest, because it embodies both the characteristic pause after reinforcement and the abrupt shift to a high rate commonly observed on *FR*, and the low terminal rate required by *DRL*. Other examples of performance on this kind of schedule are given by Ferster and Skinner; commonly, they are more variable from one reinforcement to the next, but nearly all contain frequent instances of the sort exhibited here.

This example suggests that contingencies determining the behavior at the moment of reinforcement do not suffice to determine the overall character of the performance. In any ratio schedule, faster responding produces more frequent reinforcement in time, but here, the *DRL* contingency requires that the terminal rate be fairly low The resulting performance reflects the joint action of these opposed contingencies.

The importance of contingencies in the study of behavior

To illustrate the relevance and importance of all these complexities, let us consider an experiment by Neuringer and Chung (1967). Pigeons obtained food for key-pecking on a *VI* 1-minute schedule. After a stable response rate was established, the program was changed to *percentage reinforcement*. An initial peck started an *FI* 5-second schedule, and the first peck to occur at the end of 5 seconds produced food if the *VI* program had made reinforcement available. If the *VI* program had not scheduled a reinforcement, no food was presented, and instead a 1-second blackout occurred. Brief blackouts of this sort are presumably neutral, or perhaps mildly aversive for pigeons. The next peck, after either reinforcement or blackout, started another *FI* 5-second interval. Approximately 15 percent of the intervals ended with food, and 85 percent ended with blackout. The overall frequency

of food reinforcement remained the same, but under this new program the rate of responding approximately doubled. A subsequent experiment demonstrated that the rate was about the same when food was presented after every *FI* 5-second interval. Thus, it appeared that being exposed to a blackout 85 percent of the time was functionally identical to receiving food for every completion of the 5-second interval.

In an attempt to understand this phenomenon, the same authors conducted several additional experiments with the same subjects. In one, they repeated the original procedure of giving reinforcement on a *VI* 1-minute schedule, and then introduced blackouts (or food if the programmed interval had elapsed) on *FR*-11. As before, there was a substantial increase in response rate. This increase appeared only when the contingencies for producing food and blackout were the same: If blackouts were given for every eleventh peck, but food could be obtained for a single response on the standard *VI* 1-minute schedule, the response rates were essentially the same as those without blackouts. This result suggests the following conclusion: Blackouts may function to increase rates in the same way as food, but only if given on the same schedule as food. More generally, these data suggest that the contingency between behavior and its consequences may be as important as the nature of the consequences themselves. An understanding of the contingencies of reinforcement is therefore

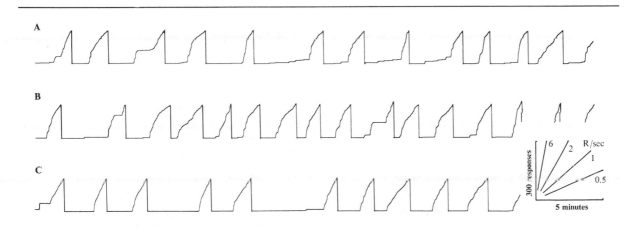

Figure 6.16 Cumulative records of responding by a pigeon on a schedule which required the completion of a fixed ratio of 160 responses, and then imposed a *DRL* 2-second contingency on reinforced responses. Samples of performance are presented from three sessions. The recorder pen reset to the baseline after each reinforcement. (From Ferster & Skinner, 1957.)

essential if one wishes to evaluate the effectiveness of different reinforcing stimuli in different situations—a problem of general significance in behavior theory.

The crucial role of the contingencies of reinforcement may also be illustrated by reference to another research area. A well-known study by Estes and Skinner (1941) demonstrated that responding maintained by fixed-interval food reinforcement was reduced or eliminated in the presence of a tone that regularly preceded an unavoidable electric shock. The effect has come to be known as *conditioned suppression* and is commonly interpreted as reflecting a conditioned emotional state (anxiety) which is incompatible with the performance of positively reinforced operant behavior (see also Chapter 8). A number of parametric determinants of conditioned suppression have been studied, and the phenomenon is currently receiving a good deal of attention.

Some recent findings have complicated the picture. Blackman (1968) demonstrated that response rates increased in the presence of a stimulus preceding a moderately intense shock when responding was maintained by a *DRL* schedule, whereas responding maintained by an alternated *FI* schedule was suppressed in the presence of the same stimulus and shock. Thus, under certain conditions, the direction of the effect depended on the schedule maintaining performance.

Related research has explored the effects of stimuli preceding response-independent food. For example, Henton and Brady (1970) found that rates of responding maintained by a *DRL* schedule increased in the presence of a stimulus preceding food—an effect that could be interpreted as reflecting a facilitative emotional or motivational effect conditioned to the prefood stimulus. However, Azrin and Hake (1969) have found that when responding was maintained on a *VI* schedule, response rate decreased in the presence of stimuli preceding response-independent positive reinforcers. Thus, once again it appears that the direction of the effect depended on the schedule maintaining performance. Moreover, the baseline schedule may be a more potent determinant of changes in responding than the nature of the reinforcer—positive or negative—with which the stimulus was paired. Therefore, an understanding of reinforcement contingencies must precede the use of maintained performances to assess conditioned emotional or motivational processes (Rescorla & Solomon, 1967; see also Chapter 8).

COMBINATIONS OF REINFORCEMENT SCHEDULES
Multiple schedules

It is often convenient to observe two different performances by a single subject within a single experimental session, especially if one is concerned with variables that may affect behavior differently depending on the contingencies of reinforcement. One possible method is to program two different reinforcement schedules in succession, each associated with a different stimulus. With a pigeon, one might program a fixed-interval schedule in the presence of a red response key. When the interval is completed and the bird obtains its food, the key color would change to green and a fixed-ratio schedule would be in effect. Red would reappear when the ratio was completed and food obtained. A procedure of this sort, termed a *multiple FI-FR* schedule, typically maintains different performances in the distinctive stimulus conditions, each appropriate to its associated schedule. This type of procedure was proposed earlier as a method for comparing ratio and interval performances in a single subject within a single session.

This advantage of multiple schedules is offset, to some extent, by complicating interactions between components. One intuitively obvious interaction is a blending of the two performances. For instance, in multiple *FI-FR,* the *FI* rate might be higher than if the same *FI* were programmed alone, indicating the influence of the high-rate *FR* performance.

Interactions of this sort—which may be thought of as *generalization* between the schedule components—are usually not important after extensive training. The opposite effect, known as *behavioral contrast* (Chapter 4), is frequently encountered but is less easy to understand intuitively. It involves behavior changes in opposite directions. An experimental example may be useful here. Reynolds (1961) trained pigeons to respond on multiple *VI-FR* schedules. The key was alternately red and green, changing every 3 minutes. Throughout the experiment, a *VI* 3-minute schedule was in effect when the key was red. Different values of the *FR* schedule, or extinction, were programmed when the key was green, each value remaining in effect until a stable performance was attained in both red and green conditions. Reynolds found that increasing the size of the *FR* from 75 to 150 produced lower rates in the presence of the green key (the *FR* stimulus). This finding is consistent with our knowledge of *FR* schedules programmed alone. Interestingly, the rate in the red condition, which was always associated with *VI*-3, did not go down, as one might expect from generalization with the *FR* performance; rather, it increased, despite constancy of obtained reinforcements in the presence of the red key.

Reynolds suggested that this contrast effect depended on changes in the relative frequency of reinforcement. When *FR*-75 was programmed for the green key, only about 20 percent of all reinforcements in the session were obtained on the *VI*-3 schedule in the red condition. When the green-key schedule was changed to *FR*-150, about 40 percent of all reinforcements were received in the red condition. The increase in response rate in the presence of the red key may therefore be attributed to an increase in relative reinforcement frequency from 0.2 to 0.4.

It is by no means clear that all instances of contrast can be explained this way (see Chapter 4). However, subsequent research with multiple schedules of reinforcement has indicated that the relative frequency of reinforcement in one schedule component is a powerful determinant of response rate in that component. The results of four multiple schedule experiments, each with pigeons as subjects and each using a constant *VI* schedule in one component, are plotted in Figure 6.17. In each case, the average rate of responding in the constant *VI* schedule component is related to the average obtained relative frequency of reinforcement in that component. In all four experiments, each subject was exposed to each of several schedule values until stable performance resulted. The durations of the schedule components were fixed and equal, so that the constant *VI* schedule was in effect for 50 percent of every session. The experiments differed widely in the contingencies used in the other component of the schedule and in the resulting behavior. Reynolds (1961), in the study just described, used various *FR* schedules; Zuriff (1970) used *VR* schedules; Bloomfield (1967) used different *DRL* schedules; and Nevin (1968) varied the frequency of reinforcement for not pecking the key, which is termed *differential reinforcement of other behavior (DRO)*. Despite these radical differences, the effects on *VI* performance are strikingly similar. It appears safe to conclude that response rate maintained by a constant *VI* component of a multiple schedule depends directly on the relative frequency of reinforcement ob-

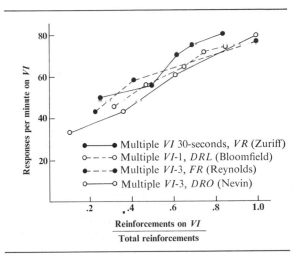

Figure 6.17 Average rates of responding by pigeons in the constant *VI* components of several multiple schedules, as a function of the relative frequency of reinforcement obtained in the *VI* components. The relative frequency varied as a consequence of variations in the reinforcement schedule in the alternated component. In Zuriff's (1970) experiment, the alternated schedule was *VR;* in Bloomfield's (1967) study, it was *DRL;* in Reynolds' (1961) work, it was *FR;* and in Nevin's (1968) research, it was *DRO.*

tained in that component, but not on the behavior required for reinforcement in the other component.

Concurrent schedules

In multiple schedules of reinforcement, two different schedules are programmed successively and are associated with different stimuli. With *concurrent* schedules, two responses are available simultaneously, each being maintained by an independent schedule of reinforcement. As in the case of multiple schedules, the performances of a single subject on two different schedules can be assessed within a single experimental session. In addition, one can obtain a measure of the subject's preference for one schedule over the other by noting the proportion of total session time spent on each of the simultaneously available alternatives.

Research on concurrent schedules, studied extensively in several species, is reviewed by Catania (1966). As he points out, analyzing the effects of simultaneously available reinforcement schedules on two concurrent responses requires that the responses be independent. At the very least, the subject must not be able to make both responses simultaneously; otherwise, reinforcement would of course affect both responses, regardless of which schedule requirement had been satisfied. This condition appears to be met for the pigeon in the standard key-pecking situation, since it cannot peck both response keys at the same time. However, if it pecks one key and then switches and obtains reinforcement on the other, that reinforcement may affect not only the final response, but also the entire pattern of pecking the first key and switching to the other. To prevent reinforcement for switching, a common procedure is to withhold reinforcement for one response if the other response has occurred within a second or two. In effect, each switch from one key to the other postpones the next reinforcement, minimizing the effects of reinforcement on pecking the other key and then switching. This procedure is termed the *change-over delay (COD)*.

A second difficulty with concurrent schedules is that the subject may not actually respond on both alternatives, but confine its behavior to the more favorable schedule. This outcome is especially likely in the case of concurrent ratio schedules. Concurrent interval schedules have a property that virtually guarantees responding on both alternatives, however. As has been indicated, interval schedules make reinforcement more probable with the passage of time since the last response. Therefore, the longer the subject persists in responding on one alternative, the more likely it is that reinforcement will be available for switching to the other. Given pretraining to insure at least occasional responding to both alternatives, this aspect of *VI* contingencies insures maintenance of performance by both schedules. For this reason, only interval schedules will be considered here.

A good deal of work has been done on concurrent *VI* schedules. Before considering some of the results, the reader should understand that the subject can obtain all available reinforcements with nearly any distribution of responses on the two keys. For example, if both schedules are *VI* with 10-second minimum intervals, and the *COD* is 1 second, the subject could obtain all available reinforcements by pecking one key for 1 second out of every 10, and responding for the remaining 9 seconds on the other key. Any less extreme departure from equal responding would be equally effective.

It is therefore of considerable interest to find, as an empirical fact, that pigeons roughly match the proportion of responses on one key to the proportion of reinforcements obtained on that key. For example, if pecks at the left-hand key are reinforced on a *VI* 2-minute schedule, while pecks at the right-hand key are reinforced on a *VI* 6-minute schedule, yielding 30 and 10 reinforcements per hour, respectively, the proportion of all reinforcements obtained on the left-hand key is 0.75. A number of studies have shown that under these conditions a pigeon will make about 75 percent of its responses on the left-hand key. This tendency to match the relative frequency of reinforcement has been observed over a wide range of *VI* schedule values; an indication of the range and precision of matching may be seen in Figure 6.18, taken from an early study of concurrent *VI* schedules by Herrnstein (1961). In this experiment, the schedule pairs were chosen so that the total number of reinforcements per hour was always 40. Data points are descriptive of terminal performances after extended training on each pair of schedules. Herrnstein also found that the total number of responses on both keys was approximately constant.

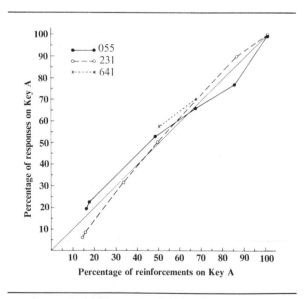

Figure 6.18 The relative frequency of responding by pigeons on one of two simultaneously available keys, as a function of the proportion of reinforcements obtained on that key. Reinforcement was programmed concurrently for responding on each key by independent variable-interval schedules chosen to give a total of 40 reinforcements per hour on both keys. (From Herrnstein, 1961.)

Herrnstein's major result was replicated and extended in an interesting way by Catania (1963a), whose experiment involved a modification of the standard concurrent schedule procedure. Pigeons confronted two keys, one of which was either red or yellow. A *VI* 2-minute schedule was always correlated with yellow, while the value of the *VI* sched ule in red was systematically varied. The pigeons could change the key color by a single peck at the other key, which was always green. Functionally, a peck at the green key was equivalent to moving the head from the left- to the right-hand key in the more common two-key procedure.

When a brief *COD* was imposed after each switching response, Catania's pigeons tended to match the number of pecks at the yellow key, relative to the total number of key-pecks when the key was red or yellow, to the relative frequency of reinforcement provided by the *VI* schedule associated with yellow. This observation is the same as Herrnstein's (1961) result, and it may be written

$$\frac{R_1}{R_1 + R_2} = \frac{r_1}{r_1 + r_2},\qquad [1]$$

where R_1 and R_2 refer to the numbers of pecks at yellow and red, respectively, while r_1 and r_2 refer to the numbers of reinforcements obtained in the presence of those stimuli.

Catania also found that the total number of pecks increased when the total number of reinforcements increased, in much the same fashion as for a single response maintained by different frequencies of reinforcement (see Figure 6.3). To describe the result, Catania used a power function with a small exponent

$$R_1 + R_2 = k(r_1 + r_2)^{1/6},\qquad [2]$$

where $R_1, R_2, r_1,$ and r_2 are defined as for Equation 1 and k is a multiplicative constant to account for individual differences in the absolute level of responding.

Combining these representations of the data, we can write

$$\frac{R_1}{k(r_1 + r_2)^{1/6}} = \frac{r_1}{r_1 + r_2}$$

or

$$R_1 = \frac{kr_1}{(r_1 + r_2)^{5/6}}.\qquad [3]$$

That is, the number of responses per session in the presence of the yellow key depends only on the frequencies of reinforcement in red and yellow

conditions, but not on the amount of responding in the red condition. This is perhaps an unexpected deduction: Most readers would probably have assumed that the pigeon responded less on the constant *VI*-2 schedule in the yellow condition when the frequency of reinforcement in the red condition was increased because of an increase in time spent responding in the presence of red and the physical impossibility of responding to both at the same time.

Catania (1963a) was able to verify this deduction experimentally by a modification of his basic procedure. Normally, the switching key was dark. Whenever a reinforcement became available on the *VI* schedule associated with red, the switching key was illuminated green, and the subject could make the switching response and collect reinforcement in the red condition as soon as the *COD* was completed. Under these arrangements, the pigeons spent very little time in the red condition—only as much as was required to obtain the available reinforcements—so that the vast majority of the session was spent in the presence of yellow. Nevertheless, the response rate in yellow depended systematically on the reinforcement frequency in red and was substantially identical with the rate in yellow when reinforcement in red was not signaled and the pigeons responded extensively. The results, averaged for the three pigeons, are summarized in Figure 6.19.

At this point, the reader should pause to consider some parallels between multiple and concurrent schedules of reinforcement. The first similarity is procedural. Although concurrent schedules are available simultaneously, the subject can respond on only one at a time if the responses are independent. This temporal succession is made especially clear in Catania's procedure, in which a single key is either red or yellow, with alternations dependent on responses to the switching key. Each key color is correlated with a different schedule of reinforcement, just as in the case of multiple schedules. The major difference is that in concurrent schedules the subject can control the length of time spent responding on each schedule, while in multiple schedules this is programmed by the experimenter.

A second point in common is that the rate of responding on one schedule depends inversely on the frequency of reinforcement obtained in the other schedule, but not on the behavior required to obtain that reinforcement. This relationship is not attributable to changes in the frequency or the contingencies of reinforcement in the first schedule, since that remains constant; nor is it attributable to

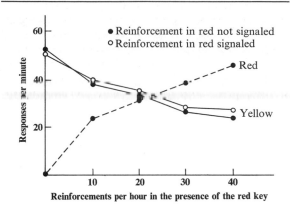

Figure 6.19 Rates of responding, calculated on the basis of total session time, in the presence of a yellow key, which was always correlated with a *VI* schedule yielding 20 reinforcements per hour, and in the presence of a red key, which was correlated with different reinforcement frequencies. The pigeons could change colors by pecking a second, switching key. Filled circles give the results when the *VI* reinforcement schedule in the red condition was conventionally programmed, without signals. The unfilled circles give the results when reinforcement availability in the red condition was signaled by illumination of the switching key, so that the rate of responding in the presence of red was essentially zero at all reinforcement frequencies. (After Catania, 1963a.)

generalization or response competition, since it is independent of performance maintained by the other schedule.

Finally, in both kinds of schedule combinations, rate of responding bears an orderly relation to the relative frequency of reinforcement. The finding that behavior may be determined by a ratio of two average reinforcement frequencies raises some new problems, since it is difficult to understand how this ratio—a mathematical transformation of two numbers, each of which can only be defined over protracted time periods—can make contact with performance. An understanding of the processes through which responding comes under the control of such remote specifications of its consequences is a major challenge for behavior theory.

However this process may ultimately be characterized, the data lend themselves to a comprehensive descriptive formulation proposed by Herrnstein (1970). He has suggested a fundamental equation relating response rate to the relative

frequency of reinforcement, as follows:

$$R_1 = k \frac{r_1}{r_1 + mr_2 + r_0}, \qquad [4]$$

where R_1 is the rate of responding in one component of a schedule, r_1 is the frequency of reinforcement obtained in that component, r_2 is the frequency of reinforcement obtained in a second component, and r_0 represents all other sources of reinforcement in the situation that are not under experimental control—e.g., the reinforcing effects of scratching, grooming, inspecting the chamber, and so forth. k is a constant that represents individual differences in the maximum rate of responding observed in a given setting. m is a constant that reflects the degree to which responding in one component is affected by reinforcement in another component. If m is 1.0, the interaction is maximal, as may be expected when components alternate rapidly in multiple schedules, or because of frequent switches between concurrent schedules. If m is 0, there is no interaction with the second component, as might be the case with wide temporal spacing between components. The formulation can incorporate the single-schedule case by simply setting r_2 equal to 0. For experiments involving two components, the rate of responding in the second component, R_2, may be described by the same equation with appropriate changes of subscript.

The reader should appreciate the following aspects of Herrnstein's equation:

1. For the single-schedule case, where $r_2 = 0$ and r_0 is greater than 0, the equation describes an increasing, negatively accelerated relation between responding and reinforcement frequency of the sort that was described earlier in connection with the parameters of interval schedules. The importance of r_0 is suggested by the fact that if r_0 is 0, R_1 always equals k, regardless of the value of r_1, which is clearly false.

2. For multiple schedules, the equation accounts for contrast: As long as m is greater than 0.0, decreases in r_2 (which would result in reductions in response rate R_2) will be accompanied by increases in R_1, because the denominator becomes smaller, and vice versa.

3. For both multiple and concurrent schedules, the equation incorporates the dependence of R_1 on *relative* reinforcement, much as does Catania's (1963a) formulation, just described (Equation 3). There is little to choose between them in this respect.

4. For concurrent schedules, where m is 1.0, the matching relation (Equation 1) is readily derived by writing the equation for R_2 and noting that its denominator is identical to that for R_1, so that the denominators cancel out, leaving

$$\frac{R_1}{R_1 + R_2} = \frac{r_1}{r_1 + r_2} \qquad [1]$$

Thus, Herrnstein's (1970) formulation seems to provide an economical, comprehensive description of maintained performance in a variety of situations. As it is extended to encompass more situations, it may be modified or replaced with other formulations, but the very possibility of providing a general, quantitative description of many aspects of maintained behavior is most encouraging.

THE DIFFERENTIATION OF RESPONDING
Free-operant behavior

In our discussion thus far, responses have been considered as binary events: They either occur or they do not occur. When a rat presses a bar, its behavior is usually recorded by means of a microswitch that operates when the bar has moved a short distance. If the bar is depressed a lesser distance, no response has occurred as far as the apparatus is concerned. Moreover, all depressions of the bar that result in switch closure are treated as identical, whether the rat presses with its right or left paw, fast or slowly, forcefully or weakly. In brief, all movements of the subject that result in a switch closure are treated as members of a single response class—bar-pressing—while all other movements are ignored (cf. Chapter 1). The reason for this neglect of the details of the subject's movement is that the resulting records of behavior bear orderly, replicable relations to the conditions of reinforcement. If the response is defined at some other level, involving a specification either too crude (e.g., any movement) or too refined (e.g., pressing with the right paw with a force between 15 and 18 grams and a duration of less than 0.20 seconds), these relations may be obsured. This point was made by Skinner (1938) and it remains a valid criterion for the definition of the behavior under study.

Merely because we often ignore dimensions of behavior other than the rate of occurrence of members of a simply defined response class does not mean that these dimensions are unaffected by the conditions of reinforcement. For example, in the standard bar-pressing situation, if reinforcement is delivered when the lever is pressed and then released, the delay of reinforcement from onset of the press will be least if the lever is released as soon as possible. This procedure provides differential reinforcement for short durations, which may indirectly affect the entire topography of the response and hence impose some limitations on its rate of emission. More importantly, the manner in which a response is made—for example, its speed— is often taken as a measure of the degree to which the response has been learned. If we are to treat measures of responding in this fashion, it is important to understand how the conditions of reinforcement may affect the way a response is made, so that the quantitative aspects of performance are not interpreted erroneously.

In thinking about how reinforcement may affect the way in which a response is made, it is convenient to consider a given response class as made up of a number of subclasses. For example, the general class *bar-pressing* may be viewed as consisting of a set of different subclasses, each with different forces or durations. Reinforcement may then be made contingent upon certain of these subclasses in a variety of ways. For example, the subject may obtain reinforcement only for forces above 30 grams—although 5 grams suffice to activate the recording equipment—or for durations greater than 2 seconds—although 10 milliseconds may be sufficient to operate the recording circuitry.

Some early work on these dimensions of bar-pressing has been described by Skinner (1938, Chapter 8). He made reinforcement contingent upon responses having either a minimum force or a minimum duration, and by gradually raising the criterion value he was able to establish and maintain unusually forceful or long bar-presses. In addition, he reported a tendency for force and duration to increase when reinforcement was discontinued. This tendency could be interpreted as an energizing effect of frustration resulting from nonreinforcement or, perhaps more simply, it may be understood in terms of the subject's history of differential reinforcement. In the past, responses that failed to meet the reinforcement criterion were, of course, not reinforced, while reinforcement was given for subsequent responses meeting the criterion. When reinforcement is terminated altogether, the subject may increase the force or duration of its responses simply because this behavior change had produced more frequent reinforcement in the past.

More recent work on response force and duration has been summarized by Notterman and Mintz

(1965). In addition to replicating and extending Skinner's observations, they examined the ways in which response force changed on various schedules of reinforcement, under conditions in which there was no force criterion in effect (other than that minimal amount required to operate the equipment). They found that forces tended to be lower immediately after reinforcement than immediately before it, the difference being greater on fixed-ratio schedules than on interval schedules. These effects were particularly clear when the fixed ratio was programmed in an unusual way, with more than one response being reinforced. For example, the subjects might be allowed to obtain reinforcement for 4 consecutive responses, after which the next 12 responses would go unreinforced. Such a schedule was designated *FR* (IV)-12. The average peak force changed systematically within each cycle of reinforcement and nonreinforcement, decreasing immediately after the first reinforcement and then increasing gradually following the first unreinforced response. It should be emphasized that these systematic shifts in force within the ratio were not the direct result of any differential reinforcement of response force. They may be understood by reference to the tendency of force to increase in extinction. When the subjects were first placed on these *FR* schedules after regular reinforcement, a tendency for force to increase with nonreinforcement was expected. Thus, the first response reinforced on an *FR* schedule was likely to be relatively forceful, even though such force was not required by the procedure. The systematic tendency for force to increase with successive nonreinforced responses may then be maintained *superstitiously*— that is, simply because this pattern of behavior was regularly followed by reinforcement.

Discrete-trial performances

The application of reinforcement contingencies to the quantitative dimensions of a single response has also received extensive study in the straight runway situation, a setting quite different from the standard free-operant situation. Rather than requiring a response that is of brief duration and readily repeated at varying rates, the runway situation involves a response that is extended in time and space and has as its various subclasses the full range of possible starting latencies and running speeds. The repetition of the entire response is strictly controlled by the experimenter, since the subject cannot run until released from a start-box, and rather long intervals are usually imposed between these opportunities. An extensive analysis of the behavior of rats in runways under various conditions of reinforcement has been given by Logan (1960), and his treatment will be followed in this section.

Consider the simple runway situation, in which food reinforcement is given in the goal-box immediately upon completion of the run. The contingencies here are analogous to those when reinforcement is given for pressing and then releasing a lever: The sooner the subject leaves the start-box and the faster it runs, the sooner reinforcement is received. Note the similarity of this contingency to the relation between response rate and reinforcement frequency on *FR* schedules. In the runway, these contingencies provide differential reinforcement for short starting latencies and high running speeds; indeed, this is the direction in which performance changes during acquisition.

This sort of contingency between speed and immediacy of reinforcement is easily changed by controlling the time at which food is given in the goal-box. For example, Logan (1960, p. 150) has described a procedure he termed "controlled interval of reinforcement," in which food is presented some fixed time after the starting door is opened. Under these conditions, faster speeds result in a longer delay of reinforcement in the goal-box than do slower speeds. Thus, slower running is differentially reinforced. This situation is analogous to an *FI* schedule, in which reinforcement is available at a fixed time without regard for response rate, but the probability of reinforcement is greater following longer *IRT*s. It differs from schedules such as *DRL* in that reinforcement is given on every trial, regardless of running speed; a runway analog to *DRL* schedules will be described later.

The controlled-interval-of-reinforcement technique appears to be more effective in maintaining slower running than are uncontrolled intervals with comparable delays of reinforcement. To demonstrate this difference, Logan (1960) used a yoked-control procedure very similar to the technique used by Ferster and Skinner (1957) in comparing *VR* and *VI* schedules. Suppose that the controlled interval of reinforcement for the experimental rat is set at 10 seconds, and the rat takes 7 seconds to traverse the runway on one trial. The delay of reinforcement in the goal-box is then 3 seconds. The yoked partner would then run its next trial with reinforcement delayed for 3 seconds after it arrived at the goal-box, regardless of how long it took to run. Thus, the yoked rats can still obtain reinforcement sooner in each trial by faster running. Comparison of performances of experimental and yoked groups of rats tested under these conditions revealed that those with the controlled interval of reinforcement ran consistently slower than the yoked controls. The analogy between this finding and the results of the yoked-control comparisons of ratio and interval performances should be clear (see earlier discussion of the Ferster & Skinner experiment in this chapter).

Logan (1960, pp. 147–148) has also worked with a procedure he termed "controlled latency of reinforcement," in which the delivery of food is determined by a timer which starts when the subject leaves the start-box, rather than when the door opens. Logan studied separate groups of rats, with subject-initiated latencies of reinforcement ranging from 2 to 20 seconds. He found that running speed decreased systematically as the latency of reinforcement increased.

Logan's method for controlling the latency of reinforcement is analogous to an *FI* schedule in which the interval begins with the first response after reinforcement. Response-initiated *FI* schedules have been studied by Chung and Neuringer (1967), with separate groups of pigeons. They found that the rate of responding after the initial response decreased as the *FI* value increased, much as speed was affected in the runway.

A final analogy between differential reinforcement of speed in the runway and rate of a free operant comes from the runway equivalent of a *DRL* schedule. Recall that the *DRL* schedule makes reinforcement available only if an *IRT* exceeds some minimum value. In the runway, one might similarly give reinforcement only if the rat runs at less than some specified speed. Logan (1960, pp. 162–166) has studied the maintained performances of rats under conditions in which reinforcement was given only if a run down the 4-foot alley took at least 5 seconds. The resulting distribution of running times was sharply peaked, with its mode just beyond the minimum time required for reinforcement. Its form was similar to the *IRT* distribution for *DRL* (Figure 6.9), except that the very short *IRTs* characteristic of *DRL* performances did not have a parallel in running times. Logan (1961) has shown that this absence of very rapid responses under *DRL*-like conditions is not unique to the runway, but appears to be characteristic of the discrete-trials situation generally.

Taken together, the similar effects of analogous contingencies of reinforcement on speed of response in the runway and the rate at which a free operant is repeated suggest the following general-

ization: A subclass of a single defined response is affected by differential reinforcement in the same way as is the rate of emission of a free operant.

THE PARAMETERS OF REINFORCEMENT

Thus far, this chapter has concentrated on the contingencies between a given response and reinforcement, and the frequency of reinforcement, as determinants of maintained behavior. In emphasizing the potency of these variables, we have ignored the reinforcing stimulus itself and its presentation in time after the response. The effects of amount and delay of reinforcement, which are commonly termed *parameters of reinforcement* and constitute a part of the conditions of reinforcement together with the prevailing schedule, will now be considered.

Amount of reinforcement

The effects of amount of reinforcement on maintained performances may be studied in the same fashion as the parameters of a schedule. Separate groups of subjects may be trained with different amounts of reinforcement and their terminal performances compared, or single subjects may be brought to steady-state performances with each of several amounts of reinforcement. Finally, single subjects may be given different amounts of reinforcement for different performances within a single session by programming either multiple or concurrent schedules of reinforcement. It will be seen that the results depend in part on the experimental design employed and the programmed contingencies of reinforcement.

In an early study of maintained free-operant performance in rats, Guttman (1953) employed sucrose solution as the reinforcing agent and related the average rate of responding by rats on an *FI* 1-minute schedule to the concentration of sucrose. He used both the independent-group and single-subject methods. First, 42 rats were divided into four groups and trained for five half-hour sessions with 4, 8, 16, or 32 percent sucrose solutions, and their average response rates determined. Then, 20 of these subjects were trained for 15 minutes per day in each of four experimental chambers, each chamber providing a different sucrose concentration. Each rat was so trained for 12 days, and the average rate of responding in each chamber was determined. Both methods gave substantially identical results, with response rates increasing systematically as a function of sucrose concentration.

In Guttman's study, training was fairly brief, and it is not likely that performances were truly stable. Some subsequent studies of asymptotic performances of rats in a runway (Logan, 1960) and of pigeons in free operant situations with variable interval reinforcement (Catania, 1963b; Keesey & Kling, 1961) have typically shown that speed of running and rate of responding are relatively insensitive to the amount of reinforcement.

In Logan's (1960, Chapter 3) discrete-trial work, independent groups of rats were typically trained for a constant number of trials in the runway, with the number of food pellets delivered in the goal-box differing across groups. In one study, for example, different groups of rats obtained 1, 3, 6, or 12 food pellets on each runway trial. Only one trial was conducted for each subject every 48 hours, in order to permit precise control of food deprivation. Average asymptotic speeds after 55 trials were .430, .453, .447, and .465 for the four groups, listed in order of increasing numbers of pellets (the speed scores are reciprocals of the time required to run 4 feet in the runway). Clearly, the effects of a twelvefold variation in amount were slight. Other runway studies have obtained larger effects, but in general the functions are shallow.

One possible reason for the small effect is that in these studies no individual subject is ever exposed to more than one amount of reinforcement. It is possible that performance is more sensitive to amount when different amounts can be compared within a reasonably short period. For example, in one portion of the study by Keesey and Kling (1961), three different amounts of reinforcement were available on identical *VI* schedules in three different stimulus conditions, which changed every 40 minutes. In essence, this was a multiple schedule with unusually long components. The data reveal a clear positive relationship between amount of reinforcement and response rate during the first minute of each component. However, the average rate of responding maintained throughout the component was little affected by amount.

The latter aspect of their results was confirmed by Catania (1963b), who also studied pigeons responding on *VI* schedules for various amounts of food—determined, in his work, by varying the duration of access to grain. When a single key was available to the pigeon, and a fixed duration of reinforcement was programmed for a number of consecutive sessions, the average rate of responding was virtually unaffected by duration. However,

when two keys were made available, and two different amounts of reinforcement were programmed concurrently on identical but independent schedules, a large and consistent difference in rates on the two keys was obtained. In fact, when the duration of reinforcement on one key was double the duration on the other, the first key commanded approximately double the rate on the second. These results are summarized in Figure 6.20. Catania suggested that concurrent performances may be unusually sensitive to variations in the parameters of reinforcement.

Multiple schedules with reasonably short components also seem to generate performances that vary systematically with amount of reinforcement, as expected from Keesey and Kling's (1961) results for responding in the first minute of each component. Again with pigeons as subjects, Shettleworth and Nevin (1965) programmed different durations of reinforcement on identical *VI* schedules in the presence of red and green lights, which alternated every 2 or 3 minutes on a single key. Their results were summarized in a plot relating the relative rate of responding in the presence of green, defined as responses in the presence of green relative to the sum of responses in the presence of red and green, to the relative duration of reinforcement in green. The results for two pigeons on five different amounts of reinforcement are shown in Figure 6.21.

In a study of multiple *VI* schedules differing in

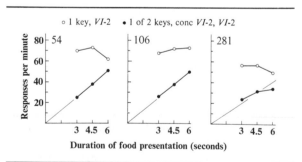

Figure 6.20 Average rates of responding by pigeons as a function of the duration of access to grain. Reinforcement was always programmed by a *VI* 2-minute schedule. The unfilled circles indicate the results when only one key was available. The filled circles show the results when two keys were available and different durations of reinforcement were programmed concurrently. (From Catania, 1963b.)

reinforcement frequency, Reynolds (1963) found an orderly relationship between the relative rate of responding in one stimulus condition and the relative frequency of reinforcement obtained in that condition. His results are plotted for comparison in Figure 6.21. Evidently, relative rates are similarly related to relative reinforcement, whether amount or frequency is varied. This agreement, coupled with Catania's results, suggests that (at least for pigeons) amount of reinforcement is functionally equivalent to frequency of reinforcement in multiple and concurrent schedules. Further confirmation of this equivalence has been provided by Rachlin and Baum (1969) in a study analogous to Catania's (1963a) research on signaled concurrent reinforcement.

Neuringer (1967) has argued that the effect of amount of reinforcement depends in part on the contingencies between responding and its consequences. In single-response, free-operant studies (such as the first phase of Catania's experiment), the amount of reinforcement obtained is constant and independent of the subject's behavior. In concurrent schedule procedures involving two responses leading to different amounts, the amount of reinforcement is contingent upon which response the subject makes. The nature of this contingency, rather than any differential effects of amount per se, may be responsible for the obtained results. In view of the known effects of the contingencies of reinforcement in the study of performance on various schedules, it is obviously important to understand and control the contingencies even when studying other determinants of maintained performance, such as amount of reinforcement. Not all effects of amount can be explained in terms of differential contingencies, however. The functions obtained by Guttman (1953), and the effects observed by Keesey and Kling (1961) and by Shettleworth and Nevin (1965) in multiple schedules, are not obviously the result of contingent relations between responding and amount of reinforcement.

Delay of reinforcement

We have seen that an understanding of the contingencies between behavior and reinforcement may be central to the understanding of the effects of amount of reinforcement. The second generally studied parameter of reinforcement, its delay with respect to the reinforced response, is even more crucially dependent on the particular contingencies for its effects. Suppose that one wished to relate the rate of responding in a free-operant situation to the delay of reinforcement. One might proceed in one of two ways. First, one might simply designate reinforced responses by some schedule, say, a VI schedule, and then present reinforcement some predetermined time after each response meeting the schedule requirement. The problem with such a procedure is that other responses might occur after the one designated for reinforcement, and the delay with respect to those subsequent responses would be shorter than the programmed value. In fact, there is no reason why the organism could not simply respond steadily at a high rate and obtain reinforcements with a very short delay. Under such a procedure, the effective delay of reinforcement is not under experimental control, but varies with the subject's behavior.

The first thought that might occur to an experimenter faced with this problem is that the programmed delay could be made effective if each

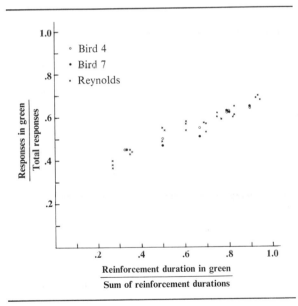

Figure 6.21 Responding by pigeons in the presence of a green key, relative to the sum of responses in the presence of green and red, as a function of the relative duration of reinforcement obtained in the presence of green. Green and red alternated regularly in time, with different reinforcement durations programmed on a VI 2-minute schedule in each key color. Also plotted are data obtained with pigeons by Reynolds (1963) in an experiment which varied the frequency, rather than the duration, of reinforcement in a similar situation. (From Shettleworth & Nevin, 1965.)

response occurring during the delay period reset the delay timer, so that when reinforcement was eventually obtained it would be given at exactly the correct time after the last response. Such a procedure would produce an extremely orderly inverse relation between the delay of reinforcement and the rate of responding, but a moment's thought will suggest that this may not be the result of losses in the effectiveness of reinforcement with increases in delay, but rather a direct effect of the contingencies built into the procedure. As the delay of reinforcement is increased, the rate of responding must decrease if the organism is to receive reinforcement at all. Another way of interpreting the effect of delayed reinforcement in such situations is that when reinforcement occurs, it will follow a period of not-responding. If not-responding is a reinforceable class of behavior, it will increase in occurrence, so that responding must necessarily decrease in frequency. Thus, functional relations describing the effects of delay of reinforcement on response rate in such procedures (e.g., Azzi et al., 1964) are in large part descriptions of the ways in which contingencies affect behavior, rather than being directly relevant to the problem at hand.

Chung and Herrnstein (1967) have examined the effects of different delays of reinforcement on two concurrently available responses in a situation that appears to avoid these difficulties. Independent but identical *VI* schedules were programmed for responding on two keys. When the programmed interval had elapsed in one schedule, responding on that key produced a blackout of fixed length, followed by food reinforcement. Responding on the other key also produced blackouts followed by food, but the blackout duration differed. Thus, different delays of reinforcement were programmed for two simultaneously available behaviors within a single session. The blackouts controlled the delay of reinforcement with respect to key-pecking, because pigeons do not peck during blackouts. The reinforcement of not-responding, which is inevitable in such procedures, should presumably lead to equivalent decrements in both response rates. Thus, differential effects on the two responses can be construed as resulting from the differential delays of reinforcement.

Chung and Herrnstein found a simple relation between the relative frequency of responding on one key and the relative value of the delay programmed on that key: The relative frequency of responding was approximately equal to the relative immediacy of reinforcement on that key, where immediacy is defined as the reciprocal of delay.

The result may be expressed by the equation,

$$\frac{R_1}{R_1 + R_2} = \frac{1/D_1}{1/D_1 + 1/D_2}.$$

The data on performances of pigeons on concurrent *VI* schedules indicate that the relative frequency of responding on one key matches the relative frequency of reinforcement on that key (Catania, 1963a; Herrnstein, 1961), the relative amount of reinforcement on that key (Catania, 1963b), and the relative immediacy of reinforcement on that key (Chung & Herrnstein, 1967). The argument put forward by Neuringer (1967) in connection with amount of reinforcement may also be applied in these other cases. However, it has also been shown that there is a similar sort of relationship between relative rate of responding and relative frequency or relative amount of reinforcement in multiple schedules, and this relationship cannot be ascribed to differential contingencies on the successive performances. Whether relative immediacy of reinforcement has comparable effects in multiple schedules remains to be seen. Pending the outcome of such an experiment, one may at least tentatively suggest that frequency, amount, and delay of reinforcement are closely interrelated parameters of maintained conditions of reinforcement, and furthermore that the effects of these parameters are not entirely dependent on the contingencies between different performances and their consequences.

MAINTAINED PERFORMANCE AND THE BEHAVING ORGANISM

Thus far, performance has been viewed as determined by the schedule of reinforcement and its implied contingencies, and the amount and/or delay of reinforcement obtained for meeting the schedule requirement. Another determinant of maintained performance is the organism itself, including at least its current state of deprivation and the history of reinforcement that it brings to the experimental situation.

Deprivation and performance

Most reinforcers are effective only under certain deprivation conditions. An obvious example is food, which does not affect responses that produce it unless the subject is at least moderately food deprived. This statement is not relevant to the theoretical controversy of whether learning can occur in the absence of relevant motivation; this chapter is concerned with performance maintained by constant conditions of reinforcement, and all theorists agree that performance depends on motivation. There are many operations that serve to induce motivational states—for example, saline injections may be functionally equivalent to water deprivation—and deprivation may have effects that are general to many situations, not merely to those involving a relevant reinforcer. However, this discussion will be confined to the effects of deprivation or satiation involving the reinforcer itself—typically food or water.

Some early work with free-operant behavior by Stebbins and Sidman (1954) examined the performances of four rats, two cats, and a monkey on various fixed-ratio schedules. The subjects were deprived of food, and progressive satiation was arranged simply by allowing the subjects to obtain many reinforcements in the course of a long session. In all subjects, the characteristic performance consisted of pauses after reinforcement, alternating with high, steady rates of responding. Late in the sessions, as the subjects became satiated, their average response rates decreased. However, the change was attributable entirely to increases in the pause after reinforcement. To show this, the time spent in pauses was subtracted from the total length of the session, and response rates in the remaining time were calculated for the first, middle, and final portions of each session. Stebbins and Sidman stated that the variation of response rate within a session was never greater than 1 percent of the initial rate. Thus, it appears that deprivation does not so much affect rate while the subject is responding as it alters the amount of time spent not engaging in the reinforced response.

Ratio schedules provide for differential reinforcement of rapid responding: The faster the subject completed a fixed ratio, the sooner reinforcement was obtained. Similar results appear when there is explicit differential reinforcement of low rates maintained on DRL schedules of reinforcement. Conrad, Sidman, and Herrnstein (1958) trained rats to respond on DRL 20-second schedules for water reinforcement until performance stabilized. For one subject, hours of water deprivation were varied systematically over a range from 9 to 70 hours, while the other four rats experienced different deprivation levels as a consequence of satiation during prolonged sessions. In all cases, the average rates of responding decreased at reduced deprivation levels. However, the distribu-

tion of interresponse times was only slightly affected. The major change in performance resulting from satiation was a marked increase in very long IRTs, which accounted for the reduction in average rates of responding.

In a standard DRL procedure, there is no direct way of separating the long pauses attributable to reduced deprivation from reductions in the general level of DRL performance. However, a modification of the procedure to require two different responses can accomplish this separation. Mechner and Guevrekian (1962) trained rats to initiate a DRL requirement on one lever and then complete it on a second lever. In particular, the rats were required to press one lever (bar A), pause 5 seconds, and then press a second lever (bar B) in order to obtain water reinforcement. Under these conditions, it was possible to measure separately the pause between responses on bar A and bar B, and the pause before the next response on bar A. After extensive training to stabilize performance, the duration of water deprivation was varied from 4 to 56 hours for each of four rats. In all cases, increasing deprivation reduced the pause between a reinforced response on bar B and the initiation of another 5-second interval on bar A. The average time from the response on bar A to that on bar B remained constant, however.

Considering all these findings together, it appears that when either rapid or slow responding is differentially reinforced, the rate of responding is not sensitive to deprivation or satiation. Only the tendency to initiate responding varies with deprivation.

The effects of deprivation on performances maintained by variable-interval schedules are of special interest in this connection. As we have seen, interval schedules indirectly impose differential reinforcement on different interresponse times, and this may affect the form of the IRT distribution. However, there is no relation between the average rate of responding and the obtained frequency of reinforcement. Also, there is little if any tendency to pause after reinforcement, and the average rate of responding may be quite constant from one reinforcement to the next. Clark (1958) has studied the effects of food deprivation on food-reinforced VI performances of rats, with the average value of the VI as a parameter of his experiment. Three rats were trained on each of three VI schedules. VI 1-, VI 2-, and VI 3-minutes. Daily sessions were conducted either 1, 3, 5, 7, 10, 20, or 23 hours after the last access to food. The performance of each rat was studied at each deprivation level for three sessions in various orders. The average rate of responding on each *VI* schedule at each deprivation time is plotted in Figure 6.22. The three functions are quite orderly and strikingly similar. They prove to bear a simple proportional relation to each other. If the average rates of responding on *VI* 3 are multiplied by 2.43, and the average rates on *VI*-2 are multiplied by 1.35, the resulting functions are identical to the function for *VI* 1-minute.

Clark does not present cumulative records of his subjects' performances. Ferster and Skinner (1957) present cumulative records of key-pecking by pigeons at various levels of food deprivation which show increasing deviations from a constant rate as deprivation is reduced; but even when the subjects respond steadily for several minutes, the rate is lower than at high levels of deprivation. It is unlikely, therefore, that Clark's results are attributable to a simple alternation between pausing and responding at a steady rate, where the major effect of deprivation is on pause length, as in ratio schedules. Evidently, *VI* schedules produce performances in which both momentary and average rates are sensitive to deprivation.

The obvious conclusion of this section is that,

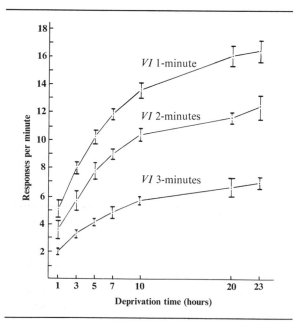

Figure 6.22 Average rates of responding by rats on three *VI* schedules of food reinforcement, as a function of the number of hours of food deprivation. (From Clark, 1958.)

as in the study of amount or delay of reinforcement, the nature of the reinforcement schedule maintaining the performance is a crucial determinant of the effect of the independent variable.

The role of the experimental history

The relevance of the subject's prior training to its maintained performance may be clear in the following example. Consider training a rat on a high-valued *FR* schedule. In the apparatus used to obtain the performances shown in Figure 6.2, rats usually make about 60 responses in extinction after regular reinforcement. An attempt to train a rat on an *FR*-100 schedule immediately after regular reinforcement would be doomed to failure: The maintained performance would be no performance at all, because extinction would be complete before the schedule requirement was met. On the other hand, a few hours' training with progressive increases in ratio size would result in a satisfactorily maintained performance. To state this more generally, reinforcement can only operate to maintain . a characteristic performance if the subject has developed a rate or pattern of responding on which reinforcement can act. The subject's reinforcement history will determine whether the necessary performance exists.

An interesting example of this comes from a study by Weissman (1961), who trained pigeons on a t^D-t^Δ schedule with a total cycle length of 90 seconds. His procedure was unusual in that an explicit discriminative stimulus was correlated with t^D. Normally, the response key was white, but it became green when the schedule made reinforcement available. The key changed back to white when a reinforcement was obtained, or at the end of t^D if the birds had not responded.

When t^D was long, the birds formed a nearly perfect discrimination: They always pecked shortly after the key turned green, but rarely when it was white. The length of t^D was gradually reduced to 0.5 seconds, at which point the latencies of responding to green were too long to obtain reinforcement, and all subjects completely stopped responding. In the next phase of Weissman's study, the key remained green continuously throughout t^D and t^Δ. Responding was reestablished with a long t^D period, after which the length of t^D was gradually reduced to 0.5 seconds, as in the first phase of the study. Since there was no change in key color correlated with t^Δ, the birds gave characteristic free-operant performances and their rates increased markedly when t^Δ was reduced.

Finally, the conditions of the first phase of the experiment were reestablished, so that the key was green only during t^D. Despite the explicit correlation of white with nonreinforcement, the birds continued to respond at high rates in t^Δ and continued to obtain food even when t^D was reduced to 0.3 seconds. This experiment provides another example of the importance of the subject's history of reinforcement in determining the performance maintained under given conditions. More importantly, it demonstrates that the reinforcement contingencies, in conjunction with a history of reinforcement for high rates, may completely override the usual effects of the discriminative stimuli.

The subject's history must also be considered in experiments relating performance to schedule parameters. For example, in determining the relation between the length of limited availability of reinforcement and performance maintained by interval schedules (e.g., Clark, 1959), one could not impose a very short limited hold initially, because the subject would rarely obtain reinforcement with the usual moderate-rate performance. This low reinforcement frequency would probably lead to further decreases in response rate, still less frequent reinforcement, and finally extinction. Therefore, the experimenter is forced to study limited-hold values in order of decreasing size, only imposing very short durations after the subject has been trained to respond at a high rate. This situation is directly analogous to shaping during response acquisition (see Chapter 2), in that the experimental variable cannot be applied until the subject is trained to emit a certain kind of behavior through reinforcing successive approximations to the final desired response.

To pursue the limited-hold example, once high rates have been established and maintained with a very short limited hold, the experimenter can remove or lengthen the hold time and attempt to recover performance maintained earlier in the experiment. He is unlikely to succeed, however, for the subject will continue to obtain all possible reinforcements if it maintains a high rate, and long *IRT*s will so rarely occur that the differential reinforcement for long *IRT*s provided by the interval schedule will probably be ineffective. This sort of irreversibility of high rates has been discussed earlier in connection with Boren's (1953) study of *FR*. Clark (1959) overcame this difficulty by withholding food reinforcement after training on the shortest limited hold. This procedure lowered rate and increased variability sufficiently to permit precise recovery of the original interval performance when the original schedule was reinstated.

Maintained performance on a schedule of reinforcement depends jointly on the properties of the schedule and the behavior the subject brings into contact with the schedule. This means that explicit control of the subject's experimental history is as necessary in the analysis of maintained behavior as in traditional studies of learning. It also means that quantitative functional relations between performance and the conditions of reinforcement may depend on the way in which those functions were obtained. Unless it can be shown that the form of the function is independent of the subjects' histories within the experimental situation—for example, by comparing functions for single subjects with those for independent groups, or by demonstrating recoverability of previous performances—the obtained relation is the result of two factors that are completely confounded. Acknowledgment of the importance of the subject's history and investigations of its influence in conjunction with the schedule of reinforcement are therefore essential to an understanding of maintained behavior.

SUMMARY AND CONCLUSIONS

In this chapter, maintained behavior has been viewed as jointly determined by the schedule of reinforcement, the way in which behavior interacts with the schedule, the parameters of reinforcement, reinforcements available in other components of the experiment and their parameters, the subject's current deprivation state, and the history of reinforcement which the subject brings to the experiment. Many of these variables are common to formulations of learning. For instance, the parameters of reinforcement and drive level figure prominently in Hullian theory. It has been shown that the effects of these latter variables are heavily dependent on the schedule of reinforcement and its resulting contingencies. Analyses of learning must therefore pay systematic attention to scheduling variables.

Most of the research on the effects of reinforcement schedules has been done with maintained free-operant performances. This chapter will therefore conclude with a review of the major results of this research, as described earlier.

First, it is necessary to distinguish two aspects of performance: the gross output of behavior, measured by the average rate of responding over long periods of time, and the patterning of behavior, measured by the distribution of responses in time. The average rate of responding clearly depends on the parameters of the reinforcement schedule. On interval schedules, rate of responding is a monotonically decreasing function of the time between reinforcements. When the schedule is specified in terms of reinforcements per hour, rate of responding is a monotonically increasing, negatively accelerated function of reinforcement frequency. On ratio schedules, an increase in the number of responses required for reinforcement leads to increases in rate at low ratio requirements, followed by decreases as the ratio size is increased to large values.

When frequency of reinforcement is equated, ratio schedules generate higher average rates than interval schedules. This difference may arise for either or both of two reasons. First, on ratio schedules, increases in rate are accompanied by increases in obtained reinforcement frequency, whereas the maximum frequency of reinforcement is fixed by interval schedules and is usually achieved at fairly low rates. Second, on interval schedules, responses separated by long periods of time are more likely to be reinforced than those spaced closely in time, whereas ratio schedules do not provide such differential reinforcement for low rates of responding. The importance of this latter factor is suggested by the precision with which rate may be controlled by specific differential reinforcement of spaced responding. Also, the imposition of a limited hold on reinforcement availability eliminates differential reinforcement for long *IRT*s on interval schedules and leads to rate increases without concomitant increases in reinforcement frequency.

When two schedules of reinforcement are programmed successively, as in multiple schedules, or simultaneously, as in concurrent schedules, the average rate of responding on one schedule depends not only on the parameters and contingencies of that schedule, but also on the frequency of reinforcement obtained in the other schedule. In particular, the rate of responding on a variable-interval schedule is directly related to the relative frequency of reinforcement obtained on that schedule, but does not depend on the behavior maintained by the other schedule. The patterning of behavior in time after a

reinforcement must be considered in addition to the gross output, because very different patterns may give rise to similar response rates. As an obvious example, fixed-interval schedules produce a systematic alternation between pauses after reinforcement and steady responding at a moderate rate, whereas variable-interval schedules maintaining a similar number of responses per hour generally do not produce systematic changes in rate between one reinforcement and the next. In temporal patterning, fixed-ratio performance is similar to fixed interval, except that ratio schedules generally maintain higher average rates. In either case, the pause after reinforcement is directly related to the time between reinforcements. This relation may result from the fact that the fixed schedules prevent the occurrence of reinforcement immediately after a preceding reinforcement.

Variable schedules arrange for reinforcement at least occasionally at short times after a preceding reinforcement, and in consequence do not produce systematic pausing. The effect is not discontinuous, however; rather, it appears that the rate of responding in any short segment of time after reinforcement is an increasing, negatively accelerated function of the frequency of reinforcement obtained at that time.

It is also important to distinguish different patterns of responding in time after previous responses, as revealed by the *IRT* distribution. Different schedules may lead to very different *IRT* distributions despite the maintenance of similar average rates. For example, *DRL* or pacing schedules produce distributions with most frequent responding at or near the time of reinforcement availability, whereas short *IRT*s predominate under *VI* reinforcement.

Various schedules may produce different *IRT* distributions because of the different frequencies of reinforcement obtained by responses terminating different *IRT*s. When responding is maintained by *VI* reinforcement, which results in different frequencies of reinforcement for different *IRT*s, the probability of responding in any short segment of time after a previous response is an increasing, negatively accelerated function of the frequency of reinforcement at that time. The generality of this function form, coupled with the pervasive control of responding by relative reinforcement, suggests the possibility of theoretical integration of much of the data on maintained performances.

REFERENCES

Anger, D. The dependence of interresponse times upon the relative reinforcement of different interresponse times. *Journal of Experimental Psychology*, 1956, **52**, 145–161. Figure 6.12: Copyright © 1956 by the American Psychological Association, and reproduced by permission.

Azrin, N. H., & Hake, D. F. Positive conditioned suppression: Conditioned suppression using positive reinforcers as the unconditioned stimuli. *Journal of the Experimental Analysis of Behavior*, 1969, **12**, 167–174.

Azzi, R., Fix, D. S. R., Keller, F. S., & Rocha e Silva, M. I. Exteroceptive control of response under delayed reinforcement. *Journal of the Experimental Analysis of Behavior*, 1964, **7**, 159–162.

Berryman, R., & Nevin, J. A. Interlocking schedules of reinforcement. *Journal of the Experimental Analysis of Behavior*, 1962, **5**, 213–223. Figure 6.7: Copyright © 1962 by the Society for the Experimental Analysis of Behavior, Inc., and reproduced by permission.

Blackman, D. Conditioned suppression or facilitation as a function of the behavioral baseline. *Journal of the Experimental Analysis of Behavior*, 1968, **11**, 53–61.

Bloomfield, T. M. Behavioral contrast and relative reinforcement frequency in two multiple schedules. *Journal of the Experimental Analysis of Behavior*, 1967, **10**, 151–158. Figure 6.17B: Copyright © 1967 by the Society for the Experimental Analysis of Behavior, Inc., and reproduced by permission.

Blough, D. S. The study of animal sensory processes by operant methods. In W. K. Honig (Ed.), *Operant behavior*. New York: Appleton-Century-Crofts, 1966. Pp. 345–379.

Blough, P. M., & Blough, D. S. The distribution of interresponse times during variable-interval· reinforcement. *Journal of the Experimental Analysis of Behavior*, 1968, **11**, 23–27.

Boren, J. J. Response rate and resistance to extinction as functions of the fixed ratio. Unpublished doctoral dissertation, Columbia University, 1953. Figure 6.4A: Reproduced by permission.

Boren, J. J. Resistance to extinction as a function of the fixed ratio. *Journal of Experimental Psychology*, 1961, **61**, 304–308.

Brandauer, C. M. The effects of uniform probabilities of reinforcement upon the response rate of the pigeon. Unpublished doctoral dissertation, Columbia University, 1958.

Catania, A. C. Concurrent performances: Reinforcement interaction and response independence. *Journal of the Experimental Analysis of Behavior*, 1963, **6**, 253–263. (a) Figure 6.19: Copyright © 1963 by the Society for the Experimental Analysis of Behavior, Inc., and reproduced by permission.

Catania, A. C. Concurrent performances: A baseline for the study of reinforcement magnitude. *Journal of the Experimental Analysis of Behavior*, 1963, **6**, 299–300. (b) Figure 6.20: Copyright © 1963 by the Society for the Experimental Analysis of Behavior, Inc., and reproduced by permission.

Catania, A. C. Concurrent operants. In W. K. Honig (Ed.), *Operant behavior*. New York: Appleton-Century-Crofts, 1966. Pp. 213–270.

Catania, A. C., & Reynolds, G. S. A quantitative analysis of the responding maintained by interval schedules of reinforcement. *Journal of the Experimental Analysis of Behavior*, 1968, **11**, 327–383. Figure 6.8: Copyright © 1968 by the Society for the Experimental Analysis of Behavior, Inc., and reproduced by permission.

Chung, S. H., & Herrnstein, R. J. Choice and delay of reinforcement. *Journal of the Experimental Analysis of Behavior*, 1967, **10**, 67–74.

Chung, S. H., & Neuringer, A. J. Control of responding by a percentage reinforcement schedule. *Psychonomic Science*, 1967, **8**, 25–26.

Clark, F. C. The effect of deprivation and frequency of reinforcement on variable-interval responding. *Journal of the Experimental Analysis of Behavior*, 1958, **1**, 221–227. Figure 6.22: Copyright © 1958 by the Society for the Experimental Analysis of Behavior, Inc., and reproduced by permission.

Clark, R. Some time-correlated reinforcement schedules and their effects on behavior. *Journal of the Experimental Analysis of Behavior*, 1959, **2**, 1–22. Figure 6.14: Copyright © 1959 by the Society for the Experimental Analysis of Behavior, Inc., and reproduced by permission.

Conrad, D. J., Sidman, M., & Herrnstein, R. J. The effects of deprivation upon temporally spaced responding. *Journal of the Experimental Analysis of Behavior*, 1958, **1**, 59–65.

Estes, W. K., & Skinner, B. F. Some quantitative properties of anxiety. *Journal of Experimental Psychology*, 1941, **29**, 390–400.

Felton, M., & Lyon, D. O. The postreinforcement pause. *Journal of the Experimental Analysis of Behavior*, 1966, **9**, 131–134. Figure 6.5B: Copyright © 1966 by the Society for the Experimental Analysis of Behavior, Inc., and reproduced by permission.

Ferster, C. B., & Skinner, B. F. *Schedules of reinforcement*. New York: Appleton-Century-Crofts, 1957. Figure 6.16: Copyright © 1957 by Appleton-Century-Crofts, Inc., and reproduced by permission of Appleton-Century-Crofts, Educational Division, Meredith Corporation.

Guttman, N. Operant conditioning, extinction, and periodic reinforcement in relation to concentration of sucrose used as reinforcing agent. *Journal of Experimental Psychology*, 1953, **46**, 213–224.

Hearst, E. The behavioral effects of some temporally defined schedules of reinforcement. *Journal of the Experimental Analysis of Behavior*, 1958, **1**, 45–55.

Henton, W. W., & Brady, J. V. Operant acceleration during a pre-reward stimulus. *Journal of the Experimental Analysis of Behavior*, 1970, **13**, 205–209.

Herrnstein, R. J. Relative and absolute strength of response as a function of frequency of reinforcement. *Journal of the Experimental Analysis of Behavior*, 1961, **4**, 267–272. Figure 6.18: Copyright © 1961 by the Society for the Experimental Analysis of Behavior, Inc., and reproduced by permission.

Herrnstein, R. J. Secondary reinforcement and rate of primary reinforcement. *Journal of the Experimental Analysis of Behavior*, 1964, **7**, 27–36.

Herrnstein, R. J. On the law of effect. *Journal of the Experimental Analysis of Behavior*, 1970, **13**, 243–266.

Kamin, L. J. Temporal and intensity characteristics of the conditioned stimulus. In W. F. Prokasy (Ed.), *Classical conditioning*. New York: Appleton-Century-Crofts, 1965. Pp. 118–147.

Keesey, R. E., & Kling, J. W.   Amount of reinforcement and free-operant responding, *Journal of the Experimental Analysis of Behavior*, 1961, **4**, 125–132.

Killeen, P.   Reinforcement frequency and contingency as factors in fixed-ratio performance. *Journal of the Experimental Analysis of Behavior*, 1969, **12**, 391–395.

Logan, F. A.   *Incentive: How the conditions of reinforcement affect the performance of rats*. New Haven. Yale University Press, 1960.

Logan, F. A.   Discrete-trials *DRL*. *Journal of the Experimental Analysis of Behavior*, 1961, **4**, 277–279.

Malott, R. W., & Cumming, W. W.   Schedules of interresponse time reinforcement. *Psychological Record*, 1964, **14**, 211–252. Figure 6.9A: Reproduced by permission of *The Psychological Record*.

Mechner, F., & Guevrekian, L.   Effects of deprivation upon counting and timing in rats. *Journal of the Experimental Analysis of Behavior*, 1962, **5**, 463–466.

Morse, W. H.   Intermittent reinforcement. In W. K. Honig (Ed.), *Operant behavior*. New York: Appleton-Century-Crofts, 1966. Pp. 52–108.

Neuringer, A. J.   Effects of reinforcement magnitude on choice and rate of responding. *Journal of the Experimental Analysis of Behavior*, 1967, **10**, 417–424.

Neuringer, A. J., & Chung, S. H.   Quasi reinforcement: Control of responding by a percentage reinforcement schedule *Journal of the Experimental Analysis of Behavior*, 1967, **10**, 45–54.

Nevin, J. A.   Differential reinforcement and stimulus control of not responding. *Journal of the Experimental Analysis of Behavior*, 1968, **11**, 715–726. Figure 6.17D: Copyright © 1968 by the Society for the Experimental Analysis of Behavior, Inc., and reproduced by permission.

Notterman, J. M., & Mintz, D. E.   *Dynamics of response*. New York: Wiley, 1965.

Rachlin, H., & Baum, W. M.   Response rate as a function of amount of reinforcement for a signalled concurrent response. *Journal of the Experimental Analysis of Behavior*, 1969, **12**, 11–16.

Rescorla, R. A., & Solomon, R. L.   Two-process learning theory: relationships between Pavlovian conditioning and instrumental learning. *Psychological Review*, 1967, **74**, 151–182.

Reynolds, G. S.   Relativity of response rate and reinforcement frequency in a multiple schedule. *Journal of the Experimental Analysis of Behavior*, 1961, **4**, 179–184. Figure 6.17C: Copyright © 1961 by the Society for the Experimental Analysis of Behavior, Inc., and reproduced by permission.

Reynolds, G. S.   Some limitations on behavioral contrast and induction during successive discrimination. *Journal of the Experimental Analysis of Behavior*, 1963, **6**, 131–139. Figure 6.21B: Copyright © 1963 by the Society for the Experimental Analysis of Behavior, Inc., and reproduced by permission.

Schneider, B. A.   A two-state analysis of fixed-interval responding in the pigeon. *Journal of the Experimental Analysis of Behavior*, 1969, **12**, 677–687.

Schoenfeld, W. N., & Cumming, W. W.   Some effects of alternation rate in a time-correlated reinforcement contingency. *Proceedings of the National Academy of Sciences*,

1957, **43**, 349–354. Figure 6.15: Copyright © 1957 by the National Academy of Sciences, and reproduced by permission.

Schoenfeld, W. N., & Cumming, W. W.   Studies in a temporal classification of reinforcement schedules: Summary and projection. *Proceedings of the National Academy of Sciences*, 1960, **46**, 753–758.

Sherman, J. C.   The temporal distribution of responses on fixed-interval schedules. Unpublished doctoral dissertation, Columbia University, 1959. Figure 6.5A: Reproduced by permission.

Shettleworth, S., & Nevin, J. A.   Relative rate of response and relative magnitude of reinforcement in multiple schedules. *Journal of the Experimental Analysis of Behavior*, 1965, **8**, 199–202. Figure 6.21A: Copyright © 1965 by the Society for the Experimental Analysis of Behavior, Inc., and reproduced by permission.

Shimp, C. P.   The reinforcement of short interresponse times. *Journal of the Experimental Analysis of Behavior*, 1967, **10**, 425–434.

Shimp, C. P.   Magnitude and frequency of reinforcement and frequencies of interresponse times. *Journal of the Experimental Analysis of Behavior*, 1968, **11**, 525–535.

Skinner, B. F.   *The behavior of organisms*. New York: Appleton-Century-Crofts, 1938. Figure 6.3B: Copyright 1938 by Appleton-Century-Crofts, Inc., and reproduced by permission of Appleton-Century-Crofts, Educational Division, Meredith Corporation.

Skinner, B. F.   Diagramming schedules of reinforcement. *Journal of the Experimental Analysis of Behavior*, 1958, **1**, 67–68. Figure 6.6: Copyright © 1958 by the Society for the Experimental Analysis of Behavior, Inc., and reproduced by permission.

Staddon, J. E. R.   Spaced responding and choice: A preliminary analysis. *Journal of the Experimental Analysis of Behavior*, 1968, **11**, 669–682.

Stebbins, W. C., & Sidman, M.   Satiation effects under fixed-ratio schedules of reinforcement. *Journal of Comparative and Physiological Psychology*, 1954, **47**, 114–116.

Teitelbaum, P.   The use of operant methods in the assessment and control of motivational states. In W. K. Honig (Ed.), *Operant behavior*. New York: Appleton-Century-Crofts, 1966. Pp. 565–608.

Weissman, A.   Impairment of performance when a discriminative stimulus is correlated with a reinforcement contingency. *Journal of the Experimental Analysis of Behavior*, 1961, **4**, 365–369.

Williams, D. R.   The structure of response rate. *Journal of the Experimental Analysis of Behavior*, 1968, **11**, 251–258.

Wilson, M. P.   Periodic reinforcement interval and number of periodic reinforcements as parameters of response strength. *Journal of Comparative and Physiological Psychology*, 1954, **47**, 51–56. Figure 6.3A: Copyright 1954 by the American Psychological Association, and reproduced by permission.

Zuriff, G. E.   A comparison of variable-ratio and variable-interval schedules of reinforcement. *Journal of the Experimental Analysis of Behavior*, 1970, **13**, 369–374. Figure 6.17A: Copyright © 1970 by the Society for the Experimental Analysis of Behavior, Inc., and reproduced by permission.

AVERSIVE CONTROL

Edmund Fantino
University of California, San Diego

The effects of aversive stimuli on behavior have been considered briefly in several of the preceding chapters together with the effects of positive reinforcement, and some similarities have been noted. In this chapter, aversive control is discussed in detail, and the question of its similarities to and differences from positive reinforcement are pursued in depth. Unlike positive reinforcement, aversive control has been viewed historically as involving two processes: the classical conditioning of fear, and the reinforcement of operant behavior that terminated fear. This view has recently been called into question and thoroughly reexamined on the basis of findings described in this chapter. New generalizations about aversive control are emerging as a result. But first, it is necessary to define aversive stimuli and to outline the procedures within which their effects are studied.

Aversive stimuli are defined in two ways: They are stimuli that the subject will work to remove or to avoid (*negative reinforcers*) and stimuli that lower the probability of a response that they follow (*punishing stimuli* or *punishers*). A stimulus that is a negative reinforcer will almost always be a punisher and vice versa. Aversive stimuli act in a manner that is precisely opposite to positive reinforcers such as food: Just as positive reinforcers increase the probability of a response they follow, punishers decrease the probability of a response they follow; just as the removal of positive reinforcers decreases the probability of responses that remove them, negative reinforcers increase the probability of responses that remove them. In other words, responses may be made more probable by following them with positive reinforcers, such as food, or with negative reinforcers, such as escape from electric shock. Responses may be made less probable by following them with punishers, such as electric shock, or with the removal of a positive reinforcer, such as food. The term *negative punishment* is suggested by this latter operation (see also Chapter 2).

The importance of aversive stimuli in the control of behavior is crucial. Imagine, for example, what the world would be like if aversive stimuli were ineffective in controlling behavior. A child would not learn to keep away from fire. A speeding motorist would not slow down when approaching a speed trap. Certainly the reader can provide many examples of his or her own behavior that are somewhat under the control of aversive stimuli.

Preparation of this chapter was supported in part by NSF Grants GB-3626, GB-6659, and GB-13418. The author wishes to thank Steven Hursh and David Myers for their thoughtful criticisms.

Therefore, it is surprising that the importance of aversive control has by no means been taken for granted by psychologists. In order to illustrate this we will briefly review the history of theoretical attitudes toward one aspect of aversive control, punishment.

EFFECTIVENESS OF AVERSIVE CONTROL
E. L. Thorndike

Our story should begin with Thorndike, whose work around the turn of this century led to his formulation of the *Law of Effect* (see also Chapters 1 and 2). Thorndike investigated the behavior of cats and other animals placed in a *puzzle box* from which food outside the box was visible. The subject's task was to escape from the box and reach the food. In order to do so it had to learn to operate a latch inside the puzzle box. On early trials the animal would make a variety of movements such as crying and scratching at the sides of the box or running within the box, but none of these helped toward a solution. Eventually, however, the subject operated the latch, escaped from the box, and obtained the food. Thorndike found that from the start of the experiment there was a gradual decrease in the amount of time required to reach the food. It was primarily the gradual nature of improvement in the cat's performance that led Thorndike to the following hypothetical account of behavior in the situation. Food reward strengthened the behavior which led to it; that is, the response that led to the food in the presence of the puzzle situation was strengthened. Responses that failed to obtain food led to discomfort that produced a weakening of the tendency to make that response. Thorndike spoke in terms of a reward trial *stamping in* the connection between the stimulus situation and the correct response, and of an incorrect trial as *stamping out* the connection between the stimulus situation and an incorrect response. He spoke in terms of *satisfaction* and *annoyance*. His operational definition of these terms show that they were quite similar to what we today call positive and negative reinforcers, respectively. For example, Thorndike (1913) said that "by a satisfying state of affairs is meant one which the animal does nothing to avoid, often doing things which maintain or renew it. By an annoying state of affairs is meant one which the animal does nothing to preserve, often doing things which put an end to it" [p. 2]. The Law of Effect, then, is the position that the connection between a stimulus and a response will be strength-ened when the consequence of that response is a satisfier (positive reinforcer) and will be weakened when the consequence of that response is an annoyer (punisher). If we ignore the emphasis on "stimulus-response connections," this statement is remarkable for its simplicity and, as we shall see, is powerful in understanding a broad spectrum of behavior.

The notion that reward and punishment are equivalent in their effects, albeit opposite in direction, did not remain in favor for very long. Indeed, Thorndike himself amended the Law of Effect to de-emphasize the role of punishment after he had conducted the series of experiments to which we now turn. These experiments involved human subjects learning lists of verbal material. For example, a subject was presented with a long list of words and was required to associate a number with each word on the list. The experimenter had a key indicating which numbers should go with which words. When the subject guessed the correct number he was told "right" by the experimenter. The phrase constituted the reward. When certain other numbers were paired with the verbal stimuli the experimenter said "wrong." This verbal response was the punishment. As one might expect, subjects tended to repeat the responses that had been followed by "right," thereby confirming one aspect of the Law of Effect. The surprising finding, however, was that the responses that had been followed by "wrong" were also more likely to be repeated than they would have been had punishment not been administered. In other words, the other aspect of the law was not confirmed: Punishment did not appear to weaken responding. On the basis of this pioneer experiment, Thorndike rejected the punishment portion of the Law of Effect.

A series of carefully controlled experiments by Stone (Stone, 1953; Stone & Walters, 1951) has shown that a subject's response is more likely to recur when followed by "wrong" than when followed by no particular consequence, and in addition, that a mild electric shock also strengthens a subject's responding. This leads to an interesting position: The verbal response "wrong" and mild electric shock appear to meet the criterion for a positive reinforcer, namely, a stimulus that increases the probability of a response that produced it. Thus, a stimulus such as electric shock or "wrong" need not always function as either a positive reinforcer or a punisher. Instead, a stimulus may increase the probability of responding in some situation, may decrease it in others, and may have no reinforcing function in still other situations. While this statement is indeed true (McKearney, 1969; Premack, 1962), it is probably not relevant for a correct understanding of Thorndike's or Stone's results. A second alternative to Thorndike's conclusion that punishment is ineffective stresses the *discriminative properties* of the punishing stimulus (cf. Azrin & Holz, 1966, pp. 420–424).

B. F. Skinner

By the 1930s Thorndike's Law of Effect was asymmetrical: Rewards could strengthen responses which produce them, but punishers were ineffective in weakening the responses which produced them. This view has not entirely passed from the psychological scene. Perhaps the most eloquent attack on the use of punishment in controlling behavior is that of Skinner (1953), who based his position on three observations: (1) the relative ineffectiveness of punishment compared to positive reward (which is similar to the Thorndike position); (2) the relatively transient effect of punishment; and (3) the unfortunate by-products of punishment which may be more troublesome and maladaptive than the behavior that was eliminated by the punishment. Skinner (1953) opened his discussion of punishment by stating,

> The commonest technique of control in modern life is punishment. The pattern is familiar: If a man does not behave as you wish, knock him down; if a child misbehaves, spank him; if the people of a country misbehave, bomb them. Legal and police systems are based upon such punishments as fines, flogging, incarceration and hard labor. Religious control is exerted through penances, threats of excommunication, and consignment to hellfire. Education has not wholly abandoned the birch rod. In everyday personal contact we control through censure, snubbing, disapproval, or banishment. In short, the degree to which we use punishment as a technique of control seems to be limited only by the degree to which we can gain the necessary power. All of this is done with the intention of reducing tendencies to behave in certain ways. Reinforcement builds up these tendencies; punishment is designed to tear them down. . . .
>
> More recently, the suspicion has also arisen that punishment does not in fact do what it is supposed to do. An immediate effect in reducing a tendency to behave is clear enough, but this may be misleading [pp. 182–183].

Skinner's treatment of punishment has been extremely influential. The first objections Skinner raised against the use of punishment were its relative ineffectiveness and the transient nature of its effects. Skinner based his conclusions on two classic experiments. Each of these experiments examined the effect of punishment on the rate of extinction of a previously reinforced response. The notion was that if punishment were effective in reducing behavior, extinction should proceed much more rapidly when responses were punished. On the other hand if punishment were relatively ineffective, extinction should proceed at more or less the same rate whether or not the extinguishing responses were also punished.

Skinner (1938) studied rats in the experimental chamber which bears his name. The chamber contained a lever which the rat pressed to obtain intermittent positive reinforcement. In the first phase of the experiment, the rats acquired the lever-pressing response. Following this training, there were two extinction sessions in which lever-pressing was no longer positively reinforced. The sessions occurred on two successive days and each was two hours long. For some rats, every lever-press in the first 10 minutes of extinction was followed by a hard slap to the foot, arranged by a spring on the lever. No further punishment was administered throughout the remaining 3 hours and 50 minutes of extinction. The other rats received no punishment at any time. The central question, of course, is whether this punishment had any effect on the rate at which lever-presses were emitted. The first result to note is that punishment did depress the rate of lever-pressing during the 10-minute period in which punishment was being administered. The more interesting finding is that after the punishment period terminated, the rate of lever-pressing was temporarily higher for the rats that had been punished than for the unpunished rats. At the end of the 2-day extinction period, there was no difference between the two groups of subjects with respect to the total number of responses emitted during extinction. Three generalizations emerged from these results: (1) Punishment is effective in reducing responding if it is continually applied after that response; (2) punishment appears to have no effect in suppressing responses after its removal; and (3) assuming that primary reinforcement builds up a "reserve" of responses, all of which will eventually be emitted in extinction, punishment serves only to delay the emission of the responses. As soon as punishment was removed, the rats emitted the responses remaining in the reserve. (Skinner subsequently abandoned the concept of the reserve.)

W. K. Estes

Estes (1944) also examined the effects of punishment on responding in extinction. The first phase of his experiment was the same as Skinner's: Rats were trained to press a lever with intermittent food reinforcement. After several hours of training, extinction began. Responses were punished with a mild electric shock in the first phase of extinction for some of the animals. The findings were similar to Skinner's: Although the electric shock had a suppressive effect on behavior while it was being applied, there was actually an increase in the rate of responding following the removal of punishment. Moreover, the total number of responses during extinction was the same whether or not the animals had been punished early in extinction.

With a more intense electric shock as a punisher, there was a far more dramatic effect on the rate of responding. Within a few minutes after the onset of extinction and intense punishment, responding was virtually eliminated. Estes then studied the animals in further extinction sessions without punishment. The first three extinction sessions without punishment were marked by a very low rate of responding; in other words, unlike the previous studies in which a marked increase in the rate of responding followed the removal of mild punishment, a more permanent suppression of responding was obtained with more intense punishment. During four additional sessions of extinction, however, the rate of responding of the previously punished subjects was as high as for the subjects which had never been punished.

Estes also found that the effects of electric shock were independent of whether the shock was received for lever-pressing or whether it was presented when the animal was not pressing the lever. In other words, he found the same degree of suppression and the same degree of recovery of the response whether or not shock was contingent upon the response. Apparently, then, the shocks created a general emotional state or state of immobilization that incidentally interfered with responding. Thus on the basis of this finding, it appeared that punishment was very different from positive reinforcement, where the effects of reinforcement in strengthening a response critically depends on the contingency between the response and the reinforcement. We will see later, however, that Estes' experiment notwithstanding, the contingency between responding and punishment is just as crucial as the contingency between a response and positive reinforcement.

On the basis of these earlier experiments, Skinner (1953) concluded that punishment "does not permanently reduce a tendency to respond ... in agreement with Freud's discovery of the surviving activity of what he called repressed wishes" [p. 184]. Having demonstrated to his satisfaction that punishment did not operate in a manner opposite that of reward, Skinner went on to analyze what effect punishment did have on behavior. He noted that the effect of punishment is confined to the immediate stimulus situation. A single speeding ticket, for example, may not influence the motorist's future driving habits. Evidence for this first effect of punishment has already been presented in the previous discussion. A second effect of punishment is attributable to *conditioned stimuli* that have been paired with or preceded punishment. For example, the speeding motorist may find his experience with the state trooper and the resultant fine and penalties somewhat harrowing. Since this experience follows driving at high speeds, a few punished occurrences of speeding may establish speeding as a conditioned aversive stimulus. The driver responds to his own speeding by slowing down, which results in the removal or reduction of the conditioned aversive stimulus, speeding. (See Chapter 5 on *negative conditioned reinforcers*, a term which is equivalent to conditioned aversive stimuli.)

Conditioned aversive stimuli thus permit punishment to exert a more long-term effect on behavior. The main problem is that the punishing agency, or the experimenter as the case may be, has very little control over the precise relation between aspects of the punishing situation and the conditioned aversive stimuli that the punishment creates in that situation. If the conditioned aversive stimuli or emotional reaction are attached precisely to the very behavior that the punishing agent would like to control, then such punishment would be very effective. Unfortunately, the conditioned aversive stimuli may be attached to aspects of the situation that should remain free of conditioned aversive stimuli. In the case of the speeding motorist, the unfortunate consequences do not appear to be too serious. Nonetheless, they will illustrate the general problem. The motorist may not only become anxious while speeding, but may become anxious whenever driving. This state of anxiety might interfere with adequate functioning while driving an automobile (or even create medical problems).

The point may be better made with an additional example. Parents with Victorian attitudes instill a daughter with a full complement of conditioned aversive stimuli related to sexual behavior. While this may be effective in curbing promiscuity, it may also backfire by carrying over into marital relations. This, of course, will not be a conscious effort on the part of the daughter. But if stimuli associated with sexual arousal are conditioned aversive stimuli, the girl may continue to respond to them by trying to remove them, perhaps by engaging in behavior incompatible with the punished behavior. Thus, these stimuli will continue to elicit that incompatible behavior. To summarize, punishment generates conditioned aversive stimuli. When these conditioned emotional stimuli arise in the future, the organism may learn a response that removes them. The problem is that the learned response, although successful in preventing the undesirable behavior, may also interfere with desirable behavior.

Although Skinner has made an impressive case against the effectiveness of aversive control, his position has not been borne out by empirical data. We will be in a better position to evaluate his and other theories of aversive control after reviewing some of the most significant and recent work in that field.

PUNISHMENT
Parameters of punishment

The most common punisher is shock applied through grid bars on the floor of an experimental chamber. Although the general principles that apply when shock is utilized as a punisher appear to be valid for other punishers as well, shock has the advantage that it can be varied over a wide range of values producing a wide range of responses in the subject, from complete insensitivity to complete suppression. In addition, the physical parameters of the shock can be precisely specified. When shock is applied to grid bars, however, the degree of shock actually received by the experimental subject is much more difficult to specify. For example, the rat may hop around and make contact with the shock grid for only a portion of the presentation of the shock. In addition, the rat may roll over on its back using its fur as an effective insulator. Finally, in most experimental chambers, the rat is able to escape the shock if it manages to stand upright with both hindpaws on the same grid bar. In other words, it is important to be able to specify precisely the characteristics of the stimulus that makes *contact* with the experimental subject.

By applying electric shock through fixed electrodes on a rat's tail (Azrin, Hopwood, & Powell,

1967), the shock actually received by the subject may be specified both reliably and accurately: "Unauthorized" escape and avoidance responses are ineffective in altering the amount of shock received by the subject. This technique not only provides an improved procedure, but also improved behavioral results. The rat's behavior in the apparatus employed by Azrin et al. is much more sensitive to the experimenter's manipulation of shock variables than it is with more conventional apparatus. Earlier work by Azrin demonstrated the effectiveness of electric shock as a punisher when shock was administered via implanted or attached electrodes in the pigeon (Azrin, 1959a; Hoffman & Fleshler, 1959) and in the monkey (Hake & Azrin, 1963). Therefore, it appears that whatever the experimental organism, shock can be used effectively in punishment research providing that it is administered through electrodes permitting control over the precise location and intensity of the administered shock.

Introduction of punishment

An important variable determining the effectiveness of punishment is the manner in which punishment is first introduced. Azrin, Holz, and Hake (1963) found that an intensity of punishment that would completely suppress responding when introduced suddenly would produce only partial and temporary suppression when punishment first consisted of a low-intensity shock but was gradually increased to the same intensity. Consequently, it is necessary to exercise utmost caution when introducing punishment. A researcher who simply uses a shock intensity that should produce moderate suppression according to a published report may be surprised to find that the subject's responding is totally suppressed after a single shock of the same intensity. Even then, the researcher's initial reaction may be to assume something is wrong with the apparatus, when, in fact, the sudden introduction of moderately intense shock was responsible.

In a similar vein, it should be noted that the order of presenting different shock intensities can greatly influence the results in a study designed to show the effects of various shock intensities on some behaviors. Care should be taken to gradually increase the punishment and then decrease it, obtaining separate curves for the ascending and descending orders, rather than randomly selecting shock values. If the latter is done, sudden increases in the shock values may produce more marked suppression than higher shock values that represent a reduction in shock intensity. Consideration of order effects was discussed with regard to schedules of positive reinforcement in Chapter 6. There it was suggested that schedules that usually generate high response rates, if introduced abruptly, did not maintain responding as well as when the schedule requirement was gradually increased. The picture appears to be much the same with punishment.

The importance of the manner in which punishment is introduced and the importance of order effects in the study of punishment intensity are significant and subtle findings, suggesting that a good deal of consideration must be given to the history of punishment in the experimental subject.

Intensity

Once we control for the manner of introduction, we can readily see that the degree of response suppression produced by a punishing stimulus depends critically on the strength of the punishing stimulus. For example, Azrin (1960a) and Appel and Peterson (1965) have demonstrated a direct relation between response suppression and punishment intensity in both the rat and the pigeon. Figure 7.1 shows the effects of mild and moderate punishment on the response rates of a single rat. A control performance of a rat without punishment is shown in the left-hand panel of Figure 7.1. In all cases, responding is maintained on a variable-interval (*VI*) 1-minute schedule of food reinforcement. Each response in the two punishment conditions produces a brief electric current through a grid floor. Note that suppression recovers upon repeated exposure to the shocks and that the moderate punishment produces more suppression and less recovery than the mild punishment. Although none of the curves in Figure 7.1 reveals complete response suppression, other punishment studies have produced total suppression (e.g., Appel, 1961).

Similar data have been obtained with pigeons. Figure 7.2 shows the effects of mild punishment on responding on a *VI* schedule of food reinforcement. Figure 7.2A illustrates typical *VI* responding maintained by food prior to the introduction of punishment. The second record of Figure 7.2A shows what occurs when every response is punished while the *VI* 1-minute schedule of food reinforcement is maintained. This record illustrates several findings of interest. In the first place, note that the rate of responding is suppressed even with this mildly punishing electric shock. Also important is the fact that the nature of the *VI* responding is unaffected; responses are emitted at a fairly uni-

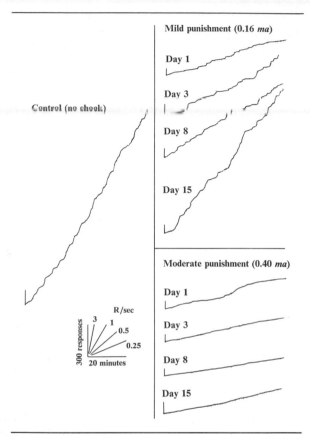

Figure 7.1 Cumulative response records showing response suppression and within-session recovery as a function of shock intensity and exposure to punishment. (From Appel & Peterson, 1965.)

form rate and are reasonably independent of the time elapsed since the previous food reinforcement. In other words, the characteristics of variable-interval behavior are unchanged by the punishment; what does occur is that the overall response rate diminishes. An additional finding of interest in this second record is the fact that the rate of responding increases during the first hour after introduction of punishment: The punished responding recovers, as in the Appel and Peterson (1965) study (see Figure 7.1). With mild punish-

Figure 7.2 Cumulative response curves for different ▶ intensities of punishment. Panel A exhibits mild, panel B exhibits moderate, panel C exhibits severe, and panel D exhibits very severe punishment. Punishment is delivered for every response (except in control conditions labeled *no punishment*), while food reinforcements are delivered on *VI* 1-minute (panel A) or *VI* 6-minute (panels B, C, and D) schedules. (From Azrin, 1960a.)

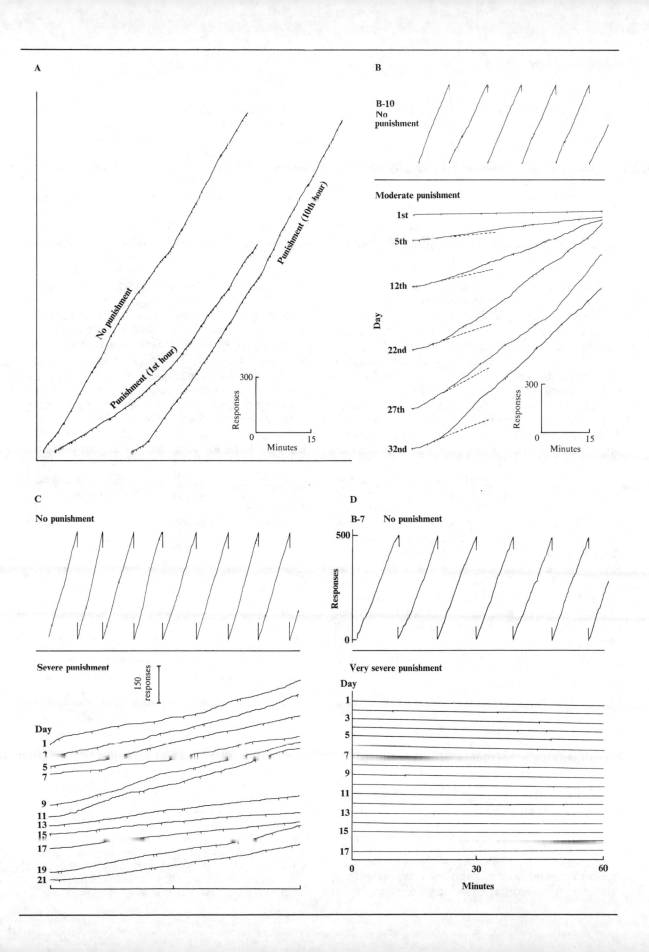

A

No punishment

Punishment (1st hour)

Punishment (10th hour)

300
Responses
0
Minutes
15

B

B-10
No
punishment

Moderate punishment

1st

5th

12th

Day

22nd

27th

32nd

300
Responses
0
Minutes
15

C

No punishment

Severe punishment

150
responses

Day
1
3
5
7
9
11
13
15
17
19
21

D

B-7   No punishment

500

Responses

0

Very severe punishment

Day
1
3
5
7
9
11
13
15
17

0   30   60
Minutes

ment the recovery is virtually complete, as illustrated in the third record of Figure 7.2A, which shows responding in the tenth hour after the introduction of punishment for every response. Note that the rate of responding is virtually identical to that in the session prior to the introduction of punishment, except at the start of the session where there is an initial suppression, indicated by the arrow in Figure 7.2A. Mild punishment appears to have no important long-term effect on ongoing behavior maintained by food reinforcement; moreover, at no time did mild punishment affect the characteristics of variable-interval responding. This has been substantiated by others (Brethower & Reynolds, 1962; Rachlin, 1966).

Figure 7.2B shows the analogous data for the case in which the punishment consists of a somewhat stronger level of electric shock (both a higher voltage and a longer duration). Note that in this case suppression is virtually complete on the first day of punishment. But even on this day, the subject continues to receive food reinforcement (on a *VI* 6-minute schedule) as indicated by the oblique blips on the record. As the days go by, recovery from punishment begins.

These data make several instructive points. The pattern of *VI*-responding is unaltered, although the rate of responding is lowered. With moderate punishment the degree of response suppression is not only greater (compare the first day of responding for Figures 7.2A and 7.2B), but recovery of responding, while substantial, is incomplete, even by the 32nd day. And responding under moderate punishment shows an initial suppression at the start of every session. The main difference between relatively mild and relatively moderate punishment, then, appears to be the degree of suppression and the relative permanence of suppression.

Frames C and D of Figure 7.2 illustrate the effects of relatively severe and very severe punishment. The trends shown in frames A and B are continued. With sufficiently severe punishment behavior is virtually eliminated. This finding, of course, is incompatible with the basic position taken by Thorndike (1932) on the relative ineffectiveness of punishment.

Schedules of punishment

One of the most widely studied topics in experimental psychology concerns schedules of reinforcement (see Chapter 6). Although there has been a tremendous development of knowledge in the area of schedules of positive reinforcement,

much less is known about schedules of punishment. The most commonly studied schedule of punishment is, of course, continuous punishment (*FR*-1), where each response is punished, as in the data shown in Figures 7.1 and 7.2. Azrin, Holz, and Hake (1963) manipulated the value of a fixed-ratio schedule of punishment. In this case, punishment was a 240-volt electric shock delivered to pigeons via implanted electrodes. In all cases, responding was also reinforced with food on a *VI* 3-minute schedule. The fixed-ratio value shown in Figure 7.3 varies from continuous punishment (*FR*-1) to a very intermittent punishment (*FR*-1000). Figure 7.3 illustrates the strikingly orderly effect of the schedule of punishment on the maintenance of responding to obtain food. When every response was punished, suppression was virtually complete; when punishment followed every thousandth response, however, punishment reduced responding by only 40 percent of the unpunished rate. Intermediate schedules of punishment produced intermediate degrees of suppression.

Thus, increasing the rate of punishment (by decreasing the *FR* value of punishment presentation) has an effect that is analogous to increasing the intensity of the punishment: The more intense or the more frequent the punishment, the greater the suppression.

Azrin (1956) has studied the effects of fixed-

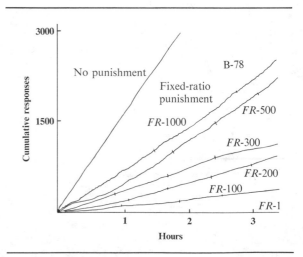

Figure 7.3 Rates of responding maintained by a *VI* 3-minute schedule of food reinforcement while punishment is delivered according to the indicated *FR* schedule. Blips indicate punishment (240 V). (From Azrin, Holz, & Hake, 1963.)

interval punishment, that is, punishment which is delivered for the first response emitted after a fixed interval of time has elapsed since the last punished response. This schedule was superimposed on a *VI* schedule of food reinforcement. With fixed-interval (*FI*) schedules of positive reinforcement, responding is generally positively accelerated after the pause following reinforcement up to the time of the reinforced response. Azrin found just the opposite with punishment: a negatively accelerated response curve. In other words, after extended exposure to the fixed-interval schedule of punishment, responding decreased as the moment for the scheduled punishment approached.

Whereas fixed-ratio and fixed-interval schedules of positive reinforcement for operant behavior are characterized by pauses following reinforcement and a subsequent period of rapid responding leading to the next reinforcement, variable-interval schedules of reinforcement are characterized by a steady, moderate rate of responding, with no noticeable pauses between reinforcements. Filby and Appel (1966) investigated the effects of variable-interval punishment superimposed on a *VI* schedule of positive reinforcement in rats. While the two schedules of reinforcement, both positive and negative, were programmed independently, the values of the two schedules were identical. For example, when the variable-interval schedule was 1 minute, food and punishment were both presented on the average of once every minute. Punishment consisted of electric shock, and positive reinforcement was a combination of milk and vitamins. Although the two reinforcing events could, in theory, occur for the same response, in practice this rarely occurred.

Filby and Appel found that with mild punishment virtually no suppression occurred for any of the three groups (*VI* 0.5-minute, *VI* 1-minute, and *VI* 3-minutes). At somewhat higher levels of punishment, however, there was complete suppression in all groups. The rat's responding was relatively insensitive to the frequency of programmed punishment. Apparently, increased frequency of punishment was offset by the commensurate increase in the rate of positive reinforcement. It would be interesting to determine whether responding would also be insensitive to the frequency of programmed punishment in the *FR* case (Figure 7.2) if the frequency of positive reinforcement underwent a commensurate change.

A crucial variable determining the effectiveness of a positive reinforcer is the immediacy of the presentation of the reinforcer following the reinforced response. The effectiveness of the reinforcement can be drastically reduced if the period of delay intervenes between execution of the response and reinforcement (Grice, 1948; Neuringer, 1969; Skinner, 1938). It is not surprising, therefore, that the same situation holds with regard to punishment. If the suppressive effects of punishment on responding are to be maximal and enduring, punishment (like reward) should be applied immediately (Azrin, 1956; Cohen, 1968).

Maintenance of punished behavior
Schedules of positive reinforcement

We have considered the schedule of punishment, the rule employed by the experimenter for presenting the punishing stimulus. Punished responses will not occur, of course, unless there is some positive reinforcement maintaining them. The most common technique for maintaining punished behavior is the concomitant scheduling of a positive reinforcer such as food. This section considers how various schedules of positive reinforcement differentially affect the extent to which punishment is effective in reducing behavior maintained by positive reinforcement.

The classic study involving effects of punishment on behavior maintained by fixed-ratio schedules of positive reinforcement is that of Azrin (1959b). Fixed-ratio schedules with sufficiently high values are characterized by a pause in the responding following reinforcement. Azrin applied punishment of different levels of intensity to behavior reinforced on an *FR*-25 schedule. Responding on *FR*-25 schedules is generally free of pausing. The curve in Figure 7.4 for 0 volts is the prepunishment baseline. It illustrates the rapid rate of responding characteristic of fixed-ratio schedules of reinforcement. The second set of records is from a complete session in which each response was followed by a 40-volt shock, and reinforcement was continued on the fixed-ratio schedule. Note that except for an initial pause in the record, responding is virtually unchanged. When the voltage was increased to 80 volts, however, there was a marked change in the behavior early in the session. By the end of the session, responding had totally recovered to the prepunishment baseline. The right-hand record indicates that, as the punishment intensity was increased, the reduction was more severe.

One striking aspect of these data is that punishment does not affect the ongoing rate of responding, which is constant. Rather, punishment affects the pause following reinforcement. In unpunished

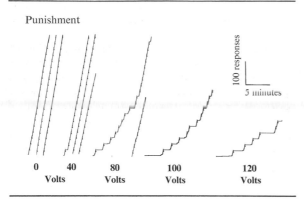

Figure 7.4 Cumulative response curves indicating the effect of different punishment intensities on responding maintained by an *FR*-25 schedule of food reinforcement (indicated by blips). Punishment was delivered following every response. (From Azrin, 1959b.)

FR schedules, the pause following reinforcement increases as the size of the *FR* requirement is increased (Chapter 6). What the punishment appears to do, then, is to change the behavior toward what would be appropriate to a larger ratio. This is still a further example of the similarity in effects between punishment and a decrease in the frequency of positive reinforcement.

The effect of punishment on behavior maintained by fixed-ratio schedules of food reinforcement is also similar to the effect of increasing satiation, as reflected by the organism's body weight. Both Stebbins and Sidman (1954) and Fantino (1964) have reported that the size of the postreinforcement pause increases as the organism's body weight increases, although when responding occurs, its rate is unaffected by changes in deprivation.

The effects of punishment on fixed-interval schedule performance have been studied in human subjects, using a somewhat different sort of punisher. Weiner (1962) noted that the "human organism seldom produces positive reinforcement without some response 'cost' (e.g., physical, monetary). Relatively few studies of operant behavior, however, have systematically investigated response cost as a determinant of the human organism's adjustment to the contingencies of positive reinforcement" [p. 201]. Weiner and his associates embarked on a series of studies to assess the effects of response-produced costs on human behavior maintained by schedules of positive reinforcement.

Weiner's subjects, who sat alone in the experimental chamber, were required to monitor a display unit for red signals. In order to observe the display, however, depression of a response lever was necessary. These lever-presses illuminated the display for 0.3 seconds. In one of his experiments, Weiner's human observers were trained for several sessions under an *FI* 1-minute schedule of presentation of the red signals. The positive reinforcer was 100 points for each detection of the red signal. After a stable baseline of responding developed under the no-cost conditions, each response cost the observer 1 point. When stable response rates were obtained on this condition, the cost was eliminated. Data from a typical subject are presented in Figure 7.5. Note the high rates of responding in the no-cost conditions and the drastically lower rates of responding in the cost conditions. During cost conditions, the response rates were extremely low, with some tendency to continue to increase ("scallop") between reinforcements. Thus, in this case the effects of punishment on behavior maintained by a schedule of positive reinforcement did alter the pattern of responding on that schedule. It did so, in the direction that made behavior more sensitive to the contingencies of positive reinforcement: Responses early in the interreinforcement interval were never reinforced, were therefore superfluous, and were easily eliminated by punishment. Figure 7.5 also shows that the rate of reinforcement obtained by the subject was not demonstrably altered by the punishment. While punishment was dramatically effective in reducing the number of responses, the effect was completely reversible. When the no-cost condition was reinstated, the pattern of responding quickly returned to that exhibited prior to the introduction of cost; the response rates were again high and uniform throughout the interreinforcement interval.

All in all, then, the effects of punishment on behavior maintained by fixed-ratio and fixed-interval schedules have in common the phenomenon that punishment exerts its greatest effect on the period following a reinforcement. In the fixed-interval case, where all responses prior to the end of the interreinforcement interval are superfluous, response suppression seemed to be much greater, although it is dangerous to generalize across studies employing different organisms and different types of punishing stimuli. In the fixed-ratio case, where every response is required to obtain reinforcement, the suppression was much less in the sense that responding, once begun, was maintained at its characteristic high rate. The effect of punishment

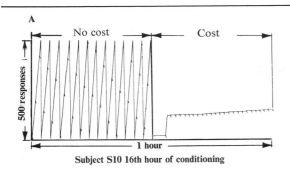

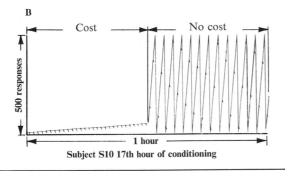

Figure 7.5 Cumulative response curves for a typical subject under cost and no-cost conditions. Responding is maintained on an *FI* 1-minute schedule. Blips indicate the occurrence of reinforcement. (From Weiner, 1962.)

on behavior maintained by both of these schedules is different from the effects on behavior maintained by variable-interval schedules of food reinforcement; as we have seen in the case of variable-interval schedules, the pattern of responding throughout the interreinforcement interval was unaffected, while the rate of responding was reduced (see Figure 7.2).

Holz, Azrin, and Ulrich (1963) maintained behavior on *differential reinforcement of low rates* of responding (*DRL*) schedules of reinforcement (see Chapter 6). Responses on this schedule were reinforced only after a period of at least 30 seconds had elapsed since the emission of the last response. In this case, as opposed to all the cases considered earlier, responses during the interreinforcement interval actually postpone the next reinforcement. Prior to the introduction of punishment, a baseline was obtained with pigeons after about 90 hours of training. Punishment, in the form of electric shock to the tail region of the subjects, was then delivered after every response. Holz et al. also varied the intensity of the punishment. After responding stabi-

lized at a particular intensity requiring at least eight sessions per intensity, a new intensity was introduced.

Figure 7.6 illustrates the effects of different levels of intensity on the rate of responding for each of the experimental subjects. Of equal interest is the fact that the figure illustrates the effect of punishment intensity on the rate of reinforcement (Figure 7.6B). It can be seen that punishment effectively lowered the rate of responding, at least with sufficiently high shock intensities, with the additional effect of increasing the number of reinforcements obtained per day by the subjects, at least up to a point. This, then, is a case in which punishment resulted in an increase in the rate of reinforcement by eliminating responses that were postponing reinforcement. When punishment was removed,

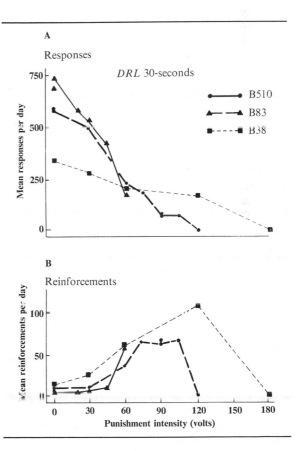

Figure 7.6 Responses and reinforcements per sessions as a function of punishment intensity for each of three subjects. Responding was maintained on a *DRL* 30-second schedule of food reinforcement. Punishment was delivered after each response. (From Holz, Azrin, & Ulrich, 1963.)

there was actually more responding than had occurred prior to punishment with, of course, a concomitant decrease in the number of reinforcements obtained. Thus, we see that the effects of punishment in this situation are equivalent to the effects with other schedules of positive reinforcement: Whether or not the suppressive effects of punishment result in a higher or lower rate of positive reinforcement, these effects are present only when punishment is being administered (at least up to moderate intensities).

The effects of punishment on the pattern of responding maintained by schedules of positive reinforcement depend very critically on the particular schedule of positive reinforcement involved. In the case of fixed-ratio schedules of food reinforcement, punishment can markedly reduce the rate of reinforcement obtained by the subject by generating long pauses following a reinforced response. Punishment during interval schedules of reinforcement, however, has virtually no effect on the obtained rate of reinforcement: Most of the responses that are eliminated are superfluous. Finally, it has been shown that with *DRL* schedules of reinforcement punishment actually increases the rate of reinforcement obtained by eliminating responses which themselves delay reinforcement.

The recoverability of responding after the removal of punishment is, of course, in accord with Skinner's position that the effects of punishment are not permanent. It should be pointed out, however, not only that punishment is very effective in eliminating behavior while it is being applied, but also that, with sufficiently severe punishment (under which behavior is virtually eliminated), recovery is incomplete.

A more important point should be made. We can concede that the effects of mild and moderate levels of punishment are transient without conceding any fundamental difference in the effects of reward and punishment. The effects of continuous positive reinforcement are transient as well. The results presented in the present section not only involved continuous punishment, but also involved a punished behavior that was being maintained by positive reinforcement. Strictly speaking, the proper comparison to assess the permanence of the effects of reward would be to discontinue reward (but not punishment) following an *FR*-1 schedule of food reinforcement and punishment. Extinction of responding would be rapid indeed. Moreover, if the reinforcement schedule were reinstated, reacquisition would be immediate. By the same token, reintroducing punishment has immediate effects.

The point is that the effects of reward would be transient as well.

Deprivation

Another factor which influences the way in which behavior is maintained on a schedule of positive reinforcement is the degree of deprivation. The interaction of this variable with the effects of punishment is shown in Figure 7.7 from a study of Azrin, Holz, and Hake (1963). This figure shows the cumulative responses of a pigeon responding on a *VR* 3-minute schedule of food reinforcement with an *FR*-100 schedule of punishment (i.e., every hundredth response produces a fairly intense electric shock). The figure shows the results for seven different levels of deprivation. Note that suppression is virtually complete at the level of deprivation that had been used with these pigeons throughout the experiment—85 percent body weight. But when the same subject was tested at more severe deprivation (60 percent body weight), the effect of punishment is minimized. We previously noted that, in the same study, rate of responding varied dramatically as a function of the schedule of punishment (see Figure 7.3). We now see that other variables are

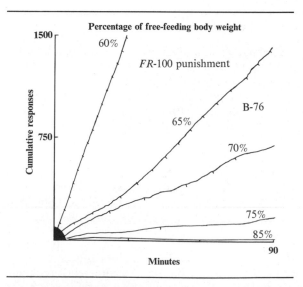

Figure 7.7 Cumulative response curves for a typical pigeon, showing the effect of food deprivation on responding maintained by a *VI* 3-minute schedule of food reinforcement and punished by an intense (160 V) shock on an *FR*-100 schedule. Delivery of shocks is indicated by blips on the record. (From Azrin, Holz, & Hake, 1963.)

involved. They, too, must be accurately specified before we can predict the effects of punishment.

Some additional effects of punishment

So far, this chapter has concentrated on situations in which a single positively reinforced response is studied under constant conditions, so that the effects of introducing punishment can be observed systematically. Before proceeding, it is necessary to appreciate some of the varied effects of punishment that may be observed when punishment is removed and when other operations are employed, such as varying the stimuli present when responding is measured, terminating positive reinforcement, and adding an alternative response.

Removal of punishment

We have already seen ample documentation of two of the most salient effects of punishment on maintained behavior: suppression and recovery of responding. We now turn to two exceptions to the generalization that behavior returns to its pre-punishment baseline following the removal of punishment. The first exception is that with sufficiently intense punishment no recovery occurs (Appel, 1961; Storms, Boroczi, & Broen, 1962). In part, this is due to the fact that with extremely intense shocks, suppression is complete; with sufficiently complete suppression, nonpunished responses do not have a chance to recur. With shock intensities less than those producing complete suppression, however, recovery is complete. As already suggested, this is analogous to the extinction of responding that occurs with the removal of positive reinforcement.

The second exception to the generalization involves a transient increase in the rate of responding following the removal of punishment. This effect is illustrated in Figure 7.8 taken from Azrin's (1960a) study. The data shown in the graph are for one of Azrin's subjects. During punishment sessions punishment was continuous, i.e., it followed every response. Throughout, behavior was maintained on a *VI* 1-minute schedule of food reinforcement. Note that the rate of responding in the first few sessions following the removal of punishment is higher than the rate that had been in effect prior to the introduction of punishment. Eventually, however, the response rates return to the baseline. These data also illustrate the effects of suppression following the introduction of punishment and the

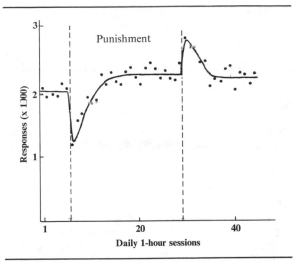

Figure 7.8 Number of responses per session for a subject responding on a *VI* 1-minute schedule of food reinforcement. During sessions in the panel marked *punishment*, each response was followed by electric shock. (From Azrin, 1960a.)

effects of recovery in subsequent punished sessions.

Punishment and stimulus control

Of great practical relevance to the use of punishment in controlling behavior is the extent to which the effects of punishment generalize to stimulus situations different from those in which the punishment was applied. We know from the study of positive reinforcement that *stimulus generalization* (cf. Chapter 4) is a common phenomenon. One of the finest studies examining stimulus generalization of the effects of punishment is that of Honig and Slivka (1964). They trained pigeons to respond to various spectral stimuli ranging in wavelengths from 490 to 610 nanometers (*nm*). Responding in the presence of any of the seven spectral stimuli used in the experiment was reinforced on a *VI* 37.5-second schedule of food reinforcement. After acquiring stable baseline data for 30 sessions, the experimenters instituted punishment whenever the subject responded in the presence of the 550-*nm* stimulus. Responding during any of the other spectral stimuli was not punished. For all stimuli, the variable-interval schedule of food reinforcement remained in effect.

The basic data obtained in this experiment are illustrated in Figure 7.9. Whereas the rates of responding were reasonably constant over all stimulus values prior to the introduction of punishment, clear gradients of generalization were obtained following the introduction of punishment. These gradients are very similar to those obtained with positive schedules of reinforcement, except that they are inverted. The extent of generalization, of course, is measured by noting how much lower the response rates are than they were when the *VI* baseline was established. Note that the more similar a stimulus is to that in which punishment is programmed, the more generalization of punishment occurs.

What happens when the punishment is removed for responding in the presence of the 550-*nm* stimulus? Results from the same study indicate that complete recovery occurs; that is, the *VI* baseline shown in Figure 7.9 is recovered within nine experimental sessions. These results demonstrate that when punishment is applied in a particular stimulus situation, some of its effects will be generalized to stimulus situations which are somewhat different from the one in which punishment occurred. Furthermore, when punishment is eliminated and the original behavior continues to receive primary reinforcement, not only does it return to its prepunishment baseline, but so do the behaviors in the presence of the other stimuli.

Punishment in extinction

In introducing the topic of punishment, we cited the classic experiments of Skinner (1938) and Estes (1944) which describe the effects of punishment on responding in extinction following positive reinforcement. We noted then that the rate of responding decreases during the brief period of punishment, but that an increase in response rate follows the termination of punishment, so that the total number of responses during extinction is roughly constant whether or not punishment is applied. These results have already been qualified in the present chapter. The basic criticism is that punishment has discriminative, as well as aversive, properties. For example, punishment in the Skinner and Estes studies was applied only in extinction and was therefore a cue for the absence of reward. When punishment was removed, therefore, conditions were identical to those in acquisition; extinction of responding in these conditions was just beginning. Indeed, it is possible to arrange the situation such that punishment may increase the rate of responding during extinction. If punishment is always associated with availability of positive reinforcement, while the absence of punishment is

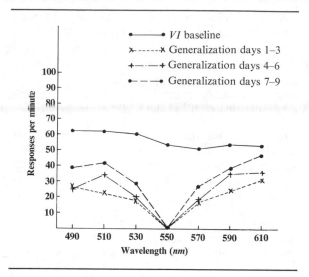

Figure 7.9 Mean rates of responding at each of seven wavelengths during nine sessions in which punishment was in effect at the central value (550 *nm*) only. Responding is maintained in the presence of all stimuli by a *VI* schedule of food reinforcement. (From Honig & Slivka, 1964.)

never associated with food, we should be able to observe a different function of punishment: punishment as a discriminative stimulus ("signal") for reward. This effect is illustrated in Figure 7.10. Prior to the extinction session shown in the figure, punishment was established as a discriminative stimulus for responding. In order to achieve this, two experimental sessions were conducted daily: In one session, both punishment and reinforcement were provided; in the other, neither punishment nor reinforcement was provided. In those sessions in which both food and punishment were provided, the pigeon received an electric shock for each key-peck and received food on a *VI* 2-minute schedule. The extinction session in Figure 7.10 shows that the introduction of punishment produced a marked increase in the rate of responding during the extinction session (during which food was never available). This finding may be somewhat obvious, but it makes a very important point: The effects of a stimulus are not invariant; without knowing the experimental history of the organism and the context of the particular experimental procedure, it is not possible to predict reliably what effect a particular stimulus, even an electric shock, will have on a particular response of a particular organism.

Similar results have been demonstrated in human subjects by Ayllon and Azrin (1968). They

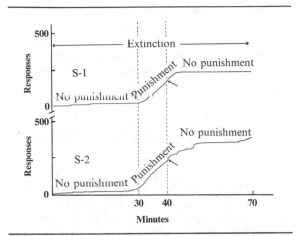

Figure 7.10 Cumulative records of responding, for each of two subjects, after maintenance on a *VI* schedule of food reinforcement with punishment. The records show that the rate of responding increased during extinction when punishment was reintroduced. The arrows indicate a transient increase in rate following the removal of punishment. (From Holz & Azrin, 1961.)

first established that a loud buzzer was a punishing stimulus by showing that it would suppress subjects' responding for token reinforcements. For example, subjects would respond at a higher rate on one response plunger that programmed tokens on an *FR*-50 schedule than on a second plunger that programmed the same *FR*-50 schedule of reinforcement, but for which each response also produced the buzzer. Following this procedure, the experimenters changed the condition so that responding on one plunger had no effect in producing either tokens or noise ("extinction, no noise" condition). On the other plunger, however, reinforcements continued to be available on an *FR*-50 schedule and every response produced the noise. Following this association of noise with positive reinforcement, the noise was transformed into a positively reinforcing stimulus. Tests for the conditioned reinforcing properties of the noise were conducted by comparing responses on a push button that had no effect with responses on a second push button whose only effect was to produce noise. Subjects produced the noise, indicating that it had acquired discriminative or conditioned reinforcing properties. Thus depending on the particular experimental history of the subject, the same stimulus can be either a punisher or a reinforcer.

Effects of punishment on choice

When a subject has an alternative response available, it will emit that response to obtain reward and will cease to perform a punished response, even at moderate intensities of punishment (Azrin & Holz, 1966, Herman & Azrin, 1964; Holz, Azrin, & Ayllon, 1963). For example, Herman and Azrin trained human subjects to respond for cigarettes on variable-interval schedules of reinforcement (see Chapter 6). There were two response devices available, a knob and a button. When responses were punished, each response activated a buzzer that produced a brief 96-decibel noise.

In the first phase of the experiment, no responses, whether on the knob or on the button, were punished. On the average of every 60 seconds, a response produced a cigarette (*VI* 60-seconds); it made no difference whether the response was a knob-pull or a button-push. This phase permitted the experimenters to assess the rate of responding on each device in the absence of punishment. Without such a baseline, of course, it would be impossible to assess whether the noise was indeed a punishing stimulus. As is generally the case in establishing a baseline, the subject was studied in this phase until the response rate appeared stable from day to day. At this point, punishment was introduced. Each knob-pull now produced the noise, while responses on the button did not produce the noise (knob-pulls were chosen for punishment because they were more frequent than button-pushes). In all other respects the procedure was the same as in the first phase.

The first question is whether or not the noise was an effective punisher. To answer this, we must examine the rate of knob-pulling by each subject in Phases I and II. The mean rate of unpunished knob-pulling for the three subjects was 27, 118, and 78 responses per minute. In Phase II, when knob-pulls produced noise, these rates were 0, 0, and 1 knob-pull per minute, respectively. Thus, the noise was dramatically effective as a punishing stimulus.

Following the demonstration that noise was a punisher in the two-response situation, the experimenters went on to test the effects of the noise in a single-response situation. Thus, in Phase III of the experiment the subjects could respond only on the knob (i.e., the button was inoperative). In this phase punishment was removed; responding was simply reinforced with cigarettes on the *VI* 60-second schedule. After this behavior stabilized, the noise was reinstated after every response. Was the effect of the noise on responding again dramatic? With only one response available, the average rate of responding for each of the three subjects was 63, 158, and 102 knob-pulls per minute. The corresponding figures after punishment was reinstated were 3, 23, and 93 responses per minute, respectively. Although in every case there was a decrease, this decrease was clear-cut for only two of the three subjects; moreover, for no subject was the decrease as marked as it was in the alternative-response condition. This study makes a point that is fairly obvious, but that has not received the degree of experimental study it warrants: Punishment is far more effective in reducing or eliminating behavior if there is an alternative nonpunished response that can be utilized by the subject to obtain positive reinforcement.

These alternative-response experiments provide that reinforcement can be obtained at the same rate by emitting nonpunished responses exclusively. It is not surprising, therefore, that punished responding is easily suppressed in these studies. If reinforcement were available on concurrent *VI* schedules (described in Chapter 6), however, the subject's rate of reinforcement would be cut in half if it were to emit one response exclusively. For example, if two discriminative stimuli are each correlated with a *VI* 1-minute schedule, an average rate of two reinforcements per minute would be attainable if responding were maintained on both schedules. But a rate of only one reinforcement per minute would be attainable if responding were maintained on one schedule. Owing to the nature of *VI* schedules, therefore, the number of reinforcements in the situation will be doubled when even a fairly low rate of responding is maintained on each of the two schedules.

How will punishment of responses on one schedule affect choice behavior in this situation? Fantino (unpublished data) studied four pigeons on a concurrent *VI* 1-minute, *VI* 1-minute schedule of rein-

forcement, in which a *VI* 1-minute schedule was associated with each of two response keys. After responding stabilized (about 24 daily sessions), electric shock (78 volts, 30 milliseconds) was introduced for all responses to the key on the right side of the apparatus, and 80 additional daily sessions were observed for each pigeon. Food continued to be available on the concurrent *VI*-1, *VI*-1 schedule of reinforcement. Each session consisted of 60 (food) reinforcements. Generally, 30 reinforcements were obtained on each key. Table 7.1 indicates the number of responses per session to each key for each pigeon averaged over (1) the last three sessions prior to punishment; (2) the first three sessions of punishment; and (3) the last three punishment sessions. Punished responses are italicized.

Each of the four subjects showed response suppression when punishment was introduced. Two pigeons, #3 and #22, showed incomplete recovery from the effect of punishment as reflected by the greater number of punished responses late in punishment. After 80 sessions, however, the data were quite stable and there is no reason to suspect that complete recovery would have occurred in further sessions. Pigeons #21 and #23 showed no recovery. On the basis of Azrin's (1960a) study with *VI* schedules of food reinforcement and moderate punishment, one would expect gradual recovery for 20 sessions in a single-response procedure. Azrin notes that this recovery was usually not complete.

The results from the choice experiment shown in Table 7.1 fall in between those obtained by Azrin (1960a) with a single key and those obtained in the several experiments utilizing an alternative response that can be emitted exclusively to obtain a maximal rate of reinforcement. These three sets of results present a picture which is consistent with analogous results from studies of positive reinforcement. In those studies, responding is less sensitive to changes in reinforcement variables when a

Table 7.1

Pigeon #	(1) Prepunishment		(2) Early punishment		(3) Late punishment	
	Left-hand key	Right-hand key	Left-hand key	Right-hand key	Left-hand key	Right-hand key
3	768	801	*125*	*171*	1335	*683*
21	1938	1702	1671	*1084*	1398	*750*
22	817	764	289	*128*	853	*380*
23	1249	1072	1178	*176*	1203	*147*

single response rather than a choice procedure is employed (Catania, 1966; Fantino & Herrnstein, 1968; Neuringer, 1967).

Finally, when a procedure is employed that enables a subject to maximize its rate of reinforcement by emitting only one of two alternative responses, the subject will tend to do so even when only a trivial difference (or even no difference) exists in terms of the consequences of responding on the two alternatives. This can be seen, for example, in the results of Herrnstein (1958); in the results of the punishment studies using the alternative response technique, cited earlier (Azrin & Holz, 1966; Herman & Azrin, 1964; Holz, Azrin, & Ayllon, 1963); and in the results of many experiments studying choice in T-mazes. A problem with all of these procedures is the fact that it is difficult to interpret the extent to which the exclusive responding to one alternative is due to the difference in the independent variable or due to the fact that once the subject displays a preference for one alternative it becomes reinforced more often for responding on that alternative; hence, the number of reinforcements for each response is confounded with the independent variable. To circumvent this problem, the subject is often forced to execute the nonpreferred alternative on some trials, for example, by blocking his entrance to the preferred goal-box in the T-maze or Y-maze. This procedure is intended to equalize the number of reinforcements associated with each choice. Whether such a forced-choice procedure in fact equalizes experience is, of course, an open question. The advantage of the type of choice procedure described—where responding on each alternative is reinforced on a variable-interval schedule of reinforcement—is that the animal, without additional prodding, responds on both alternatives, because such behavior maximizes the overall rate of reinforcement.

Conditioned punishment

Conditioned aversive stimuli are those which, while not intrinsically aversive, have acquired aversive properties because of their pairings with other aversive stimuli. We will distinguish between two types of conditioned aversive stimuli: (1) stimuli associated with primary aversive stimuli, for example, shock; and (2) stimuli associated with removal from the opportunity to obtain positive reinforcement, for example, time-out or TO-stimuli. These two types of conditioned aversive stimuli are also commonly called conditioned positive punishers and conditioned negative punishers.

One of the most thorough studies of conditioned positive punishment is that of Hake and Azrin (1965). They studied pigeons whose key-pecking was maintained by food reinforcement on a variable-interval 2-minute schedule. Presentations of a neutral stimulus were made for 15-second periods that were themselves programmed on a *VI* 6-minute schedule. Electric shocks were presented at the end of the prearranged stimulus periods. This procedure is commonly termed *conditioned suppression,* because responding is usually suppressed in the presence of the conditioned stimulus that precedes shock. Conditioned suppression in the Hake and Azrin study was shown to be a function of the intensity of the shock, that is, the higher the voltage of the electric shock, the less responding was emitted in the presence of the conditioned stimulus; responding in the absence of the conditioned stimulus was relatively unaffected. The important aspect of the study from our present point of view, however, occurred when the shock was discontinued and the conditioned-punishment procedure was introduced. For the first 30 minutes of this session, conditioned suppression was in effect as shock continued to follow conditioned-stimulus presentation. After this point the procedure was changed: Shocks were discontinued, but every response produced a stimulus for 5 seconds. If the stimulus were a conditioned punisher, the rate of responding in the absence of the stimulus should decrease. Figure 7.11 indicates that responding, in fact, decreased and also shows that the effect was transient. The transiency is not surprising since pairings of the stimulus and shock had been discontinued. Hake and Azrin also showed that the conditioned-punishment effect could be maintained indefinitely by arranging infrequent stimulus-shock pairings delivered independently of responding.

The second type of conditioned punishment involves the withdrawal of the opportunity to respond for positive reinforcement. In one experiment (Ferster, 1957), chimpanzees responded on a *VI* 6-minute schedule for food reinforcement. An overhead light in the experimental chamber was periodically turned off, during which times responses could no longer produce food. The chimpanzees soon stopped responding in the absence of the overhead lights. In the next phase of the experiment, Ferster introduced a red lamp that he termed a *pre-time-out* or *preaversive* stimulus: It appeared every 15 minutes and remained in effect for 160 to 180 seconds, depending on what the animal did after the first 160 seconds elapsed. If the animal

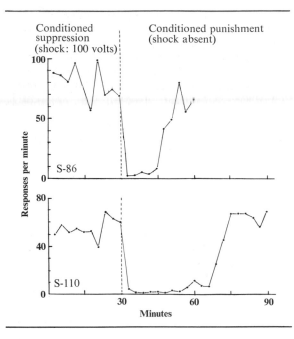

Conditioned suppression (shock: 100 volts)   Conditioned punishment (shock absent)

S-86

S-110

Minutes

Figure 7.11 Rate of responding for each of two subjects before and after introduction of conditioned punishment (dotted line at 30 minutes). Each point represents the responses per minute for consecutive 3-minute periods. (From Hake & Azrin, 1965.)

responded on the key during this 20-second period, a 60-minute time-out period followed. On the other hand, if the subject emitted no response for the duration of the 20 seconds, the red-light period terminated without a subsequent time-out. The time-out period was the same as in the first phase: The overhead lights were not illuminated and the responses were ineffective. The crucial question in this experiment is whether or not responding is suppressed during the pre-time-out stimulus. The only "punishment" in this situation was the fact that any response in the final 20 seconds of the pre-time-out stimulus produced a time-out. If the time-out were aversive, therefore, the rate of responding during the pre-time-out stimulus should be lower than the rate of responding in its absence. A clear suppression of responding during the pre-time-out stimulus occurred.

This behavior is classified as conditioned punishment, since the punishing effectiveness of the time-out is not due to any inherent properties of the time-out stimulus per se. The punishing event could also be considered as a member of the class of negative punishers, since the punishing event is a

withdrawal of a stimulus that is a conditioned positive reinforcer because of its association with food, a primary reinforcer. If a stimulus reinforces behavior that produces it, behavior that removes it should be punished; if a stimulus punishes behavior that produces it, behavior that removes it should be reinforced. These results, taken in conjunction with results on conditioned reinforcement (Chapter 5), constitute yet another instance of the symmetry of reward and punishment processes, a symmetry that will now be developed more fully.

Theories of punishment

The most popular type of punishment theory is *two-factor* or *two-process* theory (cf. Bolles, 1967; Rescorla & Solomon, 1967), which relies in part on the conditioned punishing effects that have just been discussed. Two-factor theories generally maintain that punishment involves two processes: (1) the association of stimuli preceding punishment (conditioned punishers) with the punishment itself, generally through classical conditioning; and (2) the association of a response with the removal of these conditioned punishers, generally through operant conditioning. This type of theory thus imparts a central role to conditioned punishers. For example, conditioned punishing stimuli may be temporal or spatial ones associated with the onset of punishment, or proprioceptive stimuli deriving from movements that generally precede the punished response (such as the child's incipient movements toward the cookie jar). These stimuli themselves come to elicit autonomic reactions, such as those associated with fear, that are presumed to be aversive. The subject may eliminate aversive stimuli by terminating the to-be-punished chain of behavior or by not responding at all. In either case, the behavior that occurs is actually behavior that avoids the punishment. Although in theory one could stipulate that the reinforcement for the nonpunished behavior is the avoidance of punishment, more generally, two-factor theories hypothesize that the reinforcement for the nonpunished response is the reduction of fear or other aversive stimuli. We will have more to say about this general notion when we consider theories of avoidance behavior. The two-factor theories of punishment and avoidance are often indistinguishable, particularly since two-factor theories of punishment have been concerned primarily with how punishment is avoided (avoidance behavior), rather than with the effect of punishment on ongoing behavior.

This chapter's theoretical stance is that punishment and reward are different sides of the same coin, which is the position taken by the early Thorndike, but rejected by the later Thorndike and by Skinner, as well as by most subsequent theorists. The main arguments in support of the opposing stance are contained in an excellent review by Bolles (1967), which the reader should consult. Presented here are some excerpts that will give the reader the flavor of Bolles' position.

> ... Learning theorists and educators alike were startled when Thorndike (1932) rejected the punishment half of the law of effect. Rewards still stamped in, but punishment no longer stamped out. We will consider here the sort of evidence that led Thorndike to truncate the law. We will also look at a number of studies of the effects of punishment on animal behavior. We will find that Thorndike was right, and that the effect of punishment is indeed specialized and indirect, and does indeed depend upon what it makes the animal do [pp. 416–417].
>
> We are led to the view that punishment does not itself change the strength of the response it follows, but that it provides the opportunity for other learning to occur, either directly or through the mediation of learned fear. The direct effects we have seen have been due to acquisition of competing behavior, most evident in the case of withdrawal from spatially localized shock. Fear too may cause withdrawal from fear-eliciting stimuli. However, fear has a more widespread and diffuse effect; it elicits freezing and crouching, and these kinds of behavior compete most effectively with any other kind of behavior we care to punish [p. 427].
>
> [We are brought to] the following hypothesis: *When punishment leads to learning, what is learned are the responses which the punisher elicits, including fear.* Stated another way, punishment cannot produce the learning of any behavior other than that which it elicits—e.g., withdrawal, fear, and cowering. If the punishment conditions are arranged so that punishment produces withdrawal, then the organism will withdraw. If it only produces freezing or cowering, then the organism will freeze or cower, On the other hand, if a rat is punished for running in a situation where the reaction to punishment is also running, then punishment may facilitate the behavior. ...

The elicitation interpretation of punishment has been further supported by a beautiful study by Fowler and Miller (1963). They trained rats to run an alley for food. At the goal some animals were shocked in the hindpaws and some were shocked in the forepaws. During the course of training the hindpaw subjects ran progressively faster and the forepaw subjects ran progressively slower than a group receiving no shock. This is just what would be expected if hindpaw shocks elicited running and forepaw shocks elicited startle or withdrawal [p. 428].

Different theoretical systems differ not on the question of what effect punishment has, but rather on the question of whether fear is involved, and if it is, how it is acquired. Not since Thorndike abandoned the idea that punishment weakens S-R associations has a major systematist defended it.

Curiously, even though there is this uncommon agreement about punishment there have been very few systematic statements about it, and relatively little research has been done on the phenomena of punishment. Even the textbook writers tend to slight it. This neglect of punishment is especially remarkable in view of Skinner's well-known assertions that it is probably the most common means of controlling human behavior (1953), and at the same time, ineffective and morally indefensible (1948a) [p. 429].

Bolles (1967) concludes that when punishment does have a weakening effect,

> the effect can be attributed to the acquisition of a response which is an alternative to the punished response on those occasions when the latter might occur. ... It does not seem possible to weaken the punished response itself, nor to produce by punishment competing behavior other than the particular response it elicits. Therefore punishment is not effective in altering behavior unless the reaction to punishment itself competes with the response we wish to punish [pp. 432–433].

There are several statements in Bolles' account that require clarification. One is the implication that punishment often does not have long-lasting effects. Although throughout the chapter we have seen that once punishment is removed the previously punished response rapidly recovers to its prepunishment baseline, we have also commented that behavior maintained by positive reinforcement will be eliminated in an analogous manner when positive reinforcement is omitted (extinction). Secondly, while it is certainly the case that punishment elicits responses that may in turn influence the extent to which the punished response occurs in the future, this is also true of positive reinforcement: Any salient stimulus elicits a wide range of responses. This phenomenon, in itself, is not sufficient to warrant a unique type of theory. Indeed, such effects may be subtle. For example, when a pigeon responding on a *DRL* schedule of food reinforcement emits a response with a long interresponse time which is therefore reinforced, it is likely to emit a burst of responses (i.e., unreinforced responses having short interresponse times) immediately following reinforcement. While this effect of reinforcement may complicate our understanding of behavior on *DRL* schedules, it does not necessarily mean that we should hypothesize a different type of reinforcement mechanism for behavior reinforced by *DRL* schedules than for behavior reinforced on other schedules of positive reinforcement.

Bolles' final statement that punishment will not be effective in altering behavior unless the reaction to the punishment itself competes with the punished response raises two questions: (1) How do we specify what the competing response is? and (2) How do we account for the effects of punishment on behavior maintained by fixed-ratio schedules of food reinforcement? Specification of the competing response is difficult. Very often, the only evidence that a competing response is occurring is the absence of the punished response.

The second question is equally troublesome: How might the competing-response theorist explain the fact that punishment of responding on fixed-ratio schedules of food reinforcement lengthens the pause following reinforcement, but does not change the rate of responding on the fixed ratio once such responding is initiated? It seems that the "reaction to punishment itself" must compete with the punished response only during the postreinforcement period, but it must not compete at all with the response once responding is initiated and the punisher is presented. While this may be so, there does not seem to be any necessity for postulating such a complex set of events. Moreover, the very same thing occurs without punishment, that is, with increased satiation or with an increase in the fixed-ratio requirements. In these cases, also, there is a pause after reinforcement followed by a high rate of responding. Is the pause here also somehow the result of competing behavior? While such questions may be interesting, they do not appear to be any more relevant to punishment than they are to reward.

We now turn to some evidence which affords further tests of the proposition that punishment affects behavior in a way that is analogous, but opposite in sign, to the effects of reinforcement. Rachlin (1966) examined one of the supposed differences between the consequences of reward and punishment, namely, that the high rate of responding generated by primary reinforcement is likely to be permanent, while the low rate of responding generated by introducing punishment may not be permanent. This fact has been taken as support for the asymmetrical law of effect that

we have identified with the later Thorndike and with Skinner, Estes, and Bolles. Rachlin (1966) notes that their "theory implies that the sudden suppression of responses caused by punishment is an elicited emotional disturbance which disappears as the organism becomes accustomed to the stimulus" [p. 251]. Such recovery of punished responding is hard to reconcile with the symmetrical law of effect view that we have identified with the early Thorndike and with Azrin. Rachlin conducted an extensive investigation of recovery in which pigeons were studied on a multiple schedule of food reinforcement. Two distinctive stimuli (green and orange key lights) alternated throughout the session; each was associated with a *VI* 1-minute schedule of food reinforcement. The pigeons were then punished with mild electric shock for pecking during one of the two components of the multiple schedule. As found in earlier studies, the pigeons eventually recovered so that they responded at the same rate during both components of the multiple schedule. Rachlin next introduced shock during the other component of the multiple schedule: The subjects were shocked for responding during the green period as well as during the orange period. Since responding during the orange period had recovered from the effects of punishment, if behavior during the two components of the multiple schedule were truly independent, there should now be a selective suppression during the green period which had not been previously punished and therefore could not have "recovered." Instead, the rates of responding in the two components were about equal. This leads us to an important conclusion: The recovery generalized from the orange component to the green. Next, Rachlin removed punishment during the orange period. Responding in the orange component rose well above the rate of responding in the green component, as was expected on the basis of previous work (Azrin, 1960b). What was not expected, however, was that the relative rate of responding during the orange component did not return to 50 percent; the rise following suppression appeared to be more permanent than expected on the basis of previous work. Rachlin then repeated the same cycle of events (i.e., shock in neither stimulus, shock in orange only, shock in both, shock in green only) a second and third time. The hint of a more enduring effect of punishment with more experience in the situation emerged much more clearly in the successive cycles of the experiment. This finding is schematized in Figure 7.12, which shows the asymptotic (absolute) response rates in

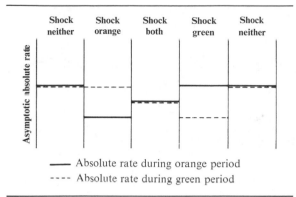

—— Absolute rate during orange period
---- Absolute rate during green period

Figure 7.12 A schematic diagram of typical asymptotic rates of responding during the orange and green periods for cycles of the experiment following the first. (From Rachlin, 1966.)

both the orange and green components for each procedure after the first. This figure shows, rather strikingly, that recovery no longer occurs: Even mild punishment, then, can be seen to have a rather permanent effect on the organism's behavior. On the basis of this experiment and others, Rachlin (1966) concluded,

> The results stress the fact that the effects of shock on the behavior of an organism depend, to a large extent, on the organism's prior experience with shock. Experience with shock tends to increase the power of shock as an instrumental suppressor.
>
> There were emotional effects consequent on punishment because the punishment used was novel whereas the reward was not. But novel reward would probably also have initial emotional effects which eventually wear out [p. 263].
>
> It is concluded that, if transient emotional states are ignored, reward and punishment are symmetrical in their effects [p. 251].

Before going on to the next important experimental finding indicating symmetry between reinforcement and punishment, it is necessary to backtrack a bit and review the dramatic and influential finding from Estes' (1944) study discussed earlier. He found that the effect of electric shock was independent of whether it was received for bar-pressing or whether it was presented when the animal was not pressing the bar. He found the same degree of suppression and the same degree of recovery of the response whether or not shock followed the response. This experiment was a major factor in generating the belief that the effects of punishment were nonspecific, that is, that punish-

ment depresses responding in the situation in general without having a specific effect on the response that produced the punishment. If this were the case, of course, we would have a dramatically different situation than we have with positive reinforcement (e.g., Ferster & Skinner, 1957). This notion fits in very well with the hypothesis that all punishment does on those occasions when it appears to reduce the probability of a response is to generate behavior that is itself incompatible with the punished response. In this case, for example, the shocks, whether or not they follow the bar-press, are believed to create a general emotional state with concomitant emotional responses, such as freezing, that interfere with an integrated response such as a bar-press. Recall, for example, the final sentence in the passage from Bolles (1967) that was quoted earlier. At that point, it was argued that the competing-response hypothesis of punishment had several drawbacks, including the fact that the competing response was often difficult to specify (and consequently could be invoked at will) and the fact that it seems hard to apply the competing-response notion to most of the results encountered throughout the chapter, for example, to those illustrating the effects of punishment on responding reinforced by different schedules of reinforcement.

It is now time to go further: We will first see that Estes' conclusion was invalid; we will then show that the effects of punishment on behavior are as specific as those of positive reinforcement; finally, we will show that while there are indeed cases in which response-independent shocks affect behavior, these cases are analogous to those in which response-independent reinforcements affect behavior. At that point we will have amassed a rather impressive case for the equivalence of reward and punishment. Moreover, it will seem at that point that there is no apparent case for the counter-argument that punishment weakens behavior only to the extent that it produces behavior that competes with the punished response.

The problem with Estes' study comparing effects of response-dependent shocks (i.e., punishment) and response-independent shocks on the suppression of bar-pressing in the rat is that shocks were applied for only a very short time (10 minutes). Punishment may create transient emotional states that could account for Estes' results. With further study, then, the different effects of response-dependent and response-independent shocks might readily be demonstrated. Estes should not be faulted for having studied the effects of response-independent shocks so little; his pioneer study was extensive and far ahead of its time.

Two studies indicate that, had Estes studied the effects of response-independent shocks further, he would have found that their effects are clearly different from that of punishment. The first study is that of Azrin (1956), who investigated the effects of presenting response-independent shocks and response-dependent shocks on similar schedules. In each case the behavior was maintained by a variable-interval 3-minute schedule of food reinforcement. There were two important conditions: In one case the shock was presented at fixed intervals; in the other, at variable intervals. Figure 7.13 indicates that response-dependent shocks had a powerful influence on ongoing behavior; response-independent shocks had a relatively local effect. For example, when shocks were presented on a variable-interval schedule, the subjects (pigeons) maintained a uniform rate of responding. The response-independent shocks did have the effect of lowering the uniform rate of responding from the baseline rate obtained in the preshock condition. This decline in rate can be attributed to the fact that many of the shocks were adventitiously correlated with responses—that is, shocks were occasionally delivered immediately following a response. Moreover, the important finding is that the decrease in responding resulting from response-independent shocks was inconsequential compared to the dramatic decrease in responding when the same shocks were presented on a response-dependent basis.

Figures 7.13A and 7.13C show a schematic representation of Azrin's results when the shocks were presented on a fixed-interval schedule. In the response-independent case, responding is maintained at a high rate, but with a negative acceleration prior to the delivery of the shock. Again, it is likely that this negative acceleration is due to the adventitious correlation of responses with shocks. Indeed, there is a perfect analogy in the case of positive reinforcement: When reinforcements are presented on a fixed-interval schedule but are uncorrelated with responding, there is a positive acceleration of responding between reinforcements (Skinner, 1948b). The only difference between the *superstitious* pattern of responding found by Azrin with response-independent shocks and that found by Skinner with response-independent reinforcements is one of direction—the two have the same effect except they are opposite in sign.

Finally, Figure 7.13 indicates that when response-dependent shocks were presented on a

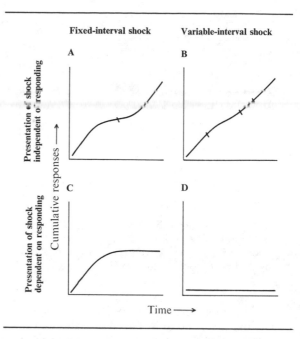

Figure 7.13 Schematic cumulative response curves showing the effects on responding of response-independent and response-dependent (punishment) shocks delivered according to *FI* or *VI* schedules. Responding is maintained by a *VI* 3-minute schedule of food reinforcement. Downward deflections indicate shock presentations. (After Azrin, 1956.)

fixed-interval schedule, there was a sharp negative acceleration of responding during each presentation of the associated orange stimulus. (Throughout the experiment, blue stimulus periods, during which shocks were never presented, alternated with orange stimulus periods, during which shocks were presented according to the procedures just described. Our discussion and the results shown in Figure 7.13 all refer to the orange stimulus.) As the time for the response-produced shock approached, responding stopped altogether, thereby avoiding the shock for the duration of the orange stimulus. Thus, the effects of the response-dependent, fixed-interval shock presentation are strikingly different from those of the response-independent, fixed-interval shock presentation: The response-dependent shock completely suppresses responding that has produced shock. The effect of fixed-interval shock presentation in the response-dependent case is again precisely what would be expected if one took the position that the effects of punishment are completely analogous to the effects of reward, except that they are opposite in sign: Food reinforcement presented at fixed intervals for responding produces positively accelerated responding; shocks presented at fixed intervals for responding produce negatively accelerated responding.

Thus, the results shown in Figure 7.13 demonstrate three important points: (1) Response-dependent shocks (punishment) produce effects that are far more dramatic than those produced by response-independent shocks; (2) the effects of punishment on behavior critically depend on the schedule of punishment; and (3) all the effects of punishment and response-independent shocks mirror those that would be expected if food reinforcement were used instead of shock—in other words, all the results are consistent with the proposition that reward and punishment are equivalent but opposite in sign.

Another convincing argument for the symmetry of reward and punishment comes from an experiment by Schuster and Rachlin (1968). They utilized the concurrent-chains procedure (Chapter 5) to test whether or not a fairly subtle and complex set of findings which held for positive reinforcement also held for punishment. A well-established finding in the study of positive reinforcement is that the correlation between a response and a reinforcement in the presence of a particular stimulus is critical in determining the subject's behavior in the presence of that stimulus. This is really just a statement that schedules of reinforcement control behavior (Ferster & Skinner, 1957). More recently, however, it has been shown that the particular correlation between a reinforcer and a response has very little effect on the reinforcing value of the stimulus as measured in a choice situation (Autor, 1960; Fantino, 1968, 1969a; Herrnstein, 1964; see also Chapter 5). For example, Neuringer (1969) showed that pigeons were indifferent between obtaining response-independent reinforcement after a delay interval and obtaining response-dependent reinforcement on a fixed-interval schedule of food reinforcement (see Chapter 6). This study, and the others cited, leads to the conclusion that choice between two stimuli depends critically on the rate of reinforcement obtained in their presence, but not on the specific correlation between the reinforcer and responding in its presence (or whatever behavior is generated by that correlation); conversely, behavior in the presence of the stimuli that have been chosen depends critically on the correlation between responding and reinforcement, but is less dependent on the rate of reinforcement in its presence (cf. Fantino, 1969b; Fantino & Herrnstein, 1968).

If the same situation held for punishment, one should find that although punishment suppresses responding to a much greater extent than response-independent shock—in keeping with Azrin's (1956) results, but not with Estes' (1944) findings—the organism should be indifferent in choosing between a stimulus in whose presence responses are punished and one in which the same number of shocks are presented on a response-independent basis. Schuster and Rachlin (1968) tested this proposition and confirmed it. They summarized their results and interpretation by stating,

> Pigeons were trained to respond under two conditions with two identical variable-interval schedules of positive reinforcement. While the schedules operated for separate response keys, they were not available concurrently. During one condition, each response was punished with electric shock. During the other condition, shocks were delivered independently of responding. The punishment suppressed responding but the free shocks did not. However, when allowed to choose, the pigeons preferred the condition associated with the lowest rate of shock regardless of whether or not the shock was dependent on responding. In general, shocks exerted their greatest effect on whichever response had the greatest influence on shocks. In this respect, punishment is instrumental in suppressing behavior and the properties of punishment are symmetrical to those of reinforcement. This empirical symmetry dictates a corresponding conceptual symmetry in terms of a positive law of effect accounting for response increments and a negative law accounting for response decrements [p. 777].

In conclusion, although punishment has not been studied as extensively as positive reinforcement, the evidence thus far obtained points to the likelihood that the principles which apply to positive reinforcement and which have been presented in other chapters of this book apply to punishment as well. Indeed, the work summarized here points to a remarkable symmetry between the effects of reward and punishment.

NEGATIVE REINFORCEMENT

Punishment, the presentation of aversive stimuli contingent on responding, is only one aspect of aversive control. Another is *negative reinforcement*, the removal of aversive stimuli contingent on responding.

The most basic experimental paradigm for negative reinforcement involves *escape:* A designated response terminates an aversive stimulus for some period of time. A closely related experimental paradigm involves *avoidance:* A designated response cancels or postpones a scheduled presentation of an aversive stimulus.

Both escape and avoidance behavior are often studied in discrete-trial procedures, which either prevent or ignore responding during intervals between trials. The relation between escape and avoidance may be appreciated most easily, though, in a widely studied free-operant procedure devised by Sidman (1953). Sidman's procedure involves the presentation of brief shocks regularly in time; the time between shocks is called the *shock-shock* or *S-S* interval. When a designated response such as bar-pressing occurs, this regular sequence of shocks is suspended, and the next shock is scheduled to occur at some other interval after the response; this time is the *response-shock* or *R-S* interval. Each additional response resets the R-S interval timer, so that maintained responding at intervals less than the R-S interval can postpone shock indefinitely.

Now, from one point of view, this is an avoidance procedure, because scheduled shocks are omitted when the response occurs. From another point of view, though, this procedure involves escape from the sequence of regular presentations of shock. Because of this ambiguity, studies of Sidman avoidance and related procedures lend themselves equally well to discussions of escape and avoidance behavior. Also, the overlap between escape and avoidance that is suggested here on procedural grounds has a parallel in theoretical accounts of avoidance behavior, as the following discussion will show.

Escape
Basic findings

A subject will rapidly learn to escape aversive stimulation. Less shaping is generally required to establish an escape response than to establish responses with positive reinforcement. While it is tempting to attribute this difference to the notion that negative reinforcers are in some sense more potent than positive reinforcers, such a conclusion would be hard to maintain. Although certain levels of aversive stimulation might be more potent than a certain amount of food in motivating a response, an experimenter could find levels of electric shock, amounts of food reinforcement, and degrees of hunger that would lead to the opposite conclusion. Moreover, there is an alternative explanation for the fact that shaping with aversive stimulation is very rapid. Aversive stimulation produces a great amount of activity, thus enhancing the probability of making the correct response in a given period of time. Consider, for example, a rat in a small box whose floor consists of grid bars through which shock is transmitted. When shock is applied through the grid bars, the rat hops up and down and moves about. The experimenter, when shaping, is thus provided with a wide selection of behavior from which to choose successive approximations to the desired behavior.

It should also be pointed out that the escape procedure differs in a fundamental way from procedures in which appetitive reinforcement is utilized. When a hungry pigeon is responding on a key to produce food, it is maintained at virtually the same level of deprivation throughout the testing session, although each reinforcement produces a slight decrement in deprivation. When an organism responds to escape from shock, however, correct responses entirely eliminate shock. In order to make the escape procedure more comparable to the typical appetitive situation, one could present continuous shock to the subject and reinforce the response by slight reductions in shock intensity; or one could maintain intermittent shock at a constant intensity and reinforce responses by providing slight reductions in the rate of shock presentation. These procedures have rarely been utilized, although Herrnstein and Hineline (1966) have performed an experiment in manipulating shock density that will be discussed later in the chapter.

These procedural differences make comparisons between behavior maintained by escape and by positive reinforcement difficult. In addition, they serve to qualify conclusions that may be drawn from these comparisons. Nonetheless, it appears that the maintenance of behavior under an escape procedure is substantially the same as it is with positive reinforcement. It should be noted, however, that much less work has been done exploring schedules of negative reinforcement. There are indications that it is more difficult to maintain behavior intermittently reinforced by escape from shock than it is to maintain behavior intermittently reinforced with food. Hendry and Hendry (1963) found that rats were unable to sustain performance when eight responses were required to escape shock (*FR*-8), although escape behavior was maintained when the schedule was *FR*-4. Hineline and Rachlin (1969) noted similar results with pigeons responding on fixed-ratio schedules of escape: Pigeons would stop responding at fixed ratios far lower (around 20) than they would when responding for positive reinforcement. Dinsmoor (1962) also had some difficulty maintaining escape behavior with rats when the schedule of escape—from a stimulus correlated with intermittent shock—was a *VI* 30-seconds. He found, for example, that when the safe period (i.e., the shock-free period following an escape response) was reduced to 30 seconds or less, the rat's performance deteriorated (cf. Kaplan, 1956, and Winograd, 1965, both of whom studied rats). On the other hand, Azrin, Holz, Hake, and Ayllon (1963) were able to maintain *FR* escape performance quite satisfactorily even with brief shock-free periods, when they employed a procedure similar to Dinsmoor's, but using squirrel monkeys as the experimental subjects.

Taken together, these experiments suggest two main generalizations: (1) Behavior maintained by schedules of negative reinforcement is appropriate to the type of schedule in the sense that the pattern of escape responding is similar to the pattern of food-reinforced responding on similar schedules; and (2) behavior is not as well maintained on the intermittent schedules of escape studied thus far as it is on intermittent schedules of positive reinforcement, at least for rats and for pigeons.

Does the second point raise any problems for our contention that reward and punishment are two sides of the same coin? The answer is "not necessarily," for at least two reasons. In the first place, as indicated earlier, it is often meaningless to try to compare the strength of two different reinforcers. This does not imply any peculiar distinction between reward and punishment, for the same argument applies to different positive reinforcers, such as intracranial self-stimulation, food, and sex. The more important point is that the quality, if not the quantity, of behavior maintained on schedules of negative reinforcement is similar to that maintained on schedules of positive reinforcement. The second argument is that there are certain features of the escape procedure that would lead one to expect that intermittently reinforced behavior would be more difficult to maintain with negative reinforcement. Hendry and Hendry (1963) speculate that during intermittent escape conditioning, "the absence of shock itself acquires aversive properties" [p. 519]. They note that in the free-responding situation subjects do not escape from the entire situation, but only from the shock; they remain in a situation in which shock will soon be reintroduced. Hendry and Hendry contrast this with discrete-trial procedures. For example, in the runway the rat escapes shock in one part of the box by running into a different box where it is not shocked. In the bar-press escape, however, the absence of shock always precedes the onset of shock, and therefore might be expected to acquire rather potent aversive properties in itself. The argument has a peculiar implication, however, recognized by Hendry and Hendry: In cases where the subject does not emit the eight responses (on *FR*-8) to escape the shock, one might conclude that in this case "a situation which regularly precedes shock will become more aversive than the shock itself" [p. 523]. While Hendry and Hendry are able to cite experiments from the literature on avoidance conditioning that lend support to their conclusion (Sidman, 1957; Sidman & Boren, 1957), an experiment by Wahlsten, Cole, Sharp, and Fantino (1968) directly tests this type of hypothesis (again, in an avoidance situation) and finds negative results. In addition, there is a more parsimonious explanation of the finding that escape behavior is difficult to maintain with intermittent schedules of reinforcement. In the intermittent escape procedure, abortive escape responses are often followed (adventitiously) by shocks; in other words, responding is adventitiously punished. The more intermittent the schedule of escape, the more often such adventitious punishment is likely to occur, and the more suppression of the escape response would in turn result; at the same time, more responding is required to escape. This interpretation of why escape behavior is poorly maintained with intermittent schedules of negative reinforcement has been raised more recently by Hineline and Rachlin (1969). Finally, it may also happen that the aversive stimulus itself elicits responses that are incompatible with the sustained emission of operant behavior (cf. Chapter 2).

The reinforcer for an escape response is the removal or reduction of shock. Two obvious parameters of the reinforcement that would be expected to have an effect on the strength of the escape response involve the *amount of reinforcement*. One is the amount of reinforcement in the sense of the amount of reduction of shock, which depends in part on the intensity of the shock; the other is the amount of reinforcement in the sense of the duration of the safe period—the time-out-from-shock period following the escape response or the intertrial interval. The shock-intensity variable is probably most analogous to degree of deprivation, while the amount of safe time is probably most analogous to amount of reinforcement in studies with positive reinforcement.

There is a positive relation between the intensity of an electric shock and the escape behavior maintained by it (Azrin, Hake, Holz, & Hutchinson, 1965; Winograd, 1965), just as there is a positive relation between the degree of food deprivation and the maintenance of responding on schedules of positive reinforcement (e.g., Clark, 1958; Dinsmoor, 1952; Fischer & Fantino, 1968). These studies utilized a single response. As indicated earlier in the chapter, evidence from studies utilizing positive reinforcement strongly indicate that choice procedures provide a far more sensitive evaluation of the effect of a reinforcement parameter than does a single-response procedure. We noted that variables that caused only a small variation in the rates of single operants cause large variations in a choice situation (e.g., Catania, 1963; see also Chapter 6). Thus we would expect the same principle to apply with negative reinforcement as well. In the case of different intensities of shock, of course, a choice procedure is difficult to implement, for the subjects cannot experience two different intensities of shock concurrently. By the same token, concurrent choice cannot be used to investigate the effects of deprivation level: The organism can be maintained at only one level of deprivation at any given time. When it comes to amount of reinforcement or of safe time, however, it is easy to use a choice procedure. Amount of reinforcement has been studied by Catania (1963) and by Rachlin and Baum (1969). Catania, for example, showed that pigeons' choice behavior was remarkably sensitive to the relative durations of reinforcements obtainable on two keys, whereas no systematic relation between duration of food reward and rate of responding was observable with the same pigeons when a single key was employed. In his single-response study of escape Dinsmoor (1962) found that, at least for safe-time values of 60 seconds or more, escape behavior was not a function of the amount of safe time. He did find, however, that when the safe period was reduced to 30 or 15 seconds, some deterioration in escape responding was observed. This conclusion is hard to evaluate, however, since the rates of escape responding maintained in Dinsmoor's experiment were very low (less than five responses per minute). Unfortunately, there are no published data comparing the effects of different safe times on choice. There is, however, an interesting study by Sidman (1954), who used a preference measure in conjunction with avoidance conditioning. In Sidman's study each

response delayed shock for a certain interval. The length of this response-shock interval was different for the two concurrently available response levers. Sidman's rats consistently showed a preference for the bar providing the longer response-shock interval. In Sidman's procedure each response was effective in producing delay of shock. Thus, the preferred response was also the more frequently reinforced response. This technique has the same weakness as the study of free choice in a T-maze: The effects of the independent variable are confounded with the effects of number of reinforced responses. In order to control for the effect of number of reinforcers without resorting to a forcing procedure, studies with positive reinforcement have used variable-interval schedules of reinforcement to program reinforcement for each response. Variable-interval schedules have the property of reinforcing each response equally often over a large range of preference (Fantino, 1967). For example, with two concurrent VI 40-second schedules, the animal could emit the preferred response exclusively and be reinforced on the average of every 40 seconds. Or the animal could occasionally emit both responses and receive reinforcement every 20 seconds. The latter alternative more closely describes the typical animal's behavior. Thus, both operants are reinforced equally often although the animal may emit one response more often. Concurrent VIs were employed by Catania (1963) in studying the effects of amount of reward in positive reinforcement. It would seem fruitful to employ a similar procedure in evaluating the effects of amount of reinforcement on responding maintained by escape from electric shock.

Initial data collected by the author in collaboration with Steven Hursh have shown that this is a feasible procedure. Rats received electric shocks delivered on the average of every 5 seconds. They could respond to escape these shocks on either of the two levers in the chamber (a modified version of the rat chamber devised by Azrin, Hopwood, & Powell, 1967). The schedule associated with each bar was a variable-interval 40-second schedule. For both rats in the initial work, the measure of choice—the proportion of responses on one bar during the shock period—was close to 50 percent when safe times were equal on both bars. For both rats, however, the choice proportions soared to about .70 for the response that produced a 60-second safe time as opposed to a 20-second safe time on the alternative bar. This finding is analogous to that of Catania's for amount of food reinforcement.

This choice study contained an additional experimental procedure that is of theoretical interest. During the shock period, for example, prior to a successful escape response, the chamber was illuminated by two lights over the response bars. Since these lights were associated with shocks, it might be hypothesized that they should themselves have acquired aversive properties. If so, the subjects should prefer a response alternative that leads to relatively less time in the light. In fact, however, the subjects were indifferent to the amount of safe time that was spent in the presence of the lights. In other words, when total safe times were equal, the choice proportions were around .50 regardless of which response led to a greater amount of darkness; when the safe times were unequal (60 seconds versus 20 seconds), the choice proportions were around .70 regardless of what proportion of the safe time was spent in darkness. Since the lights that were always on during the presence of the shock should have become conditioned aversive stimuli, these results are inconsistent with the hypothesis that the reduction in conditioned aversive stimuli is a central variable in aversive conditioning. By that hypothesis, the response that led to a longer period of offset of these conditioned aversive stimuli should have been emitted more often. The findings, however, are quite clear in indicating that this did not occur, despite the fact that the choice proportions for the same rats were sensitive to the relative amounts of safe time. The results suggest that the reinforcing value of escape from conditioned aversive stimuli is minimal, at least when compared with the effects of escape from primary aversive stimuli. These results are consistent with the position taken throughout this chapter that negative reinforcement is parallel to positive reinforcement. Although stimuli may acquire aversive properties because of classical conditioning with primary aversive stimuli such as shock, these conditioned aversive stimuli appear to play a minor or nonexistent role in the control of escape behavior.

Escape from "reinforcement" and responding for "punishment"

It is important to emphasize the fact that a given stimulus may be reinforcing in one situation and punishing in another. In other words, a stimulus does not have immutable status as a reward or punisher. Although it is certainly true that food will generally be reinforcing to a hungry organism and that an electric shock will generally be punishing to any organism, there are exceptions, and occasionally even reversals, to these generalizations. It is with the reversal that we now deal briefly. The phenomenon of *escaping from reinforcement* was first reported by Azrin (1961). He found that pigeons responding on high fixed-ratio schedules of food reinforcement would occasionally respond on a second key to remove the stimuli associated with the high ratio, thereby removing themselves from the opportunity to respond for food. Azrin's study and others showed that escape responding occurs during the pause that follows reinforcement. In other words, it appears that the pause after reinforcement is in itself a reflection of the aversiveness of the associated stimulus. Given the opportunity, therefore, the subject will respond to remove the stimulus and to remove itself from the situation.

This general finding has been embellished by showing that subjects will respond to alter stimulus conditions associated with high ratios, even when the ratio requirement itself remains unchanged (Appel, 1963). Specifically, Appel found that after receiving food reinforcement on a high fixed ratio, the subjects would respond to change the stimulus light to a different light even though that light had also been associated with the same high fixed ratio. Thompson (1965) trained pigeons on a multiple *FR, VI* schedule. He altered the value of the fixed-ratio component from 1 to 300, while the variable-interval component was kept constant (*VI* 2-minutes). After responding stabilized during the *FR* component, an additional contingency was introduced during the *VI* component; each response during the *VI* component produced a 0.3-second stimulus which was either the stimulus correlated with the fixed-ratio component or a stimulus uncorrelated with either schedule component. Thompson found that the production of the fixed-ratio stimulus produced a decrease in variable-interval responding that was proportional to the size of the fixed-ratio requirement. Thus, the stimuli associated with the high fixed-ratio requirement satisfies the definition for punishment in terms of suppressing ongoing behavior on the variable-interval schedule (and did so more than the uncorrelated stimulus).

Finally, Hutchinson, Azrin, and Hunt (1968) demonstrated that a biting response, regarded as a measure of aggression, occurred during the post-reinforcement pause among squirrel monkeys responding on high fixed-ratio schedules of food reinforcement. Related studies of the elicitation of aggressive behavior are discussed in Chapter 8. There, it is suggested that a period of nonreinforcement is functionally equivalent to presentation of shock. The studies reviewed here demonstrate that the stimuli associated with large fixed-ratio schedules, at least following reinforcement, parallel the effects of electric shock in similar conditions and qualify as aversive stimuli. The same stimuli, however, can also be shown to be positively reinforcing in the sense that a subject will respond to obtain them. For example, in chained schedules of reinforcement (cf. Chapter 5), responding on a *VI* 1-minute schedule in the initial link may be maintained by access to a stimulus correlated with a high-valued *FR* schedule (e.g., *FR*-300) in the terminal link (Ferster & Skinner, 1957). This is an excellent demonstration, therefore, that the same stimulus at different times can be both a negative and a positive reinforcer.

Just as a subject will occasionally work to remove a stimulus correlated with the opportunity to obtain food reinforcement, so will it occasionally work to obtain an electric shock sufficiently potent to maintain escape responding. This counterintuitive but well-documented finding appears to depend critically, and in a very complex way, on the organism's past history with electric shock. Although this effect has been demonstrated in a large number of studies (e.g., Byrd, 1969, 1972; Kelleher & Morse, 1968; McKearney, 1968, 1969, 1970; Morse, Mead, & Kelleher, 1967; Stretch, Orloff, & Dalrymple, 1968), a discussion of the procedure and findings of one prototype study (Byrd, 1969) suffices for our present purposes. While most of the work on response-produced shock has utilized squirrel monkeys, Byrd studied two cats initially trained in an avoidance procedure, in which responding postponed shock for 60 seconds. If the cats did not respond, shocks were delivered every 5 seconds. After the cats acquired a high degree of avoidance responding—and were rarely obtaining shocks—Byrd added response-independent shock to the procedure every 15 minutes, for example, regardless of the cats' avoidance performance. Subsequently, the avoidance schedule was omitted and the only experimental manipulation was the presentation of response-independent shock every 15 minutes. The cats' responses were now totally ineffective. Despite this, response rates increased for each cat, remaining fairly steady throughout the 15-minute intervals. After 33 sessions with this response-independent shock procedure, Byrd altered the schedule from response-independent shocks every 15 minutes to a fixed-interval 15-min-

ute schedule of shock presentation. Now, the cats' responses were actually producing the shocks (on an *FI* 15-minute schedule). Both cats maintained responding. One subject continued to respond steadily throughout the 15-minute interval with only a brief pause after shock. The second cat developed a pattern of response acceleration during the 15-minute interval, which is characteristic of behavior on fixed-interval schedules of positive reinforcement. In other words, this cat's responses were emitted at progressively higher rates until the responses produced the shocks, following which the cat emitted the postreinforcement pause that is characteristic of behavior reinforced on fixed-interval schedules. Further work permitting a systematic comparison of the effects of response-independent and response-contingent shock presentations would be most valuable in advancing our understanding of this phenomenon (see also Chapter 2).

Thus it should be clear that a given stimulus does not have immutable status as a reward or punisher. Instead, a given stimulus may be reinforcing in one situation and punishing in another. At the same time, it is not clear how electric shocks, for example, are maintaining responding to produce them. A consideration of all the studies cited fails to pinpoint the necessary and sufficient conditions for producing behavior whose only consequence is painful electric shock. Almost certainly, when a definitive explanation is obtained, the organism's experimental history with electric shock will be implicated.

Escape stimuli and conditioned reinforcers

Stimuli that are associated with the onset of positive reinforcement acquire conditioned reinforcing properties (see Chapter 5). Most experimenters who have asked whether or not a stimulus associated with the escape from shock is a positive reinforcer have met with a negative answer. This negative evidence has been ably reviewed by Beck (1961), LoLordo (1969), and Siegel and Milby (1969) and has also been discussed in Chapter 5.

Based on the literature in the area of positive reinforcement, it appears that the most efficient way for establishing the stimulus as a conditioned reinforcer is to utilize that stimulus as a discriminative stimulus for responding to obtain positive reinforcement (Dinsmoor, 1950; Keller & Schoenfeld, 1950). It is somewhat surprising, therefore, that most experimenters exploring the question of whether stimuli associated with the escape from shock are conditioned reinforcers have not first established the stimulus as a discriminative stimulus for the escape response. On those occasions when such a procedure was employed, positive results have been obtained (Dinsmoor & Clayton, 1963, 1966; Fantino & Sharp, unpublished data). In the Fantino and Sharp experiment, for example, a stimulus that had been a discriminative stimulus for the opportunity to respond (a bar-press) to escape shock later reinforced the learning of a new response (a chain-pull). In testing, inescapable shocks were presented on the average of every 30 seconds and lasted for a variable period of about 5 seconds. Responses were reinforced by the production of the discriminative stimulus (a light) for 1.5 seconds. If the chain-pull occurred during the presence of the shock, however, the shock offset was postponed at least 1.5 seconds following the light offset. This procedure was used to insure against the possibility that adventitious correlation of responding or light presentation with shock offset might account for any chain-pulling that developed. Moreover, to assess the possibility that the presence of the light elicited further responding, responses in darkness (i.e., responses that produced the light) were recorded separately from responses in the presence of the light. Fantino and Sharp found that significantly more chain-pulls were made by rats for which the light had been a discriminative stimulus to bar-press for the escape from shock than for control rats that had received identical treatment but for which there was no explicit discriminative stimulus. Although these control rats also received the light, it did not signal the opportunity to escape shock for them. The other controls insured against interpretations in terms of superstitious responding in the test situation or in terms of response elicitation. These results, in conjunction with those of Dinsmoor and Clayton (1963, 1966) and related studies described in Chapter 5, indicate that secondary reinforcers may be established on the basis of shock termination. When considered in conjunction with the many negative results that have been obtained on this question, however, the following generalization is suggested: In order to insure positive results, the stimulus should be established as a discriminative stimulus for responding to escape the shock. Moreover, it may be necessary to test for any reinforcing effects of the stimuli when the organism is properly motivated, for example, when shocks are still being presented.

Avoidance

In avoidance conditioning, the subject may avoid the shock by emitting the appropriate response prior to its onset. Most studies of avoidance conditioning have utilized a discrete-trials procedure in which a conditioned stimulus (*CS*) signals the opportunity to avoid. If the subject fails to emit the avoidance response within a specified time (the *CS-US* interval), shock (the *US*) is presented. Other studies have utilized the free-operant procedure devised by Sidman (1953) and described earlier. The acquisition of avoidance behavior often follows a more tedious course than that of escape conditioning or conditioning with positive reinforcement, owing to a wide variety of factors, some of which are poorly understood.

Response factors in avoidance conditioning

A critical factor in the acquisition of an avoidance response is the nature of the response itself. A running response, for example, is acquired rapidly. On the other hand, a lever-press response is acquired very slowly and sometimes incompletely. Indeed, if an animal must learn to press a lever to avoid shock, its behavior will be greatly facilitated if it is first required to run to the lever (Fantino, Sharp, & Cole, 1966). This somewhat surprising result is illustrated in Figure 7.14. The rats whose data are represented by the unfilled circles have just 5 seconds to avoid the shock; in that time the rats must run from one box to another when a door drops open, and then press a lever in the second box. The rats whose data are represented by the triangles start the trial in the same box with the lever and have 5 seconds to press it; since they generally stay near the lever at all times, the requirement that they press the lever within 5 seconds would appear to be trivial. The figure illustrates just the opposite result: Rats that must run and then press learn rapidly, while those that need merely press demonstrate virtually no learning. As indicated in Figure 7.14, after 80 trials the two groups were reversed. The group of rats that was now required to run acquired the response rapidly, as one would have expected from the results of the first part of the experiment. The surprising finding was that the rats which had learned to run and press no longer pressed when the requirement was made simpler. Rats in this condition showed no trace of their earlier learning when switched to the lever-press-only condition.

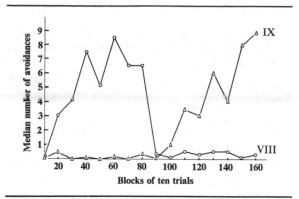

Figure 7.14 Median number of avoidance responses throughout the single session of the experiment in ten-trial blocks. For the first 80 trials, rats in Group VIII had to run and lever-press in order to avoid shock while rats in Group IX had only to lever-press. After 80 trials, these groups were switched. (From Fantino, Sharp, & Cole, 1966.)

These results indicate that by making the lever-press avoidance situation as similar as possible to that in the shuttle box, lever-press avoidance can be sharply facilitated. Why is this so? Fantino et al. (1966) favored an interpretation in terms of *response topography,* originally outlined by Meyer, Cho, and Weseman (1960). According to Meyer et al., events that disrupt freezing in response to the conditioned stimulus should facilitate lever-press avoidance since freezing is incompatible with lever-pressing. Thus, a conditioned stimulus such as the door-drop of the shuttle box should produce a startle response rather than freezing and should, therefore, facilitate lever-pressing. Indeed, control procedures showed that the main variable responsible for the differences in the rate of acquisition of the avoidance response was the door-drop. In addition to the effectiveness of the door-drop stimulus and the effectiveness of requiring a running response in facilitating avoidance performance of the experimental animals, there was a third factor in the Fantino et al. study that was also shown to be responsible for the enhanced avoidance performance of the experimental animals represented in Figure 7.14. When the rat spent the intertrial interval out of the apparatus, its performance was superior to comparable rats that had spent the intertrial intervals in the apparatus. This is compatible with the Meyer et al. interpretation in the sense that when the subject is removed from the source of noxious stimulation it

cannot spend the intertrial intervals crouching (or freezing) over the bar. Finally, the results obtained after the experimental and control groups were switched indicate that the light gained no control as a conditioned stimulus over the animal's lever-press responding during the first 80 trial training period for either group. These findings underscore the importance of the nature of the response: Rats that successfully performed the ostensibly more complex response of running and then pressing showed a total performance decrement in lever-pressing when the running part of the requirement was dropped.

An additional factor implicated in the speed of acquisition of an avoidance response is handling. Using the simple technique of picking up the animal and letting it down 10 seconds or so prior to an avoidance trial, Wahlsten, Cole, Sharp, and Fantino (1968) showed that the likelihood of a successful avoidance response was sharply increased. One possibility why handling has such a profound effect may be that it disrupts freezing behavior which may in turn be responsible for the failure of rats to avoid in the lever-press situation. Supporting this notion is the fact that tranquilizer drugs enhance avoidance in the lever-pressing situation (Krieckhaus, Miller, & Zimmerman, 1965). These results are all consistent with the hypothesis of Meyer et al.

The importance of the response utilized in avoidance has also been underscored by Bolles (1970). Taking particular note of the slow learning of avoidance responding in the laboratory, Bolles noted that in order to survive in the wild the animal must enter its environment with defensive reactions already contained in its behavioral repertoire. Bolles predicts that avoidance responses will be rapidly acquired in the laboratory only if they are part of the subject's *species-specific defense reaction (SSDR).* For the rat, the *SSDR* repertoire includes freezing, fleeing, and hiding. Thus, certain avoidance responses utilized in the laboratory, such as running in the shuttle box or jumping out of a box (Maatsch, 1959), are readily acquired because they are compatible with the behaviors in the *SSDR* repertoire. On the other hand, responses such as bar-pressing, wheel-turning, and chain-pulling are certainly not behaviors in the *SSDR* repertoire and are extremely difficult to acquire in the avoidance situation. Bolles also points out that the response requirement is the only strikingly important parameter that has thus far been uncovered despite the vast literature on avoidance learning. We should at this point, however, briefly review some of the other parameters that have been manipulated in the avoidance situation.

Nonresponse factors in avoidance conditioning

Variables affecting avoidance conditioning, other than the nature of the response, include the interval between the conditioned stimulus and the unconditioned stimulus (the *CS-US* interval); the interval between trials (the intertrial interval, or *ITI*); intensity of the *US* and the nature of the *CS*; the nature of the organism; whether or not the shock can be escaped if not avoided, and, if so, the nature of the escape response. Although each of these factors will be considered, we will see in agreement with Bolles that none has as impressive an effect on the rate of avoidance conditioning as does the nature of the avoidance response itself.

CS-US interval. The longer the *CS-US* interval, the greater chance the subject has to avoid shock (Bitterman, 1965). Therefore, it might be expected that the longer the *CS-US* interval, the more rapidly avoidance is acquired. While there is some indication that this is true (Cole & Fantino, 1966; Hoffman & Fleshler, 1962), this effect is neither very reliable nor very striking. Moreover, when tests are conducted with equal *CS-US* intervals to control for the greater opportunity to avoid with long intervals, no difference is found in the percentage of successful avoidances between groups trained with different *CS-US* intervals (Anderson, 1969, studying wheel-turning and shuttle-box avoidance; Cole & Fantino, 1966, studying lever-press avoidance). Moreover, studies using responses other than the lever-press or the wheel-turn may produce different results (cf. Solomon & Brush, 1956).

ITI. The same kind of inconclusive generalizations can be made about the effects of the intertrial interval (*ITI*). Brush (1962) reported a positive relation between shuttle-box avoidance and intertrial intervals up to 5 minutes. On the other hand, Pearl (1963) and Cole and Fantino (1966) found that shorter *ITI*s were superior in producing effective avoidance learning in the lever-press situation.

Intensity of the US. The effect of intensity of the shock on acquisition of an avoidance response is of some theoretical importance. Consider, for example, the hypothesis that the avoidance response is reinforced by fear reduction. Avoidance conditioning should be more rapid the higher the intensity of the shock, since, presumably, the more intense the shock the greater the fear that is classically conditioned to the shock. Again, the nature of the result depends on the nature of the avoidance task. For example, D'Amato and Fazzaro (1966) and Bolles and Warren (1965) found that avoidance conditioning was an *inverse function* of the shock intensity employed, thus directly disconfirming the prediction made on the basis of two-factor theory. The same result was obtained in the shuttle box by Moyer and Korn (1964) and by Theios, Lynch, and Lowe (1966). On the other hand, results in the opposite direction were obtained by Theios, Lynch, and Lowe (1966) for avoidance conditioning in the runway and by Kimble (1955) for a wheel-turning avoidance response.

Nature of the CS. As previously mentioned in discussing the results of Fantino, Sharp, and Cole (1966), the effects of the nature of the conditioned stimulus are important. In that study it was shown that the door-drop *CS* which is part of the shuttle-box procedure had an important effect in facilitating avoidance conditioning. These authors interpreted their results, however, in response terms: The effect of the loud *CS* was thought to disrupt the freezing response that otherwise interfered with lever-press avoidance. Stimulus variables have also been shown to be important—perhaps for the same reason—by other workers, especially Myers (1959).

Nature of the organism. The type of organism employed (rat, pigeon, gerbil, etc.) will affect the speed of conditioning. Moreover, it has been shown that different strains of rats have different abilities when it comes to effective avoidance learning (Nakamura & Anderson, 1962).

Nature of the escape response. One view (Solomon & Brush, 1956) suggests that the escape response is very important because it may eventually "emerge" as the avoidance response. For example, in describing a typical avoidance experiment with a panel-pushing response in the dog, Solomon and Brush note,

> On succeeding presentations of the tone-shock sequence we note that *S* escapes more quickly. His escape *latencies* decrease. After 16 presentations, averaging 3 min. apart, *S* turns his head quickly after the onset of the tone and pushes the right-hand plate with his nose. This terminates

the tone and *prevents* shock from being applied. (The first *avoidance* response has emerged.) ... Why did the first avoidance response emerge on the sixteenth trial? Why did it emerge at all [p. 217]?

It should be noted that Solomon and Brush do not maintain that this method of gradual emergence characterizes all avoidance learning.

There have been two major types of attacks against the position that the escape contingency or the nature of the escape response is crucial in avoidance conditioning. A pioneer study was performed by Mowrer and Lamoreaux (1946), who permitted their rats to escape shock that they failed to avoid; however, the escape response was different than the avoidance response. Some subjects were required to perform a running response to avoid shock but, failing that, had to jump in the air in order to escape shock. Other subjects were required to do the opposite: jump to avoid or, failing that, run to escape. Finally, control groups were run in the more conventional condition in which the escape and avoidance responses were identical: either jumping for some controls or running for the other controls. Although subjects avoided best when the avoidance response was identical to the escape response, the important finding according to Mowrer and Lamoreaux was that avoidance conditioning occurred even when the escape response was different. Obviously, then, avoidance cannot be completely dependent on the gradual emergence of the escape response since that response was ineffectual for avoiding shock. A more extensive study of this question is contained in important articles by Bolles (1969, 1970). Bolles' results support those of Mowrer and Lamoreaux in indicating that the escape contingency does not play a consistent role in the acquisition of avoidance responding. The role it does play is critically dependent on the nature of the avoidance response. For example, if the avoidance response is included in the rat's *SSDR* repertoire, then its rate of acquisition will be essentially independent of whether or not the same response is required for escape. A response that is clearly not a part of the *SSDR* repertoire, such as the lever-press, is not learned as an avoidance response regardless of the nature of the escape response. Finally, only for responses that Bolles regards as intermediate with respect to the *SSDR* dimension, such as turning, is avoidance facilitated by requiring the same response for both avoidance and escape. Bolles' results are thus compatible with, but extend, those of Mowrer and Lamoreaux.

The importance of the escape contingency has been studied in another way. Bolles, Stokes, and Younger (1966) utilized short inescapable shocks for some of their animals and compared their rate of avoidance conditioning with other animals who were required to terminate, i.e., escape from, shock. Bolles et al. found that escape from shock was not a significant factor affecting the rate of avoidance conditioning in the running-wheel. Hurwitz (1964) and D'Amato, Keller, and DiCara (1964) have obtained similar results in lever-press avoidance.

The reinforcer in avoidance: Removal of apparatus-fear?

There is a possibility that an avoidance response will be reinforced only insofar as it removes the animal from the aversive stimulus situation (Brush, 1962). We considered this hypothesis earlier when Hendry and Hendry (1963) raised it in the context of their failure to find maintained escape responding in rats on an *FR*-8 schedule of escape. They suggested the possibility that their rats were not escaping because escape from the shock left the rat in an aversive situation, i.e., in an apparatus where shock was soon to be delivered once again. Wahlsten, Cole, Sharp, and Fantino (1968) tested this hypothesis in the context of avoidance learning. Their rats could escape the apparatus by making the appropriate lever-press response. In other words, the lever-press response not only enabled the subjects to avoid the shock, but also opened a door permitting them to leave the shock chamber. On occasions when the subjects did avoid the shock they also entered the safe box. At the end of the intertrial interval, the subject was taken from the safe box and replaced in the shock box, starting the next trial. Although these subjects learned to avoid remarkably well compared to a control group that was not permitted to escape from the shock box following a successful avoidance, an important control indicated that escape from environmental cues was not the determining factor. A control group that was not allowed to escape from the shock box was handled prior to the start of a trial in the same manner as the experimental animals were handled in order to return them to the shock box at the start of a new trial. These control animals also showed a remarkable degree of avoidance. This is a case where it was very fortunate that the appropriate control was employed: Had it not been employed, the study would have shown a striking effect of escape from the cues associated with the shock box, confirming the hypothesis being tested. As it is, the experiment shows that handling an animal prior to the start of a trial greatly enhances avoidance; escape from the cues associated with the shock box does not seem to be an important additional factor.

The reinforcer in avoidance: Termination of the conditioned stimulus?

Evidence has been amassed indicating that the termination of the conditioned stimulus is not the effective reinforcer in avoidance conditioning. This evidence contradicts a crucial tenet of two-factor theory as formulated by several important theorists including Mowrer and Lamoreaux (1946), Solomon and his associates (e.g., Rescorla & Solomon, 1967), Dinsmoor (1954), Anger (1963), and others. These theorists generally assume that the conditioned stimulus acquires aversive or emotional (e.g., fearful) status because of its frequent association with the unconditioned stimulus, e.g., shock. This is the classically conditioned component of the two-process theory. The animal eventually learns to terminate the conditioned stimulus thereby avoiding the shock. The reinforcement for this response is held to be the termination of the stimulus rather than the avoidance of the unconditioned stimulus. In other words, it is felt that the avoidance response is reinforced either by a conditioned secondary reinforcer (the removal of a conditioned aversive stimulus) or by fear reduction. This is the instrumental or operant factor in two-process theory. What the animal learns is not to avoid the shock but to escape from the conditioned stimulus. What then of Sidman's avoidance procedure? Recall that in Sidman's procedure there is no exteroceptive stimulus correlated with impending shock. Any time the subject makes a response it postpones the delivery of the next shock by a fixed amount (the response-shock interval). When the subject fails to respond for a certain period of time (the shock-shock or the response-shock interval), shocks occur. How does the CS-termination hypothesis explain avoidance responses in this case? One answer is that there are covert stimuli which are serving the same function that the conditioned stimulus serves in discriminated avoidance. After a response or after a shock the stimuli associated with the situation are not aversive, since shock has never occurred soon after a response

or a shock. As time passes since the last response or shock, however, the (inferred) stimuli in the situation become increasingly aversive. They reach their aversive peak just prior to the delivery of the next shock. By responding, then, the animal escapes or removes these aversive conditioned stimuli. Anger (1963) refers to these stimuli as *conditioned aversive temporal stimuli (CATS)*. Essentially the same position was taken by Solomon and Brush (1956).

Thus, we see that even when there is no explicit conditioned stimulus, as in the Sidman procedure, the hypothesis has been advanced that it is the termination of conditioned stimuli that reinforces the avoidance response. Indeed, Sidman (1953) himself initially subscribed to such a view. More recent experimentation suggests that such a view is untenable. For example, an ingenious study by D'Amato, Fazarro, and Etkin (1968) provided strong evidence that the termination of the conditioned stimulus reinforces avoidance conditioning only insofar as it serves as a *cue* indicating that the unconditioned stimulus (the shock) will not occur. These authors utilized a cue other than prompt termination of the conditioned stimulus (CS-termination) in lever-press avoidance. For some groups an avoidance response produced a cue but did not terminate the conditioned stimulus. The crucial aspect of this procedure was that the cue occurred only on avoidance trials and therefore was never associated with the unconditioned stimulus or the shock. Therefore, it was not likely to become a powerful conditioned aversive stimulus inducing fear, since it had never been paired with the primary aversive event, the shock. Nonetheless, this cue facilitated avoidance conditioning, suggesting that the facilitation of avoidance responding by terminating the conditioned stimulus is due to its status as a discriminative cue for the avoidance of shock.

Another important study on this question is that of Bolles, Stokes, and Younger (1966). They varied whether or not responding during the CS-US interval could avoid the US and whether or not it could terminate the CS. For example, responding in one condition avoided the US without terminating the CS, while in another condition responding terminated the CS without avoiding the US. They found that avoidance of the US was the more important factor in acquiring the avoidance response; termination of the CS produced a significant but small effect. Subsequently, Bolles and Grossen (1969) performed a more extensive investigation of the role of CS-termination and were led to a somewhat different conclusion. As usual, there was a clear interaction with the nature of the avoidance response. At one extreme, for example, CS-termination had essentially no effect on the rate of acquisition of an avoidance response in a runway. Bolles and Grossen hypothesized that the avoidance response itself, running, provided a sufficient amount of feedback in that it removed the subjects from the location of the shock and was executed with effort and vigor. These results support Fantino, Sharp, and Cole (1966), who found that the conditioned stimulus (a light) in their runway acquired virtually no control over behavior. At the other extreme, a response such as a lever-press which provides very little intrinsic feedback and which is not a part of the rat's *SSDR* repertoire was very difficult to learn, supporting previous findings, and it was at the same time greatly facilitated by *CS*-termination. The important finding of Bolles and Grossen is that whenever *CS*-termination was shown to affect acquisition of the avoidance response, its effects could be attributed to the kind of cue effects shown to be important by D'Amato et al. (1968). In other words, any environmental change contingent on the avoidance response served to facilitate acquisition of the avoidance response to virtually the same degree as did *CS*-termination. These results support those of D'Amato et al. in demonstrating that *CS*-termination is not in itself an important factor in avoidance learning.

These results constitute a powerful refutation of traditional two-process theories of avoidance conditioning. It appears that previous work indicating the reinforcing nature of *CS*-termination was a reflection of the fact that *CS*-termination was a cue for the avoidance of shock and not that the *CS* was an aversive or fearful stimulus whose removal was reinforcing. Note that these findings do not invalidate the concept of conditioned negative reinforcement (cf. Miller, 1948; see also Chapter 5); they do, however, indicate that conditioned negative reinforcement may be of little importance in the acquisition of avoidance behavior.

The reinforcer in avoidance: Omission of the unconditioned stimulus?

We have seen that *CS*-termination is not the reinforcer in avoidance learning. Instead, *CS*-termination facilitates avoidance conditioning only insofar as it is a cue indicating that the *US* will not occur. This suggests that the nonoccurrence of the *US* is the basic reinforcer in avoidance conditioning. In other words, avoidance behavior is reinforced by avoidance.

We have already seen support for this notion in the studies of D'Amato et al. (1968) and of Bolles and his associates. It should be noted that Bolles (1969) has rejected the view that avoidance of the *US* reinforces avoidance behavior, maintaining instead that the avoidance response and its resultant feedback are positively reinforcing (see also Denny & Weisman, 1964). There is no clear advantage of this position over the more parsimonious one that avoidance of the shock is the reinforcer. Herrnstein (1969) has discussed the evidence favoring the view that the nonoccurrence of shock is the effective reinforcer in avoidance.

Two milestones in avoidance research were important in assessing the role of *US* avoidance. Kamin (1956, 1957) investigated the rate of avoidance conditioning when the *CS* could be terminated but the *US* could not be avoided, on the one hand, and when the *US* could be avoided but the *CS* could not be terminated, on the other hand. He found that both groups of rats learned the avoidance response, but that neither did so as quickly as control rats trained with the usual procedure in which the avoidance response both terminates the *CS* and permits *S* to avoid the *US*. While Kamin stressed the decrement shown in the group that could avoid the *US* but not terminate the *CS*, the following interpretation is suggested by his results when taken in conjunction with the results cited earlier. Avoidance of the *US* reinforces the avoidance response. The group which receives immediate feedback that the shock has been avoided acquires the avoidance response more rapidly than the group that has no stimulus bridging the gap between the response and the avoidance of the shock. This is just what one would expect based on knowledge of the effects of delay of reinforcement and of delay of punishment. In other words, if the reinforcement for the avoidance response is the nonoccurrence of shock, then procedures that help bridge the delay between the response and the reinforcement (such as *CS*-termination) should result in better avoidance. We are left to explain Kamin's other result, namely, that the *CS*-termination group that did not avoid the *US* also displayed some learning. Although much has been made of this finding, Figure 7.15 shows quite clearly that this is a very transient effect. Note that within 100

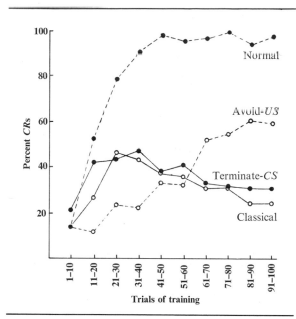

Figure 7.15 Percentage of conditioned responses in each of four groups over 100 trials. The four groups differed according to the effect of the *CR* as follows: *normal* avoided shock (*US*) and terminated *CS; avoid-US* did not terminate *CS; terminate-CS* did not avoid *US; classical* did neither, i.e., responding was ineffective. (From Kamin, 1957.)

trials the performance of the group that terminates the *CS* has deteriorated to a point where it is virtually identical to that for the classical group—a control group that neither avoids the *US* nor terminates the *CS*. At best, these results represent some conditioned reinforcement owing to the removal of a stimulus paired with shock. The most striking aspect of this facilitation, however, is not its occurrence but both the rather small size of the effect and, particularly, its impermanence. Certainly the effect of *CS*-termination does not appear to be critical in maintaining the avoidance response.

Herrnstein and Hineline (1966), in an ingenious experiment, posed the same question that has been discussed in the last two sections of this chapter: Is termination of the *CS* or a reduction in the rate of the *US* the critical factor in maintaining an avoidance response? In their procedure rats could never avoid shock in the usual sense, although responses could reduce the *shock density*, the overall rate of shocks per time. They found that response rates

were a monotonically increasing function of the degree by which the response reduced shock density. The fact that reduction in shock rate is sufficient to maintain avoidance behavior argues against two-factor theories of avoidance. Moreover, in the Herrnstein and Hineline procedure, not only were there no explicit exteroceptive stimuli that could serve as the *CS,* but the shocks were delivered randomly in time so that the kind of covert stimuli that had been invoked to play the role of the *CS* in procedures such as Sidman's (the *CATS* discussed earlier) cannot be so readily appealed to. In addition, the finding that rats will respond to decrease the frequency of shock is completely consistent with the view that positive and negative reinforcement are equivalent processes. Studies of schedules of positive reinforcement have shown that organisms will respond to reduce the expected time to food reinforcement (Fantino, 1969a, 1969b; Herrnstein, 1964; Squires & Fantino, 1971). The Herrnstein and Hineline (1966) results argue that organisms will similarly respond to increase the expected time to the next shock presentation. Whereas the studies cited on positive reinforcement utilized the concurrent-chains procedure (cf. Chapter 5) in which the organism chooses between pecking on either of two keys, Herrnstein and Hineline utilized a single response. For their subjects, the "choice" was to respond on the lever to reduce shock density or not respond and maintain the prevailing rate of shocks. They found that responding was maintained when it decreased shock density.

Herrnstein and Hineline also present some interesting data on the problem of extinction of avoidance responses. These data indicate that avoidance responses extinguish in much the same manner as do positively reinforced responses. The more similar the situation in extinction to the situation prior to extinction, the more resistant to extinction is the behavior. In the Herrnstein and Hineline study, when responses produced a sharp decrease in shock density, they extinguished rapidly after the possibility of reducing shock density was removed; at the other extreme, when the response-produced decrease in shock density was minimal, responding was extremely resistant to extinction (about 17,000 responses were made in extinction). These results are of theoretical importance in view of the emphasis that has been previously placed on the resistance of avoidance responding to extinction (Solomon, Kamin, & Wynne, 1953).

THE ETHICS OF AVERSIVE CONTROL

This chapter has surveyed the effects of aversive control procedures, with special emphasis on negative reinforcement and punishment. Direct parallels between negative and positive reinforcement, and analogous but opposite effects of punishment and positive reinforcement, have been cited frequently. Many psychologists have attempted to compare the effectiveness of these procedures, most prominently Skinner (1953), who objected to the use of punishment on several grounds, as discussed in the introduction to this chapter.

While Skinner's argument that punishment is ineffective has been overturned, we have not addressed his contention that the use of aversive control tends to be immoral and unethical. At one level, of course, this is not the province of the psychologist. Nonetheless, most of us would readily concede that it would be desirable to eliminate aversive control to the extent that alternative means could be found for controlling undesirable behavior. Unfortunately, however, there are many behaviors that do not seem to be readily amenable to alternative methods of control. This point is illustrated in the following example from Azrin and Holz (1966).

> One might insist that extinction could be made more effective than punishment by instituting complete extinction. If one never reinforced a response, then punishment would scarcely be possible since the response would rarely occur. For a large class of behavior, however, this complete absence of reinforcement is impossible. The physical world often provides reinforcement contingencies that cannot be eliminated easily. The faster we move through space, the quicker we get to where we are going, whether the movement be walking or driving an auto. Hence, running and speeding will inevitably be reinforced. Extinction of running and speeding could be accomplished only by the impossible procedure of eliminating all reinforcing events that result from movement through space. Some other reductive method, such as punishment, must be used [p. 433].

The use of punishment and negative reinforcement thus appears to be inevitable in the control of human behavior. But it is probably safe to say that the better we come to understand aversive control in the laboratory, the better we shall be able to insure that it is not abused in the control of human behavior.

SUMMARY AND CONCLUSIONS

Punishment involves the presentation of an aversive stimulus or the withdrawal of a positive reinforcer. In either case the behavior that leads to punishment is, by definition, less likely to recur. Punishment is particularly effective in suppressing behavior the more intense it is and the more suddenly it is introduced. In addition, the effects of punishment depend critically on the schedule of punishment, in much the same way as the effects of positive reinforcement depend on its scheduling. At the same time, the maintenance of punished behavior also depends on the deprivation state of the organism and on the schedule of positive reinforcement maintaining the punished behavior. The effects of punishment on the pattern of responding maintained by schedules of positive reinforcement depend on the particular schedule of positive reinforcement involved.

When punishment is removed, the previously suppressed responding generally recovers, unless the punishment had been particularly intense. While the recoverability of responding after the removal of punishment is in accord with Skinner's position that the effects of punishment are not permanent, it was pointed out that: (1) with sufficiently severe punishment, recovery is incomplete; and (2) the effects of continuous positive reinforcement are transient also (for example, discontinuing reward following an FR-1 schedule of food reinforcement would result in the rapid extinction of responding). Punishment, like reinforcement, may have immediate effects when it is reinstated following extinction.

While punished behavior generally returns to its prepunishment baseline following the removal of punishment, there are two exceptions to this rule: With sufficiently intense punishment, no recovery occurs; with less intense punishment, there is a transient increase in the rate of responding immediately following the removal of punishment. Punishment also affects behavior in the presence of stimuli that are somewhat different from those in which the punishment was applied (stimulus generalization). The effects of punishment on the extinction of behavior that had been previously maintained by positive reinforcement depend critically on both the discriminative and aversive properties of punishment. For example, it is possible to arrange a situation such that punishment may increase the rate of responding during extinction (if punishment had always been associated with the availability of positive reinforcement in the past). Experiments that have studied the effects of punishment on choice behavior indicate that responding is less sensitive to punishment parameters when a single response rather than a choice procedure is employed. This generalization is consistent with similar results from studies of positive reinforcement. When choice procedures are employed that enable subjects to maximize their rate of reinforcement (or minimize their rate of punishment) by emitting only one of the two alternative responses, subjects will tend to do so even when only a trivial difference exists in terms of the reinforcing or punishing consequences of responding on the two alternatives.

Studies of conditioned punishment have shown that stimuli associated with primary aversive stimuli such as shock and stimuli associated with removal from the opportunity to obtain positive reinforcement develop status as conditioned punishers, which themselves have punishing properties. These conditioned punishing stimuli have been implicated in two-factor or two-process theories of punishment which generally maintain that punishment involves: (1) the association of conditioned punishing stimuli which have been established by their contiguity with punishment through classical conditioning; and (2) the association of a response with the removal of these conditioned punishers, generally through operant conditioning. In other words, two-factor theorists have generally maintained that punishment is effective because organisms are reinforced for removing the conditioned punishers rather than avoiding the punishment itself. While it is clear that stimuli may acquire aversive properties due to classical conditioning with primary aversive stimuli such as shock, and that these stimuli may become effective conditioned punishers, nonetheless, such conditioned aversive stimuli appear to play a relatively

minor role in the aversive control of behavior as compared to the effects of the primary punishers. The effectiveness of punishment depends primarily on its direct suppressive effect on responses and not on the termination of conditioned punishment as two-factor theories had implied. All the results summarized in this chapter argue that punishment affects behavior in a way that is analogous but opposite in sign to the effects of positive reinforcement.

Studies of behavior maintained by escape from shock lead to the generalization that behavior maintained by schedules of negative reinforcement is appropriate to the type of schedule, in the sense that the pattern of escape responding is similar to the pattern of food-reinforced responding on similar schedules. The work of Bolles and others has shown that the nature of the response requirement is the only strikingly important parameter that has thus far been uncovered in a large number of studies on avoidance learning. The reinforcer for avoidance responding is the omission of the *US* (e.g., shock) and not the termination of the *CS*. Thus responding modified by avoidance, by escape, and by punishment procedures is most affected by the omission, termination, or presentation of the aversive stimulus, respectively, and is less dependent on conditioned aversive stimuli.

The research and theories on punishment, escape, and avoidance are all compatible with the following hypothesis: Aversive stimuli function in the same manner as do positive reinforcers. Rewards and punishments are events that are identical but opposite in sign in their effect on behavior. No separate laws need to be constructed to understand the effects of aversive stimuli. Although this conclusion is simple and is consistent with extant data, it is only very recently that it has begun to gain acceptance.

REFERENCES

Anderson, N. H. Variation of *CS-US* interval in long-term avoidance conditioning in the rat with wheel turn and with shuttle tasks. *Journal of Comparative and Physiological Psychology*, 1969, **68**, 100–106.

Anger, D. The role of temporal discriminations in the reinforcement of Sidman avoidance behavior. *Journal of the Experimental Analysis of Behavior*, 1963, **6**, 477–505.

Appel, J. B. Punishment in the squirrel monkey *Saimiri sciurea*. *Science*, 1961, **133**, 36–37.

Appel, J. B. Aversive aspects of a schedule of positive reinforcement. *Journal of the Experimental Analysis of Behavior*, 1963, **6**, 423–428.

Appel, J. B., & Peterson, N. J. Punishment: Effects of shock intensity on response suppression. *Psychological Reports*, 1965, **16**, 721–730. Figure 7.1: Reproduced by permission of author and publisher.

Autor, S. M. The strength of conditioned reinforcers as a function of frequency and probability of reinforcement. Unpublished doctoral dissertation, Harvard University, 1960.

Ayllon, T., & Azrin, N. *The token economy: A motivational system for therapy and rehabilitation*. New York: Appleton-Century-Crofts, 1968.

Azrin, N. H. Some effects of two intermittent schedules of immediate and non-immediate punishment. *Journal of Psychology*, 1956, **42**, 3–21. Figure 7.13: Copyright © 1956 by The Journal Press, and reproduced by permission.

Azrin, N. H. A technique for delivering shock to pigeons. *Journal of the Experimental Analysis of Behavior*, 1959, **2**, 161–163. (a)

Azrin, N. H. Punishment and recovery during fixed-ratio performance. *Journal of the Experimental Analysis of Behavior*, 1959, **2**, 301–305. (b) Figure 7.4: Copyright © 1959 by the Society for the Experimental Analysis of Behavior, Inc., and reproduced by permission.

Azrin, N. H. Effects of punishment intensity during variable-interval reinforcement. *Journal of the Experimental Analysis of Behavior*, 1960, **3**, 123–142. (a) Figures 7.2 and 7.8: Copyright © 1960 by the Society for the Experimental Analysis of Behavior, Inc., and reproduced by permission.

Azrin, N. H. Sequential effects of punishment. *Science*, 1960, **131**, 605–606. (b)

Azrin, N. H. Time-out from positive reinforcement. *Science*, 1961, **133**, 382–383.

Azrin, N. H., Hake, D. F., Holz, W. C., & Hutchinson, R. R. Motivational aspects of escape from punishment. *Journal of the Experimental Analysis of Behavior*, 1965, **8**, 31–44.

Azrin, N. H., & Holz, W. C. Punishment. In W. K. Honig (Ed.), *Operant behavior: Areas of research and application*. New York: Appleton-Century-Crofts, 1966. Pp. 380–447.

Azrin, N. H., Holz, W. C., & Hake, D. F. Fixed-ratio punishment. *Journal of the Experimental Analysis of Behavior*, 1963, **6**, 141–148. Figures 7.3 and 7.7: Copyright © 1963 by the Society for the Experimental Analysis of Behavior, Inc., and reproduced by permission.

Azrin, N. H., Holz, W. C., Hake, D. F., & Ayllon, T. Fixed-ratio escape reinforcement. *Journal of the Experimental Analysis of Behavior*, 1963, **6**, 449–456.

Azrin, N. H., Hopwood, J., & Powell, J. A rat chamber and electrode procedure for avoidance conditioning. *Journal of the Experimental Analysis of Behavior*, 1967, **10**, 291–298.

Beck, R. C. On secondary reinforcement and shock termination. *Psychological Bulletin*, 1961, **58**, 28–45.

Bitterman, M. E. The *CS-US* interval in classical and avoidance conditioning. In W. F. Prokasy (Ed.), *Classical conditioning*. New York: Appleton-Century-Crofts, 1965.

Bolles, R. C. *Theory of motivation*. New York: Harper & Row, 1967.

Bolles, R. C. Avoidance and escape learning: Simultaneous acquisition of different responses. *Journal of Comparative and Physiological Psychology*, 1969, **68**, 355–358.

Bolles, R. C. Species-specific defense reactions and avoidance learning. *Psychological Review*, 1970, **77**, 32–48.

Bolles, R. C., & Grossen, N. E. Effects of an informational stimulus on the acquisition of avoidance behavior in rats. *Journal of Comparative and Physiological Psychology*, 1969, **68**, 90–99.

Bolles, R. C., Stokes, L. W., & Younger, M. S. Does *CS*-termination reinforce avoidance behavior? *Journal of Comparative and Physiological Psychology*, 1966, **62**, 201–207.

Bolles, R. C., & Warren, J. A. The acquisition of bar-press avoidance as a function of shock intensity. *Psychonomic Science*, 1965, **3**, 297–298.

Brethower, D. M., & Reynolds, G. S. A facilitative effect of punishment on unpunished behavior. *Journal of the Experimental Analysis of Behavior*, 1962, **5**, 191–199.

Brush, F. R. The effects of intertrial interval on avoidance learning in the rat. *Journal of Comparative and Physiological Psychology*, 1962, **55**, 888–892.

Brush, F. R. On the differences between animals that learn and do not learn to avoid electric shock. *Psychonomic Science*, 1966, **5**, 123–124.

Byrd, L. D. Responding in the cat maintained under response-independent electric shock and response-produced electric shock. *Journal of the Experimental Analysis of Behavior*, 1969, **12**, 1–10.

Byrd, L. D. Responding in the squirrel monkey under second-order schedules of shock delivery. *Journal of the Experimental Analysis of Behavior*, 1972, **18**, 155–167.

Catania, A. C. Concurrent performances: A baseline for the study of reinforcement magnitude. *Journal of the Experimental Analysis of Behavior*, 1963, **6**, 299–300.

Catania, A. C. Concurrent operants. In W. K. Honig (Ed.), *Operant behavior: Areas of research and application*. New York: Appleton-Century-Crofts, 1966. Pp. 213–270.

Clark, F. C. The effect of deprivation and frequency of reinforcement on *VI* responding. *Journal of the Experimental Analysis of Behavior*, 1958, **1**, 221–228.

Cohen, P. S. Punishment: The interactive effects of delay and intensity of shock. *Journal of the Experimental Analysis of Behavior*, 1968, **11**, 789–799.

Cole, M., & Fantino, E. J. Temporal variables and trial discreteness in lever-press avoidance. *Psychonomic Science*, 1966, **6**, 217–218.

D'Amato, M. R., & Fazzaro, J. Discriminated lever-press avoidance learning as a function of type and intensity of shock. *Journal of Comparative and Physiological Psychology*, 1966, **61**, 313–315.

D'Amato, M. R., Fazzaro, J., & Etkin, M. Discriminated bar-press avoidance, maintenance and extinction in rats as a function of shock intensity. *Journal of Comparative and Physiological Psychology*, 1968, **63**, 351–354.

D'Amato, M. R., Keller, D., & DiCara, L. Facilitation of discriminated avoidance learning by discontinuous shock. *Journal of Comparative and Physiological Psychology*, 1964, **58**(3), 344–349.

Denny, M. R., & Weisman, R. C. Long-term discriminated avoidance performance in the rat. *Journal of Comparative and Physiological Psychology*, 1964, **57**, 123–126.

Dinsmoor, J. A. A quantitative comparison of the discriminative and reinforcing functions of stimulus. *Journal of Experimental Psychology*, 1950, **40**, 458–472.

Dinsmoor, J. A. The effect of hunger on discriminated responding. *Journal of Abnormal and Social Psychology*, 1952, **47**, 67–72.

Dinsmoor, J. A. Punishment: I. The avoidance hypothesis. *Psychological Review*, 1954, **61**, 34–46.

Dinsmoor, J. A. VI escape from stimuli accompanied by shocks. *Journal of the Experimental Analysis of Behavior*, 1962, **5**, 41–47.

Dinsmoor, J. A., & Clayton, M. H. Chaining and secondary reinforcement based on escape from shock. *Journal of the Experimental Analysis of Behavior*, 1963, **6**, 75–80.

Dinsmoor, J. A., & Clayton, M. H. A conditioned reinforcer maintained by temporal association with the termination of shock. *Journal of the Experimental Analysis of Behavior*, 1966, **9**, 547–552.

Estes, W. K. An experimental study of punishment. *Psychological Monographs*, 1944, **57**, No. 3.

Fantino, E. J. Preference for mixed- *vs* fixed-ratio schedules. Unpublished doctoral dissertation, Harvard University, 1964.

Fantino, E. J. Preference for mixed- *vs* fixed-ratio schedules. *Journal of the Experimental Analysis of Behavior*, 1967, **10**, 35–43.

Fantino, E. J. Effects of required rates of responding upon choice. *Journal of the Experimental Analysis of Behavior*, 1968, **11**, 15–22.

Fantino, E. J. Conditioned reinforcement, choice and the psychological distance to reward. In D. P. Hendry (Ed.), *Conditioned reinforcement*. Homewood, Ill.: The Dorsey Press, 1969. (a) Pp. 163–191.

Fantino, E. J. Choice and rate of reinforcement. *Journal of the Experimental Analysis of Behavior*, 1969, **12**, 723–730. (b)

Fantino, E. J., & Herrnstein, R. J. Secondary reinforcement and number of primary reinforcements. *Journal of the Experimental Analysis of Behavior*, 1968, **11**, 9–14.

Fantino, E. J., Sharp, D., & Cole, M. Factors facilitating lever-press avoidance. *Journal of Comparative and Physiological Psychology*, 1966, **62**, 214–217. Figure 7.14: Copyright © 1966 by the American Psychological Association, and reproduced by permission.

Ferster, C. B. Withdrawal of positive reinforcement as punishment. *Science*, 1957, **126**, 509.

Ferster, C. B., & Skinner, B. F. *Schedules of reinforcement*. New York: Appleton-Century-Crofts, 1957.

Filby, Y., & Appel, J. B. Variable-interval punishment during variable-interval reinforcement. *Journal of the Experimental Analysis of Behavior*, 1966, **9**, 521–527.

Fischer, K., & Fantino, E. J. The dissociation of discriminative and conditioned reinforcing functions of stimuli with changes in deprivation. *Journal of the Experimental Analysis of Behavior*, 1968, **11**, 703–710.

Fowler, H., & Miller, N. E. Facilitation and inhibition of runway performance by hind- and forepaw shock of various intensities. *Journal of Comparative and Physiological Psychology*, 1963, **56**, 801–805.

Grice, G. R. The relation of secondary reinforcement to delayed reward in visual discrimination learning. *Journal of Experimental Psychology*, 1948, **38**, 633–642.

Hake, D. F., & Azrin, N. H. An apparatus for delivering pain shock to monkeys. *Journal of the Experimental Analysis of Behavior*, 1963, **6**, 297–298.

Hake, D. F., & Azrin, N. H. Conditioned punishment. *Journal of the Experimental Analysis of Behavior*, 1965, **8**, 279–293. Figure 7.11: Copyright © 1965 by the Society for the Experimental Analysis of Behavior, Inc., and reproduced by permission.

Hendry, D. P., & Hendry, L. S. Partial negative reinforcement: Fixed-ratio escape. *Journal of the Experimental Analysis of Behavior*, 1963, **6**, 519–523.

Herman, R. L., & Azrin, N. H. Punishment by noise in an alternative response situation. *Journal of the Experimental Analysis of Behavior*, 1964, **7**, 185–188.

Herrnstein, R. J. Some factors influencing behavior in a two-response situation. *Transactions of the New York Academy of Science*, 1958, **21**, 35–45.

Herrnstein, R. J. Secondary reinforcement and rate of primary reinforcement. *Journal of the Experimental Analysis of Behavior*, 1964, **7**, 27–36.

Herrnstein, R. J. Method and theory in the study of avoidance. *Psychological Review*, 1969, **76**, 49–69.

Herrnstein, R. J., & Hineline, P. N. Negative reinforcement as shock-frequency reduction. *Journal of the Experimental Analysis of Behavior*, 1966, **9**, 421–430.

Hineline, P. N., & Rachlin, H. Notes on fixed-ratio and fixed-interval escape responding in the pigeon. *Journal of the Experimental Analysis of Behavior*, 1969, **12**, 397–401.

Hoffman, H. S., & Fleshler, M. Aversive control with the pigeon. *Journal of the Experimental Analysis of Behavior*, 1959, **2**, 213–218.

Hoffman, H. S., & Fleshler, M. A relay sequencing device for scrambling grid shock. *Journal of the Experimental Analysis of Behavior*, 1962, **5**, 329–330.

Holz, W. C., & Azrin, N. H. Discriminative properties of punishment. *Journal of the Experimental Analysis of Behavior*, 1961, **4**, 225–232. Figure 7.10: Copyright © 1961 by the Society for the Experimental Analysis of Behavior, Inc., and reproduced by permission.

Holz, W. C., Azrin, N. H., & Ayllon, T. Elimination of behavior of mental patients by response-produced extinction. *Journal of the Experimental Analysis of Behavior*, 1963, **6**, 407–412.

Holz, W. C., Azrin, N. H., & Ulrich, R. E. Punishment of temporally spaced responding. *Journal of the Experimental Analysis of Behavior*, 1963, **6**, 115–122. Figure 7.6. Copyright © 1963 by the Society for the Experimental Analysis of Behavior, Inc., and reproduced by permission.

Honig, W. K., & Slivka, R. M. Stimulus generalization of the effects of punishment. *Journal of the Experimental Analysis of Behavior*, 1964, **7**, 21–25. Figure 7.9: Copyright © 1964 by the Society for the Experimental Analysis of Behavior, Inc., and reproduced by permission.

Hurwitz, H. M. B. Method for discriminative avoidance training. *Science*, 1964, **145**, 1070–1071.

Hutchinson, R. R., Azrin, N. H., & Hunt, G. M. Attack produced by intermittent reinforcement of a concurrent operant response. *Journal of the Experimental Analysis of Behavior*, 1968, **11**, 489–495.

Kamin, L. J. The effects of termination of the CS and avoidance of the US on avoidance learning. *Journal of Comparative and Physiological Psychology*, 1956, **49**, 420–424.

Kamin, L. J. The effects of termination of the CS and avoidance of the US on avoidance learning: An extension. *Canadian Journal of Psychology*, 1957, **11**, 48–56. Figure

7.15: Reproduced by permission of the author and the *Canadian Journal of Psychology.*

Kaplan, M. The maintenance of escape behavior under fixed-ratio reinforcement. *Journal of Comparative and Physiological Psychology,* 1956, **49,** 153–157.

Kelleher, R. T., & Morse, W. H. Schedules using noxious stimuli: III. Responding maintained with response-produced electric shocks. *Journal of the Experimental Analysis of Behavior,* 1968, **11,** 819–838.

Keller, F. S., & Schoenfeld, W. N. *Principles of psychology.* New York: Appleton-Century-Crofts, 1950.

Kimble, G. A. Shock intensity and avoidance learning. *Journal of Comparative and Physiological Psychology,* 1955, **48,** 281–284.

Krieckhaus, E. F., Miller, N. E., & Zimmerman, P. Reduction of freezing behavior and improvement of shock avoidance by d-amphetamine. *Journal of Comparative and Physiological Psychology,* 1965, **60,** 36–49.

LoLordo, V. M. Positive conditioned reinforcement from aversive situations. *Psychological Bulletin,* 1969, **72,** 193–203.

Maatsch, J. L. Learning and fixation after a single shock trial. *Journal of Comparative and Physiological Psychology,* 1959, **52,** 408–410.

McKearney, J. W. Maintenance of responding under a fixed-interval schedule of electric shock presentation. *Science,* 1968, **160,** 1249–1251.

McKearney, J. W. Fixed-interval schedules of electric shock presentation: Extinction and recovery of performance under different shock intensities and fixed-interval durations. *Journal of the Experimental Analysis of Behavior,* 1969, **12,** 301–313.

McKearney, J. W. Responding under fixed-ratio and multiple fixed-interval fixed-ratio schedules of electric shock presentation. *Journal of the Experimental Analysis of Behavior,* 1970, **14,** 1–6.

Meyer, D. R., Cho, C., & Weseman, A. F. On problems of conditioning discriminated lever-press avoidance responses, *Psychological Review,* 1960, **67,** 224–228.

Miller, N. E. Studies of fear as an acquirable drive: I. Fear as motivation and fear-reduction as reinforcement in the learning of new responses. *Journal of Experimental Psychology,* 1948, **38,** 89–101.

Morse, W. H., Mead, R. N., & Kelleher, R. T. Modulation of elicited behavior by a fixed-interval schedule of electric shock presentation. *Science,* 1967, **157,** 215–217.

Mowrer, O. H., & Lamoreaux, R. R. Fear as an intervening variable in avoidance conditioning. *Journal of Comparative and Physiological Psychology,* 1946, **39,** 29–50.

Moyer, K. E., & Korn, J. Effect of *UCS* intensity on the acquisition and extinction of an avoidance response. *Journal of Experimental Psychology,* 1964, **67,** 352–359.

Myers, R. E. Interhemispheric communication through corpus callosum: Limitations under conditions of conflict. *Journal of Comparative and Physiological Psychology,* 1959, **52,** 6–9.

Nakamura, C. Y., & Anderson, N. H. Avoidance behavior differences within and between strains of rats. *Journal of Comparative and Physiological Psychology,* 1962, **55,** 740–747.

Nakamura, C. Y., & Anderson, N. H. Avoidance conditioning in wheel box and shuttle box. *Psychological Reports,* 1964, **14**(2), 327–334.

Neuringer, A. J. Effects of reinforcement magnitude on choice and rate of responding. *Journal of the Experimental Analysis of Behavior,* 1967, **10,** 417–424.

Neuringer, A. J. Delayed reinforcement versus reinforcement after a fixed interval. *Journal of the Experimental Analysis of Behavior,* 1969, **12,** 375–383.

Pearl, J. Effects of preshock and additional punishment on general activity. *Psychological Reports,* 1963, **12,** 155–161.

Premack, D. Reversibility of the reinforcement relation. *Science,* 1962, **136,** 255–257.

Rachlin, H. Recovery of responses during mild punishment. *Journal of the Experimental Analysis of Behavior,* 1966, **9,** 251–263. Figure 7.12: Copyright © 1966 by the Society for the Experimental Analysis of Behavior, Inc., and reproduced by permission.

Rachlin, H., & Baum, W. M. Response rate as a function of amount of reinforcement for signalled concurrent response. *Journal of the Experimental Analysis of Behavior,* 1969, **12,** 11–16.

Rescorla, R. A., & Solomon, R. L. Two-process learning theory: Relationships between Pavlovian conditioning and instrumental learning. *Psychological Review,* 1967, **74,** 151–182.

Schuster, R., & Rachlin, H. Indifference between punishment and free shock: Evidence for the negative law of effect. *Journal of the Experimental Analysis of Behavior,* 1968, **11,** 777–786.

Sidman, M. Avoidance conditioning with brief shock and no exteroceptive warning signal. *Science,* 1953, **118,** 157–158.

Sidman, M. Delayed-punishment effects mediated by competing behavior. *Journal of Comparative and Physiological Psychology,* 1954, **47,** 145–147.

Sidman, M. Conditioned reinforcing and aversive stimuli in an avoidance situation. *Transactions of the New York Academy of Science,* 1957, **19,** 534–544.

Sidman, M., & Boren, J. J. The relative aversiveness of warning signal and shock in an avoidance situation. *Journal of Abnormal and Social Psychology,* 1957, **55,** 339–344.

Siegel, P. S., & Milby, J. B. Secondary reinforcement in relation to shock termination: Second chapter. *Psychological Bulletin,* 1969, **72,** 146–156.

Skinner, B. F. *The behavior of organisms.* New York: Appleton-Century-Crofts, 1938.

Skinner, B. F. *Walden two.* New York: Macmillan, 1948. (a)

Skinner, B. F. "Superstition" in the pigeon. *Journal of Experimental Psychology,* 1948, **38,** 168–172. (b)

Skinner, B. F. *Science and human behavior.* New York: Macmillan, 1953.

Solomon, R. L., & Brush, E. S. Experimentally derived conceptions of anxiety and aversion. In M. R. Jones (Ed.), *Nebraska symposium on motivation,* 1956. Lincoln: University of Nebraska Press, 1956. Pp. 212–305.

Solomon, R. L., Kamin, L. J., & Wynne, L. C. Traumatic avoidance learning: The outcome of several extinction procedures with dogs. *Journal of Abnormal and Social Psychology,* 1953, **48,** 291–302.

Squires, N., & Fantino, E. A model for choice in simple concurrent and concurrent-chains schedules. *Journal of the Experimental Analysis of Behavior,* 1971, **15,** 27–38.

Stebbins, W. C., & Sidman, M. Satiation effects under fixed-ratio schedules of reinforcement. *Journal of Comparative and Physiological Psychology,* 1954, **47,** 114–116.

Stone, G. R. The effect of negative incentives in serial learning: VII. Theory of punishment. *Journal of General Psychology,* 1953, **48,** 133–161.

Stone, G. R., & Walters, N. J. The effect of negative incentives in serial learning: VI. Response repetition as a function of an isolated electric shock punishment. *Journal of Experimental Psychology*, 1951, **41**, 411–418.

Storms, L. H., Boroczi, G., & Broen, W. E., Jr. Punishment inhibits an instrumental response in hooded rats. *Science*, 1962, **135**, 1133–1134.

Stretch, R., Orloff, E. R., & Dalrymple, S. D. Maintenance of responding by fixed-interval schedule of electric shock presentation in squirrel monkeys. *Science*, 1968, **162**, 583–586.

Theios, J., Lynch, A. D., & Lowe, W. F., Jr. Differential effects of shock intensity on one-way and shuttle avoidance conditioning. *Journal of Experimental Psychology*, 1966, **72**, 294–299.

Thompson, D. M. Punishment by S^D associated with fixed-ratio reinforcement. *Journal of the Experimental Analysis of Behavior*, 1965, **8**, 189–194.

Thorndike, E. L. *Educational psychology*. Vol. 2. New York: Teacher's College, Columbia University, 1913.

Thorndike, E. L. *The fundamentals of learning*. New York: Columbia University Press, 1932.

Wahlsten, D., Cole, M., Sharp, D., & Fantino, E. J. Facilitation of bar-press avoidance by handling during the intertrial interval. *Journal of Comparative and Physiological Psychology*, 1968, **65**(1), 170–175.

Weiner, H. Some effects of response cost upon human operant behavior. *Journal of the Experimental Analysis of Behavior*, 1962, **5**, 201–208. Figure 7.5: Copyright © 1962 by the Society for the Experimental Analysis of Behavior, Inc., and reproduced by permission.

Weiner, H. Modification of "non-adjustive" human operant behavior under aversive control. *Journal of the Experimental Analysis of Behavior*, 1964, **7**(3), 277–279. (a)

Weiner, H. Response cost effects during extinction following fixed-interval reinforcement in humans. *Journal of the Experimental Analysis of Behavior*, 1964, **7**, 333–335. (b)

Winograd, E. Escape behavior under different fixed ratios and shock intensities. *Journal of the Experimental Analysis of Behavior*, 1965, **8**, 117–124.

8

EMOTION

Edmund Fantino
University of California, San Diego

Emotion, like *learning*, is a term so general as to defy definition. Earlier chapters have indicated that it may be useful to dispense with learning as an organizing concept, and to treat instead the modification of behavior according to the operations employed and the resulting processes. Here, a number of approaches to the study of emotional behavior are reviewed. It remains to be seen whether the phenomena treated here will be studied most fruitfully by grouping them all under the rubric of emotion.

At times throughout the chapter it will be necessary to discuss research and theory in motivation, another area which is poorly defined, but one which is often conceived as being closely related to emotion. Indeed some (Bindra, 1959; Young, 1961) have argued that distinctions between emotional behavior and motivated behavior are untenable. For example, Hebb (1966) suggests that emotions are all special states of motivation.

Although some of the more serious efforts at grappling with the problem of emotion have grown out of several centuries of philosophy and psychology, the emphasis in this chapter will be on more contemporary theories and their experimental underpinnings. Unfortunately, emotional behavior has not been scientifically studied with the same breadth and depth as many other fields in psychology. One reason for this dearth of knowledge and of agreement about emotion is the problem of defining what emotion is. Most people can identify what emotions are subjectively; they can recognize their own sensations. They also may have a good idea of what is meant by the terms *mind* and *psyche*, but the subjective reality of emotions or of mind does not in itself demonstrate the objective existence or the scientific usefulness of these entities or concepts. Moreover, are one person's subjective emotions the same emotions as those experienced by others? How can one tell? In any case, what causes these subjective emotions? Most people can also identify emotions objectively, usually through the behavior of others, but do these emotional behaviors correspond in any systematic fashion to subjectively experienced emotions?

Several authorities have prepared definitions of emotion, but these definitions not only indicate lack of agreement on what emotions are, but also emphasize the fact that the study of emotion can proceed along

Preparation of this chapter was supported in part by NSF Grants GB-3626 and GB-6659 and NIMH Grant MH-20752. The author gratefully acknowledges the assistance of Cheryl Logan, David Myers, Barbara Duncan, Nancy Squires, and Steven Hursh.

several very different lines. There is even the position that the study is a futile one.

EMOTION: DEFINITIONS AND GENERAL APPROACHES

The following eleven chronologically ordered definitions of, and statements about, emotion are by no means exhaustive, but they cover an expansive range. The first definition, formulated in 1928, is that of Bentley, who stated that

> emotion may be defined as a quality of excitement which accompanies operation of an instinct, or a kind of drive under which the organism whips itself into action, or a certain kind of response to a certain kind of stimulus [Plutchik, 1962, p. 174].

Bentley was suggesting that there are no unique characteristics of emotion; rather, emotion is identified by responses or bodily reactions to a stimulus situation.

"Emotion can best be characterized," according to Landis (Landis & Hunt, 1939),

> as a *relationship existing between many diverse elements of experience and reaction*. This relationship is not well specified, but, generally speaking, it is marked by pleasantness or unpleasantness and by disorganization of usually integrated behavior patterns. An emotion is the total of the experience of an individual during any period of time when marked bodily changes of feeling, surprise or upset occur [p. 184].

A third position was formulated by Duffy (1941a), who stressed the organism's adjustment to a stimulus situation, while pointing out that such adjustments characterize all behavior, not merely emotional behavior.

> I am aware of no evidence for the existence of a special condition called "emotion" which follows different principles of action from other conditions of the organism. I can therefore see no reason for a psychological study of "emotion" as such. "Emotion" has no distinguishing characteristics. It represents merely an *extreme* manifestation of characteristics found in some degree in all responses. If there is any particular point at which a difference in *degree* becomes a difference in *kind* this fact has not been demonstrated....
>
> "Emotion" is an adjustment made to a stimulating condition of such a kind that the adjustment involves a marked change in energy level. It involves, like other behavior, interpretation of the situation, or response to relationships. And from the goal-direction of the overt behavior, or of the set for response, are derived the classificatory

divisions into the particular "emotion," such as "fear" or "rage." Its characteristics—its principles of action—are those of behavior in general. It has no laws or qualities of its own. It is futile, therefore, to look for an "indicator" of "emotion." It is futile to inquire, "*What are the effects produced by 'emotion'?*" for a so-called "emotional" condition will vary in its effects, depending upon the energy level at which the behavior occurs, upon the adequacy with which direction toward the goal is maintained (or disorganization or response avoided), and upon the nature of the *response to the relationships* in the situation. Behavior not classified as "emotional" also varies with variations in these three aspects of response. Instead of investigating "emotion" per se, we could more usefully study variations in these three fundamental dimensions of behavior, determining the conditions under which such variations occur and the effects produced by their occurrence. Perhaps, when we formulate our questions better, Nature will be more obliging in her replies [pp. 292–293].

Duffy's definition has much in common with Bentley's (as well as Catania's, presented last) in that both emphasize the difficulty of identifying the distinguishing characteristics of emotion.

According to Leeper (1948),

> ... emotional processes are one of the fundamental means of motivation in the higher animal —a kind of motivation which rests on relatively complex neural activities rather than primarily on definite chemical states or definite receptor stimulation, as in the case of bodily drives of physiological motives such as hunger, thirst, toothache, and craving for salt [p. 19].

A fifth point of view is that of Skinner (1953):

> The emotions are excellent examples of the fictional causes to which we commonly attribute behavior. . . . The names of the so-called emotions serve to classify behavior with respect to various circumstances which affect its probability. The safest practice is to hold to the adjectival form. Just as a hungry organism can be accounted for without too much difficulty, although "hunger" is another matter, so by describing behavior as fearful, affectionate, timid, and so on, we are not led to look for *things* called emotions. The common idioms, "in love," "in fear," and "in anger," suggest a definition of an emotion as a conceptual state, in which a special response is a function of circumstances in the history of the individual. In casual discourse and for many scientific purposes some such way of referring to current strength in terms of the variables of which it is a function is often desirable. But so defined, an emotion, like a drive, is not to be identified with

physiological or psychic conditions [pp. 160, 162, 163].

Expressing a physiological viewpoint, Wenger (Wenger, Jones, & Jones, 1956) states:

Emotion is activity and reactivity of the tissues and organs innervated by the autonomic nervous system. It may involve, but does not necessarily involve, skeletal muscular response or mental activity....

Change in emotional behavior is altered activity or reactivity in a part of one, or more, tissue or organ innervated by the autonomic nervous system [pp. 343, 344].

"An emotion," Young (1961) explained,

is here defined as *an acutely disturbed affective state of the individual that is psychological in origin and revealed in behavior, conscious experience, and visceral functioning....*

An emotion may be defined as a strongly visceralized, affective disturbance, originating within the psychological situation, and revealing itself in bodily changes, in behavior, and in conscious experience [pp. 355–356, 597–598].

Another statement is that of Plutchik (1962):

An emotion may be defined as a patterned bodily reaction of either destruction, reproduction, incorporation, orientation, protection, deprivation, rejection or exploration, or some combination of these, which is brought about by a stimulus [p. 176].

Hebb (1966) has very simply stated that

[emotion is a] special state of arousal accompanied by mediating processes which tend to excite behavior maintaining or modifying the present state of affairs [p. 328].

More recently, Ferster and Perrott (1968) have stated,

Emotion is a state of the organism in which the form and frequency of several items of behavior in the ongoing operant repertoire are altered. The term *emotion*, as it is classically used, has the disadvantage of referring to an inner state which usually cannot be observed. The term *emotional stimulus* overcomes some of these difficulties because it describes a stimulus which alters many ongoing performances in the organism's repertoire other than those directly affected by reinforcement or extinction [p. 525].

Finally, Catania (1968) has defined emotional behavior as

correlated changes in a variety of different classes of responses as a consequence of environmental events. For example, if a pre-

aversive stimulus simultaneously alters heart rate, respiration, blood pressure, defecation and urination, and operant behavior maintained by reinforcement, the stimulus may be said to produce emotional behavior. Because this term evolved from a colloquial vocabulary that is not precise, it is impossible to provide unambiguous definitions of specific types of emotional behavior in terms of the response classes that are involved. Types of emotional behavior may be defined more consistently in terms of the experimental operations that produce them: e.g., *fear, anxiety*, or with another organism present, *anger*, produced by primary or conditioned aversive stimuli; *relief*, produced by the termination of aversive stimuli; *joy* or *hope*, produced by primary or conditioned reinforcers; and *sorrow*, produced by the termination of reinforcers. All of these cases, however, can be described in terms of experimental operations and their consequences, and because different observers are likely to disagree on the defining characteristics of the various cases (e.g., stimulus magnitude, the direction of change in different responses, etc.), the terms have not been found particularly useful in the analysis of behavior [p. 334].

Some of these approaches to the emotions are in strictly behavioral terms, others are in strictly physiological terms, and still others have sought a compromise. Some have stressed the experimental operations that define an emotion, while others have stressed the outcome of these operations. Some definitions are relatively precise, while others are quite vague. Some would restrict the term *emotion* to disturbing states of the individual, while others apply the term to a far broader range of phenomena. Some are very explicit about the distinguishing characteristics of emotional behavior, while others maintain that it is folly to try to cling to such a distinction. Although there is great diversity and disagreement, some general approaches toward the study of emotional behavior emerge.

Structuralism

Most of the approaches in this chapter deal with emotion at either the behavioral or the physiological level. Traditionally, however, there have been two other main points of view. One is the *introspective* approach to emotion. These theories go back to the pioneer of experimental psychology, Wilhelm Wundt. Wundt and his students, notably E. B. Titchener, founded a school of psychology known as *structuralism*. This was a branch of psychology that searched for the mental elements (or "structure") comprising complex experience. Much as the chemist analyzed compounds into their component elements, so the structuralist analyzed subjects' experience in terms of the elements of that experience, or sensations. When the technique was applied to emotion, therefore, the structuralist sought to analyze feelings and emotions into their conscious contents, sensations.

Wundt (1902) formulated a tridimensional view of emotion. He believed that there were three dimensions along which emotions vary: pleasantness-unpleasantness; excitement-depression; and strain-relaxation. According to Wundt, any given feeling could be located, through introspection, somewhere within the tridimensional space defined by these three dimensions. One of the problems with Wundt's theory was that other psychologists, even his own students (Titchener, 1921), did not agree on the dimensions comprising feelings. A more serious problem, however, was the dependence on introspection. With the advent of *behaviorism* and the concomitant growth in the idea that psychology should be an objective, rather than a subjective, science, introspectionism and structuralism largely withered away.

Dynamic theories

Another type of approach to emotional behavior is found in the general class of *dynamic* theories patterned after those of Freud and his followers (e.g., Freud, 1925). Freud's position was influential in the development of psychosomatic medicine and some branches of clinical psychology and psychiatry, but dynamic theories of emotion do not today have much currency in experimental psychology.

Freud's doctrine of emotion was a hedonistic one. At the center of his doctrine of emotion was the *pleasure principle*, the concept that the organism seeks self-gratification. The problem with Freud's theory of emotion was not that it was hedonistic; hedonistic theories of emotion are still somewhat influential. Rather, the problem was similar to that which plagued structuralist theories: Freud's psychology of *psychoanalysis* was very similar to the structuralists' psychology of introspection in that both relied on the individual's ability to report subjective events, that is, the contents of consciousness. In Freud's case, the difficulty was compounded by the fact that the individual's reports were also utilized to determine the contents of the unconscious.

Physiological theories

The third major approach that is historically important in the study of emotion is one that will recur throughout this chapter. The *physiological* approach, as in the theories of James and Lange and of Cannon and Bard, is very important from both a methodological and a theoretical point of view.

William James (1884) identified emotion as visceral changes. The striking aspect of his theory was that visceral changes preceded conscious emotion rather than vice versa. In other words, James believed that emotion was the product of visceral changes, not that visceral changes were a product of emotion. For James, then, feelings and emotions were our sensations and perceptions of visceral changes.

Whereas James' theory made conscious emotion the awareness of visceral reactions through sensory channels, the Cannon-Bard *thalamic* theory of emotion (e.g., Cannon 1927) made conscious emotion the result of thalamic processes mediated by thalamico-cortical tracts. Cannon's theory has also been called an *emergency* theory of emotion because of its emphasis on the homeostatic mechanisms that enable the organism to cope with emergencies. For Cannon, the centers in both the thalamus and the hypothalamus of the brain mediated an emotion, which involved both a skeletal and a visceral component. A basic distinction between the James-Lange theory and the Cannon-Bard theory of emotion is whether the bodily reactions precede the higher cortical and subcortical correlates of emotion (James-Lange) or whether the bodily reactions parallel emotion at the higher cortical levels (Cannon-Bard). There is an additional question that divides physiological theories of emotion: Where is emotion localized? This topic will be discussed more fully later on in the chapter.

Another important point is that physiological techniques may be used as tools in conducting research in an effort to measure emotion. Thus, the physiological correlates of emotion may be relevant for theories of emotion that are not primarily physiological in character.

Behavioral theories

Another class of theories of emotional behavior are the theories held by those of a behavioristic but nonphysiological persuasion. In general, these theorists believe that one can study emotional behavior, but that it is futile to study emotion in and of itself. As *behaviorists*, such theorists insist on utilizing strict operational criteria in the study and measurement of emotional behavior, which they say should be studied in the same way as behavior in general. Although there may be conscious or even unconscious components of emotion, although there are certainly physiological correlates, and although emotional behavior may often be under the control of internal stimuli, only by studying the observable behavior of the organism can a proper appreciation be gained of the lawful relations controlling emotion.

This emphasis on the behavioral viewpoint does not, however, rule out utilizing information from other approaches. Through the verbal behavior of the organism, the behaviorist can make contact with the organism's conscious experience as surely as the introspectionist who relies completely on these reports. Unfortunately, a subject's verbal behavior has not often proven to be a very useful or reliable datum. In addition, behaviorists utilize the physiological method of attack, either through physiological measuring techniques and instrumentation, or through the study of the effects on emotional behavior of direct intervention in the nervous system by *ablation* or electrical stimulation.

MEASUREMENT OF EMOTION

There are two principal methods for attacking the problem of measuring emotion: the introspective attack, which stresses the subject's reports of feeling as its basic datum, and the behavioral point of view, which emphasizes the expressions rather than the impressions of the subject. Although one may measure and even quantify emotions according to the subject's verbal reports, most progress in the study of emotion, as already implied, has come through the measurement of bodily changes and expressive movements.

Physiological measures

Perhaps the most common method of measuring emotions has been to observe or record bodily changes that are presumably related to some emotion. Bodily changes have been particularly important for those students who subscribe to *activation* theories of emotion, since they equate emotion with the level of activation of the organism.

Electrical skin conductance

An extremely popular measure of emotion has been the *galvanic skin response* (*GSR*), which is a change in the electrical resistance of the body's skin as measured by a *galvanometer*. The reason why the GSR has received such wide attention from students of emotion is that it changes swiftly and dramatically following intense stimulation, which presumably arouses emotions. For example, an unexpected loud noise, a report of bad news, and a sudden kiss on the cheek all produce changes in skin conductance. With the *GSR* the psychologist is able to identify readily the subject's reaction and to correlate it precisely with the stimulus event that gave rise to it.

The *GSR* is one of the indexes that is often used in so-called lie-detection procedures. It should be noted, however, that the change in skin conductance following a lie is far less reliable than that following strong and sudden emotional stimulation. Moreover, a given change in the *GSR* may be attributable to any one of several factors (e.g., temperature) that may be changing while the experiment is in progress. Such changes may make it difficult to interpret the effects of the independent variable.

Blood volume

Changes in blood volume are measured with a *plethysmograph*. A particular part of the body, generally an appendage such as a finger or a foot, is inserted in the instrument, which records the effects of vasoconstriction or vasodilatation. Measurement with the plethysmograph, as with the galvanometer, however, is subject to variations attributable to uncontrolled variables.

Blood pressure

Measured with a *sphygmomanometer*, blood pressure is usually recorded as a continuous mapping of the differences between the maximal pressure recorded during the heart's contraction *(systolic pressure)* and the minimal pressure reached during relaxation of the heart *(diastolic pressure)*.

Respiration

Changes in respiration are generally measured by a *pneumograph*, usually consisting of a rubber tube which is placed around the chest. As respiration occurs, the tube is expanded, and corresponding changes are recorded. These changes give measures of the rate and depth as well as the pattern of respiration.

Pulse rate

Pulse rate may be measured with a *sphygmograph*, which records the rate and intensity of the pulse.

Skin temperature

Measured by applying a *thermocouple* to the skin, skin temperature is thought to be a function of the degree of vasoconstriction, which is in turn associated with emotional stress and conflict. This method has not been widely used because it is complicated and also because skin temperature may be under the control of several other variables in addition to the particular one under study.

Pilomotor response

Closely related to changes in skin temperature is the *pilomotor reaction,* the erection of body hair often associated with rapid chilling of the skin. This response also occurs as an autonomic reaction in states of fear or anger. Although difficult to measure, pilomotor response can be recorded in motion pictures.

Eyeblink

There is some indication that strong emotions are accompanied by an increase in spontaneous eyeblinks. By attaching electrodes to the skin in the vicinity of the eye, changes in electrical potentials associated with the eyeblink may be recorded.

Tremor

Tremor is usually measured by having the subject place a finger or an arm on a plate mounted above switches and gauges which record the plate's movement. Such a device, called an *automatograph,* has confirmed the fact that emotional events are often accompanied by tremor, especially in the fingers.

Brain waves

A record of electrical changes obtained from electrodes attached to the scalp is called an *electroencephalogram (EEG).* Although this technique of measuring the electrical potential at the scalp has been successful in distinguishing between grossly different levels of activation such as sleep and wakefulness, it has not yet gained widespread use in more finely grained analyses of emotional behavior.

Although each of these physiological indexes of emotional arousal may be recorded and studied separately, the description in depth of so complex an event as an emotion always requires the simultaneous monitoring of several of these measures (Ax, 1953).

Facial expressions

Facial expressions, although commonly viewed as culturally determined, are the most obvious indicators of emotionality in our daily contacts with others. Thus, it is of considerable interest to determine whether observers belonging to a common culture agree on the emotions indicated by various expressions, and to identify the variables on which these judgments are based.

Woodworth (1938) developed a scale for judging the facial expression of emotions. He took a series of poses that had been published by a previous investigator (Feleky, 1922) and examined the distribution of judgments of these poses by 100 subjects. Woodworth developed a six-point scale which included: (1) love, happiness, mirth; (2) surprise; (3) fear, suffering; (4) anger, determination; (5) disgust; and (6) contempt.

Feleky had taken poses that intended to convey particular emotions and had asked observers to judge the emotions that they felt were being expressed. Utilizing Woodworth's scale, the correlations between the intended emotion and the judged emotion was .92, which was far better than in previous attempts. Although subjects often misjudged the intended emotion, they rarely were off by more than one scale value. For example, if the intended emotion were disgust (5 on the scale), it was most likely correctly identified as disgust; if an error were made, however, the emotion more likely to be chosen was either 4 or 6 on the scale.

Schlosberg (1941) applied the scale in a new experiment. He had subjects sort the 72 pictures of facial expressions into the six categories of the Woodworth scale. (The subjects could utilize a seventh category, *scattering,* if they could not fit a pose into one of Woodworth's.) Schlosberg's 45 subjects judged each pose three times, yielding 135 judgments of each picture. Subjects tended to agree on into which scale category a given pose should be sorted. Thus there was a clear *modal category* for each picture and a distribution of errors or deviations from this modal category. The deviations were as predicted: Subjects who did not place a pose into the modal category tended to place it into one of the two categories next to the modal category. One of the most interesting features of Schlosberg's experiment was the finding that the Woodworth scale was apparently circular. According to the subjects' judgment, the first scale category (love, happiness, mirth) was judged as being close to category 6 (contempt). Thus, for some poses whose modal category was 1 on the scale the next most frequently selected category was 6, and vice versa. On the basis of this experiment and other data, Schlosberg (1952) developed a *circular surface*. As Figure 8.1 shows, Schlosberg located each of the 72 pictures on this surface. The major axis of the circular surface was *pleasantness-unpleasantness*, extending from category 1 (love, happiness, mirth) to category 4 (anger, determination). Schlosberg named the other axis *attention-rejection*. It ranged from the border between categories 5 (disgust) and 6 (contempt) at the rejection end to the border between categories 2 (surprise) and 3 (fear, suffering) at the acceptance end of the axis. Schlosberg next had judges rate the 72 pictures on a nine-point scale for pleasantness-unpleasant-

ness and on a second nine-point scale for attention-rejection. After obtaining these scale ratings, Schlosberg was in a position to describe each of the pictures in terms of its mean rating on each of the two scales. The results of these ratings are also shown in Figure 8.1. Schlosberg then compared the predicted scale values with those that had been obtained in his 1941 study. In two separate experiments, the predictions of Schlosberg's circular surface had remarkably high correlations of .94 and .92, respectively, with the values obtained in 1941.

In order to provide a better understanding of Schlosberg's circular surface of facial expressions, Figure 8.2 shows the location on the surface of some of the typical poses. Although the individual reader may or may not agree with the ordering of the pictures along the two dimensions, Schlosberg's work proved that subjects can reliably classify facial expressions even when utilizing only two factors. Facial expressions will be considered further when reviewing the learned and cultural components of emotion (see also Chapter 9 on the ethological approach to the expression of emotion).

Figure 8.1 The location of each of the 72 pictures of the actor Frois-Wittman's poses on Schlosberg's (1952) circular surface. Picture No. 10, for example, is plotted at axis values (7,7) as determined by the rating scales. The radius drawn from the center (0,0) of the circle through the location of Picture No. 10 reaches the circumference at a scale value of 1.75. This predicted circular scale value argues well with the value of 1.65 obtained by direct sorting on the scale in Schlosberg's (1941) earlier study. (From Schlosberg, 1952.)

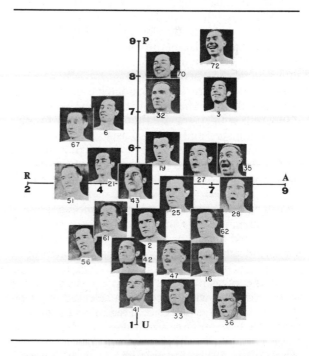

Figure 8.2 Some typical pictures of the Frois-Wittman poses located on Schlosberg's circular surface. (From Schlosberg, 1952.)

THEORIES OF EMOTION

There have been three basic theoretical approaches to the problem of emotion: hedonism, particularly the more recent and widely influential hedonistic theory of emotion developed by P. T. Young; the James-Lange theory; and the activation theories of emotion, named and developed by Lindsley. After discussing each of these three basic theoretical approaches, including evidence pertaining to each of them, some criticisms will be presented, and a synthesis of the various theories of emotion will be attempted.

Hedonism through P. T. Young

The first hedonist may well have been Aristippus, a contemporary of Socrates'. Briefly, Aristippus maintained that pleasure was the only thing in life that was worth working for; moreover, pleasure meant pleasure of the moment, while virtue, interestingly enough, referred to the ability to enjoy pleasure. The next key figure in the history of hedonism is a more familiar one: Epicurus and his followers, the Epicureans, who were active around 300 B.C., maintained that one's philosophy of life should be to be happy and to experience pleasure. The pleasures, however, should be only moderate in intensity, such as the partial fulfillment of hunger, or friendship, but not the more intense enjoyment experienced, for example, in sexual intercourse (cf. Russell, 1945).

Although interest in the doctrine of hedonism waned following the era of the Epicureans, it reappeared with vigor in the British and French associationists and empiricists. Hedonism is expressed in varying degrees in the philosophies of Hobbes, Bain, and Spencer. One of the fullest developments of hedonism was that of Bentham, who interpreted the seeking of pleasure and the avoidance or escape from pain as the basis of all human behavior. He and his followers, the Utilitarians, argued for the principle of "the greatest good for the greatest number" in applying hedonism to political behavior. Others, such as Spencer, applied the pleasure-pain principle to explain the mechanism by which evolution selected and perpetuated adaptive behavior. Hedonism has greatly influenced American psychology in this generation, particularly the psychology of motivation. Thorndike (1911) formulated his *Law of Effect* which states, in essence, that responses which lead to pleasurable events tend to be repeated, while responses that are closely accompanied by un-pleasant events will recur with diminished probability (see also Chapter 7).

Although there have been several hedonic theories of motivation (e.g., Troland, 1928), the theory that has been most extensive and influential is that of P. T. Young, who, in 1961, wrote the most recent edition of his classical book *Motivation and Emotion*. In his definition at the beginning of this chapter, Young stressed that emotion was an affective process characterized by disorganization and disturbance. In particular, Young stressed that emotion originated within a psychological situation and was manifested both in bodily changes (that is, behavior) and in conscious experience. Young saw emotion as being a cornerstone of his broader theory of behavior, which is basically a motivational theory. He distinguished emotional behavior (a subset of *motivated behavior*) from "other affective processes." For example, Young discusses the following affective processes that are to be distinguished from emotions: *simple sensory feelings, persistent organic feelings, moods, affect, sentiments, interests and aversions*, and *temperament*. Young discusses each of these other affective processes in some detail (1961, pp. 352–353) and concludes that *"an emotion is a variety of affective process distinguished from the others as an acute (brief and intense) affective disturbance."* Emotion, for Young, has three primary aspects: It is a felt, *conscious experience* that is directly reportable; it is *behavior;* it is a *physiological process*. He admits that it is "an article of scientific faith that these diverse aspects reveal a single underlying emotional event" [p. 354]. This article of faith is hard to evaluate, since it is not clear what is meant by an "underlying event," particularly when such an event must underlie the physiological process.

The aspect of Young's theory that has been widely attacked by critics and vigorously defended by Young is the statement that emotion is an "acutely disturbed affective state of the individual." For Young, emotional disruption is characterized by alterations in the smooth muscles and glands and by the appearance of reflexive response patterns, such as weeping or laughing. He maintains that these patterns are integrated at subcortical levels and that an emotional disturbance represents a shift from cortical dominance to subcortical dominance. He deals with the fact that certain states commonly classified as emotions (such as anxiety) may sometimes facilitate performance by pointing out that while mild anxiety may indeed increase efficiency of performance, mild affective states are not, by definition, emotions. Emotions are brief and intense affective disturbances. Indeed, severe anxiety lowers efficiency at most tasks. It is precisely such disruption of performance that is (by definition) indicative of the presence of emotion.

One of the most vigorous criticisms of Young's view that emotion is a disorganizing response was the polemic by Leeper (1948), who pointed out that the "disorganization theorists ... have not defined their key terms, have not written consistently and have not related their generalizations to a wide range of factual knowledge" [p. 20]. Leeper maintained that disorganization properly refers to a state in which subordinate activities are not being carried out in a coordinated manner; instead they are operating in mutually exclusive ways or in ways that are incompatible with the successful execution of the superordinate activity. But Leeper points out that emotions produce organized rather than disorganized response patterns in the organism: Like all *integrating* activities, emotion disrupts ongoing behavior that is incongruous with the desired superordinate activity. Emotion mobilizes the organism into coordinated activity in which physiological, behavioral, and experiential components are acting in consort. Leeper concedes that extreme emotion may produce disorganization, but argues that it is unfair to base an entire theory of emotion on the exceptional case. In the same paper and in subsequent articles (e.g., Leeper & Madison, 1959), Leeper developed his own theory of emotion. As indicated in his definition, Leeper's view of emotion is that it is a kind of motivation. This led him not only to a controversy with Young, but also into a controversy with Duffy, who maintained that Leeper had not gone far enough and that the term *emotion* should be eliminated altogether.

Young (1949) was quick to reply to Leeper's criticism. His attack on Leeper was launched in a manner similar to Leeper's attack on Young—by stressing that the other's definition of emotion is imprecise. In addition to demonstrating once again the great difficulty in precisely defining emotion and providing a lively controversy, the Leeper-Young papers served to clarify several points in Young's theory. Young agreed with Leeper that organized components of emotional behavior exist, acknowledging, for example, that reflexive patterns which are present during crying and in rage, organized attack and flight patterns, and other behaviors are certainly well organized from one point of view. At this point, Young makes a distinction between *emotional behavior,* which may be either organized or disorganized depending on the point of view of the observer, and *emotion,* which Young restricts in applicability to disorganized behavior. He maintains that emotional behavior, insofar as it is organized, properly belongs to the psychology of motivation, while the psychology of emotion should be restricted to emotional behavior that is disorganized. Young (1949) notes:

> Now insofar as emotional behavior can be regarded as an *organized* process its analysis, we fully agree, belongs within motivational psychology. In emotional behavior, well-integrated patterns of response appear. Why not study the motivation of these organized responses exactly as one studies reflex action, behavioral drive, social expression, and other smoothly organized activities? The writer's answer is: go ahead! Get all the light possible upon these and other integrated activities. Why not [p. 187]?

In addition to excluding organized emotional behavior from the proper study of emotion, Young underscored the fact that only contemporary affective states could be regarded within the realm of emotion. Thus, more chronic disorganizing affective states, such as persistent anxiety, depression, or any other relatively permanent affect, would not be considered as emotion.

Among the problems with Young's theory is the issue that it is easy to say that the term *emotion* should be restricted to phenomena possessing the qualities that Young requires—acute, disorganizing, contemporary affective states—but it is very difficult to maintain the distinction between emotion and nonemotional affective states when one begins to examine sample cases. Particularly troublesome is the problem of emotions such as anger that often appear to be fairly well integrated, purposive, and goal directed. Young certainly recognized that emotion, for all its disorganization, has utility for the organism. But these are responses that may be as useful, adaptive, and organized as behaviors based on food or sexual deprivation. Yet, in order to define them as emotions, Young must maintain that behaviors such as those seen in anger are disorganized and in some sense, therefore, easily distinguishable from their organized counterparts. Another example of difficulty with Young's classification is the affective reactions that accompany sexual relief. Young explicitly rules those out as emotions (classifying them instead as *persistent organic feelings*) presumably because they are not disorganizing. Yet when one studies the distinction Young makes between emotional and nonemotional forms of behavior, one is impressed that several affective states, particularly those associated with sexual relief, seem to satisfy most of the requirements for emotional behavior. Thus, in one sense, Young's theory of emotion is so specific that it makes little contact with work being done in other areas of emotion. This results from his very restrictive definition of emotion, which still has its problems. At the same time, his theory sometimes suffers by being overly general and vague. It appears, therefore, that other workers in the broad area of emotion are not likely to give up their own subject matter and their own approach to emotion in order to adopt Young's position.

Young and his collaborators have done a remarkable amount of interesting work in studying and quantifying the variables that affect gustatory palatability and choice within the context of their hedonistic theory of motivation and emotion. But Young's theoretical work on emotion, however stimulating, has had less enduring impact and is unlikely to gain general acceptance as a system of emotion.

James-Lange versus Cannon

The James-Lange theory of emotion was first formulated by William James in 1884. Carl Lange published a similar and highly detailed theory in Copenhagen in 1885. Lange's work, which emphasized changes in the small blood vessels, had some influence on James' (1890) later writings. Their theory states that visceral and somatic reactions generate the conscious component of emotion. In other words, the emotional response precedes the emotional experience; emotion is the result rather than the cause of the bodily reactions or of the behavior associated with an emotion. Fear, for example, is our awareness of bodily changes that were triggered by the fearful stimulus: We are afraid because we run; we do not run because we are afraid. This theory was one of the earliest and most influential in the history of emotion. One of the important by-products of the theory is that it generated a large number of experiments designed to refute it. Although the experiments failed to refute the James-Lange theory of emotion completely, they did generate an important catalog of information about the emotional process. The theory was important not only for generating significant research in the area of emotion, but also for being one of the first to identify emotion as a physiological event.

As indicated in the introduction to the present chapter, Walter Cannon (1927), the American physiologist, unleashed a fairly devastating attack against the James-Lange theory of emotion. One of Cannon's chief criticisms was that, although emotions were held by James and Lange to depend on preceding visceral arousal, organisms deprived of sensory input from the viscera continued to manifest emotional behavior. Sherrington (1906) had transected the afferent visceral nerves of dogs which continued to manifest rage reactions and other emotional behaviors, thus demonstrating that emotion can occur in the absence of input to the nervous system from the viscera. But, there are at least two objections with which the James-Lange theorist might counter. In the first place, although the dogs showed rage, they may not have been experiencing emotion. Of course, this objection, while underscoring the robustness of the James-Lange theory, is at the same time a sharp criticism of that theory: It appears to be untestable. The second objection to the Sherrington experiment is more sophisticated. It may well be that through the process of conditioning, rage reactions that had previously been associated with visceral input were now triggered by the stimulus that had preceded the visceral input. Indeed, this is an eminently reasonable suggestion, which will be developed later when discussing Mandler's (1962) position.

In addition to attacking the visceral reaction as unnecessary in the production of emotion, Cannon pointed out that the visceral changes accompanying emotion are too diffuse to be responsible for the clearly differentiated emotions that humans presumably experience. And although some post-Cannonic experiments have indicated that it is possible to differentiate certain emotions such as fear and anger according to their different patterns of physiological reaction (Ax, 1953), several other investigations have failed to give much support to this general approach (thereby indirectly supporting Cannon). Thus, at best, it appears that extremely subtle differences in physiological patterns must mediate rather dramatic differences in emotional experience if they mediate emotions at all. An additional difficulty with the James-Lange theory is that emotional reactions appear with a shorter latency than would be possible given the known latencies of conduction in the central nervous system. In other words, the afferent system probably cannot act fast enough to permit the physiological change to be responsible for the rapid development of consciously experienced emotion.

Finally, there is an additional criticism made by

Cannon that further weakens the tenability of the James-Lange theory. This criticism is based on an ingenious study by Marañon (1924), who injected human subjects with *adrenalin*, a natural hormone which increases autonomic and somatic activity. These subjects should, therefore, have shown signs of heightened emotionality. Although the expected physiological changes that accompany an increased discharge of adrenalin in fact occurred, the subjects, when asked to report their experiences, did not report the expected arousal of emotion. While the subjective report of human subjects is not the strongest ground for confirming or disproving a hypothesis, nonetheless there seems to be no better way to get at the conscious experience of emotion that the James-Lange theory requires be assessed. Surely, if the conscious experience of emotion were simply a reflection of visceral changes, then drugs which produce those visceral changes should in fact produce the conscious experience. There was an interesting feature of Marañon's results, however, which, as we shall see later, lends partial support to the James-Lange theory. Although the subjects did not report feeling the predicted emotion, some commented that they experienced "as if" emotions. In other words, subjects said that they felt as if they were afraid, but that they really were not.

Gellhorn

Although the reactions of the viscera are slow and do not permit a sufficient degree of differentiation to be of primary importance in determining emotion, Gellhorn (1964) observes that this type of objection cannot apply to the expressive movements of the face. Gellhorn has marshaled a fair amount of evidence implicating facial movements in emotion. For example, he points out that the sight of a smile or the sound of laughter initiates a hypothalamic discharge which, in turn, is followed by cortical excitation and alterations in muscle tone and autonomic balance. In addition, stimulation of the hypothalamus or of the limbic brain results in motor patterns of the facial muscles that resemble those seen in emotional behavior, but are different from those that are initiated by direct cortical stimulation. Gellhorn notes that no actual experiments have been performed to determine the relation of the action of facial muscles to hypothalamic discharge, and that it would be of particular interest to ascertain whether afferent stimulation of various facial muscles could generate distinct patterns of hypothalamic excita-

tion that are characteristic for different emotional expressions. He further speculates that in view of the contraction of facial muscles in typical emotional patterns as a result of hypothalamic stimulation, one should expect that

> afferent impulses arising from the face during emotional expression contribute to hypothalamic excitation and hypothalamic-cortical discharges. The great density of the cutaneous receptors in the face and the considerable variety of the patterns of the facial muscles suggest that the resulting patterns of neocortical excitation and hypothalamic-cortical discharges will match in diversity that of the emotional expression [p. 465].

This position is reminiscent of Lange's extremely astute reliance on rapid changes in the body's smallest blood vessels as the basis for emotion. Of course, Gellhorn's theory takes into account the copious evidence collected since the turn of the century on the physiology of emotion. James and Lange, in the absence of these data, had developed an intriguing notion that spurred criticism and research attempting to disprove it. While it is now believed quite unlikely that the viscera control emotion in the manner that James believed, Gellhorn's results and the extensive experiments he cites constitute a tribute to the foresight of James and Lange. Gellhorn (1964, 1968) has demonstrated that proprioceptive feedback seems to constitute an important part of the emotional complex. It appears that emotion, whether defined at the experiential level or in terms of patterns of hypothalamic discharge, is greatly influenced by preceding proprioceptive cues, including facial contraction patterns.

Activation theories

Activation theory refers to a general view that emotion represents a state of heightened arousal rather than a qualitatively unique type of psychological, physiological, or behavioral process. Arousal can be considered to lie on a continuum that extends from states of quiescence, such as deep sleep, to such extremely agitated states as rage or extreme anger. Thus, in a sense it is misleading to call activation theory a theory of emotion at all. Although there are certainly differences among these theorists, the typical activation theorist equates emotion with a state of arousal. Once this is done there is no longer much need to retain the term *emotion*.

Moreover, activation theories of emotion are often conceptually very similar to activation theories of motivation. This will be particularly clear when Hebb's (1966) theory of activation is discussed. It was already noted that Young's theory of emotion was inextricably tied to his broader theory of motivation. As indicated at the beginning of the chapter, the distinction between *motivation and emotion* is often blurred, largely because neither term is well defined and because both terms are rich in meaning for the layman.

At least one activation theorist (Duffy, 1941, 1957) has argued that the term *emotion* should be abandoned. Although the stress on physiological and behavioral arousal that is at the root of activation theory probably originated with Lange and James, the first activation theorist is generally considered to be Walter Cannon, whose theory of emotion was most influential as an attack on the James-Lange theory.

The Cannon-Bard theory of emotion (Bard, 1934) moved from criticism to a real attempt at theoretical integration. It held that the conscious correlate of emotion was the result of an upward discharge to the cerebral cortex from the thalamus which was the seat of emotions, and was not the result of impulses from the muscles and viscera as the James-Lange theory required. The problem with the debate between James and Lange and Cannon and Bard was the difficulty in trying to pinpoint the determinants of conscious experience. Indeed, as more data have been collected on the physiological and behavioral changes that constitute emotion, psychologists have become more interested in these changes rather than in the implication of these changes for conscious experience. In addition to being an attack on James and Lange, Cannon and Bard's position was a theory of emotion in its own right. We need not dwell on their theory, however, since its emphasis on the thalamus was neither correct nor useful (Lashley, 1938). The more important aspect of Cannon's theory for the present discussion, then, is neither the emphasis on the thalamus nor the attack on James and Lange, but Cannon's suggestion that emotions serve an emergency function by preparing the organism for appropriate action.

Following Cannon, other activation theorists have been more concerned with the effects of activation on efficient behavior than with explaining emotional behavior per se. One theorist who has been particularly concerned with the relation between activation and the efficiency of behavior is Hebb (1966). Figure 8.3 shows how Hebb views the relations between behavioral efficiency and activation or arousal. Note the non-

monotonic nature of the curve. Note further that only for extremely high activation does disorganization occur (presumably, it would be only this end of the continuum that would qualify as emotion according to Young).

The relation between behavioral efficiency and arousal is further complicated, according to Hebb, by the degree of difficulty of the task or how well practiced the task is. Curve A in Figure 8.4 shows that for an easy and well-learned response, maximal efficiency is attained with only a mild degree of arousal. (As an example, Hebb gives the response of giving one's name when asked.) Curve B represents a complex skill: Maximum behavioral efficiency occurs with a moderate degree of arousal; higher degrees of arousal produce a decline in behavioral efficiency. Curve C indicates a response such as running that is easy but that requires considerable mobilization and effort on the part of the organism; in this case, maximum behavioral efficiency appears with relatively high arousal.

The relation between activation or arousal and behavioral efficiency has a close parallel in motivational theory. A widely accepted generalization about motivational strength states that there is an intermediate level of motivation that is optimal in problem-solving tests. Moreover, this optimal level varies with problem difficulty: The more difficult the problem, the lower the optimal level of motivation. These relationships are collectively known as the *Yerkes-Dodson law* after the investigators who first discovered them (Yerkes & Dodson, 1908). Note that the Yerkes-Dodson law is an inverted-U curve like Hebb's arousal function shown in Figure 8.3. Similarly, the point of optimality varies with the complexity of the required behavior as shown

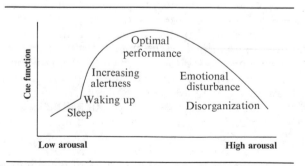

Figure 8.3   The relation between activation (*arousal*) and behavioral efficiency as seen by Hebb. *Cue function* refers to the effectiveness of stimuli in guiding behavior. (From Hebb, 1966.)

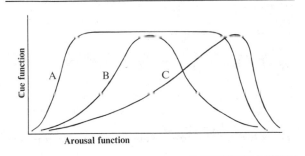

Figure 8.4 The relation between activation and behavioral efficiency for three different tasks as seen by Hebb. (From Hebb, 1966.)

by Figure 8.4. The basic rationale behind the Yerkes-Dodson law is that high motivation so intensifies goal-directed behavior that the organism cannot deal effectively with the problem.

While the Yerkes-Dodson law has been confirmed in many studies utilizing aversive stimuli such as electric shock, anxiety, and air deprivation (Broadhurst, 1957, Cole, 1911, Dodson, 1915, Hammes, 1956; Montague, 1953), confirmation of this law with aversive motivation is relatively uninteresting. In the case of sufficiently prolonged air deprivation or of sufficiently intense electric shock, for example, it is obvious that the organism will be in no condition to solve problems. The organism will, in fact, be incapacitated. Thus, it is important to confirm the Yerkes-Dodson law with appetitive motivation. One study by Fantino, Kasdon, and Stringer (1970) provided such a test, utilizing food deprivation to explore the relation between motivation and problem-solving ability. Fantino et al. utilized the detour or *Umweg* problem developed by Wolfgang Köhler. Figure 8.5 shows

sketches of the three detour problems utilized. In problem A, a pigeon must walk around and behind the wire screen to obtain food that is clearly visible through the screen. Problems B and C are progressively more difficult in that the enclosure is larger. The pigeon is said to demonstrate "insight" by temporarily moving away from the reward in order to circumvent the barrier.

The Yerkes-Dodson law requires that as the pigeon's motivation becomes sufficiently high, its tendency to move toward the barrier, hence failing to reach the food, should be enhanced; in other words, motivation should serve to strengthen the *prepotent response* of moving directly toward the food. Fantino et al. varied motivation by studying pigeons under different degrees of deprivation. In the most extreme case, the pigeons were at a level of deprivation so severe that further deprivation would have threatened their lives and resulted in serious weakness. Obviously, confirmation of the Yerkes-Dodson relation with sick or grossly weakened subjects would be trivial.

Fantino et al. (1970) found that for each of the three problems studied, increased deprivation monotonically increased the speed of problem solution. Thus, their results demonstrate two things. First, deprivation strengthens problem-solving behavior, at least with the detour problem. Second, the Yerkes-Dodson relation was not upheld; instead, increased motivation enhanced problem solving monotonically and for every level of problem difficulty studied.

Even if the Yerkes-Dodson law relating motivation to problem solving is not generally valid, there are undoubtedly cases where behavioral efficiency is in some sense enhanced by certain levels of arousal. Moreover, animals and human subjects will work to remove themselves from

Problem A   Problem B   Problem C

Figure 8.5 Sketches of three detour problems. A red food cup was placed behind the chicken-wire screen. (From Fantino, Kasdon, & Stringer, 1970.)

endpoints of the arousal continuum as shown by studies of sensory deprivation at the low end of the arousal continuum (e.g., Bexton, Heron, & Scott, 1954; Heron, 1961) and by studies of intense stimulation at the high end of the arousal continuum. There is substantial evidence, for example, that intense stimulation is aversive and will be escaped or avoided if possible (e.g., Barnes & Kish, 1957; Keller, 1941; see also Chapter 7).

Several lines of investigation have suggested a curvilinear relation between the intensity of stimulation and the reinforcing or punishing potency of such stimulation. For example, Henderson (1957) allowed rats to bar-press in order to obtain a 1-second flash of light. The rats learned to press for the light and did so at an increasing rate up to an optimal point of light intensity; at higher intensities there was a decline in the reinforcing effectiveness of the light. Sufficiently bright lights would be punishing for the rat, as shown in an earlier study by Keller (1941). This kind of evidence lends support to arousal theories such as Hebb's, as well as to activation theories of emotion and motivation in general.

The term *activation theory of emotion* was not coined by Lindsley (1951) until relatively recently in the history of research on emotion. Building on discoveries of Berger (1929) Lindsley pointed out that when subjects are in a state generally classified as emotional there are clear effects on the electroencephalogram (*EEG*). Specifically, emotion produces an *activation pattern* in which the *synchronized (alpha)* rhythms of the relaxed organism are largely replaced by low-amplitude, fast-activity brain waves. The resultant pattern, it should be noted, is similar whether the blocking is caused by emotional events, sensory stimulation, or complex problem solving. In other words, although we may concede that emotional behaviors always involve activation, it is not clear how we can distinguish between activation produced by emotional causes and activation produced by other causes. The activation concept, therefore, cannot provide us with a definition or a complete theory of emotion, except insofar as we identify emotion and activation as equivalents. If we do that, of course, then we need not retain the concept of emotion.

Emotion is, after all, an intuitive term, and it would hardly seem intuitively appealing to describe a person solving a complex calculus problem as being in a state of emotion. Or, to use an amusing example provided by Mandler (1962), a man trying to lift a two-hundred-pound weight might be in a state of high activation, but is he also experiencing intense emotion? This is the crux of the problem with the concept of emotion: Attempts to define it rigorously will fail because they will not dovetail with our intuitions.

In any case, Lindsley's activation theory of emotion points to a physiological correlate of most (gross) emotional behavior, and it provides evidence that is fairly interesting in and of itself, regardless of its direct relevance to the topic of emotion. Lindsley demonstrates that the activation pattern of the *EEG* can be reproduced by appropriate electrical stimulation of brain structures, especially in the brain stem reticular formation and in the diencephalon. When appropriate lesions are made in the reticular formation, the activation pattern of the *EEG* is abolished and the alpha rhythms are restored. In this event the organism is markedly nonexpressive or apathetic. Lindsley further points out that the "objective features of emotional expression" are caused by discharges to motor outflows from the diencephalon–brain stem reticular formation mechanism. Lindsley further speculates that this mechanism is "either identical with or overlaps" the *EEG* activating mechanism that arouses the cortex.

Figure 8.6 presents Lindsley's schematic representation of the primary structures and pathways of the central nervous system that are believed to be implicated in emotional behavior. Note that the reticular formation itself contributes impulses both upward toward the cortex and downward toward the musculature. The descending fibers provide means for impulses from the activating mechanism to influence muscular movements and visceral activity mediated by the autonomic nervous system. At the same time, the ascending fibers follow both thalamic routes (where they interact with the fibers of the diffuse thalamic projection system) and extrathalamic routes. These upward paths presumably form the basis of the activation patterns manifested in the *EEG*. Thus, electric stimulation of the activating mechanism alters the *EEG* pattern in the direction of *desynchronization* (increased activation) while, on the other hand, lesions in the same area or in its upward projection pathways can alter an activated *EEG* pattern into a *synchronized* (sleep) pattern.

The essence of Lindsley's activation theory of emotion is that the reticular system must be activated in order for significant emotional behavior to occur. Presumably the activating system serves a general energizing function, while limbic system structures are instrumental in organizing

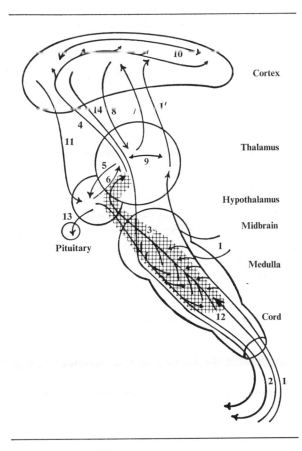

Figure 8.6 Lindsley's (1951) schematic representation of principal neural structures and pathways implicated in emotional behavior. The reticular formation is represented by crosshatching. Numbers refer to the various neural pathways. (From Lindsley, 1951.)

the input and determining the particular form of expressed emotion. While the activation mechanism must certainly be considered in a complete physiological account of emotions, and while the mechanisms of activation are of great interest in themselves, activation theory by itself is not a theory of emotion, at least as emotion has been traditionally conceived in the history of psychology.

Current status

None of the three types of theories of emotion just described has thus far gained acceptance as *the* theory of emotion, nor is it likely that any one of them will. Two of these general approaches, hedonism and activation, seem to treat emotion in such a restricted manner that each of them leaves room for other theories of emotion addressed to a different subject matter. Thus Young's hedonic theory of emotion restricts emotion to a subclass of behavior that which is disorganized that is far smaller than what is usually meant by emotion. Activation theory, too, suffers from the same problem: It involves an attempt to redefine emotion, in a way which is fairly arbitrary and not in keeping with traditional definitions. In a sense, it sidesteps the problem of emotion. The third type of approach, that of James and Lange, is implausible in many of its particulars. At the very least, the identification of an emotion as the conscious experience of visceral impulses has not been very helpful in the study of emotion, particularly since the visceral messages do not appear to contain sufficient differentiation to account for the great variety of experienced emotions.

More recently, Mandler (1962) has developed a theory of emotion that seems to be more promising than its predecessors. Mandler's theory incorporates some of the best features of the other theories, but does not incorporate their restricted natures. Before considering Mandler's theory of emotional behavior, however, it is necessary to review Marañon's (1924) study and to discuss some of the experimentation by Schachter and his associates (e.g., Schachter & Singer, 1962; Schachter & Wheeler, 1962) that were very influential in shaping Mandler's theory.

According to the James-Lange theory, drugs which produce visceral reaction should also produce emotion. But the experiment by Marañon (1924), stressed heavily by Cannon, rejected this very clear implication of the James-Lange theory. Marañon administered adrenalin injections to his experimental subjects and then asked them for their emotional reactions. The majority of the subjects reported none, although a minority of the subjects did report "as if" emotions. Taken as a whole, Marañon's results were rightly used to argue for the inadequacy of the James-Lange approach, which could only take solace in the fact that a minority of subjects reported partial reactions.

Schachter and Singer (1962) reported some experiments which give a clearer picture of what was probably going on in the minds and viscera of Marañon's subjects. They reasoned that the subjects might be attributing the tremors, palpitations, and related behaviors to the adrenalin injection and therefore discounted these cues, negating an emotional experience. If this were true, of course, uninformed subjects should experience emotion. This is the crux of half of the Schachter and Singer study. The other important variable was a manipulation of the social situation in which the injected subjects found themselves.

Some of Schachter and Singer's subjects were treated in the same way as Marañon's. They were given a drug (albeit with a phony name) and were told (veridically) what to expect in the way of side effects. Other groups of subjects in the Schachter and Singer experiment were misinformed. They were told to expect side effects, but were told incorrect side effects. For example, they were told that they might expect aching and numbness in parts of the body rather than the tremors and palpitation associated with adrenalin administration. Finally there were also control subjects who received saline injections instead of drug injections. To summarize the logic of the experiment, all of the subjects except the saline controls should have had the same degree of visceral arousal, but only some would have been able to correlate these visceral cues with their expectation of the drug-produced effects. Therefore, the misinformed subjects should have interpreted the visceral cues as emotion (not being able to discount them via knowledge of the drug's effects).

If it is true, then, that visceral cues are implicated in emotion but that their interpretation depends on other factors, for example, the social situation, the stimuli in the subject's environment might determine what emotion was felt as a result of a given visceral experience. This was the rationale for the manipulation of the subject's social environment. Subjects were told to wait for about 20 minutes so that the drug might take effect and the vision test (the sham pretext for the study) could proceed. Individual subjects were then joined by the experimenter's confederate or stooge. In one condition the stooge was high spirited; for example, he would crumple up some paper and begin shooting baskets into a wastepaper basket, and otherwise behave in an euphoric manner. Stooges in the other condition, however, were quite disagreeable and angry. The measure of emotion was twofold: observation by experimenters through a one-way mirror, and a questionnaire administered later to the subjects.

The results showed that the misinformed subjects experienced emotion more in line with the stooge's than did the correctly informed subjects, both in terms of their actions, as observed through

the one-way mirror, and in terms of their moods, as reflected in the questionnaires. The control subjects who were given saline injections were less likely than their adrenalin-injected (and equally misinformed) counterparts to act and report their emotions in the direction of those being performed by the stooges. Therefore, it appears that the internal visceral cues do play a role, otherwise the saline-injected subjects should have shown the same effect as the other misinformed subjects. These findings point to the following conclusions: Visceral cues play a role in determining emotion, as required by the James-Lange theory; and there is a striking stimulus component involved in the determination of emotions, which contradicts the contention that visceral cues alone are sufficient to account for particular emotions. This stimulus component includes not only the social situation provided by the stooge, but also the stimulus provided by the instructions. These results also enable an interpretation of Marañon's results in terms of the instructions he gave his subjects.

Schachter and his associates have done further studies that have confirmed these conclusions. For example, Schachter and Wheeler (1962) injected different drugs into different subjects with an aim toward varying the amount of activity in the sympathetic nervous system. In their experiment, the stimulus situation was held constant: All subjects observed a slapstick movie. The subjects were then observed to see whether the amount of humor they displayed was correlated with the amount of sympathetic activity due to the drug injection. Schachter and Wheeler found results in the expected direction, again underscoring the role played by visceral cues.

We are now in a position to turn to Mandler's *juke-box theory of emotion*. Mandler (1962) points out that there seem to be two stages to the production of an emotion which correspond to the two stages in selecting a tune in a juke box. The first step in the juke-box process is to insert a coin to activate the machine. This corresponds to the visceral arousal that is now seen to be implicated in producing emotion. But an additional step is required to select a tune: The appropriate button must be pressed to select the melody. This is analogous to the stimulus situation determining which emotion is in fact manifested. Mandler points out that the same stimulus situation can produce both steps simultaneously.

This view of the determinants of emotional behavior is pictured in Figure 8.7. The figure shows that both nonverbal and verbal stimuli in the en-

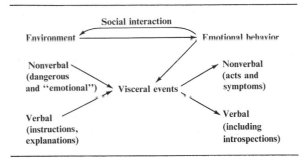

Figure 8.7 Mandler's schematic diagram of the variables implicated in emotion. Arrows refer to possible relations among antecedent and consequent variables. (From Mandler, 1962.)

vironment can affect visceral events which, in turn, can produce both nonverbal and verbal emotional behavior. In addition, the environment can act directly upon the emotional behavior which, in turn, can influence visceral events. Finally, emotional behavior can influence the environment via social interaction. Thus, in order to understand emotional behavior we must consider environmental, internal (i.e., visceral), and behavioral variables, although in order to understand the effects of these factors, each must be studied in an experimental setting that permits the controlling variables in a given situation to be determined.

In reassessing the theories of emotion of Cannon and Bard and of James and Lange, Mandler concludes with Cannon that emotions seem to be characterized by similar visceral antecedents, a conclusion well supported by Schachter's experiments. At the same time, these experiments point to the necessity of including the viscera in a complete theory of emotion. Mandler makes two interesting additional points. First, he notes that while visceral activity may not be necessary for emotional behavior to occur, an argument made by Cannon, it is probably true that visceral involvement is vital for the initial acquisition, if not the maintenance, of emotional behavior. Specifically, Mandler (1962) argues that emotional behavior "will only be present when intact visceral structures and responses have previously mediated the link between environmental conditions and emotional behavior. Emotional behavior is probably absent or minimal when visceral discharge is absent during the acquisition of the behavior" [p. 326] Indeed, Kessen and Mandler (1961) have argued that the nature of emotional behavior may change from primarily visceral representation to primarily symbolic representation, through conditioning.

Activation, then, whether from social situations, from drugs, or from other stimuli, is probably necessary but not sufficient for emotional behavior. Although it is somewhat premature to speculate on the physiological correlates of this activation, it no doubt often involves the reticular formation activating mechanism, discussed earlier, and the hypothalamus, particularly the type of proprioceptive feedback discussed by Gellhorn (1964, 1968). At the same time, the activation by itself does not produce emotional behavior; rather, these internal cues are apparently modulated by stimuli (including social stimuli) into the totality of a particular emotion. It is also premature to speculate about the physiological correlate of this mechanism, although it is likely that limbic system structures are implicated in this modulation. Given sufficient activation, a stimulus situation may generate a given emotion, with probable mediation through limbic system structures. In a very general way, this seems to be an adequate theory to deal with the present state of knowledge in the field of emotion. Whether or not the existence of such an adequate general theory justifies retention of the concept of emotion in experimental psychology is an open question.

SOME EMPIRICAL FINDINGS

Theories concern the basic nature and causes of emotion in general and specific emotions in particular. A great deal is known about emotion at an empirical level, where it is difficult or impossible to distinguish among theories.

Development of emotion

The classic study on the development and differentiation of emotions in infants and young children is that of Bridges (1932). Figure 8.8 presents data, based on an observer's ratings, that indicate how specific emotions evolved or are differentiated from their more general predecessors. Note that the first emotion is a generalized excitement reaction. As the infant grew older, its reactions to specific stimuli were observed to become more specific. Thus, soon after birth the emotion of distress was observed. After about four months, the distress reaction was itself observed to differentiate into more specific emotional reactions: anger and, later, disgust and fear (see also Chapter 9).

Learned and cultural factors

Emotion is hard enough to define without further trying to specify whether the emotional reaction is

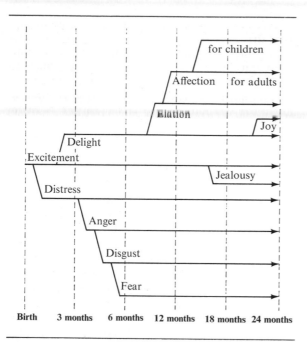

Birth · 3 months · 6 months · 12 months · 18 months · 24 months

Figure 8.8 The development and differentiation of emotions according to data based on observations of infants and young children. (After Bridges, 1932; modified by Dashiell, 1949.)

innate or learned. The distinction between innate and learned components is a thorny one in the history of psychology and not one that will be elaborated on in this chapter.

But a few generalizations are in order. Given that there is an adequate definition of the emotion *fear*, it could probably be demonstrated that behavior fitting the definition of fear can be observed in situations where it is apparently unlearned. For example, children and many other organisms show apparently fearful behavior in response to a sudden and intense stimulus, such as a clanging noise. Many organisms, particularly those high on the phylogenetic scale, show fearful reactions to strange stimuli, especially those that differ in some important characteristics from very familiar objects. A human with a mask might elicit a fear reaction from a child or a monkey. Consider Hebb's (1966) report on fear in the chimpanzee:

> Causes of [what seemed to Hebb to be] fear in the captive chimpanzee make up an almost endless list: a carrot of an unusual shape, a biscuit with a worm in it, a rope of a particular size, color and texture (but not other ropes), a doll or a toy animal, a particular piece of apparatus or part of

it, and so on. What one animal fears another may not, but as a species chimpanzees are much more susceptible than dogs to fears that do not arise from pain or threat of pain. . . .

> [A plaster of paris cast from a death mask of an adult] produced screaming, panic-stricken flight in a fifth of the adult animals who were simply shown the object, carried in the experimenter's hand as he walked up to the cage. The response of the remaining adults varied in strength, but most were very frightened and no animal failed to show erection of hair and avoidance of the test object. The same reaction was produced by a clay model of an adult chimpanzee head about half life-size. . .; an actual chimpanzee's head that had been preserved in formalin; a life-like model of a human head, sawn from a display dummy; and various related objects, such as a detached human hand (from the same dummy). With repeated testing there was some habituation . . ., but no animal got to the point of coming near any of these objects [pp. 241–242].

Several points should be made here. In the first place, the fact that the subjects had not seen the stimuli before and the fact that their fear response did not completely habituate to the stimuli both argue for the likelihood that the fear responses to the stimuli were innate. On the other hand, the gross individual differences in the responses to the stimuli argue that different histories of the various adult chimps may have contributed to the intensity and nature of the reaction. More convincing arguments for a learned component of the fear reaction come from further observations that younger chimpanzees did not exhibit a fear reaction to the same stimuli. It may well be, as Hebb points out, that the organism must first learn what is familiar before it can display fear reactions to unfamiliar-looking objects.

A discussion of innate determinants of emotional behaviors inevitably recalls Darwin's (1872) classic work on the *Expression of the Emotions in Man and Animals*. He speculated that much of man's emotional repertoire is inherited, in an evolutionary sense, from behaviors that were useful in animal life but are no longer of utility to man. Darwin, a gifted observer, supported his speculations with rich anecdotal evidence. For example, he pointed out that man's habit of curling his lips in a sneer is an evolutionary hangover from the carnivore's adaptive habit of baring its teeth in rage. A fuller discussion of the Darwinian influence is found in Chapter 9.

Although it appears that not all emotional responses are learned, it is also clear that a preponderance of the behavior that we label emotional is. This learning occurs by the principles of respondent and operant conditioning that have been enunciated throughout this volume. The classical study of the respondent conditioning of emotion, for example, is that of Watson and Rayner (1920). They studied a one-year-old boy who showed no fear reaction to the sight of a white rat, but who showed a clear emotional reaction, including crying, to a loud sound. Watson and Rayner then used the loud sound as an unconditioned stimulus and the sight of the white rat as a conditioned stimulus by pairing the sight of the white rat with the occurrence of the loud sound. After just a few pairings, the sight of the white rat was sufficient to elicit a full-blown fear reaction. In addition, the conditioned fear generalized to other stimuli, such as furry objects.

An extremely effective conditioning agent is the organism's culture. The best discussion of cultural influences on emotional expression is still Klineberg's (1940). He considered the hypothesis that members of different cultures have different emotional expressions, and the further hypothesis that these differences may be due to innate factors, such as anatomical features. For example, he discusses the supposed inscrutability of the Oriental. Klineberg points out, for example, that part of the education of the young Chinese involves the teaching of restraint. This may partially account for the reserved behavior that leads to inscrutability. In addition, however, as aliens in white America, members of this minority group might indeed have been expected to show more reserve, at least in the presence of white Americans. Klineberg notes this may be especially true because they are not "quite certain of their reception.... Much of their apparent inscrutability is merely a precaution against embarrassment.... This interpretation is borne out by the fact that when the Chinese are in an environment to which they are not alien, they give an impression of liveliness and vivacity in marked contrast to the usual stereotype" [p. 172]. Finally, Klineberg makes the further important point that our own stereotypes of the Oriental's emotional expressions may influence what we see. In other words, how we perceive emotional expression in the Oriental may tell us more about our own perceptual systems and biases than about the Oriental's emotional expressiveness.

Klineberg's account includes a wealth of anecdotal material from anthropological sources illustrating the effects of culture on emotional expressiveness. He describes several cultures in which weeping is expected in certain situations. Klineberg (1940) writes:

> Apparently with the ability to weep at will under definite conditions, there goes also the capacity of recovering quickly from this display of emotion. Among the Huichol Indians of Mexico the writer noted that when weeping occurred as part of the religious ceremonial, it was possible for the man who wept to stop at will, and as soon as it was over he returned to his usual "cheerfulness" [p. 184].

But while Klineberg stresses the learned and cultural components of emotional behavior, he also grants that there are certain emotions, primarily fear and laughter, which seem to be universal. This view is compatible with the idea that fear is probably an innate response to certain stimuli, at least in higher organisms. It should be remembered, of course, that fear can be readily conditioned to previously neutral stimuli.

Klineberg (1940) concludes his discussion by noting that

> emotional behavior is accompanied by a series of physiological changes which presumably occur in all individuals. Social factors may, however, affect the emotions in various ways. There are, for example, differences in the situations which will arouse the various emotions in different societies; the contrasting reactions to the birth of twins, to death, to sex activity may be cited in this connection. There are differences also in the amount of overt emotional behavior, as well as in the specific emotions which are permitted expression. Although it has been suggested that anatomical characteristics may play a part, it is certain that cultural influences are much more important; the variations in the emotional behavior of the Chinese under different conditions are particularly striking [p. 199].

An experimental analysis of anxiety

Facial expressions and other indicators of fear, such as crying and flight, appear to be characteristic emotional responses that are evident in many individuals without special training. As described earlier, the occurrence of such responses in various situations may be influenced by the processes of operant and respondent conditioning, and stimulus control. During the past three decades, the techniques of operant conditioning have been used extensively to study emotional behavior through the examination of responses such as lever-pressing, key-pecking, and the like, which may be chosen arbitrarily and are not in any way characteristic indicators of emotion.

Estes and Skinner (1941) first suggested a procedure for the quantitative study of anxiety in which an organism emits a standard operant response, such as a lever-press, and obtains food reinforcement on an intermittent basis. At the same time, a stimulus, which was neutral at the beginning of the experiment, is occasionally presented to the organism. Concomitant with the termination of this originally neutral stimulus, shock is delivered to the organism independent of its behavior. The effect of pairing the neutral stimulus and the shock and superimposing the two on a schedule of food reinforcement is to lower the rate of responding in the presence of the stimulus as compared with the rate of responding in its absence. This suppression of responding can be measured in several ways. One measure is a suppression ratio which divides the rate of responding in the presence of a stimulus by the rate of responding in the absence of the stimulus. Thus, if the stimulus is ineffective in suppressing behavior, the ratio is 1.0; if responding is totally suppressed in the presence of this stimulus, then the suppression ratio is zero. Since the stimulus precedes shock, it is generally called a preaversive stimulus; the suppression of responding in the presence of a preaversive stimulus is often called *conditioned suppression* or a *conditioned emotional response* or *anxiety*. The term *conditioned emotional response* is appropriate, for example, since conditioning, responding, and emotion are all implicated: responding, since that is the behavior being measured; emotion, because of the character of the reaction; and conditioning, because the stimulus that is paired with the electric shock is originally neutral. The conditioned-suppression paradigm has been used with several species of animals, including pigeons, rats, and several types of monkeys.

In their original study, Estes and Skinner maintained the behavior of rats on a *fixed-interval (FI)* 4-minute schedule of food reinforcement. They obtained suppression using a 5-minute conditioned stimulus that terminated with foot-shock. Subsequent work with the conditioned-suppression paradigm has utilized schedules of reinforcement other than the fixed interval. As with most aspects of behavior, the schedule of reinforcement is a crucial determinant of the nature of the behavior (cf. Chapter 6), and the suppression phenomenon depends in part on the schedule of positive reinforcement maintaining the suppressed behavior.

Variable-interval (VI) schedules

VI schedules of reinforcement generate a fairly uniform rate of responding and are therefore most frequently used as the baseline for conditioned suppression. Lyon (1963) found that responding on a *VI* 4-minute component of a *multiple schedule* (see Chapter 6) was suppressed more during the preshock stimulus than was responding on a *VI* 1-minute component. Blackman (1968b) has pointed out that since the *VI* 1-minute schedule generates a higher rate of responding, as well as a higher rate of reinforcement, than a *VI* 4-minute schedule of reinforcement, the differences in the amount of suppression found by Lyon could be due to either of the two factors. Blackman (1968a, 1968b) has teased apart these variables in studies which control for frequency of reinforcement and rate of responding. He found that both response rate and rate of reinforcement affected the amount of suppression obtained: Subjects equated for rate of responding showed a higher degree of suppression the lower the rate of reinforcement; subjects equated for reinforcement frequency (but with differing rates of responding) showed a greater degree of suppression with higher rates of responding.

DRL schedules

The effects of conditioned suppression on responding maintained by schedules of reinforcement that differentially reinforce low response rates (*DRL* schedules) are somewhat complex. We will restrict our discussion to a comprehensive study by Blackman (1968a). He studied conditioned suppression in rats responding on a *DRL* 15-second *limited-hold* 5-second schedule. The limited hold of 5 seconds stipulates that the organism must respond within 5 seconds after completion of the appropriate *DRL* pause in order to obtain food. Otherwise, a new 15-second pause is required before a response may be reinforced.

Response rates increased in the presence of the preaversive stimulus at low shock intensities but were suppressed at higher shock intensities. Blackman observed that the effect of low-intensity shock was to disrupt the response chain that the rats were utilizing to mediate or bridge the 15-second pause. Blackman felt that this led to the facilitation of responding that occurred with low-intensity shock. Blackman's study indicates that the extent of conditioned suppression will be a function of the intensity of the unconditioned stimulus, a finding previously reported by Annau and Kamin (1961), who maintained behavior on a *VI* schedule.

Variable-ratio (VR) schedules

Lyon and Felton (1966) studied the effects of the conditioned-suppression paradigm on responding maintained on a food-reinforced *VR* schedule (see Chapter 6) and found no systematic suppression. It would have been interesting to note whether conditioned suppression would have been obtained with high shock intensities. Nonetheless, the results obtained by Lyon and Felton are readily interpretable: Conditioned suppression occurs with variable-interval schedules, in part, because the lowering of response rate on *VI* schedules has, within limits, virtually no effect on the rate of reinforcement, whereas the lowering of response rate on *VR* schedules produces a proportional decrease in the rate of reinforcement. Therefore, one would expect *VR* behavior to be more resistant to the effects of a preaversive stimulus, just as the results obtained by Blackman and by Lyon with *VI* schedules suggest.

Fixed-ratio (FR) schedules

When behavior is maintained on an *FR* schedule of reinforcement (cf. Chapter 6), the results are somewhat more complex but are also more interesting. With *FR* schedules (Lyon, 1964) the effect of the preaversive stimulus varied depending on the position in the *FR* schedule. For example, when the preshock stimulus was presented within the first 20 responses on an *FR*-150, complete suppression was reliably produced. If the preshock stimulus was initiated during the emission of the twentieth to the sixtieth response, there was roughly a 50 percent chance of obtaining suppressed responding. Finally, when the organism was beyond the sixtieth response in the *FR*-150, no suppression occurred (that is, until the entire ratio was completed). In an *FR* schedule, as in a *VR* schedule, each response contributes to the production of reinforcement, and responding would therefore be expected to be more resistant to suppression than responding maintained by interval or *DRL* schedules. Nonetheless, Lyon's result with *FR* schedules indicates that the behavior is completely resistant only when the organism is far along in the *FR* (in the *VR* case, of course, a reinforcement may be only a few responses away at any time). Moreover, evidence has been presented in Chapter 7 to

the effect that the stimulus correlated with the early part of an *FR* schedule is aversive; therefore, very little inducement would be required to suppress responding early in an *FR* schedule.

Effect on accuracy and discrimination

A striking finding in the literature on conditioned suppression is the fact that while rate of responding is suppressed during a preshock stimulus, variables such as accuracy of timing or performance in a discrimination task are apparently not affected. For example, Migler and Brady (1964) required the organism to pause for at least 5 seconds between a response on one lever and a response on a second lever. This complex timing response was reinforced on a *VR*-2 schedule. While conditioned suppression occurred, the accuracy of timing—that is, the proportion of 5-second interresponse times between the two levers—was not affected.

Physiological correlates

It is evident from this review that the suppression of operant behavior depends on the baseline schedule of reinforcement. Does this dependency imply that the emotion of anxiety is itself related to the schedule of reinforcement? Or, to put the question more properly, to what extent is conditioned suppression related to other aspects of emotional behavior? Several investigators have measured reactions such as heart rate and blood pressure during conditioned suppression. These studies indicate that physiological correlates of emotion are often present during suppression but are by no means a reliable indicator of suppression. For example, de Toledo and Black (1966) recorded the heart rate of rats in a conditioned-suppression paradigm. They found that the change in heart rate developed more slowly than suppression, indicating that suppression preceded the physiological correlate rather than vice versa. One is tempted to say—recalling the James-Lange view—that the rats' heart rates rose because their behavior was suppressed. A more appropriate conclusion, however, is that of de Toledo and Black: The conditioning of response suppression and the conditioning of heart rate are relatively independent. De Toledo and Black also found that the change in heart rate was more variable and was of shorter duration than the suppression effect.

It would be of great interest to determine

whether or not the physiological correlates of anxiety were present in those experiments with *VR* schedules of positive reinforcement which failed to obtain suppression. If so, this dissociation between the behavioral and physiological correlates of anxiety would render the term *anxiety* less useful.

Alternatively, of course, one could speak of *physiological anxiety* and *behavioral anxiety*. Even this tortuous resolution would have problems, however. The following section discusses an experiment in which behavioral anxiety can only be attributed to positive reinforcement. In definitional terms this presents no particular problem. But, intuitively, the concept of anxiety should perhaps not apply to situations involving only positive reinforcement.

Anxiety: A reinterpretation

Until recently it was assumed that the aversive character of the unconditioned stimulus was responsible for conditioned suppression; hence, the term *anxiety*. In other words, when the stimulus that had been paired many times with the unconditioned aversive stimulus was initiated, it evoked an emotional response such as anxiety which interfered with the ongoing behavior maintained by positive reinforcement. Leitenberg (1966) found that shock resulted in suppression in the presence of the preshock stimulus as in the previous studies mentioned; he found, in addition, however, that when a loud tone, a loud noise, or a *time-out* was substituted for the shock, no suppression resulted. In other words, other stimuli that have sometimes been shown to be aversive (Chapter 7) failed to produce suppression. This result might indicate that only a strongly aversive unconditioned stimulus such as shock produces conditioned suppression. But this generalization is refuted by the results of Azrin and Hake (1969) and Meltzer and Brahlek (1970). Azrin and Hake, for example, investigated the effects of unconditioned stimuli such as food (to a hungry organism), water (to a thirsty organism), or intracranial stimulation (in the "reward" centers discussed earlier) on responding maintained by a different positive reinforcer. They found that suppression occurred with any of these unconditioned stimuli. In other words, when water reward was used instead of shock in the conditioned-suppression paradigm, it was sufficient to produce suppression in the presence of the prewater stimulus. Thus, although water and shock are totally different stimuli, they

have strikingly similar effects in suppressing behavior maintained by food reinforcement. Azrin and Hake suggest that this is probably due to some general heightened state of emotional preparedness. In any case, the finding that conditioned suppression, conditioned emotional response, or anxiety occurred whether a positive reinforcer or shock served as the unconditioned stimulus certainly demands a different perspective on the earlier work as studies of anxiety. Indeed, it appears that although suppression can be quantitatively defined (for example, a suppression ratio in the conditioned-suppression paradigm), and although many investigators have called suppression an index of anxiety, the Azrin and Hake study suggests that this inference is misleading.

Conclusion

While the general phrase *emotional behavior* in fact refers to real changes in responding correlated with various operations, the term does not seem to be particularly useful. Indeed, insofar as there will almost inevitably be a tendency to equate the changes in responding with conceptions held by laymen, such terms may actually hinder the analysis of behavior.

It may be argued, of course, that with sufficient analysis it would be possible to differentiate between the nature of the conditioned suppression found by Azrin and Hake utilizing positive reinforcers, and the conditioned suppression found by other workers utilizing shock. For example, it is likely that the physiological correlates that accompany the conditioned suppression reported by Azrin and Hake are distinct from the physiological correlates reported in studies utilizing shock. In that case one could define anxiety as a change in the suppression ratio accompanied by certain physiological correlates. This possibility is doubtful in view of the at least partial independence of suppression and its physiological correlates previously discussed. But even if such a definition were feasible, it would appear to be an unfortunate, if not futile, attempt to rescue the concept of anxiety.

Aggressive behavior

As described in Chapter 1, Ulrich and Azrin (1962) obtained aggressive behavior by administering foot shocks to two rats enclosed together in an experimental chamber. Upon receiving the shock the rats faced each other, reared up on their hind legs, and struck out at and bit one another. This type of *pain-elicited aggression* has been demonstrated for a variety of experiments, mostly by Azrin and his associates (e.g., Azrin, Hutchinson, & Hake, 1966, 1967; Azrin, Hutchinson, & Sallery, 1964). Aggression is elicited in the sense that the aggressive response reliably follows the shock providing that an appropriate object is present against which to aggress. Hence, strictly speaking, the eliciting stimulus is the shock plus an appropriate stimulus object. In order to eliminate the possible influence of social factors, subsequent studies of elicited aggression used single animals with inanimate objects to bite or attack (Azrin, Hutchinson, & Sallery, 1964). Pain-elicited aggression was obtained in these studies also. Indeed, Azrin, Hutchinson, and McLaughlin (1965) have shown that the availability of an object against which to aggress can maintain operant behavior in squirrel monkeys. In particular, squirrel monkeys would pull a chain in order to produce a ball to attack following shock.

Recent studies have also demonstrated that aggression can result from types of stimuli other than physically painful ones. Azrin, Hutchinson, and Hake (1966) found that when pigeons were responding for continuous food reinforcement and then put on an extinction schedule, they attacked restrained target birds that were located at the end of the chamber away from the response key and food magazine. Aggressive behavior ceased when the continuous-reinforcement schedule was reinstated. This extinction-induced aggression was also obtained with squirrel monkeys toward inanimate objects (Hutchinson, Azrin, & Hunt, 1968). Fixed-ratio schedules have been shown to result in aggression also. Gentry (1968) obtained aggression by a pigeon toward a restrained target bird during an *FR*-50 schedule of food reinforcement. Moreover, Hutchinson, Azrin, and Hunt (1968) found that aggression toward inanimate objects in squirrel monkeys was a function of the size of the *FR*. Thus, it seems that stimuli that will produce aggressive behavior are those which have been shown to be aversive stimuli—for example, shocks, stimuli associated with extinction, and stimuli associated with high fixed-ratio requirements (see Chapter 7).

Another example of elicited aggression, one which apparently does not involve pain, is provided by the mouse-killing phenomenon. Some rats "spontaneously" attack and kill the first mouse they ever encounter, whereas other rats of similar genetic and environmental backgrounds are never observed to kill (Karli, 1956; Myer, 1964). The percentage of killers found in a given population of rats has been shown to vary with species (Karli, 1956; Paul, Miley, & Baenninger, 1971), sex (Paul et al., 1971), and breeding and developmental experience (Heimstra & Newton, 1961; Myer, 1969, 1971). Higher percentages of killers are found among wild rats than among domesticated rats (Karli, 1956). However, among domesticated rats the incidence of killing is much lower for albinos than for hooded rats. Both wild and domesticated rats kill by repeatedly biting the mouse in the spinal cord, usually at the nape of the neck (Karli, 1956; Kreiskott, 1969), and although they differ with respect to what part of the mouse is eaten first, both wild and domesticated killers will eat the mouse after the kill (Karli, 1956).

Mouse-killing represents an instance of motivated aggression. Several investigators (Myer & White, 1965; Van Hemel, 1972) report that the opportunity to kill can serve as an adequate reinforcer for the maintenance of a learned response. Van Hemel (1972) placed killers in an operant paradigm in which mice were presented contingent upon a key-press. All subjects learned the response, killed consistently throughout training, and continued to press when shifted from continuous reinforcement to *VI*-1 schedules of reinforcement. These animals key-pressed as readily for dead and anesthetized mice as they did for live mice. Response rates for rat pups, however, were significantly lower than those exhibited in response to any form of mouse. All forms of mice elicited vigorous attack, but in no case was a rat pup injured.

Though mouse-killing is regarded as an example of elicited aggression, it is not yet clear what the eliciting stimulus actually is. Several procedures have been employed in attempts to elicit killing in animals that do not initially kill (Baenninger & Ulm, 1969; Karli, 1961; Smith, King, & Hoebel, 1970). Only those involving direct physiological manipulations such as electrical or chemical stimulation of the lateral hypothalamus (King & Hoebel, 1968; Panksepp, 1971; Smith, King, & Hoebel, 1970), or the manipulation of consummatory variables such as food deprivation or competition (Heimstra & Newton, 1961; Paul, 1972; Paul, Miley, & Baenninger, 1971; Whalen & Fehr, 1964), have been successful in inducing killing in nonkillers.

Aggression can also be maintained when it is reinforced (operant aggression). In other words, organisms will emit aggressive responses in order to obtain food reward (Reynolds, Catania, &

Skinner, 1963). Thus, aggressive responses either can be elicited by aversive stimuli or can be reinforced. It should be noted that while aggressive responses are readily manipulated in the laboratory, the emotional correlates of such behavior have not been determined. Nor is it known whether the physiological correlates of aggressive behavior are constant from experiment to experiment. Further determinants of aggressive behavior, as studied in more natural settings, are discussed in connection with the concept of instinct in Chapter 9.

Autonomic nervous system

The autonomic nervous system controls the action of the internal organs, such as the adrenal gland, the intestines, the heart, the lungs, and so forth, that are clearly implicated in the experience of emotion. The autonomic nervous system consists of two divisions: the *parasympathetic* and *sympathetic* systems. In intense emotion, the sympathetic system appears to dominate, particularly when the individual is faced with an emergency. The sympathetic nervous system controls bodily functions that mobilize the body's resources for coping with an emergency or an otherwise highly charged situation. The parasympathetic system generally acts in an opposite direction to the sympathetic system, being primarily implicated in the conservation and storage of the body's resources. The parasympathetic system stimulates the secretion of saliva and digestive fluids, and tends to slow down breathing and the pulse rate. Further discussion of the involvement of the autonomic nervous system in emotion may be found in Morgan (1965).

BRAIN MECHANISMS IN EMOTION AND MOTIVATION

It is difficult to discuss the physiology of emotion without simultaneously dealing with motivation. As noted earlier, hedonic and activation theories of emotion and motivation are closely related. Clearly, both emotion and motivation require a certain degree of activation, presumably mediated by the reticular activating system. Although many interrelated structures and physiological systems are involved in the regulation of emotion and motivation, we will focus our attention on limbic system involvement in emotion and on hypothalamic regulation of motivation. It is likely, for example, that the reactions of both the autonomic nervous system and the endocrine system are regulated by the limbic system. The hypothalamus —generally considered a portion of the limbic system—is believed to be critically involved as an integrative center for the coordination of numerous motivation states. In this section we will also review the interesting and important work on electrical self-stimulation of the brain, work which must be considered in any treatment of the physiological basis of emotion and motivation. Following a discussion of brain mechanisms in emotion and motivation, we will be in a better position to evaluate the utility of the concepts of emotion and motivation.

Limbic system structures and emotion

An anatomical circuit involving the limbic structures was first hypothesized by Papez (1937) in a highly theoretical and justly famous paper. Papez' original circuit consisted of the following principal structures: the hypothalamus, the anterior thalamic nuclei, the cingulate gyrus, the hippocampus, and their connections. This anatomical circuit, it was hypothesized, underlay emotional thought and expression. It was subsequently elaborated with the aid of some supporting data by others (Brady, 1960; MacLean, 1949; Pribram & Kruger, 1954). The exact contribution of each of these substructures to emotion (much less the even more complex interactions among them) is not well understood, but some facts are available. A representation of the limbic system is shown in Figure 8.9.

Hypothalamus

The hypothalamus, while subject to excitatory and inhibitory influences from other structures in the limbic system, appears to be central in organizing the components of emotional reactions. Several experiments involving lesions of various parts of the hypothalamus have demonstrated increases in rage and ferocity (Anand & Brobeck, 1951; Bard, 1928, 1934; Wheatley, 1944). Loss of emotional responsiveness and depression of general activity, however, have also been reported (Masserman, 1938, 1943; Ranson, 1939).

Studies employing electrical stimulation of various parts of the hypothalamus have produced both rage reactions (Hess & Brügger, 1943; Masserman, 1941) and aggressive responses (Hunsperger, 1956; Nakao, 1958), as well as flight and alarm reactions (Roberts, 1958a). The differences

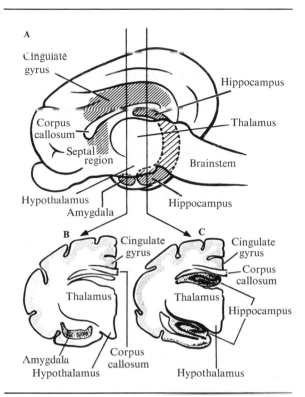

experiments involving lesions have demonstrated no emotional changes (Brady, 1958). Fear and rage reactions have been demonstrated from stimulation of both the hippocampus (MacLean & Delgado, 1953) and septal regions (Hess & Brügger, 1943).

Amygdala

Lesions in the amygdala have generally been shown to produce increased docility (e.g., Schreiner & Kling, 1953, 1956; Weiskrantz, 1956). On the other hand, some studies have failed to find changes in emotionality (Hunsperger, 1959; King, 1958), whereas still others have found drastic increases in aggression (Bard & Mountcastle, 1947; Wood, 1958).

Fear and rage in animals (Wood, 1958) and fear and anxiety in epileptics (Chapman, 1958) have been reported in studies involving stimulation of various nuclei. However, amygdaloid stimulation has also been shown to produce no emotional response (Jasper & Rasmussen, 1958), as well as reduced emotionality and decreased hostility (Egger & Flynn, 1963).

Thalamus

The dorsomedial and anterior nuclei of the thalamus connect with the granular cortex and cingulate gyrus, respectively. Ablations of the anterior nucleus have been shown to both increase the rage thresholds in cats (Schreiner, Rioch, Pechtel, & Masserman, 1953) and produce no effect (Brierley & Beck, 1958). Similarly, lesions in the dorsomedial nucleus have been demonstrated to reduce aggressiveness and anxiety in both animals and humans (Spiegel & Wycis, 1949), to produce no behavioral changes (Chow, 1954), and to increase irritability and rage (Schreiner et al., 1953).

Cingulate gyrus

Lesions and ablations in the cingulate gyrus have been shown to decrease fear reactions (Mirsky, Rosvold, & Pribram, 1957; Smith, 1944). Increased aggressiveness and general overreactivity have also been reported by some workers (Mirsky, et al., 1957).

Stimulation of the cingulate gyrus has been shown to produce convulsions, following by rage responses and somatic and autonomic reactions (Anand & Dua, 1955).

Figure 8.9 Schematic drawing of the limbic system (from a cat brain). The *cingulate gyrus* is the cortical portion of the limbic system lying just above the *corpus callosum*, which connects the two hemispheres of the brain and is not considered part of the limbic system. The principal components of the subcortical limbic system are the *septal region* (which includes the *medial forebrain bundle*, a large fiber tract connecting the septum and the hypothalamus), the *amygdala*, the *hippocampus*, and portions of the *hypothalamus* and *thalamus*. Panel A represents a medial view of the brain. Panels B and C are cross sections through the right side of the brain at the positions indicated by the vertical lines in panel A. (From McCleary & Moore, 1965.)

in these results may be due in part to the locus of the hypothalamic lesions or to the sites of stimulation.

Septum and hippocampus

Septal lesions have been shown to produce increases in emotionality (Brady & Nauta, 1953) and lowered rage thresholds in decorticated cats (Rothfield & Harmon, 1954). Nonetheless, other

Temporal lobe

Bilateral temporal lobectomy has been shown to produce a complex of behavioral changes called, collectively, the Kluver and Bucy syndrome which includes the loss of fear and rage reactions (Kluver & Bucy, 1937). Temporal ablations in human patients have produced variable results, ranging from decreased aggressiveness (Green, Duisberg, & McGrath, 1951) to postoperative increases in rage (Sawa, Ueki, Arita, & Harada, 1954).

Stimulation has evoked increases in emotionality (irritability and viciousness) in animals (Anand & Dua, 1955). On the other hand, epileptics have reported feelings of fear upon stimulation of parts of the temporal lobe (Penfield, 1958; Penfield & Jasper, 1954).

Conclusion

A more complete account of such findings is available in the standard texts on physiological psychology (e.g., Deutsch & Deutsch, 1966). But these sample data allow drawing the necessary conclusion relevant to the psychology of emotion: While the limbic system structures do appear to be implicated in emotion, the precise nature of the implication is poorly understood. One reason for the disparate results in the effects of lesions may be anatomical differences within and between the animals studied, as well as inadvertent damage to other structures. One of the difficulties in the studies involving stimulation is that different intensities of stimulation may produce different results even though the locus of stimulation is kept constant. Moreover, de Molina and Hunsperger (1959) have noted that individual differences in experimental organisms may affect the type of emotional response given to a particular stimulation.

Self-stimulation studies

The milestone work by Olds and his associates (e.g., Olds & Milner, 1954; Olds & Olds, 1961) has shown that rats will learn a response such as a bar-press in order to electrically self-stimulate certain areas of their own brains, for example, the medial forebrain bundle, a large tract of fibers that connects the septum with the hypothalamus. Differences in the rates of bar-pressing seem to be dependent on the location of the tip of the stimulating electrode. Olds defines rewarding and punishing electrode placements with reference to the operant level of responding, the amount of time spent responding when no reinforcement is provided. A rewarding placement, then, is one in which the animal will respond significantly more often; when the animal responds less often than the operant level, the electrode location is defined as a punishing location. Using this technique, Olds and his associates have reported particularly high scores for self-stimulation in several areas of the limbic system.

A rat responding to obtain intracranial self-stimulation in certain areas of the septal region is not necessarily doing so because of pleasurable qualities of such stimulation. Studies employing human patients (e.g., Heath, 1963), however, are illuminating in this respect. Verbal reports of some of these patients indicate that stimulation at certain points of the brain is indeed "pleasant," a sort of emotional reinforcement.

ICS and motivation

Intracranial self-stimulation (ICS) may also have important implications for the concept of motivation. Two different approaches to motivation are represented within the framework of research on ICS. In one, responding for ICS is taken as the behavioral representation of the direct stimulation of a neuroanatomical locus of reward. In this view ICS reflects motivation only to the extent that the processes of motivation and reward are interrelated. The other approach assumes that ICS manifests drivelike motivational properties in addition to properties generally ascribed to the concept of reward. The many investigations that have followed Olds' initial demonstration of ICS (Olds & Milner, 1954) have been generated by one or the other of these two approaches.

With certain electrode placements, a rat will press a bar as rapidly as 2000 to 7000 times per hour for as long as 24 hours at a time when each response results in the delivery of a brief electrical stimulus to the brain (Olds, 1958; Olds & Milner, 1954). The most salient characteristics of the phenomenon are the very high response rates maintained, the seeming insatiability of the reward (Valenstein & Beer, 1964), and the broad distribution of electrode placements in which stimulation sustains responding (Olds, 1956). Of all the regions in which stimulation maintains responding, the highest self-stimulation rates, and those which are most resistant to satiation, result from stimulation of the medial forebrain bundle–lateral hypothalamic area of the diencephalon (Olds, 1956; Olds & Olds, 1964).

Lesion studies indicate, however, that neither these areas nor any other discrete diencephalic area are essential for the occurrence of the phenomenon (Valenstein, 1966). Moreover, *ICS* continues unabated after the prevention of peripheral sensory feedback from visceral organs, accomplished by the interruption of outflow from all of the sympathetic division and most of the parasympathetic division of the autonomic nervous system (Ward & Hester, 1969). These findings, in conjunction with reports that rats will withstand painful electric shocks (Olds, 1955) or pass up food when hungry (Routtenberg & Lindy, 1965) in order to gain *ICS*, suggest that pleasure circuits are being stimulated and that *ICS* reflects the anatomical locus of reward.

Subsequent research, however, has pointed out several important differences between behavioral measures reflecting brain stimulation reward and those associated with more conventional rewards such as food or water (Deutsch & Deutsch, 1966). Among these are the extremely high response rates maintained by *ICS* and the animal's insatiability with certain electrode placements. In addition, despite the apparent highly rewarding quality of stimulation, rats seem to "lose interest" as soon as the current is terminated. Reflecting this loss of interest are early findings reporting the difficulty of maintaining responding for *ICS* on ratio and interval schedules of low reinforcement density (Sidman, Brady, Boren, Conrad, & Schulman, 1955); response decrements seen on the first of a series of daily trials and the consequent need for *priming* the animal with free stimulation to overcome the effects of these decrements (Olds, 1956; Wetzel, 1963); the difficulty associated with trying to establish secondary reinforcement using brain stimulation as the primary reward (Mogenson, 1965; Seward, Uyeda, & Olds, 1959; see also Chapter 5); and the rapidity with which responding maintained by *ICS* will subsequently extinguish (Howarth & Deutsch, 1962).

Largely on the basis of these differences, Deutsch (Deutsch & Howarth, 1963) has proposed that, unlike more conventional rewards, the electrical stimulus involved in *ICS* stimulates neural pathways mediating motivation or drive, as well as those mediating reward. Each current pulse simultaneously rewards the preceding response while motivating subsequent ones. Cessation of responding constitutes cessation of drive as well, and responding drops off accordingly. It is this rapid *drive decay* which accounts for the self-stimulator's quick loss of interest in the absence of stimulation.

Moreover, because *ICS* motivates as well as rewards the organism, brain stimulation reward is essentially different from more conventional forms of reward which provide no concomitant drive effects.

In support of this position, Howarth and Deutsch (1962) found that responding in extinction after training with *ICS* is a simple function of time since the last current pulse, and that it is independent of the number of unreinforced responses. The greater the amount of time since the last electrical stimulus, the greater the drive decay, and therefore the fewer responses occurring in extinction. Moreover, externally imposed deprivation states such as hunger and thirst are sufficient to prolong responding in extinction following brain stimulation reward (Deutsch & DiCara, 1967).

If two different neural elements, one underlying reward and the other underlying motivation, are in fact involved in *ICS*, it should be possible to distinguish between them on the basis of their distinctive neurophysiological properties. In support of this assumption several investigators (Deutsch, 1964; Gallistel, Rolls, & Greene, 1969) have measured what are presumed to be differing neural refractory periods for the two sets of pathways. Experiments on the effects of priming also reflect the independent motivational properties of *ICS*. Gallistel (1969) has shown that different amounts of priming presented prior to testing trials in a straight runway differentially affect *ICS* extinction responding. The aftereffect of one prime lasted no longer than 1 minute, whereas the effect of 20 primes had not dissipated even after 10 minutes.

The alternative approach to *ICS* argues that the apparent differences between *ICS* and more conventional rewards do not reflect any basic difference in the underlying mechanism of reward, but rather are attributable simply to differences in the response topographies involved in acquiring the reward. An animal receiving conventional reward typically engages in much more responding in the actual acquisition of the reward. Making the response topographies more congruent effectively dissolves many of the initially described differences. For example, Pliskoff, Wright, and Hawkins (1965) showed that responding for *ICS* can be maintained on intermittent schedules of reinforcement comparable to those ordinarily employed with food reward. They used a chaining procedure in which the *ICS* lever was retracted after 20 reinforced bar-presses for *ICS* (referred to as *CRF 20*). Responding on a second permanently available lever effectively reintroduced the *ICS* lever, and, therefore, the opportunity to self-stimulate. Performance characteristic of many different schedules of reinforcement, including *FI* 5-minutes, *FR*-65, and *DRL* 2-minutes, was maintained on the permanent lever when reinforced by access to the retractable *ICS* lever. Pliskoff et al. (1965) view this procedure as a simulation of the *consummatory chain* naturally involved in the receipt of food reward, thus rendering response topographies associated with the two kinds of reward more comparable. The addition to the *ICS* paradigm of sources of conditioned reinforcement (e.g., sound of the lever retracting, proprioceptive feedback generated by the second lever-press, etc.) normally present in some form with conventional reinforcers further supports this comparison. Pliskoff et al. conclude that "as more attention is given to the methodological aspects of *BSR* (brain stimulation reward), the need to postulate special porperties for *BSR* will begin to diminish accordingly" [p. 87]. It should be noted, however, that the *CRF* link in the chain may constitute a "self-priming" procedure in which the aftereffects of *CRF* priming facilitate responding on the permanent lever in much the same way as priming has been shown to sustain runway performance.

Extending the analogy between a succession of continuously reinforced lever-presses and the consummatory chain associated with food reward, Pliskoff and Hawkins (1967) have shown that variations in the number of *CRF* presses allowed on the *ICS* lever constitutes a variable analogous in many respects to the conventional variable of reinforcement magnitude. Further demonstrating the similarities between *ICS* and more conventional reward, Huston (1967) has used a *reinforcement reduction* method of training ratio responding for *ICS*. Rats were maintained on *FR*-50 schedules of reinforcement by gradually reducing the magnitude of reinforcement received on *CRF* for all but the terminal response in the ratio chain. Behavior was maintained on *FR*-50 even when the current made contingent on each of the first 49 responses was of subreinforcement magnitude. Huston suggests that the subreinforcement magnitude stimulation may have acquired the properties of a conditioned reinforcer.

Tests of many of the other initially recognized differences among rewards have also yielded negative evidence. Kornblith and Olds (1968) found neither performance decrement nor drive decay with long intervals between trials, and were even able to train rats to run a T-maze for *ICS* reward using a procedure which involved only one trial per day. Simi-

larly, when delivered under conditions more like those normally prevailing in *ICS*, conventional rewards yield responding more characteristic of that seen with *ICS* (Gibson, Reid, Sakai, & Porter, 1965).

On the basis of these findings it is not clear whether or not *ICS* has motivational properties that distinguish it from other rewards. Kent and Grossman's (1969) findings suggest that this issue may be improperly drawn due to the complexities of the concept of motivation. Their results indicate that there is no simple *ICS* effect. They first found that some of their experimental animals required daily priming before they would respond for *ICS*, while others did not. Animals which required priming showed evidence that the stimulation had aversive consequences in addition to rewarding ones. Though they bar-pressed to receive stimulation, the "primers" were also observed to squeal and cringe during stimulation. Some even exhibited *coordinated escape behavior* subsequent to a burst of stimulation. In contrast, animals which did not require priming gave no evidence of an aversive component to *ICS*. Brief periods of enforced nonresponding by removal of the lever had no effect on rats which did not require priming, but significantly increased latencies to respond in rats requiring priming. Finally, significant satiation effects were seen over a 2-hour period of continuous responding in rats requiring priming, but were not observed in the nonpriming animals.

Rats which had never required priming were then given tail-shock coupled with each delivery of brain stimulation reward. Following 10 days of training under these conditions the animals engaged in behavior previously seen only in the rats that had originally required priming. Included among the newly observed behavioral characteristics were increases in latencies to respond following lever removal, vocalization, and the general tendency to require priming at the beginning of a session. Thus when external aversive stimulation was added to *ICS*, the nonprimer's behavior became similar to that of the primers for whom the *ICS* itself presumably included an aversive component.

Kent and Grossman (1969) propose that many different patterns of *ICS* responding are possible, depending largely on electrode placements. Animals which initially required priming are those in which brain stimulation has concurrent rewarding and punishing effects. The resulting conflict situation which is produced in these animals produces in turn the priming requirement, the tendency to satiate, and the other behaviors described. The suggestion that *ICS* has both positive and negative properties is not a new one (Bower & Miller, 1958; Roberts, 1958b) and is substantiated by the finding that subjects which have responded to obtain *ICS* will also respond to terminate it.

The hypothalamus and motivation

Research on the physiology of motivation over the past three decades has placed recurrent emphasis on the importance of the hypothalamus as an integrative center for the coordination of motivational states. Using such techniques as the electrical stimulation and lesioning of discrete hypothalamic regions, behavior associated with each of the normally recognized biological drives can be drastically altered. Included among the list of affected behaviors are those associated with hunger, thirst, sex, sleep, defense, temperature regulation, and many others.

Nowhere are the extent and complexity of this integrative control more evident than in the hypothalamic regulation of eating and drinking. As early as the turn of the century it was suspected that some neural mechanisms were involved in the stimulation of appetite. Not until much later, however, were the effects demonstrated to be specific to the hypothalamus. Hetherington and Ranson (1940) first successfully lesioned the hypothalamus without damaging the pituitary gland. With lesions placed in the ventromedial nucleus of the hypothalamus, animals became extremely obese and often maintained weights three to four times their normal free-feeding weights. Because the immediate effect of the lesion was the production of overeating, the phenomenon was termed hypothalamic hyperphagia (Brobeck, 1946). Long-term study of hyperphagic animals (Balagura & Devenport, 1970; Brobeck, Tepperman, & Long, 1943) has revealed distinct stages of overeating. The preliminary dynamic phase, an active phase of overeating with continual weight gain, may last as long as three months. This is followed by a static phase during which the hyperphagic animals eat no more than that amount required to maintain the abnormally high stable weight. If, during the static phase, the animals are starved to their normal preoperative levels, hyperphagia resumes with refeeding and continues until the elevated plateau is again reached.

Several peculiarities of the eating behavior of chronically hyperphagic rats serve to clarify the role of the ventromedial nucleus. Miller, Bailey, and Stevenson (1950) have shown that having reached the static phase, the hyperphagic rat eats only if food is readily available. These animals will not work (e.g., press a bar, lift a weight, tolerate shock, etc.) in order to obtain food. They also more quickly reject food adulterated with quinine, indicating unusual sensitivity to the qualitative aspects of food. When placed on food deprivation, static hyperphagics show none of the hyperactivity common in normal rats on food deprivation (Teitelbaum, 1957). These findings suggest that the ventromedial nucleus normally functions not as a drive center, but as a satiety center which brings about the cessation of eating. When this area is destroyed by lesioning, overeating results not because the animals are abnormally hungry, but because they are unable to stop eating.

The function of the ventromedial nucleus may be more dependent on the action of other factors than was originally assumed. This is suggested by recent data on metabolic and regulatory changes (Han, 1967; May & Beaton, 1966; Sétáló, 1965) and the possible roles played by sex differences and circadian rhythms in determining the effectiveness of the ventromedial lesion (Balagura & Devenport, 1970; Cox, Kakolewski, & Valenstein, 1969; Gold, 1970; Rehovsky & Wampler, 1972). Falk (1961) has presented data which suggest that in addition to altering the cessation of eating, the lesions may also affect actual food motivation at least during the dynamic phase of hyperphagia.

Perhaps most perplexing are the anomalies that arise when different techniques are employed to produce the lesions. Parasagittal hypothalamic knife cuts, which produce hypothalamic hyperphagia similar in all respects to that produced by more conventional means, are effective when placed in areas that do not coincide with the location of any well-defined nucleus or fiber tract (Gold, 1970). Similarly, several investigators (Rabin & Smith, 1968; Reynolds, 1963) report that hypothalamic hyperphagia occurs reliably only when lesions produce iron deposits in the brain, as is the case with the most frequently used electrolytic lesions. Reynolds (1963) has shown that radio frequency lesions which minimize iron deposits have no reliable effect on male rats. These findings raise the possibility that the effects on eating are specific not to the ventromedial nucleus, but to the irritation produced by iron deposits. That this is not the case is suggested by the successful production of hypothalamic hyperphagia with suction lesions (Pool, 1967) and with lesions made with platinum irridium electrodes (Teitelbaum, 1955). It may be that irritation, though not necessary to produce hyperphagia, results in greater weight gains (Gold, 1970).

That the hypothalamus plays an equally complex role in the motivation or initiation—as opposed to termination—of eating was first shown by Anand and Brobeck (1951a). Bilateral lesions in the lateral hypothalamus produce total aphagia in rats and cats; that is, all animals starve to death in the presence of food. In addition to aphagia, a marked adipsia (absence of drinking) also occurs following lesions of the lateral hypothalamic area (Montemurro & Stevenson, 1957; Teitelbaum & Stellar, 1954). Stimulation of the lateral hypothalamus (Delgado & Anand, 1953; Miller, 1957) results in marked increases in food intake in the 24-hour period following stimulation. This occurs even in satiated animals. On the basis of such findings, Anand and Brobeck (1951a) have postulated the existence of a *feeding center* in the lateral hypothalamus which corresponds to the *satiety center* located in the ventromedial nucleus. When animals are given lesions in both of these areas, the effects are the same as those produced by the lateral lesions alone; e.g., the animal becomes aphagic, adipsic, and eventually dies (Anand & Brobeck, 1951b). This suggests that the normal action of these mechanisms involves the inhibition of the lateral hypothalamus by the ventromedial nucleus such that the ventromedial "regulator" after a time turns off the appetite which has resulted from lateral hypothalamic activity.

The effects of lateral hypothalamic lesions may be the result of metabolic impairment. For example, Morgane (1961) has reported that animals with lateral hypothalamic lesions do not recover even after gastric intubation with food, water, or both. Similarly, Stevenson and Montemurro (1963) found that laterally lesioned rats decreased food intake, lost weight, and died even in the face of administration of nutrients and water directly into the stomach. It is as if the animals are unable to metabolize the food for nutritional purposes even though it has been ingested. This approach, however, does not explain why animals do not try to take in food at least for a short time immediately after the lesion.

Long-term investigation of the nature of the neural deficits produced by lateral hypothalamic lesions indicates that the effects are not permanent. If kept alive, initially lesioned animals will recover (Teitelbaum & Stellar, 1954). Teitelbaum and Epstein (1962) have found that not only will adipsic-aphagic animals recover, but that the recovery follows a regular and stable course, dependent to some extent on the location and size of the lesion. Animals displaying what has come to be called the *lateral hypothalamic recovery syndrome* progress through a series of stages which, according to Teitelbaum and Epstein, reflect the regulatory as well as motivational deficits produced by the lesion. Stage I is the stage of adipsia plus aphagia. Animals refuse all forms of food as well as water and will starve if they are not forcibly fed. If food is placed in the animals' mouths they spit it out. During stage II, adipsia-anorexia, the animals eat wet palatable foods, although intragastric supplements must be continued in order to sustain life. Water is still completely refused, as are dry foods. In the third stage, adipsia–dehydration aphagia, animals will regulate their caloric intake of wet palatable foods, but will eat dry foods only if artificially hydrated by intragastric injections. They will drink no water, and in the absence of hydration, no dry food is eaten. In this stage the aphagia seems to be produced by the adipsia. Stage IV is the recovery stage. Recovered animals will drink water and regulate caloric intake of even dry foods. Body weights return to normal levels, and, at least superficially, the subjects appear recovered. Closer inspection reveals, however, that subtle differences still exist between "recovered" lateral hypothalamic animals and normal rats (Epstein & Teitelbaum, 1967; Teitelbaum, 1961; Teitelbaum & Epstein, 1962). Recovered animals will not regulate their water intake in response to dehydration produced, for example, by intragastric injections of hypertonic saline or exposure to high ambient temperatures. These rats also engage only in prandial drinking, i.e., they drink only when they eat, and therefore will not drink at all if food is removed. Eating behavior is also abnormal. Recovered animals are hypersensitive to the gustatory and textural qualities of food. They will starve to death in the presence of food containing very small amounts of quinine. Unlike the case with normal rats, injection of insulin sufficient to produce hypoglycemia does not result in increased food intake in recovered lateral hypothalamic animals. Teitelbaum has suggested that these subtle differences reflect chronic motivational deficits which remain even after metabolic function appears normal.

Attempts have been made to explain the recovery syndrome as a process of reencephalization of the neural control of behavior which for a time is relegated by the lesion to subcortical areas (Teitelbaum, Cheng, & Rozin, 1969b). This explanation is supported by the description of similarities between the development of feeding and regulation in weanling rats and the recovery occurring in the lateral hypothalamic syndrome. Thyroidectomized weanling rats, tested first at 21 days of age, displayed every stage of the lateral hypothalamic syndrome (Teitelbaum, Cheng, & Rozin, 1969a). The particular stage exhibited seemed dependent on the degree of retardation produced by thyroidectomy. For example, rats displaying the least retardation, and therefore the most advanced stage of development, immediately accepted dry food and engaged in prandial drinking. These "stage IV weanlings" also exhibited all of the subtle deficits in eating and drinking characteristic of recovered lateral hypothalamic adults. Several of the more retarded weanlings proceeded to progress slowly through the remaining stages of the syndrome. In effect, all of the consummatory deficits produced in adults by lateral hypothalamic lesions were measured in the retarded development of infants. The effects are not specific to the thyroidectomy, which was used initially solely to facilitate measurement of the rapid developmental process. Development following retardation by neonatal starvation (Cheng, Rozin, & Teitelbaum, 1971) parallels the stages of the lateral hypothalamic syndrome in a way very similar to that seen with thyroidectomy-induced retardation. Teitelbaum, (1971) maintains that the appearance of sequential stages in the infant reflects the growth and differentiation of nerve cells and the process of encephalization normally occurring immediately after birth. The lateral hypothalamic syndrome seen in lesioned adults, therefore, is the functional manifestation of the reencephalization of neural function which follows lesioning.

Presenting an alternative view, DiCara (1970) has investigated the effects of postoperative learning experience on successful recovery. Animals that had been tube fed with milk postoperatively and received preoperative feeding experience only with lab chow exhibited almost total aphagia when tested at 6 and 12 days following lesioning. In contrast, animals receiving pre- and postoperative experience feeding under conditions similar to those prevailing during the test, when given the opportunity to ingest milk from a metal spout, ingested as much as 50 percent of the amount eaten by operated controls receiving no lesions. The quality of both pre- and postoperative feeding experience seemed to affect the pattern of recovery seen in the lateral hypothalamic syndrome. It should be noted, however, that unlike most instances of the lateral hypothalamic syndrome, in this experiment adipsia was never reported in any of the lesioned animals.

Other nonneural factors affecting the pattern of lateral hypothalamic recovery have been reported. Powley and Keesey (1970), for example, have found that preoperative reductions in body weight greatly decrease the duration of postlesion periods of adipsia-aphagia and can actually produce postlesion hyperphagia. Similarly, feeding and drinking elicited by electrical stimulation of the lateral hypothalamic areas is correspondingly affected by additional factors. Preloading the animal with food decreases the amount of eating elicited by electrical stimulation, while preloading with water has no effect on eating, but decreases the amount of electrically stimulated drinking (Devor, Wise, Milgram, & Hoebel, 1970).

Such findings underscore the notion that in spite of the dramatic behavioral effects produced by the appropriate neural manipulations, motivation cannot be placed entirely within the hypothalamus. The concept must instead be taken to refer to the combined effects of the total stimulus configuration determining an organism's behavior at a given moment. That this is generally the case can be revealed by close inspection of the hypothalamic regulation of any neurally elicited behavior. Sexual behavior, for example, is profoundly affected by alterations in hypothalamic activity. Since both neural and hormonal correlates of sexual behavior are integrated at the hypothalamic level, hypothalamic lesions can abolish sexual behavior either directly or indirectly by damaging hypothalamic control of the pituitary gland. The latter effects are reversible by means of compensative hormone treatment. The former, however, produced by lesions in portions of the anterior hypothalamus, are permanent and unaffected by hormone administration. Either electrical or chemical stimulation of the same region in male rats produces increases in sexual behavior (Milner, 1970). As is the case with the hypothalamic regulation of eating, however, the effects on sexual behavior can not be considered in isolation. Madlafousek, Freund, and Grofová (1970), for example, report that prestimulation individual differences in the tendency to copulate in part determine the effectiveness of stimulation of the lateral preoptic area on the facilitation of sexual behavior.

The view that the hypothalamus cannot be considered the ultimate source of motivation in isolation from other variables has recently been formally reemphasized by Valenstein and his coworkers (Valenstein, Cox, & Kakolewksi, 1970).

These authors challenge the once widely held position that discrete hypothalamic areas underlie particular motivational states. Rather than evoking a specific motivational state, such as hunger, hypothalamic stimulation provides a general substrate of neural excitation. This sensitized substrate then becomes, in a sense, molded into particular behavioral patterns only as it interacts with the organism's species-specific response repertoire and the prevailing external environmental conditions. In this view, it then becomes meaningless to assert that the elicited behavior is maintained by the satisfaction of a stimulated drive state. The organism is motivated not by the opportunity to remove the aversive consequences of a biological state, but rather by the interaction of external and internal factors.

Several lines of research support the foregoing position. For example, many different forms of behavior can be elicited by stimulation of a particular area of the hypothalamus. Moreover, responses evoked by such stimulation can be modified without any change in the stimulus parameters (Valenstein, Cox, & Kakolewski, 1968). The same electrical stimulus which elicited eating when food was present resulted in drinking or wood gnawing when water or woodchips were available in the absence of food. Some hypothalamically elicited behaviors are, in fact, not representative of typically recognized drive states. One animal, for example, consistently picked up the end of its tail and moved it laterally into its mouth. When the tail was fastened to the animal's back, subsequent hypothalamic stimulation with identical current parameters elicited drinking (Valenstein, Cox, & Kakolewski, 1970). Valenstein et al. (1970) conclude that the particular behavior that occurs in correlation with hypothalamic stimulation is a function also of prepotent characteristics of the animal's behavioral repertoire and the prevailing external environmental conditions. Perhaps of least importance is the particular neuroanatomical site of stimulation.

EMOTION AND MOTIVATION: CONCEPTUAL ISSUES

In this section we will attempt to assess the utility of the concepts of emotion and motivation. The previous section challenged the widely held position that discrete hypothalamic areas underlie particular motivational states. Rather than evoking a specific motivational state, hypothalamic stimulation provides a general substrate of neural excita-

tion. What happens to the excitation depends critically on the prevailing external environmental conditions. Similar conclusions about motivation can be drawn at a more behavioral level. For example, the presumed reinforcing effects of brain stimulation depend critically on the particular schedule on which the stimulation is programmed. It was noted in the section on self-stimulation that the same stimulation which appeared highly reinforcing when programmed on *CRF* would not maintain responding on schedules of intermittent reinforcement.

Just as the schedule of reinforcement dictates in part the reinforcing effect of particular brain stimulation, so it helps determine how reinforcing food is, say to a hyperphagic rat. For example, Miller, Bailey, and Stevenson (1950) showed that while hyperphagic rats would eat voraciously when food was readily available, they would not press a bar to obtain food. These examples indicate that the effects of presumed motivating or reinforcing operations depend on parameters of the situation in which they are measured. To this extent, it is difficult to identify a particular behavioral effect with a motivational state of the organism. We reached the same conclusion with respect to emotion when discussing anxiety earlier.

The area of *specific hungers* is one which for years served as a classic example of particular motivational states leading to specific behavioral effects. Specific hungers illustrate the interplay of structural and environmental factors in the determination of behavior. Organisms generally develop hungers (or *subhungers*) for a deficient substance. It is convenient to assume that the bodily deficiency sets up a corresponding motivational state or drive which directs behavior toward relieving the deficiency. It was thought that the organism learned to prefer the tastes associated with recovery from the deficiency. One problem with this interpretation is that the deficiency is often not immediately remedied by ingestion of the appropriate food. It is unclear, therefore, how the system is equipped to associate recovery from the deficiency with the ingestion of the responsible food. Rozin and Kalat (1971) report a series of experiments with thiamine deficiency pointing to the conclusion that organisms do not learn to seek out foods that rectify deficiencies, but simply learn an aversion to the deficient food. They gave rats a choice of three foods: a new food that the rat had never tasted; a food that the rat had been ingesting during its deficiency (the thiamine-deficient food); and the third food which was an old familiar nondeficient food (a food that the animal had frequently ingested prior to the introduction of the thiamine-deficient regimen). These three foods may be called *new, deficient familiar*, and *safe familiar*, respectively. Rozin found that the rats preferred the familiar safe food over the new food and actively shunned the deficient food. On the basis of this and other findings, Rozin was able to conclude that the rats had developed an aversion for the deficient food. It should be stressed that it is immaterial which food actually had thiamine when rats were initially exposed to the test situation; they would still prefer the familiar safe food (even though it lacked the deficient substance), and still avoid the familiar deficient food (even if it now contained thiamine). In other words, the rats were not *thiamine-sensors*.

Thus recent research complicates the traditional view of subhungers as a (motivational) response to a physiological deficiency. Certainly, there is a complex and intriguing interaction between physiological factors associated with the deficiency and the properties of the ingested food. But whatever the factors that result in learned aversions for deficient foods, they do not appear to be an instinctual seeking-out of food to relieve a deficiency as had been previously assumed. As our knowledge of the factors controlling specific hungers increases, our conception of deficiencies as motivational states becomes increasingly unnecessary.

Motivational concepts in general, and hunger in particular, seem to be invoked most frequently in reference to phenomena that are poorly understood. In a sense motivation shares this characteristic with the concepts of emotion and instinct (see Chapter 9). Consider the case of food regulation in the blowfly (Dethier, 1969). Prior to the work of Dethier and Bodenstein (1958) showing that hunger in the blowfly could be equated with absence of stimulation from the fly's recurrent nerve, it was tempting to label the fly's food regulation as instinctive. Once the mechanism of food regulation was specified in concrete physiological terms, however, reliance on such concepts as instinct and motivation seemed less appropriate.

A similar picture emerges from the review of the theoretical and empirical underpinnings of emotion. The term *emotion,* too, is a rather amorphous one that has been used very differently by various psychologists. Not only is there no generally accepted definition of the term, but most definitions are imprecise, particularly when they attempt to fit the layman's conception. Moreover, no matter how precisely defined, the term runs the risk of being misinterpreted since it invariably conveys unintended meanings. Theories of emotion are plagued not only by the problem of definition but also by the problem of measurement, due largely to ignorance concerning the physiological factors affecting emotional behavior.

Evidence has been reviewed in this chapter indicating that emotional behavior involves the activation of both the sympathetic nervous system and the reticular activating system, and that stimulus situations determine the precise form that the behavior takes once activated. We have speculated that limbic system structures are involved in determining which emotion occurs. The physiological evidence supporting these implications is quite contradictory, however, as to the locus controlling specific emotional behaviors. Most emotional behaviors have important learned components that vary across different cultures. In general, it appears that emotional behavior is so complexly determined that a consistent characterization is at present elusive. It would appear, then, that little is gained by retaining the concept of emotion in psychology. In this respect, then, this author is in agreement with previous workers, such as Duffy, who have advocated abandonment of the term.

While the concepts of emotion and motivation tend to confuse more than to aid in the experimental analysis of behavior, the behaviors to which these terms have been traditionally applied are certainly worthy of analysis. Much of the research summarized in this chapter indicates that the analysis is being intensively undertaken by scores of experimental psychologists. The more our knowledge is enhanced about behaviors that are presently referred to as emotional or motivational, the better grasp we will have of variables controlling such behaviors, and the less need we will have for the labels *emotion* and *motivation* themselves.

SUMMARY AND CONCLUSIONS

A survey of definitions of emotion indicates a profound lack of agreement on what emotions are. While most current approaches to emotional behavior deal with it at either the behavioral or the physiological level, two traditional approaches—structuralist and dynamic theories—are also discussed. Both rely on the individual's ability to report subjective events, or the contents of consciousness. With the growth of behaviorism and the concomitant growth in the idea that psychology should be an objective rather than a subjective science, both approaches lost appeal. Physiological theorists attempt to identify emotions with their physiological concomitants. Special stress is given to the physiological approach in the section on brain mechanisms in emotion and motivation. A (nonphysiological) behaviorist approach to emotion is to study emotional behavior rather than emotion in and of itself. The behaviorists insist on utilizing strict operational criteria in the study and measurement of emotional behavior, which they say should be studied in the same way as behavior in general. Fruits of both the physiological and behavioral approaches are discussed throughout the chapter.

Measurement of emotion stresses physiological measures such as electrical skin conductance, blood volume, blood pressure, respiration, pulse rate, skin temperature, pilomotor response, eyeblink, tremor, and brain waves, as well as research on facial expressions.

Three major theories of emotion are considered before discussing the current status of theories of emotion. Young's hedonistic theory of emotion is limited by being overly specific, so that it makes little contact with work being done in other areas of emotion. The James-Lange theory of emotion states that emotion is the result rather than the cause of the bodily reactions associated with an emotion; in other words, the emotional response precedes the emotional experience. The James-Lange theory is important in being one of the first to identify emotion as a physiological event. The James-Lange theory has a modern descendant in Gellhorn's theory of emotion.

Activation theories of emotion refer to the view that emotion represents a state of heightened arousal rather than a qualitatively unique type of psychological, physiological, or behavioral process. Arousal can be considered to lie on a continuum that extends from states of quiescence, such as deep sleep, to extremely agitated states, such as rage or anger. In a sense it is misleading to call activation theory a theory of emotion at all. Although there are certainly differences among them, the typical activation theorist equates emotion with a state of arousal. Once this is done there is no longer much need to retain the term *emotion,* as one activation theorist (Duffy) has argued. Influential activation theories of emotion include the Cannon-Bard theory of emotion, which holds that the conscious correlate of emotion is the result of an upward discharge to the cerebral cortex from the thalamus. Like the James-Lange theory, the Cannon-Bard theory suffered from the difficulty of

trying to pinpoint the determinants of conscious experience. Cannon's theory was important in stressing that emotions serve an emergency function by preparing the organism for appropriate action. A modern activation theorist, Hebb, has been particularly concerned with the relation between activation and the efficiency of behavior. Hebb argues that there is a curvilinear relation between activation and behavioral efficiency. Similarly, others have argued that the relation between level of motivation and problem-solving ability is curvilinear. Behavioral evidence for this Yerkes-Dodson law of motivation is weak. Finally, Lindsley's activation theory of emotion has provided important research on one physiological correlate of most emotional behavior—the activation pattern of the *EEG* that can be reproduced by appropriate electrical stimulation of brain structures, especially in the brain stem reticular formation.

A viable current theory of emotion is that developed by Schachter and Mandler which suggests, first of all, that activation—whether from social situations, from drugs, or from other stimuli—is probably necessary but not sufficient for emotional behavior. The activation by itself does not produce emotional behavior; rather, these internal cues are apparently modulated by stimuli (including social stimuli) into the totality of a particular emotion. Given sufficient activation, a stimulus situation may generate a given emotion, with probable mediation through limbic system structures.

The investigation of emotion has stressed its development as well as learned and cultural factors that are implicated in its expression. The experimental analysis of anxiety is discussed at some length, since it provides a prototype of behaviorist research in the area of emotion. It is concluded that while the term *anxiety* (and the more general phrase *emotional behavior*) in fact refers to real changes in responding correlated with various operations, the term does not seem to be particularly useful. Indeed, insofar as there will almost inevitably be a tendency to equate the changes in responding with conceptions held by laymen, such terms may actually hinder the analysis of behavior. Research in aggressive behavior is also discussed, including recent work on mouse-killing in rats.

The physiological approach to emotion has stressed the autonomic nervous system with a particular emphasis on the involvement of brain mechanisms. The most striking conclusion drawn from a survey of limbic system structures is that while they do appear implicated in emotion, the precise nature of their involvement is poorly understood. One reason for the disparate results in the effects of lesions may be anatomical differences within and among the animals studied, as well as inadvertent damage to other structures. One of the difficulties in studies involving stimulation is that different intensities of stimulation may produce different results even though the locus of stimulation is kept constant.

Studies of self-stimulation of limbic system structures indicate that rats will learn responses such as bar-pressing in order to electrically self-stimulate certain areas of the brain. Other electrode placements produce punishing results. Research in self-stimulation also raises the possibility that the stimulation may have motivating as well as reinforcing properties.

Research on the physiology of motivation has placed recurrent emphasis on the importance of the hypothalamus as an integrative system for the coordination of motivational states. Recent research indicates, however, that rather than evoking a specific motivational state, such as hunger, hypothalamic stimulation provides a general substrate of neural excitation. This sensitized substrate then becomes molded into particular behavioral patterns only as it interacts with the organism's species-specific response repertoire and the prevailing external environmental conditions.

It is concluded that concepts such as emotion and motivation are invoked most frequently when dealing with phenomena that are poorly understood. While the concepts of emotion and motivation tend to confuse more than to aid in the experimental analysis of behavior, the behaviors to which these terms have been traditionally applied are certainly worthy of analysis.

REFERENCES

Anand, B. K., & Dua, S. Stimulation of limbic system of brain in waking animals. *Science*, 1955, **122**, 1139.

Anand, B. K., & Brobeck, J. R. Localization of a "feeding center" in the hypothalamus of the rat. *Proceedings of the Society for Experimental Biology and Medicine*, 1951, **77**, 323–324. (a)

Anand, B. K., & Brobeck, J. R. Hypothalamic control of food intake in rats and cats. *Yale Journal of Biology and Medicine*, 1951, **24**, 123–140. (b)

Annau, Z., & Kamin, L. J. The conditioned emotional response as a function of intensity of the US. *Journal of Comparative and Physiological Psychology*, 1961, **54**, 428–432.

Ax, A. F. The physiological differentiation between fear and anger in humans. *Psychosomatic Medicine*, 1953, **15**, 433–442.

Azrin, N. H., & Hake, D. F. Positive conditioned suppression: Conditioned suppression using positive reinforcers as the unconditioned stimuli. *Journal of the Experimental Analysis of Behavior*, 1969, **12**, 167–173.

Azrin, N. H., Hutchinson, R. R., & Hake, D. F. Extinction-induced aggression. *Journal of the Experimental Analysis of Behavior*, 1966, **9**, 191–204.

Azrin, N. H., Hutchinson, R. R., & Hake, D. F. Attack, avoidance, and escape reactions to aversive shock. *Journal of the Experimental Analysis of Behavior*, 1967, **10**, 131–148.

Azrin, N. H., Hutchinson, R. R., & McLaughlin, R. The opportunity for aggression as an operant reinforcer during aversive stimulation. *Journal of the Experimental Analysis of Behavior*, 1965, **8**, 171–180.

Azrin, N. H., Hutchinson, R. R., & Sallery, R. D. Pain-aggression toward inanimate objects. *Journal of the Experimental Analysis of Behavior*, 1964, **7**, 223–228.

Baenninger, R., & Ulm, R. R. Overcoming the effects of prior punishment on interspecies aggression in the rat. *Journal of Comparative and Physiological Psychology*, 1969, **69**, 628–635.

Balagura, S., & Devenport, L. D. Feeding patterns of normal and ventromedial hypothalamic lesioned male and female rats. *Journal of Comparative and Physiological Psychology*, 1970, **71**, 357–364.

Bard, P. A diencephalic mechanism for the expression of rage with special reference to the sympathetic nervous system. *American Journal of Physiology*, 1928, **84**, 490–515.

Bard, P. The neuro-humoral basis of emotional reactions. In C. A. Murchison (Ed.), *A handbook of general experimental psychology*. Worcester, Mass.: Clark University Press, 1934. Pp. 264–311.

Bard, P., & Mountcastle, V. B. Some forebrain mechanisms involved in expression of rage with special reference to suppression of angry behavior. *Research Publications of the Association for Research in Nervous and Mental Disease*, 1947, **27**, 362–404.

Barnes, G. W., & Kish, G. B. Reinforcing properties of the termination of intense auditory stimulation. *Journal of Comparative and Physiological Psychology*, 1957, **50**, 40–43.

Berger, H. Über das Elektrenkephalogramm des Menschen. *Archiv fuer Psychiatrie und Nervenkrankheiten*, 1929, **87**, 527–570.

Bexton, W. H., Heron, W., & Scott, T. H. Effects of decreased variation in the sensory environment. *Canadian Journal of Psychology*, 1954, **8**, 70–76.

Bindra, D. *Motivation: A systematic reinterpretation*. New York: Ronald Press, 1959.

Blackman, D. Conditioned suppression or facilitation as a function of the behavioral baseline. *Journal of the Experimental Analysis of Behavior*, 1968, **11**, 53–61. (a)

Blackman, D. Response rate, reinforcement frequency, and conditioned suppression. *Journal of the Experimental Analysis of Behavior*, 1968, **11**, 503–516. (b)

Bower, A. H., & Miller, N. E. Rewarding and punishing effects from stimulating the same place in the rat's brain. *Journal of Comparative and Physiological Psychology*, 1958, **51**, 669–674.

Brady, J. V. The paleocortex and behavioral motivation. In H. F. Harlow & C. N. Woolsey (Eds.), *Biological and biochemical bases of behavior*. Madison: University of Wisconsin Press, 1958. Pp. 193–235.

Brady, J. V. Emotional behavior. In J. Field, H. W. Magoun, & V. E. Hall (Eds.), *Handbook of physiology*. Vol. 3. Washington, D.C.: American Physiological Society, 1960. Pp. 1529–1552.

Brady, J. V., & Nauta, W. J. H. Subcortical mechanisms in emotional behavior: Affective changes following septal forebrain lesions in the albino rat. *Journal of Comparative and Physiological Psychology*, 1953, **46**, 339–346.

Bridges, K. Emotional development in early infancy. *Child Development*, 1932, **3**, 324–341. Figure 8.8: Copyright, 1932, by The Society for Research in Child Development, Inc.; adapted from Fig. 59, *Fundamentals of general psychology*, 1949, by J. F. Dashiell. Reproduced by permission of The Society for Research in Child Development, Inc., and Houghton Mifflin Company.

Brierley, J. B., & Beck, E. The effects upon behaviour of lesions in the dorsomedial and anterior thalamic nuclei of cat and monkey. In G. E. W. Wolstenholme & C. M. O'Connor (Eds.), *CIBA Foundation symposium on the neurological basis of behaviour*. Boston: Little, Brown, 1958. Pp. 90–104.

Broadhurst, P. L. Emotionality and the Yerkes-Dodson law. *Journal of Experimental Psychology*, 1957, **54**, 345–352.

Brobeck, J. R. Mechanisms of the development of obesity in animals with hypothalamic lesions. *Physiological Review*, 1946, **26**, 541–559.

Brobeck, J. R., Tepperman, J., & Long, C. N. H. Experimental hypothalamic hyperphagia in the albino rat. *Yale Journal of Biology and Medicine*, 1943, **15**, 831–853.

Cannon, W. B. The James-Lange theory of emotion: A critical examination and an alternative theory. *American Journal of Psychology*, 1927, **39**, 106–124.

Catania, A. C. (Ed.) *Contemporary research in operant behavior*. Glenview, Ill.: Scott, Foresman, 1968.

Chapman, W. P. Studies of the periamygdaloid area in relation to human behavior. *Research Publications of the Association for Research in Nervous and Mental Disease*, 1958, **36**, 258–277.

Cheng, M., Rozin, P., & Teitelbaum, P. Starvation retards development of food and water regulations. *Journal of Comparative and Physiological Psychology*, 1971, **76**, 206–218.

Chow, K. L. Lack of behavioral effects following destruction of some thalamic association nuclei in monkeys. *Archives of Neurology and Psychiatry*, 1954, **71**, 762–771.

Cole, L. N. The relation of strength of stimulus to rate of learning in the chick. *Journal of Animal Behavior*, 1911, **1**, 111–124.

Cox, V. C., Kakolewski, J. W., & Valenstein, E. S. Sex differences in hyperphagia and obesity. *Journal of Comparative and Physiological Psychology*, 1969, **67**, 320–326.

Darwin, C. *Expression of the emotions in man and animals.* London: Murray, 1872.

Dashiell, J. F. *Fundamentals of general psychology.* (3rd ed.) Boston: Houghton Mifflin, 1949.

Delgado, J. M. R., & Anand, B. K. Increase of food intake induced by electrical stimulation of the lateral hypothalamus. *American Journal of Physiology,* 1953, **172,** 162–168.

de Molina, A. F., & Hunsperger, R. W. Central representation of affective reactions in forebrain and brain stem: Electrical stimulation of amygdala, stria terminalis, and adjacent structures. *Journal of Physiology,* 1959, **145,** 251–265.

Dethier, V. G. Feeding behavior of the blowfly. In D. S. Lehrman, R. A. Hinde, & E. Shaw (Eds.), *Advances in the study of behavior.* Vol. 2. New York: Academic Press, 1969. Pp. 111–266.

Dethier, V. G., & Bodenstein, D. *Hunger in the blowfly.* Zeitschrift für Tierpsychologie, 1958, **15,** 129–140.

de Toledo, L. E., & Black, A. H. Heart rate: Changes during conditioned suppression in rats. *Science,* 1966, **152,** 1404–1406.

Deutsch, J. A. Behavioral measurement of the neural refractory period and its application to intracranial self-stimulation. *Journal of Comparative and Physiological Psychology,* 1964, **58,** 1–9.

Deutsch, J. A., & Deutsch, D. *Physiological psychology.* Homewood, Ill.: Dorsey Press, 1966.

Deutsch, J. A., & DiCara, L. Hunger and extinction in intracranial self-stimulation. *Journal of Comparative and Physiological Psychology,* 1967, **63,** 344–347.

Deutsch, J. A., & Howarth, C. I. Some tests of a theory of intracranial self-stimulation. *Psychological Review,* 1963, **70,** 444–460.

Devor, M. G., Wise, R. A., Milgram, N. W., & Hoebel, B. G. Physiological control of hypothalamically elicited feeding and drinking. *Journal of Comparative and Physiological Psychology,* 1970, **73,** 226–232.

DiCara, L. V. Role of post operative feeding experience in recovery from lateral hypothalamic damage. *Journal of Comparative and Physiological Psychology,* 1970, **72,** 60–65.

Dodson, J. D. The relation of strength of stimulus to rapidity of habit formation in the kitten. *Journal of Animal Behavior,* 1915, **5,** 330–336.

Duffy, E. An explanation of "emotional" phenomena without the use of the concept "emotion." *Journal of General Psychology,* 1941, **25,** 283–293. (a)

Duffy, E. The conceptual categories of psychology. A suggestion for revision. *Psychological Review,* 1941, **48,** 177–203. (b)

Duffy, E. The psychological significance of the concept of "arousal" or "activation." *Psychological Review,* 1957, **64,** 265–275.

Egger, M. D., & Flynn, J. P. Effects of electrical stimulation of the amygdala on hypothalamically elicited attack behavior in cats. *Journal of Neurophysiology,* 1963, **26,** 705–720.

Epstein, A., & Teitelbaum, P. Specific loss of the hypoglycemic control of feeding in recovered lateral rats. *American Journal of Physiology,* 1967, **213,** 1159–1167.

Estes, W. K., & Skinner, B. F. Some quantitative properties of anxiety. *Journal of Experimental Psychology,* 1941, **29,** 390–400.

Falk, J. L. Comments on Dr. Teitelbaum's paper. In M. R. Jones (Ed.), *Nebraska symposium on motivation.* Lincoln: University of Nebraska Press, 1961. Pp. 65–68.

Fantino, E., Kasdon, D., & Stringer, N. The Yerkes-Dodson law and alimentary motivation. *Canadian Journal of Psychology,* 1970, **24,** 77–84. Figure 8.5: Reproduced by permission.

Feleky, A. *Feelings and emotions.* New York: Pioneer Press, 1922.

Ferster, C. B., & Perrott, M. C. *Behavior principles.* New York: Appleton-Century-Crofts, 1968.

Freud, S. *Collected papers of Sigmund Freud.* Vols. III-IV. Hogarth: The International Psycho-analytic Library; London: The Institute of Psycho-analysis, 1925. (Republished: New York, Basic Books, 1959.)

Gallistel, C. R. The incentive of brain stimulation reward. *Journal of Comparative and Physiological Psychology,* 1969, **69,** 713–721.

Gallistel, C. R., Rolls, E., & Greene, D. Neural function inferred from behavioral and electrophysiological estimates of refractory period. *Science,* 1969, **166,** 1028–1030.

Gellhorn, E. Motion and emotion: The role of proprioception in the physiology and pathology of the emotions. *Psychological Review,* 1964, **71,** 457–472.

Gellhorn, E. *Biological foundations of emotion.* Glenview, Ill.: Scott, Foresman, 1968.

Gentry, W. D. Fixed-ratio schedule–induced aggression. *Journal of the Experimental Analysis of Behavior,* 1968, **11,** 813–817.

Gibson, W. E., Reed, L. D., Sakai, M., & Porter, P. B. Intracranial reinforcement compared with sugar-water reinforcement. *Science,* 1965, **148,** 1357–1359.

Gold, R. M. Hypothalamic hyperphagia: Males get just as fat as females. *Journal of Comparative and Physiological Psychology,* 1970, **71,** 347–356.

Green, J. R., Duisberg, R. E. H., & McGrath, W. B. Focal epilepsy of psychomotor type: Preliminary report of observations on effects of surgical therapy. *Journal of Neurosurgery,* 1951, **8,** 157–172.

Hammes, J. A. Visual discrimination learning as a function of shock-fear and task difficulty. *Journal of Comparative and Physiological Psychology,* 1956, **49,** 481–484.

Han, P. W. Hypothalamic obesity in rats without hyperphagia. *Transactions of the New York Academy of Sciences,* 1967, **30,** 229–243.

Heath, R. G. Closing remarks, with commentary on depth electroencephalography in epilepsy and schizophrenia. In G. H. Glaser (Ed.), *EEG and behavior.* New York: Basic Books, 1963. Pp. 337–393.

Hebb, D. O. *A textbook of psychology.* (2nd ed.) Philadelphia: Saunders, 1966. Figures 8.3 and 8.4: Copyright © 1966 by W. B. Saunders Company, and reproduced by permission.

Heimstra, N. W., & Newton, G. Effects of prior food competition on the rat's killing responses to the white mouse. *Behaviour,* 1961, **17,** 95–102.

Henderson, R. L. Stimulus intensity dynamism and secondary reinforcement. *Journal of Comparative and Physiological Psychology,* 1957, **50,** 339–344.

Heron, W. Cognitive and physiological effects of perceptual isolation. In P. Solomon, P. E. Kubzansky, P. H. Leiderman, J. H. Mendelson, R. Trumbull, & D. Wexler (Eds.), *Sensory deprivation.* Cambridge, Mass.: Harvard University Press, 1961. Pp. 6–33.

Hess, W. R., & Brügger, M. Das subkortikale Zentrum der affektiven Abwehrreaktion. *Helvetica Physiologica et Pharmacologia Acta,* 1943, **1,** 33–52.

Hetherington, A. W., & Ranson, S. W. Hypothalamic lesions and adiposity in the rat. *Anatomical Record,* 1970, **78,** 149.

Howarth, C. I., & Deutsch, J. A. Drive decay: The cause of fast "extinction" of habits learned for brain stimulation. *Science,* 1962, **137,** 35–36.

Hunsperger, R. W.   Affektreaktionen auf Elektrische Reizung im Hirnstamm der Katze. *Helvetica Physiologica et Pharmacologia Acta*, 1956, **14**, 70–92.

Hunsperger, R. W.   Les représentations centrales des réactions affectives dans le cerveau antérieur et dans le tranc cérébral. *Neurochirurgie*, 1959, **5**, 207–233.

Huston, J. P.   Reinforcement reduction: A method for training ratio behavior. *Science*, 1967, **159**, 444.

Hutchinson, R. R., Azrin, N. H., & Hunt, G. M.   Attack produced by intermittent reinforcement of a concurrent operant response. *Journal of the Experimental Analysis of Behavior*, 1968, **11**, 489–495.

James, W.   What is emotion? *Mind*, 1884, **9**, 188–205.

James, W.   *The principles of psychology*. Vol. 2. New York: Holt, 1890.

Jasper, H. H., & Rasmussen, T.   Studies of clinical and electrical responses to deep temporal stimulation in man with some considerations of functional anatomy. *Research Publications of the Association for Research in Nervous and Mental Disease*, 1958, **36**, 316–334.

Karli, P.   The Norway rat's response to the white mouse: An experimental analysis. *Behaviour*, 1956, **10**, 81–103.

Karli, P.   Nouvelles données expérimentales sur le comportement d'agression interspécifique rat-souris. *Journal de Physiologie*, 1961, **53**, 383–384.

Keller, F. S.   Light aversion in the white rat. *Psychological Record*, 1941, **4**, 235–250.

Kent, E., & Grossman, S. P.   Evidence for a conflict interpretation of anomalous effects of rewarding brain stimulation. *Journal of Comparative and Physiological Psychology*, 1969, **69**, 381–390.

Kessen, W., & Mandler, G.   Anxiety, pain and the inhibition of distress. *Psychological Review*, 1961, **68**, 396–404.

King, F. A.   Effects of septal and amygdaloid lesions on emotional behavior and conditioned avoidable responses in the rat. *Journal of Nervous and Mental Disease*, 1958, **126**, 57–63.

King, M. B., & Hoebel, B. G.   Killing elicited by brain stimulation in rats. *Communications in Behavioral Biology*, Part A, 1968, **2**, 173–177.

Klineberg, O.   *Social psychology*. New York: Holt, Rinehart & Winston, 1940.

Kluver, H., & Bucy, P. C.   "Psychic blindness" and other symptoms following bilateral lobectomy in rhesus monkeys. *American Journal of Physiology*, 1937, **119**, 352–353.

Kornblith, C., & Olds, J.   T-maze learning with one trial per day using brain stimulation reinforcement. *Journal of Comparative and Physiological Psychology*, 1968, **66**, 488–491.

Kreiskott, H.   Some comments on the killing response behavior of the rat. In S. Garattini & E. B. Sigg (Eds.), *Aggressive behaviour: Proceedings of the symposium on the biology of aggressive behaviour*. New York: Interscience, 1969. P. 12.

Landis, C., & Hunt, W. A.   *The startle pattern*. New York: Farrar & Rinehart, 1939.

Lange, G. C.   *Om sindsbergelser*. Copenhagen: Krønar, 1885.

Lashley, K. S.   The thalamus and emotion. *Psychological Review*, 1938, **45**, 42–61.

Leeper, R.   A motivational theory of emotion to replace "emotion as disorganized response." *Psychological Review*, 1948, **55**, 5–21.

Leeper, R. N., & Madison, P.   *Toward understanding personality*. New York: Appleton-Century-Crofts, 1959.

Leitenberg, H.   Conditioned acceleration and conditioned suppression in pigeons. *Journal of the Experimental Analysis of Behavior*, 1966, **9**, 205–212.

Lindsley, D. B.   Emotion. In S. S. Stevens (Ed.), *Handbook of experimental psychology*. New York: Wiley, 1951. Pp. 473–516. Figure 8.6: Copyright, 1951, by John Wiley & Sons, Inc., and reproduced by permission.

Lyon, D. O.   Frequency of reinforcement as a parameter of conditioned suppression. *Journal of the Experimental Analysis of Behavior*, 1963, **6**, 95–98.

Lyon, D. O.   Some notes on conditioned suppression and reinforcement schedules. *Journal of the Experimental Analysis of Behavior*, 1964, **7**, 289–291.

Lyon, D. O., & Felton, M.   Conditioned suppression and variable-ratio reinforcement. *Journal of the Experimental Analysis of Behavior*, 1966, **9**, 245–248.

MacLean, P. D.   Psychosomatic disease and the "visceral brain." *Psychosomatic Medicine*, 1949, **11**, 338–353.

MacLean, P. D., & Delgado, J. M. R.   Electrical and chemical stimulation of frontal-temporal portion of limbic system in the waking animal. *EEG and Clinical Neurophysiology*, 1953, **5**, 91–100.

Madlafousek, J., Freund, K., & Grofová, I.   Variables determining the effect of electrostimulation in the lateral preoptic area on the sexual behavior of male rats. *Journal of Comparative and Physiological Psychology*, 1970, **72**, 28–44.

Mandler, G.   Emotion. In R. M. Brown, E. Galanter, E. H. Hess, & G. Mandler (Eds.), *New directions in psychology*. Vol. 1. New York: Holt, Rinehart & Winston, 1962. Pp. 267–343. Figure 8.7: Copyright © 1962 by Holt, Rinehart and Winston, Inc., and reproduced by permission.

Marañon, G.   Contribution à l'étude de l'action émotion de l'adrenalin. *Revue française d'endocrinol*, 1924, **2**, 301–325.

Masserman, J. H.   Destruction of the hypothalamus in cats. *Archives of Neurology and Psychiatry*, 1938, **39**, 1250–1271.

Masserman, J. H.   Is the hypothalamus a center of emotion? *Psychosomatic Medicine*, 1941, **3**, 3–25.

Masserman, J. H.   *Behavior and neurosis*. Chicago: University of Chicago Press, 1943.

May, K. K., & Beaton, J. R.   Metabolic effects of hyperphagia in the hypothalamic-hyperphagic rat. *Canadian Journal of Physiology and Pharmacology*, 1966, **44**, 641–650.

McCleary, R. A.   Response-modulating functions of the limbic system: Initiation and suppression. In E. Stellar & J. M. Sprague (Eds.), *Progress in physiological psychology*. Vol. 1. New York: Academic Press, 1966. Pp. 209–272.

McCleary, R. A., & Moore, R. Y.   *Subcortical mechanisms of behavior*. New York: Basic Books, 1965. Figure 8.9: Copyright © 1965 by Basic Books, Inc., Publishers, New York. Figure 2.6 reproduced by permission.

Meltzer, D., & Brahlek, J. A.   Conditioned suppression and conditioned enhancement with the same positive *UCS*: An effect of *CS* duration. *Journal of the Experimental Analysis of Behavior*, 1970, **13**, 67–73.

Migler, B., & Brady, J. V.   Timing behavior and conditioned fear. *Journal of the Experimental Analysis of Behavior*, 1964, **7**, 247–251.

Miller, N. E.   Experiments on motivation. *Science*, 1957, **126**, 1271–1278.

Miller, N. E., Bailey, C. J., & Stevenson, J. A. F.   Decreased "hunger" but increased food intake resulting from hypothalamic lesions. *Science*, 1950, **112**, 256–259.

Milner, P. M.   *Physiological psychology*. New York: Holt, Rinehart & Winston, 1970.

Mirsky, A. F., Rosvold, H. E., & Pribram, K. H.   Effects of cingulectomy on social behavior in monkeys. *Journal of Neurophysiology*, 1957, **20**, 588–601.

Mogenson, G. J.   An attempt to establish secondary reinforcement with rewarding brain stimulation. *Psychological Reports*, 1965, **16**, 163–167.

Montague, E. K.   The role of anxiety in serial rote learning. *Journal of Experimental Psychology*, 1953, **45**, 91–96.

Montemurro, D. G., & Stevenson, J. A. F.   Adipsia produced by hypothalamic lesions in the rat. *Canadian Journal of Biochemistry and Physiology*, 1957, **35**, 31–37.

Morgan, C. T.   *Physiological psychology*. New York: McGraw-Hill, 1965.

Morgane, P. J.   Aberrations in feeding and drinking behavior of rats with lesions in globi pallidi. *American Journal of Physiology*, 1961, **201**, 420–428.

Murray, E. J.   *Motivation and emotion*. Englewood Cliffs, N.J.: Prentice-Hall, 1964.

Myer, J. S.   Stimulus control of mouse-killing rats. *Journal of Comparative and Physiological Psychology*, 1964, **58**, 112–117.

Myer, J. S.   Early experience and the development of mouse-killing by rats. *Journal of Comparative and Physiological Psychology*, 1969, **67**, 46–49.

Myer, J. S.   Experience and the stability of mouse-killing by rats. *Journal of Comparative and Physiological Psychology*, 1971, **75**, 264–268.

Myer, J. S., & White, R. T.   Aggressive motivation in the rat. *Animal Behaviour*, 1965, **13**, 430–433.

Nakao, H.   Emotional behavior produced by hypothalamic stimulation. *American Journal of Physiology*, 1958, **194**, 411–418.

Olds, J.   Physiological mechanisms of reward. In M. R. Jones (Ed.), *Nebraska symposium on motivation*. Lincoln: University of Nebraska Press, 1955. Pp. 73–139.

Olds, J.   Preliminary mapping of electrical reinforcing effects in the rat brain. *Journal of Comparative and Physiological Psychology*, 1956, **49**, 281–285.

Olds, J.   Satiation effects in self-stimulation of the brain. *Journal of Comparative and Physiological Psychology*, 1958, **51**, 320–324.

Olds, J., & Milner, P.   Positive reinforcement produced by electrical stimulation of septal area and other regions of rat brain. *Journal of Comparative and Physiological Psychology*, 1954, **47**, 419–427.

Olds, J., & Olds, M. E.   The mechanism of voluntary behavior. In R. Heath (Ed.), *The role of pleasure in behavior*. New York: Harper & Row, 1964. Pp. 23–53.

Olds, M. E., & Olds, J.   Emotional and associative mechanisms in rat brain. *Journal of Comparative and Physiological Psychology*, 1961, **54**, 120–126.

Panksepp, J.   Aggression elicited by electrical stimulation of the hypothalamus in albino rats. *Physiology and Behavior*, 1971, **6**, 321–329.

Papez, J. W.   A proposed mechanism of emotion. *Archives of Neurology and Psychiatry*, 1937, **38**, 725–743.

Paul, L.   Predatory attack by rats: Its relationship to feeding and type of prey. *Journal of Comparative and Physiological Psychology*, 1972, **78**, 69–76.

Paul, L., Miley, W., & Baenninger, R.   Mouse-killing by rats: Roles of hunger and thirst in its initiation and maintenance. *Journal of Comparative and Physiological Psychology*, 1971, **76**, 242–249.

Penfield, W.   Functional localization in temporal and deep sylvian area. *Research Publications of the Association for Research in Nervous and Mental Disease*, 1958, **36**, 210–226.

Penfield, W., & Jasper, H.   *Epilepsy and the functional anatomy of the brain*. Boston: Little, Brown, 1954.

Pliskoff, S. S., & Hawkins, T. D.   A method for increasing the reinforcement magnitude of intracranial stimulation. *Journal of the Experimental Analysis of Behavior*, 1967, **10**, 281–289.

Pliskoff, S. S., Wright, J. E., & Hawkins, T. D.   Brain stimulation as a reinforcer: Intermittent schedules. *Journal of the Experimental Analysis of Behavior*, 1965, **8**, 75–88.

Plutchik, R.   *The emotions: Facts, theories and a new model*. New York: Random House, 1962.

Pool, H.   Suction lesions and hypothalamic hyperphagia. *American Journal of Physiology*, 1967, **213**, 31–35.

Powley, T. L., & Keesey, R. E.   Relationship of body weight to the lateral hypothalamic feeding syndrome. *Journal of Comparative and Physiological Psychology*, 1970, **70**, 25–36.

Pribram, K. H., & Kruger, L.   Functions of the "olfactory brain." *Transactions of the New York Academy of Sciences*, 1954, **58**, 109–138.

Rabin, B. M., & Smith, C. J.   Behavioral comparison of the effects of irritative and nonirritative lesions in producing hypothalamic hyperphagia. *Physiology and Behavior*, 1968, **3**, 417–420.

Ranson, S. W.   Somnolence caused by hypothalamic lesions in the monkey. *Archives of Neurology and Psychiatry*, 1939, **41**, 1–23.

Rehovsky, D. A., & Wampler, R. S.   Failure to obtain sex differences in development of obesity following ventromedial hypothalamic lesions in rats. *Journal of Comparative and Physiological Psychology*, 1972, **78**, 102–112.

Reynolds, G. S., Catania, A. C., & Skinner, B. F.   Conditioned and unconditioned aggression in pigeons. *Journal of the Experimental Analysis of Behavior*, 1963, **6**, 53–59.

Reynolds, R. W.   Ventromedial hypothalamic lesions without hyperphagia. *American Journal of Physiology*, 1963, **204**, 60–62.

Roberts, W. W.   Rapid escape learning without avoidance learning motivated by hypothalamic stimulation in cats. *Journal of Comparative and Physiological Psychology*, 1958, **51**, 391–399. (a)

Roberts, W. W.   Both rewarding and punishing effects from stimulation of posterior hypothalamus of cats with same electrode at same intensity. *Journal of Comparative and Physiological Psychology*, 1958, **51**, 400–407. (b)

Rothfield, L., & Harmon, P. J.   On the relation of the hippocampal-fornix system to the control of rage responses in cats. *Journal of Comparative Neurology*, 1954, **101**, 265–282.

Routtenberg, A., & Lindy, J.   Effects of the availability of rewarding septal and hypothalamic stimulation on bar-pressing for food under conditions of deprivation. *Journal of Comparative and Physiological Psychology*, 1965, **60**, 158–161.

Rozin, P., & Kalat, J. W.   Specific hungers and poison avoidance as adaptive specializations of learning. *Psychological Review*, 1971, **78**, 459–486.

Russell, B.   *A history of Western philosophy*. New York: Simon & Schuster, 1945.

Sawa, M., Ueki, Y., Arita, M., & Harada, T.   Preliminary report on the amygdaloidectomy on the psychotic patients, with interpretation of oral-emotional manifestation in schizophrenics. *Folia Psychiatrica et Neurologica Japonica*, 1954, **7**, 309–329.

Schachter, S., & Singer, J.   Cognitive, social, and physiological determinants of emotional state. *Psychological Review*, 1962, **69**, 379–399.

Schachter, S., & Wheeler, L.   Epinephrine, chlorpromazine, and amusement. *Journal of Abnormal and Social Psychology*, 1962, **65**, 121–128.

Schlosberg, H.   A scale for judgment of facial expression. *Journal of Experimental Psychology*, 1941, **29**, 497–510.

Schlosberg, H.   The description of facial expressions in terms of two dimensions. *Journal of Experimental Psychology*, 1952, **44**, 229–237. Figures 8.1 and 8.2: Copyright 1952 by the American Psychological Association, and reproduced by permission.

Schreiner, L., & Kling, A.   Behavioral changes following rhinencephalic injury in cat. *Journal of Neurophysiology*, 1953, **16**, 643–659.

Schreiner, L., & Kling, A.   Rhinencephalon and behavior. *American Journal of Physiology*, 1956, **184**, 486–490.

Schreiner, L., Rioch, D., Pechtel, C., & Masserman, J.   Behavioral changes following thalamic injury in cat. *Journal of Neurophysiology*, 1953, **16**, 234–246.

Sétáló, G.   The mechanism of hypothalamic obesity in the rat. *Acta Physiologica Academiae Scientiarum Hungaricae*, 1965, **27**, 375–384.

Seward, J. P., Uyeda, A. A., & Olds, J.   Resistance to extinction following cranial self-stimulation. *Journal of Comparative and Physiological Psychology*, 1959, **52**, 294–299.

Sherrington, C. S.   *The integrative action of the nervous system.* New Haven, Conn.: Yale University Press, 1906.

Sidman, M., Brady, J. V., Boren, J. J., Conrad, D. G., & Schulman, A.   Reward schedules and behavior maintained by intracranial self-stimulation. *Science*, 1955, **122**, 830–831.

Skinner, B. F.   *Science and human behavior.* New York: Macmillan, 1953.

Smith, D. E., King, M. E., & Hoebel, B. G.   Lateral hypothalamic control of killing: Evidence for a cholinoceptive mechanism. *Science*, 1970, **167**, 900–901.

Smith, W. K.   The results of ablation of the cingulate region of the cerebral cortex. *Federation Proceedings*, 1944, **3**, 42–43.

Spiegel, E. A., & Wycis, H. T.   Physiological and psychological results of thalamotomy. *Proceedings of the Royal Society of Medicine Supplement*, 1949, **42**, 84–93.

Stevenson, J. A. F., & Montemurro, D. G.   Loss of weight and metabolic rate of rats with lesions of the medial and lateral hypothalamus. *Nature*, 1963, **198**, 92.

Teitelbaum, P.   Sensory control of hypothalamic hyperphagia. *Journal of Comparative and Physiological Psychology*, 1955, **48**, 158–163.

Teitelbaum, P.   Random and food-directed activity in hyperphagic and normal rats. *Journal of Comparative and Physiological Psychology*, 1957, **50**, 486–490.

Teitelbaum, P.   Disturbances of feeding and drinking behavior after hypothalamic lesions. In M. R. Jones (Ed.), *Nebraska symposium on motivation.* Lincoln: University of Nebraska Press, 1961. Pp. 39–69.

Teitelbaum, P.   The encephalization of hunger. In E. Stellar & J. Sprague (Eds.), *Progress in physiological psychology.* Vol. 4. New York: Academic Press, 1971. Pp. 319–350.

Teitelbaum, P., Cheng, M., & Rozin, P.   Stages of recovery and development of lateral hypothalamic control of food and water intake. *Annals of the New York Academy of Sciences*, 1969, **157**, 849–860. (a)

Teitelbaum, P., Cheng, M., & Rozin, P.   Development of feeding parallels its recovery after hypothalamic damage. *Journal of Comparative and Physiological Psychology*, 1969, **67**, 430–441. (b)

Teitelbaum, P., & Epstein, A. N.   The lateral hypothalamic syndrome. *Psychological Review*, 1962, **69**, 74–90.

Teitelbaum, P., & Stellar, E.   Recovery from the failure to eat, produced by lateral hypothalamic lesions. *Science*, 1954, **120**, 894–895.

Thorndike, E. L.   *Animal intelligence: Experimental studies.* New York: Macmillan, 1911.

Titchener, E. B.   *A textbook of psychology.* New York: Macmillan, 1921.

Troland, L. T.   *The fundamentals of human motivation.* New York: Van Nostrand Reinhold, 1928.

Ulrich, R. E., & Azrin, N. H.   Reflexive fighting in response to aversive stimulation. *Journal of the Experimental Analysis of Behavior*, 1962, **5**, 511–520.

Valenstein, E. S.   The anatomical locus of reinforcement. In E. Stellar & J. Sprague (Eds.), *Progress in physiological psychology.* Vol. 1. New York: Academic Press, 1966. Pp. 149–190.

Valenstein, E. S., & Beer, J.   Continuous opportunity for reinforcing brain stimulation. *Journal of the Experimental Analysis of Behavior*, 1964, **7**, 183–184.

Valenstein, E. S., Cox, V. C., & Kakolewski, J. W.   A comparison of stimulus-bound drinking and drinking induced by water deprivation. *Communications in Behavioral Biology*, 1968, **2**, 227–233.

Valenstein, E. S., Cox, V. C., & Kakolewski, J. W.   Reexamination of the role of the hypothalamus in motivation. *Psychological Review*, 1970, **77**, 16–31.

Van Hemel, P. E.   Aggression as a reinforcer: Operant behavior in the mouse-killing rat. *Journal of the Experimental Analysis of Behavior*, 1972, **17**, 237–245.

Ward, J. W., & Hester, R. W.   Intracranial self-stimulation in cats surgically deprived of autonomic outflows. *Journal of Comparative and Physiological Psychology*, 1969, **67**, 336–343.

Watson, J. B., & Rayner, R.   Conditioned emotional reactions. *Journal of Experimental Psychology*, 1920, **3**, 1–14.

Weiskrantz, L.   Behavioral changes associated with ablation of the amygdaloid complex in monkeys. *Journal of Comparative and Physiological Psychology*, 1956, **49**, 381–391.

Wenger, M. A., Jones, F. N., & Jones, M. H.   *Physiological psychology.* New York: Holt, Rinehart & Winston, 1956.

Wetzel, M. C.   Self-stimulation aftereffects and runway performance in the rat. *Journal of Comparative and Physiological Psychology*, 1963, **56**, 673–678.

Whalen, R. E., & Fehr, H.   The development of the mouse-killing response in rats. *Psychonomic Science*, 1964, **1**, 77–78.

Wheatley, M. D.   The hypothalamus and affective behavior in cats. *Archives of Neurology and Psychiatry*, 1944, **52**, 296–316.

Wood, C. D.   Behavioral changes following discrete lesions of temporal lobe structures. *Neurology*, 1958, **8**, 215–220.

Woodworth, R. S.   *Experimental psychology.* New York: Holt, Rinehart & Winston, 1938.

Wundt, W.   *Outlines of psychology.* (4th ed.) C. H. Judd (Trans.) Leipzig: Engelmann, 1902.

Yerkes, R. M., & Dodson, J. D.   The relation of strength of stimulus to rapidity of habit-formation. *Journal of Comparative Neurology and Psychology*, 1908, **18**, 459–482.

Young, P. T.   Emotion as disorganized response: A reply to Professor Leeper. *Psychological Review*, 1949, **56**, 184–191.

Young, P. T.   *Motivation and emotion: A survey of the determinants of human and animal activity.* New York: Wiley, 1961.

INSTINCT AND INNATE BEHAVIOR:
TOWARD AN ETHOLOGICAL PSYCHOLOGY

9

Gordon M. Burghardt
University of Tennessee

The previous chapter emphasized the complexity of emotional behavior, showing that it depends on both physiological arousal and external events. Sometimes, stimuli in the environment acquire their effectiveness through experience, suggesting the operation of conditioning processes; under other circumstances, stimuli produce signs of emotionality upon their very first presentation to the subject, suggesting the operation of innate mechanisms. This chapter examines a variety of behaviors that may involve innate or instinctive components, for example, the activities involved in reproduction or aggression that are characteristic of a species and are evident in the natural environment. The biological and evolutionary approach to the understanding of instinctive behavior serves to balance the emphasis of the earlier chapters on the modification of arbitrary responses by conditioning.

The concepts of instinct and innate behavior have been a concern of philosophy, biology, psychology, and related sciences for many years. The last fifty years, however, have seen the progressive elimination of the topic from psychology. The study of instinct became unfashionable, and the very use of the word was associated with ignorance or scientific charlatanism by most academic psychologists. But new findings and a more holistic and ecological concern for animals (including humans) have led to a renewed effort by psychologists to deal with instincts and innate behavior. Although approached from many viewpoints, it is safe to say that concern with so-called instinctive matters has recently been most prevalent among those who have been impressed with two things: the wide range of different activities animals engage in—activities such as courtship, feeding, fighting, and maternal care; and the diversity among species in the performance of these and many other activities. Behavioral scientists interested in such natural *species characteristic* behaviors, their causation and control, function (survival value), ontogeny, and evolution are called ethologists; their science, ethology. Most ethologists have had strong backgrounds in zoological areas and approach behavior with a biological perspective.

In recent years ethology has been termed *the biological study of be-*

Preparation of this chapter was supported in part by U.S. Public Health Service Grant MH-15707. The author wishes to thank Lori Burghardt, John A. Nevin, and William S. Verplanck for their invaluable advice and suggestions concerning the entire chapter. David Gumpper and Joel Luhan kindly read parts of the manuscript. The author is also grateful to the graduate students who studied from it and made suggestions.

havior (Tinbergen, 1963) or *the biology of behavior* (Eibl-Eibesfeldt, 1970). Earlier in its modern history it was more narrowly conceived of as *the study of instinct* (Tinbergen, 1951). Nonetheless, today the most exciting and fruitful work on instinct is taking place in ethology, although even as late as 1955 a knowledgeable animal psychologist could purport to review the area while ignoring ethology (Beach, 1955). The emphasis throughout this chapter is on conveying the importance and relevance of ethology to psychology. The converse is also true, and ethology has benefited from the experimental sophistication, conceptual rigor, and findings of comparative psychology, although more contacts are needed. While not completely independent of each other, psychological interest in ethology centers around three areas: ethological methods, ethological theory, and, perhaps most importantly, the ethological attitude.

While ethology has stressed the study of many behaviors in a wide variety of species, most psychologists have concentrated on only a few types of behavior and have studied a surprisingly limited number of organisms, the most common being the highly domesticated white rat and the white college sophomore. The research consequences of such narrow interests are presented in papers by Beach (1950), Bitterman (1965), Hodos and Campbell (1969), and Lockard (1968, 1971). A restricted number of activities (e.g., maze-running, bar-pressing), a restricted number of species (e.g., rat, pigeon, cat, dog), and a restricted set of problems (e.g., conditioning, visual perception) were used because it was believed that this approach would lead almost directly to an understanding of principles underlying most behaviors in all species, especially humans. This belief is vividly illustrated in a statement from the conclusion of the influential learning psychologist E. C. Tolman's (1938) presidential address to the American Psychological Association.

> Let me close, now, with a final confession of faith. I believe that everything important in psychology (except perhaps such matters as the building up of a super-ego, that is everything save such matters as involve society and words) can be investigated in essence through the continued experimental and theoretical analysis of the determiners of rat behavior at a choice point in a maze [p. 34].

It is interesting to note that when ethology came to the attention of psychologists, Tolman was one of the first to put his name to an experimental paper attacking the concepts involved in this new attempt to bring instinctive behavior to a respectable place in the study of behavior (Hirsch, Lindley, & Tolman, 1955).

This chapter would not appropriately fill its function if it presented modern ethology and related findings without some reference to its historical development. The more basic ethological concepts and research methods, along with some recent findings, will then be presented, in addition to the newly emerging area of human ethology. Because space precludes anything more than brief treatments of extensive research areas, the author's selectivity plays a considerable role. In addition, important topics such as social behavior, prenatal factors, perception, language, and primate behavior have had to be bypassed. It should also be noted that the last ten years have seen an enormous growth of interest and work in ethology, with the result that many concepts and methods are being challenged or revised, limited or extended, discarded or replaced—usually with no consensus. However, by emphasizing the roots of the rapidly branching (and reproducing) ethological tree, this chapter should help orient the reader to most of the current literature.

CHANGING CONCEPTIONS OF INSTINCT
Early history of instinct and its fate in psychology

Considerations of instinctive behavior, or similarly labeled phenomena, have had a long history in biological and philosophical thought. The interested reader can obtain some fascinating aspects of the story from Beach (1955), Diamond (1971), Fletcher (1957), Hess (1962), and Klopfer and Hailman (1967), as well as from the more specialized articles cited in the following discussion.

Although much of importance was written previously, the first major discussion of instinct in the context of the biology and evolution of the species was, not surprisingly, that of Charles Darwin. His chapter on instinct in *The Origin of Species* (1859) is illuminating even today. In many respects, he was more sophisticated than later writers on instinct.

Darwin began by stating that he would not attempt any definition of instinct itself, since several types of *mental actions* are embraced by the term and that everyone really understands what is meant. He provided, however, a statement which, in essence, covers many of the usual attributes of instinct.

> An action, which we ourselves should require experience to enable us to perform, when performed by an animal, more especially by a very young one, without any experience, and when performed by many individuals in the same way, without their knowing for what purpose it is performed, is usually said to be instinctive [p. 207].

He went on to state, however, that none of the characteristics just mentioned are universal.

This definition, it will be recognized, is a purely descriptive one. The term *instinct* also has been used in a more explanatory way to imply a motivational or driving force for the behavior so descriptively characterized by Darwin's definition. Darwin occasionally used instinct in an energizing fashion, such as when he stated that "instinct impels the cuckoo to migrate and to lay her eggs in other birds' nests" [p. 207]. However, Darwin was really more interested in the mechanisms which gave rise to *instinctive behavior,* a terminological change much emphasized by later writers (e.g., Lorenz, 1937). Nonetheless, the motivating aspect of instinct cannot be easily dismissed and was, in fact, destined for increased emphasis by psychologists.

A critical word in Darwin's definition is *experience,* a term not defined by him or by any of the other early writers on instinct since its meaning seemed even more obvious than that of instinct. Many current controversies stem from different meanings of the term (e.g., Lehrman, 1953). Experience is a slippery word, and if it is interpreted as encompassing all stimulative environmental effects, including physiological and biochemical factors in prenatal development (Schneirla, 1966), then obviously experience cannot be eliminated from the performance of any behavior. However, the instinct writers clearly meant that the animal had no chance to acquire the specific knowledge required to perform the behavior properly or to anticipate its consequences.

Darwin (1859) pointed out that behavior is adaptive (i.e., beneficial to the species). He did not give too many examples, since he felt that "it will be universally admitted that instincts are as important as corporeal structure for the welfare of each species, under its present conditions of life" [p. 209]. He then argued that these instinctive behaviors are inherited and that the variations found in them are also often inherited. Indeed, as Darwin recognized, in order for changed conditions of life to have an effect on instinct for subsequent genera-

tions, the instincts themselves must vary, however slightly, in order for natural selection to work. To support this conclusion, he discussed behaviors of domesticated animals and pointed to the well-known differences in the behavior of various dog breeds: pointing, retrieving, and running around a herd of sheep rather than at them.

Darwin also stressed the importance of looking at closely related species exhibiting similar types of behavior and at the evolution of behavior itself. Using this approach he discussed the probable origin of the behavior of the cuckoo, a parasitic European bird that lays its eggs in the nests of other birds, allowing the host species to rear the alien young. This behavior raises a number of questions still unanswered today (see Wickler, 1968). Another example discussed by Darwin is the evolution of the so-called slave-making instinct in ants. Some species of ants raid nests of other species, capture the young, and raise them to serve their own ends.

Some insect-behavior observers (e.g., Fabre, 1918) were very much opposed to ideas of evolution and natural selection and saw instincts as vitalistic, mystical forces that, by definition, had to appear full-blown at some precise moment in history. But Darwin's observations convinced him that instincts do not have to appear fully developed in order to be adaptive. The accumulation of slight modifications of structure or behavior over generations is sufficient to provide evolutionary divergence.

Darwin's (1859) closing sentence is an eloquent summary of his view of instinct and places him squarely opposed to *Vitalism,* whose last redoubt in science was, and in some respects still is, behavior.

> Finally, it may not be a logical deduction, but to my imagination it is far more satisfactory to look at such instincts as the young cuckoo ejecting its foster-brothers, . . . ants making slaves, . . . the larvae of ichneumonidae feeding within the live bodies of caterpillars, . . . not as specially endowed or created instincts, but as small consequences of one general law, leading to the advancement of all organic beings, namely, multiply, vary, let the strongest live and the weakest die [pp. 243–244].

Darwin made other contributions to the study of behavior. Two of his later important books were *The Descent of Man* (1871) and *The Expression of the Emotions in Man and Animals* (1872). In *The Origin of Species,* Darwin stated that he was not extending this theory to man, but in *The Descent of Man* Darwin explicitly treated human behavior and evolution. *The Expression of the Emotions in Man and Animals* is a good example of the use of the comparative method as well as of other techniques in the study of behavior, in this case emotional expression. Note again the emphasis on the overt signs of the behavior or the behavior itself, rather than a supposed internal driving force (i.e., instinct as energy).

Darwin, in his typically thorough manner, devised six methods to study emotional expression. Not all worked and some might seem naive today, but they represented an empirical approach not often found in the study of emotions until recently. The methods in brief were: (1) observations of infants; (2) observations of the insane who are less readily able to mask their emotions as compared to normal adults; (3) judgments by people of photographs of facial expressions created by electrical stimulation of certain facial muscles; (4) analyses of masterpieces of painting and sculpture; (5) cross-cultural comparisons of expressions and gestures, particularly of groups with little contact with Europeans; and (6) observations of expressions in animals, especially dogs.

Primarily concerned with how emotional expressions originated, Darwin (1872) derived three principles which anticipated concepts in learning, ethology, and physiological psychology. The first principle is that of *serviceable associated habits.* Some movements or responses become associated with "certain states of the mind" [p. 28], become fixed or habitual, and then may occur when "the same state of mind is induced . . . though they may not then be of the least use" [p. 28]. Hence responses have been *conditioned,* in the modern sense, to new stimuli. This idea is also remarkably similar to the modern ethological concept of *intention movement,* although Darwin seems not to have recognized this communicative function.

The second principle is *antithesis,* in which opposite states of mind produce incompatible opposite movements. Consider the dog in Figure 9.1. In almost every conceivable way, the postures are the antithesis of one another: archness of back, ear position, angle of head, nearness to ground, tail position, to name a few. Darwin clearly saw the importance of this principle to communication in animals and humans.

The third principle is the *direct action of the nervous system* and refers basically to the physiological—especially autonomic nervous system—effects of strong emotions. This principle includes externally apparent states such as blushing, perspiring, defecation, and respiratory changes. A

Figure 9.1 A dog expressing two different emotional states that illustrate Darwin's principle of antithesis. Panel A shows a dog approaching another dog with "hostile intentions"; panel B shows the same in a "humble and affectionate frame of mind." (From Darwin, 1872.)

good example would be extreme anger in humans.

Darwin applied these principles to many types of emotions, and many interesting behaviors were recorded in the process. He was really looking at emotional expressions as communication (Burghardt, 1970b), which would appear essential to a more detailed, even physiological, analysis of emotions. However, the psychological study of emotions has largely ignored Darwin's contributions until quite recently, while ethologists have frequently acknowledged their importance (Lorenz, in preface to Darwin, 1965; Marler, 1959).

Another important early writer on instinct was Herbert Spencer. Unlike Darwin, he viewed instinct as compound reflex action (1872), but nonetheless he felt it wise to keep the term *instinct* for those "automatic nervous adjustments...in which complex stimuli produce complex movements" [p. 432]. In addition, instincts were viewed as being accompanied by consciousness.

The later writings of Darwin also provided the framework for a somewhat different evolutionary approach to behavior which essentially ignored problems of instinct. The doctrine of evolution made the most timely problem of biology appear to be the evolution of man, and evidence of man's relationship with other animals was sought. Since man's mind and intellect seemed the most advanced of any animal, evolutionists were constrained to show that this was not an evolutionary impossibility; therefore, any evidence which showed the mental powers of animals was grasped upon and used. In other words, there was an attempt to show a continuity of *mental evolution* between animals and humans. The alternative method, showing the phylogenetic derivatives of much human behavior, was also used by Darwin, but it did not especially influence psychologists.

What did occur was that the major problem of comparative psychology became the study of the evolution of intelligence. Today, experimental psychologists speak of animal learning or conditioning rather than animal intelligence, but, except for more precision in techniques and concepts, the basic goal seems to be the same (see Holmes, 1911, for a reasoned treatment that is surprisingly modern).

The early post-Darwinian approaches in this area did not prove scientifically satisfactory for a number of reasons. One was the lack of adequate experimental evidence. Authorities, therefore, fell back on the use of anecdotes—informal stories of unusual, almost human behavior on the part of animals. Most of these anecdotes originally were related by nonscientifically trained people about pets and farm animals, a situation which allowed for personal bias and *anthropomorphism,* the attribution of human qualities to nonhuman organisms, inanimate objects, or immaterial substances. Darwin frequently relied on evidence of this kind, but he was usually cautious in his interpretation and aware of the need for further evidence. In the hands of his successors, however, the anecdotal method became almost an end in itself. Exemplifying this approach was the most well known of the early comparative psychologists, Romanes, who wrote a number of widely read books on the subject of intelligence, the most famous of which were *Mental Evolution in Animals* (1884) and *Mental Evolution in Man* (1888).

Anecdotes, properly regarded, are not entirely without value even today, since they can raise important problems and stimulate systematic research. Nonetheless, the anecdotal method did lead to serious problems, hindering the development of a more experimental and empirical approach. Washburn (1908) listed several still valid objections to the anecdotal method: "(1) The observer is not scientifically trained to distinguish what he sees from what he infers. (2) He is not intimately acquainted with the habits of the species to which the animal belongs. (3) He is not acquainted with the past experience of the individual animal concerned. (4) He has a personal affection for the animal concerned and a desire to show its superior intelligence. (5) He has the desire, common to all humanity, to tell a good story" [p. 5]. Some of these objections should be kept in mind when reading recent books on animal behavior by even well-known and reputable scientists.

Whitman (1899b) also entertainingly criticized anecdotes, but C. Lloyd Morgan is generally given credit for eliminating the anecdotal method from the more serious and scientific writings in animal behavior. His books, *An Introduction to Comparative Psychology* (1894) and *Habit and Instinct* (1896), were widely influential, and he has become famous for *Lloyd Morgan's Canon,* his statement that the best interpretation of a behavior was that based on the exercise of the lowest *psychical faculty.* While very important, this law led to the extreme reaction of attempting to explain all behavior with atomistic and mechanistic concepts such as conditioned reflexes. An early cautionary note against too literal an application of this canon was sounded by Holmes (1911).

Although the anecdotal method was limited as a technique, the interest in comparative intelligence continued. E. L. Thorndike (1899) is credited with being the father of the comparative psychology of learning because of his development of the *trial-and-error* method based on the *problem box,* an early forerunner of the Skinner box of modern learning psychology. Thorndike applied Morgan's canon with a vengeance, which perhaps was necessary at the time. Loeb (1900) was an extreme advocate of the objective approach, attempting to explain all behavior on the basis of *forced movements* (*tropisms*) caused by external stimuli, although he did allow room for *associative memory,* a learning process. Jennings (1906), working mainly with lower organisms, felt that even these animals had spontaneous behavior that could not be attributable to immediate external stimuli, thereby setting himself in opposition to Loeb. Indeed, Jennings proposed the study of the full range of activities of an animal and a consideration of internal and external causes. He anticipated present-day ethologists by emphasizing the need for a descriptive *action system* of any species whose behavior is studied. Perhaps because of Jennings' criticisms, Loeb never became popular with psychologists. But one of Loeb's students, J. B. Watson, was later to convince psychologists of the need for a reductionistic approach, based not on the tropism but on Pavlov's conditioned reflex. However, all these workers, Morgan, Loeb, Jennings, Pavlov, and Thorndike, were basically *mechanists* and were firmly opposed to the more holistic vitalists.

Returning to the development of the instinct concept, another contributor was William James (1890), whose *Principles of Psychology* contains a chapter devoted to this topic (see also Harlow, 1969). His definition of instinct is similar to that of Darwin, although not as complete. He made the point that *"every instinct is an impulse"* [p. 385] more strongly than did Darwin and discussed more extensively the performance of behavior without foresight of its results. He pointed out that if the animal had no knowledge of the ends of its behavior, it was performing the behavior for the sake of the activity itself.

James went on to say that every instinctive act in an animal with the capacity for memory *"must cease to be 'blind' after being once repeated,* and must be accompanied with foresight of its 'ends' just so far as that end may have gone under the animal's cognizance" [p. 390]. Hence, after the first performance of an activity, the dichotomy between instinct and learning becomes blurred. Clearly this dynamic interaction of instinct and experience will become more interwoven and, consequently, more difficult to unravel as the animal develops and has more experiences and more opportunities for behavioral change.

Another of James' contemporaries, Henry Rutgers Marshall (1898), discussed in similar but more extensive armchair fashion the instincts of men and animals, coming to a number of thoughtful conclusions which should be considered by the modern psychologist. Marshall extended the definition of instinct away from that of Morgan, Darwin, and others who saw instincts as complex stereotyped patterns of behavior. He emphasized the fact that the ends or results of many behaviors

are adaptive and yet the organism lacks knowledge of them. The same biological end could be obtained in many ways, however, not just through definite coordinated movements. This shift away from stereotyped activities was already seen in James' discussion of human instincts and eventually became increasingly pronounced among psychological instinct theorists. Indeed, Marshall's main interest was to show the instinctive basis of religion, perhaps exemplifying the trend to label almost all behaviors as instinctive.

William McDougall, one of the most prolific and influential writers on instinct as applied to man, distinguished two important classes of innate behavior: specific tendencies or instincts proper, and nonspecific tendencies (1908). His breakdown of behavior into the cognitive, affective, and conative anticipated much modern thought. He postulated a number of major instincts in man (most commonly thirteen) and their associated emotions. Examples are flight and fear, curiosity and wonder, pugnacity and anger, and self-abasement and subjection. Although at times McDougall used these instincts as explanations of behavior, he did not see them as rigid and unmodifiable. He went even farther than Marshall in being ultimately unconcerned with observable behavior and more concerned with internal forces, goals, and subjective emotions. He had neither the methods nor data to answer the questions he asked. But more and more, McDougall is recognized as being aware of real problems in the study of human behavior. Nonetheless, the listing of hundreds of instincts in the critical and perceptive writings of Bernard (e.g., 1924) helped eliminate the concept from scientific psychology and discredit McDougall.

Freud was a very important instinct theorist, but he too lacked an experimental orientation. He made it clear that his concern was also primarily with the impulse or energizing aspects of instinct and not instinctive behavior per se (1915). To Freud the role of the nervous system was eliminating or reducing the effects of external stimuli. The *true motive forces* were instincts based on *instinctual stimuli* originating within the organism. In discussing instincts four terms were emphasized: *Pressure* was the motor factor or measure of force or demand for work. ("Every instinct is a piece of activity" [p. 328].) The *aim* of an instinct is always satisfaction only obtainable when the instinctual stimulus is removed. The *object* of an instinct, which is highly variable and changeable, is either external or a part of the subject's own body to or through which the instinct is able to achieve its aim.

(Freud was particularly impressed with the unusual and abnormal objects that are used to satisfy sexual instincts.) The *source* of an instinct is the chemical, physiological, or mechanical process within the body that gives rise to the instinct. Although he changed his mind about specifics, Freud always claimed the number of basic instincts was small (two or three) and that they were qualitatively similar, as contrasted with McDougall's view.

It was with Freud that the use of instinct became fundamentally different from the careful descriptive approach of Darwin, since he relied on psychoanalytic techniques and ignored animal studies, even though his training was largely biological. Nonetheless, Freud made many important observations, although they had little impact on experimental psychology, with the possible exception of the recent emphasis on early experience. Fletcher (1957) extensively compares Freud, McDougall, and the early ethologists, and Bowlby (1969) attempts a modern synthesis.

The movement by psychological instinct theorists away from behavior and toward the energizing and emotional aspects of instinct came at a time when experimental psychologists were discarding all subjective or introspective methodologies and concepts as unreliable and unscientific. Behaviorism was on the rise, guided by the polemical statements of Watson (1913). Since the environment and learning were considered the causes of most, if not all, behavior, instincts were high on the list of terms to be repudiated (Watson, 1930) and the anti-instinct revolt ensued (Beach, 1955). All behavior was to be built on a few basic reflexes; the conditioned-reflex paradigm of Pavlov was just gaining currency. Kuo (1921, 1924) went so far as to attempt to banish heredity from psychology. As Lashley (1938) was later to point out, "The psychology of instincts was a dynamics of imaginary forces and the anti-instinct movement was primarily a crusade against such a conceptual dynamism. Somehow the argument got twisted. Heredity was made the scapegoat and the hypostatization of psychic energies goes merrily on" [p. 373]. Although the arguments were intellectually weak (such as banning heredity and instinct and yet retaining innate "unconditioned reflexes"), the effect was to move even farther from an evolutionary framework, although experimental psychology soon found it needed some motivating forces behind behavior which became *drives* in the 1930s and fostered much experimental work (see Bolles, 1967).

In the aftermath of the anti-instinct revolt of the 1920s, Lashley (1938) was the only major experimental psychologist who came to grips with the problems of instinct in a major paper still readable and important today. Although known primarily as a physiological psychologist, Lashley was closely associated with Watson in his early days and did some important studies on animal behavior. Aware of the anti-instinct predisposition of psychology, Lashley pointed out many striking examples of the behavior of animals which were ignored by psychologists, but which seemed to necessitate an instinct interpretation. In particular, he mentioned the need for naturalistic observation.

Post-Darwinian framers of the ethological approach

It is understandable, then, that it is not psychologists, famous as they were at the time, to whom we must give credit for present-day instinct theory as descended from the behavioral emphasis of Darwin, although they rightly discredited loose and untestable uses of the concept. One of the most neglected scientists anticipating much of modern thinking is Douglas Spalding (1873). As Haldane (1954) has noted, if Spalding had lived longer, and presumably achieved more recognition, he would undoubtedly be considered the founder of ethology. Spalding (a tutor of a young Bertrand Russell) made a number of contributions, mostly regarding chicks. He provided experimental and close observational studies of young animals that could not have acquired the abilities he noticed. He utilized the *deprivation experiment* so common today in eliminating opportunities for the animals to learn during the period before such behaviors as flying, hunting, or courting appear. For instance, he placed hoods on chicks before they opened their eyes and later found them capable of depth discrimination and other abilities. He was aware that:

> When stripped of all superfluous learning, the argument against this and every other alleged case of instinctive knowledge is simply that it is unscientific to assume an instinct when it is possible that the knowledge in question may have been *acquired* in the ordinary way. But the experiments that have been recounted are evidence that prior to experience chickens behave as if they already possessed an acquaintance with the established order of nature. A hungry chick that never tasted food is able, on seeing a fly or a spider for the first time, to bring into action muscles that were never so exercised before, and to perform a series of delicately adjusted movements that end

in the capture of the insect. This I assert as the result of careful observation and experiment; and it cannot be answered but by observation and experiment at least as extensive [p.4].

Gray (1967, 1968) has recently evaluated in some detail the contributions of Spalding and should be consulted for more details on this pioneer of ethology.

One of the persons who did have an important influence on ethology was Charles Otis Whitman, a zoologist at the University of Chicago. He observed the behavior of pigeons and doves for many years and presented a series of lectures in 1898 dealing with animal behavior. These lectures were a highly reasoned view of animal behavior by a person who was intimately connected with the field for many years. He enumerated a number of principles and cautions. However, he is most known for the statement that "instinct and structure are to be studied from the common standpoint of phyletic descent, and that not the less because we may seldom, if ever, be able to trace the whole development of an instinct" [1899, p. 328]. Ethologists tend to view Whitman as the spiritual founder of ethology, after Darwin.

In one of those ironical, yet ultimately hopeful, occurrences in science, the year after Whitman gave his lectures at Woods Hole, Edward L. Thorndike, the before-mentioned founder of comparative learning psychology, also gave two lectures at Woods Hole (1899). The first was entitled "Instinct," a very sympathetic appreciation of Whitman. His second lecture was on animal intelligence, but Thorndike made it clear that he thought of his works as fitting into the approach advocated by Whitman, and that his concern with learning carried out on the individual level complemented the process performed by evolution at the species level. Yet for a period of 50 years the intellectual descendants of each man became increasingly isolated from, and in many respects intolerant of, the other.

Jacob von Uexküll (1934) made the important observation that, of the many stimuli or environmental events occurring around an animal, the organism responds to only a few. These stimuli or signs have a releasing effect on given behaviors. The signs or stimuli to which an animal responds represent the animal's perceptual world or his *Umwelt*. How can the animal's Umwelt be represented? Von Uexküll used the concept of the *Funktionkreis*, the functional cycle or functional

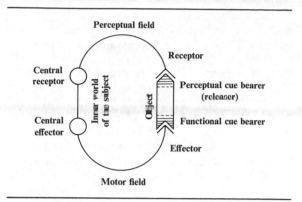

Figure 9.2 The functional circle of von Uexküll. (From von Uexküll, 1934.)

circle. Figure 9.2 presents a diagram of von Uexküll's Funktionkreis.

A perceptual cue stimulates the receptor at the periphery. This stimulation is transmitted to a central receptor, then to a central effector, and on to the peripheral effectors: the muscles, limbs, and other organs of the animal. The consequent actions of the animal may then alter the object which began the cycle by stimulating the receptor. As von Uexküll (1957) stated, "perceptual and effector worlds together form a closed unit, the *Umwelt*" [p. 6]. He also pointed out that the interpretation of the stimuli on the part of the animal could be either learned or innately known. The classic example he used was the mated female tick. Blind, the tick climbs to the top of a twig on a bush. When a mammal passes under the bush, it drops off the twig onto the animal and finds a spot on the skin at the proper temperature, burrows deep, and slowly pumps itself full of warm blood. How does the tick perform this complex act? It seems to be a succession of responses to simple stimuli. The behavior begins by the tick responding to the odor of butyric acid that emanates from the skin of all mammals. This causes her to drop off the branch. Each of the following responses is similarly mediated by a restricted cue.

The concepts of the functional cycle and the Umwelt influenced later writers such as Lorenz (1935). The Umwelt is inferred, in practice, by the stimuli to which an organism responds, which can be influenced by experience. The functional cycle is of modern interest since it contains feedback, both negative and positive. Most behaviors, such as feeding, courtship, nest building, burrowing, and fighting, can be analyzed in functional cycle terms.

Wallace Craig (1918), a student of Whitman, pointed out that an organism not only reacts to a stimulus with a fairly well-coordinated series of actions, but also seems to search for the stimulus which allows behavior of a more stereotyped nature to be performed. Craig divided instinctive behavior, therefore, into three components: *appetitive behavior, the consummatory act,* and *relative rest.*

> An appetite (or appetence, if this term may be used with purely behavioristic meaning), so far as externally observable, is a state of agitation which continues so long as a certain stimulus, which may be called the appeted stimulus, is absent. When the appeted stimulus is at length received it stimulates a consummatory reaction, after which the appetitive behavior ceases and is succeeded by a state of relative rest [p. 91].

Appetitive behavior is variable and involves opportunities for learning, such as where to hunt for food; the consummatory action, the end of the series, is always innate. Craig gave a number of examples from doves, involving drinking, locating a nest site, finding straws for building, brooding eggs, and mating. Appetitive behavior also involves a *readiness to act,* and the animal may perform low-intensity incomplete versions of the consummatory act, termed *incipient consummatory actions*, in the absence of the appropriate stimulus.

The fact that an inexperienced animal would perform the consummatory act in response to an abnormal stimulus if the normal stimulus were unavailable led to Craig's concluding that it must learn to obtain the adequate stimulus. Thus, a female dove, which has never had a nest or material to build one, lays eggs on the bare floor; but a dove that has had long experience with nests will withhold her eggs if no nest is obtainable. Similarly, the male dove, if he has never had a nest, goes through brooding behavior on the floor; but an experienced male is unwilling to do so and shows "extreme anxiety to find a nest" [Craig, 1918, p. 94].

The avoidance of stimuli was treated by Craig (1918) in a similar manner as appetitive behavior. "An aversion . . . is a state of agitation which continues so long as a certain stimulus, referred to as the disturbing stimulus, is present, but which ceases, being replaced by a state of relative rest, when that stimulus has ceased to act on the sense organs" [p. 91].

Craig noted that the same stimulus, the absence of which led to appetitive behavior and the consummatory act, could also lead to an aversion or indifference if continually present. He was also aware of the cyclic nature of the animals' activities and, in essence, elaborated on the functional circle of von Uexkull. The similarity of appetitive behavior to James' *impulse* is apparent since appetitive behavior seemingly involves an impulse, desire, drive, and so forth. Craig carried James' analysis further, especially when he reintroduced the notion that the performance of the consummatory act was reinforcing.

Craig thus attempted an empirical means of dividing and identifying the motivational (energizing), and descriptive aspects of instinct. Darwin and other writers were very clear about the descriptive aspect, but they used vague terms like *impulse* that were tied to nothing in particular and, consequently, were impossible to study. It should be pointed out that the distinction between appetitive behavior and consummatory acts cannot always be made or, if it is made, they may not be rigorously differentiated. Nonetheless, it seems clear that when psychologists such as Freud and McDougall discussed instinct they were really emphasizing the important appetitive side. Their contributions should be seen in this light and not dismissed as unscientific. Similarly, much of present-day psychology dealing with drives, motives, curiosity, exploration, and sensory reinforcement could perhaps be tied together better by using this conception. It is interesting to note the parallels between Craig's views and the discussion of reinforcement in relation to response probabilities, which is presented in Chapter 2.

The approaches discussed in this section are the ones from which ethology, as it is known today, stems. However, the term *ethology* was already in use during the nineteenth century in biology and psychology to refer to naturalistic observation and the study of character, respectively (Jaynes, 1969). Modern ethology encompasses certain conceptual, methodological, and experimental approaches in addition to an emphasis on observation.

THE CLASSICAL SYNTHESIS OF MODERN ETHOLOGY

It was not until the extensive writings of Konrad Lorenz and Niko Tinbergen that the concepts of ethology were systematized and applied to a large variety of behaviors, although many other scientists also contributed. A detailed review of the early ethological work was presented by Tinbergen (1951) and by the various authors at the Symposium of the Society for Experimental Biology (1950). A number of important early papers by von Uexküll, Lorenz, and others appeared in translation more recently (Lorenz, 1970, 1971, Schiller, 1957).

Lorenz built upon Craig's foundation in the distinction between appetitive behavior and the consummatory act, integrating it with the functional cycle of von Uexküll and the comparative and developmental approach of Heinroth (1911). Lorenz' approach is based on close observation of the normal behavior of animals. He chides many other writers for not being familiar with their subjects. It is important to have as complete a descriptive record of their activities as possible before interpretations are made. This record is termed the *ethogram* and in its early stage may read as a series of systematized but accurate anecdotes. It is necessary since ethology is an inductive antireductionistic science. From his observations Lorenz became convinced of the practical and theoretical necessity of making a sharp distinction between instinctive and learned aspects of behavior. For Lorenz, the consummatory act of Craig becomes the *fixed action pattern (FAP)*[1] and a focal point of his approach. Indeed, the FAP is the only pure instinctive movement. Appetitive behavior is the important and crucial preliminary phase of instinctive behavior. However, appetitive behavior was not emphasized in research by Lorenz nor by any of the other earlier ethologists, and it remains a relatively neglected topic today.

A rudimentary hierarchical system was envisioned by Lorenz in which appetitive behavior involved the search by the animal for the appropriate stimulus situation or *sign stimulus,* which would release the consummatory act or FAP. The emphasis of the early ethologists, then, was on fixed action patterns and the sign stimuli eliciting them. The sign stimulus was considered to be innately recognized and acted on a postulated *innate releasing mechanism (IRM).* Sign stimuli emanating from members of the same species (conspecifics) and involved in social behavior are called *releasers.* Later sections will discuss in some detail the properties of sign stimuli and fixed action patterns.

Lorenz saw appetitive behavior as a search for that situation in which the FAP could be released, while the performance of the FAP itself was rein-

[1]The standard English version of basic ethological terms is used throughout, even though the original German may have had a slightly different emphasis.

forcing. A neat example of this reinforcing effect is shown by naive squirrels who learn the most efficient manner of opening nuts even if the usual nutmeat reward has been removed (Eibl-Eibesfeldt, 1963). On the other hand, attainment of the *appeted stimulus* (Craig, 1918) or sign stimulus can be an important factor. This is not to say that only the food value of prey, for example, is rewarding, but also that mere exposure to the sign stimulus, in the absence of a released FAP, can enhance the subsequent effectiveness of a sign stimulus. For instance, the maternal response of mice to a dead baby mouse is stronger if the mice have been previously exposed to a live baby mouse, even if no response has been made to the stronger stimulus of the live baby (Noirot, 1964). In this instance, a lowered threshold is probably involved rather than any learning. Controversy abounds concerning the relative roles of perceptual and motor components to the extent that the obvious conclusion is that both can be the goal of behavior, even of the same behavior.

Lorenz noted that instinctive acts, unlike reflexes, do not always occur equally frequently or readily. There seem to be fluctuations in the animal's readiness to respond even to identical external stimuli. Indications of the animal's readiness to respond are *intention movements.* These movements are low-intensity and incomplete versions of the complete behavior pattern which a trained observer can readily interpret and are similar to the incipient consummatory action of Craig. For instance, an observer of birds can often determine when a flock will fly to a new location on the basis of the increasing intensity of flight-intention movements. Lorenz noted that every conceivable stage of intention movements could be performed up to the complete performance of the FAP itself. The increasing completeness of instinctive acts can be observed with nest-building movements in birds as the breeding season progresses (Tinbergen, 1952).

Lorenz noted that after the FAP had been performed, the animal usually was less ready to perform it again (initial warm-up effects are often found which are quite temporary). Lorenz postulated that the performance of the act discharged pent-up *action-specific energy (ASE),* which accumulated over time when the FAP was not released.

Lorenz also noted that the same stimulus does not always elicit the same reaction. In particular, he discussed escape reactions of a pair of wild swans to humans. Gradually, if no dire consequence followed the presence of a human, the animals would allow the human to come closer while the escape reaction became less intense, until the behavior of defending the nest against intruders was released rather than the escape reaction. The same stimulus released behavior that was blocked previously by an incompatible motivation. We see in this example a concern with *habituation* (the waning of a response tendency with repeated stimulation, presumably independent of sensory adaptation or motor fatigue), which Lorenz has discussed at length in his more recent writings (1965, 1969). Also intriguing to Lorenz was the fact that a fixed action pattern associated with a given functional cycle, such as a drinking movement, might also pop up as an integral part of an unrelated behavior, such as courtship. Through evolution it seemed that a behavior could be displaced from its original function. Naturally, changes in releasers as well as behaviors were involved in this phenomenon termed *ritualization*. Ritualization can also involve a change in the behavior patterns themselves: the disappearance or alteration in intensity of a movement, or even the reorganization of elemental units of a fixed action pattern.

Lorenz (1950) formulated many aspects of instinctive behavior into a model as shown in Figure 9.3. The accumulation in the reservoir, due to the constant dripping of water over time, symbolizes the accumulation of ASE, stressing the fact that the longer the period of time since the response was elicited, the more readily the response will be performed. The valve at the bottom can be released by an appropriate weight; that is, the sign stimulus will unlock the valve and allow the ASE to flow, leading to the performance of the previously blocked behavior. The strength of the response is shown by how far the water shoots. In other words, one can get varying intensities of responses depending on the stimulus used and the amount of accumulated ASE.

One particularly intriguing phenomenon that Lorenz noted was *vacuum activity*. An animal will sometimes perform a complete sequence of movements, such as hunting and attacking prey, although the adequate stimulus, such as an insect, is not present. The animal becomes so highly motivated that it will perform the activity even in the absence of the appropriate sign stimulus. This vacuum activity can be conceptionalized in the model by having the reservoir so full that the pressure exerted on the valve at the bottom is enough to open it without any weight on the pan. Although some controversy exists over whether or not a

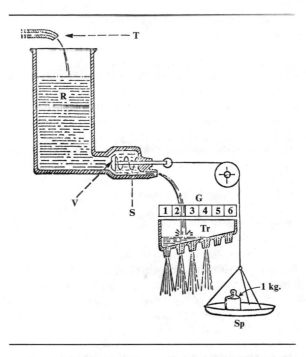

Figure 9.3 The hydraulic model of Lorenz. Symbols are: T, tap; R, reservoir; V, valve; S, spring; Sp, spring pan; Tr, trough; and G, scale measuring response strength. (From Lorenz, 1950.)

stimulus of some type is involved in the release of vacuum activities, it certainly is true that a very inappropriate stimulus can release the complex chain of activity, as earlier noted by Craig (1918). For instance, frogs and toads during the mating season will clasp a variety of completely inappropriate objects, such as rubber boots (Eibl-Eibesfeldt, 1970).

From this model Lorenz (1950) developed the *method of dual quantification:* The intensity of an act depends on two independent factors—the effectiveness of the stimulus situation and the level of internal motivation. Lorenz has always claimed that this model is a crude analogy that should not be taken too seriously, but that it is able to account for a large variety of data. However, he has been taken to task by a number of critics (e.g., Hinde, 1960; Lehrman, 1953) for implying that such hydraulic processes really occur in the organism and its nervous system. This would not seem to be a valid criticism.

One empirical weakness of the model is that it does not deal adequately with stimulus specificity. A number of studies have shown that an act can be elicited repeatedly by one stimulus until it habituates or adapts out. A second sign stimulus nonetheless elicits the same response. For example, Prechtl (1953) determined that open-beak gaping in nestling songbirds could be elicited by either shaking the nest or imitating the parental call. If either one were done repeatedly, 10 to 13 responses would be made before the reaction ceased. If the two stimuli were alternated, however, 40 to 46 respones would occur. Clearly, it does not make sense to hold that the ASE is drained off with the first stimulus. Neither does sensory adaptation or motor fatigue explain the phenomenon. Perhaps we also need the concept of stimulus-specific energy, which, of course, complicates the picture considerably.

Although Lorenz claimed that the core of instinctive behavior in the individual was impervious to learning, he also postulated the existence of the intermingling of instinctive and learned behaviors termed *instinct-conditioning intercalation* (also often referred to as *instinct-training interlocking*), which was anticipated by Craig (1918). There is certainly evidence that such things can occur. For instance, in imprinting a young bird to follow its mother, the sign stimuli (usually visual cues from the natural, foster, or artificial mother) can be largely acquired while the behavior itself (locomotion, vocalization, etc.) is innate. There is also some evidence that the naive animal may often have all the separate units of an FAP in a complex series of activities, but that it must acquire the appropriate ordering of the components through experience (Eibl-Eibesfeldt, 1963).

Tinbergen also played an important role in the development of ethology. Compared to Lorenz, he was much more experimentally inclined, performing many of the classic experiments dealing with the releaser concept (Tinbergen, 1951). Specifically, Tinbergen and his colleagues worked extensively on the behavior of a small fish called the three-spined stickleback *(Gasterosteus aculeatus).* This is a hardy, common European fish that Tinbergen found very useful for observation and experimentation in captivity. Because of the importance of this animal in the development of ethological ideas, a brief descriptive ethogram of the reproductive behavior of the stickleback will be presented (Tinbergen, 1952). We will have cause to refer to this behavior repeatedly.

The stickleback is normally a school-dwelling fish, but as the breeding season approaches in early spring, it leaves the school and stakes out in shallow, fresh water, a territory from which it will drive out any intruder, male or female. Tempera-ture, light cycles, and their effects on the hormonal condition of the animal are important *antecedent conditions.* After the boundaries of the territory are established, the male begins to dig a nest, which is primarily a shallow pit in the sandy bottom about 5 centimeters square. The pit is dug by removing sand with the mouth. Then the stickleback piles weeds, algae, and other plant material into the depression and coats it with a sticky substance from the kidney. The material is then shaped into a mound with the snout, and the fish bores a tunnel by wiggling through it. The tunnel is quite narrow and only slightly shorter than the adult fish. Construction of the nest involves a sequence of many fixed action patterns and sign stimuli. As soon as the nest is finished, the male changes color. It now possesses a bright red chin and belly, and the back turns a bluish-white. The stickleback begins to court females rather than to drive them out; however, if it meets another male (which is also now red underneath) at the border of its territory, the fish will still attack. The red belly has been shown to be a sign stimulus for this behavior. As the male invades a neighboring male's territory, the intruder seems to lose its spirit, while the territory holder becomes more aggressive. A series of attacks and retreats on the part of both fish takes place, although neither fish actually touches the other. As the intensity of the duel increases, each fish may suddenly adopt an almost vertical head-down posture, turn laterally toward its opponent, raise the ventral spines, and produce jerky movements. As if this is not enough, under certain circumstances both fish begin to dig in the sand. This behavior seems quite out of place and actually looks very much like nest digging. This sequence is a product of conflicting *functional cycles* or motivational states (fear and aggressiveness).

With females a rather different sequence of behaviors ensues. Their bellies are now swollen and shiny, containing anywhere from 50 to 100 eggs. Whenever a female approaches the male's territory, the male makes first a sideways turn away from the female and then a quick movement toward her. After each of these jerky movements, the male stops for an instant and then performs another one. This is called the zig-zag dance. It seems to be ritualized from the alternation of flight and attack movements. Eventually the female responds to the male and swims toward him in a curious head-up posture. He then turns away from her and swims toward the nest, and she proceeds to follow him. He pokes his nose into the nest opening with a series of rapid thrusts and turns on his side and raises the three dorsal spines toward the female. She then enters the nest and rests there with her head sticking out one end and her tail out the other. The male then prods her tail base with rhythmic thrusts, leading her to lay the eggs. As soon as the female lays the eggs, she swims out of the nest. The male then swims into the nest after her and quickly fertilizes the eggs. After that he drives the female away and procedes to repeat the complete sequence with another female. A given male may mate in this manner with up to five females, guiding each one through the nest in turn, prodding her to lay the eggs, and then fertilizing them. The mating behavior then rapidly ceases and his color changes to the more usual dark state, and again he becomes hostile to females as well as males. The stickleback's attention is now taken up with fanning the eggs in the nest with his pectoral fins. This seems to be important in order to insure a proper amount of oxygen and to dissipate the CO_2 which builds up. Each day the amount of time spent fanning increases until it reaches a maximum right before hatching. After the eggs hatch, the father keeps the young together for a day or two, retrieving stragglers, protecting them from predators, and so forth. However, the young stickleback soon becomes independent and associates with other young sticklebacks from other broods.

This then is a very short résumé of the actual behavior seen during reproduction in the stickleback. It is highly predictable, has a series of distinct phases, and is usually observed in captivity or in the field.

Tinbergen also derived a model for instinctive activities in which he attempted to incorporate Lorenz' approach into a broader hierarchical scheme (see Figure 9.4). Whereas Lorenz' model attempted to account for short-term changes in responsivity, Tinbergen's model attempted to deal with more long-term and cyclic changes involving a constellation of activities correlated with one another, such as in reproductive behavior. The figure shows a global instinct, reproductive behavior in the stickleback, which consists of a series of appetitive behaviors and consummatory acts which seep down to lower and lower levels. Indeed, Tinbergen felt that they can be superimposed onto the neurophysiological findings of Weiss (1941). This model is most valuable if we use it only as a descriptive classification of activities. What we have, in essence, is a hierarchical system where each drive can be divided into two or more subordinate drives that are more restrictive than the one above it.

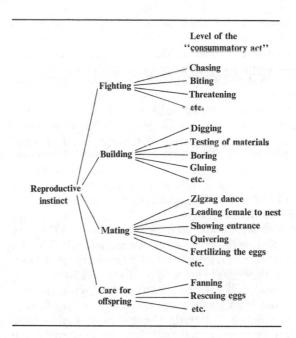

Figure 9.4   The hierarchical organization of a major instinct as illustrated by the reproductive behavior of the male three-spined stickleback. (From Tinbergen, 1951.)

Drive, as defined by Tinbergen (1952) and as used throughout this chapter, is the readiness to react to certain releasing stimuli. *Mood* is perhaps a better term for this definition and is gaining popularity (von Holst & von Saint-Paul, 1963). Each drive is not related to a specific FAP as in the ASE of Lorenz, but:

> The fighting drive, or subdrive, itself does not control merely one simple movement; it gives rise to a special form of instinctive behavior (flying aggressively towards the intruder) followed by one of several possible forms of aggression: posturing, attack or chase. The form of aggressive behavior actually shown depends on the strength of the drive in the territory owner, and on what the other male does, which means, on which external stimuli impinge upon the attacking male [p. 3].

Tinbergen speculated that specific neural centers served to integrate certain activities. He clearly stated that this theory could be proven wrong. However, he did claim that the hierarchical organization of drives was proven beyond doubt. Although this may be true, the model is somewhat misleading in that there is actually a clear sequencing of activities within and between the various levels (Guiton, 1960).

Another aspect of Tinbergen's view is that several responses may each depend on a specific stimulus, but that all of them are dependent on another state of the organism. Tinbergen uses the example of brooding, which may be induced in a bird by hormones and yet, once induced, finds the animal responding to different stimuli in specified ways. For instance, with eggs in the nest, the female sits in a characteristic manner. She will respond in a different way if the egg arrangement is disturbed and will move the eggs back and forth until the tactile stimulation is just right. She will respond in a still different way to eggs moved outside the nest, retrieving them by using a unique FAP. This retrieving behavior is central to an important ethological concept that will be discussed later.

This brief résumé of basic ethological thought cannot indicate the large amount of empirical work on which it is based. The following sections will deal in more detail with specific concepts, their analyses, and their usefulness and limitations.

Criticisms of classical ethology

We have traced the course of the instinct concept through the writings of the classical ethologists. Some American experimental psychologists immediately perceived the implications of ethology for experimental psychology, and their research developed toward a fruitful blend which had the potential of advancing both fields. For instance, Hess (1962) became interested in the experimental analysis of imprinting and Verplanck (1955) studied species differences in learning and motivation. However, the generally cautious reception of ethology by American psychology led to a delay in its psychological influence. Indeed, the early ethological position did not go unchallenged either within ethology or within psychology, and the study of behavior has benefited from the ensuing dialogue. Of the ethologists, Hinde (1970) has been the most diligent in seeking common ground with experimental and comparative psychology.

General critiques of ethology in the early 1950s were written by Hebb (1953), Lehrman (1953), Kennedy (1954), and Beach (1955). These centered around (1) the concepts of instinct and innate behavior, (2) the use of energy models and unitary motivational constructs, (3) the behavioral classifications and levels of analysis employed, and (4) the physiological correlates of ethological concepts. These are primarily theoretical issues and

will be considered at appropriate places in this chapter.

Relatively free from criticism by psychologists (but not really used by them) was the ethological insistence on (1) studying behaviors meaningful in the context of an animal's natural existence, perhaps stemming from the fact that the ethologist derives pleasure from his animals, (2) beginning an analysis with descriptive studies, (3) studying a wide range of species and behaviors, (4) comparing similar behaviors in closely related species, and (5) disparaging the exclusive use of domesticated animals. These five points tied together with an evolutionary perspective may constitute ethology's greatest contribution to psychology and what is often referred to as the *ethological attitude*. Some specific methods developed by ethologists, involving the use of social isolation and the recording of temporal sequences of behavior and preferences, have also been generally accepted.

Schneirla's alternative formulation

The problems set forth by ethologists as central to the study of behavior—that is, the understanding of the normal species-characteristic behaviors of the rich variety of animal life on our planet—have essentially been ignored by modern psychologists and even most biologists until recently. However, closely parallel in time with the development of classical ethology in Europe was the development of a quite different theoretical approach to many of the same problems by Theodore C. Schneirla in America. However, Schneirla and his students did not really formulate a systematic approach until the 1950s and 1960s when they were seemingly confronted with the challenge of the arrival of ethological ideas in the Western Hemisphere (Lehrman, 1953). The later writings of Kuo (e.g., 1967) also developed similar conclusions.

Although a complete discussion of this approach is not possible here, some of the major ideas developed by Schneirla will be presented here and at appropriate places elsewhere in this chapter (see Aronson et al., 1970, for a collection of essays by former students and others influenced by Schneirla). Schneirla eschewed ethological concepts such as innate fixed action patterns, releasing mechanisms, and energy constructs. He felt that when applied to a wide variety of animal species, there was a danger that superficially similar behaviors would be attributed to similar mechanisms. To Schneirla qualitative differences between phyletic levels were of the utmost importance. Paradoxically, however, his theory was concerned with individual behavioral development as based on differences in response to quantitative changes in stimuli. That is, Schneirla erected a theory of behavior development based on the earlier noted and important observation that animals often approach low-intensity stimuli and withdraw from high intensities of the same stimulus class. The *approach-withdrawal (A/W) theory* based on this observation relied largely on the autonomic nervous system and eventually became quite complex. Schneirla (1965) attempted to explain away many of the ethological theoretical concepts by pointing out the inordinate complexity of the interactions among the organism, its heredity, and its environment during development. He redefined experience, as mentioned earlier, to include all stimulative interactions between an organism and its environment.

Although little of Schneirla's writings have borne conclusive supportive empirical fruit, his emphasis has had a salutary effect on ethology in insuring that ethologists do not get so enamored of their concepts and generalizations that they lose their original concern with the diversity and complexity of animal behavior. But Schneirla and Lorenz both shared the essence of the ethological attitude as exemplified by the five points previously listed (Lehrman, 1971).

ETHOLOGICAL DESCRIPTION

Ethology emphasizes the normal behavior of animals and stresses the need for descriptive studies of what animals actually do before more analytical studies can begin. This descriptive record is termed the *ethogram,* a record of the activities of the organism in its normal habitat, including social interactions with members of the same species, feeding, defensive behavior, migratory behavior, grooming, preening, and so on. On the basis of the ethogram, behaviors are classified and compared with each other and rough functional groupings are made. The function, ontogeny, control (causation), and evolution of the behaviors complete the picture (Tinbergen, 1963). Control or causal analysis includes the study of movements and their stimulation, their genetic and physiological aspects, and the experimental analysis of the relationships between behaviors. The reproductive behavior of the stickleback, discussed earlier, is an example of an ethogram.

Ethology frequently has been thought of as a nonexperimental approach to behavior. This is erroneous. However, in discussing the relations of description and experiment, Lorenz (1970, original 1935) did state that "an experiment conducted in the absence of knowledge of the natural behaviour pattern is in most cases completely valueless" [p. 110]. Spalding (1873) much earlier made a similar point. "Students of animal psychology should endeavor to observe the unfolding of the powers of their subjects in as nearly as possible the ordinary circumstances of their lives. And perhaps it may be because they have not all been sufficiently on their guard in this matter that some experiments have seemed to tell against the reality of instinct" [pp. 7–8].

Ethology did not discover description, of course, but unlike many early naturalists and describers of animals, ethologists strive to separate *description* from *interpretation,* both of which are part of *observation.* The criticism of anecdotes listed earlier must be heeded. One must also be aware that our language itself hinders objectivity unless everyone attaches the same meanings to words. To say that two wolf pups greeted each other joyfully is an observation containing both description and interpretation; to say that the two pups ran toward each other wagging their tails, making certain sounds, and doing X things with their jaws, ears, etc., is pure description. While an observer can have a selective bias for seeing some things and not others (behaviors are often rapid and complex), agreement among observers is possible, especially if an observer lists the criteria used for behaviors A, B, C, etc. (Movie film records are often invaluable.)

On the other hand, initial observations should never be completely intellectual, analytical, or "cold." Lorenz (1950) maintained that the extensive observational data base of ethology would never have accumulated if ethologists did not love watching their animals. One's intuitions, insights, feelings (e.g., the phenomenological) should be recorded although the good ethologist can clearly separate what is seen from what is inferred. This point cannot be emphasized enough since experimental psychology has largely ignored it in its search for scientific respectability. Yet even in the physical sciences (which psychology modeled itself after), the intuitive, "sensuous" side of science is increasingly viewed as important (Blackburn, 1971).

There are two basic methods of describing behavior (Hinde, 1970). One is to give a detailed account of the topography (form) of behavior and its intensity, frequency, and patterning. An example would be recording what actually occurs when two elephants court and mate. The second method is to describe behavior by its function or consequences, such as retrieving pups, digging a burrow, or pressing a lever. Both can be made equally objective and most ethograms incorporate the two in varying degrees.

Although the descriptive ethogram is the beginning of the study of behavior, many of the conclusions and theories of the ethologists are based on experimental work. Ethological experiments differ from those usually performed by psychologists because they proceed initially from normal activities of organisms as seen in their natural context rather than from arbitrary and convenient responses. Furthermore, laboratory studies are ultimately evaluated in terms of how well they aid our understanding of behavior in the "real world."

Unobtrusive field observations

Ideally, unobtrusive observation in the species' natural environment should be undertaken. Many workers, especially investigators of primates and birds, have used this technique to great advantage. However, close observation frequently disturbs the animals or drives them away. One solution is the use of a blind, the technique used by Kortlandt (1962) in a field study of chimpanzees. Unfortunately, animals are often more aware of changes in their environment (e.g., odors) than observers might think, and the behavior recorded may be altered even if the subjects do not flee.

Obtrusive field observations

Another approach is to accustom the animals to the observer's presence so that they will perform the normal activities in a more-or-less uninfluenced manner. This is usually accomplished through prolonged exposure involving a gradually increasing frequency or duration of contact. It is akin to *participant observation* as employed by social psychologists, sociologists, and the FBI. Jane van Lawick-Goodall (1968), for example, was able to integrate herself literally in a troop of chimpanzees in Africa and travel with them through the bush in the Gombe Stream Reserve. The importance of ethograms was dramatically illustrated by her observations on tool making and tool using, which exposed hitherto unknown behavioral capabilities in nonhumans. She also used a food-baiting technique to keep chimps around the campsite. This *luring* method altered some normal behavior, especially that involving troop movements and

foraging, but made possible other types of observations, such as competition or "frustration behavior," if the expected dole was not forthcoming. Field experimentation can then proceed quite naturally from ideas generated in the field. For instance, by blocking normal routes, introducing models of predators, or removing individuals of known status, insight can be gained into natural behavior and its organization.

In both obtrusive and unobtrusive observations, behavior may be recorded with still and motion-picture photography, video and audio tape recordings, and written descriptions of ongoing activities. The multiple-pen event recorder, in which each event and key stands for a particular behavior, is especially valuable in obtaining exact records of behavior sequences. Hutt and Hutt (1970) offer a thorough treatment of the application of these methods. Advances in radioactive marking and biotelemetry are also making possible more precise field studies.

Semifree field observations

Another approach is to observe animals in semifree situations in large outdoor areas which may or may not simulate the natural ecology of the organisms involved. The goal is to observe the behavior of wild organisms that have grown accustomed to the presence of human observers but yet are unrestrained in a stimulus-rich environment so that they engage in the majority of their normal activities, such as feeding, courtship, and parental care. This method was used by Lorenz (1941) in his seminal study on the comparative behavior of ducks. It is one of the most frequently used techniques since the natural habitat of a species may be too far removed geographically from the investigator, the species may be very secretive, or the animal may occur with too low a frequency in its natural habitat to be adequately observed. Where animals are attracted or released and kept in large areas, there are usually no physical restraints keeping the animals together (i.e., they can move apart even if it does mean wandering among the living quarters and parking areas of the scientists). Often it is feasible to study animals in large pens in their natural areas in order to offer familiar climatic and vegetative conditions. For instance, current studies of the black bear in Tennessee utilize an enclosure in the Great Smoky Mountains National Park to study the development of bear cubs indigenous to the region (Burghardt & Burghardt, 1972).

Observations in captivity

The next step in observing animals is to try to restrict the environment even more, such as when one attempts to observe the behavior of birds in aviaries and monkeys on monkey islands. Observations in zoos usually fall into this category. Here there are even more problems in interpretation since the population densities are usually much higher than in nature and the animals have no way to spread themselves out (also sometimes a problem in the previous approach). In addition, the animals may not be in optimal health, the social structure may be altered, the sexual cycle may be changed, new behaviors may be instilled (e.g., begging), and the paucity of physical structure may produce abnormal stereotyped activities such as pacing (Hediger, 1950). Sir Solly Zuckerman (1932), studying social behavior in monkeys and apes, concluded that sexual behavior was the force holding primate societies together, since primates he studied in captivity were sexually receptive all year. This lack of reproductive cycles was, in fact, influenced by abnormalities associated with the zoo environment, including crowding and the keeping together of strangers. In the field, primates have clear reproductive cycles (Lancaster & Lee, 1965). Despite these disadvantages some fine descriptive work has been done in zoos and in other situations where the animal could not be adequately studied in its natural habitat. The trend toward large drive-through wildlife parks with fewer species and numbers of animals in naturalistic settings offers additional opportunities to adventurous psychologists interested in studying large animals in semifree situations (Eaton, 1971).

Complete environmental control

Not quite continuous with the preceding approaches are attempts to maintain a simulated natural environment, as has been most adequately done with small aquatic organisms, especially fish. Indeed, most of our ethogramic information on fish behavior has been obtained in laboratory aquariums, including all the early work on stickleback behavior by Tinbergen and his colleagues. It has recently been shown that stickleback behavior in the field is almost identical to that seen in the laboratory (Wooten, 1972). This brings out two facts which are often misrepresented by commentators on ethology. First, ethology has never been completely a field science. Second, ethologists do not claim that all findings from the laboratory

are inapplicable to the natural setting. It is the attitude and approach to behavior that is important.

The aquarium is a three-dimensional space, and it can be largely separated from the external environment: Temperature, light, and chemical factors can be controlled. These factors are impossible to control with terrestrial animals in outdoor enclosures and very difficult and expensive to control in laboratories, which necessitate the use of controlled environmental chambers. The danger in this approach, of course, is that one may not know the proper temperature, mineral content, plant life, population density, food, and other factors that are conducive to seeing the full range of an animal's activities. Fish breeders are most concerned with these problems, and a number of the difficulties they encounter and their solutions, as described by an ethologist, are found in an interesting and practical handbook for fish breeders (Wickler, 1966).

Barlow (1968a) has discussed a major attendant problem and its solution, the unfortunate tendency of "fear" to interrupt the ongoing activities of the captive subjects one is observing. There are two common alternative strategies open to the investigator. One alternative is *full exposure,* meaning that the animals are kept in a heavily trafficked area of the laboratory where, just as in zoos and in pet stores, the animals become tame and difficult to disturb. However, the situation is not ideal because certain sudden stimuli can be disturbing (door closing, quick approach by people), and this uncontrolled extraneous stimulation is intermittent.

The usual technique, therefore, is to aim for *complete isolation,* which involves reducing the environmental stimuli until the observer sits alone in front of the animals' tank or cage in a soundproof, windowless room. However, the animals often pay close attention to the observer, and the latter's slightest movements evoke orientation responses in the subject with a corresponding decrease of normal activities. Obviously this cannot do, so the observer erects blinds, uses one-way glass, or sits in the dark. The animal often seems to be able to detect the observer's presence, nonetheless. Watching the animal through binoculars at a great distance is not feasible in aquarium facilities. Television monitoring is useful but expensive. Even with a remote TV system, Barlow argues, the subjects in the isolated room are often "fearful and abnormal."

One solution is to *dither,* that is, to expose the subject(s) to a group of animals of a different species which move almost continuously. These can be separated from the subjects by a partition (dither animals in a dither compartment). This constant stimulation produces tame animals that are hard to disturb and are not sensitive to extraneous stimuli. Barlow presents some experimental evidence showing the effectiveness of this technique with fish. It would seem applicable with other animals, including birds and small mammals, and, in fact, might profitably be considered with human naturalistic studies using other people as dithers.

Limitations and extensions
of the ethogram

One can readily appreciate that it is impossible to have a complete ethogram, and no ethologist would claim that a complete ethogram is necessary before doing any other type of study. What is important to an ethologist is an appreciation that what occurs in normal behavior is central to the types of problems which one should study under more controlled and experimental situations. The ethogram, then, is an essential framework, a touchstone to which laboratory studies must be constantly related.

Much ethographic information is necessarily concerned with a limited range of the animal's activities. For instance, we may have studies on feeding behavior, courtship behavior, maternal behavior, or grooming activities of an organism in the field with little attempt to describe the totality of the organism's other activities, except those occurring concurrently with the behavior under investigation. This, of course, is a practical matter, since field studies are expensive and much behavior is seasonal.

Although descriptive studies are a major characteristic of ethology, much early ethology was not, in fact, based on observation in the species' natural environment. Lorenz (1950) pointed out that good insights into behavior are also often gathered by raising animals away from the natural environment, perhaps as pets. In such a situation one often notices movements that are incomplete or inappropriate. In the field, on the other hand, behavior may seem more adaptive and hence more purposeful than it really is. Indeed, captive animals studied in even very artificial surroundings can be valuable in that they often point out what behaviors to focus on in field studies. The secret often seems to be to offer the captive animal a varied and complex environment (such as a home) rather than the simplified and sterile environments typical of too many animal quarters in laboratories, although labora-

tories need not be this way. Hence field and lab studies can enrich each other and both are often necessary, but *the field has initial and ultimate priority.*

Since until recently the major focus of ethological research concerned units of behavior and perceptual processes such as fixed action patterns and sign stimuli, ethograms were viewed more as sources of information for detailed analysis and experiment than as ends in themselves. Surprisingly then, today the ethogram is considered more important than ever before. Ethologists are now more interested in going beyond the behavior patterns of individual animals to considerations of the entire social structure of animal societies and its relations to the environment (vegetation, climate, food) and social processes (Crook, 1970). For instance, there have been many recent field studies on primates where the social structure of the same troop is studied over years and even generations of animals and detailed individual records are kept. These studies resemble long-term anthropological investigations on little-known human groups.

Nonetheless, most ethograms are followed by some type of experimentation. Ideally, this should be manipulation in the field followed by a move to a more restricted environment, such as enclosures, and eventually to the laboratory as the need grows for precise control of parameters known to be important. However, experiments in the field do have many advantages, including the fact that the subjects do not need to be housed or fed. Birds lend themselves nicely to such studies, and surprisingly precise quantitative data can be gathered. Croze (1970) studied the cue learning and prey-searching strategy of crows by placing food under marked seashells. The birds soon learned to fly to the area on the beach where the experiments were conducted. By varying the number, type, and percentage of baited shells, he was able to show quick discrimination learning. Lea and Turner (1972) used plain and quinine-flavored pastry "worms" backed by colored cards and placed on a campus lawn to study mimicry, color preferences, and prey avoidance learning in blue tits. With imagination, almost any environment supporting wild animals can be used as an experimental laboratory.

FIXED ACTION PATTERNS

The fixed action pattern (FAP) occupies a central place in ethological theory and the analysis of behavior. Indeed, to Lorenz (1950) it was the *particulate function* of the FAP that set it apart from reflexes, tropisms, and other innate behaviors. Some examples of behaviors normally thought to be FAPs by ethologists are the burial of nuts by squirrels (Eibl-Eibesfeldt, 1963) and the covering of feces by dogs (Darwin, 1872). All these behaviors are characterized by a fairly fixed sequence of movements involving the use of many muscles and parts of the body. You will recall that the reproductive behavior of sticklebacks includes many stereotyped movements, such as sand digging, the zig-zag dance, and egg fanning. These are all FAPs in the general sense. You will also recall that these FAPs can be grouped into functional classes as illustrated in Figure 9.4.

Differences of opinion arise during discussions of FAPs, since so many behaviors of almost all multicellular animals possess some of the criteria that were advanced. Often the label *FAP* is used to loosely designate important species-characteristic behavior elements an investigator has isolated by observation. This is perhaps appropriate in ethogram construction and in comparative behavior studies of closely related species—for example, courtship in ducks. Nonetheless, FAPs deserve study in and of themselves. In this context, it is interesting to consider the critical analyses of FAPs in two recent papers. The first analysis is a presentation by a psychologist who is concerned with the ethological approach to behavior and yet is not sympathetic to its theoretical orientation (Moltz, 1965). The other analysis is by a zoologist working in fish behavior and trained in ethology (Barlow, 1968b). While the ensuing discussion emphasizes some of the problems involved in the analysis of FAPs, the lively interest in the topic today makes clear the importance and vitality of attempting to deal with the wide range of activities falling under such conceptions.

Moltz divides the properties of the FAP into empirical and theoretical aspects. The empirical properties are those upon which the identification of FAPs are based, and the theoretical properties are those processes or mechanisms inferred to exist on the basis of the empirical properties. Here we need only discuss the former. The empirical properties listed by Moltz indicate that the FAP is considered to be (1) stereotyped, (2) independent of immediate external control, (3) spontaneous, and (4) independent of individual learning.

Stereotypy

Those behavior sequences usually found as terminal components of activities such as feeding are generally considered to be quite invariable, as in Craig's consummatory act. In this way FAPs differ quite dramatically from appetitive behavior. However, FAPs often occur together in sequence as in courtship rites in many birds and fish. Furthermore, appetitive behaviors may often include stereotyped behaviors such as those involved in walking or swimming. Consequently, the common tendency to equate FAPs with consummatory acts is not altogether valid.

FAPs often appear extremely invariable among members of a species, although Barlow (1968b) points out that this invariance may be illusory because the behavior patterns occur so quickly. It was not until recently that a systematic study of variation in an FAP appeared (Dane, Walcott, & Drury, 1959). This study dealt with a film analysis of the courtship displays of goldeneye ducks and considered only the precisely measurable parameter of duration. It was found that some of the behavior units were more variable than others, although the actions were nonetheless very constant in form and duration. A later study (Dane & van der Kloot, 1964) showed that repeated performances by individuals were more stereotyped than the performance of the population as a whole. Many iguanid lizards perform a head-bobbing or "push-up" display during social communication, which is species-characteristic and differs among even closely related species. Recent studies by Ferguson (1971) and Jenssen (1971) document the fact that high degrees of stereotypy are obtained, but also that different populations of the same species can possess reliably different (if subtle) movements. Hence the term *species-characteristic* should be not given a Platonic "ideal form" interpretation. Obviously, stereotypy is relative. Natural selection can act only on variability within a population, and a display needs only to be stereotyped enough to serve its function. Many learned behaviors can become stereotyped in performance and are then commonly referred to as habits.

Independence from immediate external control

This is a less frequently encountered phenomenon, although it exists clearly in certain behaviors. The classic example is the egg-retrieving response of the graylag goose jointly investigated by Lorenz and Tinbergen (1938). In this behavior, the goose sitting on its nest will retrieve an egg displaced outside of its downy home. Upon seeing the egg, the goose will extend its neck toward the egg and roll it back into the nest with its bill. Rolling an egg is not as simple as rolling a ball or cylinder, and the goose must constantly adjust and balance the egg as it is rolled back into the nest. Hence there are two aspects of this response: the sagittal movement involved in rolling the egg under the animal's breast and the balancing *(taxic)* movements which are based on immediate feedback from stimuli associated with the rolling egg. The sagittal movement involved in the rolling of the egg is the fixed action pattern. What is interesting about this behavior is that if the egg is removed while the animal is in the process of retrieving it, the goose will continue to move its head, bill, and neck in the same manner as if the egg were still there, except that the taxic movements are absent. Indeed, the bird may continue the pattern to the point of tucking the nonexistent egg under its breast. That is, one gets a relatively pure form of the behavior. It seems to run off all by itself once it is released by the stimulus of the egg. The lateral displacement and taxic movements are not FAPs in the present sense, because they vary with existing conditions such as smooth or rough terrain.

Another example of independence from the necessity of external control is the fighting behavior of the three-spined stickleback easily elicited by models during the breeding season (Tinbergen, 1951). A male stickleback will perform a complete fight in front of an inanimate model (Sevenster, quoted in Barlow, 1968b). This behavior sequence implies some fixed internal *central patterning* by a central nervous system mechanism operating between the receptors and effectors. On the other hand, the behavior of a live opponent can continually modulate an aggressive display. It is often difficult to separate these components experimentally in many behaviors. Indeed, most FAPs appear so dependent on supplementary, taxic, or background sensory stimulation that they often will not occur completely without them. As will be shown, physiological manipulation on the subject is often necessary to answer the question of independence.

Spontaneity

The spontaneity of the FAP refers to the fact that an animal responds not only because of the immediate external stimulation. Internal factors such as hormonal and maturational states, as well as experiential and motivational factors, play an important role. Also, the longer the time period since the FAP was previously performed, the greater the readiness to perform the behavior. In other words, the threshold for the releasing stimulus becomes lower, and eventually behavior may even be exhibited in the complete absence of any identifiable releasing stimulus (vacuum activities). For example, male turkeys individually isolated under constant conditions in soundproof chambers continue to gobble in a stereotyped manner at intervals (Schleidt, 1965). Although good examples of vacuum activities are not common, it is certainly true that threshold differences exist. For instance, water extracts of the skin substances of earthworms are much more effective in releasing prey attack in food-deprived garter snakes than in more satiated ones, and less concentrated extracts become more effective as deprivation continues (Burghardt, 1970a). Such changes in responsivity, when contrasted to less changeable threshold variability for reflexes, have led to the use of this FAP characteristic to distinguish it from simple reflexes. However, it is likely that a continuum exists between isolated, rigid reflexes (knee jerk, muscle twitch) and more complex and variable responses involving the whole organism. The phenomenon of spontaneity is often used to argue for central patterning or the endogenous control of behaviors with minimal sensory input (see following section).

The deprivation experiment

A fixed action pattern is unlearned and is performed without postnatal experience of the type needed to account for its topography. The clearest examples are those behaviors shown upon birth or hatching, such as locomotion in many insects and birds, feeding behavior, head and body orientation, sucking by newborn mammals, and many other behaviors mentioned by the early instinct writers such as Spalding (1873). The technique used to show the unlearned aspect of behaviors which do not occur (mature) until later in life is the *deprivation experiment,* which is discussed in some detail by Lorenz (1965). In the deprivation experiment, the animal is tested either at birth or hatching before it has performed the activity; or, if the behavior to be tested is one which is characteristically found later in life, such as locomotor, sexual, or aggressive responses, the animal is reared in isolation from species members in order to eliminate the possibility of learning via imitation or maternal effects.

It is possible to go even further and eliminate normal sensory or effector experiences which may be factors in the final form of the behavior.

Such was the case in Carmichael's (1927) classic experiments on salamander larvae reared under constant anesthesia. Experimental animals developed the species-characteristic swimming behavior as well as normal individuals. However, even if this experiment had shown that such experience was essential for the animal to swim normally it would not explain why all salamander larvae swim in the same fashion.

Lorenz emphasizes the fact that the deprivation experiment can only show what behavior is unlearned. If a behavior is not demonstrated in animals raised in the abnormal isolation environment, one still cannot say that the behavior is learned, since abnormalities due to disease, poor diet, improper stimulus situation, and lack of social environment cannot be easily eliminated. A very well-documented example of how the social environment itself may be crucial for the occurrence of normal sexual behavior is the experiments by Harlow and Harlow (1966) showing abnormal sexual and maternal behavior in rhesus monkeys raised in social isolation. While the deprivation experiment often seems to demonstrate what is unlearned, the behavior should not therefore be labeled as innate except as a shorthand word (see following discussion). The genetic information involved may indeed be great, however.

That properly using the deprivation technique involves a subtle understanding of an animal's behavior is shown by studies of nest building in rats. Since rats reared in isolation from other rats build nests under certain conditions, the behavior had long been considered instinctive. However, Riess (1954) raised female rats not only in social isolation, but in isolation from all objects they could handle, even to the extent of feeding them powdered food. When mated and placed in cages provided with paper, they did not build nests or retrieve their young. The conclusion was that the nest-building behavior was not innate, but due to prior manipulative experience. This example was widely quoted in writings critical of ethological concepts (Beach, 1955; Hebb, 1953; Lehrman, 1953; Ross & Denenberg, 1960); Lehrman even envisioned a model for the development of nest building based on the rat's learning that piles of material conserved heat. How the precise species-characteristic movements involved in nest building became shaped was ignored, a problem similar to that in the salamander experiment just discussed. Eibl-Eibesfeldt (1961) repeated Riess' experiment after observing carefully how rats actually build

nests and the conditions in which nest building occurs. He even cut off the rats' tails so that they could not carry them in their paws as he had observed some object-deprived rats do. But the crucial difference from Riess' experiment was in testing the mated rats in their home cages where they had an established sleeping area. After giving birth these rats retrieved their babies and built good nests when offered material. In addition, Eibl-Eibesfeldt found that even rats experienced in nest building would not build nests in Riess' situation. It seems that rats in a strange environment almost inevitably explore rather than engage in other activities. Thus, a careful consideration of the species and its behavior is necessary for the proper use of the deprivation experiment, along with deliberate consideration of what the animal is deprived of (Lehrman, 1953) and what question you are seeking to answer.

Common causal factors and temporal sequencing

Barlow (1968b) is primarily concerned with the practical application of the FAP to the study of behavior. He advances three diagnostic properties of the FAP: (1) It has common causal factors distinguishing it from other FAPs; (2) it is independent from external control after being released; and (3) the components occur in predictable sequences where the intensity of components might vary but their interrelations do not. The second characteristic has already been discussed.

The first and third criteria are derived from the fact that most FAPs can be broken down into successively smaller units until reaching the level of individual muscle contractions. This brings us to the important issue of the temporal patterning of behavior, studies of which are becoming more frequent (Hinde & Stevenson, 1969). It has become apparent that it is not proper to approach behaviors such as nest building as global units, just as it was discovered that the more global instincts (e.g., maternal, reproductive) of early writers were too vague. Considering a behavior only in terms of its function can hinder analysis.

Subunits of FAPs are termed *acts*. Several acts can form an FAP, and they in turn can be grouped into *bouts*, in which a given FAP is repeated, or into *sequences,* in which a given FAP occurs with other FAPs. How, then, can acts be distinguished from FAPs and FAPs from sequences? Close analysis can determine whether the supposed acts of an FAP always occur as ABCD, or if on occasion only

A or B occurs, while at increasing levels of completeness ABC or ABCD would occur but never BCAD or CDA. Thus, the third criterion can be objectively and readily measured by observing the temporal ordering of behavior. In other words, if two behaviors are always associated, they are considered as two acts of an FAP; if they can be disassociated, then two FAPs in sequence are involved. The difficulty in application is seen in the fact that nature rarely provides correlations of 1.00. Is a correlation of 0.90 sufficient?

Barlow (1968b) cites his own observations on the courtship movements of orange chromides, a cichlid fish, to illustrate the problem. This courtship movement consists of two components, *quivering* of the head from side to side and *flickering* caused by the opening and closing of the pelvic fins. The behavior is controlled by a single releaser, the approach of the mate. Certainly, the quivering and flickering components seem to be part of an FAP, yet Barlow discovered that if the relative size of the mate is varied, the two behaviors are influenced differentially. Hence closer analysis shows that the two acts are really two FAPs. Barlow claims that threshold differences for the component behaviors are not sufficient to explain his results. Quantitative studies of temporal sequencing of behavior are also important, although these studies have been unavailable until recently. Dane and van der Kloot (1964) found no rigid sequence of actions in the precopulatory display of the male goldeneye duck. Eight male behaviors are involved which do, however, tend to follow each other more than chance would predict. Nelson's (1964) study of courtship behavior in species of fish was even more quantitative and dealt with intervals between behaviors as well as their duration and frequency. A *sequence* was defined as male actions that were statistically dependent. Such sequences were separated from each other by intervals and were statistically independent of one another. Within a sequence, an action was found dependent upon only the immediately preceding action. Delius (1969) has utilized even more sophisticated quantitative techniques in the study of the various maintenance and comfort movements of skylarks and the relations between them.

While Barlow insists that an invariable sequence is critical to temporal patterning, he neglects the possible role of experience. Fromme (1941) replicated Carmichael's salamander work with tadpoles (frog larvae, quite distantly related to salamanders) and found that the anesthetized subjects did not swim quite as well as the controls. This experiment, along with many others, supports the notion that often normal sensory or "practice" experiences are helpful, if not essential, in providing the context in which the species-characteristic movements are expressed. Traditional learning or conditioning interpretations are certainly not very helpful. In the nest-building studies in rats, discussed earlier, Eibl-Eibesfeldt (1961) found that the behavior of nest building is composed of a sequence of FAPs, each with its own releasing stimuli and, perhaps, appetitive phases as well. He discovered a number of movements involved in the nest construction of a variety of rodents, including such different behaviors as *grasping* nest material with the teeth, *pulling* it free with biting if necessary, *carrying* it to the nest site, *depositing* it, *pushing* it into a heap, *scratching* out a hollow in the middle, and *pushing* material to the sides. The animals may also *split* material such as straw into finer material with characteristic movements. Clearly, nest building is no simple reflexive behavior. In rats deprived of manipulation experience, all of the necessary movements occurred, but the sequence was less coordinated and efficient because behaviors appeared at the wrong times. Here, then, is an instance where FAPs are integrated through experience into a highly functional sequence. A similar integrating role was found in nut-opening behavior of squirrels and sexual behavior of polecats (Eibl-Eibesfeldt, 1967). Therefore, to ask simply whether such behaviors are unlearned is inadequate.

Further, the ontogeny of a unitary FAP may reveal that it can be dissected into smaller units. Fox and Apelbaum (1969) have analyzed the orienting-jump response of rabbits and found it to be composed of a number of elements including vocalizations which develop at different rates postnatally, although in the adult an integrated FAP is observed. These complications should warn against overinterpretation of FAPs and the distinction from smaller units.

As should be apparent by now, the FAP represents a variety of relatively stereotyped activities to which the various criteria discussed here cannot always be applied unambiguously. Certain FAPs have properties which allow better analysis of some problems than others. If properly used, the FAP allows one to formalize and to investigate behaviors by clarifying the kinds of attributes which need investigation and their potential as sources of ontogenetic and evolutionary change. Barlow suggests the term *modal action pattern (MAP)* as a substitute for fixed action pattern, since the latter focuses more attention on fixedness than on the often important variability. At the same time, *MAP*, as a term, maintains needed emphasis on the species-characteristic form of the behavior.

PHYSIOLOGICAL INVESTIGATIONS OF INSTINCTIVE MOVEMENTS

Ethological views in the 1930s concerning instinctive behavior and the concept of action-specific energy were not congruent with current physiological thinking. Early criticisms of ethology made much of the fact that there appeared to be little physiological evidence to support ethological conceptions of fairly complex behaviors. The notion then was that the central nervous system was basically a switchboard connecting external stimuli and motor responses. This was incompatible with the idea of spontaneous behavior and the performance of behavior sequences without constant and detailed sensory feedback. The ethologists were concerned with understanding behavior and were not about to succumb to reductionistic limitations set by physiologists who had inadequately studied the nervous system. However, being biologists, ethologists readily admitted that instinctive movements must have a physiological base. Therefore, in order to support their ideas on the physiological level, earlier ethologists were forced to rely on work devoted to less complex behaviors such as locomotion and the role of feedback. In particular they referred to the work of von Holst (see discussions in Hess, 1962, and Tinbergen, 1951), whose observations on worms and fish did not support classic chain reflex theory and suggested the operation of more central (endogenous) factors. By recording fin movements of spinal fish that had been deafferentated (the sensory nerves to the brain were cut), he found that rhythmical locomotor impulses as well as coordinated fin movements survive even in the absence of sensory feedback. Later experiments by Lissman and Gray using the dogfish and amphibians (Gray, 1950) showed similar results with the exception that some small amount of afferent input was needed to maintain the coordination.

Dependence upon sensory feedback, however, seemed more important in mammals in light of the several studies, beginning with Mott and Sherrington (1895), which showed no "purposeful" movements of a limb in monkeys after it had been deafferented. Taub and Berman (1968) report an extensive series of experiments which question the interpretation of such studies. They found that if one deafferents *both* forelimbs of a monkey, for instance, it walks and climbs using all limbs in near normal fashion and can even pick up small objects between the thumb and forefinger. Blindfolded monkeys also climb and ambulate, indicating that the ability is not visually mediated in the absence of proprioceptive feedback. Total spinal cord deafferentation also did not abolish forelimb use. These studies show that central nervous system factors can be almost exclusively involved in coordinated movements in mammals and, by the way, pose problems for learning theories based on response-produced stimulation, not to say any general cybernetic theory of behavior. A view gaining currency (Wilson, 1972) is that the main function of sensory feedback in locomotion, for example, is to superimpose error correction reflexes upon a "fundamental control scheme" in the CNS that "develops under strong genetic limitation" [p. 365], as do the peripheral mechanisms (muscles, bones).

It was not until quite recently, however, that physiological investigations of more complex instinctive movements have been performed, and a rather large literature is rapidly accumulating (e.g., Roeder, 1963). A few samples of the type of phenomena, animals, and methods used follow.

Electrical stimulation

W. R. Hess (1954) was the first person to perform an extended series of studies devoted to the effect of electrical stimulation of the more primitive areas of the brain (ESB) on normal ongoing activities. Hess found that he was able to elicit well-coordinated, virtually complete movement sequences identical with normal behavior by electrically stimulating the cat's brain. He was able to elicit almost at will "rage" behavior. An interesting sequence was seen in sleep activity involving the search for an appropriate place, the circular movements involved in patting down the nonexistent materials on the hard floor, curling up, closing the eyes, and going to sleep.

Von Holst and von Saint-Paul (1962, 1963) did a similar but more extensive series of studies eliciting the behavior of chickens by stimulating the lower brain centers. They were able to show sequences such as feeding, brooding, alerting, cackling, fleeing, and crowing. Antipredator activity could even be distinguished into behavior patterns directed against an aerial or a ground predator, illustrating the specificity involved. One of the important findings of their studies was the need to provide appropriate external stimuli such as food or a predator. Without the proper stimuli, the animal became restless exhibiting a searching behavior of the sort described by Craig. The stimulation acted like the antecedent conditions (setting factors) of behavior, such as food deprivation and similar motivators. These workers also discovered the need for good basic knowledge of the normal patterns of chicken behavior. They discovered that they had to utilize the services of a chicken expert in order to appropriately understand the behaviors that they were eliciting with the stimulation.

Another important aspect of the technique was that they could stimulate more than one area simultaneously and in this way study the interaction between different behavior patterns and moods. This is clearly similar to the study of conflict behavior under the more normal situations described later, but it permits a means of investigating the physiological factors involved. Table 9.1 gives the various kinds of interactions found. The careful reader should be able to note the similarity of some of these categories to the subsequently described conflict classes of successive and simultaneous ambivalent behavior, displacement activity, and redirected behavior.

This research shows that to a considerable extent fixed action patterns can be centrally organized, offering verification of the ethologist's contentions on this point. They also show that the interaction of drives or *moods*, as von Holst and von Saint-Paul prefer to term them, are capable of being looked at physiologically. Hence, the strength and timing of the motivational states can be more precisely studied than under normal conditions.

Von Holst and von Saint-Paul were not overly interested in the precise localization of their stimulating points in the chicken brain although they had a collaborator working on that aspect. They did begin a telemetering approach involving radio frequency stimulation of the chicken brain without any wires or constraints whatsoever. More precise localization and electrical stimulation studies of chickens are becoming available (Phillips & Youngren, 1971). These show considerable variability in response along with fragmented sequences of FAPs rather than rigidly programmed ones. Therefore, it is important to keep in mind that ESB does not simply trigger a discrete center which completely controls behavior.

This approach—brain stimulation of natural behaviors—is being taken up by more recent investigators within a wide variety of species. Studies have been performed by electrically stimulating such behaviors as vocalization in crickets (Huber, 1962); reproductive and defensive behavior in pigeons (Åkerman, 1966a, 1966b); nest building, courtship, feeding, and biting in bluegills (Demski & Knigge, 1971); mating, attacking, threatening, grooming, eating, and other behaviors in the opossum (Roberts, Steinberg, & Means, 1967); and gnawing in rats (Roberts & Carey, 1965). Ingenious use of brain stimulation has also altered social hierarchies in primates (Delgado, 1967).

Interpreting the elicitation of well-coordinated movement sequences in animals as evidence for ethological concepts, such as action-specific energy and innate fixed action patterns, has been contested by Moltz (1965), who points out that sequences of learned behavior can also be elicited through brain stimulation. In fact, brain stimulation may be rewarding for learned responses which produce it, such as lever-pressing in rats (Olds & Milner, 1954; see also Chapter 8). Therefore, the study of the elicitation of specific action patterns in newborn or deprived animals is certainly to the point.

An example of this approach is the experiment

Table 9.1   Types of Interaction of Different Behavior Patterns

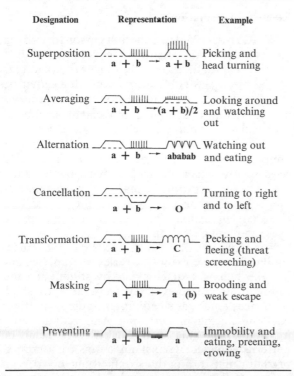

Designation	Representation	Example
Superposition	a + b → a + b	Picking and head turning
Averaging	a + b → (a + b)/2	Looking around and watching out
Alternation	a + b → ababab	Watching out and eating
Cancellation	a + b → O	Turning to right and to left
Transformation	a + b → C	Pecking and fleeing (threat screeching)
Masking	a + b → a (b)	Brooding and weak escape
Preventing	a + b → a	Immobility and eating, preening, crowing

(From von Holst & von St.-Paul, 1963.)

by Roberts and Bergquist (1968), who tested hypothalamically elicited attack in cats raised in social isolation. They found that the basic elements of the attack occurred in the absence of contact with either prey or species members. Experience may improve the efficiency of performance and its environmental stimulus control, however. Experimental cats attacked a sponge as quickly and for as long as they attacked a rat, while control subjects responded more quickly and for a longer time to the rat. The central nervous system seems to have the behavior essentially "wired in," but it must be refined and developed by ontogenetic events.

More critical than these deprivation studies are those involving the brain stimulation of newborn animals which avoid the possible detrimental effects of isolation. Precocial animals like chicks which have a rich behavioral repertoire at hatching are ideal. Septal, preoptic, and diencephalic stimulation produced alertness, head shaking, pecking attack, distress calling, flight, crouching, and other behaviors in newly hatched chicks (Meyer & Salzen, 1970). These certainly are good indications of some innate central control of motor activities. Again, however, sustained invariant sequences of behavior were not found, as is also the case in normal chicks.

Electrical brain stimulation is far from natural, of course, so other forms of stimuli must be acting in normal activity. Although technically more difficult to present and to control, work has been done with localized warming of parts of the brain which elicited grooming, panting, and sleeplike relaxation in the opossum (Roberts, Bergquist, & Robinson, 1969). The central nervous system has a chemical structure also, with some complex molecules more prevalent in some parts of the brain than others. Chemical substances, such as presumed neural transmitters and their inhibitors (acetylcholine, epinephrine, etc.), when injected into parts of the brain, such as the hypothalamus, elicit eating, drinking, and other behaviors, as well as affect learned responses (Grossman, 1967). Hormones seem to elicit more complex behaviors and will be discussed briefly later in the chapter.

Ablation

Another technique which is often used is ablation, the removal or making disfunctional certain areas of the nervous system followed by looking at the effects on behavior. This is a classic technique of physiological psychology and has been especially studied in relationship to learning and primary motivations such as hunger, thirst, and sex (for a good review see Grossman, 1967).

Investigators are beginning, however, to assess the effects of brain lesions on more discrete fixed action patterns and their autonomic correlates (Randall, 1964). Representative of some recent studies are those of Lakso and Randall (1969) and Ursin (1969). Lakso and Randall studied fishing behavior in cats after midbrain lesions. A subject was placed in a chamber with a number of openings of several sizes, dry or water filled, and with or without fish (in water). Normal and lesioned cats fished in a similar manner only when a sunfish was in the large water-filled chamber, but the lesioned animals would also fish if no prey were present but a fairly large hole (8.5-inch diameter) was. One is reminded of fishermen lining the banks of a fished-out stream. Analysis of the stimuli from the fish that elicit normal fishing (form, movement, shimmering, etc.) and a precise determination of the lesion effect should be done. In experiments with cats, Ursin (1969) discussed the fact that ablation of the cingulate gyrus did not alter flight or defensive behavior, whereas amygdala lesions reduced these behaviors. Such studies indicate how species-characteristic behaviors can be used to trace out neural networks of behavior more clearly than learned responses (e.g., avoidance) that are influenced by many procedural parameters, making interpretation difficult.

Work on brain mechanisms has certainly moved in the direction of being more important for the understanding of normal ongoing activities. It is interesting, however, that while von Holst began his studies with the hope of using brain stimulation to understand behavioral drive interactions, few present investigators are interested in using these techniques to investigate ethological concepts (but see Brown & Hunsperger, 1963).

Physiological work will become more relevant to ethology, however, as physiologists discover the need to describe and to classify the behaviors affected by their manipulations more precisely. A sign of the results of such behavioral sophistication is seen in a study by Randall, Lakso, and Littschwager (1969), who found lesion-induced dissociation of the appetitive and consummatory phases of grooming. The appetitive behaviors in this situation include all orienting or social invitation movements. The consummatory phase includes the grooming scratch, lick, or bite. A normal cat, if petted, shows both phases, while a cat with a brain stem lesion may only show the consummatory phase, "completely divorced from the normally preceding appetitive components" [p. 476]. This phenomenon not only supports the ethologists' behavioral conceptions, but also aids in neurological analysis, an example of the mutual interaction benefiting our understanding of behavior.

Invertebrate studies

In lower organisms the neurophysiology of complex behavior may be more readily studied and the appropriateness of ethological models evaluated. In the sea slug (*Aplysia*), Peretz (1969) has found specific neurons which initiate spontaneous gill movements. He severed all nerves between the abdominal ganglion and the gill and discovered that the endogenous activity (one response per 5 minutes) occurred only when the ctenidiogenital nerve was intact, although peripheral factors are also important (Kupfermann et. al., 1971). In barnacles, endogenous rhythmic patterns of activity occur since they are found "in the totally isolated central nervous system at a periodicity consistent with the behavior of the intact animal" (Gwilliam & Bradbury, 1971, p. 512). In the marine snail (*Tritonia*), it has been shown that very brief electrical or even mechanical stimulation of a small group of cells in the pleural ganglion triggers an escape response involving a "fixed action pattern of moderate complexity" (Willows & Hoyle, 1969). This result accords well with the classical ethological view that many FAPs, once triggered, are independent of immediate external control.

Alexander (1968) has reviewed stridulation (sound production via a structure on the forewings) in male crickets as based on his and Huber's work and reaches a number of clear conclusions. Only males produce sounds, one of which is a species-characteristic calling song to attract females. Normally light-dark cycles trigger singing bouts, but they can occur without any known external cue (Bentley, 1971). Some conclusions are:

1. Environmental manipulations (such as deafening, exposure to foreign sounds, including songs of related species) during development do not alter some aspects of the songs. Indeed, no conclusive evidence of long-term changes has been reported.

2. The genotype-phenotype correlation is very high. (This finding is supported by hybridization experiments, which will be discussed later.)

3. Aspects of the pattern of all stridulations are independent of external stimuli and probably also of proprioceptive feedback. The form of some is completely independent. For example, male crickets deafened either before hearing their calls (as juveniles) or as experienced adults still stridulated normally. Severing wings or otherwise altering proprioceptive feedback also had no effect.

4. The nature of the patterns depends on *pacemakers,* either single or small groups of neurons, in various parts of the cricket's body. These have been studied by both ablation and electrical stimulation. "The structures responsible for the pattern are located in the CNS and reflect genetic differences more or less directly in their functional variations" [p. 210]. A recent extension of the genetic-physiological approach is discussed in the behavior-genetics section.

5. If a male cricket is prevented from calling, the intensity of stimuli needed to elicit calling is reduced and the class of effective stimuli broadened. On the other hand, once calling is started it is difficult to stop. Calling is often spontaneous in that no known external stimulus is present.

Alexander looks at those results in terms of the Lorenzian model as presented by one of its leading critics (Lehrman, 1953) and concludes:

> I can think of no significant way that cricket stridulation deviates from the criteria of Lorenz's original "hydraulic" model, constructed in a time of almost complete ignorance of CNS function and apparently largely discarded now as a useful construct, perhaps even by Lorenz himself. The similarity is certainly close enough to justify the model and its use, even now, as a baseline in the search for extremes and kinds of resistance to environmental variations among behavior patterns, whether essentially complete "units" of behavior in an arthropod or obscure fractions of behavioral responses in higher vertebrates. ... The data given here not only prove that behavior essentially fitting Lorenz's model does exist, they explain its biological significance and, to a significant degree, they describe its neurophysiological, developmental, and hereditary correlates [pp. 212–213].

That a conception of behavior (highly simplified by Lorenz himself) derived from pure observation of free-ranging and hand-reared animals is that useful on a physiological level is indeed encouraging at a time when most physiological research seems unrelated to the normal activities of animals. However, the goal of such research should not be to prove or disprove anyone's model, but to explore the mechanisms of meaningful (to the subject) behaviors uncovered by description and functional and ontogenetic analysis.

Behavioral endocrinology

Another area of investigation that is certainly relevant to instinctive behavior includes the role of hormones. Endocrinology is one of the basic sciences with which a broadly based ethological scientist should be acquainted, since many behaviors are influenced by hormone levels. The most extensive work in this area has been with sexual behavior. Typically, androgens (testosterone) enhance male sexual behavior and estrogens enhance female sexual behavior and responsiveness. This has been shown for all classes of vertebrates. Other hormones are involved, too, such as pituitary gonadotrophins. The usual method is to castrate organisms and then replace the hormones to assess their effects.

Beach, the most influential worker in the field, especially with mammals, has attempted to derive evolutionary trends in the evolution of sexual behavior. Beach's (1956) theory concerning rats involves two factors: the arousal mechanism (AM) and the copulatory mechanism (CM). Both of these are very similar to the appetitive and consummatory behaviors of the early ethologists. Beach's (1958) evolutionary approach is based on observations that indicate that as one goes from lower to higher mammals (1) the hormonal control of sexual behavior decreases, (2) the cortical involvement increases, and (3) female sexual behavior is generally less dependent on the cortex than is the male's. Recent work indicates that although Beach's generalizations are too broad (e.g., McGill, 1965) and even simplistic, they facilitated the synthesis of many studies. Recent work (Krames, 1971) does support the idea that the AM and CM are distinct mechanisms. Fresh and used female rats did not affect the male rat's AM threshold but did affect the CM threshold.

That the brain is involved in hormonal influences on sex behavior is nicely shown by the studies of Harris and Michael (1964). They injected estrogen into the hypothalamus of castrated cats and obtained clear indications of estrous behavior. This was true even though the reproductive system was undeveloped and hence peripheral feedback was not crucial. Injections into other parts of the brain had no effect.

Barfield (1964), who looked at sexual as well as agonistic testosterone-elicited behavior in chickens and doves, found different areas of the brain involved in the two behaviors as well as in species differences. Komisaruk (1967) found that brain hormones induced sexual behavior in doves. That

many important possibilities exist in the area of brain and hormonal interactions is also shown by the study of Kling (1968), who found interaction effects between amygdalectomy and testosterone injections (noncentral) in the sexual behavior of young male monkeys.

Sexual behavior, however, involves much more than the arousal and completion of copulation. Courtship and nest building are important associated activities, as is parental care. Indeed, the term *reproductive behavior* is to be preferred, since the sex hormones influence these other behaviors as well.

Hinde (1965) reports on the many factors involved in nest building, egg laying, and brood patch development in canaries. The brood patch is an area of the ventral surface of the female canary that becomes featherless and highly vascularized in the interval between the onset of nest building and the laying of the first egg. It increases in tactile sensitivity during this period and serves the function of its name. The relations among hormonal and external stimuli are complex.

Lehrman (1965) reports an extensive series of studies on the role of internal and external factors in reproduction of the ring dove (*Streptopelia risoria*). Looking at nest-building behavior and incubation, he and his colleagues discovered that the external stimuli (mate and nesting material) can actually stimulate the secretion of hormones. Hence social stimuli can influence hormonal control of behavior in a complex feedback manner, as suggested by von Uexküll's functional cycle.

A final study to be mentioned indicates the pervasiveness of hormonal effects. Emlen (1969) investigated the stellar orientation of birds. It is known that under an artificial planetarium sky many species, such as the indigo bunting (*Passerina cyanea*), orient in a northward direction in spring and southward in autumn. Perhaps this is due to a selective orientation to the spring and autumn night skies, which differ somewhat. Yet buntings oriented northward in the spring even if they were shown an autumn sky. Emlen then brought groups of buntings into either spring or autumn migratory condition and tested them in a planetarium displaying the spring sky. Although the external stimulus (i.e., sky) was the same, birds in spring condition oriented northward and those in autumn condition oriented southward. Since hormones play an important role in the physiology of migratory readiness, "differences in hormonal state may determine the manner in which an orientational cue will be used" [p. 718].

Other approaches

The study of the effects of drugs on species-characteristic behavior is still in its infancy. Sample studies include those of Silverman (1966) on the effects of drugs on social behavior of rats and of Kovach (1964) on the effects of drugs on imprinting.

Another promising area is the use of physiological correlates of ongoing activity. Candland et al. (1969) studied telemetered heart rate before and during the pairing of roosters. In the before stage, the roosters could see each other but they could not fight. They found that heart rate could be used not only to predict whether aggression would occur but also to predict which rooster would win. Those which ended up losing showed greater heart-rate increases before competition than those which were to win. This approach should be very useful in the study of behavior. However, it would especially seem appropriate in the study of relations among social organization, overt behavior, and the emotions and their autonomic correlates. A true physiological psychology of naturalistic behaviors is finally in the offing.

SIGN STIMULI

Although the writings of von Uexküll and Lorenz were of importance in creating interest in sign or key stimuli and releasers, the early systematic discussions of sign stimuli were by Tinbergen (cf. 1948, 1951). Considerations of the role of the external environment by ethologists is not limited to these aspects; however, it has been one of the most characteristic of their interests and will be emphasized here.

Sensitivity and selectivity

It is important to know the sensory capacities of animals. Experimenters are often surprisingly anthropomorphic in frequently assuming that the organism with which they are working responds to the same type of stimuli that they do. This is a two-edged error, cutting both ways.

First, experimenters often do not control an aspect of the environment to which the animal is sensitive. For instance, many maze and runway studies use rats without even considering the possibility that rats might be responding to odors in the apparatus. As far as rats are concerned, two kinds of evidence indicate that much of the learning literature may be seriously questioned. Experi-

ments have shown that the odor of one small food pellet can lead to a differential discrimination on the part of a rat at a choice point in a T-maze (Southall & Long, 1969), casting some doubt on the many experiments where food is placed out of sight only in the designated compartment. Other evidence has shown that a rat trained in a maze in which another rat has been tested previously responds differently depending on whether the rat which preceded it was rewarded or not. A different odor trail is left by a rat depending on whether it expects or does not expect to be rewarded, and this chemical cue is picked up by the succeeding rats (Ludvingson, 1969).

The sword also cuts the other way. An experimenter often decides to study a sensory capacity that is important to humans but which may not be very relevant to the animal under study. Consider again the rat: Even a gross consideration of its natural habitat and life history in the wild should lead to a conclusion that visual perception is not ideally studied in this nocturnal organism (Barnett, 1963). The use of visual stimuli in learning, discrimination, and physiological studies of rats would be difficult to understand unless rats were really the objects of interest, rather than tools for discovering general principles. The pink-eyed albino rat should be even more convincing on this score, yet thousands of experimental studies have been done utilizing visual stimuli in the white rat (Munn, 1950). If one is really interested in studying the abilities of rats *qua* rats, then why was not equal effort expended on the other sensory modalities, in which case the rat's remarkable abilities of olfaction would have been recognized?

The purpose of this example is to demonstrate the danger of neglecting *sensitivity*. Perceptual abilities are set in the first instance by the structure of the sense organs which are largely inherited. The manner in which the receptor cells are connected to the central nervous system is also largely innate (Sperry, 1951). The ability of the organism to discriminate is part of its biological heritage. We cannot see unaided into the ultraviolet range of light energy, but bees can. The sensory apparatus sets outer limits to perceptual abilities. Psychologists should certainly be aware of the sensory capacities of their subjects.

Animals also demonstrate *selectivity:* They do not respond equally to all aspects of their environment to which they are sensitive. Such selectivity does not need to be learned; newly born or hatched animals often show distinct preferences. For instance, Hess (1956) showed that newly hatched ducklings and chicks peck differentially at discs of different colors. In addition, ducklings and chicks have different preferences which presumably are related to their natural habitats. Ducklings peck more at green discs and chicks more at orange and blue ones.

However, the objects that an animal must recognize in the world are not simple discs. They are complex stimulus objects such as predators, food, sexual partners, nest material, and species members of different status. These objects involve many possible aspects of stimulation to which the animal could respond, including a variety of visual, chemical, tactile, and auditory characteristics. In some cases, thermal stimuli are crucial, as in rattlesnakes (Noble & Schmidt, 1937) and the tick discussed earlier. This sort of selectivity is also discussed in Chapter 4 in connection with the concept of attention.

Basic properties of sign stimuli

One might expect that if stimulus objects present a variety of stimuli which the animal is physiologically able to receive and respond to, then a balanced combination of those stimuli should be involved in releasing behavior. Nonetheless, this is not usually the case when specific responses are observed. Tinbergen (1951) lists many examples. For instance, a carnivorous water beetle (*Dystiscus marginalis*) has well-developed eyes and can be trained to respond to visual stimuli, yet it appears not to use visual stimuli to any great extent in capturing prey. It would completely ignore a moving prey presented in a glass tube; yet placing a dilute meat extract into the water will release frantic hunting movements, and the beetle will attempt to capture every solid object it encounters. Hence, chemical and tactile stimuli are most crucial, and visual stimuli, which are important in other behaviors, are not necessary in prey catching.

There are many other examples. In the breeding season, male three-spined sticklebacks have special *nuptial markings*, an intensely red throat and belly, which release an attack on the part of a male stickleback if another male enters its territory. A very crude model of a fish is an effective stimulus if it has a red belly, yet a highly accurate model of a stickleback without the red belly presented in the same way is ineffective. Certainly, however, the stickleback can see the other characteristics. Indeed, the swollen belly of the female seems to act as the releaser for courtship behavior.

These two examples demonstrate the phenomenon of *sign* or *key stimuli* and dramatically illustrate the role of selectivity by the animal in responding to a limited part of the total stimuli available. It should be emphasized that the term *stimulus* is used by the ethologist in a rather different manner than by the physiologist. For the latter (as for the early mechanists such as Loeb), the actual energy for the response is contained in the stimulus.

The lack of insight by an animal in its behavior controlled by sign stimuli is shown by the hen and chicks studied by Brückner (Tinbergen, 1951). Normally when a chick is separated from its mother, the hen proceeds to search for and retrieve it. If a chick is removed from the hen and placed out of her vision, the mother, upon hearing the chick's high-pitched distress call, immediately begins searching for the missing chick. If, however, one of her young was placed near her under a clear glass dome which prevented her from hearing but not from seeing the chick, the hen would completely ignore it during her frantic search. Here again the importance of one aspect of the total stimulus situation is clear. Schleidt (1961), in studies with turkey hens and their poults, found that the hen would attack any intruder in her nest area, although she would not attack her own young, or, if breeding for the first time, any object giving the proper call. When deafened, however, she would attack even her own young, visual characteristics notwithstanding. In this case, given the introduction of an object, an attack is released unless inhibited by another sensory cue, the young turkey's call.

Various sign stimuli can also be presented in such a way that their relative effectiveness can be ranked. For instance, Burghardt (1969a) has shown that many species of newborn snakes will respond to water extracts of the skin substances of species-characteristic prey. Extracts from prey such as earthworms, fish, frogs, mice, and insects are prepared in warm water in an identical fashion. They are then presented to isolated snakes that have never before eaten. A cotton swab is dipped into the colorless extract and introduced into the snake's cage. If a common garter snake (*Thamnophis sirtalis*) is offered a swab dipped in worm extract, it will often show increased tongue flicking and even attack and attempt to swallow the swab, whereas distilled water or extracts prepared from nonspecies-characteristic prey such as insects elicit only a few exploratory tongue flicks and never an open mouth attack. Newborn snakes of different species may respond to different as well as similar prey extracts with more-or-less attack behavior or none at all. Such species differences in relative preference can be quantified and comparative conclusions drawn.

In these examples can be seen the basic methods used in sign-stimulus analysis: using inanimate models, eliminating various cues emanating from the stimulus object, restricting the ability of the subject to resolve certain stimuli, and comparing closely related species. Preferences or differential responsivity are assessed under the different experimental conditions.

It will be recalled that releasers are a restricted subset of sign stimuli involving other members of the same species. The earlier examples concerning chickens and sticklebacks involve social releasers (or simply releasers) because the response is dependent upon stimuli given by conspecifics. This contrasts with the example of the water beetle and its prey. In that instance, as well as with sign stimuli involving such objects as nest-building material, food objects, and predators, the responding organism has, through evolution, acquired the ability to recognize either a beneficial or a potentially harmful object on the basis of one or more stimuli. There is, however, usually no evolutionary pressure for the prey, predator, or nest-building material to cooperate. A one-way adaptation mechanism is involved. If anything, the living sources of such sign stimuli have selective pressures acting upon them to reduce the effectiveness of the cues they emanate. With social releasers, however, it is mutually beneficial for the signaler (the animal which gives the response to which the other responds) and the responder to cooperate in the evolution of the signaling system. In other words, social releasers represent part of an animal communication system (Burghardt, 1970b).

Although sign stimuli typically involve only one aspect of the entire stimulus situation, current research is demonstrating that the specificity is not always as rigid as in some of the more classic examples. A careful reading of even these studies, however, shows that the elucidated sign stimuli were not operating necessarily alone or exclusively. Tinbergen (1951) notes that a stickleback model without a red belly sometimes, although very rarely, released an attack by a male. These exceptions could, of course, be due to a number of reasons, including threshold lowering (in vacuo) or conditioning. Another property of sign stimuli is that they usually release only one reaction. Indeed, another criterion for the fixed action pattern is that it is a unit of behavior under the control of one specific sign stimulus. The one reaction–one sign-stimulus equivalence is most apparent in naive or inexperienced animals. However, the fact that many adult animals, such as the hen and the stickleback, still respond to isolated cues demonstrates that much experience often does not lead to the animal responding to the stimulus object as a whole. Indeed, the reverse phenomenon can occur, a finding not uncommon in learning studies.

Because psychologists tend toward the view that releasers may occur in fish and birds but not in the mammals in which they are really the most interested, a final example from primate behavior is appropriate. Sackett (1966) studied rhesus monkeys raised in isolation from all other monkeys. The isolated monkeys reacted differentially to slides of monkeys involved in different species-characteristic behaviors. Nonmonkey control slides elicited little response. Slides of threatening monkeys released the most vocalization and disturbance in the naive monkeys. The sign stimulus here appeared to be the facial expression. The monkeys could also present pictures to themselves by pressing levers, and different pictures were preferred over others at certain ages. This study also demonstrated the age-related responsivity of animals to sign stimuli. Hence, deprivation experiments in monkeys demonstrate not only fixed action patterns and vocalizations but innate recognition of species-characteristic stimuli as well.

Sign stimuli have a number of properties and interact in a variety of ways. The discussion in this chapter is only meant to give a tentative classification and should not be thought of as final pigeonholes. Indeed, the careful reader will note the incompatibility of some of the properties with each other, emphasizing the point that a variety of mechanisms are involved.

Heterogeneous summation

Various sign stimuli may be attached to the same object and, when this occurs, their combined effect is sometimes found to be additive in response intensity or frequency. In the stickleback male, aggressive responses to a model are released not only if it has a red belly, but also if the head is facing downward in a *threat posture*. The effects of color and posture are additive; that is, the sum of the responses to either characteristic alone equals the response to both appearing simultaneously. This phenomenon is termed the *rule of heterogeneous summation* and provides a marked contrast to a *Gestalt* where the complete stimulus is more effective than the sum of its parts.

The recognition of this phenomenon originated

with Seitz (1940), who studied the releasers of fighting in male cichlid fish (*Astatotilapia strigigena*). He discovered that five different stimuli, such as color, size, and tail beating from another male, presented singly, produced about the same level of fighting and were additive when mixed in any combination, two released more marked fighting than one, and four were more effective than two. Weidmann and Weidmann (1958) tested food-begging pecks in black-headed gull chicks with models of different shapes and colors and found the rule to predict quite accurately their quantitative results as measured by number of pecks. Further studies need to be done. Heterogeneous summation may generally hold, but it is hard to conceive of it as being more than a first approximation, considering the vast number of behaviors and diversity of organisms responding to sign stimuli. Indeed, the visual modality seems to have been looked at exclusively in tests of summation. Nonetheless, it has been argued that there has been a shift through evolution from additive responding to the more complex Gestalt or configurational effects that will be described later.

Skinner's (1938) *law of spatial summation* for reflexes is defined in a manner similar to heterogeneous summation. However, he held the rather rigid view of stimuli and responses such that "two stimuli define separate reflexes even though the response is the same" [p. 31]. The responses of interest to ethologists are not usually the simple reflexes, such as eyeblinking, discussed by Skinner.

Supernormal stimuli

The sign stimulus and its corresponding internal releasing mechanism was originally analogized by Lorenz to a key and lock, an analogy which can be questioned in light of the phenomenon known as *supernormal* sign stimuli (also called *superoptimal* or *supranormal*). In this situation, one finds that artificial stimuli can be prepared which are even more effective than the natural stimulus and which will be preferred by the organism. The ringed plover will prefer to incubate an artificial egg with black spots on a white background rather than its own natural egg, which has dark brown spots on a light brown background (Koehler & Zagarus, 1937). The contrast of spots versus background is the crucial factor, and the artificial egg provides a greater instance of the sign stimulus. Indeed, an oystercatcher was found by Tinbergen (1951) to prefer a five-egg clutch over the normal three-egg clutch and, even more dramatically, to prefer a giant normally marked egg over the normal-sized egg.

Magnus (1958) has provided a particularly interesting example of supernormal stimuli. He measured the rate of response of a male silver-washed fritillary butterfly to a female. The yellow-orange in the female's wings, when fluttered, release courtship responses in the male. Hypothesizing that alternation between color and dark released the behavior, Magnus was able to induce courtship responses in the male by placing yellow-orange and dark strips on a revolving cylinder. The more rapid the stripe alternation, the greater its effectiveness in releasing courtship, even when it was faster than that of a normal female. Increasing effectiveness was found up to a speed which appears, on the basis of physiological studies, to be the limit of the male's ability to detect alternating lights.

An example from mammals can also be given. Golden hamsters have two dark patches on the chest that are involved in agonistic behavior which takes place in upright postures. A hamster exposes the patches when on the offensive and covers them with its forelimbs when submissive or on the defensive. The patches operate as a threat stimulus. If the patches of a hamster are made larger and darker than normal by dyeing, intense flight behavior is released in other hamsters, even more dominant ones (Grant, MacKintosh, & Lerwill, 1970). Even more interesting is the finding that weanling hamsters provided with the supernormal stimulus and paired with littermates of the same sex not only were dominant over their partners, but also were more aggressive in general and had a higher growth rate (Payne & Swanson, 1972).

More studies on supernormal stimuli should be performed, as such stimuli probably play an important role in behavioral evolution. For instance, in mimicry situations the mimic often imitates and exaggerates the stimulus characteristic of the host or mimicked species (Wickler, 1968). Ritualized displays also often involve behaviors and releasers exaggerated from their presumed ancestral or developmental sources.

Setting factors

Sign stimuli do not always have the same effectiveness, which may be due to many reasons. Naturally, seasonal factors play a role in responses to stimuli involved in nest building, courtship, territoriality, responses to young, and other behaviors. Such responsivity differences may be a function of hormonal changes and other physiological mechanisms ultimately caused by external factors. However, even within a period of time in which the animal is responsive to sign stimuli of a given type, changes in responsivity can often occur. Very important factors are differences due to motivational states, which are usually related to antecedent conditions and functional cycles. Obviously a hungry animal responds more to sign stimuli from prey than will a sated animal. Less obviously, Schaefer and Hess (1959) found an inverse relationship between pecking preferences for various colors and color preferences in imprinting objects. Tinbergen et al. (1942) found that grayling butterflies (*Eumenis semele*) approach flower blossoms on the basis of color when feeding, but that approach of females by males during courtship is not released by color but by factors of brightness, movement, and distance. Also, repeated presentations of the same sign stimulus eventually lead to response waning, although the process is neither simple nor similar across all species and behaviors (Hinde, 1970).

Configurational sign stimuli

Although most sign stimuli seem to be isolated aspects of the stimulus object, more complex relational factors can also be involved. Of course, the fact that the red patch on a model must be on the belly to be most effective in eliciting fighting in a male stickleback implies some relational aspect. A more complex configurational stimulus is involved in the gaping response of young thrushes to cardboard models (Tinbergen & Kuenen, 1939). A round cardboard body had two heads attached; the heads were also round but of different sizes (Figure 9.5B). They found that the larger head was the one to which the young thrushes directed their gaping. However, if the same two heads were attached to a smaller body (Figure 9.5A), then the gaping responses were oriented toward the smaller head. Hence, the *configuration* (Gestalt) rather than the parts were most important. Such *relational* releasers may be involved in supernormal stimuli.

Many so-called configurational or gestalt-like releasers involve movement as a critical variable. Such is true for the most famous configurational sign stimulus—the hawk-goose silhouette. Early experiments by Lorenz and Tinbergen (Tinbergen, 1951) indicated that short-necked (hawk) models were more effective in eliciting freezing and other fearful behavior than were long-necked (goose) models when passed over young turkeys, geese, or

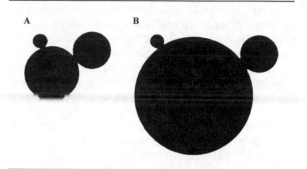

Figure 9.5 Two double-headed dummies used to release gaping in thrushes. Gaping was directed at the smaller head with model A and the larger head with model B. The body in A is 4 centimeters in diameter; B is 8 centimeters in diameter. The heads were 1 and 3 centimeters in diameter, respectively. (From Tinbergen & Kuenen, 1939.)

ducks. A short-necked, long-tailed hawk model could, if moved in the reverse direction, simulate a goose.(Figure 9.6), and therefore, different effects were found depending on merely the direction of movement of the same model. These and other early studies were not very sophisticated experimentally, nor was the prior experience of the young animals adequately controlled. Hirsch, Lindley, and Tolman (1955) tested naive birds under more stringent conditions and found no differential effects of shape in eliciting fear. They then concluded that the innate sign stimuli interpretation was "untenable," although they had studied young domesticated leghorn chickens rather than the wild species used by previous workers.

Schleidt (1961) found a simpler explanation for the hawk-goose model effect. Using turkey chicks

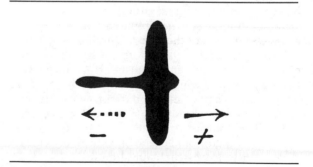

Figure 9.6 The hawk-goose model. (From Tinbergen, 1951.)

with controlled experience, he found that both the hawk and the goose initially released strong fear responses, but that the effectiveness of either rapidly decreased with repeated exposure. Differential responsivity could be built into the animal by arranging for selective habituation of the response to one of the stimuli. Thus, since the pen-reared birds used in most previous studies saw hawks flying overhead much less frequently than they saw harmless long-necked birds, he concluded that the hawk-goose phenomenon is not based on an innate configurational stimulus. However, Green, Green, and Carr (1966) in a careful experiment found that mallard ducklings not only responded to the hawk model more than to the goose, but that the response to the latter did not differ from that to a triangle moved either point (apex) or base forward. This latter test with the triangle is important because Schneirla (1965), in his attempt to explain away all innate configurational sign stimuli, argued that any differential responding in naive birds to hawk and goose models has nothing to do with shape but with the suddenness of contrast change caused by the model moving into the visual field when moved with the short neck first. Indeed, Schneirla suggested the triangle experiment as a test of the usefulness of his *approach-withdrawal (A/W) theory* (see earlier discussion in this chapter).

One of the most widely quoted releaser studies was that of Tinbergen and Perdeck (Tinbergen, 1951), who showed that the red spot on the parent herring gull's bill released begging in the newly hatched chick. By using parent dummies that were identical except that the red spot was either on the tip of the bill or moved to the forehead and that were presented in the same manner, they were able to show that the "normal" head (in relation to the bill spot) released four times as many begging pecks. The conclusion was that a configurational stimulus was involved. But Schneirla (1956) proposed that movement was a critical factor and that in the method of presentation used by Tinbergen and Perdeck the bill spot moved more quickly and prominently than the forehead spot. Hailman (1967) followed up this hypothesis and showed that if amount of movement was equalized, bill and forehead spots received the same number of pecks.

The conclusion about configurational (Gestalt) sign stimuli that most fits the objective evidence is that they can be genetically based, that experience plays an important role, and that careful experimentation is necessary before concluding that they exist.

The innate releasing mechanism

The existence of sign stimuli (as discrete from physical stimuli discussed in the previous section) led to the postulation of the *innate releasing mechanism (IRM)*. If one accepts that there is selectivity on the part of animals and that this can occur in absence of prior specific experience, then one can accept most of what the classical ethologist meant by the IRM. To quote Tinbergen (1951): "The strict dependence of an innate reaction on a certain set of sign stimuli leads to the conclusion that there must be a special neuro-sensory mechanism that releases the reaction and is responsible for its selective susceptibility to such a very special combination of sign stimuli. This mechanism we will call the Innate Releasing Mechanism (IRM)..." [p. 41–42]. Therefore, any selective responsivity by the organism leads us to conclude that some internal factor is involved. More theoretically, the IRM is postulated to prevent the discharge of endogenous energy, as in the hydraulic model (Figure 9.3) discussed earlier.

The history of the IRM concept has been reviewed by Schleidt (1962). He finds that there has been misuse of the term, particularly the assumption of innateness without the appropriate deprivation experiments. Many releasing mechanisms, as in imprinting, may be largely based on acquired sign stimuli. Certainly, all IRMs seem to be modified by postnatal experience. For instance, sign stimuli can lose effectiveness through habituation, or experience can sharpen or enhance responses to even highly specific, innately recognized sign stimuli. For example, selective feeding of newborn snakes can drastically alter the relative effectiveness of worm and fish prey extracts in favor of those substances which were experienced (Fuchs & Burghardt, 1971). In general, sign stimuli seem much more easily modified than fixed action patterns (Weidmann, 1971). Further, it is more accurate to speak of stimulus preferences than of all-or-none exclusivity in controlling behavior.

Another controversy over the IRM theory concerns the fact that many ethologists felt that the location of many IRMs is central rather than peripheral. That is, central nervous system mechanisms were considered more important than peripheral sensory filtering mechanisms, although some critics have argued for the overriding importance of peripheral structural mechanisms to explain perceptual preferences (e.g., Lehrman, 1953). However, there is evidence that both are involved (Konishi, 1971; Marler, 1961). Recent physiological results are surprisingly congruent with the sign stimuli findings of ethologists and support the view that the sensory systems filter and select information from the environment that might be particularly relevant. The general method is to record from various parts of the sensory system while presenting external stimuli to see whether or not neural cells fire or alter responding in some way. The visual system has been most studied with recordings made from the retina to the cortical projection areas. In the frog (*Rana pipiens*) five types of peripheral responses seem to exist (Maturana et al., 1960) Some cells are selectively responsive to movements of certain-sized contrasting objects. One type of response seems ideally suited to be a "bug detector." In cats, Hubel and Wiesel (1962) have found cells in the visual cortex that selectively respond to complex stimuli. A cell may have a *receptive field* in which such stimuli as narrow bars elicit firing only when oriented at a certain angle or when moving in a given direction. Are the receptive fields in the cat innately wired or is visual experience necessary for their formation? Raising kittens from birth in visually deprived settings does produce animals in which receptive field units are practically nonexistent (Wiesel & Hubel, 1963). Such results do not argue for the formative role of experience, for newborn kittens have functioning receptive fields (Hubel & Wiesel, 1963). Here again, however, visual experience can improve on the basal innate ability.

Little evidence is yet available on whether an IRM exists which actually inhibits nerve cell firing from reaching the motor areas until the proper stimuli are present. Nonetheless, while the early ethologists could only assume the existence of releasing mechanisms, physiological work is beginning to uncover them and determine how they function.

ANALYSIS OF MOTIVATION: THE ANTECEDENTS OF BEHAVIOR

As we have seen, the problem of instinct is two-sided, involved with both behavior directly observed, the primary emphasis of this chapter, and the push, urge, drive, mood, or energy behind the overt response. Classical ethology dealt with both. However, ethologists' views of the internal determinants of behavior were largely based on inferences from observed behavior. In this section we will briefly consider the value and current status of the ethological views of motivation and then consider the important area of conflicts between two or more motivational states.

Criticism of energy models and unitary drives

The endogenous energy models of Lorenz and Tinbergen have been heavily criticized. One criticism is that the models do not allow for feedback; that is, in none of the models is provision made for the stimulus consequences of the activities of the organism to modify the ongoing behavior. In the original energy model, only the performance of the activity itself could reduce the amount of stored energy and hence the tendency to respond. This was a reaction toward the extreme drive-reduction approach of the time (e.g., Hull, 1943), which held that the cessation, as well as instigation, of behavior is due to the direct intervention of physiological factors (tissue needs). For instance, a dog stops eating or drinking because of distension of the stomach or changes in internal chemical factors due to the water ingested rather than because it performed so many consummatory movements. In point of fact, both internal and behavioral factors are involved. This lack of feedback is certainly a serious drawback, probably resulting from the early ethological view that peripheral stimulation was less important than central coordination. Nonetheless, the early model of von Uexküll (1934) certainly allowed for feedback. His functional circle is just that: a circle between the organism and the stimulus object. Somehow during the development of their models, Lorenz and Tinbergen neglected this aspect.

A second important criticism deals with the endogenous or innate aspects of drives. An influential view in psychology is that most, if not all, drives are acquired (i.e., derived and maintained by learning and reinforcement associated with a few so-called primary drives such as hunger, thirst, and sex). Sucking behavior in mammals has long been a battleground for this argument. Koepke and Pribram (1971) recently analyzed sucking in kittens and showed that endogenous factors play an important role in this drive. Kittens that had never received milk for sucking (over a period of six months) initiated sucking as often as controls, although they did not suck as long.

Other criticisms of ethological models were directed toward the energy construct itself (Kennedy, 1954; Lehrman, 1953). Ideas of action-specific energy (ASE) seemed to hark back to the energy views of Freud and McDougall and were used to attack the ethological views with a guilt-by-association tactic. The attack succeeded because there were enough similarities to cover up the potential value of the concepts. Hinde (1956, 1960), in particular, has presented detailed critiques of the ethological energy and drive conceptions based mainly on the limitations of the early Lorenz-Tinbergen model. However, even Hinde (1960) admits they have been very successful in accounting for a great deal of behavior.

An important criticism, also common to psychological views of drive, is that one cannot talk about a drive for a given class of behavior since different parameters of that behavior are not highly correlated. "Fear" in rats, as measured in an open field apparatus, is a case in point. The various measures (e.g., urination, activity) do not covary. Hence, there is no value and indeed harm in referring to changes in an animal's motivational state. As Hinde (1960) puts it: "Factors such as stimuli and hormones which affect specific patterns of behaviour are to be thought of as controlling this activity, of increasing the probability of one pattern rather than another. Changes in strength or threshold can thus be thought of as changes in the probability of one pattern of activity rather than another, and not as changes in the level of energy in a specific neural mechanism" [p. 212]. Indeed, the concept of ASE was largely replaced in the 1950s by *specific-action potential (SAP)*, and today *response tendency*, which is admittedly more operational and less theoretical, is the stylish euphemism.

In retrospect, the most important contribution of the energy models was to provide a framework for the reintroduction of "spontaneous" behavior and behavior cycles into behavioral study. Still, the critics of energy or drive models of behavior have yet to go beyond a descriptive operationism (probability of response A, given condition X), as eventually we must.

The energy concept, along with many ethological terms such as *releasers, innate releasing mechanisms, displacement behavior, fixed action patterns,* etc., have been criticized because a level of discourse can be reached for which the concepts are sometimes vague, unhelpful, or downright misleading. This is true of any scientific language, however, that attempts to make sense out of many observations. Hinde used this technique in his early criticisms but now is more constructive and emphasizes repeatedly throughout his recent book (Hinde, 1970) that while such concepts need to be used carefully, they are useful relative to the type of analysis engaged in. This is an important truism.

When ethological ideas are considered from the viewpoint of what the early ethologists were interested in, they were most successful and useful. Certainly they fostered much research. On the other hand we now know much more and can qualify, elaborate, or limit them.

In fact, recent work indicates that the burial of the ethological motivational views was somewhat hasty. Wooten (1971) measured aggression in sticklebacks in a variety of ways and found the postulation of a unitary drive most parsimonious in explaining his high correlations between measures. McFarland (1970) has attempted to apply control theory to behavioral homeostasis. He finds many similarities between physical and behavioral systems in terms of work and acting on the environment. He concludes that not only can motivational state be given a rigorous meaning, but that the energy concept is inevitable. Further,

> by introducing a motivational energy concept at this stage, the way is opened for a *post hoc* identification of the energy changes involved. For example, the vacillations observed in a conflict situation immediately suggest a reciprocal exchange of potential and kinetic energy, and even if it is not possible to analyze the system in a conventional manner, it may be possible to work backward from this supposition. Finally, the energy concept has considerable intuitive appeal, as evidenced by its frequent use in the past. Concepts such as energy storage, and behavioral inertia and momentum, need not be used vaguely, and can be given a precise meaning in terms of the observed and postulated variables involved [p. 25].

This approach has yet to be systematically applied, but in the following sections conflict situations of the type referred to will be reviewed.

Conflict behavior

We have already discussed the three major concepts of the early ethological approach: the analysis of behavior into the appetitive phase, the consummatory acts and fixed action patterns, and the releaser or stimulus factors. Nevertheless, many behaviors did not lend themselves to ready analysis using the concepts in their original limited sense.

Perhaps the most well-studied and interesting complication is *conflict behavior,* which is considered to be the simultaneous activation of more than one drive, and usually two. Here we are using *specific drives* in the classic ethological theoretical sense, that is, behaviors motivated by their own action-specific energy. As pointed out earlier, the less loaded term *response tendency* more clearly ties the concept to direct observables. The simultaneous activation of the antecedents to two incompatible sets of behaviors might seem to be quite rare, but the reverse is true. Consider the extreme measures that are often needed to keep an animal working for food in a learning apparatus, such as reducing a pigeon's weight to 80 percent of normal.

Most conflict behaviors fall into four categories (Hess, 1962). These categories are *successive ambivalent behavior, simultaneous ambivalent behavior, redirected behavior,* and *displacement activity.* In all of them, the role of intention movements (subtle and incomplete preliminaries to full-blown performance) is pronounced (Daanje, 1951).

Successive ambivalent behavior

Successive ambivalent behavior occurs when an animal alternates between incomplete performances of movements appropriate to two conflicting response tendencies belonging to different functional cycles or subsets of the same functional cycle. Another term for this conflict is *alternation.* An example is the frequently observed intention movements of attack and flight elicited in animals at territorial boundaries. At the boundary of two nest-site territories, a gull's motivation to attack an intruder decreases the farther the resident moves from the center, and the tendency to flee at the sight of an intruder increases (Tinbergen, 1953). Two males at the border of a territory may be seen to alternately attack and flee. Such situations are more naturalistic versions of a classic paradigm in experimental psychology, the approach-avoidance situation analyzed extensively by Miller (1959). In this situation, a rat is placed in an apparatus where approaching and eating food is accompanied by electric shock. Consequently, an approach-avoidance conflict is established, and the animal may eventually vacillate between approach and avoidance at a given distance from the goal.

Simultaneous ambivalent behavior

This conflict situation often occurs when the two conflicting functional cycles or moods can be simultaneously expressed. For example, a sparrow at a bird feeder may both approach and peck at food and fluff its feathers in preparation to leave

if danger approaches. This is similar to *blending* as used by Skinner (1938).

It is with aggressive and courtship behavior, however, that simultaneous ambivalent behavior has been most thoroughly studied. With aggressive behavior, the attempt is made to independently vary the motivation to attack (aggressiveness) and the tendency to flee (fear). If the tendencies to attack and flee reach certain stages simultaneously, then threat behavior occurs, combining elements found otherwise only in attack or fearful behavior. Thus, threat is interpreted as a result of a simultaneous arousal of aggressiveness and fear. This has been shown in the facial expression and bodily posture, including tail position, of cats (Leyhausen, 1956), wolves (Schenkel, 1947), and dogs (Lorenz, 1966). Leyhausen argues that the arched back of the cat seen in Halloween pictures is a product of the tendency to withdraw, expressed by backward movement of the front paws, and the tendency to attack, evidenced by the forward movement or nonmovement of the rear limbs. Figure 9.7 shows some examples of postures in the black-

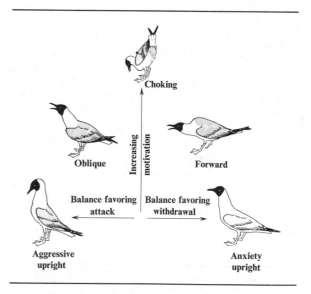

Figure 9.7 The displays of the black-headed gull used in courtship and fighting are thought to involve degrees of attack and withdrawal. In the "oblique" and "aggressive upright" positions aggression predominates, but the oblique is relatively more intense. In the "forward" and "anxiety upright" positions the balance favors withdrawal motivation. The "choking" display seems to represent a balance of attack and withdrawal elements, also with very strong motivation. (After Moynihan, 1955; from Marler & Hamilton, 1966.)

headed gull that illustrate aggressive and flight tendencies and their changes with intensity of arousal. The use of such postures to determine the state of aggressiveness, fearfulness, or threat has been extended to elephants by Kuhme (1963), who interpreted these and other motivational-emotional states on the basis of trunk position

Related to simultaneous ambivalent behavior is *compromise behavior* (Andrew, 1956), in which the animal displays a behavior element common to both tendencies. This can be seen most easily in the bodily orientation of aquatic animals where an intermediate position often occurs. Gravity from below and light (usually from above) are both involved in the upright orientation of fish in water. The response factors are termed the *ventral earth reaction* and the *dorsal light reaction,* respectively. If the light comes from the side at a 90-degree angle to gravity rather than from above at the usual 180 degrees, the fish takes a position intermediate to its normal upright posture and the sideways posture dictated by light. If one destroys the ability of the animal to orient to one of the two factors, for instance by destroying the labyrinth involved in orientation toward gravity, the fish will orient in the direction dictated by the light, since the gravity cues are unavailable to it (von Holst, 1950).

A more complex example is tail flicking which occurs in many birds. This is an intention movement of takeoff which occurs in an approach-avoidance conflict when a bird is seemingly attracted toward food but remains wary. In this case, vigorous tail flicking is an intention movement of incipient flight that would be involved in approaching the food as well as in its avoidance.

Redirected behavior

Redirected activity occurs when an animal performs the behavior appropriate to the motivational state but directs that behavior toward an inappropriate object in the presence of the proper stimulus. This type of conflict response is seen most often in aggressive behavior where an organism (a bird, for example) may have a tendency to attack an intruder (such as a cat or human). Yet as the resident approaches the interloper, it seems to reconsider the desirability of attacking it and attacks instead an innocent bystander (e.g., a bird sitting on a branch) or even an inanimate object. In this instance, it is fairly easy to gauge the tendencies to attack and to flee. Psychoanalytic displacement is similar to redirected behavior and should not be confused with *displacement activity.*

Displacement activity

It often occurs that the behavior seen in a conflict situation is inappropriate to either of the two conflicting response tendencies. Two sticklebacks at a territorial boundary may be involved in the successive ambivalent behavior mentioned earlier. Both of the responses involved (flight and attack) are clearly related to the conflicting motivations. However, suddenly one or both of the fish engage in sand-digging behavior which is associated with nest building (Tinbergen & van Iersel, 1947). Roosters involved in encounters often begin pecking at the ground in feeding movements even in the absence of any food. Other examples involve displacement grooming, drinking, and other responses (Tinbergen, 1952).

Such apparently irrelevant behaviors were dramatic and seemingly inexplicable. Yet the fact that they occurred in certain contexts involving the nearly equal arousal of two motivational states led to the view that this was due to the sparking over of energy from the conflicting drives, resulting in the term *displacement*. Since displacement activities appear to be what the name implies (i.e., behaviors outside their normally relevant motivational context), they are termed *allochthonous*. When motivated by their own drives or, more descriptively, when occurring in the normal context, then the behaviors are termed *autochthonous*. Nest digging during a fight is clearly not occurring in its normal context.

Tinbergen (1952) formalized the early ethological interpretation of displacement activities, which was derived from the energy model. The analysis of displacement behaviors indicated that they occur during intense conflicts between two drives. At lower arousal levels of conflicting drives, ambivalent behavior occurs, but when the drives become too strong, the mere alternation of intention movements is not a sufficient outlet and displacement activities result. The fact that displacement activities usually occur after ambivalent behavior was adduced as evidence for the existence of intense conflicts.

But how did this theoretical model deal with the fact that the fixed action patterns observed were not associated with the action-specific energy of the FAPs in conflict? The seemingly irrelevant displacement activities "are outlets through which the thwarted drives can express themselves in motion" [Tinbergen, 1952, p. 12]. The pent-up motivational energy discharges through an outlet provided by another instinctive center which, by definition, would mean that the behavior that occurs is out of context or irrelevant.

Tinbergen also noted that the behaviors usually performed as displacement activities, such as grooming, pecking, drinking, and preening, were performed repeatedly and frequently in the life of the animal and had low thresholds. In addition, displacement activities could be influenced by the posture of the animal at the time the sparking over occurred and by the external stimuli present. For example, displacement feeding in turkeys could be increased if food was present, and displacement drinking could be increased if water was available (Räber, 1948). Further examples of the effect of external stimuli on the displacement activity rapidly accumulated. Morris (1954) showed that displacement behavior in a conflict between courtship and male fighting in the zebra finch might be either feeding, grooming, mounting, or sleeping. Nonetheless, usually one behavior predominates in a given kind of conflict in a species.

The next major advance in the study of displacement activities came in studies by Andrew (1956), Sevenster (1960, 1961), and van Iersel and Bol (1958). They gathered support for the *disinhibition hypothesis*. Working with snow buntings, Andrew (1956) argued that the peripheral stimuli that elicited grooming were almost always present, but that grooming was usually suppressed by other activities. If two conflicting response tendencies, both of which were suppressing grooming, were blocked, then the competing responses usually inhibiting grooming were removed (disinhibition) and the grooming would occur in response to the usual peripheral stimuli. Van Iersel and Bol (1958), working with terns, developed this idea more theoretically. In their view, if any two hypothetical centers controlling given behaviors were mutually inhibitory so that both behaviors could not be simultaneously performed, their mutual inhibition would remove any inhibition of other centers controlling easily inhibited patterns such as grooming. Rowell (1961) has confirmed many of the elements of the disinhibition hypothesis in the behavior of chaffinches. The disinhibition hypothesis has also been applied to mammals as in Fentress' (1968) study on grooming in voles.

Certainly the disinhibition hypothesis is supported in many instances and represents an advance in knowledge. However, some questions are necessary. For example, the hypothesis does not explain why only one displacement activity is usually associated with a given conflict between two tendencies. Since such activities as feeding and grooming are not the only activities with low thresholds that the animal performs a great deal of the time, it is not easy to explain why one particular behavior occurs in the displacement act in response-probability terms alone.

One answer to the question of why a particular activity always occurs in a given conflict situation is that it may have acquired some signal value in and of itself. In other words, ritualization may have occurred as a result of evolution so that displacement feeding, for instance, is a commonly understood symbol (social releaser) for the conflict between a given pair of motivations. This process of ritualization is of great importance to the study of the evolution of behavior. A displacement behavior can serve as a stimulus for other individuals and thus evolves with their behavior, giving it adaptive value.

Recent review and theoretical contributions to displacement activity have been made by Zeigler (1964) and McFarland (1966). McFarland focuses on the crucial distinction between behaviors classified as relevant (autochthonous) and irrelevant (allochthonous) and points out the need for a rigorous discrimination. He argues that it is impossible for a behavior to be truly irrelevant in the causal sense, but it is possible for it to be functionally irrelevant. McFarland modified the disinhibition theory utilizing inputs from American behavioristic psychologists, particularly Hull (1943), and the physiological findings on the reticular activating system. He notes that the disinhibition theory can only apply to displacement activities caused by conflict situations. This is only one of the original conditions for displacement activities as described by Tinbergen (1952) and Bastock, Morris, and Moynihan (1953). The others were physical thwarting of appetitive behavior and the thwarting of consummatory behavior by the removal of the consummatory stimulus or the goal of an activity. The apparent motivating effects of removing a consummatory reinforcer are also discussed in connection with learned behaviors in Chapters 5 and 7. The disinhibition theory has recently come under severe criticism (Wilz, 1970) as it applies to displacement fanning during courtship in sticklebacks, indicating that much more needs to be done on such strange and fascinating phenomena.

Staddon and Simmelhag (1971) in their analysis of the Skinnerian superstition phenomenon find that many of the actual behaviors observed are remarkably similar to the ethological categories of conflict behavior. Reynierse et al. (1970) have observed the same in extinction of classical conditioning. Their work thus points toward an integration of conditioning and naturalistic approaches to the study of behavior.

THE QUESTION OF THE INNATE: BEHAVIOR GENETICS AND EVOLUTION

Perhaps the most criticized aspect of ethology is its supposed revival of an outmoded dichotomy variously termed innate and acquired, unlearned and learned, heredity and environment, instinct and intelligence, nature and nurture, nativism and empiricism, and so forth. To the ethologist, all these appositions emphasize the same distinctive feature. That is, one of the members of each pair of terms refers to inherited phylogenetic mechanisms, while the other refers to the acquisition or modification of characteristics throughout ontogeny.

Marler and Hamilton (1966) point out that it was Lorenz who took the reasonable middle-of-the-road position between a strict instinct, or even *vitalistic,* position and an exclusively environmentalist or *mechanistic* view (Lorenz, 1950).

Innate, inherited, and genetic are becoming common words in the psychological literature. This section attempts to classify some of the concepts, methods, and arguments encountered. Slowly emerging is a consensus view which neither verbally eliminates the problem nor chooses sides between those theoretically or philosophically inclined to favor genetics or environment.

Part of the problem stems from the terms *instinct* and *innate,* which are too often used interchangeably. The two terms are not synonymous. Instinct or preferably instinctive behavior, refers to fairly complete sequences of species-characteristic responses usually performed frequently in the normal existence of the individual. These behaviors are of widespread occurrence throughout the species and its relatives. Further, once aroused by external and internal factors (day length, hormone levels, food deprivation, etc.), instinctive behaviors, unlike reflexes, seem to have a certain motivating force or drive behind them. Instincts often do seem to be refractory to a fairly large number of environmental manipulations. Nonetheless, instinctive behaviors can have important components greatly influenced by traditional types of learning as well as by more subtle environmental and physiological events. While originally some ethologists held that instinctive movements, viewed strictly as fixed action patterns, could not be modified, this

involved a confusion with the term *innate,* as Lorenz (1965) was later to admit.

The term *innate* is both more prevalent and more theoretical than *instinct.* It refers not only to behaviors, but to all characteristics of organisms, including skeletal structure, eye color, the circulatory system—in short, everything we consider part of an organism's genetic heritage and what are often called inborn or inherited characters. As Lorenz (1965) has pointed out, behaviors themselves (the phenotype) are not innate; it is the information encoded in the genes (the genotype) that is innate. This is true, of course, for all inherited characters, including structure. Currently it is thought that the sequence of several molecules in nuclear DNA contains this information (Thorpe, 1963). To use the term *innate* in reference to structure or behavior is a shorthand way of referring to phenomena which we consider to be shaped and influenced strongly, although perhaps indirectly, by specific genetic information.

But no animal exists without either heredity or an environment. Even an animal's ability to learn or adapt to environmental events is based on evolved (innate) factors (Lorenz, 1969). On the other hand, the expression of genetic information is influenced by the internal and external conditions of the animal. Going even further, Dobzhansky (1972) stated: "In flies, as well as in men, the genetic endowment determines the entire range of reactions, realized and unrealized, of the developing organism in all possible environments" [p. 530].

The problem is a difficult one. Since innate factors enter into everything, how can some behaviors be more innate than others? Conversely, how can we say that some behaviors are acquired, learned, or conditioned? It is important, therefore, to note which aspects of a structure or behavior are based on specific genetic or environmental factors. Nonetheless, all concepts dealing with portioning evolutionary or environmental factors in a given behavior, whether they are called innate, genetic, conditioning, learning, imprinting, stimulation, or reinforcement, are abstractions, in spite of how operational we become. The organism, by existing, is a reflection of many interacting and coalesced processes. Yet classification and analysis are necessary.

At this stage, the primary question is how genetic information is to be identified. There are two major methods used: the ontogenetic or developmental approach and the genetic approach. Advocates of either one have a tendency to denigrate the efficacy of the other (e.g., Lorenz, 1965; Whalen, 1971).

However, both are important, useful, and, in fact, complementary.

Individual development

A major method of the developmental approach is the deprivation experiment, previously discussed, where the animal is tested before it has been exposed to the situation whose importance in shaping a behavior or perceptual process is being evaluated. A newborn iguanid lizard's head bobs in the species-characteristic manner, even if hatched in isolation from all other lizards. A duck raised to sexual maturity away from all other animals (the Kasper Houser experiment) possesses many of the species-characteristic social behaviors. One goal of this method is to identify units of structures, behaviors, and the like, which are found to be so resistant to the usual environmental stimuli that at least their basal structure is shaped by genetic information.

Obviously, all animals are normally exposed to many stimulative factors pre- and postnatally, which can affect the expression of behavior. Some experiences, including reciprocal structure-function interactions, may be necessary in order for a behavior to be manifested at all (a threshold effect), or they may be necessary for the behavior to be perfected (as in rat nest building). However, the "knowledge" possessed by the animal could not have originated in such a fashion. For instance, if prior manipulative experience were necessary for rats to build nests, such experience alone cannot explain the topography of the nest-building movements.

But the deprivation experiment does have limitations. One is that the scientist decides, almost intuitively, what nongenetic factors could possess the required adaptive knowledge and transmit it to the animal. That is, the experimenter tries to eliminate possible sources of environmental information and tests whether the animal still performs and how well it does so. Second, the deprivation experiment alone cannot tell us about the modifiability of the behaviors seen. Certain experiences may easily alter a process that is highly specific at birth or, conversely, firmly establish a behavior only weakly demonstrated under deprivation conditions, if at all. In the deprivation experiment, genetic factors are considered operative if withholding or altering environmental information does not abolish the behavior. This has led to the argument that innate factors are synonymous with unlearned behaviors, and that since experimental psychologists do not know many things about learning, learning can never be excluded as a factor

from any behavior (Beach, 1955). This position is illogical. One could just as easily define learned behavior as not innate and claim that our lack of knowledge concerning innate behavior precludes learning. Such criticisms are semantic nitpickings and reflect a false dichotomy. Just as *learning* or *experience* can stand for many types of processes, *innate* can also stand for the many ways in which genetic factors operate. They are not mutually exclusive.

This discussion points up some of the difficulties surrounding this issue. Many critics of classical ethology stated that a behavior itself cannot be shown to be innate and, to be consistent, they also claimed that learned, conditioned, or environmental were equally suspect as labels and should always be placed in quotes. So far, so good; even classically oriented ethologists will accept this today. But these same scientists would go on to praise enthusiastically experiments that showed "innate" behaviors were *really* acquired, learned, shaped through reinforcement, and so forth (but not then using quotes). The experiments on rat nest-building, which have been previously discussed, are one example. Another is Lehrman's (1955) studies of parental feeding in doves, which is used as evidence even though his conclusions on this point were later shown to be wrong and based on inadequate controls (Klinghammer & Hess, 1964). It seems that those who favor a behavioristic-learning bias, although masking it by criticizing a "false instinct-learning dichotomy," have yet to learn the lesson themselves. The genetic methods outlined in the next section more clearly help us out of the innate-learned bind. But this is no reason not to use studies on individual animals to identify shaping influences on behavior.

While the deprivation experiment is often used to discover the source of information contained in a response, it can also be the starting point for studies unraveling the myriad steps and interactions between genes, structure, and behavior from conception to birth to adulthood. This is the *epigenetic* phase of ethological study, which is becoming increasingly important.

An excellent example of developmental research on a behavior that would clearly be considered innate by the usual deprivation experiment criteria is the recognition of species-characteristic maternal calls by newly hatched ducks and chicks (Gottlieb, 1971). Newly hatched mallard ducklings, for instance, will approach the maternal call of their own species in preference to that of other species. Indexes of prenatal behavior, such as bill clapping and heart-rate changes, showed that the embryo can respond selectively to its own maternal call five days before hatching. Modifying "the amount and time of normally occurring auditory stimulation" [p. 121] led to temporal changes in the embryonic response. Similarly, devocalized embryos incubated in auditory isolation showed some delay and deficiency in their ability to discriminate the species-characteristic maternal call after hatching. Such experiments show that normal sensory stimulation is needed for the proper manifestation of innate behavior. It should also be realized that the genetic constitution of an animal is ultimately tied to its ancestors' experiences and environment.

Strictly speaking, the term *innate* can only be used in reference to differences among individuals or species (Hinde & Tinbergen, 1958; Verplanck, 1957) and, therefore, it is not possible to state what is innate in an individual or species. In other words, a series of deprivation experiments with related species reared in identical fashion is necessary, and then only the differences between characters, and not the characteristics themselves, can be discussed. This is in essence true of any genetic character, including eye color or color blindness in humans. However, after studying a group it is often possible to state rather precisely the probability of even an unborn individual possessing a certain genetic or innate character, a skill which is used, in fact, as the basis for genetic counseling of prospective parents. Remember that innate, when used in reference to behavior, is a shorthand term for specifying a constellation of adaptive information sources ultimately genetic. It also seems somewhat artificial to make a determination of innate characteristics contingent upon comparing two strains of mice, a mouse with a rat, or a mouse with a zebra. In fact, the early ethologists' view that behaviors were characteristics of organisms like teeth, skin color, and bone structure and that they develop in ontogeny through more or less the same processes has been heavily criticized. Yet on the genetic level this view has been supported (Dobzhansky, 1972) and it is to genetic studies we now turn.

Genetic aspects of behavior

The second method of measuring innate information is through formal genetic studies. The area of behavioral genetics has shown remarkable growth in the last two decades. Many of these studies deal with the inheritance or heritability of characteristics such as intelligence, emotionality, seizures, and so forth. This area has been reviewed by Hall (1951) and more recently by Fuller and Thompson (1960), Hirsch (1967), and Thiessen (1972). In this section, however, we will be concerned with the genetic analysis of those behaviors which are clearly definable in terms of the evolution and life history of the species. Such behavioral characteristics can usually be measured with greater precision and validity than can psychological units. With all the controversy concerning the measurement of intelligence, learning, and emotionality in animals and man, it is hard to fathom why one would begin to look at the genetics of a character one cannot readily measure in an agreed-upon fashion. However, when such behaviors as nest-building movements, facial expressions, or courtship postures are concerned, the very character in which one is interested is observed.

Ethological studies of genetics, although still infrequent, are increasingly important. While the deprivation experiment alone is very informative, genetic studies are theoretically needed before concluding that certain traits or behaviors are dependent upon specific inherited information that is innate in the ethological sense (Konishi, 1966). Remember, however, that this is true of all morphological aspects of all species also. Genetic experimentation was not part of the operational definitions outlined by early writers (e.g., Darwin, James) or by the early ethologists. In this sense, genetic techniques introduce a new emphasis.

As previously emphasized, all characteristics of organisms are the products of genetic and developmental factors. The real question is whether the characters seen in the animal, the *phenotype*, are closely correlated with the genetic factors, the *genotype*. Rarely, if ever, is there a 100 percent correlation. However, it is possible to inquire into the relative contributions of heredity and environment to the *variability* found in the phenotype. The usual formula is

$$\sigma_P^2 = \sigma_G^2 + \sigma_E^2 + \sigma_{GE}^2$$

where σ_P^2 is the phenotypic variance, σ_G^2 is the genetic variance, σ_E^2 is the environmental variance, and σ_{GE}^2 is the interaction variance between heredity and environment. This formula is applicable to populations and never to individuals. Indeed, the genetic diversity within a species is great and it is the basis of heritability and evolution (Dobzhansky, 1972). The ultimate conclusion is that we can speak only of genetic or environmental (including conditioning) factors as producing differences between groups or individuals with known genetic and experiential backgrounds but never in relation to one group or individual. That is, we can never state for an individual either what is genetically determined or what is environmental, learned, conditioned, and so on. While theoretically acceptable, this view seems too restrictive in practice to apply in most studies, and the operational approaches of the ethologists (e.g., deprivation experiments) and learning psychologists (e.g., operant conditioning) are presently more practical (Beck, 1967a) and should not be discarded. However, the preceding message must never be forgotten.

It is important to again point out that with any genetic trait there is a certain variability in its expression phenotypically within the individual regardless of its genotype. More than that, the same environment may interact differently with different genotypes and vice versa, as we will see later. The modern view is that for every character influenced genetically there is a *range of reaction norm* (Mayr, 1963), a setting of potentials, as it were, for the development of the behavior. Usually this is seen in a two-dimensional way, such as a maximum or minimum number of units of either scales on a snake, points on an IQ exam, or head bobs during courtship in ducks. However, this is a too limited view. The range of reaction norm should be seen in a multidimensional framework, influencing behavior not only in one direction but in many others—for instance, the number of head bobs, the duration of head bobs, and the conditions under which head bobbing occurs. In spite of this added complication, the range of reaction norm is helpful in envisioning one source of variability, encompassing the biochemical and structional events from DNA to the temporal ordering of behavior involved in the realization of biological inheritance.

There are a number of approaches open to the investigator of genetic factors in behavior, some of which were even used by Darwin. The first three are also variants of the developmental approach.

1. *Comparison of inbred strains of animals presumably homozygous at every gene locus*. For example, inbred strains of mice and fruitflies (*Drosophila*) are widely used. The method is common and is certainly valuable in the initial stages of study. For instance, Thompson (1953) compared 15 inbred strains of mice on a variety of behavioral measures. Large differences were found in exploratory activity. Conversely, differences among individuals within an inbred strain will be largely environmental, since each individual will have the same genotype except for random mutations.

2. *Comparison of different strains not necessarily homozygous or highly inbred*, such as laboratory rats, chicken breeds, dog breeds, and other domesticated animals. A most extensive study on breed differences in dogs has been performed by Scott and Fuller (1965).

3. *Comparison of naturally occurring varieties, subspecies, or populations (demes) of wild organisms*, such as finches, deer mice, and frogs. This is another method that actually moves toward evolutionary studies. In the eastern garter snake (*Thamnophis sirtalis*) the response to chemical cues from prey by newborn young differs in various populations. For instance, offspring from a female captured in Wisconsin responded much more to fish than to earthworm extracts, offspring from an Iowa litter responded with more attacks to worm than to fish extracts, and litters from near Chicago responded about equally well to both. These chemical preference differences are undoubtedly genetic (innate) since the snakes had never eaten previously (Burghardt, 1970c). Furthermore, the one possible nongenetic source of this knowledge would be the maternal diet. Yet offspring of garter snake females on controlled diets (fish or earthworms) responded similarly (Burghardt, 1971). On the other hand, population differences can be nongenetic or cultural as in the song dialects of white-crowned sparrows. Sparrows from different areas have distinct versions of the species-characteristic song. Deprivation studies have shown that the differences must be acquired between two weeks and two months of age (Marler & Tamura, 1964).

4. *Comparison of animals with a known mutant gene with normal subjects to determine the effects of the single gene on behavior*. This approach is exemplified by the study of Bastock (1956) who showed that male *Drosophila melanogaster*, which possess the gene *yellow,* are less effective in courtship than normal males. She further showed that this less effective courtship in yellow males is due to lesser amounts of vibration and licking than for normal males, resulting in less stimulation of the female.

5. *Breeding and hybridization studies*. Eventually needed to make any firm conclusions about the genetic mechanisms involved in behavior, breeding and hybridization studies are made by crossing strains or species and backcrossing offspring to the parental strains or by inbreeding the hybrids, F_1 (first generation) and F_2 (second generation). This

often allows a determination of whether one, two, or more genes are involved (polygenic inheritance). A number of interesting examples could be cited; however, we will limit ourselves to two.

Dilger (1960, 1962) found that nine species of the lovebird genus *Agapornis* differ in a number of activities, especially in nest building. Two species differ drastically in their nest-building movements: Fischer's lovebird (*A. personata fischeri*) carries nest material in its bill; and the peach-faced lovebird (*A. roseicallis*) carries nest material by tucking it in its feathers. The behavior involved in tucking the nesting materials, which are cut into strips by the birds, is complex and utilizes a sequence of movements. Experience during ontogeny seems to affect the behavior little except to make it less variable. Dilger crossed the two species and studied the behavior of the F_1 hybrids. These birds were unsuccessful in building nests because they would attempt to both tuck strips under the feathers and carry them in the bill. They seemed confused about what to do. If they put them in the feathers, they were not tucked in properly and would fall out in the trip to the nest. After several months the hybrids became more experienced and carried more of the nest strips in their bills, but they still showed many of the intention movements involved in the tucking behavior and would only fly with the material in their bills after first attempting to tuck. Although tucking behavior diminished to a fairly great extent after two years, the birds still performed many of the movements associated with tucking. In general, the hybrids moved toward the behavior seen in *fischeri*, which, according to Dilger's work, is the more recently evolved of the two species. Since these birds produced infertile hybrids, the next step, the backcrossing or inbreeding of the F_1 generation, is impossible, and we need to move to another example to demonstrate this method.

Bentley (1971) has performed a genetic analysis of calling in male crickets, the physiology of which was discussed previously. By the use of F_1 hybrids between two species with distinctly different calls (A & F, Figure 9.8), he was able to determine that most hybrid song parameters, such as number of sound pulses per trill and number of trills per phase, were intermediate between the parents' (C & D, Figure 9.8). However, the hybrid songs of the males differed from each other depending on which species was the male parent and which the female. This phenomenon indicates that some of the song characteristics are sex-linked, that is, carried on the X chromosome, as male crickets do not have

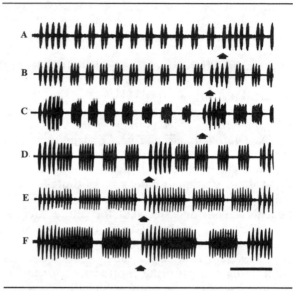

Figure 9.8   Sound pulse patterns in the calling song of male crickets of two species of *Teleogryllus* and hybrids. Each record begins with a single 4- to 6-pulse *chirp*, followed by a series of *trills* containing 2 to 14 sound pulses, depending on genotype. Chirps and trills are arranged in a repeating *phrase*. Records start with a complete phrase. Arrows mark the onset of the second phrase. (A) wild type *T. oceanicus*; (B) backcross of *T. oceanicus* female (♀) X F_1 male (♂) shown in C; (C) F_1 *T. commodus* ♀ X *T. commodus* ♂; (D) F_1 *T. commodus* ♀ X *T. oceanicus* ♂; (E) backcross of *T. commodus* ♀ X F_1 ♂ shown in D; (F) wild type *T. commodus*. Song patterns are strictly determined by genotype. Most hybrid features are intermediate between corresponding parental features, for example, number of pulses per trill and number of trills per phrase. The bar at bottom indicates 0.5 second. (From Bentley, 1971.)

the Y chromosome. Further analysis showed that the intertrill interval was the only feature influenced by sex-linked genes. For example, this aspect of the song in hybrids was more similar to the males of the maternal species. Further, when both F_1 males are crossed to females of their maternal species, the difference largely disappeared (B & E, Figure 9.8) Nonetheless, some differences persisted. Consequently, the genetic control of calling in crickets is based on genes on several chromosomes, even though a precise feature is located on the sex chromosome. Bentley then went on to record muscle action potentials reflecting the discharge of single motor neurons subserving calling from wild-type, hybrid, and backcrossed males. He concluded that in addition to showing that some features of male calls are located on the X chromosome, "the genetic information is precise enough to specify a difference of a single impulse between trill patterns of homologous motor neurons from different genotypes" [p. 1141].

6. *Selection for certain characteristics to determine the range of genetic variability and its ability to be fixed through selection in the population.* This may be done with inbred, domesticated, or wild species. There have been many attempts along these lines, particularly dealing with intelligence, emotionality, and other factors (see Hall, 1951). Specific behaviors selected for study include phototaxis and geotaxis (Hirsch, 1967) and mating speed in *Drosophila* (Manning, 1961).

7. *Pedigree analysis.* Tracing characteristics from parents to offspring is often used, especially in slow breeding organisms such as humans and livestock. This has allowed the determination of such hereditary and sex-linked factors in humans as eye color, color blindness, hemophilia, and handedness (Fuller & Thompson, 1960).

8. *Twin studies.* This approach is widely used in human behavior genetic studies, especially the comparison of monozygotic (identical) twins and dizygotic (fraternal) twins to determine the variance attributable to genetic factors in a number of behaviors (see Vandenberg, 1968, for a review).

The use of these methods promises to elucidate many of the old unanswerable heredity-environment questions that have been sources of controversy for years. They may also help clarify the origins of behavior and the units of behavior that are most evolutionarily meaningful.

In closing, the issues raised by the forceful reintroduction into psychology of the innate concept and genetic factors are real; they cannot be ignored and will be resolved only by more sophisticated analyses (e.g., Kovach, 1971). Actually, much of the confusion concerning the concept of the innate is due to both semantic difficulties and the fact that scientists contributing to the debate are interested in different problems in behavior (Lehrman, 1970). Since genetic factors can be expressed in variable ways depending on the interaction of the developing organism with its environment, developmental fixity, stereotypy, or even the results of the deprivation experiment do not absolutely prove the involvement of specific genetic information. Here the genetic breeding experiments prove valuable. But many behaviors considered innate on the basis of studies of individual development have proven to be under strong genetic control from breeding experiments, and it is highly probable that other behaviors considered innate from the deprivation experiment will also be found so from genetic studies and vice versa. Hence the two methods are complementary, necessary, and usually reach the same conclusions about the importance of specific genetic or environmental information (e.g., male cricket calls).

The evolution of behavior

Evolution is involved in all the behavioral characteristics that are seen in the diversified organic world around us. However, the study of the evolution of behavior is an important field in its own right and emphasizes certain methods which can only be touched on here. Evolution is a process by which natural selection favors a more adaptive genotype by allowing some phenotypes to have more offspring than others. This necessitates genetic variation within a population. The ultimate source of such variability is mutation.

Taxonomy

Behavior can often be used as a guide to the *taxonomic* classification of an organism. There are many instances where the behavior of an animal has given important clues as to its systematic position within a group. Barlow (1962) uses behavioral evidence to argue that a species of fish, *Badis badis,* has been placed not only in the wrong genus but also in the wrong family and suborder. He observed the spawning behavior of this species and noted that it is remarkably similar to that of the Anabantoid species and not similar to that of any other species to which it was thought related. Indeed, the behavioral similarity of this species to Anabantoid fish also manifests itself in locomotion, color changes, and feeding behavior.

Another instance of the value of behavior to taxonomy is shown by the calls of morphologically very similar species of frogs that have been shown to be different, particularly at the zone of overlap of the two species. Experimental studies support the view that the two species are reproductively isolated by the mating calls, meaning that hybridization does not easily occur (Blair, 1964).

The use of such evidence necessarily implies that some behavioral characteristics are as constant or as much representative of the species as are the physical characteristics usually used in classifying animals. Not all behavior, of course, is equally suitable for such studies. One needs to use behaviors that are well buffered against environmental events, and fixed action patterns are usually prime candidates as the behavioral characteristics to be used. Songs and vocalizations are also important, as shown by the frog example. In birds, many calls and songs are performed without experience and with little or no learning involved, while other species are very much dependent upon either general or specific experience (Marler & Hamilton, 1966). In insects, on the other hand, songs and calls seem to be impervious to experiential effects (Alexander, 1968). Although it has been argued that the use of behavior as a taxonomic tool does not imply a genetic shaping of the differences between the species involved (Moltz, 1965), it would appear that the evidence indicates the opposite. Naturally, the further one gets from the genes themselves—that is, the more pathways or mechanisms, biochemical and physiological, that are interspersed between DNA and the character seen (i.e., between the genotype and the phenotype)—the greater the opportunity for environmental events to modify the phenotype. Nonetheless, it is conceivable that in some behavioral characteristics the number of steps from gene to behavior is less than with some morphological or physiological characteristics.

Behavioral evolution

The preceding section discussed the role that behavior can play in understanding the systematics and evolution of a given species. However, we can also be concerned with how behavior evolves and use comparative study to elucidate some of the mechanisms by which behavior changes throughout phylogeny. An excellent review of this area is presented by Manning (1971). There has been a long history of interest in the evolution of some behavioral characteristics. For instance, we have already discussed how since Darwin's time comparative psychologists have been especially interested in the evolution of intelligence. There are great difficulties in obtaining even an approximation of the course of the evolution of intelligence let alone any good ideas of how learning and intelligence evolved. It would appear that the question is just too complex to answer at this time. Who is to say that an earthworm in its environment is not behaving more intelligently than man is in his?

The ethologist has started out with more modest goals, utilizing directly observable and more easily measurable behaviors that an organism performs, as ethology has also done in relation to behavior genetics discussed earlier. Ethology has also emphasized the study of closely related forms for generating hypotheses about how specific behaviors change through evolution.

Since behaviors do not fossilize, with the exception of certain records of behavior such as tracks, prey remains, and structures built by a limited number of species, it might be thought that the study of the evolution of behavior would be an almost impossible task considering the additional problem that many intermediary links between the species have become extinct. Although these are indeed problems, they are not completely formidable (Romer, 1958). One must, at present, be satisfied with different magnitudes of precision in studying different levels of behavior.

A distinction must first be made between *homologous* behaviors that are derived from a common ancestor and *convergent* or *analogous* behaviors that, although functionally similar, are derived from unrelated elements. Wings in insects and birds are analogous in function, but they are not homologous since no common ancestor of both groups had either wings or extremities which became wings. Wings of birds and bats are only analogous as wings, since the common reptilian ancestor did not fly. But wings of bats and birds are homologous if they are considered "forelimbs," which the reptilian ancestor possessed and which independently evolved as flight structures in birds and bats. Since the question is complicated for structures and the anatomy of animals, how are behaviors determined to be homologous rather than analogous or convergent? Ethologists use a number of techniques for this difficult task (Atz, 1970). First consider the topography of the FAP, that is, the various acts and muscle coordinations involved with the fixed action pattern. For instance, most birds scratch their heads by raising one leg over the wing rather than by directly lifting the claw to the head. This behavior, in fact, is taken as homologous for groups of vertebrates, since mammals and lizards scratch with their rear limbs in a similar manner, raising the hind limb over the shoulder to scratch the head (Heinroth, 1930). Most often, however, ethologists study closely related species in order to discover reasonable hypotheses as to how behaviors originate and evolve.

The order of the behavioral acts of FAPs also may give a clue to the evolutionary relationships among species. For instance, at identical places in

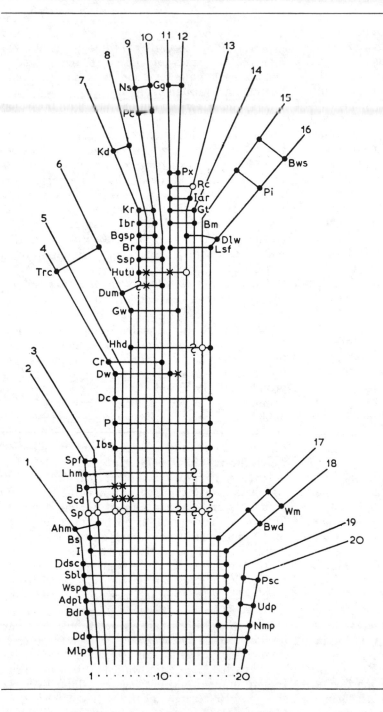

courtship behavior two species of fish may perform different tail-wagging movements. The fact that they occurred in the same point in the sequence indicates that they are homologous (Baerends, 1958).

It is also frequently possible to order a number of

species in such a way that a gradation in movements is found. Although the two extremes have very different behaviors unlikely to be considered homologous when considered alone, the fact that a series of connecting stages or links can be found illustrates a conceivable way in which the behavior

Characters

Mlp	monosyllabic "lost-piping"	Dc	decrescendo call of the female	Px	Pintail-like extension of the median tail-feathers
Dd	display drinking	Br	Bridling		
Bdr	bony drum on the drake's trachea	Cr	chin-raising	Rc	R-calls of the female in incitement and as social contact call
Adpl	Anatine duckling plumage	Hhd	hind-head display of the drake		
Wsp	wing speculum	Gw	grunt-whistle	Iai	incitement with anterior of body raised
Sbl	Sieve bill with horny lamellae	Dum	down-up movement		
Ddsc	disyllabic duckling social contact call	Hutu	head-up-tail-up	Gt	graduated tail
		Ssp	speculum same in both sexes		
I	incitement by the female	Wm	black-and-white and red-brown wing markings of Casarcinae	Bm	bill markings with spot and light-colored sides
Bs	body-shaking as a courtship or demonstrative gesture			Dlw	drake lacks whistle
		Bgsp	black-gold-green teal speculum	Lsf	lancet-shaped shoulder feathers
Ahm	aiming head-movements as a mating prelude	Trc	chin-raising reminiscent of the triumph ceremony	Bws	blue wing secondaries
Sp	sham-preening of the drake, performed behind the wings			Pi	pumping as incitement
		Ibr	isolated bridling not coupled to head-up-tail-up	Dw	drake whistle
Scd	Social courtship of the drakes			Bwd	black-and-white duckling plumage
B	"burping"	Kr	"Krick"-whistle		
Lhm	lateral head movement of the inciting female	Kd	"Koo-dick" of the true teals	Psc	polysyllabic gosling social contact call of Anserinae
		Pc	post-copulatory play with bridling and nod-swimming		
Spf	specific feather specializations serving sham-preening			Udp	uniform duckling plumage
		Ns	nod-swimming by the female	Nmp	neck-dipping as mating prelude
Ibs	introductory body-shaking	Gg	*Geeeeegeeeee*-call of the true pintail drakes		
P	pumping as prelude to mating				

Figure 9.9 Ducks arranged by courtship movements and social releasers showing possible evolutionary relationships. The vertical lines represent species; the horizontal lines represent the characters common among them. A cross indicates the absence of a character, a circle indicates a special emphasis and differentiation of the character, and a question mark indicates the author's uncertainty. (From Lorenz, 1941.)

change between species A and Z could occur and hence be homologous. Differences among species in the stimulus threshold for releasing homologous behaviors, or the relative frequency with which homologous behaviors are performed, are also informative (Manning, 1971). One of the first thorough evolutionary studies showing the power of behavioral information was the study of Lorenz on courtship movements in ducks (Figure 9.9).

Homologous sign stimuli effects can also be utilized in evolutionary studies. For instance, we have already pointed out that there are clear differences found in the chemicals from prey eliciting tongue flicking and attack in newborn snakes, even among closely related species of the same genus. Similar responses to the same prey extract given by closely related species most likely involve homologous chemical sign stimuli. However, a number of less closely related species from different genera and different families may respond to the same extract, and chemical analysis will be needed in differentiating homologous and convergent chemical prey recognition.

Differences in overt behavior have been found most useful in evolutionary studies. Fixed action patterns associated with courtship and other social behaviors in particular are employed since they are less likely to show adaptation to specific ecological factors as feeding behavior often does. That is to say, social behavior more often indicates evolutionary relationships (homologies) than many other types of behavior such as feeding, habitat preference, and predator defense.

Social behavior is often more stylized, formal, and less variable than many other behaviors. That is, it is often ritualized since mutual understanding (predictability) is necessary. One form of ritualization involving the incorporation of diverse FAPs into social behaviors such as fighting and courtship has been referred to earlier. This phenomenon, while vaguely understood, has been seen as highly significant by many people (see papers in Huxley, 1966) and has many parallels to human rituals from smoking peace pipes to church services (Lorenz, 1966). The latter are much less specifically innate and are clearly culturally shaped, but all cultures have them for social interactions, indicating their functional significance.

IMPRINTING

The phenomenon of imprinting is the aspect of ethology that most effectively brought it to the attention of experimental psychology. In point of fact, imprinting had been described not only by Spalding (1873), but also by Sir Thomas More in *Utopia* in 1516. Other people have also noticed that a newly hatched chick or gosling will often follow and treat as its mother the first moving object that it sees. The fixation is quite rapid, and the natural mother may be ignored forever. Spalding's (1873) observations anticipated modern research on imprinting. He noted that as soon as chicks could locomote, they followed any moving object and would readily follow a duck or a human instead of a hen. On the other hand, the chick would ignore and run away from its mother if first exposed to her at ten days of age, even if the hen tried to entice it. Thus, there seemed to be a certain optimal time for imprinting to occur. Further experiments with chicks raised in the dark showed that between three and four days of age the onset of fear prevented the formation of the imprinting bond. Heinroth (1911), who raised many birds in captivity, extended these observations on the formation of such social bonds by imprinting to many species. William James (1890) used work such as Spalding's to articulate two principles by which instinctive behaviors can be modified and which apply particularly cogently to imprinting. The first is that "when objects of a certain class elicit from an animal a certain sort of reaction, it often happens that the animal becomes partial to the first specimen of the class on which it has reacted, and will not afterward react to any other specimen" [p. 394].

The important implications of this dramatic behavior were articulated by Lorenz (1935, 1937), who extensively described imprinting and, furthermore, stated a variety of its attributes that seemed to differentiate it from standard learning. This, of course, was a challenge to the psychologists' attempts to explain all behavior acquisition on the basis of one or two processes, usually respondent and operant conditioning. Nonetheless, twenty years were to pass before the experimental investigation of imprinting came into prominence, and many questions remain yet unanswered.

Lorenz (1935) conceptualized imprinting as "the process of acquisition of the object of instinctive behaviour patterns oriented towards conspecifics, which are initially incorporated without the object" [1970, p. 246]. Thus imprinting fit his theory of instinct. Lorenz used the example of the greylag goose, which, upon hatching, follows the first moving object that it sees, which was often Lorenz himself. Lorenz did not have to reward the gosling in any obvious or conventional way for following him. The first attribute, therefore, is that imprinting does not proceed according to trial and error, nor does it involve reward and punishment. The mere exposure to a broad class of stimuli at a certain time determines subsequent stimulus control of behavior.

Lorenz also refers to the fact that imprinting may affect future mate choice. Of course, at the time the bird becomes imprinted, it is incapable of performing courtship behavior. Hence, the second attribute is that the behaviors whose releasers the animal learns do not always have to be performed at the time imprinting occurs.

The third point is that imprinting can only take place during a brief *critical period* in the life of the individual. As Lorenz (1970) states, imprinting "depends upon a *quite definite physiological developmental condition* in the young bird" [p. 127]. The limits of the period were set by physiological maturational factors. This recalls James' (1890) second principle—the *Law of Transitoriness:* "Many instincts ripen at a certain age and then fade away" [p. 398].

Fourth, imprinting is irreversible. In other words, the effects of imprinting cannot be forgotten. This is the aspect of imprinting, as described by Lorenz, that has been most controversial. Lorenz (1970), even in his early writings, was not dogmatic on this point, saying, "Of course, it is not yet permissible, in the light of the relative novelty of all observations on this process, to make a final statement about the permanence of these acquired objects" [p. 127].

The last attribute of imprinting that Lorenz mentions is that the imprinting centers on supraindividual characters. In other words, during the imprinting phase proper, the young bird learns to recognize the class of objects (i.e., the species) to which it belongs. Only later, perhaps via more typical learning, does the bird distinguish its parents from others.

Early experimental studies

Little further work was performed until the experimental studies of the early 1950s, particularly those of Fabricius (1951), Ramsay (1951), and Ramsay and Hess (1954). Since imprinting is one of the most investigated phenomena in ethology, it serves as an indication of what might develop in other areas of ethological analysis; it also pinpoints some of the problems which, hopefully, workers will avoid in the future.

Ramsay and Hess (1954) used as an imprinting stimulus a decoy male mallard duck fitted with a heating element and an internal speaker that played a tape of a human voice saying: GOCK, gock, gock, gock. The decoy was moved in a circular runway, and the animal to be imprinted could follow after it. Ducklings were hatched in the dark and placed in individual light-tight boxes until the imprinting period. No food or water was given until after the complete experiment to eliminate the more obvious primary reinforcers and because of the chicks' and ducklings' limited ability to feed and drink in the dark. This poses no hardship on the animals for the first several days because the yolk sac provides a source of nutrition. Imprinting periods during which the ducklings could follow the decoy were 10 and 30 minutes in length. Twenty-four hours later the animal was presented with a choice situation containing both the male target stimulus and a decoy of the female mallard that rendered the taped sound of a female mallard calling her young. In other words, the preference test was biased in favor of the characteristics of the natural mother in terms of both visual and auditory cues. Several types of measures showed that the ducklings preferred the target stimulus and that the mean strength of imprinting sharply peaked between 13 and 16 hours.

The past fifteen years have seen a tremendous increase in the experimental study of imprinting, and a comprehensive review of the experimental findings is not possible. Sluckin (1965) has reviewed the material up to that date in a book which could do no more than briefly cite most of the entries. Other briefer treatments of imprinting are those of Hinde (1970), Marler and Hamilton (1966), Moltz (1963), Hess (1959a, 1964), Bateson (1966), and Sluckin (1972), among others.

Methodology and controversy

There is some disagreement on the interpretation of collected data. Many of the disagreements are due to differences in species and in theories rather than data. For example, studies on chicks only questionably disprove another's findings with ducks. Even within the same species there are marked differences in imprintability. Vantress broiler chicks are good imprinters, whereas white leghorn chicks are not (Hess, 1959a). Individual differences within a breed are also common and can further vary according to the season of the year.

Other conflicting evidence can be traced to the large variety of procedures used to imprint animals and the measures taken to assess whether imprinting occurred. Sluckin (1972) lists five methods of measuring short-term filial imprinting alone. Also, although it is important to constantly improve the apparatus, some of the changes in the methods employed do not allow for the easy comparison of results. For instance, some investigators use animals imprinted in straight runways, while others use circular arenas; some investigators use naturalistic stimuli, such as duck decoys, while other workers employ more unnatural stimuli, such as balls, cubes, and cylinders in various colors and sizes; some investigators use visual stimuli alone, while others add heat and/or auditory stimuli. Although in early studies it was felt, even by Lorenz, that the naive bird could be imprinted to almost anything, there is increasing evidence that imprinting stimuli vary considerably in their effectiveness.

Another area in which methodology leads to much conflicting evidence has to do with how the animals are maintained prior to being imprinted and between imprinting and the test period which assesses whether imprinting occurred. Some investigators keep their animals visually isolated from others and place them in dark, individual boxes. They are, of course, exposed to the sounds of other chicks. Some investigators maintain the chicks in groups until they are imprinted. Still other investigators keep the animals socially isolated in the light until the imprinting experience. These various methods affect imprinting in chicks and ducklings. For instance, Polt and Hess (1964) found that during the critical period (16 hours of age) socialized chicks followed the model more in the imprinting situation than did isolated chicks. But when tested 24 hours later in a choice test between the imprinting model and a group of four chicks, the socialized group preferred the chicks while the isolated chicks preferred the model. This study indicates several things: (1) Animals kept together before the imprinting experience can imprint on each other; (2) such imprinting or other aspects of the social experience can facilitate the following of a novel stimulus; and (3) the amount of following during imprinting is not necessarily correlated with the amount of imprinting.

There is, then, many a source of conflicting data.

Indeed, Klopfer (1971) was led to exclaim in one of the more staid journals: "In moments of extreme frustration one is also tempted to explain results in terms of delusions and demons" [p. 378]. The most important lesson to be gained from this state of affairs is that the natural context of a behavior cannot be ignored. Imprinting investigators prematurely brought the phenomenon into the laboratory without having enough ethogramic information as to relevant and meaningful conditions and procedures, thus ignoring a basic tenet of ethology in the process. Hess (1972), a pioneer in the laboratory analysis of imprinting, has readily admitted this and has reoriented his entire research to the field. The next few years should see many more papers based on field observations and experiments. One important aspect of imprinting that has been especially ignored has been the parental behavior toward the young, including maternal calls. It is amazing that it was felt that a dynamic social process, such as imprinting certainly is, could be understood adequately by studying (albeit intensively) only one of the two classes of participants.

Major findings in filial imprinting

A coherent picture of imprinting is currently impossible because of the aforementioned problems, but with chicks and ducks (particularly mallard ducks and their domesticated descendants, the white pekin) the following statements can be supported, at least under some experimental conditions.

1. *Imprinting occurs only, or occurs most easily, over a quite restricted period in the early posthatch stages of the animal's life.* The earliest experiments in imprinting supported Lorenz' contention of a critical period for imprinting (e.g., Ramsay & Hess, 1954). Hess (1959a) has argued that with ducklings and chicks the critical period is terminated at the end of the first day of life and that any attachments that can be made after that time are not due to imprinting in the classical sense but are due to more conventional associative conditioning.

The term *critical period* has been criticized on several grounds (e.g., Bateson, 1966; Caspari, 1967; Sluckin, 1965), and less restrictive substitutes such as *sensitive* or *optimal period* have been advocated. However, the concept itself remains and the other terms are used interchangeably by most workers. Whether or not they should be is another issue (Evans, 1970). In any event, what is the nature of the critical period? The early view of Lorenz was that it was a physiological, maturationally delimited

period. The Ramsay and Hess (1954) study and others verified the narrow time span involved.

However, the maturational view is to some extent challenged by findings that certain types of posthatch experience can delay the end of the critical period. Part of this evidence is negated by the confusion between following an object and imprinting to it. However, Moltz and Stettner (1961) showed that a restriction of patterned-light experience could extend the period to 48 hours posthatch but not to 72 hours. These workers put hoods on ducklings that allowed only diffuse light to reach the eyes until the imprinting session. Control animals wore hoods with holes allowing patterned visual experience. After imprinting all animals were hoodless until the following day when the imprinting test occurred.

The prevention of all social experience can also extend the attachment phase. For instance, Sluckin (1962) found that chicks could still be imprinted at eight days as determined by a test at fifteen days, but birds isolated until fifteen days could not be imprinted. In this instance, however, one is working with imprinting periods measured in hours rather than in minutes, and an organism so deprived is likely to be abnormal in many respects in addition to not having formed a *filial bond*. The point remains that a narrowly defined critical period for initial attachments exists, whatever initiates and terminates it.

Research has also been directed at the factors responsible for the end of the critical period. There are two aspects to this problem. First, when an animal is imprinted to an object, why is it not easily imprinted to another object also presented within the critical period? This is termed the *primacy effect*, considered by Hess (1959a) to be a basic attribute of imprinting. In some manner, being imprinted to one stimulus prevents responsivity to a new one, a characteristic also discussed by William James (1890).

The second question concerns the broader limits of the critical period within a population of animals without prior experience. These two questions are quite different, and much of the writing on imprinting confuses them. Since the answers are not yet in and the evidence we do have is controversial, only a brief discussion will be given here.

We will first consider the limits of the critical period itself, which may be self-terminating through maturation or terminated by the occurrence of some other event. According to the purely maturational view, the end of the period is based on an endogenous waning of the tendency to follow; that is, following just naturally disappears (Fabricius, 1951). Although difficult to disprove, this view has two points against it: (1) It cannot be the complete reason since posthatch experience has some effect on the length of the period; and (2) it specifies no mechanism through which the decrease in following is mediated. The next view was that the development of fear to novel objects conflicted with the approach and following of the imprinting stimulus (Verplanck, 1955). Insofar as this growth of fear was endogenous, this theory runs into the first objection listed for the maturational view, but it did offer a mechanism. Hess (1959b) performed a very neat experiment showing that the peak of the critical period occurred at the intersect between increasing locomotor ability and decreasing fear. He found that a chick's speed of locomotion was low until 13 to 16 hours after hatching and that at this age, fear, as measured by the bird's distress calls or movements away from the model, was just beginning to develop. Fear affected all animals by age 33 to 36 hours. The fear hypothesis is probably the most tenable today, although it has been noted that following may cease, even in the absence of such objective signs of fear as distress calls (Jaynes, 1956; Weidmann, 1958), and alternative but less well supported theories have been advanced (e.g., Moltz, 1960).

The problem of what causes the decrease in imprintability to a new stimulus as soon as the animal becomes imprinted on one object has been less studied (a phenomenon similar to proactive interference). One view is that socialization itself inhibits imprintability to new objects (Sluckin, 1965). The question is, how? In the natural situation where the first imprinted object is constantly presented, competing responses to the original object could lead to little imprinting to other objects in the environment. But in the laboratory the original object is typically no longer available.

The existence of the critical period, then, has been amply demonstrated, but the details of its parameters need further study.

2. *More than one modality can be involved in establishing the imprinting bond.* While most investigators have worked with visual stimuli, the early studies by Ramsay and Hess (1954) involved visual, auditory, and thermal stimuli. Most experimenters removed the thermal stimulus on the bases that it is not too important and that it may provide a primary reinforcement. Results generally show that while imprinting can occur to auditory and visual stimuli, if both types of stimuli are presented to-

gether, the effectiveness of an imprinting stimulus is increased. Most evidence indicates that auditory stimuli are more potent than visual stimuli if presented alone (Fischer, 1966; Gottlieb, 1971), although there is some disagreement as to whether imprinting is to the sound per se (Sluckin, 1972).

3. *Not all visual or auditory stimuli are equally effective in establishing an imprinting bond.* A number of studies have established this fact beyond doubt in ducks and chicks. Some of the visual parameters studied were color (Gray, 1961; Schaefer & Hess, 1959), shape (Hess, 1959a), pattern (Klopfer, 1967), and type of stimulus movement (Sluckin & Salzen, 1961; Smith, 1962; Smith & Bird, 1963). In early experimentation, it was generally felt that although stimulus preferences were a factor, they were easily overridden by the imprinting experience. That this is not always the case was shown by Klopfer (1967). Birds imprinted to either a plain white model or a patterned varicolored one chose the latter regardless of which one they were imprinted to. Of course, rather extreme stimulus differences were involved.

Stimulus movement was once considered crucial for imprinting to occur, but this is not the case. Hess (1959a) was able to imprint a mallard duckling to a model merely by having the animal in a dim environment with two identical models that were alternately illuminated. The duckling ran back and forth between the two and became imprinted. A motionless flickering light is also an effective imprinting stimulus (James, 1959). Relative conspicuousness from the background might then be an important factor (Bateson, 1966), or perhaps just visual change.

While visual stimuli vary in effectiveness, little evidence indicates that species-characteristic visual cues are prepotent, although the positive results of Hess and Hess (1969) should lead to the reevaluation of this conclusion. With auditory cues the evidence is more clear-cut (Gottlieb, 1971). In wood, mallard, and Peking ducklings, as well as in domestic chicks, the species-characteristic maternal call is preferred. Further, such calls are preferred over species-characteristic visual stimuli.

4. *Mere exposure to an imprinting stimulus is sufficient to establish the imprinting bond.* A number of studies have found that the organism does not necessarily need to make an overt motor response in order for imprinting to occur (see Baer & Gray, 1960). However, it is extremely difficult to prevent an animal from making some responses (e.g., orienting, attempts to follow) to a stimulus even if it is prevented from approaching it.

5. *The greater the effort expended by an animal, the greater the imprinting*. To show that imprinting can occur in complete absence of overt responses is not to prove that overt responses by the animal do not play an important role in addition to perceptual factors. Hess (1959a) found that the longer the distance traversed by a bird or the more difficult it was for the organism to follow the stimulus during the imprinting period, the stronger the imprinting at a later time. Hess even formulated this relationship into the *law of effort:* The strength of imprinting is a function of the logarithm of the effort involved. This law has come under much critical scrutiny. One problem is to equate the periods of exposure. Attempts to repeat it or to find it under slightly different conditions have generally been negative, casting doubt on the validity of the law (see Sluckin, 1965). In any event, the relationship between the amount of effort expended during imprinting and the strength of imprinting is bound to be complex, as shown by the Polt and Hess (1964) study which found that although socialized chicks followed the imprinting stimulus more than isolated chicks, only the latter were imprinted.

6. *Punishment facilitates imprinting during the critical period*. Anecdotal accounts indicated that if an animal imprinted to a human was accidentally stepped on while following, it would follow the human even closer and apparently with more enthusiasm than previously (Hess, 1964). Kovach and Hess (1963) put fine wires around the wings of chicks before placing them in the imprinting apparatus. They found that the following of an imprinting stimulus by chicks was increased by giving the animals electric shocks through the wires during the critical period at age 18 hours. If animals were shocked after the critical period (32 and 48 hours, respectively), they followed less. It appears that painful or at least arousing stimuli can facilitate the imprinting response. While it has been argued (Sluckin, 1965) that punishment is "an entirely extraneous factor in imprinting" [p. 105], this necessitates a completely romantic view of life outside the laboratory. It would certainly be adaptive to run to the imprinted object if anything aversive happens, since in the natural situation the imprinted object serves as protector and security. Interestingly enough, baby monkeys punished by "bad" mothers (that is, those reared under deprivation) attempt to cling even closer to the source of their discomfort (Harlow & Harlow, 1966). This phenomenon indicates that simplistic notions of pain and punishment need to be avoided in behavioral research (see also Chapter 7). Arousal of

various kinds may turn out to be an important concomitant of imprinting.

7. *Imprintability is under genetic control*. Different breeds of domestic chicks differ in the ease and strength of imprinting, which indicates, as discussed in the preceding section, a genetic factor. Hess (1959a) reported some pilot studies on selective breeding for imprintability, but formal genetic studies did not appear until relatively recently. Graves and Siegel (1969) performed an extensive genetic analysis of the initial approach response of chicks to an imprinting object (a plastic dome with flickering colored lights emitting the tape-recorded call of a broody hen). They selected both for and against the speed of approach to the object. The fast-response line (FRL) showed a marked decrease in that after five generations the response time was cut to about one third of the initial time. Consequently, a significant heritability for approach exists. Curiously, the slow-response line (SRL) was not altered, indicating the negative selection was ineffective. Graves and Siegel discuss their results in terms of *threshold traits*; that is, "selection in the SRL was an attempt to delay responsiveness, but, if responsiveness per se is a threshold trait, it has to be triggered before it can be delayed" [p. 690]. Consequently, their use of a quantitative measure would be inappropriate if the behavior is an all-or-none phenomenon at the phenotypic level with which they were working. One can see from these data that studying the intricacies of genetic factors on behavior rivals the complications found in the study of conditioning.

8. *The imprinted stimulus can act as a reinforcing stimulus for arbitrarily chosen behaviors*. Hoffman et al. (1966) discovered that ducklings readily learned a key-peck response when the reinforcer was the presentation of the imprinted object (a plastic milk bottle). This effect was found only with ducklings imprinted during the first 24 hours after hatching, demonstrating a clear optimal or critical period. A further study showed that responses to the key still occurred at 60 days of age, although at a much reduced frequency (Hoffman & Kozma, 1967). Bateson and Reese (1969) have shown that naive chicks will learn to stand on a pedal in a cage that triggers the lighting and rotates a box placed outside the cage. The chicks acted as if they became attached to the stimulus and later would choose the color stimulus (red or blue) with which they had been reinforced. Perhaps this should be called *autoimprinting*. In any event the interaction between operant conditioning and imprinting needs more attention.

The physiology of imprinting has also been looked at with mixed results. One intriguing study is by Schulman (1972), who found that, not surprisingly, imprinted turkey chicks would key-peck in order to be exposed to the imprinted stimulus. But if naive birds were injected intraperitoneally with brain homogenates of imprinted chicks, they would peck for the imprinted stimulus much more than did controls.

Sexual imprinting

One of the major originally postulated properties of imprinting was that the animal learned the releasers of behavior patterns that it was not capable of performing at that time. Whether this occurs in other learning situations has not really been researched although it should be. Investigation of this attribute of imprinting has been largely limited to ducks.

In the precocial birds that we have been discussing, there is considerable descriptive evidence to support the notion that the object of sexual choice at maturity can be altered from the normal species-characteristic sex object (see Hess, 1959a). Lorenz (1935) himself mentions a number of such examples. The phenomenon does appear to be a real and a very dramatic one. For instance, Hess records a human-imprinted jungle fowl that courted only humans even after many years in captivity. However, the question of what the specific role of early experience is in the establishment of sexual choice cannot easily be decided. The anecdotal evidence suggests that the sexual choice of an animal, usually a male, can become altered, but many of these cases are themselves open to a number of questions. For example, often the animal was reared by humans as a pet at home, and then it later made sexual overtures to humans. It is necessary, however, to have a free choice between the imprinted and the normal sexual objects in order to show that the behavior is released more by the imprinted object than by the normal object (Klinghammer, 1967).

Another methodological problem is that while one may get the animal at a very young age and imprint it to oneself or another animal at the critical period, the subject is, nonetheless, in the company of humans or the other animal involved not just during the early critical period but throughout its life until sexual maturity. In order to assess properly whether the early experience is responsible for the altered mate choice, the early experience period needs to be experimentally isolated.

The most extensive and detailed long-term experiments have been performed by Schutz (1965), who mainly used mallard ducks, although he also studied other species of ducks and domestic fowl. He raised ducklings with either their natural mothers, siblings, a foster mother of a different species, or foster siblings of different species. His effects were enhanced by rearing with the mother rather than siblings. But before discussing his results, it is useful to consider the implications of one aspect of Lorenz' original notions on imprinting. If imprinting to the mother figure is responsible for the determination of later mate choice, it should hold for both males and females. This would seem to work adequately for those species in which the males and females look the same, that is, in visually *monomorphic* species. However, in many species, including the mallard, the male is considerably different visually (*dimorphic*) from the female, particularly during the courtship season. In the mallard the male has a dark green neck and head, whereas the female is brownish all over. In this species it would be appropriate for males to learn what females look like on the basis of their mothers, but certainly it would not do for females to choose their sexual partners on the basis of what their mothers looked like. A finding related to this problem is the observation by Hess (1959a) that male mallard ducklings imprinted to a male model paired with males when they became sexually mature rather than with females. In other words, homosexual bonds were formed. Possible sex differences in odors, vocalizations, and so forth, do not appear too important in ducks, but are possible and should not be ignored, of course.

The work of Schutz has begun to clear up this problem. Schutz found that female and male mallards reared with their own species paired only with the opposite sex of their own species as one would expect. Female mallards always mated with their own kind regardless of what species they were reared with, indicating that although they could become imprinted to a mother object of a wide variety of species, filial imprinting was divorced from sexual choice. On the other hand, mallard drakes would pair under many circumstances with the foster species rather than with conspecific females. In the female, then, determination of a sexual partner is largely innate, based on the recognition of certain markings, whereas experience was important for males. In the monomorphic species, sexual imprinting occurs in both sexes.

Schutz found that compared to the imprinting of the following reaction the optimal period for sexual imprinting occurs later in life and lasts for weeks rather than hours. For instance, about one third of the birds reared with their own species for the first three weeks and then reared with a different species for the next five to six weeks showed themselves to be sexually imprinted to the foster species.

Even with the males Schutz found that not all members of the species could become imprinted sexually. Those individuals that did not choose to mate with the foster species always chose their own species. Related evidence comes from the fact that male or female mallards reared under complete visual and auditory isolation from all other ducks for nine weeks paired at the normal time with their own species. Other ducks were the best foster species for mallards. It was very difficult to imprint mallards on chickens and coots. On the other hand, domestic or wild fowl and coots were easily imprinted on mallards. Hess and Hess (1969) have shown that mallards imprint more strongly to mallard decoys than to humans. This suggests some mechanism of innate recognition which interacts more or less with postnatal experience.

Species of birds in which the young are not mobile at birth are termed *altricial* (e.g., songbirds). Altricial birds are obviously not suited for following-response imprinting. They remain in the nest and their parents bring them food, clean out the nest, protect them from predators, and so forth. The young play a relatively passive role in the relationship. Imprinting studies with altricial birds by necessity deal almost exclusively with future mate choice rather than with parental imprinting. Klinghammer (1967) found that in mourning doves and ring doves early experience (over a period of days, not hours) with either humans or their own species had a potent effect on later mate choice and that a critical period existed for this phenomenon. However, the later postweaning experience of the animal was also important. Both females and males could become imprinted to the human hand and would give the species-characteristic sexual responses to the hand even in preference to the natural object. Interestingly enough, both of these species of doves are monomorphic. Early experience can have an effect on mate choice, but the effect is not irreversible by any means.

Immelmann (1966) has gathered quite convincing evidence for the long-term irreversibility of sexual choice in male zebra finches, a dimorphic species. As for mammals, there is evidence that imprinting of the following response can occur in precocial species such as guinea pigs and sheep (Hess, 1959a; Scott, 1962). Evidence that such early experience modifies sexual choice is not yet con-clusive (but see Beauchamp & Hess, 1971). In altricial tree shrews (*Tupaia longipes*) sexual imprinting to humans does seem to occur (Sorenson, 1970).

Parental imprinting

Most imprinting studies emphasize the behavior of the neonate toward the parent. It is obvious that the behavior of parents toward the young also plays important roles in the development of behavior. Noble and Curtis (1939) found that if pairs of jewel fish (*Hemichromis bimaculatus*) breeding for the first time were given eggs of cichlid species other than their own, they would rear them and subsequently kill young of their own species. However, pairs of jewel fish that had previously reared their own young would eat the young of the foster species (see also Greenberg, 1963; Myrberg, 1964).

In mammals, parental imprinting seems to occur in goats (Klopfer, Adams, & Klopfer, 1964). If a mother is not allowed access to her kid within one hour after its birth, she will reject it. This carries the fish studies further in that individual, rather than just species, recognition is involved. Individual recognition of their parents and siblings by young can also occur, as shown in experiments on ring-billed gulls (Evans, 1970).

EARLY EXPERIENCE

The area of study that is entitled *early experience* is a broad one which should include the area of imprinting. However, because classical imprinting is a rather specialized ethological topic dealing with specific effects, we have considered it separately and in more detail than we will other areas of early experience research.

The relatively recent emphasis on early experience—those events occurring early in the organism's life which have a greater or more potent effect than the same experiences occurring later in its life—has evolved due to the work of the ethologists on imprinting and the interest in psychology engendered thereby. Another area of influence on experimental work in early experience comes from the theories and observations of Sigmund Freud. His emphasis on early sexual experience in shaping adult habits, especially abnormal functioning, is certainly one reason for focusing on the exact role of early experience.

Early experience effects can be considered from many viewpoints and methodologies. In this section, however, we will emphasize several studies selected from the multitude now available that deal with variables in early experience phenomena. Several recent volumes (e.g., Newton & Levine, 1968; Sluckin, 1972) provide comprehensive reviews.

The area that has received the most experimental attention concerns the effects of neonatal handling on later emotional and learning abilities. In accord with the ethological emphasis on species-characteristic behavior, we will limit the discussion to behavior measured with a fair naturalistic validity, dealing in turn with food selection, fighting, habitat selection, social choice, and social behavior in primates.

Food preferences

Raising animals from birth on restricted diets can lead to strong food preferences or even fixations. Kuo (1967) discusses the fixation of dietary preferences after six months on a single food in cats, dogs, and birds. There are surprisingly few studies of less extreme dietary restrictions involving equated experience with more than one food. Burghardt and Hess (1966) showed that raising three groups of naive snapping turtles (*Chelydra serpentina*) on either fish, earthworms, or horsemeat for 12 daily feedings channeled a subsequent free-choice preference test in favor of the food experienced. Giving the turtles an equivalent 12 days of experience on a different one of the three foods did not alter the preference for the first fed diet. In other words, the primacy attribute of imprinting seemed to be satisfied. A further experiment (Burghardt, 1967) showed that the primacy effect could be obtained after only one feeding on each of two foods. In both experiments, however, all foods were not equal in their ability to be "fixated," implying that the early experience interacted with innate preferences. A similar situation has been shown to occur in chicks with natural seeds (Burghardt, 1969b) and colored mash (Capretta, 1969).

Aggression

One of the first hints that early experience factors were playing a role in later rodent behavior arose from the studies by Scott (1942) and Ginsburg and Allee (1942) on strain differences in the aggressive and fighting behavior of inbred mice. In both studies, the experimenters were looking for genetic factors by comparing strains in dominance and fighting ability. What happened, however, was that of the three strains studied in both experiments, the

most aggressive strain from Ginsburg and Allee was the least aggressive according to Scott's experiments, and vice versa. Clearly something was wrong, and further experimentation and an analysis of the experimental designs themselves were performed. Ginsburg (1967) has recently evaluated these experiments and concludes that a major factor in the different results concerns how the animals were handled in their early lives. In one procedure the mice were transferred by being picked up by the tail with a forceps. In the other the mice were allowed to walk from one cage to the other or, if necessary, were scooped up into a container. The strain (C57BL/10), most aggressive when nonhandled, was least aggressive when forceps handled. Therefore, early handling differences explain most of the conflicting results of Scott and Ginsburg and Allee. But the answer is not quite that simple since the other two strains (C$_3$H and C) were unaffected by the differential handling as far as aggressive behavior was concerned. Hence, a new complication arises. The early experience variable interacts with the genotype. The C57BL/10 strain is more labile—that is, more affected by environmental events—than are the other strains. This very lability or plasticity, however, is based on genetic differences: "The genotype demonstrably and predictably refracts experiential input according to its own biological properties" [Ginsburg, 1967, p. 149].

The lesson from these experiments should be kept in mind when comparisons between, as well as within, species are made.

Habitat selection

Wecker (1963) has demonstrated the variable way in which experience and heredity can interact. His study involved the selection of habitats (fields or woods) by deer mice of the same species (*Peromyscus maniculations*) but of different subspecies. The wild-caught woodland form (*P. m. gracilis*) will choose a wooded area over a field, whereas a wild-caught prairie form (*P. m. bairdi*) will choose the field over the woods. Laboratory-reared mice from the same populations (F$_1$) choose the appropriate area, and one may conclude that the selection is innate. Since Wecker was interested in determining the effect of early experience in the field or woods environment on the habitat preference, he took offspring of the wild-caught field variety and raised them in a wooded habitat. Nonetheless, they still chose the field. Early experience does not seem to play a large role in the habitat preference of natural populations of these mice, although the microclimate basis for the preference is not clear. What is it about the field that made it preferred: more light, different vegetation or temperature, less humidity, etc.?

Wecker also tested offspring of a laboratory population of the field form (*bairdi*) twelve to twenty generations removed from the field environment. These laboratory-reared offspring evidenced no preference for the field or woods. The altered environment had a dramatic effect in less than 20 years of domestication. Wecker then reared the laboratory stock in a pen in the field. The field was chosen over the woods. But if he reared the laboratory stock in a pen in the woods, the latter showed no preference for the wooded over the field environment. What seems to have occurred is that although no innate preference for the field exists in the laboratory stock, they are nonetheless programmed to learn to prefer only their ancestral habitat. This is important support for the view that evolutionary processes direct the learning or modification of behavior in subtle ways.

Social choice

A similar study by Kilham, Klopfer, and Oelke (1968) shows that such a process is not restricted to either rodents or habitat learning. Taking their cue from an earlier study by Howells and Vine (1940), these workers tested the social preference of naive Vantress-cross chicks (yellow) and naive sex-linked chicks (black) by allowing them to approach either their own or the alien breed. They found no initial preference. However, if newly hatched chicks of either breed were raised with a companion (*Kumpan*) of either breed and then were tested for social preference, the process uncovered was similar to that discovered by Wecker. Yellow chicks housed with yellow chicks preferred their own kind, as did black chicks raised with a black Kumpan. Black chicks raised with yellow chicks and yellow chicks reared with black chicks showed no preference for either black or yellow chicks. Here again we see a bias toward learning certain things, in this case a preference for characteristics of their own breed. But color itself was not a crucial characteristic. Yellow Vantress chicks raised with their own kind did not discriminate between normal Vantress chicks and Vantress chicks dyed blue. But if blue-dyed Vantress chicks were reared with other blue-dyed chicks, they preferred the blue chicks. Other evidence even indicated a slight prepotency for blue. Nonetheless, behavioral factors not yet identified were more important to the chicks than color, the difference most easily noted by humans. The authors conclude, "Preferences for own-kind are immanent, but require activation by a particular experience" [p. 243].

Social behavior in primates

The work of H. F. Harlow and associates on the effects of social deprivation on various social behaviors of rhesus monkeys is well known and will not be thoroughly reviewed here (see reviews in Harlow & Harlow, 1965, 1966; Harlow, Harlow, & Hansen, 1963). A few of their interesting findings can be listed. Three months of total social isolation after birth puts young monkeys in a state of emotional shock and makes them appear similar to autistic children. However, if they survive this trauma, socialization with peers of the same age for 30 minutes a day leads to complete social recovery and future normal sexual behavior. Six months of total social isolation led to some permanent social deficiencies and 12 months of isolation even more so. Learning ability appears unaffected. There appears to be a critical period, not rigidly defined, for the socialization of the monkey.

Missakian (1969) has reported a detailed comparative analysis of the social behavior of wild-reared rhesus monkeys, naive socially deprived monkeys raised without any physical contact with other monkeys for six years, and experienced socially deprived monkeys that had periodic exposure to females during the three years preceding the experiment. All monkeys were at least six years old. Introducing females to each of the monkeys in a test situation had clear results. None of the socially deprived males executed a normal mount. Further, no single aspect of reproductive behavior was differentially affected since grooming and threatening were also radically altered. Since the experienced socially deprived monkeys were indistinguishable from the totally deprived group, the author argues that the early experience effect is irreversible.

LEARNING

Learning is a major research area in experimental psychology. Indeed, an up-to-date review of this important and highly sophisticated field is excellently presented in this volume. However, since learning, conditioning, or indeed any modification of behavior cannot occur apart from the organism and its evolutionary heritage, it is also valuable to look at such phenomena in the context of the organism's total life history and its evolved capacities. The results of even minor environmental manipulations were shown to be influenced by the genotype in the preceding section. Some aspects of the learning involved in species-characteristic behavior have also been discussed. Presented here will be a few comments on the psychological study of animal learning from an ethological perspective. It should be borne in mind that unless learning is equated with all environmentally induced modifications in behavior, learning is a far less prevalent phenomenon in the animal kingdom than is indicated by present research emphases. Also interesting to note is that problems in conceptualizing, defining, or categorizing learning (learned behavior) have not led to the abandonment of the topic, as has been suggested in the case of instinct and innate behavior. However, it does imply that new approaches are necessary.

One very important phenomenon in the modification of behavior is *habituation,* the waning of a response tendency under repeated stimulation. We have already seen in an earlier section how selective habituation was invoked to account for the hawk-goose sign-stimulus effect in turkeys. Hinde (1970) has been an active worker in this area, and through his studies of mobbing behavior by chaffinches to owl models, he has argued for at least two distinct types of habituation, long and short term. Habituation is probably the most pervasive type of learning, entering into almost all behaviors including unconditioned reflexes, and deserves much more investigation.

However, as pointed out earlier, the goal of comparative and animal learning psychologists has been to understand and compare more complex learning abilities of different species. Over the years three major approaches to the problem have been advanced and are currently influential. These are the *ethological* approach which emphasizes the species-characteristic and situation-specific factors, the *general process* view which emphasizes the generality across species of basic "laws of learning," and the *phyletic discontinuity* approach which emphasizes the qualitative differences in learning abilities across different evolutionary levels. Although they emphasize different aspects of learning, they are not mutually exclusive.

The ethological approach

The ethologist views learning from the perspective of the animal's normal behavior. In analyzing such behavior, an attempt is made to discover

where learning plays a role. A monkey may be more "intelligent" than a dog or cat, but try to housebreak the former and one realizes the limitations of such comparisons. The difference between the monkey and cat on this particular task can be readily traced to the different life histories of the animals' wild ancestors. In other words, learning is often specific to certain situations, as influenced by the organism's evolution.

A dramatic example concerns the *delayed-reaction* technique in which an animal is tested on the length of time it can remember a specific fact, such as under which of several dishes food has been placed. Even dogs and primates have their retention usually measured in minutes (Maier & Schneirla, 1935), while Baerends (1941; see also Tinbergen, 1951) has shown that a digger wasp (*Ammophilia campsetris*) can remember how many food items (i.e., caterpillars) to bring to her larvae in her several nests for up to 15 hours in the natural environment. Since a wasp is clearly inferior to a dog or monkey on many learning tasks, the point is that learning can be highly specific to certain evolutionary adapted situations. The innate bases for learning have recently been treated by Lorenz (1969).

It is also important to consider the sensory and motor abilities of the subject. That is, one does not expect a rat to peck a disc nor a pigeon to open a lock. A monkey or raccoon can easily do the latter because of their manipulatory digits. Although this seems obvious, it has not always been remembered in the design or comparison of animal learning studies. Chimpanzees do better than the arboreal gibbon on learning and insight problems, not necessarily because of greater intelligence, motivation, or interest, but because the experimental conditions are not suitable for an animal with long digits that cannot pick up items resting on a flat surface (Beck, 1967b). One must also keep in mind the sensory limitations of the animal. Rats learn brightness discriminations more slowly than chicks under similar conditions not because chicks are more intelligent but because the chick is a more "visual" animal.

The Brelands, who were trained in a traditional animal conditioning paradigm (in this case Skinnerian), set out to apply the principles they had learned to training a wide variety of animals for acts and commercials (Breland & Breland, 1951). They discovered that their trained animals had the unfortunate tendency to begin incorporating species-characteristic responses into the trained sequences of behavior (pigs would root, raccoons would wash, etc.). This phenomenon they termed *instinctive drift*. They were literally forced to accept the ethological position that any general laws of behavior must be imposed on species with different genetically based behavioral repertoires (Breland & Breland, 1961, 1966). Ethologists hold, then, that all learning and conditioning must be looked at in light of the animal's evolutionary and individual history. Further, the more important principles will arise from the use of tasks and testing environments suited to the species. For example, shortlived species, such as many insects, may have less opportunity to learn individually; hence, they have developed more reliance on specific innate factors. Consider, for example, those insects which mate once in their lives and then die. Also animals in narrow and more stable ecological niches may have less need to learn certain behaviors than species living in broader and more varying environments. Predators may be predisposed to learn different behaviors in different ways than prey species; carnivores may learn differently from vegetarians; and ground-dwelling species may learn differently from arboreal ones, etc. Generalizations may best lie along these lines rather than brain structure, phylogenetic relationships, or our intuitions. Again, convergent rather than homologous abilities may be involved. In any event, generalizing beyond a species should be cautiously done.

Ethologists are also interested in assessing the relationships between phenomena seen in their studies and those seen in more typical laboratory and learning situations. For example, Baerends, Bril, and Bult (1965) trained a pig-tailed macaque to locate food under a cover marked with a fairly complex distinctive design. They then altered various components of the design to assess whether the rule of heterogeneous summation would hold. It did, but they were unable to design a supernormal stimulus.

The general process approach

After allowing for sensory and motor limitations, however, the traditional view has been that learning processes in all organisms are essentially the same and differ only in their quantitative aspects. If this is so, we really might as well study only one or two convenient organisms. Then when we know enough about them, we will be able to apply the derived laws, principles, or functional relationships between stimulus and response to any organism that we wish. This position is essentially the one advocated by Skinner (1956) and is certainly the implicit, if not explicit, rationale for most of the

studies relying on the rat or pigeon (e.g., Hull, 1943). This approach is explicit in several of the preceding chapters and can be traced back to such early animal learning psychologists as Thorndike and Watson (Bitterman, 1969) and Pavlov (Seligman, 1970).

The pervasiveness of this attitude among psychologists and its research consequences has been excellently handled by Seligman (1970). The question he poses is "whether sufficient evidence exists to challenge the *equivalence of associability*" [p. 408, italics mine]. The evidence from ethology and from the Brelands should be enough to show its inadequacy, and Seligman acknowledges that they "have gathered a wealth of evidence to challenge the general process view of learning" [p. 408]. He claims, however, that these data have had little effect on psychologists. While Seligman is charitable in his reasons, it seems more accurate to claim that there has been a general bankruptcy of thought in comparative psychology for years in its inability to look beyond its own array of apparatus and narrow theories. Seligman goes on to give evidence against the "general process psychologist" from "findings which have sprung up within his own tradition" [p. 408]. He ignores, however, the findings of Verplanck (1955) who was certainly influenced by the animal learning tradition.

The point seems to be that until very recently no evidence would dissuade the traditional animal conditioner. What is now occurring is that younger experimental psychologists have slowly become interested in different types of learning processes and have discovered that the old "laws" and assumptions need serious qualifications. For instance, Glickman and Schiff (1967) proposed a biological theory of reinforcement based on the activation of underlying neural systems involved in the performance of species-characteristic consummatory acts. Using recent physiological and ethological findings, as well as experimental psychology, they consider the adaptive and evolutionary aspects of learning. Seligman (1970) classifies conditioning on a "preparedness" scale. Some animals can easily learn some things but not others: there is a predisposition involved (cf. the deer mice and chick examples in the previous section). In some cases, responses are contraprepared. It is difficult if not impossible to condition certain tasks. Bolles (1970) in his treatment of avoidance learning similarly considers the important role of species-characteristic responses and asks, "Is it possible that some responses in S's repertoire actually are not acquirable as R_as? Such a conception defies one of the principal tenets of operant conditioning theory. The present paper argues for just this conclusion" [p. 33]. He argues that innate species-specific defense reactions are involved in almost all avoidance learning, especially those involving rapid acquisition.

Rozin and Kalat (1971) came to similar conclusions in discussions of poison avoidance and specific hungers in rats. It seems that the traditional views do not even hold for all kinds of learning in this most studied animal. Rats learn to associate vitamin deficiencies and poison-induced illnesses with the taste of foods experienced hours earlier, which leads to the discarding of the .5 second *CS-UCS* interval as any kind of general law. Further studies have shown that visual cues cannot be the *CS* for this behavior in rats; but in quail the reverse holds since visual cues are more salient than gustatory ones (Wilcoxon, Dragoin, & Kral, 1971). Garter snakes have been shown to readily acquire an illness-induced aversion in one trial, yet snakes have traditionally been considered stupid and virtually incapable of learning (Burghardt, Wilcoxon, & Czaplicki, in preparation).

Rozin and Kalat (1971) conclude that "biologically speaking, there is no reason to assume that there should exist an extensive set of generally applicable laws of learning, independent of the situation in which they are manifested" [p. 460]. While some generalizations might exist because of similar environmental demands and nervous system structures, this can never be determined until many species are studied in many different contexts. They specifically acknowledge the similarity and priority of the ethologists' position but make a notable advance in the discussion of mechanisms and theory, since they are familiar with both the ethological and psychological evidence. Indeed, this seems to be the secret. Older psychologists trained in virtual ignorance of ecology, evolutionary biology, and naturalistic animal behavior usually responded to ethological views either with defensive attacks based on semantic quibbling or by completely ignoring it, usually by claiming that ethology was almost beneath contempt methodologically ("hip boot naturalists") or that it dealt with species and behaviors irrelevant to psychological concerns. Tracing Skinner's writings illuminates the transition from the latter view to a concern with both the phylogeny and ontogeny of behavior (1966), which are areas his system virtually ignores in its emphasis on operant processes in adult animals. Even this paper is marred at the end by a self-serving and irrelevant attack on some ethologists

Staddon and Simmelhag (1971) are workers in the operant tradition who have indeed gone beyond the cumulative record. Their reappraisal of the superstition experiment with pigeons (discussed in Chapters 2 and 3) is a model of both close observation of what animals really do in the Skinner box and theoretical integration. Of interest here is their use of concepts such as appetitive behavior, consummatory acts, evolution, displacement behavior, and species-characteristic responses. Similarly, Reynierse, Scavio, & Ulness (1970) systematically observed rats in a classical fear-conditioning situation. They put forward a conflict theory of extinction after noting that some shock-elicited behaviors were not conditionable, while others, such as licking which suddenly appeared during extinction, were allochthonous and fit other criteria of displacement activities.

The phyletic discontinuity approach

A reaction against the concentration on a limited number of species in the comparative psychology of learning and the assumption of a general theory has been eloquently made by Bitterman (1960, 1965). Bitterman is attempting to develop, particularly for vertebrates, a phylogeny of learning. His method is to study one or several species from certain classes of vertebrates. He has particularly concentrated on fish, reptiles, birds, and mammals, ignoring amphibians. Certainly, we are very far from a true comparative or ethological psychology of learning. Outside of imprinting, for instance, there have been few studies on the learning abilities of ducks and geese. In fact, as Bitterman has pointed out, the reliance on a limited number of species makes it difficult to test the assumption that learning processes are indeed similar across phyla.

Bitterman argues that in comparative studies one cannot look at such types of learning as simple discriminations, classical conditioning, or even operant conditioning. Indeed, most animals trained on such tasks show only quantitative differences; only the rate varies. But what if more complex tasks are involved? Bitterman uses problems involving repeated learning called *habit reversals*.

Reversal learning involves training an animal to discriminate between two stimuli, one of which is positive (reinforcement) and the other negative (punishment or no reinforcement). After criterion is reached, the positive and negative stimuli are switched and the animal must learn now to respond to the previously punished or unreinforced stimulus and not to respond to the previously reinforced stimulus. After criterion is reached, the stimuli are switched again. By switching the stimuli from positive to negative repeatedly, one can determine whether there is successive reduction in the number of trials it takes the animal to switch to the new positive stimulus. This sort of problem may be said to involve "learning to learn" and is related to the work in conceptual behavior and learning sets described in Chapter 4.

Bitterman utilizes two basic problems of successive habit reversal. One is the *spatial* problem in which two identical stimuli are presented, one to the left and one to the right, and the animal must respond to position cues. The second successive habit reversal is a *visual* problem, which involves two different colored patches of light that are random as far as position is concerned but for which the color is the discriminative stimulus. Bitterman's other basic procedure involves *probability learning* in which the stimuli or positions are correlated with different reinforcement probabilities (e.g., 0.75, 0.25). Some subjects match (i.e., respond to the alternatives with probabilities of 0.75 and 0.25), while others maximize (i.e., respond consistently to the favored side or stimulus). The situation is closely related to concurrent schedules (Chapter 6).

Bitterman tests his animals using operant-type apparatus modified for use with fish, turtles, and other animals unusual in psychological research. He claims to find that from fish to mammal there are qualitative jumps in the ability to learn these relatively complex problems. Indeed, animals are classified on the basis of being fishlike or ratlike. For example, Bitterman has found that rats exhibit progressive improvement in discrimination reversals, whether the alternatives are defined spatially or by visual stimuli. Fish, by contrast, do not seem to improve in their mastery of either spatial or visual problems during a series of reversals. The turtle improves over a series of reversals with spatial problems, like the rat, but does not improve on visual-problem reversals, like the fish. Interestingly, similar results are obtained with the probability learning experiments. Rats tend to maximize, regardless of whether the alternatives are defined by spatial or visual characters, whereas fish tend to match, again for both spatial and visual problems. The turtle is like the rat on spatial problems, exhibiting a tendency to maximize, but like the fish on visual problems, matching its responding to the possibility of reinforcement. Apparently, qualitative performance differences are consistent to the

type of problem, and the turtle may be classed with the rat on spatial problems and with the fish on visual problems, thus being in some sense intermediate between those species. Bitterman's work with pigeons indicates that they maximize on spatial problems, like the rat, but match on visual problems, like turtles and fish. Thus, the pigeon may be viewed as intermediate between turtle and rat.

At first glance such results look convincing, particularly since they support our usual notions of progressive improvement the more advanced (i.e., closer to humans) we get on the evolutionary scale. An ethologist, however, would urge caution in interpreting the results on several grounds. One would be the unrepresentativeness of the one or two species from each class of vertebrates compared. For example, turtles differ widely among themselves, let alone among other reptiles, such as snakes and crocodiles. Another criticism would be the suitability of the stimuli, responses, and reinforcers employed. They all should allow equally for the learning-to-learn phenomenon to be demonstrated. Motivational factors are also important and Bitterman has tried to control for them, but the problem is complex.

Other, more fundamental questions have to be asked about the interpretation of the experimental results themselves. The decision about whether an animal shows improvement or not turns out to be based on minor differences in the reversal learning curve slope, as well as on seemingly minor procedural differences, such as whether a correction or noncorrection method is employed. In addition, there is the problem of premature acceptance of results if they confirm what one expects. What Bitterman has done, however, is to revitalize interest in the comparative intelligence issue that excited psychologists early in the century (Holmes, 1911; Washburn, 1908).

Even if we accept Bitterman's results, it is evident that his procedure does not differentiate among mammals. However, the learning-set approach (of which the habit reversal is a simple variant) has shown promise of differentiating the learning capacities of mammals (Harlow, 1959). The learning-set task involves teaching the animal successive similar, but not identical, problems, such as discriminating among shapes. A monkey, for instance, will readily learn to solve the problem in fewer and fewer trials until it responds correctly after the first error. This method not only seemed to discriminate primates from other advanced mammals such as raccoons and cats, but even to discriminate primates according to their phylogenetic rank. However, recent evidence tends to throw serious doubt on the general validity of the method for mammals since a mere rodent, the gerbil (*Meriones unguiculates*), performs very well indeed on learning-set problems (Blass & Rollin, 1969). It is much closer to higher mammals such as raccoons than it is to its rodent relatives. Again, there are questions about the appropriateness of different kinds of stimuli for various species.

The conclusion from these attempts is that one needs much more information before solid evidence for qualitative levels of ability can be gathered. Clearly, there are gross differences between Human and Fish. The question is whether qualitative jumps are involved in the intermediate organisms. Even if such is eventually shown to be the case, it tells us nothing about the extinct transition species involved between present qualitatively different groups (e.g., reptiles and birds).

In another sense, however, even the above discussion is irrelevant, for recently Bovet, Bovet-Nitti, & Oliverio (1969) presented results indicating dramatic qualitative differences in the avoidance learning of various inbred strains of mice. If qualitative differences can occur within the same species, then arguments about fish and rats are beside the point. In essence, the results support Bitterman's contention (à la Skinner) even more than he expected. Genetic experiments on learning have advanced greatly in recent years. The review by Wahlsten (1972) excellently covers material of interest to all conditioners.

These three approaches differ greatly in their initial assumptions. It would appear that integration of the valid points of each one is necessary. Indeed, ethologists are using conditioning techniques and even operant apparatus with greater frequency and are finding them useful. However, when all is said and done, the results will need to be placed in an evolutionary context, and the main point of the ethologists will be vindicated. Comparative psychologists try to eliminate evolutionary and situation specificity by looking at presumed general tasks in artificial environments. It is fair to ask whether animal learning psychologists have thereby eliminated the really important problems in comparative studies. An ethologist might well say, Watch an animal develop, raise it as a pet, observe it interacting in a complex structural and social environment, and, if you then still study it as learning psychologists have studied it before, you will at least be extremely wary about saying anything about the animal's behavior outside the apparatus. You may perhaps even question the importance of what takes place inside the apparatus.

The comparative imperative

It should be clear that the detailed analysis of behavior in closely related species is a necessary part of any study of the ontogeny and evolution of behavior. Comparative studies, however, are often time consuming and may tend to show little immediate payoff. This is surely one reason most students of behavior concentrate on a few well-known domesticated species such as rats, pigeons, cats, dogs, rhesus monkeys, or goldfish. It has been argued that because of the enormous work already done on several species with their backlog of parametric data we should, for scientific reasons, limit our study to those few animals which are already commonly used. Further, although it is nice to have some supplementary information from those odd souls preferring to work with a wild rodent instead of the white rat or with bluejays instead of pigeons, in the long run breakthroughs in comparative studies will come through the use of a few well-chosen species. There is some validity to this argument, since a scientist's time and resources are definitely finite. However, one can question whether the choice of animals that psychologists have settled on is indeed the best. Do they represent a broad enough range of behaviors and evolutionary steps? This point has been discussed at some length by Hodos and Campbell (1969), who reached negative answers and argue that the reliance on such limited and poorly chosen species has prevented any breakthroughs in comparative psychology. In studying the evolution of behavior many tactics can be used, all necessitating close comparison. For instance, man-made variance in a domestic species can be studied as noted earlier. More such studies may uncover important clues about how these behaviors arose and were shaped, particularly those behaviors not deliberately selected for by man.

Moreover, comparative information gathered not only in the field but under the more constant environment of zoos and laboratories should be collected for many wild species. This is a true imperative for several reasons. One is the heuristic importance for our science itself. Another is the probability that many of these species may cease to exist in their natural state in the near future; even if they do continue to survive, they may be so altered through environmental disruption that they no longer provide good clues to existing fairly stable differences among species. Hence, there are scientific as well as aesthetic, ecological, and moral reasons for maintaining as great a species diversity in the world as possible. Of course, it may just be possible that man does not really want to learn about himself and his evolution (Lorenz, 1966). It is to the question of human behavior that we now turn. If the ethological approach can help us understand animal behavior from sea slugs to chimps, and if, as all evidence indicates, man is also a product of evolution, then an ethological psychology of people is certainly possible.

HUMAN ETHOLOGY

We have looked at a number of ways in which behavior of animals can be studied, emphasizing the biological ethological approach. The task in this section will be to look briefly at human behavior from the perspective offered by the methods and theories of the ethologists. It should be emphasized again that one can utilize ethological methods without ascribing to ethological concepts or theories.

In the first text of ethology, Tinbergen (1951) devoted five pages to human ethology. He was mainly concerned with presenting evidence to support ethological concepts in human behavior. For instance, he mentioned von Holst's study on the coordination between limbs and the superposition of various rhythms that are not controllable (try reversing the direction or frequency of your arm swings as you walk at a constant speed). Gesell's (1946) and McGraw's (1946) studies on the maturational (innate) aspect of locomotion in man were cited. Tinbergen also cited Lorenz (1943) on the *babiness releasers* of human infants and baby animals that involve such characteristics as a foreshortened face, large forehead, and protruding cheeks. In short, stimuli that mean *cuteness* in a young animal might act as an innately recognized releaser for parental reactions, in much the same way as the immediate response to a bug crawling on one's skin is held to be a fixed action pattern with an orientation component. Finally, Tinbergen discussed displacement reactions, such as scratching behind the ear and yawning, that may also be innate. Such was human ethology 20 years ago. There were some interesting notes, but no systematic studies.

Recognition of the potential role of ethology in the study of human behavior was not readily apparent in the scientific community until the appearance of semipopular books that attempted to apply the ethological perspective toward human behavior

in dramatic and perhaps overstated ways. Included are books by Lorenz (1966), Ardrey (1961, 1966, 1970), Morris (1967, 1969), Storr (1968), Hass (1970), and Tiger (1969). These books present much ethological information, some more accurately and completely than others. Much of the criticism directed toward them has been unwarranted and based on emotional, social, and political grounds rather than on the scientific adequacy of the writings themselves (Bressler, 1968). The most telling criticism of all the books, however, is that they attempt to tell us something about human behavior largely by relying on behavior of other animals. Now this has been done by many people, and experimental psychologists are no less likely to do so than others and more likely than most. Studies based on rats and pigeons have led to such things as teaching machines, utopian projects, behavior therapy, and other innovations. Although such extrapolation has had criticism, it has never reached the pitch of the criticism directed toward the popularization of ethology. This is probably due to several factors, resistance to evolutionary thinking by educated people being a major one, and the significance of the derived behaviors being another.

There are certain dangers in interpreting human behavior on the basis of the behavior of even the most advanced nonhuman primates, largely because man is a specialized and unique animal in at least the same sense that an elephant or a water moccasin is a unique, specialized animal. One does not apply the results of the work on another species to these organisms and expect a very high percentage of correct predictions. The question is, first, whether the ethological approach and its methods can be applied effectively to human behavior, and, secondly, whether the findings of ethology on other organisms share some continuum with findings on human behavior. The writings cited in most part deal with the second question, and Lorenz (1966) makes it clear that his discussion of human behavior is speculative and based largely on evidence derived from other species. A recent symposium volume (Eisenberg & Dillon, 1971) is devoted to a careful examination of this problem. What is needed now are ethological studies of human behavior.

Much more extensive and controlled work needs to be done before human ethology is at a scientific level comparable to more classic ethology and experimental psychology. This statement should come as a surprise. Why has the study of human behavior been so shortchanged? There seem to be two major reasons. One is the bypassing in psychology of the naturalistic, descriptive period essential to the development of most sciences. The other is the neglect of the evolutionary biology of the human organism. A danger, however, in emphasizing human as contrasted to animal ethology is that we will again make the mistake of separating man from nature. In any case, the picture is rapidly changing. While this chapter was in various stages of preparation, much important work appeared— too much material to even begin to cover here (e.g., Blurton-Jones, 1972; Hinde, 1972; McGrew, 1972; Wickler, 1972).

Ethological concepts and human behavior

Eibl-Eibesfeldt (1970) wrote the first extensive review of the evidence for the relevance to human behavior of such classical ethological ideas as fixed action patterns and releasing mechanisms. Much of human ethology as presented by Eibl-Eibesfeldt and other ethologists is concerned with showing that human behavior has genetic (innate) components independent of or interacting with acquired (cultural) aspects of behavior. It is indeed necessary to show that human behavior has a far-reaching evolutionary aspect as advocated by Darwin (1871), since this possibility has been ignored, if not actually denied, by many social scientists who argue that virtually all human behaviors are completely acquired (e.g., Montagu, 1968). Therefore, ethologists did see a need to show that, as in other animals, human behavior has some direct innate components. It is obvious that this can best be demonstrated in human infants, who have had less experience and fewer opportunities to learn than human adults. Obviously, with humans we cannot do the deprivation experiments or other manipulations that can be done in other species, although some behavior genetic techniques, such as twin studies and pedigree analysis, are useful. Although the human infant is extremely helpless and is able to do little when compared to human adults, ethologists have studied human infants to see what fixed action patterns and sign stimuli or releasers are present that are similar to those seen in other animals, where the question of their being innate is less controversial.

Certainly, infants do a number of things at birth that are innate or unconditioned. These are commonly called reflexes and include the grasp and sucking reflexes. Although the grasp reflex is well known, the extent of it has been demonstrated by Pieper (Eibl-Eibesfeldt, 1970) in his studies of premature human infants, who could hang by their front hands or even by all fours from cords strung out in space.

There are other behaviors that are less well known and more complex. For example, Prechtl and Schleidt (1950) have shown that newborn infants will spontaneously turn their heads left and right in a rhythmic manner, presumably seeking the nipple. This also occurs in response to a touch to the mouth region. When the nipple does get into the mouth, the lips close firmly upon it. This rhythmic seeking of the breast is observed only shortly after birth. Later it is replaced by an oriented search for the breast; when the mouth region is touched, the infant turns directly toward the stimulus object so that it can grab hold of it.

There is also evidence of well-coordinated climbing, walking, swimming, and crawling behavior in newborn children (Eibl-Eibesfeldt, 1970; Zelazo, Zelazo, & Kolb, 1972). Crying, smiling, and laughing are expressive behaviors found in young infants. The work of Freedman (1965), who studied the motor and mental abilities of identical and fraternal twins, concentrating on such behaviors as smiling and fear of strangers, is relevant here. He recorded much of his material on film so that it could be analyzed and reanalyzed repeatedly by naive observers. The fact that a behavior genetic method as well as early observational techniques was used gives Freedman's work added support. Certainly, very early in life the infant recognizes the smile, which is a social response with some evolutionary importance. The recognition of smiling also goes along with the ability to smile. Although many persons have argued that smiles are learned responses based on the association of positive reinforcement with smiling, happy parents and subsequent imitation (e.g., Sullivan, 1953), some very elementary observations would seem to clearly disprove the position that the smile per se is totally learned. For instance, blind and blind-deaf infants smile at the proper age although they could never have seen another person smile at them. They smile in the proper pleasurable situations also. There are several types of smiles, e.g., the *pleasure smile* which appears first and the so-called *social smile* which comes later. The fact that experience may alter the form and frequency of smiling and the situations in which it will occur does not disprove the fact that the smile itself is an innate response.

The perceptual side of infant behavior has also been experimentally studied, again with results that strongly indicate the operation of innate factors. Young, even newborn, infants possess the ability to perceive differences in color, form, and visual complexity as shown by preference tests (Fantz, 1967; Kagen, 1970) and space and constancy effects as shown by conditioning experiments (Bower, 1965, 1966b). Bower (1966a) has shown that the law of heterogeneous summation holds for infants up to three months of age and is gradually replaced by Gestalt-type responses to stimuli. Clearly, the human infant is not born a near *tabula rasa,* as tenaciously held by many experimental psychologists (e.g., Hebb, 1949). The actual study of the perception in infants, rather than the speculation from inadequate animal and adult human studies, was due to the influence of ethological ideas, as in Fantz' work.

Thus, we see that studies of newborn and young infants show that behaviors occur which in function certainly resemble responses seen in young organisms of many species, that is, behaviors which lead to attention by the mother, show rejection of unpleasant stimuli, help form bonds, serve as a basis of locomotion, and so forth. To deny an evolutionary basis for these behaviors can be no more than to deny the evolutionary heritage for the human species, a position not in accord with present scientific knowledge.

Such studies only demonstrate that innate factors are involved in human behavior; at some level, human behavior derives from an instinctive base. However, the behaviors of the infant, no matter how preprogrammed, are limited in scope. Are these reflexes and fixed action patterns of infants all that is determined by evolution? Are there other evolutionary components to human behavior that do not make themselves evident until years later? Behaviors such as fighting, courtship, and language would fall into this category. This is a much more difficult question to answer, but it must not be ignored (Callan, 1970). The next section can only touch on this problem because of our limited knowledge.

Ethological methods and human behavior

It is perhaps more useful at this stage to apply ethological methods and approaches, rather than ethological concepts, to the study of adult behavior. Indeed, Tinbergen (1968) has argued that the most important application of ethology to humans lies with ethological methods rather than with the specific theoretical constructs. There is no implication, however, that humans will not differ in important ways from other animals. This is obvious when

we look at our libraries, religions, and wars. Yet behind our symbolic and cognitive abilities lies an evolutionary history. Even if this be disputed, the descriptive methods of ethology may greatly aid the analysis of those aspects of our lives which we often arrogantly feel place us above mere nature and alone to the angels.

It is certainly surprising that we know much less about what people do in the real world than we do about the private lives of many of our fellow creatures. This is certainly due to the neglect of description as the crucial first step in studying behavior. Anthropologists, of course, have studied primitive peoples in what appears to be a descriptive context for many years and have gathered invaluable data. But, as Eibl-Eibesfeldt and Hass (1967) have pointed out, most anthropological studies neglect those aspects of human behavior common to all mankind, such as facial expressions. This is not to say that important information has not been gathered. Some anthropologists have dealt with the problems in their field in a way very reminiscent of an ethologist trying to study a foreign species (e.g., Malinowski, 1922). But it is with psychology that we are concerned, and "psychology appears to stand alone as a science without a substantial descriptive, naturalistic, ecological side" [Wright, 1967, p. 3]. Today, however, even experimental psychologists are calling for a return to description (Verplanck, 1970).

For convenience, observational studies can be classified into five categories: (1) studies which describe as completely as possible most of the behavior of a person or group in pursuing their normal activities, in an attempt, in essence, to construct an ethogram; (2) studies which narrow down the ethogram to one particular setting, such as the school, the home, or the psychotherapy session; (3) studies which consider functional groupings of behavior, such as courtship, aggression, or maternal care; (4) studies which examine elements common to many behaviors, such as facial expressions, grouping patterns (as on a beach), or problem solving; and (5) studies which investigate the fine grain of behavior or perception based on an extremely detailed analysis.

Naturally there is considerable overlap, but this classification has its value. It is an alternative one to that used in the earlier discussion of animal descriptive studies. Manipulations are often incorporated into these studies, although sometimes prematurely. Hutt and Hutt (1970) present a useful compendium of observational techniques with the emphasis on human behavior.

Complete coverage

Many studies (e.g., Barker, 1968; Barker & Wright, 1951, 1955) have tried to deal with the total behavior of children in their natural settings. Barker and Wright call this approach *ecological psychology,* and adherents of the approach see its similarity to ethology and natural history (Willems, 1965; Willems & Rausch, 1969).

This approach certainly has made important steps in the direction of a naturalistic psychology. However, an ethologist would have to criticize it on several grounds. Perhaps the most telling criticism is that the written *specimen records* contain too much interpretation ("Anne motioned urgently.... Anne watched Miss Madison solemnly" [Barker, 1968, p. 13]) and not enough on the actual movements, gestures, or words. It is, in fact, not very objective, which is perhaps a reason this last redoubt of naturalistic description in psychology had so little impact.

The complete ethogram approach is ultimately desirable. Nonetheless, the task involved in describing one small community, let alone a representative sample, is immense and demands many years of dedicated study. Such an undertaking has not been done from an ethological point of view.

The restricted-setting ethogram

It is often more feasible to study behavior in a restricted setting, such as an institution or classroom, where unobtrusive recording (observation through one-way glass, tape recordings, filming) can be accomplished more easily than physically following the subject. In other words, the techniques can be similar to the use of blinds in animal observation. Examples of studies in a restricted setting are the work of Gump (1969) who analyzed behavior within a third-grade classroom, Blurton-Jones (1967) who studied nursery-school children ethologically, and Kelly (1969) who compared behaviors within high schools. The last makes it clear that the observational method employed can greatly influence the results. Indeed, the method and strategy in naturalistic studies need to be chosen with at least as much care as the amount of shock given to rats in laboratory studies. Naturalistic studies are not professional escape routes for the lazy, the undisciplined, or the dilettante.

Analysis of a functional grouping

The work of Scheflen (1965) is a good example of the analysis of a functional grouping of behaviors

in the restricted setting, in this case the psychotherapy session. Scheflen was not the first to notice that much important nonverbal behavior occurs in psychotherapy (see review by Mehrabian, 1969), but his approach is more systematic than that of his predecessors, in addition to being concerned with a functional classification of behavior. What it lacks is precise quantification.

In his study Scheflen noted that much of the behavior shown by both patients and psychotherapists was strongly reminiscent of early phases of courtship in America. This was evidenced by specific patterns of behavior classified into *courtship readiness, courtship positioning,* and *invitational movements.*

Courtship readiness is indicated by, among other things, preening movements. Preening movements of a male psychotherapist are seen in Figure 9.10. Preening movements of women include stroking their hair, glancing at their makeup in a mirror, rearranging their clothing, and so on. Courtship positioning involves mainly the seating arrangement of the individuals, which is often simply face to face in didactic therapy but which can be more complicated in groups. Invitational movements are, of course, sexual, as seen in Figure 9.11, which gives some of the invitational behaviors of women patients. Through close observation Scheflen was able to show that such movements, although similar to real courtship, had really nothing to do with courtship because of the interposition of various *qualifiers* or *declaimers* that break off the interaction at certain definite points. Therefore, Scheflen uses the term *quasi courtship.* This process of withdrawal from courtship or quasi courtship is termed *decourting.*

Of special interest is the fact that in addition to

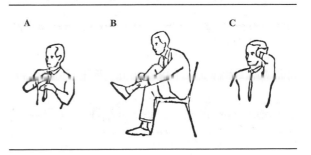

Figure 9.10 Some preening behavior of male psychotherapists. Panel A is the tie preen; panel B is the sock preen; and panel C is the hair preen. (From Scheflen, 1965.)

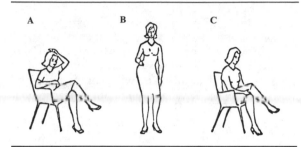

Figure 9.11 Appealing or invitational behaviors of women patients. Panel A shows presenting the palm, with hair preening; panel B shows rolling the hip; and panel C shows presenting and caressing the leg. (From Scheflen, 1965.)

working out the behavior patterns, Scheflen derived from them a functional grouping or sequence of activities that has adaptive value. He shows how the proper use of quasi courting by a male therapist can serve to keep the group acting as a unit and bring back distracted members to the group.

The analysis of specific behavior components

A number of investigators have studied the occurrence of behavior elements in natural settings. For instance, Eibl-Eibesfeldt and Hass (1967) have looked at facial expression cross-culturally and have studied a number of isolated tribes which had never seen white men previously. Theirs is a more detailed version of the approach advocated by Darwin (1872), who wrote to people throughout the world asking for direct observational reports on both emotional expression and what today would be referred to as *nonverbal communication* in various human groups. "Observations on natives who have had little communication with Europeans would be of course the most valuable . . ." [p. 16]. He asked for details of the expression of astonishment, shame, defiance, deep thought, contempt, laughter, disgust, fear, good spirits, and so forth. Darwin reasoned that those gestures or expressions common to distinct races were most probably innate or instinctive. Finding a great deal of such commonality led to his concluding "that the same state of mind is expressed throughout the world with remarkable uniformity; and this fact is in itself interesting as evidence of the close similarity in bodily structure and mental disposition of all the races of mankind" [p. 17].

However, detailed analysis of facial expressions cannot be made from written descriptions alone. Eibl-Eibesfeldt and Hass made motion pictures of expressions and recorded the context in which they occurred. Because people do not behave naturally when being photographed, the experimenters fitted their camera with a false front lens that contained prisms so that pictures were taken from the side of the camera. In this way they recorded the behavior of bystanders and others rather than that of the person ostensibly being photographed. This technique might be useful in animal photography also, particularly in the case of large mammals such as black bears, which the writer has personal reason to believe are threatened by cameras. Eibl-Eibesfeldt and Hass filmed flirting, greeting, smiling, begging, praying, and other patterns.

The general result is the observation that all these behaviors contain some elements that are invariable across all the cultures examined. For example, in all the cultures studied flirting girls showed similar behavior. Initial contact is made by a smile followed by a quick "eyebrow flash" (a rapid lift of the eyebrows), a pattern which occurs in greeting generally. If the male shows some interest, usually by his approach, she responds by turning and lowering her head, covering her face with a hand, and giggling. This is characterized as *ritualized withdrawal* and may alternate with the smile phase (approach) several times. This latter case can be described as *ambivalent behavior*. Such observations indicate that Darwin was correct and that more recent reviews of the evidence concluding that there were no universal (and therefore innate) patterns of expression (Bruner & Taguiri, 1954) were premature. This reassessment is supported by recent studies of the recognition of facial expressions from photographs in five literate and preliterate cultures (Ekman & Friesen, 1971; Ekman, Sorenson, & Friesen, 1969). All cultures significantly picked the preferred label for the six expressions used: happiness, fear, disgust-contempt, anger, surprise, and sadness. It should, of course, be understood that invariances in expressive reaction are not incompatible with cultural determination of situations producing that reaction (see Chapter 8).

Using a different method, Guthrie (1970) has thoroughly reviewed the evolution and ontogeny of human threat display organs (e.g., hair, chin, nose). While he concludes that the "physical pattern of human threat structure does not differ remarkably from that of other species" [p. 299], he also points out the flexibility and ontogenetic change that occurs in our species. He speculates that the physical differences among races may be related to social forces that operated during their evolution.

Species-characteristic responses are not necessarily innate. However, the danger in considering similarities as being instinctive is greater the more similar the condition in which the animals are raised. Since humans live in the most varied ecological and social environments, invariances or universals across cultures are more suggestive of phylogenetic programming than in other animals, but are not, of course, completely conclusive.

Another approach in the same category is to look at other types of nonverbal communication, such as the role of individual distances between people, or *proxemics,* as discussed at length by Hall (1966). The individual distance or space maintained between persons during social intercourse is remarkably constant and seems to involve a mutually understood language, even though the participants may be unaware of it. Similar phenomena have been noted in many species (Hediger, 1950). Cross-cultural studies, however, indicate that the preferred distance differs between cultures (e.g., Italian and Scandinavian) and that such differences can contribute to the frequent discomfort felt by people in sudden contact with persons from different areas of the world. Cultural differences in the *personal space* of individuals certainly indicate that environmental rather than innate factors are involved in the specific dimension of the space, although the need for some distance may be innate.

One can also study posture, position, gestures, or nonlinguistic aspects of vocalizations, such as intonation, as reviewed by Mehrabian (1969) and Duncan (1969). The methods employed usually depend on close analysis of movements, sounds, or spatial arrangements gathered in either natural or laboratory situations. They can blend into the experimental studies when stooges are utilized or social groupings are deliberately manipulated.

Related to these studies are those dealing with the role of physical space in human behavior. For instance, the way buildings are designed has a great influence on the type of interactions that can take place within them. Even the shape of tables influences who sits where and when (Sommer, 1969). A recent symposium volume deals exclusively with the multifaceted use of space by animals and humans (Esser, 1971).

The atomistic approach

Behavior and perceptual responses can be studied in fine detail. Birdwhistell (1952, 1970), who termed his approach *kinesics,* looks at even the movements of the fingers very closely. One of his goals is to compare gestures with linguistic terms, that is, to find parallels between gestures and verbal expressions. An area called *paralinguistics* is opening in which the parallel of behavior with verbal language is pushed to the extreme. A potentially unfortunate effect of an immediate analysis of overt behavior in atomistic detail is to bypass the functional organization of behavior patterns and the context in which they occur. We have seen an emphasis on organization and context throughout the research and theorizing on animal behavior.

Perceptual studies in human adults from an ethological perspective are rare. An exception is the work of Hess and his colleagues on size changes in the pupil of the eye in response to normal everyday stimuli (Hess, 1965; Hess, Seltzer, & Shlien, 1965). They found that the size of the pupil reflects, among other things, the degree of interest in visual material such as pictures. Males, for instance, show increased pupils in response to nude females and vice versa. Indeed, it is even possible to separate heterosexual from homosexual males with this method. This technique, *pupillometrics,* can also be used as an indicator of positive or negative attitudes, which is particularly valuable in situations where subjects cannot or will not state their opinions. Pupil size may also act as a releaser. Identical female portraits that differ only in pupil size were tested on males. It was found that the picture with large pupils elicited increased pupil size in subjects, as well as more favorable verbal assessments. The subjects, by the way, could not articulate how the two pictures differed. Perhaps there is a rational explanation for eye makeup after all.

The influence of ethology on general thinking in the behavioral and biological sciences is beginning to be felt in many ways, much more so than has ever been true of any previous approach to scientific psychology. We have already discussed biological areas such as evolution, genetics, and physiology. However, the effect on the behavioral sciences will be no less dramatic. Bowlby (1969) and Storr (1968) attempt to synthesize psychoanalysis and ethology. Goffman (1969, 1971) uses ethology extensively in his sociological writings. Callan (1970) considers the mutual relations of anthropology and ethology. Tiger and Fox (1971) attempt a balanced integration of evolutionary and ethological thinking with all the social sciences. Even human speech is being looked at with the concepts and methods of ethology (Mattingly, 1972). Coming shortly will be detailed in-depth studies of innumerable aspects of human behavior. In short, an ethological approach to human behavior is seen by many as offering a way of looking at man in a holistic and dynamic manner, preserving scientific precision, and placing man squarely in nature as part of the web of living things, all distinct yet interdependent. It is nothing less than an attempt to view man as inextricably part of the natural world, a product of its evolution, dependent upon its laws, and to be studied by the same approaches so useful in studying the behavior of other species. Human distinctiveness in language, symbolism, emotion, art, and society is best studied in a naturalistic context. This is the new terrain ethology offers the study of our species.

SUMMARY AND CONCLUSIONS

The modern study of instinct originates primarily from the work of ethologists who observed carefully and experimented with the many natural behaviors of animals. Conditioning or learning approaches to behavior that did not actively investigate the role of evolutionary and ecological factors on behavior were seen as sorely inadequate. This chapter has attempted to review the historical development and current status of ethological theories, methods, and their biological approach.

The methodological core of ethology is based on detailed observation of animal behavior either in the field or in stimulus-rich environments in captivity. The repertoire of species-characteristic behaviors (the ethogram) is studied in this way. After description, the ethologist is interested in studying the function (adaptive value both to the individual and species), the causation (both internal and external), the ontogeny (from prenatal development to conditioning in adults), and the evolution of behaviors. Social behavior has been the focus of much, but certainly not all, of the ethologists' attention. Laboratory and experimental studies are seen as important primarily since they help to elucidate behavior in the field.

The concept of instinct entails both behavioral and motivational concepts which are not to be viewed today as excluding environmental, developmental, or conditioning factors. Nonetheless, instinctive behaviors, such as courtship, fighting, and hunting, are frequently involved in adaptive, normal activities of organisms. The evolutionary heritage of the individual animal seems responsible for many behaviors and their motivation.

Innate processes are those directly or indirectly influenced by the genetic background of the individual. Both developmental (deprivation) and genetic studies can indicate the role of such phylogenetic information. Innate behavior is a shorthand term referring to the genetic factors underlying the adaptive function of behavior. Since even the ability to learn, imprint, or solve problems is ultimately related to evolved abilities, it is clear that genetic processes enter into almost all behavior. A continuum exists as to the specificity of the genetic information involved. Further, the study of the ontogeny of behavior from genes through structure (epigenesis) shows that the expression of genetic factors is influenced by the pre- and postnatal environment of the organism. However, the degree of environmental modifiability, the types of factors involved, and the relevance of such experimental modification for the normal life history of the species are highly variable.

The primary behavioral unit for the level of analysis used by ethologists is the fixed action pattern, a stereotyped species-characteristic response relatively refractory in its topographical modifiability. Stimuli are important in many ways, but most ethological interest has focused on sign stimuli from natural objects that release fixed action patterns. Instinctive behaviors are roughly divided into two phases, appetitive behavior and consummatory acts, the former leading to the latter. Fixed action patterns and stimuli are important in both, but appetitive behavior is the more variable, arousal is an important factor, and it is more likely the focus of traditional learning operations (e.g., the rat learning where to find food or what to do to get it, not how to eat once it has the food). Ethological research has focused more on the consummatory acts, the behaviors occurring at the end of a behavior sequence. Conflicts can occur between different motivational states or moods of an animal, leading to ambivalent, redirected, and displacement behaviors.

Physiological studies have generally supported ethological concepts and give encouragement to the view that they may be giving us a tentative but more realistic glimpse of the organization, structure, and development of behavior. Experimental psychologists are also increasingly finding ethological views to be of value and are beginning to incorporate them into their theories and methods.

Ethology focused its interest on the overt and normal behavior of organisms and instigated interest in the development of behavior. In addition, ethology made psychology face up to the limitations of narrow laboratory studies and the use of a limited species diversity. This and other aspects of the ethological attitude are most important and can, and hopefully will, greatly enrich psychology.

In human behavior the methods of ethology are becoming popular and enlarge the range of behaviors studied. The ultimate value of ethological concepts in the study of human behavior is less known at this time, but certainly has considerable applicability. The goal of ethology, to look at man naturalistically and as a biological product of evolution, is of great value, regardless of the fate of specific ethological theories.

So now we come to the final question. What has become of instinct? Perhaps discussions of instincts are passé. Yet the phenomena that instinct theorists attempted to deal with have not disappeared. They were merely ignored. But genetics and evolution are not mythological, and ethology has provided psychology with a means of taking account of them in an objective and scientific manner. In this chapter, the attempt has been to argue provocatively for the importance of innate factors in behavior. Such an alternative view needs a fair hearing in the context of modern psychology.

REFERENCES

Åkerman, B. Behavioural effects of electrical stimulation in the forebrain of the pigeon: I. Reproductive behaviour. *Behaviour,* 1966, **26,** 323–338. (a)

Åkerman, B. Behavioural effects of electrical stimulation in the forebrain of the pigeon: II. Protective behaviour. *Behaviour,* 1966, **26,** 339–350. (b)

Alexander, R. D. Arthropods. In T. A. Sebeok (Ed.), *Animal communication.* Bloomington: Indiana University Press, 1968. Pp. 167–216.

Andrew, R. J. Some remarks on behaviour in conflict situations, with special reference to *Emberiza* Spp. *British Journal of Animal Behaviour,* 1956, **4,** 85–91.

Ardrey, R. *African genesis.* New York: Atheneum, 1961.

Ardrey, R. *The territorial imperative.* New York: Atheneum, 1966.

Ardrey, R. *The social contract.* New York: Atheneum, 1970.

Aronson, L. R., Tobach, E., Lehrman, D. S., & Rosenblatt, J. S. (Eds.) *Development and evolution of behavior.* San Francisco: W. H. Freeman, 1970.

Atz, J. W. The application of the idea of homology to behavior. In L. R. Aronson, E. Tobach, D. S. Lehrman, & J. S. Rosenblatt (Eds.), *Development and evolution of behavior.* San Francisco: W. H. Freeman, 1970. Pp. 53–74.

Baer, D. M., & Gray, P. H. Imprinting to a different species without overt following. *Perceptual and Motor Skills,* 1960, **10,** 171–174.

Baerends, G. P. Fortpflanzungsverhalten und Orientierung der Grabwespe *Ammophilia campestris* Jur. *Tijdschrift voor Entomologie,* 1941, **84,** 68–275.

Baerends, G. P. Comparative methods and the concept of homology in the study of behaviour. *Archives Neerlandaises de Zoologie,* 1958, **13,** Suppl. 1, 401–417.

Baerends, G. P., Bril, K. A., & Bult, P. Versuche zur Analyse einer erlernten Reizsituation bei einen Schueinsaffen *(Macaca nemestrina).* *Zeitschrift für Tierpsychologie,* 1965, **22,** 394–411.

Barfield, R. J. Induction of copulatory behavior by intracranial placement of androgen in capons. *American Zoologist,* 1964, **4,** 133.

Barker, R. G. *Ecological psychology.* Stanford, Calif.: Stanford University Press, 1968.

Barker, R. G., & Wright, H. F. *One boy's day.* New York: Harper & Row, 1951.

Barker, R. G., & Wright, H. F. *Midwest and its children: The psychological ecology of an American town.* New York: Harper & Row, 1955.

Barlow, G. W. Ethology of the Asian teleast, *Badis badis:* IV. Sexual behavior. *Copeia,* 1962, 346–360.

Barlow, G. W. Dither: A way to reduce undesirable fright behavior in ethological studies. *Zeitschrift für Tierpsychologie,* 1968, **25,** 315–318. (a)

Barlow, G. W. Ethological units of behavior. In D. Ingle (Ed.), *The central nervous system and fish behavior.* Chicago: University of Chicago Press, 1968. Pp. 217–232. (b)

Barnett, S. A. *The rat: A study in behavior.* Chicago: Aldine, 1963.

Bastock, M. A gene mutation which changes a behavior pattern. *Evolution,* 1956, **10,** 421–439.

Bastock, M., Morris, D., & Moynihan, M. Some comments on conflict and thwarting in animals. *Behaviour,* 1953, **6,** 66–84.

Bateson, P. P. G. The characteristics and context of imprinting. *Biological Reviews,* 1966, **41,** 177–220.

Bateson, P. P. G., & Reese, E. P. The reinforcing properties of conspicuous stimuli in the imprinting situation. *Animal Behaviour,* 1969, **17,** 692–699.

Beach, F. A. The snark was a boojum. *American Psychologist,* 1950, **5,** 115–124.

Beach, F. A. The descent of instinct. *Psychological Review,* 1955, **62,** 401–410.

Beach, F. A. Characteristics of masculine sex drive. In M. R. Jones (Ed.), *Nebraska symposium on motivation.* Lincoln: University of Nebraska Press, 1956. Pp. 1–32.

Beach, F. A. Evolutionary aspects of psychoendocrinology. In A. Roe & G. G. Simpson (Eds.), *Behavior and evolution.* New Haven: Yale University Press, 1958. Pp. 81–102.

Beauchamp, G. K., & Hess, E. H. The effects of cross-species rearing on the social and sexual preferences of guinea pigs. *Zeitschrift für Tierpsychologie,* 1971, **28,** 69–76.

Beck, B. B. Review of *Mechanisms of animal behavior. Psychology Today,* 1967, **1**(3), 14–15. (a)

Beck, B. B. A study of problem solving by gibbons. *Behaviour,* 1967, **28,** 95–109. (b)

Bentley, D. R. Genetic control of an insect neuronal network. *Science,* 1971, **174,** 1139–1141. Figure 9.8: Copyright © 1971 by the American Association for the Advancement of Science, and reproduced by permission.

Bernard, L. L. *Instinct: A study in social psychology.* New York: Holt, 1924.

Birdwhistell, R. L. *Introduction to kinesics.* Louisville: University of Louisville Press, 1952.

Birdwhistell, R. L. *Kinesics and context.* Philadelphia: University of Pennsylvania Press, 1970.

Bitterman, M. E. Toward a comparative psychology of learning. *American Psychologist,* 1960, **15,** 704–712.

Bitterman, M. E. Phyletic differences in learning. *American Psychologist,* 1965, **20,** 396–410.

Bitterman, M. E. Thorndike and the problem of animal intelligence. *American Psychologist,* 1969, **24,** 444–453.

Blackburn, T. R. Sensuous intellectual complementarity in science. *Science,* 1971, **172,** 1003–1007.

Blair, W. F. Isolating mechanisms and interspecies interactions in anuran amphibians. *Quarterly Review of Biology,* 1964, **39,** 334–344.

Blass, E. M., & Rollin, H. R. Formation of object-discrimination learning sets by Mongolian gerbils *(Meriones unguiculates).* *Journal of Comparative and Physiological Psychology,* 1969, **69,** 519–521.

Blurton-Jones, N. G. An ethological study of some aspects of social behaviour of children in nursery school. In D. Morris (Ed.), *Primate ethology.* Chicago: Aldine, 1967. Pp. 437–563.

Blurton-Jones, N. (Ed.) Ethological studies of child behaviour. Cambridge, England: Cambridge University Press, 1972.

Bolles, R. C. *Theory of motivation.* New York: Harper & Row, 1967.

Bolles, R. C. Species-specific defense reactions and avoidance learning. *Psychological Review,* 1970, **77,** 32–48.

Bovet, D., Bovet-Nitti, F., & Oliverio, A. Genetic aspects of learning and memory in mice. *Science,* 1969, **163,** 139–149.

Bower, T. G. R. Stimulus variables determining space perception in infants. *Science,* 1965, **149,** 88–89.

Bower, T. G. R. Heterogeneous summation in human infants. *Animal Behaviour,* 1966, **14,** 395–398. (a)

Bower, T. G. R.   Slant perception and shape constancy in infants. *Science,* 1966, **151,** 832–834. (b)

Bowlby, J.   *Attachment and loss.* Vol. 1. *Attachment.* New York: Basic Books, 1969.

Breland, K., & Breland, M.   A field of applied animal psychology. *American Psychologist,* 1951, **6,** 202–204.

Breland, K., & Breland, M.   The misbehavior of organisms. *American Psychologist,* 1961, **16,** 681–684.

Breland, K., & Breland, M.   *Animal behavior.* New York: Macmillan, 1966.

Bressler, M.   Sociology, biology, and ideology. In D. C. Glass (Ed.), *Genetics.* New York: Rockefeller University Press, 1968. Pp. 178–210.

Brown, J. L., & Hunsperger, R. W.   Neuroethology and the motivation of agonistic behavior. *Animal Behaviour,* 1963, **4,** 439–448.

Bruner, J. S., & Taguiri, R.   The perception of people. In G. Lindzey & E. Aronson (Eds.), *Handbook of social psychology.* Vol. 2. *Research methods.* Reading, Mass.: Addison-Wesley, 1954. Pp. 634–654.

Burghardt, G. M.   The primacy effect of the first feeding experience in the snapping turtle. *Psychonomic Science,* 1967, **7,** 383–384.

Burghardt, G. M.   Comparative prey-attack studies in newborn snakes of the genus *Thamnophis. Behaviour,* 1969, **33,** 77–114. (a)

Burghardt, G. M.   Effects of early experience on food preference in chicks. *Psychonomic Science,* 1969, **14,** 7–8. (b)

Burghardt, G. M.   Chemical perception in reptiles. In J. W. Johnston, Jr., P. G. Moulton, & A. Turk (Eds.), *Communication by chemical signals.* New York: Appleton-Century-Crofts, 1970. Pp. 241–308. (a)

Burghardt, G. M.   Defining communication. In J. W. Johnston, Jr., P. G. Moulton, & A. Turk (Eds.), *Communication by chemical signals.* New York: Appleton-Century-Crofts, 1970. Pp. 5–18. (b)

Burghardt, G. M.   Intraspecific geographical variation in chemical food cue preferences of newborn garter snakes *(Thamnophis sirtalis). Behaviour,* 1970, **36,** 246–257. (c)

Burghardt, G. M.   Chemical-cue preferences of newborn snakes: Influence of prenatal maternal experience. *Science,* 1971, **171,** 921–923.

Burghardt, G. M., & Burghardt, L. S.   Notes on the behavioral development of two female black bear cubs: The first eight months. In S. Herrero (Ed.), *Bears—their biology and management.* Morges, Switzerland: International Union for the Conservation of Nature & Natural Resources, 1972, New Series No. 23, 207–220.

Burghardt, G. M., & Hess, E. H.   Food imprinting in the snapping turtle, *Chelydra serpentina. Science,* 1966, **151,** 108–109.

Burghardt, G. M., Wilcoxon, H. C., & Czaplicki, J. Z.   Conditioning in garter snakes: Aversion to palatable prey indicated by delayed illness. In preparation.

Callan, H.   *Ethology and society.* Oxford: Clarendon Press, 1970.

Candland, D. K., Taylor, D. B., Dresdale, L., Leiphart, J. M., & Salow, S. P.   Heart rate, aggression and dominance in the domestic chicken. *Journal of Comparative and Physiological Psychology,* 1969, **67,** 70–76.

Capretta, P. J.   The establishment of food preferences in chicks *Gallus gallus. Animal Behaviour,* 1969, **17,** 229–231.

Carmichael, L.   A further study of the development of behavior in vertebrates experimentally removed from the influence of external stimulation. *Psychological Review,* 1927, **34,** 34–47.

Caspari, E. W.   Gene action as applied to behavior. In J. Hirsch (Ed.), *Behavior-genetic analysis.* New York: McGraw-Hill, 1967. Pp. 112–134.

Craig, W.   Appetites and aversions as constituents of instincts. *Biological Bulletin,* 1918, **34,** 91–107.

Crook, J. H.   Social organization and the environment: Aspects of contemporary social ethology. *Animal Behaviour,* 1970, **18,** 197–209.

Croze, H.   *Searching image in carrion crows.* Berlin: Paul Parey, 1970.

Daanje, A.   On locomotory movements in birds and the intention movements derived from them. *Behaviour,* 1951, **3,** 48–98.

Dane, B., & Van der Kloot, W. G.   An analysis of the display of the goldeneye duck *(Bucephala clangula* [L.] *). Behaviour,* 1964, **22,** 282–328.

Dane, B., Walcott, C., & Drury, W. H.   The form and duration of the display actions of the goldeneye *(Bucephala clangula). Behaviour,* 1959, **14,** 265–281.

Darwin, C.   *On the origin of species.* London: 1859. (Facsimile edition: New York, Atheneum, 1967.)

Darwin, C.   *The descent of man and selection in relation to sex.* London: Murray, 1871. 2 vols.

Darwin, C.   *The expression of the emotions in man and animals.* London: Murray, 1872. (Republished: Chicago, University of Chicago Press, 1965.)

Delgado, J. M. R.   Social rank and radio-stimulated aggressiveness in monkeys. *Journal of Nervous and Mental Disorders,* 1967, **144,** 383–390.

Delius, J. D.   A stochastic analysis of the maintenance behavior of skylarks. *Behaviour,* 1969, **33,** 137–178.

Demski, L. S., & Knigge, K. M.   The telencephalon and hypothalamus of the bluegill *(Lepomis macrochirus):* Evoked feeding, aggressive and reproductive behavior with representative frontal sections. *Journal of Comparative Neurology,* 1971, **143,** 1–16.

Diamond, S.   Gestation of the instinct concept. *Journal of the History of the Behavioral Sciences,* 1971, **7,** 323–336.

Dilger, W. C.   The comparative ethology of the African parrot genus *Agapornis. Zeitschrift für Tierpsychologie,* 1960, **17,** 649–685.

Dilger, W. C.   The behavior of lovebirds. *Scientific American,* 1962, **206,** 88–98.

Dobzhansky, T.   Genetics and the diversity of behavior. *American Psychologist,* 1972, **27,** 523–538.

Duncan, S., Jr.   Nonverbal communication. *Psychological Bulletin,* 1969, **72,** 118–137.

Eaton, R. L.   The animal parks: The new and valuable biological resource. *BioScience,* 1971, **21,** 810–811.

Eibl-Eibesfeldt, I.   The interactions of unlearned behaviour patterns and learning in mammals. Symposium presented at meetings of C.I.O.M.S. In J. F. Delafresnaye (Ed.), *Brain mechanisms and learning.* Oxford: Blackwell, 1961. Pp. 53–73.

Eibl-Eibesfeldt, I.   Angeborenes und Erworbenes im Verhalten einiger Saüger. *Zeitschrift für Tierpsychologie,* 1963, **20,** 705–754.

Eibl-Eibesfeldt, I.   Concepts of ethology and their significance in the study of human behavior. In H. W. Stevenson, E. H. Hess, & H. L. Rheingold (Eds.), *Early behavior: Comparative and developmental approaches.* New York: Wiley, 1967. Pp. 127–146.

Eibl-Eibesfeldt, I.   *Ethology: The biology of behavior.* New York: Holt, Rinehart & Winston, 1970.

Eibl-Eibesfeldt, I., & Hass, H. Film studies in human ethology. *Current Anthropology,* 1967, **8,** 477–479.

Eisenberg, J. F., & Dillon, W. S. *Man and beast: Comparative social behavior.* Washington: Smithsonian Institution Press, 1971.

Ekman, P., & Friesen, W. V. Constants across cultures in the face and emotion. *Journal of Personality and Social Psychology,* 1971, **17,** 124–129.

Ekman, P., Sorenson, E. R., & Friesen, W. V. Pan-cultural elements in facial displays of emotions. *Science,* 1969, **164,** 86–88.

Emlen, S. T. Bird migration: Influence of physiological state upon celestial orientation. *Science,* 1969, **165,** 716–718.

Esser, A. H. (Ed.) *Behavior and environment.* New York: Plenum Press, 1971.

Evans, R. M. Imprinting and mobility in young ring-billed gulls, *Larus delawarensis. Animal Behaviour Monographs,* 1970, **3,** 193–248.

Fabre, J. H. *The wonders of instinct.* London: T. Fisher Unwin, 1918.

Fabricius, E. Zur Ethologie junger Anatiden. *Acta Zoologica Fennica,* 1951, **68,** 1–178.

Fantz, R. L. Visual perception and experience in early infancy: A look at the hidden side of behavior development. In H. W. Stevenson, E. H. Hess, & H. L. Rheingold (Eds.), *Early behavior: Comparative and developmental approaches.* New York: Wiley, 1967. Pp. 181–224.

Fentress, J. C. Interrupted ongoing behaviour in two species of vole (*Microtus agrestis* and *Clethrionomys britannicus*): I. Response as a function of preceding activity and the context of an apparently "irrelevant" motor pattern. *Animal Behaviour,* 1968, **16,** 135–153.

Ferguson, G. W. Variation and evolution of the push-up displays of the side-blotched lizard genus *Uta* (Iguanidae). *Systematic Zoology,* 1971, **20,** 79–101.

Fischer, G. J. Auditory stimuli in imprinting. *Journal of Comparative and Physiological Psychology,* 1966, **61,** 271–273.

Fletcher, R. *Instinct in man in the light of recent work in comparative psychology.* New York: International Universities Press, 1957.

Fox, M. W., & Apelbaum, J. Ontogeny of the orienting-jump response of the rabbit. *Behaviour,* 1969, **35,** 77–83.

Freedman, D. G. An ethological approach to the genetical study of human behavior. In S. G. Vandenberg (Ed.), *Methods and goals in human behavior genetics.* New York: Academic Press, 1965. Pp. 141–161.

Freud, S. Instinct and their vicissitudes, 1915. In E. Jones (Ed.), *The collected papers of Sigmund Freud.* Vol. 4. New York: Basic Books, 1959. Pp. 60–83.

Fromme, A. An experimental study of the factors of maturation and practice in the behavioral development of the embryo of the frog, *Rana pipiens. Genetic Psychology Monographs,* 1941, **24,** 219–256.

Fuchs, J. L., & Burghardt, G. M. Effects of early feeding experience on the response of garter snakes to food chemicals. *Learning and Motivation,* 1971, **2,** 271–279.

Fuller, J. L., & Thompson, W. R. *Behavior genetics.* New York: Wiley, 1960.

Gesell, A. The ontogenesis of infant behavior. In L. Carmichael (Ed.), *Manual of child psychology.* New York: Wiley, 1946. Pp. 295–331.

Ginsburg, B. E. Genetic parameters in behavioral research. In J. Hirsch (Ed.), *Behavior-genetic analysis.* New York: McGraw-Hill, 1967. Pp. 135–153.

Ginsburg, B. E., & Allee, W. C. Some effects of conditioning on social dominance and subordination in inbred strains of mice. *Physiological Zoology,* 1942, **15,** 485–506.

Glickman, S. E., & Schiff, B. B. A biological theory of reinforcement. *Psychological Review,* 1967, **74,** 81–109.

Gottlieb, G. *Development of species identification in birds: An inquiry into the prenatal determinants of perception.* Chicago: University of Chicago Press, 1971.

Grant, E. C., MacKintosh, J. H., & Lerwill, C. J. The effect of a visual stimulus on the agonistic behaviour of the golden hamster. *Zeitschrift für Tierpsychologie,* 1970, **27,** 73–77.

Graves, H. B., & Siegel, P. B. Bidirectional selection for responses of *Gallus domesticus* chicks to an imprinting situation. *Animal Behaviour,* 1969, **17,** 683–691.

Gray, J. The role of peripheral sense organs during locomotion in the vertebrates. In Society for Experimental Biology, *Physiological mechanisms in animal behavior.* Symposium No. 4. New York: Academic Press, 1950. Pp. 112–126.

Gray, P. H. The releasers of imprinting: Differential reactions to color as a function of maturation. *Journal of Comparative and Physiological Psychology,* 1961, **54,** 597–601.

Gray, P. H. Spalding and his influence on research in developmental behavior. *Journal of the History of the Behavioral Sciences,* 1967, **3,** 168–179.

Gray, P. H. Prerequisite to an analysis of behaviorism: The conscious automation theory from Spalding to William James. *Journal of the History of the Behavioral Sciences,* 1968, **4,** 365–376.

Green, M., Green, R., & Carr, W. J. The hawk-goose phenomenon: A replication and an extension. *Psychonomic Science,* 1966, **4,** 185–186.

Greenberg, B. Parental behavior and imprinting in cichlid fishes. *Behaviour,* 1963, **21,** 127–144.

Grossman, S. P. *A textbook of physiological psychology.* New York: Wiley, 1967.

Guiton, P. On the control of behavior during the reproductive cycle of *Gasterosteus aculeatus. Behaviour,* 1960, **15,** 163–184.

Gump, P. V. Intra-setting analysis: The third-grade classroom as a special but instructive case. In E. P. Willems & H. I. Rausch (Eds.), *Naturalistic viewpoints in psychological research.* New York: Holt, Rinehart & Winston, 1969. Pp. 200–220.

Guthrie, R. D. Evolution of human threat display organs. In T. Dobzhansky, M. K. Hecht, & W. C. Steere (Eds.), *Evolutionary biology.* Vol. 4. New York: Academic Press, 1970. Pp. 257–302.

Gwilliam, G. F., & Bradbury, J. C. Activity patterns in the isolated central nervous system of the barnacle and their relation to behavior. *Biological Bulletin,* 1971, **141,** 502–513.

Hailman, J. P. The ontogeny of an instinct. *Behaviour Supplement,* 1967, No. 15.

Haldane, J. B. S. Introducing Douglas Spalding. *British Journal of Animal Behaviour,* 1954, **2,** 1.

Hall, C. S. The genetics of behavior. In S. S. Stevens (Ed.), *Handbook of experimental psychology.* New York: Wiley, 1951. Pp. 304–329.

Hall, E. T. *The hidden dimension.* New York: Doubleday, 1966.

Harlow, H. F. Learning set and error factor theory. In S. Koch (Ed.), *Psychology: A study of a science.* Vol. 2. New York: McGraw-Hill, 1959. Pp. 492–537.

Harlow, H. F. William James and instinct theory. In R. B. Macleod (Ed.), *William James: Unfinished business.* Washington D.C.: American Psychological Association, 1969. Pp. 21–30.

Harlow, H. F., & Harlow, M. K. The affectional systems. In A. M. Schrier, H. F. Harlow, & F. Stollnitz (Eds.), *Behavior of nonhuman primates.* Vol. 2. New York: Academic Press, 1965. Pp. 287–334.

Harlow, H. F., & Harlow, M. K. Learning to love. *American Scientist,* 1966, **54,** 244–272.

Harlow, H. F., Harlow, M. K., & Hansen, E. W. The maternal affectional system of rhesus monkeys. In H. L. Rheingold (Ed.), *Maternal behavior in mammals.* New York: Wiley, 1963. Pp. 254–281.

Harris, G. W., & Michael, R. P. The activation of sexual behavior by hypothalamic implants of oestrogen. *Journal of Physiology,* 1964, **171,** 275–301.

Hass, H. *The human animal.* New York: Putnam, 1970.

Hebb, D. O. *The organization of behavior: A neuropsychological theory.* New York: Wiley, 1949.

Hebb, D. O. Heredity and environment in mammalian behaviour. *British Journal of Animal Behaviour,* 1953, **1,** 43–47.

Hediger, H. *Wild animals in captivity.* London: Butterworth, 1950.

Heinroth, O. Beiträge zur Biologie, namentlich Ethologie und Psychologie der Anatiden. *Verhandlungen des V. Internationalen Ornithologen-Kongresses,* Berlin, 1911, 589–702.

Heinroth, O. Über bestimmte Bewegungsweisen der Wirbeltiere. *Sitzungsberichte der Gesellschaft naturforschender Freunde zu Berlin,* 1930, 333–342.

Hess, E. H. Natural preferences of chicks and ducklings for objects of different colors. *Psychological Reports,* 1956, **2,** 447–483.

Hess, E. H. Imprinting. *Science,* 1959, **130,** 133–141. (a)

Hess, E. H. Two conditions limiting critical age of imprinting. *Journal of Comparative and Physiological Psychology,* 1959, **52,** 515–518. (b)

Hess, E. H. Ethology: An approach toward the complete analysis of behavior. In R. Brown, E. Galanter, E. H. Hess, & G. Mandler, *New directions in psychology.* New York: Holt, Rinehart & Winston, 1962. Pp. 157–266.

Hess, E. H. Imprinting in birds. *Science,* 1964, **146,** 1128–1139.

Hess, E. H. Attitude and pupil size. *Scientific American,* 1965, **212**(4), 46–54.

Hess, E. H. "Imprinting" in a natural laboratory. *Scientific American,* 1972, **227**(8), 24–31.

Hess, E. H., & Hess, D. R. Innate factors in imprinting. *Psychonomic Science,* 1969, **14,** 129–130.

Hess, E. H., Seltzer, A. L., & Shlien, J. M. Pupil response of hetero- and homosexual males to pictures of men and women. *Journal of Abnormal Psychology,* 1965, **70,** 165–168.

Hess, W. R. *Diencephalon: Autonomic and extrapyramidal functions.* New York: Grune & Stratton, 1954.

Hinde, R. A. Ethological models and the concept of drive. *British Journal of Philosophical Science,* 1956, **6,** 321–331.

Hinde, R. A. Energy models of motivation. *Symposium of the Society for Experimental Biology.* Cambridge: Cambridge University Press, 1960. Pp. 199–213.

Hinde, R. A. Interaction of internal and external environments in the regulation of the reproductive cycle of the ring dove. In F. A. Beach (Ed.), *Sex and behavior.* New York: Wiley, 1965. Pp. 381–415.

Hinde, R. A. *Animal behaviour: A synthesis of ethology and comparative psychology.* (2nd ed.) New York: McGraw-Hill, 1970.

Hinde, R. A. (Ed.) *Nonverbal communication.* Cambridge, England: Cambridge University Press, 1972.

Hinde, R. A., & Stevenson, J. G. Sequences of behavior. In D. S. Lehrman, R. A. Hinde, & E. Shaw (Eds.), *Advances in the study of behavior.* Vol. 2. New York: Academic Press, 1969. Pp. 267–296.

Hinde, R. A., & Tinbergen, N. The comparative study of species-specific behavior. In A. Roe & G. G. Simpson (Eds.), *Behavior and evolution.* New Haven: Yale University Press, 1958. Pp. 251–268.

Hirsch, J. *Behavior-genetic analysis.* New York: McGraw-Hill, 1967.

Hirsch, J., Lindley, R. H., & Tolman, E. C. An experimental test of an alleged innate sign stimulus. *Journal of Comparative and Physiological Psychology,* 1955, **48,** 278–280.

Hodos, W., & Campbell, C. B. Scala naturae: Why there is no theory in comparative psychology. *Psychological Review,* 1969, **76,** 337–350.

Hoffman, H. S., & Kozma, F., Jr. Behavioral control by an imprinted stimulus: Long-term effects. *Journal of the Experimental Analysis of Behavior,* 1967, **10,** 495–501.

Hoffman, H. S., Searle, J. L., Toffey, S., & Kozma, F., Jr. Behavioral control by an imprinted stimulus. *Journal of the Experimental Analysis of Behavior,* 1966, **9,** 177–189.

Holmes, S. J. *The evolution of animal intelligence.* New York: Holt, 1911.

Howells, T. H., & Vine, D. O. The innate differential in social learning. *Journal of Abnormal and Social Psychology,* 1940, **35,** 537–548.

Hubel, D. H., & Wiesel, T. N. Receptive fields, binocular interaction, and functional architecture in the cat's visual cortex. *Journal of Physiology,* 1962, **160,** 106–154.

Hubel, D. H., & Wiesel, T. N. Receptive fields of cells in striate cortex of very young visually inexperienced kittens. *Journal of Neurophysiology,* 1963, **26,** 994–1002.

Huber, F. Central nervous control of sound production in crickets and some speculations on its evolution. *Evolution,* 1962, **16,** 429–442.

Hull, C. L. *Principles of behavior.* New York: Appleton-Century-Crofts, 1943.

Hutt, S. J., & Hutt, D. *Direct observation and measurement of behavior.* Springfield, Ill.: Charles C Thomas, 1970.

Huxley, J. S. (Ed.) Ritualization of behaviour in animals and men. *Philosophical Transactions of the Royal Society,* London, 1966, 251 (Whole No. 772).

Immelmann, K. Zur Irreversibilität der Prägung. *Die Naturwissenschaften,* 1966, **53**(8), 209.

James, H. Flicker: An unconditioned stimulus for imprinting. *Canadian Journal of Psychology,* 1959, **13,** 59–67.

James, W. *Principles of psychology.* Vol. 2. New York: Holt, 1890.

Jaynes, J. Imprinting: The interaction of learned and innate behavior: I. Development and generalization. *Journal of Comparative and Physiological Psychology,* 1956, **49,** 201–206.

Jaynes, J. The historical origins of "ethology" and "comparative psychology." *Animal Behaviour,* 1969, **17,** 601–606.

Jennings, H. S. *Behavior of the lower organisms.* New York: Columbia University Press, 1906.

Jenssen, T. A. Display analysis of *Anolis nebalosus* (Sauria, Iguanidae). *Copeia,* 1971, 197–209.

Kagen, J. Attention and psychological change in the young child. *Science,* 1970, **170,** 826–832.

Kelly, J. G. Naturalistic observations in contrasting social environments. In E. P. Willems & H. L. Rausch (Eds.), *Naturalistic viewpoints in psychological research.* New York: Holt, Rinehart & Winston, 1969. Pp. 183–189.

Kennedy, J. S. Is modern ethology objective? *British Journal of Animal Behaviour,* 1954, **2,** 12–19.

Kilham, P., Klopfer, P. H., & Oelke, H.   Species identification and colour preferences in chicks. *Animal Behaviour,* 1968, **16,** 238–244.

Kling, A.   Effects of amygdalectomy and testosterone on sexual behavior of male juvenile macaques. *Journal of Comparative and Physiological Psychology,* 1968, **65,** 466–471.

Klinghammer, E.   Factors influencing choice of mate in altricial birds. In H. W. Stevenson, E. H. Hess, & H. L. Rheingold (Eds.), *Early behavior: Comparative and developmental approaches.* New York: Wiley, 1967. Pp. 5–42.

Klinghammer, E., & Hess, E. H.   Parental feeding in ring doves *(Streptopelia roseogrisea):* Innate or learned. *Zeitschrift für Tierpsychologie,* 1964, **21,** 338–347.

Klopfer, P. H.   Stimulus preferences and imprinting. *Science,* 1967, **156,** 1394–1396.

Klopfer, P. H.   Imprinting: Determining its perceptual basis in ducklings. *Journal of Comparative and Physiological Psychology,* 1971, **75,** 378–385.

Klopfer, P. H., Adams, D. K., & Klopfer, M. S.   Maternal "imprinting" in goats. *Proceedings of the National Academy of Sciences,* 1964, **52,** 911–914.

Klopfer, P. H., & Hailman, J. P.   *An introduction to animal behavior: Ethology's first century.* Englewood Cliffs, N.J.: Prentice-Hall, 1967.

Koehler, O., & Zagarus, A.   Beiträge zum Brutverhalten des Halsbrandregenpfeifers *(Charadrius hiaticula* L.). *Beiträge zur Fortpflanzung der Vögel,* 1937, **13,** 1–9.

Koepke, J. E., & Pribram, K. H.   Effects of milk on the maintenance of sucking behavior in kittens from birth to six months. *Journal of Comparative and Physiological Psychology,* 1971, **75,** 363–377.

Komisaruk, B. R.   Effects of local brain implants of progesterone on reproductive behavior in ring doves. *Journal of Comparative and Physiological Psychology,* 1967, **64,** 219–224.

Konishi, M.   The attributes of instinct. *Behaviour,* 1966, **27,** 316–328.

Konishi, M.   Ethology and neurobiology. *American Scientist,* 1971, **59,** 56–63.

Kortlandt, A.   Chimpanzees in the wild. *Scientific American,* 1962, **206** (5), 128–138.

Kovach, J. K.   Effects of autonomic drugs on imprinting. *Journal of Comparative and Physiological Psychology,* 1964, **57,** 183–187.

Kovach, J. K.   Interaction of innate and acquired: Color preferences and early exposure learning in chicks. *Journal of Comparative and Physiological Psychology,* 1971, **75,** 386–398.

Kovach, J. K., & Hess, E. H.   Imprinting: Effects of painful stimulation upon the following response. *Journal of Comparative and Physiological Psychology,* 1963, **56,** 461–464.

Krames, L.   Sexual responses of polygamous female and monogamous male rats to novel partners after sexual cessation. *Journal of Comparative and Physiological Psychology,* 1971, **77,** 294–301.

Kuhme, W.   Erganzende Beobachtungen an Afrikanischen Elefanten *(Loxodonta africana* Blumenbach 1797) im Freigehege. *Zeitschrift für Tierpsychologie,* 1963, **20,** 66–79.

Kuo, Z. Y.   Giving up instincts in psychology. *Journal of Philosophy,* 1921, **17,** 645–664.

Kuo, Z. Y.   A psychology without heredity. *Psychological Review,* 1924, **31,** 427–451.

Kuo, Z. Y.   *The dynamics of behavior development: An epigenetic view.* New York: Random House, 1967.

Kupferman, I., Pinsker, H., Castellucci, V., & Kandel, E. R.   Central and peripheral control of gill movements in Aplysia. *Science,* 1971, **174,** 1252–1256.

Lakso, V., & Randall, W.   Fishing behavior after lateral midbrain lesions in cats. *Journal of Comparative and Physiological Psychology,* 1969, **68,** 467–475.

Lancaster, J. B., & Lee, R. B.   The annual reproductive cycle in monkeys and apes. In I. De Vore (Ed.), *Primate behavior: Field studies of monkeys and apes.* New York: Holt, Rinehart & Winston, 1965. Pp. 486–513.

Lashley, K.   Experimental analysis of instinctive behavior. *Psychological Review,* 1938, **45,** 445–471. Reprinted in F. A. Beach, D. O. Hebb, C. T. Morgan, & H. W. Nissen (Eds.), *The neuropsychology of Lashley.* New York: McGraw-Hill, 1960. Pp. 372–392.

Lea, R. G., & Turner, J. R. G.   Experiments on mimicry: II. The effect of a Batesian mimic on its model. *Behaviour,* 1972, **42,** 119–130.

Lehrman, D. S.   A critique of Konrad Lorenz's theory of instinctive behavior. *Quarterly Review of Biology,* 1953, **28,** 337–363.

Lehrman, D. S.   The physiological basis of feeding in ring doves *(Streptopelia risoria).* *Behaviour,* 1955, **7,** 241–286.

Lehrman, D. S.   Interaction between internal and external environments in the regulation of the reproductive cycle of the ring dove. In F. A. Beach (Ed.), *Sex and behavior.* New York: Wiley, 1965. Pp. 355–380.

Lehrman, D. S.   Semantic and conceptual issues in the nature-nurture problem. In L. R. Aronson, E. Tobach, D. S. Lehrman, & J. S. Rosenblatt (Eds.), *Development and evolution of behavior.* San Francisco: W. H. Freeman, 1970. Pp. 17–52.

Lehrman, D. S.   Behavioral science, engineering, and poetry. In E. Tobach (Ed.), *The biopsychology of development.* New York: Academic Press, 1971. Pp. 459–472.

Leyhausen, P.   Verhaltensstudien an Katzen. *Zeitschrift für Tierpsychologie,* Beiheft 2, 1956.

Lockard, R. B.   The albino rat: A defensible choice or bad habit? *American Psychologist,* 1968, **23,** 734–742.

Lockard, R. B.   Reflections on the fall of comparative psychology: Is there a message for us all? *American Psychologist,* 1971, **26,** 168–179.

Loeb, J.   *Comparative physiology of the brain and comparative psychology.* New York: Putnam, 1900.

Lorenz, K.   Der Kumpan in der Umwelt des Vögels. *Journal für Ornithologie,* 1935, **83,** 137–213. Translated in K. Lorenz, *Studies in animal and human behaviour.* Vol. 1. Cambridge: Harvard University Press, 1970. Pp. 101–258.

Lorenz, K.   Uber dis Bildung des Instinkbegriffes. *Die Naturwissenschaften,* 1937, **25,** 289–300, 324–331. Translated in K. Lorenz, *Studies in animal and human behaviour.* Vol. 1. Cambridge: Harvard University Press, 1970. Pp. 259–315.

Lorenz, K.   Vergleichende Bewegungsstudien an Anatiden. *Journal für Ornithologie,* 1941, **89,** 194–294. Translated in K. Lorenz, *Studies in animal and human behaviour.* Vol. 2. Cambridge: Harvard University Press, 1971. Pp. 14–114. Figure 9.9: Copyright, 1971, by Konrad Lorenz. Reproduced by permission of Harvard University Press and Methuen & Co. Ltd., London.

Lorenz, K.   Die angeborenen Formen möglicker Erfahrung. *Zeitschrift für Tierpsychologie,* 1943, **5,** 235–409.

Lorenz, K.   The comparative method in the study of innate behavior patterns. *Symposia of the Society for Experimental Biology,* 1950, **4,** 221–268. Figure 9.3: Reproduced by permission.

Lorenz, K.   *Evolution and modification of behavior.* Chicago: University of Chicago Press, 1965.

Lorenz, K.   *On aggression.* New York: Harcourt Brace Jovanovich, 1966.

Lorenz, K.   Innate bases of learning. In K. Pribram (Ed.), *On the biology of learning.* New York: Harcourt Brace Jovanovich, 1969. Pp. 13–93.

Lorenz, K. *Studies in animal and human behaviour.* Cambridge: Harvard University Press, 1970–71. 2 vols.

Lorenz, K., & Tinbergen, N. Taxis und Instinkthandlung in der Eirollbewegung der Graugans. *Zeitschrift für Tierpsychologie,* 1938, **2**, 1–29. Translated in C. H. Schiller (Ed.), *Instinctive behavior.* New York: International Universities Press, 1957. Pp. 176–208.

Ludvingson, H. W. Runway behavior of the rat as a function of intersubject reward contingencies and consistency of daily reward schedule. *Psychonomic Science,* 1969, **15**, 41–43.

Magnus, D. Experimentelle Untersuchungen zur Bionomie und Ethologie des Kaisermantels *Argynnis paphia* L. (Lep. Nymph): I. Über optische Auslöser von Angliergereaktionen und ihre Bedeutung für das Sichfinden der Geschechter. *Zeitschrift für Tierpsychologie,* 1958, **15**, 397–426.

Maier, N.R., & Schneirla, T.C. *Principles of animal psychology.* (Rev. ed.) New York: Dover Publications, 1964. (Orig. pub. 1935.)

Malinowski, B. *Argonauts of the western Pacific.* New York: E. P. Dutton, 1922.

Manning, A. The effects of artificial selection for mating speed in *Drosophila melanogaster. Animal Behaviour,* 1961, **9**, 82–92.

Manning, A. Evolution of behavior. In J. L. McGaugh (Ed.), *Psychobiology: Behavior from a biological perspective.* New York: Academic Press, 1971. Pp. 1–52.

Marler, P. Developments in the study of animal communication. In P. R. Bell (Ed.), *Darwin's biological work.* Cambridge, England: Cambridge University Press, 1959. Pp. 150–206.

Marler, P. The filtering of external stimuli during instinctive behavior. In W. H. Thorpe & O. L. Zangwill (Eds.), *Current problems in animal behaviour.* Cambridge, England: Cambridge University Press, 1961. Pp. 150–166.

Marler, P., & Hamilton, W. J., III. *Mechanisms of animal behavior.* New York: Wiley, 1966.

Marler, P., & Tamura, M. Culturally transmitted patterns of vocal behavior in sparrows. *Science,* 1964, **146**, 1483–1486.

Marshall, H. R. *Instinct and reason.* New York: Macmillan, 1898.

Mattingly, I. G. Speech cues and sign stimuli. *American Scientist,* 1972, **60**, 327–337.

Maturana, H. R., Lettvin, J. Y., McCulloch, W. S., & Pitts, W. H. Anatomy and physiology of vision in the frog (*Rana pipiens*). *Journal of General Physiology,* 1960, **43**, 129–175.

Mayr, E. *Animal species and evolution.* Cambridge, Mass.: Belknap, Harvard University Press, 1963.

McDougall, W. *An introduction to social psychology.* London: Methuen, 1908.

McFarland, D. J. On the causal and functional significance of displacement activities. *Zeitschrift für Tierpsychologie,* 1966, **23**, 217–235.

McFarland, D. J. Behavioral aspects of homeostasis. In D. S. Lehrman, R. A. Hinde, & E. Shaw (Eds.), *Advances in the study of behavior.* Vol. 3. New York: Academic Press, 1970. Pp. 1–26.

McGill, T. E. Studies of the sexual behavior of male laboratory mice: Effects of genotype, recovery of sex drive, and theory. In F. Beach (Ed.), *Sex and behavior.* New York: Wiley, 1965. Pp. 76–88.

McGraw, M. B. Maturation of behavior. In L. Carmichael (Ed.), *Manual of child psychology.* New York: Wiley, 1946. Pp. 332–369.

McGrew, W. C. *An ethological study of children's behavior.* New York: Academic Press, 1972.

Mehrabian, A. Significance of posture and position in the communication of attitude and status relationships. *Psychological Bulletin,* 1969, **71**, 359–372.

Meyer, C. C., & Salzen, E. A. Hypothalamic lesions and sexual behavior in the domestic chick. *Journal of Comparative and Physiological Psychology,* 1970, **73**, 365–376.

Miller, N. E. Liberalization of basic S-R concepts. In S. Koch (Ed.), *Psychology: A study of a science.* Vol. 1. New York: McGraw-Hill, 1959. Pp. 196–292.

Missakian, E. A. Reproductive behavior of socially deprived male rhesus monkeys (*Macaca mulatta*). *Journal of Comparative and Physiological Psychology,* 1969, **69**, 403–407.

Moltz, H. Imprinting: Empirical basis and theoretical significance. *Psychological Bulletin,* 1960, **57**, 291–314.

Moltz, H. Imprinting: An epigenetic approach. *Psychological Review,* 1963, **70**, 123–138.

Moltz, H. Contemporary instinct theory and the fixed action pattern. *Psychological Review,* 1965, **72**, 27–47.

Moltz, H., & Stettner, L. J. The influence of patterned-light deprivation on the critical period for imprinting. *Journal of Comparative and Physiological Psychology,* 1961, **54**, 279–283.

Montagu, M. F. A. (Ed.) *Man and aggression.* London: Oxford University Press, 1968.

Morgan, C. L. *An introduction to comparative psychology.* London: Edwin Arnold, 1894.

Morgan, C. L. *Habit and instinct.* London: Edwin Arnold, 1896.

Morris, D. The reproductive behavior of the zebra finch (*Poephila gutata*), with special reference to pseudofemale behavior and displacement activities. *Behaviour,* 1954, **6**, 271–322.

Morris, D. *The naked ape.* New York: McGraw-Hill, 1967.

Morris, D. *The human zoo.* New York: McGraw-Hill, 1969.

Mott, F. W., & Sherrington, C. S. Experiments upon the influence of sensory nerves upon movement and nutrition of the limbs. *Proceedings of the Royal Society,* London, 1895, **57**, 481–488.

Moynihan, M. Some aspects of reproductive behavior in the black-headed gull (*Larus ridibundus ridibundus L.*) and related species. *Behaviour Supplement,* 1955, **4**, 1–201. Figure 9.7: Reproduced by permission of author and publishers.

Munn, N. L. *Handbook of psychological research on the rat.* New York: Houghton Mifflin, 1950.

Myrberg, A. A., Jr. An analysis of preferential care of eggs and young by adult cichlid fishes. *Zeitschrift für Tierpsychologie,* 1964, **21**, 53–98.

Nelson, K. The temporal patterning of courtship behavior in the glandulocaudine fishes (*Ostariophysis, Characidae*). *Behaviour,* 1964, **24**, 90–146.

Newton, G., & Levine, S. (Eds.) *Early experience and behavior.* Springfield. Ill.: Charles C Thomas, 1968.

Noble, G. K., & Curtis, B. The social behavior of the jewel fish, *Hemichromis bimaculatus* (Gill). *Bulletin of the American Museum of Natural History,* 1939, **76**, 1–46.

Noble, G. K., & Schmidt, A. Structure and function of the facial and labial pits of snakes. *Proceedings of the American Philosophical Society,* 1937, **77**, 263–288.

Noirot, E. Changes in responsiveness to young in the adult mouse. IV. The effects of an initial contact with a strong stimulus. *Animal Behaviour,* 1964, **12**, 442–445.

Olds, J., & Milner, P. Positive reinforcement produced by electrical stimulation of septal area and other regions of rat brain. *Journal of Comparative and Physiological Psychology,* 1954, **47**, 419–427.

Payne, A. P., & Swanson, H. H.   The effects of a supranormal threat stimulus on the growth rates and dominance relationships of pairs of male and female golden hamsters. *Behaviour,* 1972, **42**, 1–7.

Peretz, B.   Central neuron initiation of periodic gill movement. *Science,* 1969, **166**, 1167–1172.

Phillips, R. E., & Youngren, O. M.   Brain stimulation and species-typical behaviour: Activities evoked by electrical stimulation of the brains of chickens *(Gallus gallus). Animal Behaviour,* 1971, **19**, 757–779.

Polt, J. M., & Hess, E. H.   Following and imprinting: Effects of light and social experience. *Science,* 1964, **143**, 1185–1187.

Prechtl, H. F. R.   Zur physiologie der angeborenen auslösenden Mechanismen: I. Quantitative Untersuchungen über die Sperrbewegung junger Singvögel. *Behaviour,* 1953, **5**, 32–50.

Prechtl, H. F. R., & Schleidt, W. M.   Auslösende und steuernde Mechanismen des Saugaktes: I. *Zeitschrift für Vergleichende Physiologie,* 1950, **32**, 252–262.

Räber, H.   Analyse des Balzverhalten eines domestizierten Truthahas *(Meleagris). Behaviour,* 1948, **1**, 237–266.

Ramsay, A. O.   Familial recognition in domestic birds. *Auk,* 1951, **68**, 1–16.

Ramsay, A. O., & Hess, E. H.   A laboratory approach to the study of imprinting. *Wilson Bulletin,* 1954, **66**, 196–206.

Randall, W. L.   The behavior of cats *(Felis Catus L.)* with lesions in the caudal midbrain region. *Behaviour,* 1964, **23**, 107–139.

Randall, W., Lakso, V., & Liittschwager, J.   Lesion-induced dissociations between appetitive and consummatory grooming behaviors and their relationship to body weight and food intake rhythms. *Journal of Comparative and Physiological Psychology,* 1969, **68**, 476–483.

Reynierse, J. H., Scavio, M. J., Jr., & Ulness, J. D.   An ethological analysis of classically conditioned fear. In J. H. Reynierse (Ed.), *Current issues in animal learning.* Lincoln: University of Nebraska Press, 1970. Pp. 33–54.

Riess, B. F.   Effect of altered environment and of age in the mother-young relationships among animals. *Annals of the New York Academy of Sciences,* 1954, **57**, 606–610.

Roberts, W. W., & Bergquist, E. H.   Attack elicited by hypothalamic stimulation in cats raised in social isolation. *Journal of Comparative and Physiological Psychology,* 1968, **66**, 590–595.

Roberts, W. W., Bergquist, E. H., & Robinson, T. C. L.   Thermoregulatory grooming and sleep-like relaxation induced by local warming of preoptic area and anterior hypothalamus in opossum. *Journal of Comparative and Physiological Psychology,* 1969, **67**, 182–188.

Roberts, W. W., & Carey, R. J.   Rewarding effect of performance of gnawing aroused by hypothalamic stimulation in the rat. *Journal of Comparative and Physiological Psychology,* 1965, **59**, 317–324.

Roberts, W. W., Steinberg, M. L., & Means, L. W.   Hypothalamic mechanisms for sexual, aggressive, and other motivational behaviors in the opossum, *Didelphis virginiana. Journal of Comparative and Physiological Psychology,* 1967, **64**, 1–15.

Roeder, K. D.   Ethology and neurophysiology. *Zeitschrift für Tierpsychologie,* 1963, **20**, 434–440.

Romanes, G. J.   *Mental evolution in animals.* London: Kegan Paul, Trench & Co., 1884.

Romanes, G. J.   *Mental evolution in man.* London: Kegan Paul, Trench & Co., 1888.

Romer, H. S.   Phylogeny and behavior with special reference to vertebrate evolution. In A. Roe, & G. G. Simpson (Eds.), *Evolution and behavior.* New Haven: Yale University Press, 1958. Pp. 48–75.

Ross, S., & Denenberg, V. H.   Innate behavior: The organism in its environment. In R. M. Waters, D. A. Rethlingshafer, & W. E. Caldwell (Eds.), *Principles of comparative psychology.* New York: McGraw-Hill, 1960. Pp. 43–73.

Rowell, C. H. F.   Displacement grooming in the chaffinch. *Animal Behaviour,* 1961, **9**, 38–63.

Rozin, P., & Kalat, J. W.   Specific hungers and poison avoidance as adaptive specializations of learning. *Psychological Review,* 1971, **78**, 459–486.

Sackett, G. P.   Monkeys reared in isolation with pictures as visual input: Evidence for an innate releasing mechanism. *Science,* 1966, **154**, 1468–1473.

Schaefer, H. H., & Hess, E. H.   Color preferences in imprinting objects. *Zeitschrift für Tierpsychologie,* 1959, **19**, 161–172.

Scheflen, A. E.   Quasi-courtship behavior in psychotherapy. *Psychiatry,* 1965, **28**, 245–257. Figures 9.10 and 9.11: Copyright © 1965 by the William Alanson White Psychiatric Foundation, and reproduced by permission.

Schenkel, R.   Ausdrucks-Studien an Wölfen. *Behaviour,* 1947, **1**, 81–130.

Schiller, C. H. (Ed.)   *Instinctive behavior.* New York: International Universities Press, 1957.

Schleidt, W.   Reaktionen von Truthühnern auf fliegende Raubvögel und Versaiche zur Analyse ihrer AAM's. *Zeitschrift für Tierpsychologie,* 1961, **18**, 534–560.

Schleidt, W.   Die historische Entwicklung der Begriffe "Angeborener Auslösemechanismus" in der Ethologie. *Zeitschrift für Tierpsychologie,* 1962, **19**, 697–722.

Schleidt, W.   Gaussian interval distributions in spontaneously occurring innate behaviour. *Nature,* 1965, **206**, 1061–1062.

Schneirla, T. C.   Interrelationships of the "innate" and the "acquired" in instinctive behavior. In *L'Instinct dans le comportement des animaux et de l'homme.* Paris: Mason and Cie, 1956. Pp. 387–452.

Schneirla, T. C.   Aspects of stimulation and organization in approach/withdrawal processes underlying vertebrate behavioral development. In D. S. Lehrman, R. A. Hinde, & E. Shaw (Eds.), *Advances in the study of behavior.* Vol. 1. New York: Academic Press, 1965. Pp. 1–74.

Schneirla, T. C.   Behavioral development and comparative psychology. *Quarterly Review of Biology,* 1966, **41**, 283–302.

Schulman, A. H.   Transfer of behavior controlled by an imprinted stimulus via brain homogenate injections in turkeys. *Psychonomic Science,* 1972, **27**, 48–50.

Schutz, F.   Sexuelle Prägung bei Anatiden. *Zeitschrift für Tierpsychologie,* 1965, **22**, 50–103.

Scott, J. P.   Genetic differences in the social behavior of inbred strains of mice. *Journal of Heredity,* 1942, **33**, 11–15.

Scott, J. P.   Critical periods in behavioral development. *Science,* 1962, **138**, 949–958.

Scott, J. P., & Fuller, J. L. (Eds.)   *Genetics and the social behavior of the dog.* Chicago: University of Chicago Press, 1965.

Seitz, A.   Die Paarbildung bei einigen Cichliden: I. Die Paarbildung bei *Astatotilapia strigigena* (Pfeffer). *Zeitschrift für Tierpsychologie,* 1940, **4**, 40–84.

Seligman, M. E.   On the generality of the laws of learning. *Psychological Review,* 1970, **77**, 406–418.

Sevenster, P.   The mechanism of a displacement activity. *Archives Neerlandaises de Zoologie,* 1960, **13**, 576–579.

Sevenster, P.   A causal analysis of a displacement activity (fanning in *Gasterosteus aculeatus* L.), *Behaviour,* 1961, Suppl. 9, 1–170.

Silverman, A. P. Social behaviour of laboratory rats and the action of chlorpromazine and other drugs. *Behaviour,* 1966, **27,** 1–38.

Skinner, B. F. *The behavior of organisms.* New York: Appleton-Century-Crofts, 1938.

Skinner, B. F. A case study in scientific method. *American Psychologist,* 1956, **11,** 221–233.

Skinner, B. F. The phylogeny and ontogeny of behavior. *Science,* 1966, **153,** 1205–1213.

Sluckin, W. Perceptual and associative learning. *Proceedings of the Zoological Society of London,* 1962, **8,** 193–198.

Sluckin, W. *Imprinting and early learning.* Chicago: Aldine, 1965.

Sluckin, W. *Early learning in man and animal.* Cambridge, Mass.: Schenkman, 1972.

Sluckin, W., & Salzen, E. A. Imprinting and perceptual learning. *Quarterly Journal of Experimental Psychology,* 1961, **13,** 65–77.

Smith, F. V. Perceptual aspects of imprinting. *Proceedings of the Zoological Society of London,* 1962, **8,** 171–191.

Smith, F. V., & Bird, M. W. Varying effectiveness of distant intermittent stimuli for the approach response in the domestic chick. *Animal Behaviour,* 1963, **11,** 57–61.

Society for Experimental Biology. *Physiological mechanisms in animal behavior.* Symposium No. 4. New York: Academic Press, 1950.

Sommer, R. *Personal space: The behavioral basis of design.* Englewood Cliffs, N.J.: Prentice-Hall, 1969.

Sorenson, M. W. Behavior of tree shrews. In L. A. Rosenblum (Ed.), *Primate behavior: Developments in field and laboratory research.* Vol. 1. New York: Academic Press, 1970. Pp. 141–193.

Southall, P. F., & Long, C. J. Odor cues in a maze discrimination. *Psychonomic Science,* 1969, **16,** 126–127.

Spalding, D. A. Instinct with original observations on young animals. *MacMillan's Magazine,* 1873, **27,** 282–293. Reprinted in *British Journal of Animal Behaviour,* 1954, **2,** 2–11.

Spencer, H. *The principles of psychology.* Vol. 1. (2nd ed.) London: Williams & Norgate, 1872.

Sperry, R. W. Mechanisms of neural maturation. In S. S. Stevens (Ed.), *Handbook of experimental psychology.* New York: Wiley, 1951. Pp. 236–280.

Staddon, J. E. A., & Simmelhag, V. L. The "superstition" experiment: A reexamination of its implications for the principles of adaptive behavior. *Psychological Review,* 1971, **78,** 3–43.

Storr, A. *Human aggression.* New York: Atheneum, 1968.

Sullivan, H. S. *The interpersonal theory of psychiatry.* New York: W. W. Norton, 1953.

Taub, E., & Berman, A. J. Movement and learning in the absence of sensory feedback. In S. J. Freedman (Ed.), *The neuropsychology of spatially oriented behavior.* Homewood, Ill.: Dorsey Press, 1968. Pp. 173–192.

Thiessen, D. D. *Gene organization and behavior.* New York: Random House, 1972.

Thompson, W. R. The inheritance of behavior: Behavioral differences in fifteen mouse strains. *Canadian Journal of Psychology,* 1953, **7,** 145–155.

Thorndike, E. L. Instinct. *Biological Lectures from the Marine Biological Laboratory of Woods Hole, 1899,* 1900, **7,** 57–67. (a)

Thorndike, E. L. The associative processes in animals. *Bio-*

logical Lectures from the Marine Biological Laboratory of Woods Hole, 1899, 1900, **7,** 67–91. (b)

Thorpe, W. H. Ethology and the coding problem in germ cell and brain. *Zeitschrift für Tierpsychologie,* 1963, **20,** 529–551.

Tiger, L. *Men in groups.* New York: Random House, 1969.

Tiger, L., & Fox, R. *The imperial animal.* New York: Holt, Rinehart & Winston, 1971.

Tinbergen, N. Social releasers and the experimental method required for their study. *Wilson Bulletin,* 1948, **60,** 6–51.

Tinbergen, N. *The study of instinct.* Oxford: Clarendon Press, 1951. Figures 9.4 and 9.6: Reproduced by permission of The Clarendon Press, Oxford.

Tinbergen, N. "Derived" activities. Their causation, biological significance, origin, and emancipation during evolution. *Quarterly Review of Biology,* 1952, **27,** 1–32.

Tinbergen, N. *Social behaviour in animals.* London: Methuen, 1953.

Tinbergen, N. On aims and methods of ethology. *Zeitschrift für Tierpsychologie,* 1963, **20,** 410–433.

Tinbergen, N. On war and peace in animals and man. *Science,* 1968, **160,** 1411–1418.

Tinbergen, N., & Kuenen, D. J. Über die auslösenden und die richtunggebenden: Reizsituationen der Sperrbewegung von jungen Drosseln (*Turdus m. merula* L. *und T. E. ericetorum* Turton). *Zeitschrift für Tierpsychologie,* 1939, **3,** 37–60. Translated in C. H. Schiller (Ed.), *Instinctive behavior.* New York: International Universities Press, 1957. Pp. 209–238. Figure 9.5: Copyright 1957 by International Universities Press, Inc., and reproduced by permission.

Tinbergen N., Meeuse, J. D., Boerema, L. K., & Varossieau, W. W. Die Balz des Samtfalters, *Eumenis* (= *Satyrus*) *semele* (L.). *Zeitschrift für Tierpsychologie,* 1942, **5,** 182–226.

Tinbergen, N., & van Iersel, J. J. A. "Displacement reactions" in the three-spined stickleback. *Behaviour,* 1947, **1,** 56–63.

Tolman, E. C. The determiners of behavior at a choice point. *Psychological Review,* 1938, **45,** 1–35.

Ursin, H. The cingulate gyrus: A fear zone? *Journal of Comparative and Physiological Psychology,* 1969, **68,** 235–238.

Vandenberg, S. G. (Ed.) *Progress in human behavior genetics.* Baltimore: Johns Hopkins Press, 1968.

van Iersel, J. J. A., & Bol, A. C. Preening of two tern species: A study of displacement activities. *Behaviour,* 1958, **13,** 1–88.

van Lawick-Goodall, J. The behavior of free-living chimpanzees in the Gombe Stream Reserve. *Animal Behaviour Monographs,* 1968, **1,** 161–311.

Verplanck, W. S. Since learned behavior is innate, and vice versa, what now? *Psychological Review,* 1955, **62,** 139–144.

Verplanck, W. S. A glossary of some terms used in the objective science of behavior. *Psychological Review,* 1957, **64** (6), Part 2, 1–42. (a)

Verplanck, W. S. An hypothesis on imprinting. *British Journal of Animal Behaviour,* 1957, **5,** 123. (b)

Verplanck, W. S. An "overstatement" on psychological research: What is a dissertation? *Psychological Record,* 1970, **20,** 119–122.

von Holst, E. Quantitative Messung von Stimmungen im Verhalten der Fische. In Society for Experimental Biology. *Physiological mechanisms in animal behavior.* Symposium No. 4. New York: Academic Press, 1950. Pp. 143–172.

von Holst, E., & von Saint-Paul, U. Electrically controlled behavior. *Scientific American,* 1962, **206**(3), 50–59.

von Holst, E., & von Saint-Paul, U. On the functional organization of drives. *Animal Behaviour,* 1963, **11,** 1–20. Table 9.1: Reproduced by permission of the author and Baillière Tindall, Ltd., London.

von Uexküll, J. *Streifzüge durch die Umwelten von Tieren und Menschen.* Berlin: Springer, 1934. Translated in C. H. Schiller (Ed.), *Instinctive behavior.* New York: International Universities Press, 1957. Pp. 5–80. Figure 9.2: Copyright 1957 by International Universities Press, and reproduced by permission.

Wahlsten, D. Genetic experiments with animal learning. *Behavioral Biology,* 1972, **7**, 143–182.

Washburn, M. F. *The animal mind.* New York: Macmillan, 1908.

Watson, J. B. Psychology as the behaviorist views it. *Psychological Review,* 1913, **20**, 158–177.

Watson, J. B. *Behaviorism.* Chicago: University of Chicago Press, 1930.

Wecker, S. C. The role of early experience in habitat selection by the prairie deer mouse, *Peromyscus maniculatus bairdi. Ecological Monographs,* 1963, **33**, 307–325.

Weidmann, R., & Weidmann, U. An analysis of the stimulus situation releasing food-begging in the black-headed gull. *Animal Behaviour,* 1958, **6**, 114.

Weidmann, U. Verhaltensstudien an der Stockente: II. Versuche zur Auslösung und Prägung der nachfolge und Anschlussreaction. *Zeitschrift für Tierpsychologie,* 1958, **15**, 277–300.

Weidmann, U. Innate behavior. In *Topics in animal behavior.* New York: Harper & Row, 1971. Pp. 3–12.

Weiss, P. Self-differentiation of the basic patterns of coordination. *Comparative Psychology Monographs,* 1941, **17**, 1–96.

Whalen, R. E. The concept of instinct. In J. L. McGaugh (Ed.), *Psychobiology: Behavior from a biological perspective.* New York: Academic Press, 1971. Pp. 53–72.

Whitman, C. O. Animal behavior. *Biological Lectures from the Marine Biological Laboratory of Woods Hole, 1898,* 1899, **6**, 285–338. (a)

Whitman, C. O. Myths in animal psychology. *The Monist,* 1899, **9**, 524–537.(b)

Wickler, W. *Breeding aquarium fish.* New York: Van Nostrand Reinhold, 1966.

Wickler, W. *Mimicry in plants and animals.* New York: McGraw-Hill, 1968.

Wickler, W. *The sexual code.* Garden City, N.Y.: Doubleday, 1972.

Wiesel, T. N., & Hubel, D. H. Single-cell responses in striate cortex of kittens deprived of vision in one eye. *Journal of Neurophysiology,* 1963, **26**, 1003–1017.

Wilcoxon, H. C., Dragoin, W. B., & Kral, P. A. Illness-induced aversions in rat and quail: Relative salience of visual and gustatory cues. *Science,* 1971, **171**, 826–828.

Willems, E. P. An ecological orientation in psychology. *Merrill-Palmer Quarterly,* 1965, **11**, 317–343.

Willems, E. P., & Rausch, H. L.(Eds.) *Naturalistic viewpoints in psychological research.* New York: Holt, Rinehart & Winston, 1969.

Willows, A. O. D., & Hoyle, G. Neuronal network triggering a fixed action pattern. *Science,* 1969, **166**, 1549–1551.

Wilson, D. M. Genetic and sensory mechanisms for locomotion and orientation in animals. *American Scientist,* 1972, **60**, 358–365.

Wilz, K. J. The disinhibition interpretation of the "displacement" activities during courtship in the three-spined stickleback, *Gasterosteus aculaetus. Animal Behaviour,* 1970, **18**, 682–687.

Wooten, R. J. Measures of the aggression of parental male three-spined sticklebacks. *Behaviour,* 1971, **40**, 228–262.

Wooten, R. J. The behaviour of the male three-spined stickleback in a natural situation: A quantitative description. *Behaviour,* 1972, **41**, 232–241.

Wright, H. F. *Recording and analyzing child behavior.* New York: Harper & Row, 1967.

Zeigler, H. P. Displacement activity and motivational theory: A case study in the history of ethology. *Psychological Bulletin,* 1964, **61**, 362–376.

Zelazo, P. R., Zelazo, N. A., & Kolb, S. "Walking" in the newborn. *Science,* 1972, **176**, 314–315.

Zuckerman, S. *The social life of monkeys and apes.* London: Routledge, 1932.

10

POSTSCRIPT

John A. Nevin
Columbia University

The careful reader will have noted many instances of overlap in the preceding chapters. Similar experimental operations that give rise to related behavioral effects are interpreted in different ways, depending on the context in which they are considered. In the same vein, similar behavioral effects are discussed in quite different ways, depending on the operations that give rise to them and the topics they are related to by a given author. It is perhaps inevitable that such overlaps should exist: Behavior has many aspects and is complexly determined, so that there can be no one-for-one relationship between operations and effects. It may be instructive to review some basic experimental operations that have been treated in a number of the chapters and a few behavioral phenomena that have been noted in different connections in order to appreciate the richness of the interrelations among operations and effects in the study of behavior.

Consider the operation of experimental extinction—the discontinuation of a reinforcing consequence for a specified response. The direct effect of this operation is a decrease in the rate or speed of the response, or the probability that the response will recur (Chapters 1, 2, and 3). If extinction is arranged in the presence of one stimulus while reinforcement continues in the presence of another, the reduction in responding is generally confined to the stimulus correlated with extinction (Chapters 3 and 4).

This simple operation of nonreinforcement has a number of other behavioral effects, however. For example, the termination of reinforcement in the presence of one stimulus (S-) is likely to produce behavioral contrast —an increase in response rate in the presence of an alternated stimulus that is correlated with reinforcement ($S +$). It is also likely to produce peak shift when generalization gradients are obtained by presenting stimuli along a dimension that includes both $S +$ and $S -$, and inhibitory stimulus control may be observed when stimuli are presented along an independent dimension that includes $S -$ but not $S +$. In Chapter 4 these observations are discussed in conjunction with the concept of inhibition; however, other effects of stimuli correlated with extinction are more in keeping with the notion of aversion. For example, Chapter 5 describes experiments that demonstrate escape from or avoidance of stimuli that signaled nonreinforcement. These observations define such stimuli as negative reinforcers. In a similar vein, Chapter 7 shows that such stimuli can function as punishers: When a response produces a signaled time-out from positive reinforcement, responding is suppressed.

The effects of extinction have also been discussed in terms that relate to various concepts of motivation and emotion. Chapters 2 and 5 mention the frustration effects of extinction that are suggested by the enhanced vigor of conditioned behavior and by the increases in general activity that are often observed at least briefly after reinforcement is terminated. As described in Chapters 2 and 8, the termination of reinforcement may elicit aggressive behavior against another organism.

Finally, in the vocabulary of ethology in Chapter 9, thwarting of appetitive behavior—that is, behavior that usually leads to a given releasing stimulus and its correlated fixed action pattern—is often observed to generate unrelated displacement activities. For example, when the female stickleback does not respond to the courtship dance of the male, the male may engage in fanning movements that characteristically occur after mating and the laying of eggs. Although the lack of response by a female does not qualify as nonreinforcement of courtship for the male if there is no prior history of reinforcement for the behavior, the effect is analogous to extinction in that a strong response is not followed by its normal consequence. If appropriate conditions are arranged, the extinction of conditioned behavior may also lead to displacement activities.

So far, then, it appears that a given operation can generate quite a broad spectrum of behavioral effects, depending on the circumstances in which the organism is observed. One is reminded of recent findings in the areas of emotion and motivation: As described in Chapter 8, an injection of adrenalin may give rise to angry or euphoric behavior depending on the stimulus conditions in which the subject is placed, and stimulation of a single hypothalamic area may lead to eating if food is present, or drinking if water is present. In like fashion, the effects of extinction seem to depend on the available stimuli in the situation and their relation to responding. Of at least equal importance is the way in which the investigator examines behavior: If only one response is measured, in the presence of one stimulus condition alone, one may observe nothing more than the basic decrease in response rate; but as the number of stimuli and responses studied in relation to each other increases, the richness of even the simplest behavioral process becomes evident.

A different experimental operation that is also treated in a number of chapters—presentation of electric shock—can have many of the same effects. It was noted in Chapter 7 that response-contingent electric shock decreases the rate of emission of a response that is maintained by a constant schedule of reinforcement (see also Chapter 2). By-products of this basic effect of punishment in studies of stimulus control are much the same as those of extinction: Contrasting rate increases may occur in the presence of an alternated stimulus that is not correlated with punishment, and peak shift is observed in subsequent generalization gradients (Chapter 4). Moreover, the effects of punishment generalize in much the same way as those of extinction (Chapter 7). In studies of reinforcement and aversive control, pairing of electric shock with a neutral stimulus can be shown to establish that stimulus as a conditioned negative reinforcer (Chapter 5) or as a conditioned punisher (Chapter 7). Finally, shocks occasion aggressive behavior in much the same way as the abrupt termination of reinforcement (Chapters 1 and 8).

Because electric shocks rarely occur in natural settings, their effects have been explored rather little from an ethological point of view. However, analogous effects may appear in naturally occurring behaviors as well. The imposition of punishment on positively reinforced responding is often viewed as establishing an approach-avoidance conflict. The same type of conflict between approach and flight is often noted in natural settings as a condition that gives rise to displacement behavior (Chapter 9). The similar effects of thwarting and conflict in occasioning displacement may be seen as paralleling the similarity between extinction and punishment.

The seeming equivalence of terminating reinforcement and presenting electric shock is likely to suggest that both experimental operations induce in the organism a state that might be called aversion, frustration, inhibition, conflict, or some combination of these terms and their connotations, and that one should move on from the direct study of behavior to the examination of inferred internal states of this sort. There are two kinds of problems involved in this shift away from behavioral observations toward internal states. The first is that one is led to expect that additional effects of one of these variables will also be produced by the other. For example, as described in Chapter 8, a stimulus that is followed by electric shock will suppress ongoing positively reinforced operant behavior—an effect that has been identified with the concept of anxiety. If nonreinforcement generates internal conditions like those produced by shock, one would expect that a stimulus that precedes a period of nonreinforcement would also suppress ongoing behavior. However, it has been shown that stimuli preceding unavoidable periods of time-out from positive reinforcement do not suppress responding (Chapter 8).

Now, as Chapters 6 and 8 have pointed out, conditioned suppression produced by electric shock depends importantly on the schedule of reinforcement maintaining the baseline performance; indeed, under some conditions, increases rather than decreases in rate may be observed. Suppression may also be produced by pairing a stimulus with a positive reinforcer, as well as by pairing with an aversive stimulus (Chapter 8). This latter effect also depends on parameters such as the baseline schedule of reinforcement. Thus, it would be a mistake to identify either a stimulus event (shock or time-out from reinforcement) or a behavioral effect (suppression or facilitation) with the presence of any particular state within the organism.

One possible reaction to this sort of difficulty is to ignore the conditioned-suppression paradigm on the grounds that it is too complex to give consistent data for the assessment of a state of aversion within the organism. The effects of conditioned suppression procedures are indeed complex, but they are orderly and replicable. Thus, this reaction would in effect be a decision to restrict the study of behavior to those situations which generate data fitting our preconceptions—scarcely a way to advance empirical science.

The second problem that may arise from a shift of interest from behavior to an inner event is that investigators are more likely to ignore the situational determinants of the effects on which their inferences are based. One of the safest generalizations in the study of behavior is that the magnitude and even the direction of any given effect depends on the specific situation within which it is studied. Even the basic process of reinforcement is parametrically determined: A stimulus that has reinforcing effects on one response may not serve as a reinforcer for a different response, or may be ineffective under different deprivation conditions (Chapter 2). In like fashion, the effect of a stimulus as a punisher depends on the particular conditions that are arranged and on the history of the behaving organism. As noted in the discussion of escape and avoidance conditioning in Chapter 7, not all responses appear to be equally conditionable (see also Chapter 2). Perhaps even more striking are findings that under certain conditions electric shock may not suppress a response that produces it, but rather maintains responding even in the absence of other reinforcers. Nonreinforcement

may also fail to have its characteristic effects on stimulus control when special training procedures are used (Chapter 4), and stimuli correlated with extinction may function like positive reinforcers if scheduled in the same relation to responding as primary reinforcement (Chapter 6). As a final example, the elicitation of fighting by electric shock depends on a number of parameters such as shock intensity, shock frequency, and chamber size (Chapter 1); extinction-induced aggression is likely to prove to be at least as heavily dependent on situational parameters.

When it is recognized that the presence, magnitude, and direction of a given effect depend on the combined operation of numerous experimental variables, it becomes scientifically uneconomical to talk about unitary events that are internal to the organism but are revealed in different ways depending on the situation. This difficulty was appreciated by Tolman, whose approach to learning theory was considered in Chapter 1. His system had always concerned itself with the objective definition and evaluation of constructs that otherwise had the flavor of purely private mental phenomena: expectancy, value, and the like. This was to be accomplished by setting up standard defining experiments that would permit the separate evaluation of each of the constructs in his theoretical system, on the assumption that the independent variable that was identified with a certain value of each construct or intervening variable would have the same effect in a new, nonstandard situation as well. However, as Tolman (1959) wrote near the end of his career,

> I wish now to emphasize that this last assumption might well prove to be invalid. For there may be all sorts of interactions between the variables (independent as well as intervening), in the new nonstandard situations, interactions which could not have been predicted from the results obtained in the standard defining situations by themselves. . . . Hence, I have considerable doubt concerning not only the practical feasibility but also the validity of the proposal [p. 148].[1]

This difficulty is not unique to Tolman's system, but extends to all systems that view behavior as a manifestation of events at some other level. If such hypothesized events are not entirely consistent with orderly, reliable data in a variety of situations

---

[1]E. C. Tolman, Principles of purposive behavior. In S. Koch (Ed.), *Psychology: A study of a science.* Vol. 2. New York: McGraw-Hill, 1959. Pp. 92–157.

and over broad ranges of parameter values, one might just as well dispense with them and concentrate on the analysis of the behavioral processes themselves.

As analysis proceeds, the findings may suggest new kinds of theoretical integration that have little in common with traditional conceptions. The constructs and classifications that we now use are themselves the result of our own behavioral histories. They have provided rough-and-ready guides to the prediction and control of behavior in many everyday encounters, and they have served adequately as organizing rubrics for a great deal of experimentation in this century. However, there is no guarantee that they will correspond to the groupings of behavioral phenomena that may be suggested by further careful study.

Learning, motivation, emotion, instinct—these and more specific constructs, such as expectancy, drive, inhibition, or frustration, may well have served their purpose in bringing the study of behavior to its present state. Now, we can see diverse behaviors as determined by the combined action of many variables, and we can analyze the role of each variable by careful experimentation. A number of broad empirical generalizations have emerged from the experimental analysis of behavior, as described in the various chapters of this volume. At last, perhaps, such debates as those over the nature of instinct and its difference from learning, or the attempts to separate the contributions of learning from those of motivation, will be forgotten as we concentrate on new ways to comprehend the order and diversity of behavior.

NAME INDEX

SUBJECT INDEX